THE ORCHID STUD-BOOK

THE ORCHID STUD-BOOK:

An Enumeration of Hybrid Orchids of Artificial Origin,

WITH THEIR PARENTS, RAISERS, DATE OF FIRST FLOWERING, REFERENCES TO DESCRIPTIONS AND FIGURES, AND SYNONYMY.

With an Historical Introduction and 120 Figures and a Chapter on Hybridising and raising Orchids from Seed.

BY

ROBERT ALLEN ROLFE, A.L.S.

AND

CHARLES CHAMBERLAIN HURST. F.L.S.

A Companion Volume to the Orchid Review.

GYAN

Published by

GYAN

Gyan Publishing House
5, Ansari Road
Daryaganj, New Delhi-110002
Phone: 011-47034999, 9811692060
E-mail: books@gyanbooks.com

Distribution Network
gyanbooks.com
India, USA, Canada, UK, Australia, France

ISBN : 978-81-212-2253-2 (HB)
First Published, 1909

2nd Impression 2021

Printed at: Gyan Press, Delhi.

The Orchid Stud-Book
Author: Robert Allen Rolfe, Charles Chamberlain Hurst

THE ORCHID STUD-BOOK:

An Enumeration of Hybrid Orchids of Artificial Origin,

WITH THEIR PARENTS, RAISERS, DATE OF FIRST FLOWERING, REFERENCES TO DESCRIPTIONS AND FIGURES, AND SYNONYMY.

With an Historical Introduction and 120 Figures and a Chapter on Hybridising and raising Orchids from Seed.

BY

ROBERT ALLEN ROLFE, A.L.S.

AND

CHARLES CHAMBERLAIN HURST. F.L.S.

A Companion Volume to the ORCHID REVIEW.

Kew:

FRANK LESLIE & CO., 12, LAWN CRESCENT.

1909.

CALANTHE × DOMINYI, THE FIRST HOME-RAISED HYBRID ORCHID.

See pages vii *and* 50.

Grown at Kew. *Photo by F. W. Rolfe.*

Preface.

THE object of the present work is to provide an authentic list of existing Orchid hybrids of artificial origin, arranged on a uniform system, so as to show at a glance the crosses that have already been made, the adopted name of the hybrids, the works in which they have been described and figured, the original raiser or exhibitor, and the date of first flowering—in short it is intended as a guide to the already vast literature of the subject, and a standard of nomenclature. No apology is necessary for its production—a glance at the synonymy of some of the more popular hybrids enumerated should convince anyone of the need of such a Text Book.

Many difficulties have been met with during its execution. These have partly arisen through the same hybrid having been raised independently in different collections, but chiefly through want of a uniform system. Some raisers have considered all the seedlings from the same cross as forms of one, while others have given distinct names to different seedlings out of the same seed-pod. Some hybrids have received Latin or classical names, in accordance with the rules of binomial nomenclature, or have been distinguished by the joint names of the two parents, while others have been named in the vernacular. A few have been recorded without names. In addition to this there are many hybrids whose parentage has been lost, or whose records are incomplete, contradictory, or erroneous. Stray seedlings, loss or absence of record of parentage, change of ownership of unflowered seedlings, the contemporaneous flowering of the same hybrid in different collections, and the naming of hybrids without reference to the work of earlier operators, have all contributed their quota to the confusion arising from the multiplicity of systems of nomenclature, and the result may be seen in the following pages. The object of the work is to provide a remedy for this confusion, so far as possible, and we may now proceed to describe the plan of the work.

The work is divided into two parts:—

PART I. contains an enumeration of the species and hybrids which have been used as parents, these being arranged in alphabetical sequence, followed by the name of the resulting hybrid. The name of the first parent (in the alphabetical series) is given in heavy type in the centre of the column, and all the species with which it has been crossed are arranged alphabetically on the left, with the resulting hybrid on the right. Each parent appears again in its own alphabetical position, and thus the hybrids of any given species appear all together (those of a later date, of course appearing in the Addenda, which should also be consulted). Take Brassavola Digbyana, for example:—Eighteen hybrids of it appear on page 1—where also are found the eighteen species with which it has been crossed, in alphabetical order—but there are nineteen additions on page 239, so popular is this species as a parent. The name of the hybrid appears to the right of the second parent, and necessarily occurs twice, as may be seen under Aërides on page 1, where the two parents of A. × hybridum follow each other immediately, but in the very next case, *Zygonisia* × Rolfeana, they are separated by the whole width of the alphabet. Having found the name of the hybrid by means of its parents, one turns to Part II., where its history and other details are given. Part I. serves the double purpose of indicating the name of any given hybrid whose parents are known, and of shewing with what others a given species has been crossed.

PART II. contains, (1) an alphabetical enumeration of existing hybrids, each under its adopted name, followed by (2) the names of its parents, (3) references to descriptions and figures, (4) the name of the raiser or exhibitor, (5) date of first flowering, and (6) synonymy, these being followed in a few cases by (7) a short additional note. A few explanatory details must now be given under these several headings.

1. NAMES.—In all cases we have aimed at adopting the earliest correct name, but this is not invariably the name first published. Part II. commences with a few suggestions for securing greater uniformity of practice than at present exists, and the following paragraph may be repeated, as it has been our guide throughout:—

" Hybrids raised between species should receive specific names, Latin or classical, consisting of a single word—the use, however, of two short words being permissible where they can be connected with a hyphen. Short names should be used for preference, those exceeding six syllables being considered inadmissible."

Where the earliest name agrees with this proposition it has been adopted unmodified, but if not in agreement an attempt has been made to amend it. Thus the hybrid between Cattleya Dowiana and C. Eldorado appears as C. × Ingramiæ, not as C. × Lady Ingram, the earlier form of the name, and this in spite of the fact that another name, C. × Suzannæ, is already in correct form. The latter appeared five years later, and remains, as it has always been, a synonym. Similar names in the vernacular have been treated in the same way, where they could not conveniently be joined by a hyphen, but those consisting of a single word have been adopted. For the same reason Brassocattleya × Veitchii is preferred to the earlier B.-c. × Digbyano-Mossiæ, which consists of seven syllables, and B.-c. × Maronæ to B.-c. × Madame Charles Maron, which consists of three distinct words. Names formed by joining the specific appellations of the two parents without abbreviation have generally been avoided, as too long, though this does not always apply. Further, such names have often been used in some particular sense. Thus we have Odontoglossum × crispo-Hallii and O. × Hallio-crispum, the latter being the reversed cross, but both are here included under O. × Cooksoni. In a similar way O. × spectabile includes both O. × crispo-Harryanum and O. × Harryano-crispum. Names formed by combining portions of the names of the parents have been adopted.

2. Parents.—The names of the parents are given in their alphabetical sequence, and in most cases where the seed parent is definitely recorded the sign ♀ follows the name. But in many cases the record is not clear, and where doubt exists the sign has been omitted. Raisers might help to fill up some of these blanks, and to correct any that are known to be erroneous.

3. References.—We have aimed at giving a reference to the original record in all cases, though the remark may not always apply to reports of the same meeting in different papers. The hybrids exhibited at meetings of the Royal Horticultural Society are taken from the *Gardeners' Chronicle,* the records being continuous from the time of the epoch-making Calanthe × Dominyi. Those exhibited at meetings of the Société Nationale d' Horticulture de France are mostly taken from the Society's *Journal,* though some of the records appear a little earlier in contemporary publications, which are also cited in many cases. The *Orchid Review* is cited regularly, so far as the first reference and any additional information is concerned. Owing to the appearance in the first volume of the "History of Orchid Hybridisation," and the continuous records since, the information is in a very available form. Other works are cited where the information found appears to be of sufficient importance.

Figures.—Except in cases where they are unduly numerous, an attempt has been made to give a complete list of published figures, (avoiding, however, mere repetitions in the same work), and these are indicated by the letters "t" and "f." Any varietal names of the plants figured are given within brackets, immediately following the figure, as (v. oculata), (v. aureo-marginata), and (v. magnifica), which indicate varieties of Cattleya × Iris (p. 59). This point is mentioned, because it was found impracticable to include the multitudinous varieties which have appeared within the scope of the work, and a selection would have been both difficult and unsatisfactory.

LIST OF WORKS CITED.—Space has been economised by a great abbreviation of the titles of works that are frequently cited, but a detailed list is given at the end of the Introduction.

4. RAISER OR EXHIBITOR.—The names following the list of references are those of the Raiser or Exhibitor, for the two are sometimes different, and in such cases the actual raiser is often not on record. Where the two are known to be different the name of the actual raiser is given first, within brackets, followed by that of the exhibitor or introducer, as, for example, "Brassocattleya × heatonensis.—(Charlesworth) Hye."

5. DATE.—The date is intended to indicate the period of first flowering, but this is not always known with certainty. The date of the first record is taken unless there is information to the contrary, as in the case of Cattleya × Apollo, which flowered six years before it was recorded. It may be added here that seedlings which are recorded as unflowered are not included.

6. SYNONYMY.—This has proved an unusually difficult subject. A glance at page 97 will show that the well-known hybrid between Cattleya Mossiæ and Lælia purpurata (Læliocattleya × Canhamiana) has been recorded under nineteen distinct names, while Paphiopedilum × aureum has nearly forty synonyms. The latter may be an exceptional case, and a good example of the wide diversity of character often shown by secondary hybrids (even out of the same capsule), which seem to defy all attempts to name them satisfactorily, but generally speaking there has been a careless and even reckless multiplication of synonymy. But hybrids with imperfect or contradictory records have proved still more difficult. It was impossible to ascertain whether they should be regarded as distinct or as forms of something else, and many such have had to be omitted because of the sheer impossibility of knowing where to put them. The records or the plants may exist somewhere, and if so we hope that the absence of the names will be detected, and that such information will be forthcoming as will serve to clear up their history. A similar difficulty may have led to some of them being inserted in the wrong place, and if so we hope the errors will be pointed out. The synonyms are arranged as far as possible chronologically, which shows the history of any given hybrid better than an alphabetical arrangement.

ILLUSTRATIONS.—The text is illustrated with 120 figures of hybrids in half tone, which can well be left to speak for themselves. In two or three cases the parents are also shown.

7. ADDITIONAL NOTES.—These explain themselves, and it is only necessary to add that they either contain information not included else-

where, or call attention to points requiring elucidation. They might easily have been extended, but for the fear that the work might outgrow the limits assigned.

Addenda.—The Addenda has outgrown its intended limits, because the work has taken so much longer to complete than was anticipated. Roughly speaking, it may be said to contain three years additions, up to the end of 1907. As the plan is uniform throughout, it is only necessary to add that the numbers indicate the position in the body of the work. Numbers followed by letters, a, b, c. &c., indicate actual additions, but the remainder indicate additional information respecting names previously enumerated. It is intended to give later and future additions in the *Orchid Review*, so as to prevent the work from falling out of date. Particulars of this appear on page 326, after the Index.

Index.—As the adopted names of the hybrids, as well as those of their parents, follow a strict alphabetical sequence, it has been thought necessary to give only an Index of Synonyms. The Addenda, however, of both Parts I. and II. should not be overlooked by those who consult the work. Finally appears a List of Illustrations, 120 in number.

Omissions.—A few remarks under this head appear necessary. The absence of many hybrids of unknown or doubtful parentage has already been explained as unavoidable, but the omission of many well-known natural hybrids, as Odontoglossum × Andersonianum and Læliocattleya × elegans, may occasion surprise, especially as they appear in the list of parents. But a careful examination of the programme will show that, strictly speaking, natural hybrids do not come within the limits of the work, and can only be included when they have been raised artificially. They are more numerous than is generally realised, and their inclusion would have greatly extended the bulk and difficulty of the work. Many are also not in cultivation. It was necessary to draw the line somewhere, and it may yet be possible to deal with them elsewhere. The inclusion of the multitudinous named varieties was impossible, and a selection would have been both difficult and unsatisfactory, but we have been able to indicate those that have been figured, by the inclusion of the varietal name within brackets after the figure cited. The only other matter which occurs to us is the omission of Awards. They had been included, but it was found that there was such an utter want of uniformity between the systems of the different Societies, and the value of their awards at different periods, that the record was not worth the space required, and they were again cancelled. The records of the different Societies must be consulted for them.

Secondary and more Complex Hybrids.—A great deal of difficulty has been experienced in dealing with secondary hybrids and those of more complex parentage. Although we have treated them the same as primary hybrids it is felt that the plan is not satisfactory. Primary hybrids usually combine the characters of their parents in such a way that they can easily be recognised, and the variations assumed by different individuals from the same seed pod or the same cross are seldom great enough to prevent them from being recognised, and had the matter gone no further most of the difficulties could have been got over with very little trouble. But we now have hybrids of almost every degree of complexity—primary hybrids recrossed with their own parents, or crossed with other species or hybrids; hybrids derived from two species in which the parents are combined in equal and in unequal proportions; hybrids derived from three species, from four, and one even from five species; and while some of these complex hybrids vary enormously between themselves they also in some cases resemble others that are known to have been derived from different crosses. In short there are hybrids whose parentage cannot be fixed with any degree of certainty by an analysis of their characters, because of the amount of reversion that has taken place. Then there is that curious complication that certain crosses which from their parentage appear to be distinct, yet on analysis prove identical. To put the case differently, the same hybrid may be obtained in two different ways. For example, Odontoglossum nobile crossed with O. × spectabile would appear to be a distinct hybrid from O. × Rolfeæ crossed with O. × armainvillierense, but an analysis of parentage shows that both are composed of half O. nobile, a quarter O. crispum, and a quarter O. Harryanum. The two have been left under their respective names of O. × percultum and O. × Ossultoni, but it is at least a question whether they ought not to have been regarded as forms of one. And this is only a type of a series. Owing to these perplexing facts it becomes a question whether secondary and more complex hybrids may not in the future have to be treated in a different way from primary ones, or at all events have to be classified separately. The species in certain genera are now becoming so completely linked up by chains of hybrids that we may have to treat these complex forms purely as florists' flowers, selecting and naming only such as show distinct improvements on their predecessors and ignoring the remainder. Some such selective method seems almost inevitable in the near future.

With these remarks we commend the work to our readers, in the hope that their friendly criticism and kindly help will lead to its improvement in the event of another edition being called for.

To Messrs. R. T., G. B. and F. W. Rolfe our thanks are due for help in reading the proof and in some other details.

R. A. Rolfe,
C. C. Hurst.

September, 1908.

THE HISTORY OF ORCHID HYBRIDISATION.

"On the 28th of October, 1856," writes Dr. Lindley (*Gard. Chron.*, 1858, p. 4), "Mr. James Veitch, jun., of the Exotic Nursery, Chelsea, brought to the writer of this memorandum a flower of a Calanthe which combined the peculiar hairy forked spur and deeply lobed lip of the white Calanthe furcata, with the violet colour and broad middle lobe of the lip of C. Masuca. One might have said that the flowers were just intermediate between the two. . . . It appears that it had been raised in the Exotic Nursery, by Mr. Dominy, Messrs. Veitch's indefatigable and very intelligent foreman, between C. Masuca and C. furcata. The seed was obtained in 1854 by crossing these two species, was immediately sown, and in two years the seedlings were in flower. Nor is it the least remarkable circumstance connected with this production that it grows and flowers freely, while C. Masuca is a 'shy' plant. We therefore propose, with much pleasure, that the name of the hybrid be Calanthe Dominii, in order to put upon record the name of the first man who succeeded in this operation. He is indeed specially entitled to this distinction, not only in consequence of having produced other Orchidaceous mules, among which we understand are Cattleyas, but because of his eminent success in raising such plants from seed, as a matter of horticultural business." This was over a year after the event, but it is upon record that when Mr. Veitch first showed him the plant the Doctor exclaimed, "Why, you will drive the botanists mad!" This historic plant is figured as the frontispiece to the present work.

It was Mr. John Harris, a surgeon, of Exeter, who suggested to Dominy the possibility of muling Orchids, and who pointed out to him the reproductive organs seated in the column, and showed that the application of the pollinia to the stigmatic surface was analagous to the dusting of the stigma of other flowers with pollen.

The Rev. W. Herbert, Dean of Manchester, had previously suggested the possibility of raising hybrid Orchids. In a paper entitled "On Hybridisation among Vegetables," published in 1847 (*Journ. Hort. Soc.*, ii. p. 104), he remarked, "Cross breeding among Orchidaceous plants would perhaps lead to very startling results; but, unfortunately, they are not easily raised by seed. I have, however, raised Bletia, Cattleya, Orchis (Herminium) Monorchis and Ophrys aranifera from seed; and if I were not during the greater part of the year absent from the place where my plants are deposited, I think I could succeed in obtaining crosses in that order. I had well-formed pods last spring of Orchis by pollen of Ophrys as well as of other species of Orchis which had been forced; and if I had remained on the spot I think I should have obtained some cross-bred Orchidaceous seed. An intelligent gardener may do much for science by attempts of this kind, if he keeps accurate notes of what he attempts, and does not jump at immature conclusions." This is interesting as the earliest note on the subject that we have met with, and because it appeared at a time when there was a prevalent notion among gardeners that muling among Orchids was an impossibility. The results, however, must be classed among the "might-have-beens," and we may return to Dominy.

Dominy is said to have commenced his hybridising operations in 1853, with the genus Cattleya, and six years later the first flowers appeared. In August 1859, five seedling plants were exhibited at a meeting of the Horticultural Society by Messrs. Veitch, which were noted as extremely interesting, and as affording the first examples of well-marked and really showy new forms of Orchids produced by hybridisation. They were ultimately named Cattleya × hybrida, and it is unfortunate that Dominy did not carry out Dean Herbert's injunction to keep accurate records, for the parentage of this Cattleya was given first as C. granulosa and C. Harrisoniana, then as C. granulosa and C. Leopoldi, and finally as C. guttata and C. intermedia. C. guttata and Loddigesii are now accepted as the parents.

A second Cattleya, C. × Dominiana, obtained from C. maxima and C. intermedia, was exhibited in the November following.

In December, 1859, the beautiful Calanthe × Veitchii, a hybrid between C. rosea and C. vestita, made its appearance, and received a First-class Certificate from the Horticultural Society. This is one of the most popular hybrids yet raised, and is now largely cultivated as a very useful autumn-flowering plant.

In June, 1861, a fifth hybrid appeared, and also received a First-class Certificate, under the name of Goodyera × Dominii. Its parents were recorded as Goodyera discolor and Anœctochilus Lowii, now known as Hæmaria discolor and Dossinia marmorata, and thus was the first generic cross. It was afterwards called Dossinimaria × Dominii, and now seems to have been lost sight of.

In July, 1862, another ornamental-leaved Orchid was exhibited, under the name of Goodyera × Veitchii, also receiving a First-class Certificate. It was another generic hybrid, its parents being Hæmaria discolor and Macodes Petola. It is now known as Macomaria × Veitchii.

In September, 1863, the first Læliocattleya flowered, though the name did not appear till long afterwards. It was exhibited as Cattleya × exoniensis, and its parents were at first given as Cattleya Mossiæ and Lælia purpurata, but the second parent was afterwards corrected to L.

crispa. This parentage was ultimately confirmed by a repetition of the cross.

In May, 1864, the first hybrid Lælia appeared, though it was exhibited under the name of Cattleya × Pilcheri. Its parents were Lælia crispa and L. Perrinii, and it must have been one of Dominy's earliest hybrids, for it is said to have been raised in 1853. It is now known as Lælia × Pilcheri.

In May, 1865, another ornamental-leaved hybrid appeared, and received a First-class Certificate under the name of Anœctochilus × Dominii. Its parents were Hæmaria discolor and Anœctochilus Roxburghii (xanthophyllus), and the plant has since been named Anœctomaria × Dominii, being the third generic hybrid in the Anœctochilus group.

Early in 1867 another interesting generic hybrid flowered, its parents being Phaius grandifolius and Calanthe vestita. It was described by Reichenbach under the name of Phaius × irroratus, as "one of the beautiful evidences of Mr. Dominy's unrivalled talent in hybridising Orchids."

It was not until 1869 that a hybrid Cypripedium appeared, when C. × Harrisianum flowered for the first time. It was raised from C. villosum, fertilized with the pollen of C. barbatum, and was named by Prof. Reichenbach after Dr. Harris, of Exeter, who first gave Mr. Dominy the idea of hybridising Orchids. It is now called Paphiopedilum × Harrisianum, the tropical species being generically distinct.

In 1870 Cypripedium × Dominianum was described by Reichenbach, as a hybrid derived from C. caricinum fertilized with the pollen of C. caudatum. The author gave the alternative name of Selenipedium × Dominianum, thus adding a new genus to the list. It has since, however, been called Phragmopedilum × Dominianum, for it is now known that the genus Selenipedium proper is not in cultivation.

In the same year the first hybrid of Cypripedium Fairrieanum flowered, and was described by Reichenbach under the name of C. × vexillarium, as "one of the surprises which Mr. Dominy prepares for the Messrs. Veitch." C. barbatum was the seed parent. It is now referred to Paphiopedilum.

Early in 1871, Mr. Burbidge published in the *Gardeners' Chronicle* a list of the Hybrid Orchids raised up to that period, in which occurs the name of Aërides × hybridum, raised from A. affine and A. Fieldingii, thus adding another genus to the list. There is no clue to the date, and we do not know of another record, nor yet what became of the plant.

The first successful follower of Mr. Dominy appears to have been Mr. Cross, gardener to Lady Ashburton, of Melchet Court, Hampshire, who obtained Cypripedium × Ashburtoniæ by crossing C. barbatum with the pollen of C. insigne. It flowered and was described in 1871. Two years later he added C. × Crossianum, obtained from C. insigne crossed with the pollen of C. venustum. They were the first hybrids from C. insigne, and both were distributed by Messrs. Veitch. They are now referred to Paphiopedilum.

Mr. Seden next appeared upon the scene, having succeeded Mr. Dominy in the work at the Royal Exotic Nursery. His first hybrid was described as Cypripedium or Selenipedium × Sedeni. It was obtained by crossing Selenipedium longifolium with the pollen of S. Schlimii, and *vice versa*, both crosses flowering for the first time in 1873, and proving absolutely identical. It is a handsome hybrid, combining the best characters of both parents, and is now known as Phragmopedilum × Sedenii.

In 1873, also, what was really the first secondary hybrid appeaed, through it was described under the name of Cattleya × fausta. It was said to be "just intermediate between C. Loddigesii, as the ♀, or seed parent, and C. × exoniensis, as the ♂, or pollen parent. Two forms were described at the outset—the typical form, with rosy-lilac sepals and petals and a paler lip, and the variety radicans, distinguished by the presence of a number of dark purplish veins and streaks on the anterior part of the lip. Thus it afforded an indication of what has since been repeatedly confirmed, namely, that secondary hybrids are especially variable, plants raised from the same seed-pod often exhibiting great dissimilarity between themselves. It is now known as Læliocattleya × fausta.

The genus Dendrobium was next added to the list. In February, 1874, Dendrobium × Ainsworthii flowered for the first time, and received a First-class Certificate. It was raised in the collection of Dr. Ainsworth, of Lower Broughton, near Manchester, by Mr. Mitchell, between D. aureum ♀ and D. nobile ♂, and the seed is said to have been sown about seven years previously. It has since been recorded that plants of the same cross were raised by Mr. West, at the Fairfield Nursery, near Manchester, at about the same time.

The year 1874 also saw the additions of two other genera, Chysis and Zygopetalum, to the list, as the result of Mr. Seden's industry.

Chysis × Sedeni was recorded as a hybrid seedling between C. Limminghei ♀ and C. bractescens ♂, but Reichenbach suggested C. lævis as the pollen parent, which is clearly corrrect.

Zygopetalum × Sedeni was described as a hybrid between Z. Mackayi and Z. maxillare, the latter being the seed parent. It received a First-class Certificate from the Horticultural Society.

Hybrid Orchids were now decidedly on the increase, for at least ten were recorded during 1876, three of which were the work of new operators.

The first hybrid raised in the collection of John C. Bowring, Esq Forest Farm, Windsor, was Cypripedium × stenophyllum, its parents being C. Schlimii and C. caricinum. It is now referred to Phragmopedilum.

Mr. W. Swan, gardener to W. Leech, Esq., Oakley, Fallowfield, Manchester, made his debut with a hybrid between Cypripedium Dayanum ♀ and C. barbatum ♂, which was named C. × Swanianum by Reichanbach, in honour of the raiser.

Later in the year Messrs. Rollisson & Sons, of Tooting, flowered a hybrid which was said to have been raised by Mr. Mylam, from Cattleya granulosa crossed with the pollen of Lælia crispa, and was named Lælia × Mylamiana. It is said to have been raised in 1863, and is now known as Læliocattleya × Mylamiana.

The following year revealed the existence of another recruit, when Zygopetalum × Clayi flowered in the collection of Colonel Clay, of Birkenhead. Its parents were *Z.* crinitum and *Z.* maxillare, and it received a First-Class Certificate from the Manchester Botanical and Horticultural Society in April, 1877.

The event of 1878 was the flowering of a very handsome hybrid from Cattleya Dowiana, which was described under the name of Lælia × Dominiana. The second parent was said to be "some Lælia, probably elegans," but long afterwards it was proved by the repetition of the cross to be L. purpurata. It was the last of Mr. Dominy's hybrids, and a fitting climax to his labours, for if depth and richness of colouring be the criterion of excellence it is not only unrivalled among this raiser's productions, but is scarcely surpassed at the present day. It is now known as Læliocattleya × Dominiana.

It is evident that some of Mr. Dominy's hybrids were not recorded when they flowered for the first time, for Dendrobium × Dominyanum (D. nobile ♀ × Linawianum ♂), which was described in 1878, was said to have been obtained by Mr. Dominy "a very long time ago," and although not recorded until four years after D. × Ainsworthii it was evidently the first hybrid in the genus. Cattleya × felix also, described in 1876, was said to be one of the oldest seedlings raised by Mr. Dominy. Its parents were Lælia crispa and Cattleya Schilleraiana, and it was afterwards named Læliocattleya × felix. Again, Cypripedium × calophyllum, which was described in 1880, was said to be "one of the oldest artificial hybrids, having been gained at the Royal Exotic Nursery a long time ago." It was a seedling from C. barbatum and C. venustum, and is now called Paphiopedilum × calophyllum.

As we have been unable to mention all Mr. Dominy's hybrids individually we may here remark that they number twenty-five, and comprise six Cattleyas, one Lælia, six hybrids between the two genera, two Calanthes, one hybrid between Calanthe and Phaius, three Cypripediums, one Selenipedium, one Dendrobium, one Aërides (probably lost), and three hybrids of the Anœctochilus group. They extended over a period of more than twenty years. Mr. Dominy's name will always be remembered as the pioneer of this interesting branch of horticulture. In 1880, on the occasion of his retirement from Messrs. Veitch's service, the Royal Horticultural Society presented him with a Gold Medal in recognition of his services to horticulture.

The genus Lycaste was added to the list in 1878, when a hybrid between L. Skinneri and L. Deppei flowered in the collection of Mr. W. Marshall, of Enfield. It was recorded without a name, but was afterwards called Lycaste × hybrida.

Hybrids now began to increase rapidly in number, and we shall only be able to indicate a few of the more prominent landmarks. Half-a-dozen novelties appeared in 1879, belonging to genera already mentioned.

In 1880 another genus was added to the list, when the handsome Masdevallia × Chelsoni flowered for the first time. It was obtained by Mr. Seden from M. amabilis crossed with the pollen of M. Veitchiana, and the flowers exhibit a charming combination of orange and scarlet.

In 1880 a batch of four hybrids raised by a new operator appeared, and were described together as Cypripedium × meirax, × chloroneurum, × politum, and × melanophthalmum. Reichenbach spoke of them as a lot of fresh hybrids, raised by Mr. Robert Warner, of Broomfield, whose history is not known, probably in consequence of a lost pocket book. All of them he believes had C. venustum for one parent. Their history was discussed some time ago (*Orch. Rev.*, 1905, pp. 291-293).

In 1881 a hybrid Anguloa flowered, in the collection of John C. Bowring, Esq., Forest Farm, Windsor. It was named Anguloa × media by Reichanbach, who spoke of it as no doubt derived from A. Clowesii and A. Ruckeri.

The existence of two new hybridists was also revealed, for Calanthe × Barberiana flowered in the collection of John T. Barber, Esq., Spondon, Derby, having been raised from C. Turneri nivalis crossed with the pollen of C. vestita, while C. × Sandhurstiana was raised by P. H. Gosse, Esq., of Sandhurst, Torquay, from C. rosea crossed with the pollen of C. vestita, and thus is a form of C. × Veitchii.

For a quarter of a century English hybridists appeared to monopolise the field, but in 1881 a French hybrid flowered. In the *Revue Horticole* for that year (p. 346), the flowering of two unnamed seedling Cattleyas is recorded by M. Bergman. They were raised by M. Alfred Bleu, of Paris, from C. intermedia crossed with the pollen of C. Aclandiæ. The cross afterwards received the name of C. × calumnata. Whether this was its first flowering is not quite clear, for another hybrid which afterwards received the name of Cattleya × fimbriata has been confused with it, under the same record, and Mr. Bleu is said to have flowered this in 1878. The latter appears to have been the first French hybrid, and is now considered to be a form of the natural hybrid C. × Isabella.

The next hybridist which we find evidence of was Mr. Fraser, of Derncleugh, near Aberdeen, who raised Masdevallia × Fraseri. It was derived from M. ignea ♀ and M. coccinea ♂, and flowered in 1882.

In 1882 also Cypripedium × Dauthieri was described, from the establishment of Messrs. Van Houtte, of Ghent. Its origin was a mystery, but it was soon identified as a form of C. × Harrisianum, and, curiously enough, it has since been traced as a stray seedling from Messrs. Veitch's establishment (See *Orch. Rev.*, 1899, p. 71).

In the following year we find Sir Trevor Lawrence, Bart., included in the ranks of the hybridists, he having raised the brilliant Calanthe × porphyrea from C. vestita and C. labrosa.

In 1884 the flowering is recorded of Cypripedium × Laforcadei, raised by M. Bauer, of Paris, but it is a form of the earlier C. × Ashburtonæ.

In 1885 the first hybrid Thunia appeared, and, curiously enough, the same hybrid was raised by two different operators—first by Mr. Toll, of Manchester, and shortly afterwards by Mr. Seden, in both cases from T. Marshalliana ♀ and T. Bensonæ ♂. Plants were exhibited simultaneously at one of the Royal Botanical Society's Shows, in 1885, the former as T. × Wrigleyana, the latter as T. ×. Veitchiana. Under the latter name it was eventually described.

In 1886, a very striking novelty appeared, and was described by Reichenbach under the name of Lælia × Batemaniana. It was raised by Mr. Seden from Sophronitis grandiflora crossed with the pollen of Cattleya intermedia, and flowered in August, 1886, when a little over five years old. Reichenbach called it "a lovely gem, a miniature Lælia" and added:—"This novelty offers a wide field for considerations of nomenclature. Are all hybrids between what we call genera to get intermediate names? . . . The effect of mixing a Sophronitis and a Cattleya is a Lælia; hence I must reduce Sophronitis to Lælia, except S. violacea, with a remodelled character." It was dedicated to the veteran Orchidist, James Bateman, Esq., of Worthing, whose name had been known in connection with Orchids for upwards of half a century. The plant is now called Sophrocattleya × Batemaniana.

Another generic hybrid might have been added to the list, for Messrs. Veitch flowered a hybrid whose origin had been lost, and Reichenbach could only suggest Zygopetalum maxillare as one parent, and called it Zygopetalum × leopardinum. A year later the flowering of a hybrid from Colax jugosus afforded a clue, and the present plant was transferred to Zygocolax.

The first artificial hybrid Phalænopsis flowered in 1886, and possesses a double interest, being the first successful experiment undertaken to prove the origin of a wild plant. When in 1853, Phalænopsis intermedia first appeared, as a single plant in an importation of Phalænopsis Aphrodite (then called P. amabilis) received from the Philippines, Dr. Lindley suggested that it might be a natural hybrid between that species and P. rosea. With a view to prove this hypothesis, Mr. Seden crossed P. rosea with the pollen of P. Aphrodite, and when the resulting progeny flowered for the first time, in 1886, it proved absolutely identical with the wild P. × intermedia.

In 1886, the work of two other hybridists appeared. Cypripedium × Io was raised in the collection of Norman C. Cookson, Esq., Oakwood, Wylam-on-Tyne, from C. Argus and C. Lawrenceanum, and C. × apiculatum in that of D. O. Drewett, Esq., of Riding Mill-on-Tyne, from C. barbatum and C. Boxallii.

The work was now being rapidly extended over a wider field, for in 1887 hybrids raised by at least seven new operators flowered for the first time, and Reichenbach remarked "All Orchidic England is engaged in the procreation of mules." We may briefly mention them, but the great extension of the work will prevent us from giving more than a selection in future. Dr. Harris, of Lamberhurst, Kent (a namesake of the gentleman who gave Dominy the idea of hybridising Orchids), flowered Cattleya × Harrisii, raised from C. Leopoldi and C. Mendelii, C. × Miss Harris, from C. Mossiæ and C. Schilleriana, and Lælia × Novelty, from L. pumila and Læliocattleya × elegans. W. Vanner, Esq., Camden Wood, Chislehurst, flowered Dendrobium × Vannerianum, raised from D. moniliforme (japonicum) and D. Falconeri. Captain Hincks, of Breckenbrough, Thirsk, Yorks, raised Masdevallia × Hincksiana, from M. tovarensis and M. ignea. Mr. F. Horn, gardener to Baron N. Rothschild, of Vienna, flowered Cypripedium × Hornianum from C. superbiens and C. Spicerianum. Messrs. F. Sander & Co., St. Albans, flowered Masdevallia × Geleniana, raised from M. caudata and M. xanthina, Reichenbach remarking "This is the *debut* of Mr. F. Sander in Orchid hybridising, and very many more are forthcoming." Lastly, we find two Cypripediums, × Charles Canham and × Mrs. Canham, said to have been raised by an amateur, whose name was not divulged, but has since been recorded as Mr. James Douglas. They were obtained from C. superbiens and C. villosum, and the reverse cross, and were sent out by Messrs. Veitch.

Among the numerous hybrids of 1887 the most interesting was Zygocolax × Veitchii, raised by Mr. Seden from Zygopetalum crinitum fertilised with the pollen of Colax jugosus, which flowered when a little over five years old. It marks the commencement of a new era in the nomenclature of generic Orchid hybrids. Hitherto such plants had been referred to one or the other of the parent genera, but with very unsatisfactory results, and the precedent adopted in another group of compounding a new name from the joint names of the parent genera was now extended to Orchids (See Rolfe, "On bigeneric Orchid Hybrids," *Journ. Linn. Soc.* xxiv. pp. 156-170, t. 48). Seven names for generic hybrids were there established.

In 1888 the genus Epidendrum was added to the list, when E. × O'Brienianum flowered in Messrs. Veitch's establishment, having been raised by Mr. Seden by crossing E. evectum with the pollen of E. radicans. The first hybrid from Cattleya citrina also flowered when 6½ years old. It was raised by Dr. Harris, of Lamberhurst, the seed parent being C. intermedia. It was called C. × citrino-intermedia. About thirty other new hybrids were recorded, including the work of at least four new operators.

The first artificial hybrid Miltonia flowered in 1889. Various experiments are said to have been made with this and the allied genus Odontoglossum, and young seedlings had been raised, though none survived until reaching the flowering stage. It was M. Alfred Bleu, of Paris, who first attained success, M. × Bleuana flowering for the first time in January, 1889, when rather under five years old. Its parents were M. vexillaria ♀ and M. Roezlii ♂.

The first hybrid of Brassavola Digbyana, then known as Lælia Digbyana, also appeared. It was raised by Messrs. Veitch, Cattleya Mossiæ being the seed parent, and received an Award of Merit from the R. H. S. in April, 1889, under the name of Lælia × Digbyano-Mossiæ. It was afterwards referred to Læliocattleya, and ultimately to Brassocattleya.

In 1889 the first hybrid Cymbidium also flowered, having been raised by Messrs. Veitch from C. Lowianum and C. eburneum. It received a First-class Certificate from the R. H. S. on March 12th, 1889, under the name of Cymbidium × eburneo-Lowianum. It is now called C. × Veitchii.

The most noteworthy addition to the list recorded during 1890 was Epiphronitis × Veitchii, a new generic cross, raised by Mr. Seden from Sophronitis grandiflora crossed with the pollen of Epidendrum radicans. It received a First-class Certificate from the R. H. S. on June 24th, 1890. It is remarkable for having the habit of a greatly dwarfed edition of the pollen parent, the influence of the seed parent being chiefly seen in its larger flower and slightly darker colour.

In 1890 also an artificially-raised hybrid Odontoglossum first reached the flowering stage, in the collection of Baron Edmond de Rothschild, of Armainvilliers, near Paris. About the end of 1884, M. Leroy fertilised O. crispum with the pollen of O. luteopurpureum, and in May, 1890, one out of a batch of five seedlings flowered, and was named O. × Leroyanum, though it was immediately afterwards referred to O. × Wilckeanum, a natural hybrid with the same parentage.

The first hybrid Phaius of pure parentage also flowered during 1890, though the genus had previously been crossed with Calanthe. Phaius × Cooksoni was raised in the collection of Norman C. Cookson, Esq., Oakwood, Wylam-on-Tyne, where it was raised from P. Wallichii, crossed with the pollen of P. simulans (formerly confused with P. tuberculosus). The seed was sown in December, 1887, and a plant flowered in March, 1890, when only two years and a quarter old.

The first hybrid Stanhopea was raised in Germany, in the collection of Herr Spindler, of Spindlersfeld, from S. oculata crossed with the pollen of S. tigrina. It flowered in the summer of 1890, and was described and figured as S. × Spindlerianum.

Disa × Veitchii, the first hybrid in the genus, was raised by Messrs. James Veitch and Sons, from D. racemosa crossed with the pollen of D. grandiflora, and flowered when only a year and nine months old, thus creating a record for quickness of flowering. It received a First-class Certificate and a Silver-gilt Flora Medal from the Royal Horticultural Society on June 9th, 1891.

The second artificially-raised Odontoglossum flowered in 1891, and is interesting because the plant was raised to prove the parentage of a wild hybrid. Odontoglossum × excellens had been described by Reichenbach, in 1881, as a natural hybrid between O. Pescatorei and O. tripudians, but it was soon suggested that the second parent must have been O. triumphans. Mr. Seden accordingly crossed O. Pescatorei with the pollen of O. triumphans, and when the resulting seedling flowered it proved to be identical with the wild plant.

In 1892 a hybrid having three genera in its composition flowered. It was raised by Messrs. James Veitch & Sons from Sophronitis grandiflora ♀ and Læliocattleya × Schilleriana ♂, and received the name of Sophrocattleya × Veitchiana. The plant is now known as Sophrocatlælia × Veitchiana, which indicates its parentage more correctly.

The first hybrid Vanda was described in 1893, under the name of Vanda × Miss Joaquim. It was raised at Singapore, by the lady whose name it bears, from V. Hookeriana and V. teres, which species are said to be cultivated in every garden in Singapore. It is a very handsome hybrid.

In 1894 a hybrid Sobralia appeared, namely, S. × Veitchii, raised by Messrs. James Veitch & Sons, from S. macrantha crossed with the pollen of S. xantholeuca. It received a First-class Certificate from the R. H. S. in July, 1894.

In 1894 Sophrolælia was also added to the list. Messrs. Veitch flowered a hybrid between Lælia Dayana ♀ and Sophronitis grandiflora ♂, which was exhibited by them under the name of Sophrocattleya × læta, but shortly afterwards it was described as Sophrolælia × læta (*O. R.* 1894, p. 334).

The third generic hybrid recorded in 1894 was Epilælia × Hardyana, a plant being exhibited at a meeting of the R. H. S. in November, 1894, by Messrs. Sander. It had, however, according to a letter from Mr. Sander, previously flowered, in February, 1891. It was raised in the collection of Baron N. Rothschild, of Vienna, by M. Joly, from Epidendrum ciliare ♀ and Lælia anceps ♂.

In November, 1896, another hybrid Odontoglossum appeared, and received a First-class Certificate from the R.H.S. under the name of O. × crispo-Hallii. It was raised in the collection of N. C. Cookson, Esq., Oakwood, Wylam-on-Tyne, from O. Hallii ♀ and O. crispum ♂, and was afterwards called O. × Cooksoni.

About the same time Calanthe × albata flowered in the establishment of Messrs. Sander, at St. Albans, and is remarkable as the first hybrid between the deciduous and evergreen sections of the genus. Its parents are C. veratrifolia ♀ and C. × Cooksoni (a form of C. × Sedeni) ♂. Many unsuccessful attempts to unite the two sections had previously been made.

In 1897 a genuine Epicattleya appeared—for the earlier natural hybrid Epicattleya × guatemalensis had been referred to Cattleya. The novelty was raised by Messrs. James Veitch and Sons, from Cattleya Bowringiana crossed with the pollen of Epidendrum radicans, and received the name of Epicattleya × matutina. In its reed-like stems it most resembles the pollen parent.

The genus Spathoglottis was also added to the list, Messrs. Veitch flowering the handsome S. × aureo-Vieillardii, said to have been raised from S. aurea ♀ and S. Vieillardii ♂. It has, however, since been pointed out that the seed parent was S. Kimballiana, which at that time was thought to be synonymous with S. aurea, but is now known to be different. The hybrid is now called S. × Veitchii, and is figured at page 311.

A second hybrid having three genera involved in its parentage also appeared during 1897, receiving an Award of Merit from the R.H.S. under the name of Brassocatlælia × Lindleyano-elegans. It was raised in the collection of Sir Trevor Lawrence, Bart., from Brassocattleya × Lindleyana and Læliocattleya × elegans, both parents being themselves generic hybrids. It is now called Brassocatlælia × Lawrencei.

The most interesting hybrids of 1898 were three Odontoglossums raised in the establishment of M. Charles Vuylsteke, of Loochristi, Ghent. First came O. × loochristiense, raised from O. crispum and O. triumphans, and afterwards O. × crispo-Harryanum, from O. crispum and O. Harryanum, the latter receiving a First-class Certificate at the Temple Show. In both cases O. crispum was the seed parent. The former has since proved identical with the natural hybrid O. × harvengtense, and the latter is now known as O. × spectabile. The third of the series was O. × Rolfeæ, obtained by crossing O. nobile (Pescatorei) with the pollen of O. Harryanum.

In 1899 another generic hybrid appeared, being raised by Messrs. Linden, of Brussels, from Zygopetalum crinitum fertilised with the pollen of Batemannia Colleyi. It was described under the name of Zygobatemannia × Mastersii, in compliment to the late Dr. Maxwell T. Masters, F.R.S.

The genus Angræcum was added to the list in 1899, Messrs. Veitch flowering a handsome hybrid from A. sesquipedale ♀ and A. superbum ♂, which received a First-class Certificate from the R.H.S. under the name of A. × Veitchii. At the same time a Silver Flora Medal was given to the raiser, Mr. John Seden.

A hybrid between Lælia cinnabarina ♀ and Brassavola Digbyana ♂ was also raised by Messrs. Veitch, and received an Award of Merit from the R.H.S. under the name of L. × Mrs. M. Gratrix, for the pollen parent was then referred to Lælia. The hybrid is now known as Brassolælia × Gratrixiæ.

In 1902 three new generic hybrids were recorded. Leptolælia × Veitchii was raised by Messrs. Veitch from Leptotes bicolor ♀ and Lælia cinnabarina ♂. Zygonisia × Rolfeana was raised by Messrs. Sander, from Zygopetalum maxillare (Gautieri) ♀ and Aganisia lepida ♂, and received an Award of Merit at the Holland House Show. Phaiocymbidium × chardwarense was raised in the collection of G. F. Moore, Esq., Chardwar, Bourton-on-the-Water, Glos., it is said from Phaius Wallichii (P. grandifolius was at first recorded) ♀ and Cymbidium giganteum ♂, but the point requires confirmation, for the plant has entirely the character of the Phaius parent, except as regards colour.

In 1903 the genus Cynorchis was added to the list, when C. × kewensis flowered for the first time at Kew, where it was raised from C. Lowiana fertilised with the pollen of C. purpurascens. The cross was made in the spring of 1901, and the seed sown in the following autumn, and germinated very quickly, while in May, 1903, two of the seedlings flowered, when little over two years had elapsed from the time that the cross was made.

A hybrid from Schomburgkia tibicinis ♀ and Cattleya Mossiæ ♂ also appeared, having been raised by Messrs. Dallemagne and Co. It is known under the name of Schombocattleya × spiralis, and is figured at page 233.

Vanda × Maronæ was another interesting addition, which was raised by M. Ch. Maron from V. teres ♀ and V. suavis ♂, and exhibited at the Temple Show. It was the second hybrid in the genus, and the first raised in Europe.

The year 1904 produced a sensational hybrid when the six-flowered inflorescence of Odontioda × Vuylstekeæ appeared at the Temple Show, and received both a First-class Certificate and a Silver-gilt Lindley Medal. It was raised by M. Charles Vuylsteke, of Ghent, from Cochlioda Nœtzliana and Odontoglossum nobile (Pescatorei), and is figured at page 281.

Other interesting hybrids of the year were the beautiful albino Cattleya × Peetersiæ, raised by M. Peeters, of Brussels, from C. Gaskelliana alba × C. Warneri alba, Sophrocattleya × Doris, raised by Messrs. William Bull & Sons, from S. grandiflora and C. Dowiana aurea, and S.-c. × Atreus, by Messrs. Veitch, from S. grandiflora and C. Lawrenceana.

In 1905 three new generic hybrids appeared. Dialælia × Veitchii was raised by Messrs. James Veitch & Sons, from Diacrium bicornutum and Lælia cinnabarina, and received a Botanical Certificate from the Scientific committee of the R.H.S. in the spring of the year. It was described as most resembling the Diacrium in habit, as well as in the colour of the flowers.

Odontioda × Lairesseæ was raised by M. A. de Lairesse, of Liége, Belgium, from Odontoglossum crispum crossed with the pollen of Miltonia Warscewiczii, and received an Award of Merit from the R.H.S. on July 20th, 1905. It is most like the pollen parent in habit, as well as in the colour of the flowers, which, however, are larger and modified in shape. It is figured on page 217.

Epidiacrium × gattonense is a hybrid raised in the collection of Jeremiah Colman, Esq., Gatton Park, Reigate, from Diacrium bicornutum and Epidendrum radicans. It was described as most like a dwarf form of the latter, and bearing a terminal head of reddish scarlet flowers. It was exhibited without a name on May 9th, 1905.

The genus Promenæa was also added to the list in 1905, a seedling from P. stapleioides ♀ and P. xanthina ♂ having flowered in the collection of De Barri Crawshay, Esq., Rosefield, Sevenoaks, which received an Award of Merit from the R.H.S. in May, 1905, under the name of P. × Crawshayana. It is now believed to be a form of the natural hybrid P. × Rollissoni.

The first two hybrids of Odontoglossum Edwardii were also recorded, namely O. × Lairessei, raised by M. A. de Lairesse, of Liége, from O. Cervantesii ♀ and O. Edwardii ♂, and O. × Thompsonianum, which flowered in the collection of W. Thompson, Esq., of Stone, and received a First-class Certificate from the R.H.S., from O. Edwardii ♀ and O. crispum ♂. This, however, was raised in the collection of D. B. Rappart, Esq., of Liscard.

A handsome hybrid from O. Rossi crossed with the pollen of O. × spectabile flowered in 1905 with Messrs. Charlesworth & Co., and received a First-class Certificate from the R.H.S. on December 5th under the name of O. × Smithii. It was the first successful attempt to unite the Mexican Odontoglossums with those of the O. crispum group. It is figured on page 290.

In 1906 an additional generic hybrid appeared, namely Brassoepidendrum × stamfordiense, which was exhibited by H. T. Pitt, Esq., Rosslyn, Stamford Hill. It is said to have been derived from Epidendrum Parkinsonianum × Brassavola glauca.

The first hybrid Cœlogyne also appeared in 1906, in the collection of Col. Brymer, Ilsington House, Dorchester. It is said to have been raised from C. Dayana × C. asperata, and received the name of C. × Brymeriana. It bore a pendulous raceme of nineteen flowers.

Several interesting hybrids appeared in 1907, one of the earliest being the beautiful Odontioda × Bradshawiæ, which received a First-class Certificate from the R.H.S. on January 19th. It was raised by Messrs. Charlesworth & Co., from Cochlioda Nœtzliana ♀ and Odontoglossum crispum ♂, and is figured on page 280. Later in the year came the brilliant Odontioda × Devossiana, raised by M. H. Graire, of Amiens, France, from Odontoglossum Edwardii fertilised with the pollen of Cochlioda Nœtzliana, which received a First-class Certificate on October 29th. Another hybrid from Odontoglossum Edwardii was raised by Messrs. William Bull & Sons, and received an Award of Merit on January 8th, under the name of O. × Aliciæ. O. × spectabile was the pollen parent. It is figured on page 282. Odontonia × Elwoodii was raised by Messrs. Charlesworth & Co. from Odontoglossum cirrhosum and Miltonia Roezlii. Cœlogyne × Colmanii was raised in the collection of Jeremiah Colman, Esq., Gatton Park, Reigate, from C. speciosa and C. cristata alba, and received an Award of Merit from the R.H.S. It is figured at page 265. Lastly may be mentioned Brassocattleya × Alexanderi, a striking hybrid from Cattleya citrina crossed with the pollen of Brassavola Digbyana, which was raised in the collection of Major G. L. Holford, at Westonbirt, and received an Award of Merit from the R.H.S. in March, 1907.

This hasty survey, while indicating how the work was being constantly extended over a wider field, fails to show what was being done with the earlier genera, but in the following pages may be seen what substantial progress was being made. The genus Paphiopedilum heads the list, with over 750 hybrids; Læliocattleya follows with over 360, Cattleya has over 230, Dendrobium and Odontoglossum have each over 90 (and the latter is growing very rapidly), Lælia and Masdevallia muster over 40, Phragmopedilum over 30, and Phalænopsis over 20, from which the numbers dwindle down to units in the case of Aërides, Angræcum, Cynorchis, Promenæa and Thunia.

Generic Hybrids.

The number of generic hybrids enumerated is 25, of which the following 23 are bigeneric :—

Anœctomaria,	from Anœctochilus and Hæmaria.
Brassocattleya,	,, Brassavola and Cattleya.
Brassoepidendrum,	,, ,, and Epidendrum.
Brassolælia,	,, ,, ,, Lælia.
Dialælia,	,, Diacrium and Lælia.
Dossinimaria,	,, Dossinia and Hæmaria.
Epicattleya,	,, Cattleya and Epidendrum.
Epidiacrium,	,, Diacrium ,, ,,
Epilælia,	,, Epidendrum and Lælia.
Epiphronitis,	,, ,, ,, Sophronitis.
Læliocattleya,	,, Cattleya and Lælia.
Leptolælia,	,, Lælia and Leptotes.
Macomaria,	,, Hæmaria and Macodes.
Odontioda,	,, Cochlioda and Odontoglossum.
Odontonia,	,, Miltonia ,, ,,
Phaiocalanthe,	,, Calanthe and Phaius.
Phaiocymbidium,	,, ? Cymbidium and Phaius.
Schombocattleya,	,, Cattleya and Schomburgkia.
Sophrocattleya,	,, ,, ,, Sophronitis.
Sophrolælia,	,, Lælia and Sophronitis.
Zygobatemannia,	,, Batemannia and Zygopetalum.
Zygocalyx,	,, Colax ,, ,,
Zygonisia,	,, Aganisia ,, ,,

Two others have three genera in their composition, these, of course, being secondary hybrids. They are :—

Brassocatlælia, from Brassavola, Cattleya and Lælia.

Sophrocatlælia, ,, Cattleya, Lælia and Sophronitis.

An analysis of the parentage of these trigeneric hybrids may be interesting. Brassocatlælia includes ten distinct hybrids, seven of which were derived from the intercrossing of Brassavola and Læliocattleya, one from Brassocattleya and Lælia, one from Brassolælia and Cattleya, and one from Brassocattleya and Læliocattleya. Of Sophrocatlælia four hybrids are known, two of these being derived from the intercrossing of Cattleya and Sophrolælia, and two from Læliocattleya and Sophronitis. The arrangement may seem puzzling at first sight, but a moment's consideration will show that in each case the same three genera are represented, though in slightly different proportions. This brings out the curious fact that the same result may be reached by several different ways, and it may be added that when hybrids between Brassocattleya and Brassolælia appear, also between Brassolælia and Læliocattleya, they will also have to be included under Brassocatlælia, which will exhaust the possible ways of obtaining this artificial or hybrid genus.

In one of these fourteen trigeneric hybrids, namely Brassocatlælia × Lawrencei, both the parents were themselves hybrids, and an analysis shows that it has four species in its composition, Brassavola tuberculata, Cattleya intermedia, C. Leopoldi, and Lælia purpurata.

Specific Composition of Hybrids.

An analysis of the specific composition of the hybrids enumerated would give some curious results. Hybrids may be divided into primary and secondary, and the latter include hybrids of various degrees of complexity. There are hybrids derived from two species, from three, from four, and in one case even from five, and a brief consideration of these several classes will be interesting.

Primary Hybrids are the result of crossing distinct species, sometimes belonging to different genera, and necessarily represent the first stage in the process. Primary hybrids almost invariably show a blend of the parental characters, and can usually be fairly described as intermediate, though in a few cases one parent is apparently prepotent over the other, and thus may be described as dominant. The seedlings, even out of the same capsule, often vary slightly between themselves, and the variation is increased when different varieties of the same species are used, but the differences are seldom great, and no difficulty is experienced in assigning all as forms of the same hybrid. Reversing the cross seldom makes any difference, for in many cases where the reverse cross has been made the result is practically identical.

Prepotency, already mentioned, sometimes exhibits itself in a very peculiar way. Either parent may exert this prepotent character. In the case of Cattleya × lamberhurstensis it is the seed parent, C. intermedia, which is dominant, but in Epiphronitis × Veitchii it is the pollen parent, Epidendrum radicans, and the character is so marked, both in habit and floral structure, that without actual evidence no one would suspect that it was a seedling from Sophronitis grandiflora. Epicattleya × matutina, Epilælia × Charlesworthii and a few others exhibit the same kind of prepotency. All are suspected to be cases of partial reversion, the hybrids resembling the more ancestral of the two parents. The idea is borne out by the disappearance of other characters which may be considered as of comparatively recent development. For example, the peculiar beak-like staminode of Paphiopedilum Rothschildianum is invariably lost in its hybrids, the organ reverting to the more typical shield-shaped form.

FALSE HYBRIDS.—There is another kind of prepotency—if the term is indeed applicable—in which the seedlings resemble the seed parent entirely, the influence of the pollen parent being apparently lost. Zygopetalum Mackayi furnishes one of the best known examples, for it has been crossed with more than one species of Odontoglossum, also with such diverse plants as Lycaste Skinneri, Oncidium tigrinum, and Lælia anceps, and yet the seedlings in each case resembled the seed parent entirely. It is not a case of self-fertilisation, for in each case the pollen of the Zygopetalum was carefully removed (and unless the foreign pollen is applied to the stigma no capsule is produced). It is suspected to be a case of parthenogenesis, the stimulus of pollination sufficing to cause the ovules to develop into buds. These and other similar cases are worthy of further investigation from a biological standpoint, but they are outside the scope of the present work. The very term "false" hybrids implies a doubt whether they are hybrids at all in a true sense.

SECONDARY HYBRIDS form a very numerous class. They have arisen from the intercrossing of primary hybrids, either with their own parent species, with different species, or with each other. Their existence necessarily involves the question of the fertility of hybrids, which we have not touched upon, but which for the present may, in the majority of cases, be taken for granted. The one striking difference between secondary and primary hybrids is the much greater variability of the former. It may not be equally apparent in all cases, especially where the original parents are very closely allied, but it is so common as to have attracted universal attention, and various attempts have been made to explain it. The facts are beyond dispute, and the controversial side of the question may be omitted.

This great variability was noticed when the very first batch of secondary hybrids flowered, as already mentioned (p. x.), and it may be interesting to record an observation made at the time. Five of the seedlings of Lælio-cattleya × fausta (then called Cattleya × fausta) were painted by Mr. John Day, who remarked as follows (*Orch. Draw.* xxx. t. 31): "Mr. Seden tells me that they raised seven plants of it only (or that only seven have flowered), and they were all different. This he attributes to the fact that the pollen parent, Cattleya exoniensis, is itself a hybrid between C. Mossiæ and Lælia crispa, and some of the offspring have run back to their grandparents, and some have taken more to their mamma, C. Loddigesii." The remark is interesting on another account, for it shows that Mr. Seden had then correctly diagnosed the much-disputed parentage of the pollen parent.

SECONDARY HYBRIDS DERIVED FROM TWO SPECIES are necessarily primary hybrids intercrossed with one of their own parents, and these now form a very numerous class. Phragmopedilum × Sedenii re-crossed with

P. longifolium and P. Schlimii, and yielding respectively P. × Ainsworthii (calurum), and P. cardinale, may be mentioned as two familiar examples. In each case they exhibit a partial return to the characters of the original species. One of them has been carried further, for P. × cardinale has been re-crossed with P. Schlimii, yielding P. × Ada (see p. 226), in which P. Schlimii is represented three times over, thus giving seven-eighths of that species and only one-eighth P. longifolium. In a similar way Dendrobium × Ainsworthii has been re-crossed with D. × nobile, yielding D. × Rubens, and with D. aureum, yielding D. × Gem; while Læliocattleya × Schilleriana has been re-crossed with Cattleya intermedia, yielding L.-c. × Zampa, and with Lælia purpurata yielding L.-c. × Horniana. There are even smaller degrees of difference. For example, Phragmopedilum × Sedenii has been crossed with both P. × Ainsworthii and P. × cardinale, and although the parents are themselves separated by only a fractional difference (one eighth) the respective hybrids have received separate names. We have left them as P. × Lemoinierianum and P. × Rosy-Gem, but it will be seen that the interval separating the original P. longifolium and P. Schlimii has been almost filled up by a series of slightly differing intermediate forms, involving a very difficult question of nomenclature.

Secondary Hybrids combining Three Species may result from the intercrossing of primary hybrids with a third species, as in the case of Læliocattleya × fausta, just mentioned, or from the union of primary hybrids that have one parent in common, as in the variable Paphiopedilum × Charlesianum, whose parents, P. × Leeanum and P. × nitens, are both partly derived from P. insigne. Combinations of three species may also be formed by crosses of increased complexity. It is among hybrids formed by the union of three distinct species that the remarkably wide range of variation observed among secondary hybrids is first met with. Paphiopedilum × aureum and P. × Hera may be mentioned as two of the most familiar examples, but many others could be enumerated.

Hybrids combining four species result from the intercrossing of primary hybrids whose original parents are all different; also from more complex crosses. For example Paphiopedilum × Harri-Leeanum was derived from P. × Harrisianum and P. × Leeanum, and thus is composed of equal parts of P. barbatum, villosum, insigne and P. Spicerianum, but the same four species were combined when P. Spicerianum and P. × œnanthum were united to form P. × Figaro, though the proportions are different. In this the amount of P. Spicerianum blood is doubled, while that of P. barbatum and P. villosum is reduced by one-half. Again, in P. × Brunianum, raised from P. × Leeanum and P. × œnanthum, the same four species appear, but here we get half P. insigne and a quarter of P. Spicerianum, while P. barbatum and P. villosum are represented as in P. ×

Figaro. Other combinations between the same four species are possible, it not actually in existence. But the complexity does not end here, for a similar result may be reached in three different ways. P. × Boyleanum was raised from P. × Crossianum and P. × Harrisianum, but the union of P. × nitens with P. × calophyllum, also that of P. × Ashburtonæ with P. × Measuresianum would agree on analysis, each being composed of equal parts of P. barbatum, insigne, venustum and villosum. The second cross is called P. × Patria, but the arrangement is not satisfactory. The third cross has not been raised.

HYBRIDS FROM FIVE SPECIES are at present rare. The first was Paphiopedilum × Kubele, raised from P. × œnanthum ♀ and P. × Youngianum ♂, which flowered in 1901. Two years later, P. × Kohinoor appeared, raised from P. × œnanthum ♀ and P. × Haywoodianum ♂, and in 1906 P. × Seraphis, from P. × Orpheus ♀ and P. × œnanthum ♂. All were raised by the late Mr. Reginald Young, of Liverpool, and it will be noticed that in each case P. × œnanthum was one of the parents, so that all have three species in common. In fact P. × Kubele and P. × Kohinoor possess four species in common, for both P. × Youngianum and P. × Haywoodianum are half derived from P. superbiens, and thus the difference between them is in respect of only one out of the five original species.

Hybrids of still greater complexity are clearly possible, but we do not remember one having flowered yet.

VARIABILITY OF HYBRIDS.—An excellent example of the wide range of variation seen in secondary hybrids is afforded by the case of Paphiopedilum × Hera, derived from P. × Leeanum ♀ and P. Boxallii ♂, of which a series of thirty flowers, arranged in three groups, have been figured (*Journ. Roy. Hort. Soc.* xxvii. pp. 614-624, fig. 167-169: *Orch. Rev.* 1903, pp. 71-73, fig. 16-18). They were selected from a series of forty-nine flowers, of which no two were exactly alike. The thirty figured show great variation both in shape and colour, some being profusely spotted and blotched with purple-brown, and others much suffused with the same colour, while in a few the purple markings are very much reduced. These differences may be attributed to the varying influence in the offspring of the original species, P. Boxallii, P. insigne and P. Spicerianum, and it emphasises the importance of keeping accurate records, for their common origin would never have been guessed.

Still more remarkable is the case of P. aureum, a hybrid from P. Spicerianum ♀ and P. nitens (Sallieri Hyeanum) ♂, which has been described under nearly forty different names. We cannot give the whole range of variation, but may mention the differences seen in the six varieties figured by M. Goossens (*Dict. Ic. Orch.*, Paph. hyb.). P. × aureum (t. 24) has the petals, lip and the lower half of the dorsal sepal greenish yellow, with the upper half of the latter white, the only other colour being a few minute brown lines at the base of the petals and a few brown dots inside the lip. In var. virginale (t. 24 a) there is a slight suffusion of brown in the flower, and some purple veining on the petals and base of the dorsal sepal. In var. Marie Closon (t. 24 e) the purple on the dorsal sepal takes the form of a band, which extends to beyond the middle of the dorsal sepal. In var. Cyrus (t. 24 d) the band on the dorsal sepal is broader and extends right to the apex, while traces of lateral bands occur, with many brown dots on the base of the dorsal sepal and petals. In var. Œdippe (t. 24 c) the greater part of the dorsal sepal is suffused and veined with purple, and the whole flower is darker in colour. Lastly, in var. Hebe (t. 24 b) both the petals and dorsal sepal are closely spotted with dark brown all over, the spots on the latter being purple where they extend into the white area. These remarkably diverse forms came out of the same capsule.

The case of Dendrobium × Blackianum (*Orch. Rev.* 1904, p. 104) is equally remarkable. It was obtained from D. Findlayanum crossed with the pollen of D. × Wiganiæ, and exhibits a remarkable range of variation. There are buff yellow forms, with the disc of the lip reddish maroon, and varying considerably in size, others in which the coloured disc is greatly reduced in size or almost absent, some with white ground colour and purple tips to the sepals and petals, and a purple disc to the lip; in short there are forms approaching each parent in general character.

Among Dendrobiums, Cattleyas, Odontoglossums and others cases could be mentioned where a wide range of variation has been observed between the offspring from the same capsule, and the more distinct the original species the greater the possibilities of variation. This variation affords materials for selection, and for great improvements in the future.

THE LITERATURE OF ORCHID HYBRIDS.

THE literature of Orchid Hybrids is becoming rather extensive, and the following list of works and papers dealing with various phases of the subject will probably be found useful. It does not profess to be exhaustive, but contains most of the principal works that were readily accessible at the time it was compiled, and includes many papers on Natural Hybrids belonging to cultivated genera.

1847. On Hybridisation among Vegetables. By the Hon. and Very Rev. William Herbert, LL.D. Orchids.—*Journ. Hort. Soc.* vol. ii. p. 104.

1858. Calanthe × Dominii (with a few general remarks). By Dr. Lindley. —*Gard. Chron.* 1858, p. 4.

1871. Seedling Orchids. By F. W. Burbidge.—*Gard. Chron.* 1871, pp. 43-44, fig. 9.

1873. Hybridising Orchids. By F. W. Burbidge.—*The Garden*, iii. pp. 163-164.

1876. Cultivated Plants, their propagation and improvement. By F. W. Burbidge. The Orchid family, pp. 414-424.

1883. Hybrid Cypripediums. By W. Goldring.—*Gard. Chron.* 1883, i. p. 787.

1886. The Hybridisation of Orchids. By H. J. Veitch, F.L.S.—*Journ. Roy. Hort. Soc.* vii. pp. 22-36, with five plates.

1887. On Bigeneric Orchid Hybrids. By R. A. Rolfe, A.L.S.—*Journ. Linn. Soc.* xxiv. pp. 156-170, t. 4.

1887-1894. A Manual of Orchidaceous Plants cultivated under glass in Great Britain. By James Veitch & Sons. (Includes most of the hybrids then in existence).

1888. On the fertilisation of Cattleya labiata var. Mossiæ, Lindl. By Harry James Veitch, F.L.S.—*Journ. Linn. Soc.* xxiv. pp. 395-406, fig. 1-14.

1892. Les Orchidées de Semis. By Ernest Bergman.—*Journ. Soc. Nat. d'Hort. de France*, xiv. pp. 41-43, 85-93, 159-169, 211-223, 274-292, 422-446, 494-506.

1893 The History of Orchid Hybridisation. By R. A. Rolfe.—*Orch. Rev.* i. pp. 3-6, 35-40, 67-71, 99-103, 131-134, 195-197, 227-229, 259-263, 291-295, 323-328, 356-360.

1893-1904. Hybrid Odontoglossums. By R. A. Rolfe.—*Orch Rev.* i. pp. 142-144, 170-174, 201-206, 275-278, 331-334; ii. pp. 139-141, 200-201, 328-330; iii. pp. 325-329; v. pp. 74-75; vi. pp. 179-180;

vii. pp. 167-169; viii. pp. 299-301; ix. pp. 56, 260-264; xi. pp. 197-198; xii. p. 176. (A series of papers relating to the Natural Hybrids in the genus).

1893. Lælio-cattleya × elegans and L.-c. × Schilleriana. By R. A Rolfe.—*Orch. Rev.* i. pp. 235-238.

1893. Hybrid Oncidiums. By R. A. Rolfe.—*Orch. Rev.* i. pp. 298-302.

1893. Lælio-cattleya × Gottoiana and L.-c. × albanensis. By R. A. Rolfe.—*Orch. Rev.* i. pp. 338-339.

1893. The Nomenclature of Hybrids. By R. A. Rolfe.—*Orch. Rev.* i. pp. 340-343.

1894. Some Results of the Hybridisation of Orchids. By James Veitch & Sons.—*Veitch Man. Orch.* x. pp. 138-154.

1894. Orchid Hybridisation.—*Orch. Rev.* ii. pp. 50-52, 83-86, 116-118, 166-168.

1894. Hybrids between Cypripedium and Selenipedium. By W. Swan.—*Orch. Rev.* ii. p. 171.

1894. Catasetum × splendens. By R. A. Rolfe.—*Orch. Rev.* ii. pp. 355, 357; iii. pp. 85-86.

1895. The Orchid Hybrids (with first supplement). By Geo. Hansen. Second Supplement, 1899.

1895. A List of Hybrid Cypripediums. By H. J. Chapman.—*Gard. Chron.* 1895, ii. pp. 199-201.

1895. Les Cypripediums hybrides d'origine Francaise. By H. Martinet.—*Le Jardin*, 1895, pp. 52-53. Repeated in *Gard. Chron.* 1895, ii. p. 370.

1895. American Hybrid Cypripediums.—*American Gardening*, March 23rd, 1895. Repeated in *Gard. Chron.* 1895, i. p. 550.

1895. Dictionnaire des Orchidées Hybrides.—By E. Bohnhof.

1895. Cypripedium × siamense. By Reginald Young.—*Orch. Rev.* iii. pp. 20-21.

1895. Mexican Hybrid Lælias. By R. A. Rolfe.—*Orch. Rev.* iii. pp. 45-48.

1895. Hybrid Selenipediums.—*Orch. Rev.* iii. pp. 75-80.

1895. Oncidium × hæmatochilum. By Thomas T. Potter.—*Orch Rev.* iii. pp. 174-175, 230; vii. pp. 273-274, fig. 15, p. 293.

1895. Cypripedium × Littleanum. By R. A. Rolfe.—*Orch. Rev.* iii. pp. 209-210, fig. 8.

1896. Natural Hybrid Orchids. By R. A. Rolfe.—*Gard. Chron.* 1896, i. pp. 105-106, 198-199, 232-234.

1896. Cypripediums with identical names. By Reginald Young.—*Orch. Rev.* iv. pp. 11-14, 37-39.

1896. A Hybridist's Notes. By Theodore L. Mead.—*Orch. Rev.* iv. pp. 41-43, 169-171, 326.

1896. Notes on periods of ripening Orchid seed. By Norman C. Cookson. —*Orch. Rev.* iv. p. 112.

1896. Nomenclature of Orchids. By the Right Hon. J. Chamberlain.—*Orch. Rev.* iv. pp. 133-135.

1896. Nomenclature of Orchids. By C. C. Hurst.—*Orch. Rev.* iv. pp. 165-166.

1896. Regarding certain supposed Hybrid Orchids. By Emeric S. Berkeley.—*Orch. Rev.* iv. pp. 167-168.

1896. Quick hybridisation of Orchids. By Alex. Hodgkinson.—*Orch. Rev.* iv. p. 334.

1896. Complex Cypripedium Hybrids. By Reginald Young.—*Orch. Rev.* iv. pp. 361-362.

1897. The raising of Orchid seedlings. By R. Eichel.—*Orch. Rev.* v. pp. 38-40, 82-84, 114-116, 138-140.

1897. Curious Crosses. By C. C. Hurst.—*Orch. Rev.* v. pp. 179-180, 365-367.

1897. Curious Cypripedium Seedlings. By E. A. Orpet.—*Orch. Rev.* v. pp. 242-243.

1897. Epidendrum radicans as a parent.—*Orch. Rev.* v. pp. 274, 301.

1897. Closely allied hybrids. By Reginald Young.—*Orch. Rev.* v. p. 275.

1897. Cattleya × hybrida. By R. A. Rolfe.—*Orch. Rev.* v. pp. 333-335.

1898. Notes on Some Curiosities of Orchid Breeding. By C. C. Hurst.—*Journ. Roy. Hort. Soc.* xxi. pp. 442-486, fig. 105-112; *Orch. Rev.* v. pp. 326-328; vi. pp. 202-204.

1898. Paphiopedilum seed and the time to sow it. By Reginald Young.—*Orch. Rev.* vi. pp. 6-8; vii. p. 16. By E. C. H. Pidsley.—*l.c.* p. 34.

1898. Zygopetalum crossed with Odontoglossum.—*Orch. Rev.* vi. p. 19.

1898. Hybridising Dendrobiums. By F. H. Moore.—*Orch. Rev.* vi. pp. 52-54, 108-109.

1898. Hybrid Orchids. By James O'Brien.—*Journ. Roy. Hort. Soc.* xxi. pp. 178-185; *Orch. Rev.* vi. p. 221.

1898. Cypripedium niveum as a parent. By Reginald Young.—*Orch. Rev.* vi. pp. 362-365; vii. pp. 28-29.

1898. Curiosities of Orchid Breeding. By C. C. Hurst.—*Nature*, Dec. 22nd, 1898, pp. 178-181; *Orch. Rev.* vii. pp. 11-12.

1899. Curious Crosses. By C. C. Hurst.—*Orch. Rev.* vii. pp. 13-15.

1899. Spontaneous Hybrids of Hardy Orchids. By C. Wolley Dod.—*Gard. Chron*, 1899, i. p. 179; *Orch. Rev.* vii. p. 105.

1899. Nomenclature of Hybrids.—*Orch. Rev.* vii. pp. 106-109.

1900. Notes on some Experiments in Hybridisation and Cross-breeding. By C. Chamberlain Hurst, F.L.S.—*Journ. Roy. Hort. Soc.* xxiv. pp. 90-126, fig. 9-41. This paper is largely devoted to Orchids).

1900. Hybridisation viewed from the standpoint of Systematic Botany. By R. Allen Rolfe, A.L.S.—*Journ. Roy. Hort. Soc.* xxiv. pp. 181-202, fig. 93-102. (Includes Natural Hybrid Orchids whose parentage has been proved by experiment).

1900. Fertility of Paphiopedilum Fairrieanum Hybrids. By J. E. Rothwell.—*Orch. Rev.* viii. p. 74. By Reginald Young. –*l. c.* pp. 103-104.

1900. Hybrid Dendrobiums. By R. A. Rolfe.—*Orch. Rev.* viii. pp. 161-164.

1900. Lælia cinnabarina as a parent. By E. O. Orpet.—*Orch. Rev.* viii. pp. 202-203.

1900. Raising Orchids from seed. By E. O. Orpet.—*Orch. Rev.* viii. pp. 356-357.

1900. Sur les unités des Caractères spécifiques et leur application à l'étude des Hybridees. By Hugo de Vries.—*Rev. Gén. Bot.* 1900, pp. 257-271; *Gard. Chron.* 1900, ii. pp. 391-392, 432. (Though not dealing with Orchid hybrids the principle is applicable to them, and the paper is therefore included).

1900. The Evolution of Plants. By R. Irwin Lynch.—*Journ. Roy. Hort. Soc.* xxv. pp. 17-37. (Includes a few Orchid hybrids).

1901. Sander's Orchid Guide. By F. Sander & Co. Addenda, 1903 (includes lists of hybrid Orchids).

1901. Fertility of Hybrids. By E. O. Orpet.—*Orch. Rev.* ix. pp. 103-104.

1901. Raising Orchids from seed. By E. O. Orpet.—*Orch. Rev.* ix. pp. 110-112.

1901. Natural Hybrid Lycastes. By R. A. Rolfe.—*Orch. Rev.* ix. pp. 99-102, 309-310.

1901. Natural Hybrid Miltonias. By R. A. Rolfe.—*Orch. Rev.* ix. pp. 289-295.

1901. Hybridisation and raising of Orchids. By James O'Brien.—*Gard. Chron.* 1901, ii. pp. 317-318.

1902. Mendel's Law applied to Orchid Hybrids. By C. C. Hurst, F.L.S., F.R.H.S.—*Journ. Roy. Hort. Soc.* xxvi. pp. 688-695; *Orch. Rev.* x. pp. 187-188.

1902. List of Orchids used in the fertilisation of Hybrids which have received either First-class Certificates or Awards of Merit from the R.H.S. By J. Gurney Fowler.—*Journ. Roy. Hort. Soc.* xxvi. pp. 696-723.

1902. Mendel's Law of Inheritance.—*Orch. Rev.* x. pp. 11-13, 45, 107, 187-189, 236-239.

1902. Nomenclature of Hybrids. By L. Cappe.—*Orch. Rev.* x. pp. 38-40.

1902. Experiments in Plant Hybridisation. By C. C. Hurst.—*Orch. Rev.* x. p. 45.

1902. Variation in Secondary Hybrids. By C. C. Hurst.—*Orch. Rev.* x. pp. 74-76.

1903. Epidendrum × kewense. By R. A. Rolfe.—*Orch. Rev.* xi. pp. 6-7.

1903. Fertility of Hybrids. By C. C. Hurst.—*Orch. Rev.* xi. pp. 23-24.

1903. Paphiopedilum × siamense. By Reginald Young.—*Orch. Rev.* xi. pp. 44-46.

1903. Orchid Hybridisation.—*Orch. Rev.* xi. pp. 61-62, 122-123, 216-217, 253-254, 277-278, 316-318.

1903. Mendel's Law applied to Orchid Hybrids. By C. C. Hurst, F.L.S. —*Journ. Roy. Hort. Soc.* xxvii. pp. 614-624, fig. 167-169; *Orch. Rev.* xi. pp. 71-74, fig. 16-18, pp. 97-99.

1903. Calanthes and Mendel's Law. By H. J. Chapman.—*Orch. Rev.* xi. pp. 116-117. By C. C. Hurst.—*l. c.* xi. p. 158.

1903. Recent Experiments in the Hybridisation of Orchids. By C. C. Hurst, F.L.S.—*Report. Brit. Assoc.* 1903, p. 353; *Gard. Chron.* 1903, ii. pp. 226-227; *Orch. Rev.* xi. pp. 314-316.

1903. Orchids, their culture and management. By H. J. Chapman. Contains a chapter on Orchid Hybridisation (pp. 21-32).

1904. Orchid hybridising in Florida. By T. L. Mead.—*Orch. Rev.* xii. p. 72; xiii. pp. 160-161.

1905. Paphiopedilum Fairrieanum and its hybrids. By Francis Wellesley and R. A. Rolfe.—*Orch. Rev.* xiii. pp. 11-18, 38-44, 68-73, 103-108, 135-138, with 18 figures.

1905. Mr. Warner's Hybrid Cypripedes.—*Orch. Rev.* xiii. pp. 291-293, 348-349.

1905. Curiosities of Hybridisation. By Emily Thwaites.—*Orch. Rev.* xiii. pp. 353-354.

1905. A propos des Semis d'Orchidées. By Louis Cappe.—*Le Jardin*, 1905, pp. 40-41; 362-363.

1905. Recherches experimentales sur les semis des Orchidées. By Albert Maumené.—*Le Jardin*, 1895, pp. 158-159, fig. 83-86; *Gard. Chron.* 1905, ii. p. 22, fig. 83-85.

1905. Action des microorganismes sur la germination des Orchidées. By Noel Bernard.—*Journ. Soc. Nat. Hort. France*, 1905, pp. 434-439; *Gard. Chron.* 1905, ii. p. 104.

1906. List of Orchid Hybrids. By Sander & Sons. Addenda, 1907.

1906. Curiosities of Hybridisation. By F. Denis.—*Orch. Rev.* xiv. p. 28.

1906. The Mendelian Laws of Inheritance.—*Orch. Rev.* xiv. pp. 97-99.

1906. Hybrid Orchids. By H. J. Chapman.—*Orch. Rev.* xiv. pp. 99-101.

1906. Hybridising with mixed pollen.—*Orch. Rev.* xiv. pp. 284-285; xv. p. 375.

1906. The late Reginald Young's Hybridisation Experiments.—*Orch. Rev.* xiv. pp. 321-324.

1907. Dendrobium seedlings and Mendel's Law. By J. M. Black.—*Orch. Rev.* xiv. pp. 100-102.

1907. Epidendrum × kewense: a Mendelian Experiment. By R. A. Rolfe.—*Orch. Rev.* xv. pp. 58-59. By C. C. Hurst.—*l. c.* pp. 122-123.

1907. Natural Hybrids of the Cattleya group. By R. Allen Rolfe, A.L.S.—*Rep. third Internat. Conf. Genetics*, pp. 222-241, fig. 51-55 (Includes the natural hybrids that have also been raised artificially).

1907. Hybrid Odontoglossa. By de Barri Crawshay, F.R.H.S.—*Rep. third Internat. Conf. Genetics*, pp. 242-272, fig. 56-88.

1907. Natural Hybrid Cattleyas. By L. Forget.—*Orch. Rev.* xv. pp. 293-296.

1907. Cattleya × bahiensis and C. × Frankeana. By R. A. Rolfe.—*Orch. Rev.* xv. pp. 279-280, 316.

1907. Hybridisation and Crossing in Orchids. By F. Ledien.—*Moller's Deutsche Gartner Zeitung*; *Gard. Chron.* 1907, i. pp. 333-334.

Additional information may be found by the references given in the body of the work, which includes a nearly complete enumeration of published figures of hybrid Orchids.

A list of the principal works cited is given at pp. xlvii.-xlviii.

HYBRIDISING AND RAISING ORCHID SEEDLINGS.

THE Orchid Stud-Book would not be complete without a chapter on hybridising and the raising of Orchid seedlings, and as the work will doubtless appeal to beginners as well as to the expert hybridist, we will commence with the most elementary details.

HYBRIDISING is one of the most fascinating phases of Orchid culture. Every stage in the work is interesting—the pollination of the flower, the development of the capsule, the sowing and germination of the seeds, and the gradual development of the seedlings from the tiniest atom up to the time when the scape pushes up and the flower at length unfolds. Few Orchidists can resist the attempt to raise at least a few seedlings, but one must be prepared for disappointments, and it is this particular stage of the process which generally proves the most difficult. Once surmounted the rest is easy, and the next difficulty may be that of finding the necessary space for the plants as they approach the flowering stage. But we will not anticipate.

THE MATERIALS.—No elaborate preparations are necessary. Such materials as are ready to hand will serve as a commencement, but it would be well to begin with some easy subject, proceeding to more difficult ones as experience is gained. A Cypripede or Cattleya is easily manipulated, but an Epidendrum of the radicans group, though more troublesome to cross, is an ideal subject in other respects, for the seedlings can be raised almost with certainty, as they germinate quickly, and begin to flower when under three years old. Two or three subjects might very well be tried together for a commencement, using whatever subjects are available. Later on a rigid selection of parents will be found desirable, but even at the outset the best possible forms should be used.

METHOD OF PROCEDURE.—Before commencing it is advisable that the operator should thoroughly understand the floral structure, by pulling a few flowers to pieces and identifying the pollen masses and stigma. In the majority of Orchids the pollen masses will be found under a little case at the apex of the column, and they may be easily removed with a pencil, a piece of stick, or in some cases with a finger, by lifting the case gently but firmly upwards and then withdrawing it, when the pollen masses will generally be found adhering to it. In the case of a Cypripede two pollen masses will be found—not enclosed in a case at the apex of the column—but one opposite to each lateral opening at the base of the lip. The pollen is viscous, and is easily removed with a pencil or piece of stick, but if the flower is to be fertilised both the anthers should be cut clean away. The stigma is generally situated in a shallow cavity in front of the column, just below the anther, but in Cochlioda there are two stigmas, which thus become partially lateral, while in the Cypripedium group the stigma is the shield-shaped body situated on the underside of the column inside the lip, on the opposite side to the staminode. The stigma may generally be recognised by its shiny viscous surface, but in the Cypripedium group it is dry, the pollen here being viscous. Having identified the parts we may proceed to describe the details.

POLLINATION OF THE FLOWER.—Having selected the flower that is intended to be fertilised, the first thing to be done is to remove its own pollen—generally a very simple task, but in those genera which have powdery pollen care should be taken that no grains are left behind, or the flower might be self-fertilised. Next take the pollen that is intended to be used and apply it to the stigma, to which it will adhere, and the process of pollination is complete. The reverse cross may be effected at the same time, if the pollen from the first flower is then applied to the stigma of the second. In fertilising small flowers with pollen from larger ones it is sometimes found that the pollen masses are too large to enter the stigma entire, and then it is necessary to cut them, and use only a portion, and conversely in reversing the operation the pollen of more than one flower is sometimes used. Crosses between Cochlioda and Odontoglossum and between Sophronitis and similar large flowers are examples.

RECORDING THE CROSS.—The details of the cross should now be entered in a note-book, with a number, which latter should be written on a small tag, and tied loosely on to the pedicel of the flower. Crosses should be numbered consecutively, and carefully entered, space being left under each for future use, as success or failure, the sowing of the seed, &c. All records should be carefully kept, as the correct parentage is of great importance when the seedlings flower. One should not trust to memory for these details.

EFFECT OF POLLINATION.—The effect of pollination—if the cross has taken—will soon be apparent, in the floral segments fading prematurely and the column and ovary beginning to swell, and the chief thing to be done is to keep the plant healthy, and avoid checks and over-stimulation, so that the capsule may develop properly. A matter which sometimes perplexes beginners at this stage is that capsules will swell to a considerable size and then go off prematurely, or when they open they may be empty or contain only a mass of chaff without good seeds. The reason is frequently that fertilisation proper has not taken place, and an explanation of the process will make this point clear.

FERTILISATION proper does not take place immediately. When an Orchid flower opens the ovules are undeveloped, and, in this state, are incapable of being fertilised. An example will make this point clear. If the ovary of an ordinary flower—a lily for example—be examined as soon as the flower opens, the ovules will be found in a developed condition, so that when the pollen is applied to the stigma the pollen tubes grow rapidly, making their way down the tissue of the style, and into the ovary, when they enter the micropyle (or mouth) of the ovule, and unite with the contents of the egg-cell, this latter constituting the act of fertilisation, after which union the ovule develops into a perfect seed. But if an Orchid flower be examined at this stage the ovarian cavity and ovules will be found quite rudimentary, and if the flower is not pollinated they will progress no further, the flower at length shrivelling and falling off. But when pollinated a rapid change takes place. The column and ovary begin to swell and the segments to fade or change colour. The ovary often looks like a simple pedicel when the flower expands, but after pollination it gradually takes on a capsule-like appearance. The act of pollination applies a stimulus to the ovary, causing it to swell, and the ovules to develop, after which only can fertilisation take place. This retarded development of the ovary is one of the points in which Orchids differ so markedly from most other plants, and is, of course, correlated with the slow development of the pollen tubes.

Cattleya Mossiæ.—In the case of Cattleya Mossiæ the whole process has been worked out by Mr. Harry J. Veitch, who, by a series of experiments, ascertained the fact that fertilisation does not take place until a period of from 75 to 90 days after pollination. The process is briefly as follows: A few hours after pollination the floral segments become flaccid, and show signs of withering. In a couple of days the pollinia are seen to be disintegrating, forming, with the viscid secretion from the stigma, a gelatinous mass that quite fills up the stigmatic cavity. At the same time the pollen tubes have commenced to grow, and in eight days they have reached the base of the column, being found in vast numbers among the conducting tissues. At the end of a month the ovary has become considerably enlarged, and the placentæ and ovules are beginning to assume a definite form, while the pollen tubes are pushing downwards along the sides of the placentæ and among the ovules. In two months, though the pollen tubes are present in countless numbers, and have even reached the base of the ovary, the ovules are not yet developed, but soon afterwards they rapidly undergo a change of form, and at the end of about three months the long looked-for event takes place. The pollen tubes now enter the micropyle of the ovule, and fertilisation of the egg-cell is effected. It is noteworthy that before this event takes place the ovary has developed from a terete body, less than a quarter of an inch in diameter, to a six-angled one, more than seven times as broad, entirely through the stimulus given by the act of pollination, and it enables one to realise to some extent why a seed pod may make considerable progress, and yet go off, if for any reason the ovules should fail to be fertilised.

CAUSES OF FAILURE.—The period required for the development of the pollen tubes and ovules varies considerably in different Orchids, and this may represent one of the causes of failure when very distinct species are intercrossed. When a species is fertilised with its own pollen all the forces at work are in complete harmony, but when the pollen is derived from a widely distinct species the rhythm may be completely upset. The pollen may be capable of causing the development of the ovary and ovules, and yet fail to effect fertilisation when the proper time comes. The pollen tubes from a very distinct species may mature too soon or too late. Or they may be too large to effect an entrance into the micropyle of the ovule of the other species. Again, they may sometimes fail to reach the necessary length, or there may be some other incompatibility or obstacle to their proper development in the new combination. There are good reasons for the belief that in most cases where the ovary develops as the result of pollination without fertilisation being subsequently effected that the difficulty is largely a mechanical one, and one of them is the fact that in many cases a few good seeds are produced. There is also the well-known fact that in the case of Cattleya crossed with Sophronitis, and of Brassavola crossed with Cattleya, the fertile seeds are only found at the apex of the capsule. Again, Cattleya can be crossed with Epidendrum, but the reverse cross fails, and the reason is believed to be that the pollen tubes of Cattleya, and similar large-flowered Orchids, are too large to enter the micropyle of the ovule.

MATURING OF THE CAPSULE.—If the capsules survive the period just mentioned—technically they cannot be called seed-capsules until after the ovules are fertilised—they will probably mature and ripen. The period of maturing varies greatly in different Orchids, and to some extent also under varying conditions, but as this stage approaches it is advisable to watch for the first sign of splitting, otherwise some of the seed may be lost. If the capsule then appears mature it may be cut at once, or tied up securely in a piece of loose tissue paper for a few days, so as to allow the seeds time to mature fully. In practice it is a general custom to tie up the capsule when nearly mature to prevent loss of the seeds before splitting is noticed, also to prevent the seeds from falling and germinating where not wanted.

GATHERING THE SEED.—When the capsule is cut it should be removed to a dry shed, and as soon as ready may be opened, or the seed removed by tapping the capsule gently over a piece of tissue paper. As soon as any seeds fall they should be examined with a good lens to see if they appear perfect. If they appear plump in the centre and diminish considerably towards the pointed ends, they may be considered good, but if they look like hairs or chaff, without any thickening in the middle they are generally bad, that is to say the embryo has not developed. The presence or absence of an embryo can be ascertained with certainty if the lens is sufficiently powerful. In the latter case the chaff may be thrown away at once, but in doing this one should be careful to see that *all* the seed is bad, for occasionally a few good seeds will be present amongst a multitude of chaff (generally near the apex of the capsule), and these might be easily overlooked. It should be remembered that any good seeds are likely to fall first, so that it is possible to see very quickly whether any good seeds are present, and proceed accordingly. It is useless to sow a lot of chaff, and if that can be left behind so much the better, for one can seldom deal with the whole, so numerous are the seeds in a capsule. If most of them appear good one need not trouble about separating the chaff. It is scarcely necessary to add that the number on the capsule should be preserved, and that any necessary entry should be made in the record book.

SOWING THE SEED will be the next stage of the process, and this too is best done outside the house, because the minute seeds are so easily blown about by light currents of air, and germinate where not wanted to. In most cases the seed, or some of it, is best sown at once, though if the capsules ripen in late autumn or winter they may be kept in paper in a dry place until the days begin to lengthen, so that when they begin to germinate circumstances may be favourable to their development. A label should be added containing the number.

WHERE TO SOW.—The old custom was to sow the seed on the parent plant, or on some adjacent one that will not require to be disturbed for some time, and for Cypripedes and terrestrial Orchids generally, also for Odontoglossums this plan is still the best. Care should be taken to choose a plant that will not want potting for some time, and one where the compost is in a healthy condition. The plant should be removed to the shed, and the seeds sprinkled thinly over the compost, after which a label should be inserted containing the number of the cross. A light sprinkling with a sprayer should now be given to settle the seeds, after which the plant may be returned to the house. When once the seed has been sown the compost must never be allowed to become dry, or the young embryo will shrivel and quickly die.

EPIPHYTIC ORCHIDS.—In the case of certain epiphytic Orchids, particularly those of the Cattleya group, another method of sowing is now generally adopted. Blocks of soft wood (both pine and willow have been recommended) are cut across the grain with a rough saw into thin blocks, which are placed on a layer of crocks in a smallish pot, and the seeds are sown on the rough surface of the wood. The blocks are sunk below the rim of the pot, which is then covered with a piece of glass, and the seeds kept constantly moist, by the use of a sprayer as often as necessary.

Another method is to strain a piece of coarse canvas over a bunch of sphagnum moss, and then squeeze it into a pot, below the rim, then sowing the seeds and covering with glass as before. The germination can now be watched, for there is no compost for the seeds to sink down into and get lost. Once sown the seeds must never be allowed to get dry, but care should be taken not to wash them off in spraying. Of course they must be placed in a suitable temperature, and be shaded from direct sunshine. The pots are often placed in a small frame, where they are less likely to get dry, which would be quickly fatal. The method is unsuitable for Cypripedes and other terrestrial Orchids. Until experience has been gained it is best to sow a few seeds under different conditions, noting the result, and in case of failure, if any seed is left over, a second sowing may be made a few weeks later.

GERMINATION usually commences at once, and under the conditions last mentioned its progress can be followed. The first sign of germination is that the seeds begin to swell and turn green, then they lose the seed coat and gradually become globular. At length a growing point appears, with some root-hairs, and then the first true root begins to push.

PRICKING OFF.—The pricking off of the young seedlings requires to be done with care and discretion, especially if, as sometimes happens, they come up too thickly. A small pan of compost should be prepared, and the tiny globes may be removed with a pointed stick carefully pushed beneath them, care being taken not to injure them. They should be placed in a minute cavity in the new compost, giving a slight spraying to settle them. A similar procedure may be followed when the seeds are sown direct on the compost, but here, if not too crowded, they may be left until rather larger, when they may be handled more easily. Care must always be taken not to damage the roots. After pricking off, the young seedlings are best returned to the case for a time. A sharp watch must be kept for the presence of slugs, or other pests, which would make short work of the young seedlings.

POTTING ON.—When the young seedlings get a little larger they should be potted off into thimble pots, about an inch in diameter. The compost will vary according to the class of Orchid, and should be similar to that required by the parents, but will be required to be chopped fine, and the dust should be removed with a fine sieve. A few finely broken crocks should be placed at the bottom of the pots, and on these a little compost is placed. The plant is then placed in position, and the compost made moderately firm with the fingers, after which a light spraying may be given. The compost should be just moist, not too wet or too dry, and it should be of about the same temperature as the house, being placed there for a day or two before use if necessary. The water used should be rain or soft water, and of the same temperature as the house. After potting the tiny pots may be bedded in pans or baskets of peat, and placed in a light position in the house, not too far from the glass. Potting on as required is all that now remains to be done, but the seedlings should be encouraged to make vigorous growth, without any attempt to rest them during the winter.

THE FLOWERING PERIOD.—When the seedlings become strong enough the first scape may be expected, and the grower will be able to see the result of his labour. But it will be well to remember that the plants have seldom reached their full development at this period, and the flowers may be expected to improve as the plants become stronger. The quickness with which they flower will depend to some extent upon the way they are grown, and for this reason it is best to keep them moving as much as possible, so as to get them large enough to flower early. We have in a few cases seen great differences between seedlings out of the same capsule when grown under different conditions, and time may be gained by not resting them in the winter while they remain small. Some genera flower much sooner than others, the period varying from about two years, in a few cases, up to five or six years, or occasionally even longer—the date being calculated from the time the seed is sown. Calanthes, Disas, and a few other terrestrial Orchids are among the quickest to flower with a few Epidendrums, there being quite a number of cases on record of seedlings which have flowered under two years old. A few Cypripedes have also flowered very early, but generally speaking they are of slower growth, and the same may be said of Cattleyas and their allies. A few may flower the third year, but more in the fourth and fifth. In every group, however, there appear to be a few precocious individuals, while others seem to lag behind, some of the latter being of weak constitution. The only way of hastening the period of blooming in any group is to get them strong as early as possible by liberal treatment.

SELECTION OF PARENTS.—Although this is a subject which naturally comes at the very beginning of the work, it is not likely to receive much attention until some progress has been made in raising seedlings. It is a matter on which a great deal might be written, but in many small collections the choice of parents is limited, and most of the popular species that flower at the same time have already been hybridised together, as well as many of the earlier hybrids. And there are many crosses which are not worth making, because the characters of certain species neutralise each other. Generally, plants having strongly opposed characters are not worth crossing. For example a hybrid between the darkest and lightest coloured species in a genus is likely to be of a pale undecided tint, which would justify a remark sometimes made about two species being spoilt. Although one cannot always forsee what the result of a given cross may be, it is generally possible to give a very good guess, especially at the present time, when the result of so many crosses is known. And it is here that the following pages should be specially useful. The hybridist having certain species in flower, and wishing to know whether they have already been crossed, has only to turn to Part I. of the work, where the crosses which have flowered are recorded, with the name of the resulting hybrid, and if it is there, on referring to Part II. he will find the clue to its history. Of course, crosses not recorded may have been made, but not yet reached the flowering stage. It should be useful in another way, for certain crosses are worth repeating, especially if the best varieties of the parents can be used, and this is particularly the case with rare hybrids, or those that can only be propagated very slowly. A batch of any good hybrid raised from the best varieties of the parents attainable is sure to yield a few good forms, the best of which can be selected and grown on.

Hybrids as Parents.—In one respect hybridisation is always likely to remain progressive, for the best of the hybrids can be crossed together, or re-crossed with the original parents, with the object of emphasising desirable qualities or of developing new breaks of colour, and if such further crossing is done with definite objects in view, and the worst forms constantly weeded out, progress is sure to result. One cannot expect more than a certain percentage of superior forms, and the worst should be discarded after being proved. In this work the great variability of secondary hybrids will usually afford plenty of scope for selection. Much has been accomplished already, and the rate of progress is likely to be accelerated in the future.

It now remains to say something about the individual genera and their peculiarities.

The Cypripedium group first claims our attention, for its hybrids far outnumber any other, and this is largely due to the ease and certainty with which the seedlings can be raised. Though generally known as Cypripedium in gardens, they really belong to Paphiopedilum, for Cypripedium proper comprises the hardy deciduous species, of which no hybrids have been raised artificially, though wild ones are known. The plants known as Selenipedium in gardens also belong to another genus, Phragmopedilum, for Selenipedium proper comprises three tall reed-like plants which are not cultivation.

Paphiopedilum seedlings are very easily raised. Having obtained capsule of seed, one has only to scatter it over the compost of some plant that will not require potting for some considerable time, keep the compost moist, and await the appearance of the seedlings, which, if the seeds are good and the treatment right, is generally only a matter of time. In the latter respect they are rather erratic, sometimes appearing very quickly, and at others not until the lapse of several months, or even more. The late Mr. Reginald Young has recorded the appearance of seedlings as long as two years after the seed was sown, and in the case of P. × Quirinus a single seedling appeared nine months after the seed was sown, and then three or four others just three years later. This, however, is quite exceptional, and is only mentioned to show that a cross need not necessarily be written off as a failure because the seedlings do not appear almost immediately. After sowing the seeds one naturally watches their progress through a good lens, but some of the seeds sink into cavities in the compost or get covered over, and are lost sight of until the point of a tiny leaf emerges from the compost. It is useless to sow the seeds of these and other terrestrial Orchids on blocks of wood. When the young seedlings are large enough to handle they may be pricked off, as already described. The capsules generally take from nine to fifteen months to ripen, and the seedlings will generally begin to flower when about three years old—in exceptional cases a little earlier—but more during the next two years. A good deal depends on the way they are grown, but some mature much more quickly than others.

PHRAGMOPEDILUM capsules ripen much more quickly than those of the preceding genus, and are unique among cultivated Orchids. in being three-celled. The seedlings, however, require similar treatment and reach the flowering stage at about the same age.

CALANTHE capsules ripen in about three to five months, and some of the seedlings begin to flower when two to three years old. The deciduous species of the C. vestita group are the most popular subjects, but a few of the evergreen species have also been crossed, and in one case the deciduous and evergreen sections have been united. Calanthe has also been crossed with Phaius grandifolius and its allies, yielding the generic hybrids known as Phaiocalanthe. Calanthe seedlings require careful handling when small, but are easily grown and succeed under ordinary treatment.

PHAIUS is a near ally of Calanthe, and the seedlings are equally easy to raise, and also flower comparatively early. The hybrids between P. simulans and the species of the P. grandifolius group are very beautiful and floriferous, and a similar remark applies to those between the latter and P. Humblotii. P. × Cooksoni, the first of the series, flowered within the short period of two years and a quarter from the time seed was sown, and the seedlings generally are easily grown and flower at a very early period. They require warm house treatment, and are highly decorative. The yellow P. maculatus has also yielded several beautiful hybrids when combined with the species of the P. grandifolius group.

SPATHOGLOTTIS is another genus of terrestrial Orchids which is very easily manipulated, and the seedlings flower very quickly. S. × kewensis flowered within eighteen months after the seed was sown, and other seedlings have flowered very quickly. The genus contains several beautiful hybrids, and is worthy of more attention.

DISAS.—Hybrids between Disa grandifolia and a few allied species are also very easily raised, and flower very quickly. D. × Veitchii, the first of the series, flowered when only twenty-one months old, and D. × kewensis, which came next, only eighteen months after the seed was sown. They are easily grown under suitable treatment, but sometimes do not succeed in the Orchid house, requiring rather a position in a cool frame.

CYNORCHIS.—Only one Cynorchis is known, namely C. × kewensis, derived from C. Lowiana and C. purpurascens, but it almost holds the record for quickness of flowering, for the seedlings are said to have flowered within about two years from the date when the cross was made. Seedlings of this genus are of the easiest possible culture, and anyone having a warm house and requiring an easy subject to commence with, could not find a better one. It may be mentioned, as showing the ease with which seedlings of this genus are raised, that a plant of C. fastigiata in the Clare Lawn collection produced a capsule (possibly fertilised by some insect), which was allowed to mature, and afterwards the seedlings came up all over the place, and were pulled up like weeds.

ZYGOPETALUM, LYCASTE, CHYSIS and other soft-leaved Orchids are easily raised, but the capsules do not mature so quickly, nor the seedlings flower so early as the genera previously mentioned. The first-named has been crossed with several other genera, but the seedlings in many cases have resembled the mother almost entirely, so that the attempt to reverse the crosses might be made. With Colax, however, true hybrids have resulted.

MASDEVALLIA capsules mature rather quickly, but the seedlings do not flower so early as some of the soft-leaved genera previously mentioned. Several beautiful hybrids have been raised, but the genus has been rather neglected of late.

CYMBIDIUMS are very easily raised, but take longer to mature, and the seedlings are sometimes rather erratic in making their appearance. There is a case on record of a batch of seeds obtained by crossing C. Lowianum and C. eburneum, and sown on the compost of the parent plant, which continued to germinate for years, so that some of them had reached the flowering stage while others were still tiny seedlings. Hybrid Cymbidiums contain some highly decorative plants, and there is plenty of scope for further development.

CATTLEYA may be regarded as typical of a group of allied genera of epiphytic Orchids, which succeed best under the special treatment described on p. xxxvii., though the old system of sowing on the compost of the parent plants, or on that of young growing seedlings, may also be followed.

When sown on canvas or blocks of wood the germination may be watched from the very commencement, and the process is most interesting. Shortly after sowing the seed begins to swell, and gradually acquires a greenish tinge. Next the testa ruptures, and the minute embryo gradually assumes a globular form, and steadily increases in size. Then some minute root-hairs appear, and a growing point is seen at the apex of the young seedling, from which a minute leaf begins to push. Soon afterwards the first true root appears, after which, with ordinary care, the seedlings may be considered safe, and will gradually develop until the flowering stage is reached. The most critical period seems to be what is termed the thalloid stage, for the seeds will sometimes swell and assume a greenish tinge, and then make no further progress, finally shrivelling up and disappearing, for no apparent reason. The researches of M. Noel Bernard seem to show that the cause of this is the absence of certain microscopic fungi which live in the plant, a point we may go into presently. When sown on blocks of wood or canvas the tiny globules sometimes almost cover the surface, and some of them should be pricked off before they choke each other, and in any case this should be done as soon as the first true root begins to push, so that a supply of food is at once available. Thin sowing should be practiced, even if some of the seeds have to be left unused. Cattleyas usually flower from four to six years old, though some mature earlier under favourable treatment, and others, especially among the earlier hybrids, have taken much longer to bloom. The tendency is to shorten the period by growing the seedlings on rapidly. The species of Cattleya which have been intercrossed are very numerous, as may be seen by the following pages, but other combinations are possible, and the utilisation of the hybrids themselves as parents offers endless possibilities for the future. Cattleya has also been united with Lælia, Brassavola, Epidendrum, Sophronitis, Diacrium and Schomburgkia, and there is still plenty of scope for further experiments.

LÆLIA may be bracketed with Cattleya as regards treatment, and the remark applies to the allied genera, which cross with each other very freely.

SOPHRONITIS GRANDIFLORA crosses freely with Cattleya and Lælia, but the seedlings are rather delicate, and grow very slowly. The Sophronitis is generally used as the seed-bearer, and the pollen masses of the larger parent have to be cut, being too large for the stigma.

EPIDENDRUM flowers are rather difficult to manipulate, owing to their small size, and to the fact that the lip is united to the column, but the seedlings are among the easiest to raise, and they begin to flower in the second or third year. The capsules mature very quickly, and no easier subject could be found for a beginner.

DENDROBIUM seedlings are not difficult to raise, and begin to flower when three or four years old. The popular D. nobile has been crossed with many of the allied species, and some of these with each other, but there is plenty of scope for further experiments, especially in the way of securing greater variety among the hybrids.

ODONTOGLOSSUM.—For a long period the genus Odontoglossum furnished the apparent paradox that although natural hybrids were common all attempts to raise them artificially resulted in failure. At length, in 1890, one seedling flowered in the collection of Baron Edmond de Rothschild, at Armainvilliers, near Paris, and a year later a second with Messrs. Veitch. A few other single examples followed, and then M. Ch. Vuylsteke, of Loochristi, Ghent, took the genus in hand, and his remarkable success is now known to every hybridist. At the present time they are being raised in numerous collections, with great success. It is probable that the early experiments were conducted on wrong lines, for the seedlings are not difficult to raise where Odontoglossums are well grown, only requiring a little additional care while very small. A slight increase in the amount of heat, shade and moisture seems to be the most important cultural modification to aim at. The seeds should be scattered over the surface of the compost of an established plant, and kept constantly moist and shaded from direct sunlight, when the seeds will soon assume a greenish tinge, and pass through the ordinary stages of germination. It is best to sow seeds on several plants in different positions, and if seedlings do not result some error in treatment may be suspected. When the tiny seedlings are pricked off, the protection of a small hand light is useful until they become well established. A point to remember is that the minute seedlings are very delicate in their earlier stages, and liable to be ruined by a few hours neglect, which would have no effect on older plants. On the opposite page is given a photographic illustration of a group of 600 seedlings raised in the collection of W. Thompson, Esq., Walton Grange, Stone, by Mr. W. Stevens. The suspended pots contain the tiny seedlings, potted in thimble pots and plunged in moss, while the larger ones stand on the stage beneath, one of them (in the back row on the right) being in flower, so that plants in every stage are represented. As regards their culture Mr. Stevens remarks:—

"I find that seeds germinate pretty freely almost anywhere in a cool house, on pots with other plants, or on calico or flannel placed in pots stuffed tight with moss, but as soon as they have formed a little corm they want to be moved on to pots of moss, and hung up near the light. During winter they require all the light they can get, but as the sun gets more power they require plenty of care and watching, so as not to over-water or shrivel them up. When large enough I single them out into finger pots, and plunge them in larger pots filled with moss, so as to keep them in an equable condition as regards moisture, and when they begin to root they may be considered safe, always with the exception of insect pests. Thrips will soon make work with the tiny plants, and must be kept down, but I consider the greatest pest of all is a small black midge, which lays its eggs in the compost, and the grub when hatched out feeds on all it can find in the

GROUP OF SEEDLING ODONTOGLOSSUMS AT WALTON GRANGE.

pots." For other details we must refer the reader to the original article (*Orch. Rev.* 1903, pp. 41-43, fig. 10).

Odontoglossum has also been united with the allied genera, Cochlioda and Miltonia, yielding the hybrids known under the names of Odontioda and Odontonia, the former including some of the most brilliant hybrids that have yet appeared. An enormous number of seedlings are now in existence, and some striking developments may be anticipated. In using Cochlioda as the seed parent it should be remembered that the genus possesses two lateral stigmas. The seedlings should be treated like Odontoglossums.

PHALÆNOPSIS.—Several beautiful Phalænopsis hybrids have been raised, but they grow slowly, and require a good deal of care. The capsules mature early, and the seeds should be sown on the compost of the parent plants, and the seedlings, when large enough, should be carefully pricked off and placed in the best position in the house, after which, with proper care, they will gradually progress till the flowering stage is reached. The behaviour of the flowers after fertilisation is curious. The sepals and petals do not fade, but gradually lose their original colour, becoming green, and doubtless act like leaves in assimilating food for the benefit of the maturing capsule. Vanda is an allied genus of which two hybrids have been raised, and the seedlings should receive similar treatment to Phalænopsis.

SEEDLING ORCHIDS AND FUNGI.—The question of fungus co-operation in Orchid roots is interesting. By a series of experiments M. Noel Bernard has ascertained that the presence of certain microscopic fungi is indispensable for the germination of Orchid seeds. He has always found these fungi on the seedlings sent to him, as well as in those collected in their native homes; also that when the seeds are sown in sterilised tubes germination cannot progress beyond a certain stage. But if the fungi are then added growth proceeds, and he comes to the conclusion that these fungi elaborate a supply of food which the young seedlings are not able to obtain for themselves. How far this information can be utilised by Orchid growers is not quite clear, for these fungi are present wherever the parent plants are grown, and so the seedlings may be left to take care of themselves. A photograph of M. Bernard's cultures, with details, may be found in the *Orchid Review* (1906, pp. 201, 203).

GENERAL CONCLUSIONS.—It may be added, in conclusion, that Orchid seedlings, whatever the genus, require the same treatment as their parents, and where the latter are well grown, no difficulty should be experienced. A little additional care is necessary during their infantile stages, because from their minute size a few hours neglect may injure them beyond all hope of recovery, while the effect upon older plants might scarcely be noticed. For the same reason special attention should be paid by the grower to cleanliness, and to the keeping down of insect pests. In a wild state seedlings receive no special attention, but the conditions are suitable for old and young alike, and the plants pass through their different stages accordingly. If similar conditions can be secured at home the grower may embark on this most fascinating phase of Orchid culture with confidence.

LIST OF PRINCIPAL WORKS CITED.

Amer. Flor. . . . . . American Florist.
Amer. G. . . . . . American Gardening.
Amer. G.C. . . . . . Gardeners' Chronicle of America.
B.M. . . . . . Botanical Magazine.
Bohnh. Dict. O. Hyb. . . Bohnhof, Dictionnaire des Orchidées Hybrides.
Boyle Woodl. O. . . . Boyle, Woodlands Orchids.
Bull Cat. . . . . . . Wm. Bull & Sons' Catalogue.
Bull. Soc. Tosc. Ort. . . Bulletino della R. Società Toscano di Orticultura.
Charlesw. Cat. . . . Charlesworth & Co.'s Catalogue.
Chron. O. . . . . . Chronique Orchidéenne.
Day. O. Draw. . . . Day, Orchid Drawings (at Kew).
Desb. Cyp. . . , . Desbois, Monographie des Cypripedium, Selenipedium et Uropedium.
Dict. Ic. O. . . . . . Dictionnaire Iconographique des Orchidées.
Die Gart. . . . . . Die Gartenwelt.
Flora and Sylva. . . . .
Fl. d. Ser. . . . . . Flore des Serres.
Fl. Exch. . . . . . Florist's Exchange.
Fl. M. . . . . . . Floral Magazine.
Fl. and Pom. . . . . Florist and Pomologist.
Gard. . . . . . . Garden.
G. Alb. . . . . . . Garden Album.
Gard. & For. . . . . Garden and Forest.
G.C. . . . . , . Gardeners' Chronicle.
G.M. . . . . . . Gardeners' Magazine.
G. World. . . . . . Gardening World.
Gtfl. . . . . . . Gartenflora.
Gartenz. . . . . . . Wittmack, Garten-Zeitung.
Godefr. & Br. Cyp. . . Godefroy-Lebeuf and N. E. Brown, Les Cypripedées.
Hans. O. Hyb. . . . Hansen, The Orchid Hybrids.
Ill. H. . . . . . . Illustration Horticole.
Jard. . . . . . . Le Jardin.
Jenn. O. . . . . . . Jennings, Orchids and how to grow them in India.

J. d. O.	Journal des Orchidées.
J. H.	Journal of Horticulture.
J. L. Soc.	Journal of the Linnean Society.
J. R. H. S.	Journal of the Royal Horticultural Society.
J. S. H. Fr.	Journal de la Société Nationale d'Horticulture de France.
J. S. H. Rhone.	(This work we have not seen.)
Kerch. Liv. d'O.	Kerchove, Livre des Orchidées.
Kew Bull.	Kew Bulletin.
Lind.	Lindenia.
Monit. H.	Moniteur Horticole.
Nich. Dict.	Nicholson's Dictionary of Gardening.
O. A.	Orchid Album.
O. R.	Orchid Review.
Orchidoph.	L'Orchidophile.
Proc. H. S.	Proceedings of the Horticultural Society.
Puydt. O.	Puydt, Les Orchidées.
Pucci Cyp.	Pucci, Cypripedium.
Reichenb.	Reichenbachia.
Rep. Miss. Bot. G.	Report of the Missouri Botanic Garden.
Rep. R.H.S. Conf. Genet.	Report of the Royal Horticultural Society's Conference on Genetics.
Rev. H.	Revue Horticole.
Rev. H. Belge.	Revue d'Horticulture Belge et Étrangére.
R. H. Meas. Cyp.	R. H. Measures, Collection of Cypripediums at The Woodlands, Streatham.
R. I. Meas. Cyp.	R. I. Measures, List of Cypripediums in the collection of Mr. R. I. Measures, Cambridge Lodge, Camberwell.
Sand. Cat.	Sander & Co.'s Catalogue.
Sand. O. Guide.	Sander's Orchid Guide.
Sem. Hort.	Semaine Horticole.
Stein. O.	Stein, Orchideenbuch.
Thompson Sale Cat.	Thompson's Sale Catalogue.
V. Man. O.	Veitch's Manual of Orchidaceous Plants.
Warn. Sel. O.	Warner's Select Orchidaceous Plants.
Wien. Ill. G. Zeit.	Wiener Illustrirte Garten-Zeitung.
Will. O. Gr. Man.	Williams' Orchid Growers' Manual.
Wochenschr.	Koch und Fintelmann, Wochenschrift fur Gartnerei und Pflanzenkunde.

The Orchid Stud-Book.

PART I.

ALPHABETICAL enumeration of species and hybrids which have been intercrossed, with the names of the resulting hybrids. The name of the first parent is given in heavy type in the centre of the column, the second parent on the left, with the resulting hybrid opposite. The parents are arranged in alphabetical sequence throughout.

The detailed information respecting the hybrids is given in Part II. of the work.

1. AËRIDES.

1. **A. affine.**

A. Fieldingii.	A. × hybridum.

2. **A. Fieldingii.**

A. affine.	A. × hybridum.

2. AGANISIA.

1. **A. lepida.**

Zygopetalum maxillare.	Zygonisia × Rolfeana.

3. ANGRÆCUM.

1. **A. sesquipedale.**

A. superbum.	A. × Veitchii.

2. **A. superbum.**

A. sesquipedale.	A. × Veitchii.

4. ANGULOA.

1. **A. Clowesii.**

A. Ruckeri.	A. × media.

2. **A. Ruckeri.**

A. Clowesii.	A. × media.
A. uniflora.	A. × Madouxiana.

3. **A. uniflora.**

A. Ruckeri.	A. × Madouxiana.

5. ANŒCTOCHILUS.

1. **A. Roxburghii.**

Hæmaria discolor.	Anœctomaria × Dominyi.

6. BATEMANNIA.

1. **B. Colleyi.**

Zygopetalum crinitum.	Zygobatemannia × Mastersii.

7. BRASSAVOLA.

1. **B. Digbyana.**

Cattleya Dowiana.	Brassocattleya × Leemanniæ.
C. Eldorado.	B.-c. × Pocahontas.
C. Gaskelliana.	B.-c. × Thorntoni.
C. × Hardyana.	B.-c. × heatonensis.
C. labiata.	B.-c. × Fournieræ.
C. Mendelii.	B.-c. × Maroni.
C. Mossiæ.	B.-c. × Veitchii.
C. quadricolor.	B.-c. × Chamberlainæ.
C. Schrœderæ.	B.-c. × langleyensis.
C. Trianæ.	B.-c. × Sedenii.
C. Warneri.	B.-c. × Mariæ.
C. Warscewiczii.	B.-c. × Maronæ.
Lælia cinnabarina.	Brassolælia × Gratrixiæ.
L. crispa.	B.-l. × Rolfei.
L. purpurata.	B.-l. × Veitchii.
L. tenebrosa.	B.-l. × Helen.
Læliocattleya × Aphrodite.	Brassocatlælia × Wiganii.
L.-c. × elegans.	B.-c.-l. × Mackayi.

2. **B. fragrans.**

Cattleya intermedia.	Brassocattleya × nivalis.
C. Mossiæ.	B.-c. × striata.

Brassavola—(*continued*).

3. **B. glauca.**

C. Leopoldi.	B.-c. × conspicua.
C. Lueddemanniana.	B.-c. × Milton.
C. Schrœderæ.	B.-c. × Sanderi.
C Trianæ.	B.-c. × Orpheus.
Lælia cinnabarina.	Brassolælia × Clio.
L. harpophylla.	B.-l. × Bouteletii.

4. **B. Perrinii.**

Cattleya Leopoldi.	Brassocattleya × belairensis.

8. BRASSOCATTLEYA.

1. **B.-c. × Lindleyana** (nat. hyb.).

Læliocattleya × elegans.	Brassocatlælia × Lawrencei.

9. CALANTHE.

1. **C. × bella.**

C. × Veitchii.	C. × Florence.

2. **C. Darblayana.**

C. rosea.	C. × splendens.
C. × Ruby.	C. × atrorubens.
Phaius grandifolius.	Phaiocalanthe × grandis.

3. **C. furcata.**

C. Masuca.	C. × Dominyi.

4. **C. × gigas.**

Phaius grandifolius.	Phaiocalanthe × Niobe.
P. Wallichii.	P.-c. × Schrœderiana.

5. **C. grandiflora.**

C. Regnieri.	C. × gigas.

6. **C. labrosa.**

C. × Veitchii.	C. × lentiginosa.
C. vestita.	C. × porphyrea.

7. **C. Masuca.**

C. furcata.	C. × Dominyi.
C. tricarinata.	C. × Harryana.
C. veratrifolia.	C. × Rollissoni.
Phaius grandifolius.	Phaiocalanthe × inspirata.
P. Humbloti.	P.-c. × Berryana.

8. **C. Regnieri.**

C. grandiflora.	C. × gigas.
C. rosea.	C. × Aurora.

Calanthe Regnieri—(*continued*).

C. × Veitchii.	C. × Winnii.
C. veratrifolia.	C. × Elwesii.
C. vestita.	C. × Darblayana.
Phaius grandifolius.	Phaiocalanthe × Arnoldæ.

9. **C. rosea.**

C. × Darblayana.	C. × splendens.
C. Regnieri.	C. × Aurora.
C. × Veitchii.	C. × Victoria-Regina.
C. vestita.	C. × Veitchii.

10. **C. × Ruby.**

C. × Darblayana.	C. × atrorubens.
Phaius Wallichii.	Phaiocalanthe × Ruby.

11. **C. Sanderiana.**

C. veratrifolia.	C. × Laucheana.

12. **C. × Sedenii.**

C. veratrifolia.	C. × albata.
C. vestita.	C. × Ruby.

13. **C. tricarinata.**

C. Masuca.	C. × Harryana.

14. **C. Turneri.**

C. × Veitchii.	C. × bella.
C. vestita.	C. × Barberiana.

15. **C. × Veitchii.**

C. × bella.	C. × Florence.
C. labrosa.	C. × lentiginosa.
C. Regnieri.	C. × Winnii.
C. rosea.	C. × Victoria-Regina.
C. Turneri.	C. × bella.
C. vestita.	C. × Sedenii.
Phaius grandifolius.	Phaiocalanthe × Sedeniana.
P. Wallichii.	P.-c. × Brandtiæ.

16. **C. veratrifolia.**

C. Masuca.	C. × Rollissoni.
C. Regnieri.	C. × Elwesii.
C. Sanderiana.	C. × Laucheana.
C. × Sedenii.	C. × albata.

17. **C. vestita.**

C. labrosa.	C. × porphyrea.
C. Regnieri.	C. × Darblayana.
C. rosea.	C. × Veitchii.
C. × Sedenii.	C. × Ruby.
C. Turneri.	C. × Barberiana.
C. × Veitchii.	C. × Sedenii.
Phaius grandifolius.	Phaiocalanthe × irrorata.

10. CATTLEYA.

1. C. Aclandiæ.

C. bicolor.	C. × Fascelis.
C. Dowiana.	C. × Clementinæ.
C. Forbesii.	C. × quinquecolor.
C. granulosa.	C. × Bleui.
C. intermedia.	C. × calummata.
C. labiata.	C. × Eurydice.
C. Loddigesii.	C. × Brabantiæ.
C. maxima.	C. × Rooseveltiæ.
C. Mendelii.	C. × Niobe.
C. Mossiæ.	C. × Apollo.
C. Schilleriana.	C. × peckaviensis.
C. Schrœderæ.	C. × Saint-Benoit.
C. superba.	C. × Selfridgei.
C. Trianæ.	C. × Lottie.
C. Warscewiczii.	C. × Fernandii.
Lælia cinnabarina.	Læliocattleya × Adolphus.
L. pumila.	L.-c. × Dallemagnei.
L. purpurata.	L.-c. × Emiliæ.
L. superbiens.	L.-c. × Humberti.
L. tenebrosa.	L.-c. × Remula.
Læliocattleya × elegans.	L.-c. × Philbrickiana.
Sophronitis grandiflora.	Sophrocattleya × Hardyana.

2. C. amethystoglossa.

C. granulosa.	C. × granuglossa.
C. intermedia.	C. × interglossa.
C. Lueddemanniana.	C. × Thorntoni.
C. Trianæ.	C. × Miranda.
Epidendrum × O'Brienianum.	Epicattleya × Orpetii.
Lælia cinnabarina.	Læliocattleya × Marica.
L. harpophylla.	L.-c. × Ghislainæ.

3. C. aurantiaca.

C. intermedia.	C. × aurantimedia.

4. C. bicolor.

C. Aclandiæ.	C. × Fascelis.
C. Bowringiana.	C. × Chesnelliana.
C. Dowiana.	C. × Iris.
C. labiata.	C. × Clarkiæ.
C. Leopoldi.	C. × Mahleræ.
C. Lueddemanniana.	C. × Geleniana.
C. Rex.	C. × Tankervilleæ.
C. Trianæ.	C. × Pandora.
C. velutina.	C. × Frasquita.
C. Warscewiczii.	C. × Ella.
Lælia crispa.	Læliocattleya × Terentia.

Cattleya bicolor (*continued*).

L. Dayana.	L.-c. × Hamiltoni.
L. harpophylla.	L.-c. × leucasta.
L. pumila.	L.-c. × Binoti.
L. tenebrosa.	L.-c. × La-France.
L. xanthina.	L.-c. × elsteadensis.
Læliocattleya × elegans.	L.-c. × Gazelle.
L.-c. × Schilleriana.	L. c. × Andreana.

5. C. Bowringiana.

C. bicolor.	C. × Chesnelliana.
C. Dormaniana.	C. × Firefly.
C. Dowiana.	C. × Mantinii.
C. Eldorado.	C. × Rothwelliæ.
C. Gaskelliana.	C. × Ariel.
C. × Hardyana.	C. × Whiteleyæ.
C. × Harrisii.	C. × Fabiola.
C. Harrisoniana.	C. × Browniæ.
C. labiata.	C. × Portia.
C. Leopoldi.	C. × Bactia.
C. Loddigesii.	C. × Minerva.
C. maxima.	C. × Chloris.
C. superba.	C. × Charlesworthii.
C. Trianæ.	C. × Barbara.
C. velutina.	C. × Clytie.
C. Warneri.	C. × Chapmanii.
C. Warscewiczii.	C. × Wendlandiana.
Epidendrum × O'Brienianum.	Epicattleya × O'Brieniæ.
E. radiatum.	E.-c. × Sedenii.
E. radicans.	E.-c. × matutina.
Lælia albida.	Læliocattleya × Bowrialbida.
L. anceps.	L.-c. × Wrigleyi.
L. autumnalis.	L.-c. × belairensis.
L. Dayana.	L.-c. × Meteor.
L. pumila.	L.-c. × Parysatis.
L. tenebrosa.	L.-c. × Irene.
Læliocattleya × Clive.	L.-c. × decora.
L.-c. × Dominiana.	L.-c. × Illione.
L.-c. × elegans.	L.-c. × Tiresias.
L.-c. × Ingramii.	L.-c. × Robsonæ.
L.-c. × Leeana.	L.-c. × Hera.
Sophronitis grandiflora.	Sophrocattleya × eximia.

6. C. × Brymeriana (nat. hyb.).

C. labiata.	C. × Viceroy.
Lælia tenebrosa.	Læliocattleya × Milleri.
Læliocattleya × elegans.	L.-c. × princeps.

Cattleya—(*continued*).

7. **C. × calummata.**

Sophronitis grandiflora.	Sophrocattleya × Nydia.

8. **C. citrina.**

C. intermedia.	C. × lamberhurstensis.
Læliocattleya × elegans.	Læliocattleya × Seraph.

9. **C. × Claesiana.**

Epidendrum × O'Brienianum.	Epicattleya × Nebo.

10. **C. dolosa.**

C. labiata.	C. × rubescens.
C. Trianæ.	C. × Mariannæ.
Lælia Boothiana.	Læliocattleya × Praeti.
L. Dayana.	L.-c. × Maynardi.
L. purpurata.	L.-c. × radiata.

11. **C. Dormaniana.**

C. Bowringiana.	C. × Firefly.
C. Dowiana.	C. × Doinii.
C. luteola.	C. × Arthuriana.
Lælia xanthina.	Læliocattleya × Sanderæ.
Læliocattleya × Schilleriana.	L.-c. × claptonensis.

12. **C. Dowiana.**

Brassavola Digbyana.	Brassocattleya × Leemanniæ.
C. Aclandiæ.	C. × Clementinæ.
C. bicolor.	C. × Iris.
C. Bowringiana.	C. × Mantinii.
C. Dormaniana.	C. × Doinii.
C. Eldorado.	C. × Ingramæ.
C. Forbesii.	C. × fulvescens.
C. Gaskelliana.	C. × Rothschildiana.
C. granulosa.	C. × Pittiana.
C. Harrisoniana.	C. × Pittiæ.
C. labiata.	C. × Fabia.
C. Leopoldi.	C. × Chamberlainiana.
C. Lueddemanniana.	C. × Kienastiana.
C. luteola.	C. × Aurora.
C. maxima.	C. × vestalis.
C. Mendelii.	C. × Octavia.
C. Mossiæ.	C. × Frederickiæ.
C. × Patrocinii.	C. × Saint-Gilles.
C. Percivaliana.	C. × Leda.
C. Schilleriana.	C. × Wiganii.
C. Schrœderæ.	C. × Zephyra.
C. Trianæ.	C. × Raphaelæ.

Cattleya Dowiana—(*continued*).

C. velutina.	C. × Maroni.
C. Warneri.	C. × Comet.
C. Warscewiczii.	C. × Hardyana.
Lælia cinnabarina.	Læliocattleya × Charlesworthii.
L. crispa.	L.-c. × Pallas.
L. Dayana.	L.-c. × Ingrami.
L. × Euterpe.	L.-c. × Astræa.
L. × Gravesiæ.	L.-c. × Clytie.
L. Perrinii.	L.-c. × Decia.
L. pumila.	L.-c. × Clive.
L. purpurata.	L.-c. × Dominiana.
L. tenebrosa.	L.-c. × Truffautiana.
L. xanthina.	L.-c. × Ophir.
Læliocattleya × callistoglossa.	L.-c. × Colmaniana.
L.-c. × elegans.	L.-c. × Fournieræ.
L.-c. × Schilleriana.	L.-c. × Lucilia.

13. **C. Eldorado.**

Brassavola Digbyana.	Brassocattleya × Pocahontas.
C. Bowringiana.	C. × Rothwelliæ.
C. Dowiana.	C. × Ingramæ.
C. Gaskelliana.	C. × Nymph.
C. labiata.	C. × Maronæ.
C. Leopoldi.	C. × Mitchellii.
C. Warscewiczii.	C. × Marriottiæ.
Lælia crispa.	Læliocattleya × Pisandra.
L. harpophylla.	L.-c. × Maroni.
L. xanthina.	L.-c. × odorata.

14. **C. elongata.**

C. labiata.	C. × Rembrandt.

15. **C. Forbesii.**

C. Aclandiæ.	C. × quinquecolor.
C. Dowiana.	C. × fulvescens.
C. Gaskelliana.	C. × Winniana.
C. intermedia.	C. × Isabella.
C. Mendelii.	C. × Melpomene.
C. Mossiæ.	C. × Heloisiæ.
C. superba.	C. × superforbesii.
C. velutina.	C. × Juno.
Lælia purpurata.	Læliocattleya × Reginæ.

16. **C. Gaskelliana.**

Brassavola Digbyana.	Brassocattleya × Thorntoni.
C. Bowringiana.	C. × Ariel.
C. Dowiana.	C. × Rothschildiana.

Cattleya Gaskelliana—(*continued*).

C. Eldorado.	C. × Nymph.
C. Forbesii.	C. × Winniana.
C. Harrisoniana.	C. × Williamsiæ.
C. Leopoldi.	C. × Doris.
C. Loddigesii.	C. × Greavesiæ.
C. Lueddemanniana.	C. × Cybele.
C. maxima.	C. × Milleri.
C. Rex.	C. × Pearl.
C. Schilleriana.	C. × Goossensiana.
C. superba.	C. × mollis.
C. Warscewiczii.	C. × Harold.
Epidendrum costaricense.	Epicattleya × Lilianæ.
Lælia anceps.	L.-c. × novissima.
L. Boothiana.	Læliocattleya × Ethelwald.
L. crispa.	L.-c. × Bryan.
L. Dayana.	L.-c. × Eunomia.
L. Perrinii.	L.-c. × Semiramis.
L. purpurata.	L.-c. × Roeblingii.
L. tenebrosa.	L.-c. × Eva.
L. xanthina.	L.-c. × Astoræ.
Læliocattleya × elegans.	L.-c. × Herga.
L.-c. × Proserpine.	L.-c. × Tyro.

17. C. granulosa.

C. Aclandiæ.	C. × Bleui.
C. amethystoglossa.	C. × granuglossa.
C. Dowiana.	C. × Pittiana.
C. × Hardyana.	C. × Germania.
C. Harrisoniana.	C. × Gratrixiæ.
C. labiata.	C. × Imperator.
C. Leopoldi.	C. × Titus.
C. Mendelii.	C. × weedoniensis.
C. Mossiæ.	C. × Dallemagneæ.
C. Rex.	C. × Shakespeare.
C. Schilleriana.	C. × resplendens.
C. superba.	C. × Nephthys.
C. velutina.	C. × Greyæ.
C. Walkeriana.	C. × Leucothoe.
C. Warscewiczii.	C. × Wavriniana.
Lælia cinnabarina.	Læliocattleya × Milleræ.
L. crispa.	L.-c. × Mylamiana.
L. Dayana.	L.-c. × Galatea.
L. purpurata.	L.-c. × burbagensis.
L. tenebrosa.	L.-c. × Magnei.
L. xanthina.	L.-c. × Robinii.
Læliocattleya × Schilleriana.	L.-c. × Noel.

18. C. guttata.

C. Loddigesii.	C. × hybrida.

Cattleya—(*continued*).

19. C. × Hardyana.

Brassavola Digbyana.	Brassocattleya × heatonensis.
C. Bowringiana.	C. × Whiteleyæ.
C. granulosa.	C. × Germania.
C. labiata.	C. × Peetersii.
C. Leopoldi.	C. × Fowleri.
C. Mendelii.	C. × Roehrsiana.
Lælia cinnabarina.	Læliocattleya × Edwardi.
L. pumila.	L.-c. × rubens.
L. tenebrosa.	L.-c. × Haroldiana.
Læliocattleya × albanensis.	L.-c. × dellensis.
L.-c. × elegans.	L.-c. × Chantinii.
L.-c. × Schilleriana.	L.-c. × Greenwoodii.

20. C. × Harrisii.

C. Bowringiana.	C. × Fabiola.

21. C. Harrisoniana.

C. Bowringiana.	C. × Browniæ.
C. Dowiana.	C. × Pittiæ.
C. Gaskelliana.	C. × Williamsiæ.
C. granulosa.	C. × Gratrixiæ.
C. Leopoldi.	C. × Lucianiana.
C. Mossiæ.	C. × highburiensis.
C. Schilleriana.	C. × Daphne.
Lælia cinnabarina.	Læliocattleya × Gladys.
L. Dayana.	L.-c. × Groganiæ.
L. harpophylla.	L.-c. × Luna.
L. pumila.	L.-c. × confusa.
L. purpurata.	L.-c. × Whitiniæ.
L. tenebrosa.	L.-c. × Cranstouniæ.
Sophronitis grandiflora.	Sophrocattleya × Chamberlaini.

22. C. intermedia.

Brassavola fragrans.	Brassocattleya × nivalis.
C. Aclandiæ.	C. × calummata.
C. amethystoglossa.	C. × interglossa.
C. aurantiaca.	C. × aurantimedia.
C. citrina.	C. × lamberhurstensis.
C. Forbesii.	C. × Isabella.
C. Leopoldi.	C. × intricata.
C. Loddigesii.	C. × Claesiana.
C. Lueddemanniana.	C. × Claridiana.
C. maxima.	C. × Dominiana.
C. Mendelii.	C. × suavior.

Cattleya intermedia—(*continued*).

C. Mossiæ.	C. × Mackayi.
C. Percivaliana.	C. × brunoyensis.
C. Schilleriana.	C. × Bertheauana.
C. Schrœderæ.	C. × Thayeriana.
C. Skinneri.	C. × belairensis.
C. superba.	C. × porphyrophlebia.
C. Trianæ.	C. × Olivia.
Lælia cinnabarina.	Læliocattleya × Amelia.
L. flava.	L.-c. × Fournieri.
L. grandis.	L.-c. × Ella.
L. purpurata.	L.-c. × Schilleriana.
Læliocattleya × elegans.	L.-c. × Cicero.
L.-c. × Hippolyta.	L.-c. × Santiago.
L.-c × Schilleriana.	L.-c. × Zampa.
Sophronitis grandiflora.	Sophrocattleya × Batemanniana.

23. **C. × intricata.**

C. superba.	C. × Burberryana.

24. **C. iricolor.**

C. Mossiæ.	C. × Philo.

25. **C. × Isabella.**

C. Mossiæ.	C. × Parthenia.

26. **C. labiata.**

Brassavola Digbyana.	Brassocattleya × Fournieræ.
C. Aclandiæ.	C. × Eurydice.
C. bicolor.	C. × Clarkiæ.
C. Bowringiana.	C. × Portia.
C. × Brymeriana.	C. × Viceroy.
C. dolosa.	C. × rubescens.
C. Dowiana.	C. × Fabia.
C. Eldorado.	C. × Maronæ.
C. elongata.	C. × Rembrandt.
C. granulosa.	C × Imperator.
C. × Hardyana.	C. × Peetersii.
C. Lawrenceana.	C. × Mars.
C. Leopoldi.	C. × Victoria-Regina.
C. Loddigesii.	C. × Mastersonæ.
C. Mossiæ.	C. × Œnone.
Lælia anceps.	Læliocattleya × Liptoni.
L. autumnalis.	L.-c. × cornuta.
L. cinnabarina.	L.-c. × Coronis.
L. crispa.	L.-c. × Veitchiana.
L. Dayana.	L. c. × Wilsonæ.

Cattleya labiata—(*continued*).

L. Perrinii.	L.-c. × Statteriana.
L. pumila.	L.-c. × Cornelia.
L. purpurata.	L.-c. × bella.
L. tenebrosa.	L.-c. × Lucasiana.
Læliocattleya × Clive.	L.-c. × Cooksonæ.
L.-c. × elegans.	L.-c. × Schulzeana.
L.-c. × exoniensis.	L.-c. × Leonæ.
L.-c. × Gottoiana.	L.-c. × Jeanette.
L.-c. × Schilleriana.	L.-c. × Scottiana.

27. **C. Lawrenceana.**

C. labiata.	C. × Mars.
C. Lueddemanniana.	C. × Preciosa.
C. Mendelii.	C. × Murrayi.
C. Mossiæ.	C. × Lawre-mossiæ.
C. Percivaliana.	C. × Sedenii.
C. Schilleriana.	C. × Firebrand.
C. Schrœderæ.	C. × Jussieu.
C. Trianæ.	C. × Cecilia.
C. Warscewiczii.	C. × Jupiter.
Lælia Boothiana.	Læliocattleya × Hilda.
L. cinnabarina.	L.-c. × highburiensis.
L. harpophylla.	L.-c. × Ida.
L. Perrinii.	L.-c. × Minerva.
L. purpurata.	L.-c. × Hyeana.
L. tenebrosa.	L.-c. × Baden-Powellii.
Læliocattleya × elegans.	L.-c. × Ruby.

28. **C. Leopoldi.**

Brassavola Digbyana.	Brassocattleya × conspicua.
B. Perrinii.	B.-c. × belairensis.
C. bicolor.	C. × Mahleræ.
C. Bowringiana.	C. × Bactia.
C. Dowiana.	C. × Chamberlainiana.
C. Eldorado.	C. × Mitchellii.
C. Gaskelliana.	C. × Doris.
C. granulosa.	C. × Titus.
C. × Hardyana.	C. × Fowleri.
C. Harrisoniana.	C. × Lucianiana.
C. intermedia.	C. × intricata.
C. labiata.	C. × Victoria-Regina.
C. Loddigesii.	C. × Patrocinii.
C. Mendelii.	C. × Harrisii.
C. Mossiæ.	C. × Cyane.

Cattleya Leopoldi (*continued*).

C. Schrœderæ.	C. × Gautheriniana.
C. superba.	C. × Feuillatii.
C. Trianæ.	C. × Zeo.
C. Warscewiczii.	C. × Atalanta.
Lælia cinnabarina.	Læliocattleya × Diogenes.
L. crispa.	L.-c. × devoniensis.
L. harpophylla.	L.-c. × Osyana.
L. pumila.	L.-c. × olivetensis.
L. tenebrosa.	L.-c. × Issy.
Læliocattleya × elegans.	L.-c. × La-Fresnaie.
L.-c. × Schilleriana.	L.-c. × aurelianensis.
Sophronitis grandiflora.	Sophrocattleya × Cleopatra.

29. **C. Loddigesii.**

C. Aclandiæ.	C. × Brabantiæ.
C. Bowringiana.	C. × Minerva.
C. Gaskelliana.	C. × Greavesiæ.
C. guttata.	C. × hybrida.
C. intermedia.	C. × Claesiana.
C. labiata.	C. × Marstersonæ.
C. Leopoldi.	C. × Patrocinii.
C. Lueddemanniana.	C. × Manglesii.
C. maxima.	C. × olivetensis.
C. Mendelii.	C. × Clarissa.
C. Skinneri.	C. × Astræa.
C. superba.	C. × Breauteana.
C. Trianæ.	C. × Albertiana.
C. Warscewiczii.	C. × Minucia.
Lælia crispa.	Læliocattleya × Tresederiana.
L. Dayana.	L.-c. × Aurora.
L. Perrinii.	L.-c. × amœna.
L. pumila.	L.-c. × Leeana.
L. purpurata.	L.-c. × Sallieri.
Læliocattleya × elegans.	L.-c. × Zenobia.
L.-c. × exoniensis.	L.-c. × fausta.
L.-c. × fausta.	L.-c. × leucoglossa.
L.-c. × Schilleriana.	L.-c. × Behrensiana.
Sophronitis grandiflora.	Sophrocattleya × Calypso.

30. **C. Lueddemanniana.**

C. amethystoglossa.	C. × Thorntoni.
C. bicolor.	C. × Geleniana.
C. Dowiana.	C. × Kienastiana.
C. Gaskelliana.	C. × Cybele.
C. intermedia.	C. × Claridiana.
C. Lawrenceana.	C. × Preciosa.

Cattleya Lueddemanniana—(*contd.*).

C. Loddigesii.	C. × Manglesii.
C. Schilleriana.	C. × Claudian.
C. Trianæ.	C. × Princess.
C. velutina.	C. × Measuresiæ.
Lælia Dayana.	Læliocattleya × Timora.
L. Perrinii.	L.-c. × Hermione.
L. pumila.	L.-c. × porphyrea.
L. purpurata.	L.-c. × Duvaliana.
Læliocattleya × devoniensis.	L.-c. × Mardellii.
L.-c. × Schilleriana.	L.-c. × Ada.

31. **C. luteola.**

C. Dormaniana.	C. × Arthuriana.
C. Dowiana.	C. × Aurora.
C. × Parthenia.	C. × exquisita.
C. Trianæ.	C. × flavescens.

32. **C. Marstersoniæ.**

Lælia pumila.	Læliocattleya × Isis.

33. **C. maxima.**

C. Aclandiæ.	C. × Rooseveltiæ.
C. Bowringiana.	C. × Chloris.
C. Dowiana.	C. × vestalis.
C. Gaskelliana.	C. × Milleri.
C. intermedia.	C. × Dominiana.
C. Loddigesii.	C. × olivetensis.
C. Skinneri.	C. × Eclipse.
Lælia crispa.	Læliocattleya × Amesiana.
L. pumila.	L.-c. × Measuresii.
L. purpurata.	L.-c. × Amazone.
Læliocattleya × elegans.	L.-c. × Darwiniana.

34. **C. Mendelii.**

Brassavola Digbyana.	Brassocattleya × Maroni.
C. Aclandiæ.	C. × Niobe.
C. Dowiana.	C. × Octavia.
C. Forbesii.	C. × Melpomene.
C. granulosa.	C. × weedoniensis.
C. × Hardyana.	C. × Roehrsiana.
C. intermedia.	C. × suavior.
C. Lawrenceana.	C. × Murrayi.
C. Leopoldi.	C. × Harrisii.
C. Loddigesii.	C. × Clarissa.
C. Rex.	C. × Halevy.
C. Warscewiczii.	C. × armainvillierensis.
Lælia cinnabarina.	Læliocattleya × Lucia.
L. × Latona.	L.-c. × Cora.
L. purpurata.	L.-c. × Aphrodite.

Cattleya Mendelii—(*continued*).

L. tenebrosa.	L.-c. × Acis.
L. xanthina.	L.-c. × Zephyra.
Læliocattleya × Schilleriana.	L.-c. × Powellii.

35. C. Mossiæ.

Brassavola Digbyana.	Brassocattleya × Veitchii.
B. fragrans.	B.-c. × striata.
C. Aclandiæ.	C. × Apollo.
C. Dowiana.	C. × Frederickiæ.
C. Forbesii.	C. × Heloisiæ.
C. granulosa.	C. × Dallemagneæ.
C. Harrisoniana.	C. × highburiensis.
C. intermedia.	C. × Mackayi.
C. iricolor.	C. × Philo.
C. × Isabella.	C. × Parthenia.
C. labiata.	C. × Œnone.
C. Lawrenceana.	C. × Lawre-mossiæ.
C. Leopoldi.	C. × Cyane.
C. Rex.	C. × Faerie-Queene.
C. Schilleriana.	C. × Harrisiæ.
C. superba.	C. × Gertrude.
C. Walkeriana.	C. × Eros.
C. Warneri.	C. × intertexta.
C. Warscewiczii.	C. × Adonis.
Lælia Boothiana.	Læliocattleya × mollis.
L. cinnabarina.	L.-c. × Hippolyta.
L. crispa.	L.-c. × exoniensis.
L. grandiflora.	L.-c. × Juno.
L. grandis.	L.-c. × Hebe.
L. harpophylla.	L.-c. × Hodgkinsonæ.
L. Perrinii.	L.-c. × Beranekii.
L. purpurata.	L.-c. × Canhamiana.
L. superbiens.	L.-c. × Choletiana.
L. tenebrosa.	L.-c. × Martinetii.
L. xanthina.	L.-c. × Norba.
Læliocattleya × Amesiana.	L.-c. × Nephelia.
L.-c. × elegans.	L.-c. × Krænzlinii.
L.-c. × Gottoiana.	L.-c. × Wiganiæ.
L.-c. × Hippolyta.	L.-c. × Ceres.
L.-c. × Schilleriana.	L.-c. × Fortuna.
Schomburgkia tibicinis.	Schombocattleya × spiralis.
Sophronitis grandiflora.	Sophrocattleya × Imperatrix.

36. C. × O'Brieniana.

Læliocattleya × elegans.	Læliocattleya × Herode.

Cattleya—(*continued*).

37. C. × Parthenia.

C. luteola.	C. × exquisita.
C. Warneri.	C. × Wellsiæ.

38. C. × Patrocinii.

C. Dowiana.	C. × Saint-Gilles.
C. Warscewiczii.	C. × mirabilis.

39. C. Percivaliana.

C. Dowiana.	C. × Leda.
C. intermedia.	C. × brunoyensis.
C. Lawrenceana.	C. × Sedenii.
C. quadricolor.	C. × Knightii.
C. Trianæ.	C. × Adela.
Lælia cinnabarina.	Læliocattleya × Percibarina.
L. flava.	L.-c. × Ernesti.
L. Perrinii.	L.-c. × Homere.
L. purpurata.	L.-c. × Electra.
Læliocattleya × elegans.	L.-c. × Venus.

40. C. quadricolor.

Brassavola Digbyana.	Brassocattleya × Chamberlainæ.
C. Percivaliana.	C. × Knightii.
Lælia cinnabarina.	Læliocattleya × Leopoldi.

41. C. Rex.

C. bicolor.	C. × Tankervilleæ.
C. Gaskelliana.	C. × Pearl.
C. granulosa.	C. × Shakespeare.
C. Mendelii.	C. × Halevy.
C. Mossiæ.	C. × Faerie-Queene.
C. velutina.	C. × Lloydiæ.
C. Warscewiczii.	C. × Clymene.
Lælia crispa.	Lælio-cattleya × Bievreana.
L. tenebrosa.	L.-c. × Doinii.
L. xanthina.	L.-c. × Constance.

42. C. Schilleriana.

C. Aclandiæ.	C. × peckaviensis.
C. Dowiana.	C. × Wiganii.
C. Gaskelliana.	C. × Goossensiana.
C. granulosa.	C. × resplendens.
C. Harrisoniana.	C. × Daphne.
C. intermedia.	C. × Bertheauana.
C. Lawrenceana.	C. × Firebrand.
C. Lueddemanniana.	C. × Claudian.
C. Mossiæ.	C. × Harrisiæ.
C. Trianæ.	C. × Elvina.
C. Warneri.	C. × Whitei.
C. Warscewiczii.	C. × Edwardi.

Cattleya Schilleriana—(*continued*).

Lælia cinnabarina.	Læliocattleya × Helena.
L. crispa.	L.-c. × felix.
L. purpurata.	L.-c. × Antigone.
L. tenebrosa.	L.-c. × Massangeana.
L. xanthina.	L.-c. × Gemma.
Læliocattleya × Schilleriana.	L.-c. × Morrisii.

43. C. Schrœderæ.

Brassavola Digbyana.	Brassocattleya × langleyensis.
B. glauca.	B.-c. × Sanderi.
C. Aclandiæ.	C. × Saint-Benoit.
C. Dowiana.	C. × Zephyra.
C. intermedia.	C. × Thayeriana.
C. Lawrenceana.	C. × Jussieu.
C. Leopoldi.	C. × Gautheriniana.
C. Trianæ.	C. × Cappei.
C. Warneri.	C. × Katherinæ.
C. Warscewiczii.	C. × Leoni.
Lælia cinnabarina.	Læliocattleya × Ballii.
L. flava.	L.-c. × Mercia.
L. grandis.	L.-c. × Bertha.
L. purpurata.	L.-c. × Fascinator.
L. tenebrosa.	L.-c. × Lycidas.
Læliocattleya × Hippolyta.	L.-c. × Dora.

44. C. Skinneri.

C. intermedia.	C. × belairensis.
C. Loddigesii.	C. × Astræa.
C. maxima.	C. × Eclipse.
Lælia cinnabarina.	Læliocattleya × Dido.
L. flava.	L.-c. × Marriottiana.
L. purpurata.	L.-c. × Speranskyæ.

45. C. superba.

C. Aclandiæ.	C. × Selfridgei.
C. Bowringiana.	C. × Charlesworthii.
C. Forbesii.	C. × superforbesii.
C. Gaskelliana.	C. × mollis.
C. granulosa.	C. × Nephthys.
C. intermedia.	C. × porphyrophlebia.
C. × intricata.	C. × Burberryana.
C. Leopoldi.	C. × Feuillatii.
C. Loddigesii.	C. × Breauteana.
C. Mossiæ.	C. × Gertrude.
C. Warscewiczii.	C. × Macænas.

Cattleya superba—(*continued*).

Lælia cinnabarina.	Læliocattleya × Sunray.
L. pumila.	L.-c. × Wavrinii.
L. tenebrosa.	L.-c. × Pharos.
Læliocattleya × devoniensis.	L.-c. × Sedenii.
L.-c. × Doris.	L.-c. × Vesta.
L.-c. × elegans.	L.-c. × Robsoni.
L.-c. × exoniensis.	L.-c. × triophthalma.

46. C. Trianæ.

Brassavola Digbyana.	Brassocattleya × Sedenii.
B. glauca.	B.-c. × Orpheus.
C. Aclandiæ.	C. × Lottie.
C. amethystoglossa.	C. × Miranda.
C. bicolor.	C. × Pandora.
C. Bowringiana.	C. × Barbara.
C. dolosa.	C. × Mariannæ.
C. Dowiana.	C. × Raphaelæ.
C. intermedia.	C. × Olivia.
C. Lawrenceana.	C. × Cecilia.
C. Leopoldi.	C. × Zeo.
C. Loddigesii.	C. × Albertiana.
C. Lueddemanniana.	C. × Princess.
C. luteola.	C. × flavescens.
C. Percivaliana.	C. × Adela.
C. Schilleriana.	C. × Elvina.
C. Schrœderæ.	C. × Cappei.
C. Warscewiczii.	C. × Ballantiniana.
Lælia anceps.	Læliocattleya × Boylei.
L. cinnabarina.	L.-c. × warnhamensis.
L. crispa.	L.-c. × massiliensis.
L. flava.	L.-c. × Myra.
L. grandiflora.	L.-c. × Eumæa.
L. harpophylla.	L.-c. × Doris.
L. Jongheana.	L.-c. × Schrœderæ.
L. pumila.	L.-c. × Tydea.
L. purpurata.	L.-c. × Wellsiana.
L. tenebrosa.	L.-c. × Mabel.
L. xanthina.	L.-c. × Ascania.
Læliocattleya × bella.	L.-c. × Alexandræ.
L.-c. × Dominiana.	L.-c. × Rosalind.
L.-c. × Sallieri.	L.-c. × Clementinæ.
L.-c. × Schilleriana.	L.-c. × Cybele.
Sophronitis grandiflora.	Sophrocattleya × Saxa.

47. C. velutina.

C. bicolor.	C. × Frasquita.

Cattleya velutina—(*continued*).

C. Bowringiana.	C. × Clytie.
C. Dowiana.	C. × Maroni.
C. Forbesii.	C. × Juno.
C. granulosa.	C. × Greyæ.
C. Lueddemanniana.	C. × Measuresiæ.
C. Rex.	C. × Lloydiæ.
C. Warneri.	C. × Paynteri.
Lælia Dayana.	Læliocattleya × Proserpine.
L. purpurata.	L.-c. × Alberti.
Læliocattleya × elegans.	L.-c. × Lutetia.

48. C. Walkeriana.

C. granulosa.	C. × Leucothoe.
C. Mossiæ.	C. × Eros.

49. C. Warneri.

Brassavola Digbyana.	Brassocattleya × Mariæ.
C. Bowringiana.	C. × Chapmanii.
C. Dowiana.	C. × Comet.
C. Mossiæ.	C. × intertexta.
C. × Parthenia.	C. × Wellsiæ.
C. Schilleriana.	C. × Whitei.
C. Schrœderæ.	C. × Katherinæ.
C. velutina.	C. × Paynteri.
Lælia cinnabarina.	Læliocattleya × Topaz.
L. crispa.	L.-c. × Cowperi.
L. grandis.	L.-c. × albanensis.
L. pumila.	L.-c. × hybrida.
L. purpurata.	L.-c. × eximia.
L. tenebrosa.	L.-c. × Gottoiana.
Læliocattleya × callistoglossa.	L.-c. × wisetonensis.
L.-c. × elegans.	L.-c. × Deweyi.

50. C. Warscewiczii.

Brassavola Digbyana.	Brassocattleya × Maronæ.
C. Aclandiæ.	C. × Fernandii.
C. bicolor.	C. × Ella.
C. Bowringiana.	C. × Wendlandiana.
C. Dowiana.	C. × Hardyana.
C. Eldorado.	C. × Marriottiæ.
C. Gaskelliana.	C. × Harold.
C. granulosa.	C. × Wavriniana.
C. Lawrenceana.	C. × Jupiter.
C. Leopoldi.	C. × Atalanta.
C. Loddigesii.	C. × Minucia.
C. Mendelii.	C. × armainvillierensis.
C. Mossiæ.	C. × Adonis.

Cattleya Warscewiczii—(*continued*).

C. × Patrocinii.	C. × mirabilis.
C. Rex.	C. × Clymene.
C. Schilleriana.	C. × Edwardi.
C. Schrœderæ.	C. × Leoni.
C. superba.	C. × Macænas.
C. Trianæ.	C. × Ballantiniana.
Lælia cinnabarina.	Læliocattleya × Cappei.
L. crispa.	L.-c. × Nysa.
L. Dayana.	L.-c. × Euphrosyne.
L. Perrinii.	L.-c. × Rothschildiæ.
L. pumila.	L.-c. × epicasta.
L. purpurata.	L.-c. × callistoglossa.
L. tenebrosa.	L.-c. × bletchleyensis.
L. xanthina.	L.-c. × Phryne.
Læliocattleya × amanda.	L.-c. × Brymeriana.
L.-c. × Canhamiana.	L.-c. × Britannia.
L.-c. × Dominiana.	L.-c. × Antimachus.
L.-c. × elegans.	L.-c. × Clonia.
L.-c. × Leeana.	L.-c. × Stepmanii.
L.-c. × Sallieri.	L.-c. × Scylla.
L.-c. × Schilleriana.	L.-c. × Marguerite.

11. CHYSIS.

1. C. bractescens.

C. × Chelsoni.	C. × langleyensis.
C. Limminghei.	C. × Sedenii.

2. C. Chelsoni.

C. bractescens.	C. × langleyensis.

3. C. lævis.

C. Limminghei.	C. × Chelsoni.

4. C. Limminghei.

C. bractescens.	C. × Sedenii.
C. lævis.	C. × Chelsoni.

12. COLAX.

C. jugosus.

Zygopetalum crinitum.	Zygocolax × Veitchii.
Z. intermedium.	Z.-c. × Wiganianus.
Z. Mackayi.	Z.-c. × Amesianus.
Z. maxillare.	Z.-c. × leopardinus.

13. CYMBIDIUM.

1. C. eburneum.

·C. Lowianum.	C. × Veitchii.
·C. Tracyanum.	C. × Wiganianum.

2. C. giganteum.

C. Mastersii.	C. × Winnianum.
C. Tracyanum.	C. × Bennett-Poei.
Phaius Wallichii.	Phaiocymbidium × chardwarense.

3. C. grandiflorum.

·C. Lowianum.	C. × Sedenii.
·C. Mastersii.	C. × Maroni.

4. C. Lowianum.

C. eburneum.	C. × Veitchii.
·C. grandiflorum.	C. × Sedenii.
C. Mastersii.	C. × Charlesworthii.
·C. tigrinum.	C. × Lowgrinum.

5. C. Mastersii.

C. giganteum.	C. × Winnianum.
C. grandiflorum.	C. × Maroni.
C. Lowianum.	C. × Charlesworthii.

6. C. tigrinum.

·C. Lowianum.	C. × Lowgrinum.

7. C. Tracyanum.

C. eburneum.	C. × Wiganianum.
C. giganteum.	C. × Bennett-Poei.

14. CYNORCHIS.

1. C. Lowiana.

·C. purpurata.	C. × kewensis.

2. C. purpurata.

·C. Lowiana.	C. × kewensis.

15. DENDROBIUM.

1. D. × Ainsworthii.

Dendrobium aureum.	D. × Gem.
D. × Cassiope.	D. × Andromeda.
D. Findlayanum.	D. × melanodiscus.
D. moniliforme.	D. × Doris.
D. nobile.	D. × Rubens.
D. primulinum.	D. × Achilles.
·D. signatum.	D. × Melpomene.
D. Wardianum.	D. × Lutwycheanum.
D. × Wiganiæ.	D. × Thwaitesiæ.

2. D. albosanguineum.

D. nobile.	D. × Murrayi.

Dendrobium—(*continued*).

3. D. aureum.

D. × Ainsworthii.	D. × Gem.
D. × Cassiope.	D. × Curtisii.
D. × euosmum.	D. × Cordelia.
D. Falconeri.	D. × Benita.
D. Findlayanum.	D. × Schneiderianum.
D. Hildebrandii.	D. × Elwesii.
D. Linawianum.	D. × dulce.
D. luteolum.	D. × cheltenhamense.
D. moniliforme.	D. × endocharis.
D. nobile.	D. × Ainsworthii.
D. × Rubens.	D. × Ariel.
D. signatum.	D. × Ophir.
D. superbum.	D. × Gemma.
D. Wardianum.	D. × Aspasia.

4. D. Bensonæ.

D. × Cassiope.	D. × Staffordi.
D. Maccarthiæ.	D. × Kenneth.
D. moniliforme.	D. × Virginia.
D. nobile.	D. × Florence.

5. D. bigibbum.

D. Linawianum.	D. × Sibyl.

6. D. Brymerianum.

D. nobile.	D. × Hunteri.

7. D × Cassiope.

D. × Ainsworthii.	D. × Andromeda.
D. aureum.	D. × Curtisii.
D. Bensonæ.	D. × Staffordi.
D. × Dominyanum.	D. × Domicassio.
D. Findlayanum.	D. × Minos.
D. Wardianum.	D. × Berkeleyi.

8. D. × cheltenhamense.

D. nobile.	D. × Thompsonianum.

9. D. × chlorostele.

D. nobile.	D. × Wilsoni.
D. Wardianum.	D. × Vulcan.

10. D. chrysotoxum.

D. pulchellum.	D. × illustre.

11. D. crassinode.

D. Findlayanum.	D. × Cypheri.
D. luteolum.	D. × Astræa.
D. Wardianum.	D. × Waltoni.

12. D. crepidatum.

D. nobile.	D. × Sedenii.

Dendrobium—(*continued*).

13. D. crystallinum.

D. moniliforme. D. × Æneas.

14. D. × Cybele.

D. moniliforme. D. × Scylla.

15. D. × Dominyanum.

D. × Cassiope. D. × Domicassio.
D. Findlayanum. D. × Burberryanum.
D. × Schneiderianum. D. × Holmesianum.

16. D. × endocharis.

D. nobile. D. × euosmum.

17. D. × euosmum.

D. aureum. D. × Cordelia.
D. signatum. D. × Imogen.

18. D. Falconeri.

D. aureum. D. × Benita.
D. moniliforme. D. × Vannerianum.
D. nobile. D. × Venus.

19. D. fimbriatum.

D. nobile. D. × Mantinii.

20. D. Findlayanum.

D. × Ainsworthii. D. × melanodiscus.
D. aureum. D. × Schneiderianum.
D. × Cassiope. D. × Minos.
D. crassinode. D. × Cypheri.
D. × Dominyanum. D. × Burberryanum.
D. Linawianum. D. × Harold.
D. nobile. D. × Cybele.
D. signatum. D. × clarense.
D. Wardianum. D. × harefieldiense.

21. D. formosum.

D. Lowii. D. × Lawrencei.

22. D. hercoglossum.

D. moniliforme. D. × Isis.

23. D. Hildebrandii.

D. aureum. D. × Elwesii.
D. nobile. D. × Ellisii.
D. Wardianum. D. × Haywoodiæ.

24. D. Huttoni.

D. pulchellum. D. × porphyrogastrum.
D. sanguinolentum. D. × rhodostoma.

Dendrobium—(*continued*).

25. D. Kingianum.

D. speciosum. D. × Spyersii.

26. D. Linawianum.

D. aureum. D. × dulce.
D. bigibbum. D. × Sibyl.
D. Findlayanum. D. × Harold.
D. nobile. D. × Dominyanum.
D. Wardianum. D. × chlorostele.

27. D. lituiflorum.

D. nobile. D. × Corningianum.
D. Wardianum. D. × micans.

28. D. Lowii.

D. formosum. D. × Lawrencei.

29. D. luteolum.

D. aureum. D. × cheltenhamense.
D. crassinode. D. × Astræa.
D. Wardianum. D. × Bryan.

30. D. Maccarthiæ.

D. Bensonæ. D. × Kenneth.

31. D. × melanodiscus.

D. nobile. D. × Magda.

32. D. moniliforme.

D. × Ainsworthii. D. × Doris.
D. aureum. D. × endocharis.
D. Bensonæ. D. × Virginia.
D. crystallinum. D. × Æneas.
D. × Cybele. D. × Scylla.
D. Falconeri. D. × Vannerianum.
D. hercoglossum. D. × Isis.
D. nobile. D. × Cassiope.
D. × Pitcherianum. D. × Galatea.
D. pulchellum. D. × Stratius.
D. Wardianum. D. × Veitchii.

33. D. nobile.

D. × Ainsworthii. D. × Rubens.
D. albosanguineum. D. × Murrayi.
D. aureum. D. × Ainsworthii.
D. Bensonæ. D. × Florence.
D. Brymerianum. D. × Hunteri.
D. × cheltenhamense. D. × Thompsonianum.
D. × chlorostele. D. × Wilsoni.
D. crepidatum. D. × Sedenii.
D. × endocharis. D. × euosmum.
D. Falconeri. D. × Venus.

Dendrobium nobile—(*continued*).

D. fimbriatum.	D. × Mantinii.
D. Findlayanum.	D. × Cybele.
D. Hildebrandii.	D. × Ellisii.
D. Linawianum.	D. × Dominyanum.
D. lituiflorum.	D. × Corningianum.
D. × melanodiscus.	D. × Magda.
D. moniliforme.	D. × Cassiope.
D. primulinum.	D. × Pitcherianum.
D. pulchellum.	D. × Whitei.
D. Ruckeri.	D. × Roeblingianum.
D. × Schneiderianum.	D. × Acis.
D. signatum.	D. × Wiganiæ.
D. suavissimum.	D. × Lotus.
D. thyrsiflorum.	D. × Backhousei.
D. tortile.	D. × Niobe.
D. Wardianum.	D. × murrhiniacum.

34. **D. Parishii.**

D. superbum.	D. × Nestor.

35. **D. Pierardi.**

D. superbum.	D. × Adrastus.

36. **D. × Pitcherianum.**

D. moniliforme.	D. × Galatea.

37. **D. primulinum.**

D. × Ainsworthii.	D. × Achilles.
D. nobile.	D. × Pitcherianum.
D. superbum.	D. × Mentor.

38. **D. pulchellum.**

D. chrysotoxum.	D. × illustre.
D. Huttoni.	D. × porphyrogastrum.
D. moniliforme.	D. × Stratius.
D. nobile.	D. × Whitei.

39. **D. × Rubens.**

D. aureum.	D. × Ariel.

40. **D. Ruckeri.**

D. nobile.	D. × Roeblingianum.

41. **D. sanguinolentum.**

D. Huttoni.	D. × rhodostoma.

42. **D. × Schneiderianum.**

D. × Dominyanum.	D. × Holmesianum.
D. nobile.	D. × Acis.

Dendrobium—(*continued*).

43. **D. signatum.**

D. × Ainsworthii.	D. × Melpomene.
D. aureum.	D. × Ophir.
D. × euosmum.	D. × Imogen.
D. Findlayanum.	D. × clarense.
D. nobile.	D. × Wiganiæ.

44. **D. speciosum.**

D. Kingianum.	D. × Spyersii.

45. **D. suavissimum.**

D. nobile.	D. × Lotus.

46. **D. superbum.**

D. aureum.	D. × Gemma.
D. Parishii.	D. × Nestor.
D. Pierardi.	D. × Adrastus.
D. primulinum.	D. × Mentor.

47. **D. thyrsiflorum.**

D. nobile.	D. × Backhousei.

48. **D. tortile.**

D. nobile.	D. × Niobe.

49. **D. Wardianum.**

D. × Ainsworthii.	D. × Lutwycheanum.
D. aureum.	D. × Aspasia.
D. × Cassiope.	D. × Berkeleyi.
D. × chlorostele.	D. × Vulcan.
D. crassinode.	D. × Waltoni.
D. Findlayanum.	D. × harefieldiense.
D. Hildebrandii.	D. × Haywoodiæ.
D. Linawianum.	D. × chlorostele.
D. lituiflorum.	D. × micans.
D. luteolum.	D. × Bryan.
D. moniliforme.	D. × Veitchii.
D. nobile.	D. × murrhiniacum.

50. **D. × Wiganiæ.**

D. × Ainsworthii.	D. × Thwaitesiæ.

16. DISA.

1. **D. grandiflora.**

D. × kewensis.	D. × Watsoni.
D. racemosa.	D. × Veitchii.
D. tripetaloides.	D. × kewensis.
D. × Veitchii.	D. × Diores.

2. **D. × kewensis.**

D. grandiflora.	D. × Watsoni.
D. × Veitchii.	D. × Elwesii.

3. **D. racemosa.**

D. grandiflora.	D. × Veitchii.

Disa racemosa—*(continued).*

D. tripetaloides.	D. × langleyensis.
D. × Veitchii.	D. × Luna.

4. **D. tripetaloides.**

D. grandiflora.	D. × kewensis.
D. racemosa.	D. × langleyensis.
D. × Veitchii.	D. × Premier.

5. **D. × Veitchii.**

D. grandiflora.	D. × Diores.
D. × kewensis.	D. × Elwesii.
D. racemosa.	D. × Luna.
D. tripetaloides.	D. × Premier.

17. DOSSINIA.

1. **D. marmorata.**

Hæmaria discolor.	Dossinimaria × Dominyi.

18. EPIDENDRUM.

1. **E. × Burtoni.**

E. radicans.	E. × Boundii.

2. **E. ciliare.**

E. Wallisii.	E. × Sedenii.
Lælia anceps.	Epilælia × Hardyana.
L. autumnalis.	E.-l. × belairensis.
L. Dayana.	E.-l. × Eros.

3. **E. cinnabarinum.**

E. × O'Brienianum.	E. × Acis.
E. radicans.	E. × Galatea.

4. **E. cochleatum.**

E. cucullatum.	E. × Cuco.

5. **E. Cooperianum.**

E. × O'Brienianum.	E. × heatonense.
Lælia cinnabarina.	Epilælia × Sylvia.

6. **E. costaricense.**

Cattleya Gaskelliana.	Epicattleya × Lilianæ.

7. **E. cucullatum.**

E. cochleatum.	E. × Cuco.

8. **E. elegantulum.**

E. Wallisii.	E. × Clarissa.

9. **E. elongatum.**

E. × O'Brienianum.	E. × Orpetii.

Epidendrum—*(continued).*

10. **E. Endresii.**

E. Wallisii.	E. × Veitchii.

11. **E. evectum.**

E. radicans.	E. × O'Brienianum.
E. xanthinum.	E. × kewense.

12. **E. Frederici-Gulielmi.**

E. radicans.	E. × Charlesworthii.

13. **E. fucatum.**

Lælia cinnabarina.	Epilælia × Whitei.

14. **E. ibaguense.**

E. × O'Brienianum.	E. × Burtoni.

15. **E. × O'Brienianum.**

Cattleya amethystoglossa.	Epicattleya × Orpetii.
C. Bowringiana.	E.-c. × O'Brieniæ.
C. × Clæsiana.	E.-c. × Nebo.
E. cinnabarinum.	E. × Acis.
E. Cooperianum.	E. × heatonense.
E. elongatum.	E. × Orpetii.
E. ibaguense.	E. × Burtoni.
E. pristes.	E. × Delphi.
E. radicans.	E. × Thayeri.
E. Stamfordianum.	E. × Berkeleyi.
E. vitellinum.	E. × Phœbus.
Lælia cinnabarina.	Epilælia × heatonensis.
Sophronitis violacea.	Epiphronitis × Orpetii.

16. **E. Parkinsonianum.**

Lælia grandis.	Epilælia × Margaritæ.

17. **E. pristes.**

E. × O'Brienianum.	E. × Delphi.

18. **E. pseudepidendrum.**

E. Wallisii.	E. × langleyense.

19. **E. radiatum.**

Cattleya Bowringiana.	Epicattleya × Sedenii.

20. **E. radicans.**

Cattleya Bowringiana.	Epicattleya × matutina.
E. × Burtoni.	E. × Boundii.
E. cinnabarinum.	E. × Galatea.

Epidendrum radicans (*continued*).

E. evectum.	E. × O'Brienianum.
E. Frederici-Gulielmi.	E. × Charlesworthii.
E. × O'Brienianum.	E. × Thayeri.
E. Stamfordianum.	E. × Olenus.
E. vitellinum.	E. × Cassiope.
E. xanthinum.	E. × dellense.
Lælia cinnabarina.	Epilælia × Charlesworthii.
L. purpurata.	E.-l. × Veitchii.
Sophronitis grandiflora.	Epiphronitis × Veitchii.

21. **E. Stamfordianum.**

E. × O'Brienianum.	E. × Berkeleyi.
E. radicans.	E. × Olenus.

22. **E.** × **Veitchii.**

E. × Wallisii.	E. × elegantulum.

23. **E. vitellinum.**

E. × O'Brienianum.	E. × Phœbus.
E. radicans.	E. × Cassiope.
Lælia tenebrosa.	Epilælia × Lawrencei.

24. **E. Wallisii.**

E. ciliare.	E. × Sedenii.
E. × elegantulum.	E. × Clarissa.
E. Endresii.	E. × Veitchii.
E. pseudepidendrum.	E. × langleyense.
E. × Veitchii.	E. × elegantulum.

25. **E. xanthinum.**

E. evectum.	E. × kewense.
E. radicans.	E. × dellense.

19. HÆMARIA.

1. **Hæmaria discolor.**

Anœctochilus Roxburghii.	Anœctomaria × Dominyi.
Dossinia marmorata.	Dossinimaria × Dominyi.
Macodes Petola.	Macomaria × Veitchii.

20. LÆLIA.

1. **Lælia albida.**

Cattleya Bowringiana.	Læliocattleya × Bowrialbida.

Lælia—(*continued*).

2. **L. anceps.**

Cattleya Bowringiana.	Læliocattleya × Wrigleyi.
C. Gaskelliana.	L.-c. × novissima.
C. labiata.	L.-c. × Liptoni.
C. Trianæ.	L.-c. × Boylei.
Epidendrum ciliare.	Epilælia × Hardyana.
L. pumila.	L. × amœna.
L. purpurata.	L. × Edissa.
L. superbiens.	L. × Nemesis.

3. **L. autumnalis.**

Cattleya Bowringiana.	Læliocattleya × belairensis.
C. labiata.	L.-c. × cornuta.
Epidendrum ciliare.	Epilælia × belairensis.
L. cinnabarina.	L. × Stanislaus.
L. purpurata.	L. × Omen.

4. **L. Boothiana.**

Cattleya dolosa.	Læliocattleya × Praeti.
C. Gaskelliana.	L.-c. × Ethelwald.
C. Lawrenceana.	L.-c. × Hilda.
C. Mossiæ.	L.-c. × mollis.
L. purpurata.	L. × pulcherrima.
L. tenebrosa.	L. × Mozart.

5. **L. cinnabarina.**

Brassavola Digbyana.	Brassolælia × Gratrixiæ.
B. glauca.	B.-l. × Clio.
Cattleya Aclandiæ.	Læliocattleya × Adolphus.
C. amethystoglossa.	L.-c. × Marica.
C. Dowiana.	L.-c. × Charlesworthii.
C. granulosa.	L.-c. × Milleræ.
C. × Hardyana.	L.-c. × Edwardi.
C. Harrisoniana.	L.-c. × Gladys.
C. intermedia.	L.-c. × Amelia.
C. labiata.	L.-c. × Coronis.
C. Lawrenceana.	L.-c. × highburiensis.
C. Leopoldi.	L.-c. × Diogenes.
C. Mendelii.	L.-c. × Lucia.
C. Mossiæ.	L.-c. × Hippolyta.
C. Percivaliana.	L.-c. × Percibarina.
C. quadricolor.	L.-c. × Leopoldi.
C. Schilleriana.	L.-c. × Helena.
C. Schrœderæ.	L.-c. × Ballii.
C. Skinneri.	L.-c. × Dido.
C. superba.	L.-c. × Sunray.

Lælia cinnabarina—(*continued*).

C. Trianæ.	L.-c. × warnhamensis.
C. Warneri.	L.-c. × Topaz.
C. Warscewiczii.	L.-c. × Cappei.
Epidendrum Cooperianum.	Epilælia × Sylvia.
E. fucatum.	E.-l. × Whitei.
E. × O'Brienianum.	E.-l. × heatonensis.
E. radicans.	E.-l. × Charlesworthii.
L. autumnalis.	L. × Stanislaus.
L. flava.	L. × Icarius.
L. grandiflora.	L. × Dutremblayi.
L. grandis.	L. × Ragotiana.
L. harpophylla.	L. × Coronet.
L. × Pilcheri.	L. × flammea.
L. purpurata.	L. × Latona.
L. tenebrosa.	L. × cinnabrosa.
Læliocattleya × bella.	Læliocattleya × Iberia.
L.-c. × callistoglossa.	L.-c. × Lowii.
L.-c. × Pallas.	L.-c. × Picanus.
Leptotes bicolor.	Leptolælia × Veitchii.
Sophronitis grandiflora	Sophrolælia × Psyche.

6. **L. crispa.**

Cattleya bicolor.	Læliocattleya × Terentia.
C. Dowiana.	L.-c. × Pallas.
C. Eldorado.	L.-c. × Pisandra.
C. Gaskelliana.	L.-c. × Bryan.
C. granulosa.	L.-c. × Mylamiana.
C. labiata.	L.-c. × Veitchiana.
C. Leopoldi.	L.-c. × devoniensis.
C. Loddigesii.	L.-c. × Tresederiana.
C. maxima.	L.-c. × Amesiana.
C. Mossiæ.	L.-c. × exoniensis.
C. Rex.	L.-c. × Bievreana.
C. Schilleriana.	L.-c. × felix.
C. Trianæ.	L.-c. × massiliensis.
C. Warneri.	L.-c. × Cowperi.
C. Warscewiczii.	L.-c. × Nysa.
L. Dayana.	L.-c. × Euterpe.
L. Perrinii.	L. × Pilcheri.
L. pumila.	L. × Gravesiæ.
L. purpurata.	L. × splendens.
L. tenebrosa.	L. × crispabrosa.
L. xanthina.	L. × Olivia.

Lælia crispa—(*continued*).

Læliocattleya × Dominiana.	Læliocattleya × Victoria.
L.-c. × Schilleriana.	L.-c. × Stella.

7. **L. Dayana.**

Cattleya bicolor.	Læliocattleya × Hamiltoni.
C. Bowringiana.	L.-c. × Meteor.
C. dolosa.	L.-c. × Maynardi.
C. Dowiana.	L.-c. × Ingrami.
C. Gaskelliana.	L.-c. × Eunomia.
C. granulosa.	L.-c. × Galatea.
C. Harrisoniana.	L.-c. × Groganiæ.
C. labiata.	L.-c. × Wilsonæ.
C. Loddigesii.	L.-c. × Aurora.
C. Lueddemanniana.	L.-c. × Timora.
C. velutina.	L.-c. × Proserpine.
C. Warscewiczii.	L.-c. × Euphrosyne.
Epidendrum ciliare.	Epilælia × Eros.
L. crispa.	L. × Euterpe.
L. Perrinii.	L. × Exquisite.
L. purpurata.	L. × Diana.
L. tenebrosa.	L. × Iona.
L. xanthina.	L. × Oweniana.
Sophronitis grandiflora.	Sophrolælia × læta.

8. **L. × Euterpe.**

Cattleya Dowiana.	L.-c. × Astræa.

9. **L. flava.**

Cattleya intermedia.	Læliocattleya × Fournieri.
C. Percivaliana.	L.-c. × Ernesti.
C. Schrœderæ.	L.-c. × Mercia.
C. Skinneri.	L.-c. × Marriottiana.
C. Trianæ.	L.-c. × Myra.
L. cinnabarina.	L.-c. × Icarius.
L. pumila.	L.-c. × Flavina.
Sophronitis grandiflora.	Sophrolælia × Marriottiana.

10. **L. grandiflora.**

Cattleya Mossiæ.	Læliocattleya × Juno.
C. Trianæ.	L.-c. × Eumæa.
L. cinnabarina.	L. × Dutremblayi.

11. **L. grandis.**

Cattleya intermedia.	Læliocattleya × Ella.
C. Mossiæ.	L.-c. × Hebe.
C. Schrœderæ.	L.-c. × Bertha.
C. Warneri.	L.-c. × albanensis.

Lælia grandis—(*continued*).

Epidendrum Parkinsonianum.	Epilælia × Margaritæ.
L. cinnabarina.	L. × Ragotiana.
L. purpurata.	L. × Mantinii.

12. L. × Gravesiæ.

Cattleya Dowiana.	Læliocattleya × Clytie.

13. L. harpophylla.

Brassavola glauca.	Brassolælia × Bouteletii.
Cattleya amethystoglossa.	Læliocattleya × Ghislainæ.
C. bicolor.	L.-c. × leucasta.
C. Eldorado.	L.-c. × Maroni.
C. Harrisoniana.	L.-c. × Luna.
C. Lawrenceana.	L.-c. × Ida.
C. Leopoldi.	L.-c. × Osyana.
C. Mossiæ.	L.-c. × Hodgkinsonæ.
C. Trianæ.	L.-c. × Doris.
L. cinnabarina.	L. × Coronet.
L. purpurata.	L. × Briseis.
L. tenebrosa.	L. × stellata.
Læliocattleya × Sallieri.	L.-c. × ochracea.
Sophronitis grandiflora.	Sophrolælia × Valda.

14. L. Jongheana.

Cattleya Trianæ.	Læliocattleya × Schrœderæ.

15. L. × Latona.

Cattleya Mendelii.	L.-c. × Cora.
L. tenebrosa.	L. × Minerva.

16. L. longipes.

Læliocattleya × Schilleriana.	L.-c. × Ira.

17. L. Perrinii.

Cattleya Dowiana.	L.-c. × Decia.
C. Gaskelliana.	L.-c. × Semiramis.
C. labiata.	L.-c. × Statteriana.
C. Lawrenceana.	L.-c. × Minerva.
C. Loddigesii.	L.-c. × amœna.
C. Lueddemanniana.	L.-c. × Hermione.
C. Mossiæ.	L.-c. × Beranekii.
C. Percivaliana.	L.-c. × Homere.
C. Warscewiczii.	L.-c. × Rothschildiæ.
L. crispa.	L. × Pilcheri.
L. Dayana.	L. × Exquisite.

Lælia Perrinii—(*continued*).

L. pumila.	L. × juvenilis.
L. purpurata.	L. × Ingramæ.
Læliocattleya × elegans.	Læliocattleya × Diarmid.

18. L. × Pilcheri.

L. cinnabarina.	L. × flammea.

19. L. pumila.

Cattleya Aclandiæ.	L.-c. × Dallemagnei.
C. bicolor.	L.-c. × Binoti.
C. Bowringiana.	L.-c. × Parysatis.
C. Dowiana.	L.-c. × Clive.
C. × Hardyana.	L.-c. × rubens.
C. Harrisoniana.	L.-c. × confusa.
C. labiata.	L.-c. × Cornelia.
C. Leopoldi.	L.-c. × olivetensis.
C. Loddigesii.	L.-c. × Leeana.
C. Lueddemanniana.	L.-c. × porphyrea.
C. × Marstersonæ.	L.-c. × Isis.
C. maxima.	L.-c. × Measuresii.
C. superba.	L.-c. × Wavrinii.
C. Trianæ.	L.-c. × Tydea.
C. Warneri.	L.-c. × hybrida.
C. Warscewiczii.	L.-c. × epicasta.
L. anceps.	L. × amœna.
L. crispa.	L. × Gravesiæ.
L. flava.	L. × Flavina.
L. Perrinii.	L. × juvenilis.
L. tenebrosa.	L. × nigrescens.
Læliocattleya × elegans.	Læliocattleya × Novelty.
L.-c. × exoniensis.	L.-c. × Cassiope.
Sophronitis grandiflora.	Sophrolælia × Orpetii.

20. L. purpurata.

Brassavola Digbyana.	Brassolælia × Veitchii.
Cattleya Aclandiæ.	Læliocattleya × Emiliæ.
C. dolosa.	L.-c. × radiata.
C. Dowiana.	L.-c. × Dominiana.
C. Forbesii.	L.-c. × Reginæ.
C. Gaskelliana.	L.-c. × Roeblingii.
C. granulosa.	L.-c. × berbagensis.
C. Harrisoniana.	L.-c. × Whitiniæ.
C. intermedia.	L.-c. × Schilleriana.
C. labiata.	L.-c. × bella.
C. Lawrenceana.	L.-c. × Hyeana.
C. Loddigesii.	L.-c. × Sallieri.

Lælia purpurata—(*continued*).

C. Lueddemanniana.	L.-c. × Duvaliana.
C. maxima.	L.-c. × Amazone.
C. Mendelii.	L.-c. × Aphrodite.
C. Mossiæ.	L.-c. × Canhamiana.
C. Percivaliana.	L.-c. × Electra.
C. Schilleriana.	L.-c. × Antigone.
C. Schrœderæ.	L.-c. × Fascinator.
C. Skinneri.	L.-c. × Speranskyæ.
C. Trianæ.	L.-c. × Wellsiana.
C. velutina.	L.-c. × Alberti.
C. Warneri.	L.-c. × eximia.
C. Warscewiczii.	L.-c. × callistoglossa.
Epidendrum radicans.	Epilælia × Veitchii.
L. anceps.	L. × Edissa.
L. autumnalis.	L. × Omen.
L. Boothiana.	L. × pulcherrima.
L. cinnabarina.	L. × Latona.
L. crispa.	L. × splendens.
L. Dayana.	L. × Diana.
L. grandis.	L. × Mantinii.
L. harpophylla.	L. × Briseis.
L. Perrinii.	L. × Ingramæ.
L. tenebrosa.	L. × Pacavia.
Læliocattleya × callistoglossa.	Læliocattleya × Birkbeckiæ.
L.-c. × Dominiana.	L.-c. × Wiganiana.
L.-c. × elegans.	L.-c. × Pringiersii.
L.-c. × Schilleriana.	L.-c. × Horniana.
Sophronitis grandiflora.	Sophrolælia × heatonensis.

21. L. superbiens.

Cattleya Aclandiæ.	Læliocattleya × Humberti.
C. Mossiæ.	L.-c. × Choletiana.
L. anceps.	L. × Nemesis.

22. L. tenebrosa.

Brassavola Digbyana.	Brassolælia × Helen.
Cattleya Aclandiæ.	Læliocattleya × Remula.
C. bicolor.	L.-c. × La-France.
C. Bowringiana.	L.-c. × Irene.
C. × Brymeriana.	L.-c. × Milleri.
C. Dowiana.	L.-c. × Truffautiana.
C. Gaskelliana.	L.-c. × Eva.
C. granulosa.	L.-c. × Magnei.
C. × Hardyana.	L.-c. × Haroldiana.
C. Harrisoniana.	L.-c. × Cranstounæ.
C. labiata.	L.-c. × Lucasiana.
C. Lawrenceana.	L.-c. × Baden-Powellii.
C. Leopoldi.	L.-c. × Issy.
C. Mendelii.	L.-c. × Acis.
C. Mossiæ.	L.-c. × Martinetii.
C. Rex.	L.-c. × Doinii.
C. Schilleriana.	L.-c. × Massangeana.
C. Schrœderæ.	L.-c. × Lycidas.
C. superba.	L.-c. × Pharos.
C. Trianæ.	L.-c. × Mabel.
C. Warneri.	L.-c. × Gottoiana.
C. Warscewiczii.	L.-c. × bletchleyensis.
Epidendrum vitellinum.	Epilælia × Lawrencei.
L. Boothiana.	L. × Mozart.
L. cinnabarina.	L. × cinnabrosa.
L. crispa.	L. × crispabrosa.
L. Dayana.	L. × Iona.
L. harpophylla.	L. × stellata.
L. × Latona.	L. × Minerva.
L. pumila.	L. × nigrescens.
L. purpurata.	L. × Pacavia.
L.-c. × callistoglossa.	L.-c. × Ivernia.
L.-c. × Canhamiana.	L.-c. × Kathleen.
L.-c. × Hippolyta.	L.-c. × Vinesiæ.
L.-c. × Schilleriana.	L.-c. × Celestinæ.
Sophronitis grandiflora.	Sophrolælia × Gratrixiæ.

23. L. xanthina.

Cattleya bicolor.	Læliocattleya × elsteadensis.
C. Dormaniana.	L.-c. × Sanderæ.
C. Dowiana.	L.-c. × Ophir.
C. Eldorado.	L.-c. × odorata.
C. Gaskelliana.	L.-c. × Astoræ.
C. granulosa.	L.-c. × Robinii.
C. Mendelii.	L.-c. × Zephyra.
C. Mossiæ.	L.-c. × Norba.
C. Rex.	L.-c. × Constance.
C. Schilleriana.	L.-c. × Gemma.
C. Trianæ.	L.-c. × Ascania.
C. Warscewiczii.	L.-c. × Phryne.
L. crispa.	L. × Olivia.
L. Dayana.	L. × Oweniana.

21. LÆLIOCATTLEYA.

1. L.-c. × albanensis.

Cattleya × Hardyana.	L.-c. × dellensis.

2. L.-c. × amanda.

C. Warscewiczii.	L.-c. × Brymeriana.

3. L.-c. × Amesiana.

C. Mossiæ.	L.-c. × Nephelia.

4. L.-c. × Aphrodite.

Brassavola Digbyana.	Brassocatlælia × Wiganii.

5. L.-c. × bella.

Cattleya Trianæ.	L.-c. × Alexandræ.
Lælia cinnabarina.	L.-c. × Iberia.

6. L.-c. × callistoglossa.

Cattleya Dowiana.	L.-c. × Colmaniana.
C. Warneri.	L.-c. × wisetonensis.
Lælia cinnabarina.	L.-c. × Lowii.
L. purpurata.	L.-c. × Birkbeckiæ.
L. tenebrosa.	L.-c. × Ivernia.
L.-c. × Canhamiana.	L.-c. × Henri.
L.-c. × elegans.	L.-c. × Senarti.
L.-c. × Gottoiana.	L.-c. × Lily.
L.-c. × Schilleriana.	L.-c. × Agnes.

7. L.-c. × Canhamiana.

Cattleya Warscewiczii.	L.-c. × Britannia.
Lælia tenebrosa.	L.-c. × Kathleen.
L.-c. × callistoglossa.	L.-c. × Henri.

8. L.-c. × Clive.

Cattleya Bowringiana.	L.-c. × decora.
C. labiata.	L.-c. × Cooksonæ.

9. L.-c. × devoniensis.

Cattleya Lueddemanniana.	L.-c. × Mardellii.
C. superba.	L.-c. × Sedenii.

10. L.-c. × Dominiana.

Cattleya Bowringiana.	L.-c. × Illione.
C. Trianæ.	L.-c. × Rosalind.
C. Warscewiczii.	L.-c. × Antimachus.
Lælia crispa.	L.-c. × Victoria.
L. purpurata.	L.-c. × Wiganiana.

Læliocattleya—(*continued*).

11. L.-c. × Doris.

Cattleya superba.	L.-c. × Vesta.

12. L.-c. × elegans.

Brassavola Digbyana.	Brassocatlælia × Mackayi.
Brassocattleya × Lindleyana.	B.-c.-l. × Lawrencei.
Cattleya Aclandiæ.	L.-c. × Philbrickiana.
C. bicolor.	L.-c. × Gazelle.
C. Bowringiana.	L.-c. × Tiresias.
C. × Brymeriana.	L.-c. × princeps.
C. citrina.	L.-c. × Seraph.
C. Dowiana.	L.-c. × Fournieræ.
C. Gaskelliana.	L.-c. × Herga.
C. × Hardyana.	L.-c. × Chantinii.
C. intermedia.	L.-c. × Cicero.
C. labiata.	L.-c. × Schulzeana.
C. Lawrenceana.	L.-c. × Ruby.
C. Leopoldi.	L.-c. × La-Fresnaie.
C. Loddigesii.	L.-c. × Zenobia.
C. maxima.	L.-c. × Darwiniana.
C. Mossiæ.	L.-c. × Krænzlinii.
C. × O'Brieniana.	L.-c. × Herode.
C. Percivaliana.	L.-c. × Venus.
C. superba.	L.-c. × Robsoni.
C. velutina.	L.-c. × Lutetia.
C. Warneri.	L.-c. × Deweyi.
C. Warscewiczii.	L.-c. × Clonia.
Lælia Perrinii.	L.-c. × Diarmid.
L. pumila.	L.-c. × Novelty.
L. purpurata.	L.-c. × Pringiersi.
L.-c. × callistoglossa.	L.-c. × Senarti.
Sophronitis grandiflora.	Sophrocatlælia × Eros.

13. L.-c. × exoniensis.

Cattleya labiata.	L.-c. × Leonæ.
C. Loddigesii.	L.-c. × fausta.
C. superba.	L.-c. × triophthalma.
Lælia pumila.	L.-c. × Cassiope.

14. L.-c. × fausta.

Cattleya Loddigesii.	L.-c. × leucoglossa.

15. L.-c. × Gottoiana.

C. labiata.	L.-c. × Jeanette.
C. Mossiæ.	L.-c. × Wiganiæ.
L.-c. × callistoglossa.	L.-c. × Lily.

Læliocattleya—(*continued*).

16. **L.-c. × Hippolyta.**

Cattleya intermedia.	L.-c. × Santiago.
C. Mossiæ.	L.-c. × Ceres.
C. Schrœderæ.	L.-c. × Dora.
Lælia tenebrosa.	L.-c. × Vinesiæ.

17. **L.-c. × Ingrami.**

Cattleya Bowringiana.	L.-c. × Robsonæ.

18. **L.-c. × Leeana.**

C. Bowringiana.	L.-c. × Hera.
C. Warscewiczii.	L.-c. × Stepmanii.

19. **L.-c. × Pallas.**

Lælia cinnabarina.	L.-c. × Picanus.

20. **L.-c. × Proserpine.**

Cattleya Gaskelliana.	L.-c. × Tyro.

21. **L.-c. × Sallieri.**

C. Trianæ.	L.-c. × Clementinæ.
C. Warscewiczii.	L.-c. × Scylla.
Lælia harpophylla.	L.-c. × ochracea.

22. **L.-c. × Schilleriana.**

Cattleya bicolor.	L.-c. × Andreana.
C. Dormaniana.	L.-c. × claptonensis.
C. Dowiana.	L.-c. × Lucilia.
C. granulosa.	L.-c. × Noel.
C. × Hardyana.	L. c. × Greenwoodii.
C. intermedia.	L.-c. × Zampa.
C labiata.	L.-c. × Scottiana.
C. Leopoldi.	L.-c. × aurelianensis.
C. Loddigesii.	L.-c. × Behrensiana.
C. Lueddemanniana	L.-c. × Ada.
C. Mendelii.	L.-c. × Powellii.
C. Mossiæ.	L.-c. × Fortuna.
C. Schilleriana.	L.-c. × Morrisii.
C. Trianæ.	L.-c. × Cybele.
C. Warscewiczii	L.-c. × Marguerite.
Lælia crispa.	L.-c. × Stella.
L. longipes.	L.-c. × Ira.
L. purpurata.	L.-c. × Horniana.
L. tenebrosa.	L.-c. × Celestinæ.
L.-c. × callistoglossa.	L.-c. × Agnes.
Sophronitis grandiflora.	Sophrocatlælia × Veitchii.

22. LEPTOTES.

1. **L. bicolor.**

Lælia cinnabarina.	Leptolælia × Veitchii.

23. LYCASTE.

1. **L. aromatica.**

L. Deppei.	L. × Groganii.

2. **L. cruenta.**

L. Skinneri.	L. × Imschootiana.

3. **L. Deppei.**

L. aromatica.	L. × Groganii.
L. Skinneri.	L. × hybrida.

5. **L. macrophylla.**

L. Skinneri.	L. × Balliæ.

4. **L. Rossiana.**

L. Skinneri.	L. × Janetæ.

6. **L. Schilleriana.**

L. Skinneri.	L. × schœnbrunnensis.

7. **L. Skinneri.**

L. cruenta.	L. × Imschootiana.
L. Deppei.	L. × hybrida.
L. macrophylla.	L. × Balliæ.
L. Rossiana.	L. × Janetæ.
L. Schilleriana.	L. × schœnbrunnensis.

24. MACODES.

1. **M. Petola.**

Hæmaria discolor.	Macomaria × Veitchii.

25. MASDEVALLIA.

1. **M. abbreviata.**

M. Veitchiana.	M. × Acis.

2. **M. amabilis.**

M. ignea.	M. × Rebecca.
M. tovarensis.	M. × Measuresiana.
M. Veitchiana.	M. × Chelsoni.

3. **M. Arminii.**

M. Estradæ.	M. × Leda.

4. **M. × Asmodia.**

M. Veitchiana.	M. × Alceste.

Masdevallia—(*continued*).

5. **M. Barlæana.**

M. infracta. M. × glaphyrantha.
M. Veitchiana. M. × splendida.

6. **M. caudata.**

M. coccinea. M. × Shuttryana.
M. Estradæ. M. × Sedenii.
M. × Gairiana. M. × Hincksiæ.
M. ignea. M. × Henrietta.
M. rosea. M. × Courtauldiana.
M. Veitchiana. M. × Kimballiana.
M. xanthina. M. × Geleniana.

7. **M. × Chelsoni.**

M. peristeria. M. × Ajax.
M. Reichenbachiana. M. × Asmodia.

8. **M. Chimæra.**

M. tovarensis. M. × Eric.

9. **M. coccinea**

M. caudata. M. × Shuttryana.
M. Estradæ. M. × Stella.
M. Gairiana. M. × Pluto.
M. ignea. M. × Fraseri.
M. tovarensis. M. × McVittiæ.
M. triangularis. M. × Cassiope.
M. Veitchiana. M. × falcata.

10. **M. coriacea.**

M. Veitchiana. M. × Hebe.

11. **M. cucullata.**

M. Veitchiana. M. × bockingensis.

12. **M. Davisii.**

M. tovarensis. M. × Winniæ.
M. Veitchiana. M. × Gairiana.

13. **M. Estradæ.**

M. Arminii. M. × Leda.
M. caudata. M. × Sedenii.
M. coccinea. M. × Stella.
M. ignea. M. × Whitei.
M. Veitchiana. M. × langleyensis.

14. **M. × Gairiana.**

M. caudata. M. × Hincksiæ.
M. coccinea. M. × Pluto.

15. **M. ignea.**

M. amabilis. M. × Rebecca.
M. caudata. M. × Henrietta.
M. coccinea. M. × Fraseri.
M. Estradæ. M. × Whitei.
M. racemosa. M. × Rushtoni.
M. tovarensis. M. × Hincksiana.
M. Veitchiana. M. × Heathii.

Masdevallia—(*continued*).

16. **M. infracta.**

M. Barlæana. M. × glaphyrantha.

17. **M. macrura.**

M. tovarensis. M. × Curlei.

18. **M. peristeria.**

M. × Chelsoni. M. × Ajax.

19. **M. racemosa.**

M. ignea. M. × Rushtoni.
M. triangularis. M. × Doris.

20. **M. Reichenbachiana.**

M. × Chelsoni. M. × Asmodia.

21. **M. rosea.**

M. caudata. M. × Courtauldiana.

22. **M. Schlimii.**

M. Veitchiana. M. × Imogen.

23. **M. Schrœderiana.**

M. Veitchiana. M. × Circe.

24. **M. tovarensis.**

M. amabilis. M. × Measuresiana.
M. Chimæra. M. × Eric.
M. coccinea. M. × McVittiæ.
M. Davisii. M. × Winniæ.
M. ignea. M. × Hincksiana.
M. macrura. M. × Curlei.
M. Veitchiana. M. × Amesiana.

25. **M. triangularis.**

M. coccinea. M. × Cassiope.
M. racemosa. M. × Doris.

26. **M. Veitchiana.**

M. abbreviata. M. × Acis.
M. amabilis. M. × Chelsoni.
M. × Asmodia. M. × Alceste.
M. Barlæana. M. × splendida.
M. caudata. M. × Kimballiana.
M. coccinea. M. × falcata.
M. coriacea. M. × Hebe.
M. cucullata. M. × bockingensis.
M. Davisii. M. × Gairiana.
M. Estradæ. M. × langleyensis.
M. ignea. M. × Heathii.
M. Schlimii. M. × Imogen.
M. Schrœderiana. M. × Circe.
M. tovarensis. M. × Amesiana.
M. Wageneriana. M. × Sanderi.
M. xanthina. M. × Lawrencei.

27. **M. Wageneriana.**

M. Veitchiana. M. × Sanderi.

Masdevallia—(*continued*).

28. **M. xanthina.**

M. caudata.	M. × Geleniana.
M. Veitchiana.	M. × Lawrencei.

26. MILTONIA.

1. **M. Roezlii.**

M. vexillaria.	M. × Bleuana.

2. **M. vexillaria.**

M. Roezlii.	M. × Bleuana.

27. ODONTOGLOSSUM.

1. **O. × Andersonianum.**

O. Harryanum.	O. × Bradshawiæ.

2. **O. cirrhosum.**

O. Hallii.	O. × elegans.
O. sceptrum.	O. × Juno.

3. **O. crispum.**

O. × Denisonæ.	O. × mirum.
O. Hallii.	O. × Cooksoni.
O. Harryanum.	O. × spectabile.
O. Kegeljani.	O. × waltonense.
O. luteopurpureum.	O. × Denisonæ.
O. nobile.	O. × armainvillierense.
O. sceptrum.	O. × mirificum.
O. tripudians.	O. × bellatulum.
O. triumphans.	O. × harvengtense.

4. **O. × Denisonæ.**

O. crispum.	O. × mirum.
O. triumphans.	O. × Vuylstekei.

5. **O. × elegans.**

O. nobile.	O. × beardwoodiense.

6. **O. Hallii.**

O. cirrhosum.	O. × elegans.
O. crispum.	O. × Cooksoni.
O. Harryanum.	O. × Crawshayanum.

7. **O. Harryanum.**

O. × Andersonianum.	O. × Bradshawiæ.
O. crispum.	O. × spectabile.
O. Hallii.	O. × Crawshayanum.
O. Lindleyanum.	O. × Wattianum.
O. luteopurpureum.	O. × Hyeanum.
O. nobile.	O. × Rolfeæ.
O. triumphans.	O. × Charlesworthii.

Odontoglossum—(*continued*).

8. **O. Kegeljani.**

O. crispum.	O. × waltonense.

9. **O. Lindleyanum.**

O. Harryanum.	O. × Wattianum.

10. **O. luteopurpureum.**

O. crispum.	O. × Denisonæ.
O. Harryanum.	O. × Hyeanum.

11. **O. nobile.**

O. crispum.	O. × armainvillierense.
O. × elegans.	O. × beardwoodiense.
O. Harryanum.	O. × Rolfeæ.
O. sceptrum	O. × amœnum.
O. triumphans.	O. × excellens.

12. **O. sceptrum.**

O. cirrhosum.	O. × Juno.
O. crispum.	O. × mirificum.
O. nobile.	O. × amœnum.

13. **O. tripudians.**

O. crispum.	O. × bellatulum.

14. **O. triumphans.**

O. crispum.	O. × harvengtense.
O. × Denisonæ.	O. × Vuylstekei.
O. Harryanum.	O. × Charlesworthii.
O. nobile.	O. × excellens.

28. PAPHIOPEDILUM.

1. **P. × almum.**

P. concolor.	P. × Hollidayanum.
P. niveum.	P. × Rothwelliæ.
P. × Swanianum.	P. × Mantinii.

2. **P. Appletonianum.**

P. barbatum.	P. × westoniense.
P. callosum.	P. × siamense.
P. × chloroneurum.	P. × Xuthus.
P. Spicerianum.	P. × Quirinus.

3. **P. Argus.**

P. × Arthurianum.	P. × Argutus.
P. barbatum.	P. × turpe.
P. bellatulum.	P. × Madeline.
P. Boxallii.	P. × Murillo.
P. callosum.	P. × calloso-Argus.
P. Charlesworthii.	P. × Ian.
P. concolor.	P. × Evenor.
P. Curtisii.	P. × Hurrellianum.
P. Dayanum.	P. × Pandora.
P. × Harrisianum.	P. × Jean.

Paphiopedilum Argus—(*continued*).

P. hirsutissimum.	P. × punctatissimum.
P. insigne.	P. × Swinburnei.
P. Lawrenceanum.	P. × Io.
P. × marmorophyllum.	P × prestonense.
P. × Morganiæ.	P. × Argo-Morganiæ.
P. × nitens.	P. × leopardinum.
P. niveum.	P. × Gravesiæ.
P. × œnanthum.	P. × Descombesiæ.
P. philippinense.	P. × burfordiense.
P. purpuratum.	P. × Batalinii.
P. Rothschildianum.	P. × Rehderæ.
P. Sanderianum.	P. × Wilsonæ.
P. × selligerum.	P. × aspasioides.
P. Spicerianum.	P. × Crethus.
P. Stonei.	P. × Rothwellianum.
P. tonsum.	P. × Iphis.
P. villosum.	P. × vernixium.

4. P. × **Arthurianum.**

P. Argus.	P. × Argutus.
P. × Harrisianum.	P. × Osyanum.
P. × Leeanum.	P. × Leeæ.
P. Spicerianum.	P. × Minos.

5. P. × **Ashburtonæ.**

P. barbatum.	P. × Philene.
P. × calophyllum.	P. × Imperatrix.
P. callosum.	P. × Zenobia.
P. × Harrisianum.	P. × Wiganianum.
P. insigne.	P. × Annærtii.
P. × Leeanum.	P. × Louisæ.
P. × Numa.	P. × whitefieldiense.
P. purpuratum.	P. × Atropos.
P. Spicerianum.	P. × Donatii.
P. Stonei.	P. × Clarkiæ.
P. × vernixium.	P. × Lowryanum.

6. P × **auroreum.**

P. × Harrisianum.	P. × grandiflorum.
P. insigne.	P. × Ephialtes.

7. P. **barbatum.**

P. Appletonianum.	P. × westoniense.
P. Argus.	P. × turpe.
P. × Ashburtonæ.	P. × Philene.
P. bellatulum.	P. × Richmanii.
P. Boxallii.	P. × apiculatum.
P. callosum.	P. × calloso-barbatum.
P. × Canhami.	P. × Eros.
P. Charlesworthii.	P. × Lumsdenii.
P. × chloroneurum.	P. × festum.

Paphiopedilum barbatum (*contd.*).

P. ciliolare.	P. × Descombesii.
P. concolor.	P. × tessellatum.
P. × Crossianum.	P. × Margaritæ.
P. Curtisii.	P. × Kerchoveanum.
P. Dayanum.	P. × Swanianum.
P. Druryi.	P. × orphanum.
P. × Euryale.	P. × Abessa.
P. Fairrieanum.	P. × vexillarium.
P. Godefroyæ.	P. × Sirius.
P. × Harrisianum.	P. × Ensign.
P. Haynaldianum	P. × Orissa.
P. hirsutissimum.	P. × porphyrochlamys.
P. Hookeræ.	P. × marmorophyllum.
P. insigne.	P. × Ashburtonæ.
P. Lawrenceanum.	P. × almum
P. × Lathamianum.	P. × Dakinii.
P. × Leeanum.	P. × Cardosoanum
P. Lowii.	P. × calanthum.
P. Mastersianum.	P. × Endymion.
P. niveum.	P. × Tautzianum.
P. × œnanthum.	P. × plumosum.
P. philippinense.	P. × selligerum.
P. præstans.	P. × barbato-præstans.
P. purpuratum.	P. × Pitcheri.
P. Rothschildianum.	P. × tringiense.
P. × selligerum.	P. × Joiceyi.
P. Spicerianum.	P. × Eyermanianum.
P. Stonei.	P. × euryandrum.
P. superbiens.	P. × superciliare.
P. × superciliare.	P. × Vigerianum.
P. × Swanianum.	P. × gandavense.
P. tonsum.	P. × Rossianum.
P. venustum.	P. × calophyllum.
P. × vexillarium.	P. × Singletonianum.
P. villosum.	P. × Harrisianum.
P. virens.	P. × pleistochlorum.

8. P. **bellatulum.**

P. Argus.	P. × Madeline.
P. barbatum.	P. × Richmanii.
P. × Bleui.	P. × Asmodia.
P. Boxallii.	P. × Berkleyanum.
P. callosum.	P. × Wottoni.
P. Chamberlainianum.	P. × Rowena.
P. Charlesworthii.	P. × Dora.
P. ciliolare.	P. × Olenus.
P. concolor.	P. × conco-bellatulum.

Paphiopedilum bellatulum —(*contd.*).

P. × Crossianum.	P. × Jacobianum.
P. Curtisii.	P. × Chapmanii.
P. Dayanum.	P. × Annie.
P. × enfieldense.	P. × Buckinghami.
P. Godefroyæ.	P. × Gratrixii.
P. × Gowerianum.	P. × Mary-Beatrice.
P. × Harrisianum.	P. × southgatense.
P. Haynaldianum.	P. × Ariel.
P. hirsutissimum.	P. × Schofieldianum.
P. Hookeræ.	P. × Youngiæ.
P. insigne.	P. × Helena.
P. Lawrenceanum.	P. × Lawrebel.
P. × Mabeliæ.	P. × Ameliæ.
P. niveum.	P. × Psyche.
P. philippinense.	P. × Phœbe.
P. Rothschildianum.	P. × Rolfei.
P. Spicerianum.	P. × Enid.
P. superbiens.	P. × Measuresiæ.
P. × superciliare.	P. × Arnoldiæ.
P. × Swanianum.	P. × Cycnides.
P. tonsum.	P. × Hunteri.
P. venustum.	P. × Venubel.
P. × vexillarium.	P. × Gratrixiæ.
P. villosum.	P. × allertonense.
P. × Youngianum.	P. × Beranekii.

9. P. × **Bleui**.

P. bellatulum.	P. × Asmodia.
P. × superciliare.	P. × Alfredianum.

10. **P. Boxallii**.

P. Argus.	P. × Murillo.
P. barbatum.	P. × apiculatum.
P. bellatulum.	P. × Berkleyanum.
P. callosum.	P. × Bartelsii.
P. × calophyllum.	P. × Pluto.
P. × Calypso.	P. × Menelik.
P. × Canhami.	P. × Lendyanum.
P. Chamberlainianum.	P. × Kamilii.
P. Charlesworthii.	P. × Elsie.
P. × chloroneurum.	P. × Burberryanum.
P. Curtisii.	P. × Saint-Hilda.
P. Dayanum.	P. × Scylla.
P. Druryi.	P. × Gordoni.
P. exul.	P. × Irene.
P. × gemmiferum.	P. × Heloisianum.
P. × Germinyanum.	P. × eximium.
P. × Harrisianum.	P. × Eismannianum.
P. Haynaldianum.	P. × Proetus.
P. hirsutissimum.	P. × Godseffianum.

Paphiopedilum Boxallii—(*continued*).

P. insigne.	P. × Schlesingerianum.
P. × Io.	P. × Behrensianum.
P. javanicum.	P. × vernixioides.
P. × Lathamianum.	P. × Bala.
P. Lawrenceanum.	P. × Thayerianum.
P. × Leeanum.	P. × Hera.
P. Lowii.	P. × Beatrice.
P. × Morganiæ.	P. × Frederico-nobiie.
P. × nitens.	P. × Parkerianum.
P. niveum.	P. × Graceæ.
P. × œnanthum.	P. × rubescens.
P. × Orpheus.	P. × Juturna.
P. philippinense.	P. × Metis.
P. Rothschildianum.	P. × Edith.
P. Spicerianum.	P. × Calypso.
P. Stonei.	P. × Georgii.
P. superbiens.	P. × Adela.
P. tonsum.	P. × Zeno.
P. venustum.	P. × pavoninum.
P. villosum.	P. × Reynaldi.

11. **P. × Bruno**.

P. × Leeanum.	P. × Leemanni.

12. **P. Bullenianum**.

P. insigne.	P. × corbeillense.
P. purpuratum.	P. × Remus.
P. venustum.	P. × Fitchianum.

13. **P. callosum**.

P. Appletonianum.	P. × siamense.
P. Argus.	P. × calloso-Argus.
P. × Ashburtonæ.	P. × Zenobia.
P. barbatum.	P. × calloso-barbatum.
P. bellatulum.	P. × Wottoni.
P. Boxallii.	P. × Bartelsii.
P. × calophyllum.	P. × Pallas.
P. Chamberlainianum.	P. × Alcippe.
P. Charlesworthii.	P. × Rosita.
P. ciliolare.	P. × Zeus.
P. concolor.	P. × conco-callosum.
P. Curtisii.	P. × Goultenianum.
P. Druryi.	P. × Smithianum.
P. exul.	P. × Conwayi.
P. Fairrieanum.	P. × Juno.
P. Godefroyæ.	P. × Finetii.
P. × Harrisianum.	P. × Ledouxiæ.
P. hirsutissimum.	P. × Doncasterianum.
P. Hookeræ.	P. × Fortuna.

Paphiopedilum callosum—(*contd.*).

P. insigne. P. × Leonæ.
P. × Lathamianum. P. × Calliope.
P. Lawrenceanum. P. × Maudiæ.
P. × Leeanum. P. × Angeliæ.
P. Mastersianum. P. × Pytho.
P. niveum. P. × calloso-niveum.
P. × œnanthum. P. × Bagshaweæ.
P. philippinense. P. × Millmanii.
P. Rothschildianum. P. × Fowleri.
P. Sanderianum. P. × May.
P. × Sementa. P. × aurelianense.
P. Spicerianum. P. × Moensiæ.
P. Stonei. P. × Fordianum.
P. superbiens. P. × Moussetianum.
P. × superciliare. P. × Moreauanum.
P. × Tautzianum. P. × Nandii.
P. tonsum. P. × Felicity.
P. venustum. P. × Orpheus.
P. villosum. P. × Indra.

14. **P. × calophyllum.**

P. × Ashburtonæ. P. × Imperatrix.
P. Boxallii. P. × Pluto.
P. callosum. P. × Pallas.
P. × Harrisianum. P. × Fausianum.
P. insigne. P. × Northumbrian.
P. × Leeanum. P. × Boltonianum.
P. × nitens. P. × Patria.
P. × œnanthum. P. × Pollettianum.
P. Spicerianum. P. × Macfarlanei.
P. superbiens. P. × polychromum.
P. × vexillarium. P. × liegense.

15. **P. × Calypso.**

P. Boxallii. P. × Menelik.
P. Chamberlainianum. P. × Vanneri.
P. insigne. P. × Melia.
P. × Lathamianum. P. × Stevensii.
P. × Leeanum. P. × Evelyn.
P. × nitens. P. × Sanderi.
P. × regale. P. × Adamsii.
P. Rothschildianum. P. × calypsoides.
P. tonsum. P. × Œnomaus.

16. **P. × Canhami.**

P. barbatum. P. × Eros.
P. Boxallii. P. × Lendyanum.
P. × Colossus. P. × Cobbiæ.
P. Curtisii. P. × Savageæ.

Paphiopedilum × Canhami (*contd.*).

P. × Harrisianum. P. × Vidor.
P. Haynaldianum. P. × Ino.
P. × Leeanum. P. × Straeteni.

17. **P. Chamberlainianum.**

P. bellatulum. P. × Rowena.
P. callosum. P. × Alcippe.
P. concolor. P. × Eira.
P. × Calypso. P. × Vanneri.
P. exul. P. × Bullii.
P. × Germinyanum. P. × Ajax.
P. × Harrisianum. P. × Manto.
P. Haynaldianum. P. × Myra.
P. hirsutissimum. P. × Merope.
P. insigne. P. × Fowleræ.
P. × Lathamianum. P. × Wrightiæ.
P. Lawrenceanum. P. × Hiero.
P. × Leeanum. P. × Chamber-Leeanum.
P. × nitens. P. × Polkii.
P. niveum. P. × Suttonæ.
P. × œnanthum. P. × Zurigo.
P. Parishii. P. × Keelingii.
P. philippinense. P. × Helvetia.
P. Rothschildianum. P. × Transvaal.
P. Spicerianum. P. × Deedmanianum
P. superbiens. P. × Thyades.
P. villosum. P. × Madiotianum.

18. **P. × Chapmanii.**

P. × Cycnides. P. × Balfouriæ.
P. × Harrisianum. P. × stamfordiense.

19. **P. Charlesworthii.**

P. Argus. P. × Ian.
P. barbatum. P. × Lumsdenii.
P. bellatulum. P. × Dora.
P. Boxallii. P. × Elsie.
P. callosum. P. × Rosita.
P. ciliolare. P. × Villeboisii.
P. concinnum. P. × Favarger.
P. × Creon. P. × Robertsii.
P. Curtisii. P. × Rachel.
P. × Cymatodes. P. × woodfordiense.
P. Dayanum. P. × Helen.
P. Druryi. P. × Rogersoni.
P. × enfieldense. P. × Rhodopsis.
P. × Euryale. P. × wyndhurstense.
P. exul. P. × Daphne.

Paphiopedilum Charlesworthii—(*continued*).

P. × Gowerianum.	P. × Vitazo.
P. × Harrisianum.	P. × bingleyense.
P. hirsutissimum.	P. × erubescens.
P. insigne.	P. × Hitchinsiæ.
P. × Io.	P. × Urania.
P. × Lathamianum.	P. × Rappartii.
P. Lawrenceanum.	P. × decipiens.
P. × Leeanum.	P. × longwoodense.
P. × macropterum.	P. × Cardosoæ.
P. niveum.	P. × Eos.
P. × œnanthum.	P. × Stottianum.
P. × Savageanum.	P. × Braeckmanii.
P. Spicerianum.	P. × Memnon.
P. superbiens.	P. × Evadne.
P. × superciliare.	P. × Decia.
P. tonsum.	P. × Nellie.
P. villosum.	P. × Wrigleyi.

20. **P. chloroneurum.**

P. Appletonianum.	P. × Xuthus.
P. barbatum.	P. × festum.
P. exul.	P. × Tia.
P, insigne.	P. × Ridolfianum.
P. × vexillarium.	P. × Zalmoxis.

21. **P. ciliolare.**

P. barbatum.	P. × Descombesii.
P. bellatulum	P. × Olenus.
P. callosum.	P. × Zeus.
P. Charlesworthii.	P. × Villeboisii.
P. Curtisii.	P. × simile.
P. Druryi.	P. × Greyanum.
P. × Harrisianum.	P. × Appletoniæ.
P. hirsutissimum.	P. × Eurylochus.
P. Hookeræ.	P. × Rimbertianum.
P. insigne.	P. × Bleui.
P. Lawrenceanum.	P. × Lucie.
P. × nitens.	P. × Duvalii.
P. niveum.	P. × Aylingii.
P. philippinense.	P. × Finetianum.
P. Rothschildianum.	P. × Amesii.
P. × selligerum.	P. × Ashtoni.
P. × Sementa.	P. × Iris.
P. Spicerianum.	P. × Bookeri.
P. Stonei.	P. × Truffautiæ.
P. superbiens.	P. × Lachmee.
P. × superciliare.	P. × exoptatum.
P. villosum.	P. × Pygmalion.

22. **P. × Cleopatra.**

P. Lawrenceanum.	P. × resplendens.

Paphiopedilum—(*continued*).

23. **P. × Coffinetii.**

P. Fairrieanum.	P. × Princess.

24. **P. × Colossus.**

P. × Canhami.	P. × Cobbiæ.

25. **P. × concinnum.**

P. Charlesworthii.	P. × Favarger.

26. **P. concolor.**

P. × almum.	P. × Hollidayanum.
P. Argus.	P. × Evenor.
P. barbatum.	P. × tessellatum.
P. bellatulum.	P. × conco-bellatulum.
P. callosum.	P. × conco-callosum.
P. Chamberlainianum.	P. × Eira.
P. Curtisii.	P. × Minnie.
P. Dayanum.	P. × Burbidgeanum.
P. × Harrisianum.	P. × Watsonianum.
P. insigne.	P. × Orion.
P. Lawrenceanum.	P. × concolawre.
P. × Leeanum.	P. × Whitei.
P. Spicerianum.	P. × Arete.
P. Stonei.	P. × platycolor.
P. superbiens.	P. × Arnoldianum.
P. × superciliare.	P. × Marchandii.
P. venustum.	P. × Marshallianum.
P. villosum.	P. × conco-villosum.

27. **P × conspicuum.**

P. insigne.	P. × Ridolfianum.

28. **P. × Creon.**

P. Charlesworthii.	P. × Robertsii.

29. **P. × Crossianum.**

P. barbatum.	P. × Margaritæ.
P. bellatulum.	P. × Jacobianum.
P. × Harrisianum.	P. × Boyleanum.
P. insigne.	P. × Rafaeli.
P. × Leeanum.	P. × Clusia.
P. × marmorophyllum.	P. × Lachesis.
P. Spicerianum.	P. × Malyanum.

30. **P. Curtisii.**

P. Argus.	P. × Hurrellianum.
P. barbatum.	P. × Kerchoveanum.

Paphiopedilum Curtisii (*continued*).

P. bellatulum.	P. × Chapmanii.
P. Boxallii.	P. × Saint-Hilda.
P. callosum.	P. × Goulteni-anum.
P. × Canhami.	P. × Savageæ.
P. Charlesworthii.	P. × Rachel.
P. ciliolare.	P. × simile.
P. concolor.	P. × Minnie.
P. Dayanum.	P. × Curtia.
P. Druryi.	P. × Fairy-Queen.
P. × Harrisianum.	P. × Gaudianum.
P. hirsutissimum.	P. × Adonis.
P. Hookeræ.	P. × Quies.
P. insigne.	P. × miniatum.
P. Lawrenceanum.	P. × Gowerianum.
P. Lowii.	P. × Joliboisii.
P. × Morganiæ.	P. × Warburtoni.
P. × nitens.	P. × colombense.
P. niveum.	P. × Cowleyanum.
P. philippinense.	P. × Clinkaberry-anum.
P. praestans.	P. × Holtii.
P. purpuratum.	P. × Oakesianum.
P. Rothschildi-anum.	P. × Lairessei.
P. Sanderianum.	P. × Cooksonæ.
P. × selligerum.	P. × Vanneræ.
P. Spicerianum.	P. × Allenianum.
P Stonei.	P. × Constance.
P. superbiens.	P. × Cymatodes.
P. villosum.	P. × Helios.

31. **P. × Cycnides.**

P. × Chapmanii.	P. × Balfouriæ.

32. **P. × Cymatodes.**

P. Charlesworthii.	P. × woodfordiense.
P. Rothschildi-anum.	P. × Premier.

33. **P. Dayanum.**

P. Argus.	P. × Pandora.
P. barbatum.	P. × Swanianum.
P. bellatulum.	P. × Annie.
P. Boxallii.	P. × Scylla.
P. Charlesworthii.	P. × Helen.
P. concolor.	P. × Burbidge-anum.
P. Curtisii.	P. × Curtia.
P. Fairrieanum.	P. × Constable-anum.
P. Godefroyæ.	P. × Colesii.
P. × Harrisianum.	P. × Lewisii.
P. Lowii.	P. × Patersoni.
P. insigne.	P. × Gayotiæ.
P. niveum.	P. × Lily.
P. × œnanthum.	P. × Tennyson.

Paphiopedium Dayanum- (*contd.*).

P. Spicerianum.	P. × pallens.
P. superbiens.	P. × Kittelii.
P. × superciliare.	P. × Coffinetii.
P. × Swanianum.	P. × Artemis.
P. × Tautzianum.	P. × Pittii.
P. venustum.	P. × caligare.
P. villosum.	P. × Iago.
P. virens.	P. × Petri.

34. **P. Druryi.**

P. barbatum.	P. × orphanum.
P. Boxallii.	P. × Gordoni.
P. callosum.	P. × Smithianum.
P. Charlesworthii.	P. × Rogersoni.
P. ciliolare.	P. × Greyanum.
P. Curtisii.	P. × Fairy-Queen.
P. × Godseffianum.	P. × Castalia.
P. × Harrisianum.	P. × Florence.
P. hirsutissimum.	P. × Dallemagnei.
P. Hookeræ.	P. × Druryo-Hookeræ.
P. insigne.	P. × Æson.
P. Lawrenceanum.	P. × Cybele.
P. × nitens.	P. × medium.
P. niveum.	P. × microchilum.
P. × Sementa.	P. × Josephianum.
P. Spicerianum.	P. × Buchanianum.
P. superbiens.	P. × Haywoodi-anum.
P. tonsum.	P. × Piercei.
P. villosum.	P. × Winnianum.

35. **P. × enfieldense.**

P. bellatulum.	P. × Bucking-hami.
P. Charlesworthii.	P. × Rhodopsis.

36. **P. × Euryale.**

P. barbatum.	P. × Abessa.
P. Charlesworthii.	P. × wyndhurst-ense.

37. **P. exul.**

P. Boxallii.	P. × Irene.
P. callosum.	P. × Conwayi.
P. Chamberlaini-anum.	P. × Bullii.
P. Charlesworthii.	P. × Daphne.
P. × chloroneurum.	P. × Tia.
P. × Harrisianum.	P. × Harri-exul.
P. Lawrenceanum.	P. × Julia.
P. villosum.	P. × vill-exul.

38. **P. Fairrieanum.**

P. barbatum.	P. × vexillarium.
P. callosum.	P. × Juno.
P. × Coffinetii.	P. × Princess.
P. Dayanum.	P. × Constable-anum.

Paphiopedilum Fairrieanum— *(continued).*

P. insigne.	P. × Arthurianum.
P. Lawrenceanum.	P. × streatham-ense.
P. × Leeanum.	P. × Reginæ.
P. × œnanthum.	P. × Schrœderi.
P. purpuratum.	P. × Ballantinei.
P. Spicerianum.	P. × Niobe.
P. superbiens.	P. × Edwardii.
P. × Swanianum.	P. × Aasenii.
P. tonsum.	P. × Amesiæ.

39. P. × **Fitchianum.**

P. insigne.	P. × Huttiæ.

40. P. × **gemmiferum.**

P. Boxallii.	P. × Heloisianum.

41. P. × **Germinyanum.**

P. Boxallii.	P. × eximium.
P. Chamberlainianum.	P. × Ajax.
P. insigne.	P. × Chouvetii.

42. P. **Godefroyæ.**

P. barbatum.	P. × Sirius.
P. bellatulum.	P. × Gratrixii.
P. callosum.	P. × Finetii.
P. Dayanum.	P. × Colesii.
P. × Harrisianum.	P. × Harrisi-froyæ.
P. insigne.	P. × Ettyi.
P. × nitens.	P. × Alexandræ.
P. niveum.	P. × Greyi.
P. venustum.	P. × Lloydiæ.
P. villosum.	P. × Una.

43. P. × **Godseffianum.**

P. Druryi.	P. × Castalia.
P. hirsutissumum.	P. × Clytie.
P. × Leeanum.	P. × Hiawatha.
P. Sanderianum.	P. × Cassandra.

44. P. × **Gowerianum.**

P. bellatulum.	P. × Mary-Beatrice.
P. Charlesworthii.	P. × Vitazo.
P. niveum.	P. × Sophie.
P. Rothschildianum.	P. × Shillianum.
P. × Youngianum.	P. × Mapleæ.

45. P. × **Hanseni.**

P. Rothschildianum.	P. × Miranda.

46. P. × **Harrisianum.**

P. Argus.	P. × Jean.
P. × Arthurianum.	P. × Osyanum.
P. × Ashburtonæ.	B. × Wiganianum.

Paphiopedilum × Harrisianum— *(continued).*

P. × auroreum.	P. × grandiflorum.
P. barbatum.	P. × Ensign
P. bellatulum.	P. × southgatense.
P. Boxallii.	P. × Eismannianum.
P. callosum.	P. × Ledouxiæ.
P. × calophyllum.	P. × Fausianum.
P. × Canhami.	P. × Vidor.
P. Chamberlainianum.	P. × Manto.
P. × Chapmanii.	P. × stamfordiense.
P. Charlesworthii.	P. × bingleyense.
P. ciliolare.	P. × Appletoniæ.
P. concolor.	P. × Watsonianum.
P. × Crossianum.	P. × Boyleanum.
P. Curtisii.	P. × Gaudianum.
P. Dayanum.	P. × Lewisii.
P. Druryi.	P. × Florence.
P. exul.	P. × Harri-exul.
P. Godefroyæ.	P. × Harrisifroyæ.
P. Haynaldianum.	P. × Wincqzianum.
P. hirsutissimum.	P. × Belandorffii.
P. Hookeræ.	P. × loochristiense.
P. insigne.	P. × œnanthum.
P. javanicum.	P. × Colmanii.
P. × Lathamianum.	P. × Pryorianum.
P. × Lawrebel.	P. × Unxia.
P. Lawrenceanum.	P. × gigas.
P. × Leeanum.	P. × Harri-Leeanum.
P. Mastersianum.	P. × Belus.
P. × nitens.	P. × giganteum.
P. niveum.	P. × Marwoodii.
P. × œnanthum.	P. × Creon.
P. × orphanum.	P. × Gabrieli.
P. purpuratum.	P. × concinnum.
P. Rothschildianum.	P. × Excelsior.
P. Sanderianum.	P. × Harrisander.
P. × Schrœderi.	P. × Little-Gem.
P. × selligerum.	P. × Paulii.
P. Spicerianum.	P. × Savageanum.
P. superbiens.	P. × Tryonianum.
P. × Swanianum.	P. × Rossiæ.
P. tonsum.	P. × orangense.
P. venustum.	P. × chloroneurum
P. × vernixium.	P. × bellinum.
P. villosum.	P. × conspicuum.

Paphiopedilum—(*continued*).

47. **P. Haynaldianum.**

P. barbatum.	P. × Orissa.
P. bellatulum.	P. × Ariel.
P. Boxallii.	P. × Prœtus.
P. × Canhami.	P. × Ino.
P. Chamberlainianum.	P. × Myra.
P. × Harrisianum.	P. × Wincqzianum.
P. Hookeræ.	P. × Æneas.
P. insigne.	P. × Pelias.
P. × Lathamianum.	P. × nobilior.
P. × Leeanum.	P. × Clotilde.
P. philippinense.	P. × Lebaudyanum.
P. Spicerianum.	P. × Carnusianum.
P. × Swanianum.	P. × gracile.
P. villosum.	P. × Hanseni.

48. **P. × Haywoodianum.**

P. × œnanthum.	P. × Koh-i-noor.
P. × Swinburnei.	P. × Goodsoni.

49. **P. × Hera.**

P. × superciliare.	P. × Thomyris.

50. **P. hirsutissimum.**

P. Argus.	P. × punctatissimum.
P. barbatum.	P. × porphyrochlamys.
P. bellatulum.	P. × Schofieldianum.
P. Boxallii.	P. × Godseffianum.
P. callosum.	P. × Doncasterianum.
P. Chamberlainianum.	P. × Merope.
P. Charlesworthii.	P. × erubescens.
P. ciliolare.	P. × Eurylochus.
P. Curtisii.	P. × Adonis.
P. Druryi.	P. × Dallemagnei.
P. × Godseffianum.	P. × Clytie.
P. × Harrisianum.	P. × Ollendorffii.
P. insigne.	P. × Alcides.
P. Lawrenceanum.	P. × Mulus.
P. × Leeanum.	P. × Zampa.
P. × Morganiæ.	P. × Durbar.
P. × nitens.	P. × Erato.
P. × selligerum.	P. × Carderi.
P. Spicerianum.	P. × Medeia.
P. superbiens.	P. × Castleanum.
P. × Swanianum.	P. × Bondii.
P. venustum.	P. × Deception.
P. × vexillarium.	P. × Jenseni-anum.

Paphiopedilum hirsutissimum—(*continued*).

P. villosum.	P. × Germinyanum.

51. **P. Hookeræ.**

P. barbatum.	P. × marmorophyllum.
P. bellatulum.	P. × Youngiæ.
P. callosum.	P. × Fortuna.
P. ciliolare.	P. × Rimbertianum.
P. Curtisii.	P. × Quies.
P. Druryi.	P. × Druryo-Hookeræ.
P. × Harrisianum.	P. × loochristiense.
P. Haynaldianum.	P. × Æneas.
P. insigne.	P. × Echo.
P. Lawrenceanum.	P. × enfieldense.
P. × marmorophyllum.	P. × fulgens.
P. Mastersianum.	P. × xanthophyllum.
P. × nitens.	P. × Edmundii.
P. × œnanthum.	P. × Cleopatra.
P. purpuratum.	P. × gemmiferum.
P. Rothschildianum.	P. × Jupiter.
P. × Sementa.	P. × amabile.
P. Spicerianum.	P. × Eurydice.
P. Stonei.	P. × Melanthus.
P. superbiens.	P. × Pageanum.
P. × superciliare.	P. × amethystinum.
P. venustum.	P. × Atys.
P. villosum.	P. × Schusterianum.

52. **P. insigne.**

P. Argus.	P. × Swinburnei.
P. × Ashburtonæ.	P. × Annærtii.
P. × auroreum.	P. × Ephialtes.
P. barbatum.	P. × Ashburtonæ.
P. bellatulum.	P. × Helena.
P. Boxallii.	P. × Schlesingerianum.
P. Bullenianum.	P. × corbeillense
P. callosum.	P. × Leonæ.
P. × calophyllum.	P. × Northumbrian.
P. × Calypso.	P. × Melia.
P. Chamberlainianum.	P. × Fowleræ.
P. Charlesworthii.	P. × Hitchinsiæ.
P. × chloroneurum.	P. × Ridolfianum.
P. ciliolare.	P. × Bleui.

Paphiopedilum insigne—(*continued*).

P. concolor.	P. × Orion.
P. × Crossianum.	P. × Rafaeli.
P. Curtisii.	P. × miniatum.
P. Dayanum.	P. × Gayotiæ.
P. Druryi.	P. × Æson.
P. Fairrieanum.	P. × Arthurianum.
P. × Fitchianum.	P. × Huttiæ.
P. × Germinyanum.	P. × Chouvetii.
P. Godefroyæ.	P. × Ettyi.
P. × Harrisianum.	P. × œnanthum.
P. Haynaldianum.	P. × Pelias.
P. hirsutissimum.	P. × Alcides.
P. Hookeræ.	P. × Echo.
P. × Io.	P. × Tryanowskyanum.
P. javanicum.	P. × Mandæ.
P. × Lathamianum.	P. × Hobartii.
P. Lawrenceanum.	P. × Eucharis.
P. × Leeanum.	P. × Simonii.
P. Lowii.	P. × Rossii.
P. × Luciæ.	P. × Redversii.
P. × Lynchianum.	P. × Ilione.
P. × marmorophyllum.	P. × Gem.
P. Mastersianum.	P. × albanense.
P. × Niobe.	P. × Priam.
P. × nitens.	P. × Romulus.
P. niveum.	P. × Venus.
P. × œnanthum.	P. × Milo.
P. × Petri.	P. × Petri-insigne.
P. × Pollettianum.	P. × magnificum.
P. purpuratum.	P. × regale.
P. × Schrœderi.	P. × Thalia.
P. × selligerum.	P. × burbagense.
P. × Sementa.	P. × Vibilia.
P. × siamense.	P. × Reginaldianum.
P. Spicerianum.	P. × Leeanum.
P. superbiens.	P. × Thorntoni.
P. × Swanianum.	P. × Comus.
P. tonsum.	P. × Krishna.
P. venustum.	P. × Crossianum.
P. × vexillarium.	P. × Daedalus.
P. villosum.	P. × nitens.

53. P. × Io.

P. Boxallii.	P. × Behrensianum.
P. Charlesworthii.	P. × Urania.
P. insigne.	P. × Tryanowskianum.
P. Lawrenceanum.	P. × Vanninii.
P. purpuratum.	P. × modestum.

Paphiopedilum × **Io**—(*continued*).

P. Rothschildianum.	P. × Neptune.
P. Spicerianum.	P. × Lœwegrenianum.
P. × vexillarium.	P. × vexill-Io.
P. × Youngianum	P. × Brandtiæ.

54. P. javanicum.

P. Boxallii.	P. × vernixioides.
P. × Harrisianum.	P. × Colmanii.
P. insigne.	P. × Mandæ.
P. × Leeanum.	P. × Uriel.
P. Spicerianum.	P. × lutescens.

55. P. × Lathamianum.

P. barbatum.	P. × Dakinii.
P. Boxallii.	P. × Bala.
P. callosum.	P. × Calliope.
P. × Calypso.	P. × Stevensii.
P. Chamberlainianum.	P. × Wrightiæ.
P. Charlesworthii.	P. × Rappartii.
P. exul.	P. × Persephone.
P. × Harrisianum.	P. × Pryorianum.
P. Haynaldianum.	P. × nobilior.
P. insigne.	P. × Hobartii.
P. Lawrenceanum.	P. × Pynaertii.
P. × Leeanum.	P. × Grovesianum.
P. × nitens.	P. × illustre.
P. purpuratum.	P. × rotundum.
P. × Savageanum.	P. × Bollerillæ
P. Spicerianum.	P. × Salomonæ.
P. Victoria-Mariæ.	P. × Brunhild.
P. villosum.	P. × chrysotoxum.

56. P. × Lawrebel.

P. × Harrisianum.	P. × Unxia.

57. P. Lawrenceanum.

P. Argus.	P. × Io.
P. barbatum.	P. × almum.
P. bellatulum.	P. × Lawrebel.
P. Boxallii.	P. × Thayerianum.
P. callosum.	P. × Maudiæ.
P. Chamberlainianum	P. × Hiero.
P. Charlesworthii.	P. × decipiens.
P. ciliolare.	P. × Luciæ.
P. × Cleopatra.	P. × resplendens.
P. concolor.	P. × concolawre.
P. Curtisii.	P. × Gowerianum.
P. Druryi.	P. × Cybele.
P. exul.	P. × Julia.
P. Fairrieanum.	P. × streathamense.
P. × Harrisianum.	P. × gigas.

Paphiopedilum Lawrenceanum *(continued).*

P. hirsutissimum.	P. × mulus.
P. Hookeræ.	P. × enfieldense.
P. insigne.	P. × Eucharis.
P. × Io.	P. × Vanninii.
P. × Lathamianum.	P. × Pynaertii.
P. × Leeanum.	P. × Magnei.
P. Lowii.	P. × Macfarlaneanum.
P. × Marshallianum.	P. × Gravesii.
P. Mastersianum.	P. × Matthewsii.
P. × Morganiæ.	P. × Venetia.
P. × nitens.	P. × decorum.
P. niveum.	P. × Aphrodite.
P. × Numa.	P. × standense.
P. × œnanthum.	P. × Bijou.
P. Parishii.	P. × Elizabethæ.
P. philippinense.	P. × Hobsoni.
P. × Poliettianum.	P. × Fabia.
P. Rothschildianum.	P. × Mahleræ.
P. Sanderianum.	P. × Ultor.
P. × selligerum.	P. × Llangattockiæ.
P. × Sementa.	P. × crassifolium.
P. Spicerianum.	P. × radiosum.
P. Stonei.	P. × Numa.
P. superbiens.	P. × Euryale.
P. × superciliare.	P. × augustum.
P. × Swanianum.	P. × Rogersii.
P. tonsum.	P. × Barbeyæ
P. venustum.	P. × auroreum.
P. × vernixium.	P. × Coffigniezii.
P. villosum.	P. × luridum

58. P. × Leeanum.

P. × Arthurianum.	P. × Leeæ.
P. × Ashburtonæ.	P. × Louisæ.
P. barbatum.	P. × Cardosoanum.
P. Boxallii.	P. × Hera.
P. × Bruno.	P. × Leemanni.
P. callosum.	P. × Angeliæ.
P. × calophyllum.	P. × Boltonianum.
P. × Calypso.	P. × Evelyn.
P. × Canhami.	P. × Straeteni.
P. Chamberlainianum.	P. × Chamber-Leeanum.
P. Charlesworthii.	P. × longwoodense.
P. concolor.	P. × Whitei.
P. × Crossianum.	P. × Clusia.
P. Fairrieanum.	P. × Reginæ.
P. × Godseffianum.	P. × Hiawatha.

Paphiopedilum × Leeanum *(continued).*

P. · Harrisianum.	P. × Harri-Leeanum.
P. Haynaldianum.	P. × Clotilde.
P. hirsutissimum.	P. × Zampa.
P. insigne	P. × Simonii.
P. javanicum.	P. × Uriel.
P. × Lathamianum.	P. × Grovesianum.
P. Lowii.	P. ∴ roseum.
P. Lawrenceanum.	P. × Magnei.
P. × Lynchianum.	P. × Coronis.
P. × Morganiæ.	P. × Pegasus.
P. × Niobe.	P. × Niobe-Leeanum
P. × nitens.	P × Charlesianum.
P. niveum.	P. × Jeanette.
P × œnanthum.	P. × Brunnianum.
P. purpuratum.	P. × Norrisianum.
P. × Romulus.	P. × Olbia.
P. × Schlesingerianum.	P. × Lasellei.
P. × Simonii.	P × Christopher.
P. Spicerianum.	P. × Bruno.
P. Stonei.	P. × Harveyanum.
P. superbiens.	P. × Woden.
P. tonsum.	P. × maculatum.
P. venustum.	P. × Ashworthiæ
P. Victoria-Mariæ.	P. × Glonerianum.
P. villosum.	P. × Leander.

59. P. Lowii.

P. barbatum.	P. × calanthum.
P. Boxallii.	P. × Beatrice.
P. Curtisii.	P. × Joliboisii.
P. Dayanum.	P. × Patersoni.
P. insigne.	P. × Rossii.
P. Lawrenceanum.	P. × Macfarlaneanum.
P. × Leeanum.	P. × roseum.
P. niveum.	P. × Drewettii.
P. × œnanthum.	P. × Daisyæ.
P. Parishii.	P. × Robinsianum.
P. philippinense.	P. × Berenice.
P. Sanderianum.	P. × Reginaldiæ.
P. Spicerianum.	P. × Wittii.
P. superbiens.	P. × macropterum.
P. venustum.	P. × pycnopterum.
P. × vexillarium.	P. × Opoixii.
P. villosum.	P. × lucidum.

Paphiopedilum—(*continued*).

60. P × Lucie.

P. insigne.	P. × Redversii.
P. tonsum.	P. × Omphale.

61. P. × Lynchianum.

P. insigne	P. × Ilione.
P. × Leeanum.	P. × Coronis.

62. P. × Mabeliæ.

P. bellatulum.	P. × Ameliæ.

63. P. × macropterum.

P. Charlesworthii.	P. × Cardosoæ.

64. P. × marmorophyllum.

P. Argus.	P. × prestonense.
P. × Crossianum.	P. × Lachesis.
P. Hookeræ.	P. × fulgens.
P. insigne.	P. × Gem.
P. Spicerianum.	P. × Parksianum.

65. P. × Marshallianum.

P. Lawrenceanum.	P. × Gravesii.

66. P. Mastersianum.

P. barbatum.	P. × Endymion.
P. callosum.	P. × Pytho.
P. × Harrisianum.	P × Belus.
P. Hookeræ.	P. × xanthophyllum.
P. insigne.	P. × albanense.
P. Lawrenceanum.	P. × Matthewsii.
P. tonsum.	P. × Tantalus.

67. P. × Measuresianum.

P. Spicerianum.	P. × Ashworthii.
P. tonsum.	P. × Tacita.

68. P. × Medeia.

P. villosum.	P. × Hanningtoni.

69. P. × Morganiæ.

P. Argus.	P. × Argo-Morganiæ.
P. Boxallii.	P. × Frederico-nobile.
P. Curtisii	P. × Warburtoni.
P. hirsutissimum.	P. × Durbar.
P. Lawrenceanum.	P. × Venetia.
P. × Leeanum.	P. × Pegasus.
P. Rothschildianum.	P. × l'Ansoni.
P. × selligerum.	P. × Nansen.
P. Spicerianum.	P. × Charpinianum.
P. superbiens.	P. × Penelope.

Paphiopedilum—(*continued.*)

70. P. × Niobe.

P. insigne.	P. × Priam.
P. × Leeanum.	P. × Niobe-Leeanum.
P. × orphanum.	P. × Lincolnii.
P. × Sementa.	P. × Pelops.
P. Spicerianum.	P. × Norma.

71. P. × nitens.

P. Argus.	P. × leopardinum.
P. Boxallii.	P. × Parkerianum.
P. × calophyllum.	P. × Patria.
P. × Calypso.	P. × Sanderi.
P. Chamberlainianum.	P. × Polkii.
P. ciliolare.	P. × Duvalii.
P. Curtisii.	P. × colombense.
P. Druryi.	P. × medium.
P. Godefroyæ.	P. × Alexandræ.
P. × Harrisianum.	P. × giganteum.
P. hirsutissimum.	P. × Erato.
P. Hookeræ.	P. × Edmundii.
P. insigne.	P. × Romulus.
P. × Lathamianum.	P. × illustre.
P. Lawrenceanum.	P. × decorum.
P. × Leeanum.	P. × Charlesianum.
P. niveum.	P. × La-France.
P. × œnanthum.	P. × triumphans.
P. × selligerum.	P. × nitidum.
P. Spicerianum.	P. × aureum.
P. Stonei.	P. × whalleyense.
P. venustum.	P. × Violetta.
P. villosum.	P. × Colossus.

72. P. niveum.

P. × almum.	P. × Rothwelliæ.
P. Argus.	P. × Gravesiæ.
P. barbatum.	P. × Tautzianum.
P. bellatulum.	P. × Psyche.
P. Boxallii.	P. × Graceæ
P. callosum.	P. × calloso-niveum.
P. Chamberlainianum.	P. × Suttonæ.
P Charlesworthii.	P. × Eos.
P. ciliolare.	P. × Aylingii.
P. Curtisii.	P. × Cowleyanum.
P. Dayanum.	P. × Lily.
P. Druryi.	P. × microchilum.
P. Godefroyæ.	P. × Greyi.
P. × Gowerianum.	P. × Sophie.
P. × Harrisianum.	P. × Marwoodii.
P. insigne.	P. × Venus.
P. Lawrenceanum.	P. × Aphrodite.

Paphiopedilum niveum—(*contd.*).

P. × Leeanum.	P. × Jeanette.
P. Lowii.	P. × Drewettii.
P. × nitens.	P. × La-France.
P. philippinense.	P. × Vipanii.
P. Spicerianum.	P. × Spicero-niveum.
P. superbiens.	P. × Georgeanum.
P. × superciliare.	P. × Opoixiæ.
P. tonsum.	P. × Olivia.
P. venustum.	P. × Saron.

73. **P. × Numa.**

P. × Ashburtonæ.	P. × whitefieldiense.
P. Lawrenceanum.	P. × standense.

74. **P. × œnanthum.**

P. Argus.	P. × Descombesiæ.
P. barbatum.	P. × plumosum.
P. Boxallii.	P. × rubescens.
P. callosum.	P. × Bagshaweæ.
P. × calophyllum.	P. × Pollettianum.
P. Chamberlainianum.	P. × Zurigo.
P. Charlesworthii.	P. × Stottianum.
P. Dayanum.	P. × Tennyson.
P. Fairrieanum.	P. × Schrœderi.
P. × Harrisianum.	P. × Creon.
P. × Haywoodianum.	P. × Koh-i noor.
P. Hookeræ.	P. × Cleopatra.
P. insigne.	P. × Milo.
P. Lawrenceanum.	P. × Bijou.
P. × Leeanum.	P. × Brunnianum.
P. Lowii.	P. × Daisyæ.
P. × nitens.	P. × triumphans.
P. Spicerianum.	P. × Figaro.
P. superbiens.	P. × œno-superbiens.
P. tonsum.	P. × Ganymedes.
P. venustum.	P. × Wendlandianum.
P. villosum.	P. × Krameri-anum.
P. × Youngianum.	P. × Kubele.

75. **P. × orphanum.**

P. × Harrisianum.	P. × Gabrieli.
P. × Niobe.	P. × Lincolnii.

76. **P. × Orpheus.**

P. Boxallii.	P. × Juturna.

77. **P. × Pageanum.**

P. Spicerianum.	P. × Picardianum.

Paphiopedilum—(*continued*).

78. **P. × Pallas.**

P. Rothschildianum.	P. × Elise.

79. **P. Parishii.**

P. bellatulum.	P. × Statteri.
P. Chamberlainianum.	P. × Keelingii.
P. Lawrenceanum.	P. × Elisabethæ.
P. Lowii.	P. × Robinsianum.
P. Rothschildianum.	P. × Treleasei.

80. **P. × pavonium.**

P. villosum.	P. × Cahuzacii.

81. **P. × Petri.**

P. insigne.	P. × Petri-insigne.

82. **P. philippinense.**

P. Argus.	P. × burfordiense.
P. barbatum.	P. × selligerum.
P. bellatulum.	P. × Phœbe.
P. Boxallii.	P. × Metis.
P. callosum.	P. × Millmanii.
P. Chamberlainianum.	P. × Helvetia.
P. ciliolare.	P. × Finetianum.
P. Curtisii.	P. × Clinkaberryanum.
P. Haynaldianum.	P. × Lebaudyanum.
P. Lawrenceanum.	P. × Hobsoni.
P. Lowii.	P. × Berenice.
P. niveum.	P. × Vipanii.
P. purpuratum.	P. × Philo.
P. Rothschildianum.	P. × Johnsoni.
P. × selligerum.	P. × Danervaliæ.
P. Spicerianum.	P. × Astræa.
P. superbiens.	P. × Youngianum.
P. tonsum.	P. × Bryan.
P. venustum.	P. × Alfred.
P. villosum.	P. × Priapus.

83. **P. × Pollettianum.**

P. insigne.	P. × magnificum.
P. Lawrenceanum.	P. × Fabia.

84. **P. præstans.**

P. barbatum.	P. × barbato-præstans.
P. Curtisii.	P. × Holtii.
P. Spiceranum.	P. × Janet.

85. **P. purpuratum.**

P. Argus.	P. × Batalinii.
P. × Ashburtonæ.	P. × Atropos.
P. barbatum.	P. × Pitcheri.

Paphiopedilum purpuratum—(*contd.*).

P. Bullenianum.
P. Curtisii.
P. Fairrieanum.
P. × Harrisianum.
P. Hookeræ.
P. insigne.
P. × Io.
P. × Lathamianum
P. × Leeanum.
P. philippinense.
P. × Savageanum.
P. Spicerianum.
P. Stonei.
P. superbiens.
P. venustum.
P. × Remus.
P. × Oakesianum.
P. × Ballantinei.
P. × concinnum.
P. × gemmiferum.
P. × regale.
P. × modestum.
P. × rotundum.
P. × Norrisianum.
P. × Philo.
P. × Rehderianum.
P. × Cythera.
P. × Wynniæ.
P. × Dacia.
P. × Symondsiæ.

86. **P. × regale.**

P. × Calypso.
P. tonsum.
P. × Adamsii.
P. × Garfieldii.

87. **P. × Romulus.**

P. × Leeanum.
P. × Olbia.

88. **P. Rothschildianum.**

P. Argus.
P. barbatum.
P. bellatulum.
P. Boxallii.
P. callosum.
P. × Calypso.
P. Chamberlainianum.
P. ciliolare.
P. Curtisii.
P. × Cymatodes.
P. × Gowerianum.
P. × Hanseni.
P. × Harrisianum.
P. Hookeræ.
P. × Io.
P. Lawrenceanum.
P. × Morganiæ.
P. × Pallas.
P. Parishii.
P. philippinense.
P. Sanderianum.
P. × selligerum.
P. Spicerianum.
P. superbiens.
P. × superciliare.
P. × Swanianum.
P. tonsum.
P. venustum.
P. villosum.
P. × Youngianum.
P. × Rehderæ.
P. × tringiense.
P. × Rolfei.
P. × Edith.
P. × Fowleri.
P. × calypsoides.
P. × Transvaal.
P. × Amesii.
P. × Lairessei.
P. × Premier.
P. × Shillianum.
P. × Miranda.
P. × Excelsior.
P. × Jupiter.
P. × Neptune.
P. × Mahleræ.
P. × l'Ansoni.
P. × Elise.
P. × Treleasei.
P. × Johnsoni.
P. × Prince.
P. × Nebula.
P. × Faroultii.
P. × Mabeliæ.
P. × Massaianum.
P. × Adrien.
P. × Solon.
P. × bruxellense.
P. × Vacuna
P. × Sutherlandiæ.

Paphiopedilum—(*continued*).

89. **P. Sanderianum.**

P. Argus.
P. callosum.
P. Curtisii.
P. × Gowerianum.
P. × Harrisianum.
P. Lawrenceanum.
P. Lowii.
P. Rothschildianum.
P. × selligerum.
P. superbiens.
P. × Wilsonæ.
P. × May.
P. × Cooksonæ.
P. × Cassandra.
P. × Harrisander.
P. × Ultor.
P. × Reginaldiæ.
P. × Prince.
P. × Dido.
P. × Andromeda.

90. **P. × Savageanum.**

P. × Lathamianum.
P. Charlesworthii.
P. purpuratum.
P. × Bollerillæ.
P. × Braeckmanii.
P. × Rehderianum

91. **P. × Schlesingerianum.**

P. × Leeanum.
P. × Lasellei.

92. **P. × Schrœderi.**

P. × Harrisianum.
P. insigne.
P. × Little Gem.
P. × Thalia.

93. **P. × selligerum.**

P. Argus.
P. barbatum.
P. ciliolare.
P. Curtisii.
P. × Harrisianum.
P. hirsutissimum.
P. insigne.
P. javanicum.
P. Lawrenceanum.
P. × Leeanum.
P. × Morganiæ.
P. × nitens.
P. philippinense.
P. Rothschildianum.
P. Sanderianum.
P. Spicerianum.
P. superbiens.
P. tonsum.
P. × aspasioides.
P. × Joiceyi.
P. × Ashtoni.
P. × Vanneræ.
P. × Paulii.
P. × Carderi.
P. × burbagense.
P. × illustre.
P. × Llangattockiæ.
P. × Ashworthiæ.
P. × Nansen.
P. × nitidum.
P. × Danervaliæ.
P. × Nebula.
P. × Dido.
P. × Lynchianum.
P. × Elinor.
P. × Aspasia.

94. **P. × Sementa.**

P. callosum.
P. ciliolare.
P. Druryi.
P. Hookeræ.
P. insigne.
P. Lawrenceanum.
P. × Niobe.
P. × aurelianense.
P. × Iris.
P. × Josephianum.
P. × amabile.
P. × Vibilia.
P. × crassifolium.
P. × Pelops.

Paphiopedilum—(*continued*).

95. P. × siamense.

P. insigne.	P. × Reginaldianum.

96. P. × Simonii.

P. × Leeanum.	P. × Christopher.

97. P. Spicerianum.

P. Appletonianum.	P. × Quirinus.
P. Argus.	P. × Crethus.
P. × Arthurianum.	P. × Minos.
P. × Ashburtonæ.	P. × Donatii.
P. barbatum.	P. × Eyermanianum.
P. bellatulum.	P. × Enid.
P. Boxallii.	P. × Calypso.
P. callosum.	P. × Moensiæ.
P. × calophyllum.	P. × Macfarlanei.
P. Chamberlainianum.	P. × Deedmanianum.
P. Charlesworthii.	P. × Memnon.
P. ciliolare.	P. × Bookeri.
P. concolor.	P. × Arete.
P. × Crossianum.	P. × Malyanum.
P. Curtisii.	P. × Allanianum.
P. Dayanum.	P. × pallens.
P. Druryi.	P. × Buchanianum.
P. Fairrieanum.	P. × Niobe.
P. × Harrisianum.	P. × Savageanum.
P. Haynaldianum.	P. × Carnusianum
P. hirsutissimum.	P. × Medeia.
P. Hookeræ.	P. × Eurydice.
P. insigne.	P. × Leeanum.
P. × Io.	P. × Lœwegrenianum.
P. javanicum.	P. × lutescens.
P. × Lathamianum.	P. × Solomonæ.
P. Lawrenceanum.	P. × radiosum.
P. × Leeanum.	P. × Bruno.
P. Lowii.	P. × Wittii.
P. × marmorophyllum.	P. × Parksianum.
P. × Measuresianum.	P. × Ashworthii.
P. × Morganiæ.	P. × Charpinianum.
P. × Niobe.	P. × Norma.
P. × nitens.	P. × aureum.
P. niveum.	P. × Spiceroniveum.
P. × œnanthum.	P. × Figaro.
P. × Pageanum.	P. × Picardianum.
P. philippinense.	P. × Astræa.
P. præstans.	P. × Janet.

Paphiopedilum Spicerianum (*con.*).

P. purpuratum.	P. × Cythera.
P. Rothschildianum.	P. × Faroultii.
P. × selligerum.	P. × Lynchianum.
P. Stonei.	P. × Alice.
P. superbiens.	P. × Hornianum.
P. tonsum.	P. × Celia.
P. venustum.	P × polystigmaticum.
P. × vernixium.	P. × Claudii.
P. × vexillarium.	P. × Statterianum.
P. Victoria-Mariæ.	P. × Zollingeri.
P. villosum.	P. × Lathamianum.

98. P. Stonei.

P. Argus.	P. × Rothwellianum.
P. × Ashburtonæ.	P. × Clarkiæ.
P. barbatum.	P. × euryandrum.
P. Boxallii.	P. × Georgei.
P. callosum.	P. × Fordianum.
P. ciliolare.	P. × Truffautiæ.
P. concolor.	P. × platycolor.
P. Curtisii.	P. × Constance.
P. Hookeræ.	P. × Melanthus.
P. Lawrenceanum.	P. × Numa.
P. × Leeanum.	P. × Harveyanum.
P. × nitens.	P. × whalleyense.
P. purpuratum.	P. × Winniæ.
P. Spicerianum.	P. × Alice.
P. superbiens.	P. × Morganiæ.
P. × superciliare.	P. × Comet.
P. venustum.	P. × Doris.
P. × vexillarium.	P. × Apollo.
P. villosum.	P. × Abas.

99. P. superbiens.

P. barbatum.	P. × superciliare.
P. bellatulum.	P. × Measuresiæ.
P. Boxallii.	P. × Adela.
P. callosum.	P. × Moussetianum.
P. × calophyllum.	P. × polychromum
P. Chamberlainianum.	P. × Thyades.
P. Charlesworthii.	P. × Evadne.
P. ciliolare.	P. × Lachmee.
P. concolor.	P. × Arnoldianum.
P. Curtisii.	P. × Cymatodes.
P. Dayanum.	P. × Kittelii.
P. Druryi.	P. × Haywoodianum.
P. Fairrieanum.	P. × Edwardii.
P. × Harrisianum.	P. × Tryonianum.

Paphiopedilum superbiens—(*contd.*).

P. hirsutissimum. P. × Castleanum.
P. Hookeræ. P. × Pageanum.
P. insigne. P. × Thorntoni.
P. Lawrenceanum. P. × Euryale.
P. × Leeanum. P. × Woden.
P. Lowii. P. × macropterum.
P. × Morganiæ. P. × Penelope.
P. niveum. P. × Georgeanum.
P. × œnanthum. P. × œno-superbiens.
P. philippinense. P. × Youngianum.
P. purpuratum. P. × Dacia.
P. Rothschildianum. P. × Mabeliæ.
P. Sanderianum. P. × Andromeda.
P. × selligerum. P. × Elinor.
P. Spicerianum. P. × Hornianum.
P. Stonei. P. × Morganiæ.
P. × Swanianum. P. × Hecla
P. venustum. P. × Carrierei.
P. villosum. P. × Canhami.
P. virens. P. × Sementa.
P. × Youngianum. P. × Ira.

100. **P. × superciliare.**

P. barbatum. P. × Vigerianum.
P. bellatulum. P. × Arnoldiæ.
P. × Bleui. P. × Alfredianum.
P. callosum. P. × Moreauanum.
P. Charlesworthii. P. × Decia.
P. concolor. P. × Marchandii.
P. ciliolare. P. × exoptatum.
P. Dayanum. P. × Coffinetii.
P. × Hera. P. × Thomyris.
P. Hookeræ. P. × amethystinum.
P. Lawrenceanum. P. × augustum.
P. niveum. P. × Opoixiæ.
P. Rothschildianum. P. × Massaianum.
P. Stonei. P. × Comet.
P. villosum. P. × Lauræ.

101. **P. × Swanianum.**

P. × almum. P. × Mantinii.
P. barbatum. P. × gandavense.
P. bellatulum. P. × Cycnides.
P. Dayanum. P. × Artemis.
P. Fairrieanum. P. × Aasenii.
P. × Harrisianum. P. × Rossiæ.
P. Haynaldianum. P. × gracile.
P. hirsutissimum. P. × Bondii.
P. insigne. P. × Comus.
P. Lawrenceanum. P. × Rogersii.
P. Rothschildianum. P. × Adrien.
P. Susperbiens. P. × Hecla.

Paphiopedilum × Swanianum—(*con.*).

102. **P. × Swinburnei.**

P. × Haywoodianum. P. × Goodsoni.
P. venustum. P. × buryense.

103. **P. × Tautzianum.**

P. callosum. P. × Nandii.

104. **P. tonsum.**

P. Argus. P. × Iphis.
P. barbatum. P. × Rossianum.
P. bellatulum. P. × Hunteri.
P. Boxallii. P. × Zeno.
P. callosum. P. × Felicity.
P. × Calypso. P. × Œnomaus.
P. Charlesworthii. P. × Nellie.
P. Druryi. P. × Piercei.
P. Fairrieanum. P. × Amesiæ.
P. × Harrisianum. P. × orangense.
P. insigne. P. × Krishna.
P. Lawrenceanum. P. × Barbeyæ.
P. × Leeanum. P. × maculatum.
P. × Lucie. P. × Omphale.
P. Mastersianum. P. × Tantalus.
P. × Measuresianum. P. × Tacita.
P. niveum. P. × Olivia.
P. × œnanthum. P. × Ganymedes.
P. philippinense. P. × Bryan.
P. × regale. P. × Garfieldii.
P. Rothschildianum. P. × Solon.
P. × selligerum. P. × Aspasia.
P. Spicerianum. P. × Celia.
P. venustum. P. × Polyphemus.
P. villosum. P. × Bullieri.
P. × Youngianum. P. × Syrinx.

105. **P. venustum.**

P. barbatum. P. × calophyllum.
P. bellatulum. P. × Venubel.
P. Boxallii. P. × pavoninum.
P. Bullenianum. P. × Fitchianum.
P. callosum. P. × Orpheus.
P. concolor. P. × Marshallianum.
P. Dayanum. P. × caligare.
P. Godefroyæ. P. × Lloydiæ.
P. × Harrisianum. P. × chloroneurum.
P. hirsutissimum. P. × deceptum.
P. Hookeræ. P. × Atys.
P. insigne. P. × Crossianum.
P. Lawrenceanum. P. × auroreum.
P. × Leeanum. P. × Ashworthiæ.
P. Lowii. P. × pycnopterum.

Paphiopedilum venustum—(*contd.*).

P. × nitens.	P. × Violetta.
P. niveum.	P. × Saron.
P. × œnanthum.	P. × Wendlandianum.
P. philippinense.	P. × Alfred.
P. purpuratum.	P. × Symondsiæ.
P. Rothschildianum.	P. × bruxellense.
P. Spicerianum.	P. × polystigmaticum.
P. Stonei.	P. × Doris.
P. superbiens.	P. × Carrierei.
P. × Swinburnei.	P. × buryense.
P. tonsum.	P. × Polyphemus.
P. villosum.	P. × Measuresianum.

106. **P. × vernixium.**

P. × Ashburtonæ.	P. × Lowryanum.
P. × Harrisianum.	P. × bellinum.
P. Lawrenceanum.	P. × Coffigniezii.
P. Spicerianum.	P. × Claudii.

107. **P. × vexillarium.**

P. barbatum.	P. × Singletonianum.
P. bellatulum.	P. × Gratrixiæ.
P. × calophyllum.	P. × liegense.
P. × chloroneurum.	P. × Zalmoxis.
P. hirsutissimum.	P. × Jensenianum.
P. insigne.	P. × Daedalus.
P. × Io.	P. × vexill-Io.
P. Lowii.	P. × Opoixii.
P. Spicerianum.	P. × Statterianum.
P. Stonei.	P. × Apollo.

108. **P. Victoria-Mariæ.**

P. × Lathamianum.	P. × Brunhild.
P. × Leeanum.	P. × Glonerianum.
P. Spicerianum.	P. × Zollingeri.

109. **P. villosum.**

P. Argus.	P. × vernixium.
P. barbatum.	P. × Harrisianum.
P. bellatulum.	P. × allertonense.
P. Boxallii.	P. × Reynoldi.
P. callosum.	P. × Indra.
P. Chamberlainianum.	P. × Madiotianum
P. Charlesworthii.	P. × Wrigleyi.
P. ciliolare.	P. × Pygmalion.
P. concolor.	P. × conco-villosum.
P. Curtisii.	P. × Helios.
P. Dayanum.	P. × Iago.

Paphiopedilum villosum (*contd*)

P. exul.	P. × villexul.
P. Druryi.	P. × Winnianum.
P. × Harrisianum.	P. × conspicuum.
P. Godefroyæ.	P. × Una.
P. Haynaldianum.	P. × Hanseni.
P. hirsutissimum.	P. × Germinyanum.
P. Hookeræ.	P. × Schusterianum.
P. insigne.	P. × nitens.
P. × Lathamianum.	P. × chrysotoxum.
P. Lawrenceanum.	P. × luridum.
P. × Leeanum.	P. × Leander.
P. Lowii.	P. × lucidum.
P. × Medeia.	P. × Hanningtoni.
P. × nitens.	P. × Colossus.
P. × œnanthum.	P. × Kramerianum.
P. × pavoninum.	P. × Cahuzacii.
P. philippinense.	P. × Priapus.
P. purpuratum.	P. × concinnum.
P. Rothschildianum.	P. × Vacuna.
P. Spicerianum.	P. × Lathamianum.
P. Stonei.	P. × Abas.
P. superbiens.	P. × Canhami.
P. × superciliare.	P. × Lauræ.
P. tonsum.	P. × Bullieri.
P. venustum.	P. × Measuresianum.

110. **P. virens.**

P. barbatum.	P. × pleistochlorum.
P. Dayanum.	P. × Petri.
P. superbiens.	P. × Sementa.

111. **P. × Youngianum.**

P. bellatulum.	P. × Beranekii.
P. × Gowerianum.	P. × Mapleæ.
P. × Io.	P. × Brandtiæ.
P. × œnanthum.	P. × Kubele.
P. Rothschildianum.	P. × Sutherlandiæ.
P. superbiens.	P. × Ira.
P. tonsum.	P. × Syrinx.

29. PHAIUS.

1. **P. × amabilis.**

P. Blumei.	P. × Joiceyanus.
P. grandifolius.	P. × Brownii.

2. **P. bicolor.**

P. Humblotii.	P. × Owenianus.

Phaius—(*continued*).

3. P. Blumei.

P. × amabilis. P. Humblotii. P. simulans. P. × Joiceyanus. P. × Crawshawianus. P. × Marthæ.

4. P. × Cooksonæ.

P. Humblotii. P. × Ruby.

5. P. × Cooksoni.

P. Humblotii. P. simulans. P. Wallichii. P. × oakwoodiensis. P. × Clive. P. × Harold.

6. P. grandifolius.

Calanthe × Darblayana. C. × gigas. C. Masuca. C. Regnieri. C. × Veitchii. C. vestita. P. × amabilis. P. Humblotii. P. maculatus. P. × Marthæ. P. simulans. P. Wallichii. Phaiocalanthe × grandis. P.-c. × Niobe. P. c. × inspirata. P.-c. × Arnoldiæ. P.-c. × Sedeniana. P.-c. × irrorata P. × Brownii. P. × Cooksonæ. P. × Veitchii. P. × orphanus. P. × amabilis. P. × hybridus.

7. P. Humblotii.

Calanthe Masuca. P. bicolor. P. Blumei. P. × Cooksoni. P. × Cooksonæ. P. grandifolius. P. × Phœbe. P. Wallichii. P. × Owenianus. Phaiocalanthe × Berryana. P. × Owenianus. P. × Crawshawianus. P. × oakwoodiensis. P. × Ruby. P. × Cooksonæ. P. × Chapmanii. P. × Phœbe. P. × Wiganianus.

8. P. maculatus.

P. grandifolius. P. Wallchii. P. × Veitchii. P. × Ashworthianus.

9. P. × Marthæ.

P. grandifolius. P. × orphanus.

10. P. × Phœbe.

P. Humblotii. P. × Chapmanii.

11. P. × Owenianus.

P. Humblotii. P. × Wiganianus.

Phaius—(*continued*).

12. P. × simulans.

P. Blumei. P. × Cooksoni. P. grandifolius. P. Wallichii. P. × Marthæ. P. × Clive. P. × amabilis. P. × Cooksoni.

13. P. Wallichii.

Calanthe × gigas. C. × Ruby. C. × Veitchii. Cymbidium giganteum. P. × Cooksoni. P. grandifolius. P. Humblotii. P. maculatus. P. simulans. Phaiocalanthe × Schrœderiana. P.-c. × Ruby. P.-c. × Brandtiæ. Phaiocymbidium × chardwarense. P. × Harold. P. × hybridus. P. × Phœbe. P. × Ashworthianus. P. × Cooksoni.

30. PHALÆNOPSIS.

1. P. amabilis.

P. × intermedia. P. Lueddemanniana. P. rosea. P. Schilleriana. P. Stuartiana. P. violacea. P. × Amesii. P. × Sedeni. P. × Artemis. P. × Rothschildiana. P. × Leda. P. × Harriettæ.

2. P. Aphrodite.

P. rosea. P. Schilleriana. P. Stuartiana. P. × intermedia. P. × leucorrhoda. P. × Ariadne.

3. P. × intermedia.

P. amabilis. P. × leucorrhoda. P. Sanderiana. P. × Amesii. P. × Schrœderæ. P. × Rothschildæ.

4. P. × leucorrhoda.

P. × intermedia. P. × Schrœderæ.

5. P. Lueddemanniana.

P. amabilis. P. Mannii. P. Sanderiana. P. Stuartiana. P. violacea. P. × Sedeni. P. × Hymen. P. × Veitchiæ. P. × Hermione. P. × Luedde-violacea.

6. P. Mannii.

P. Lueddemanniana. P. Stuartiana. P. × Hymen. P. × langleyensis.

Phalænopsis—(*continued*)

7. **P. rosea.**

P. amabilis. P. × Artemis.
P. Aphrodite. P. × intermedia.
P. Sanderiana. P. × Hebe.
P. Schilleriana. P. × Veitchiana.
P. Stuartiana. P. × Cassandra.

8. **P. Sanderiana.**

P. × intermedia. P. × Rothschildiæ.
P. Lueddemanniana. P. × Veitchiæ.
P. rosea. P. × Hebe.
P. Stuartiana. P. × Amphitrite.

9. **P. Schilleriana.**

P. amabilis. P. × Rothschildiana.
P. Aphrodite. P. × leucorrhoda.
P. rosea. P. × Veitchiana.
P. Stuartiana. P. × Wiganiæ.

10. **P. Stuartiana.**

P. amabilis. P. × Leda.
P. Aphrodite. P. × Ariadne.
P. Lueddemanniana. P. × Hermione.
P. Mannii. P. × langleyensis.
P. rosea. P. × Cassandra.
P. Sanderiana. P. × Amphitrite.
P. Schilleriana. P. × Wiganiæ.

11. **P. violacea.**

P. amabilis. P. × Harriettæ.
P. Lueddemanniana. P. × Lueddeviolacea.

31. PHRAGMOPEDILUM.

1. **P × Ainsworthii.**

P. caudatum. P. × Hardyanum.
P. × Sedenii. P. × Lemoinierianum.

2. **P. Boissierianum.**

P. cardinale. P. × Hanischianum.
P. Schlimii. P. × Cleola.
P. × Sedenii. P. × Brysa.

3. **P. × cardinale.**

P. Boissierianum. P. × Hanischianum.
P. caudatum. P. × Finetianum.
P. Lindleyanum. P. × Cupid.
P. longifolium. P. × Eva.
P. Schlimii. P. × Ada.
P. × Sedenii. P. × Rosy-Gem.

Phragmopedilum—(*continued*).

4. **P. caricinum.**

P. caudatum. P. × Dominianum.
P. longifolium. P. × conchiferum.
P. Schlimii. P. × stenophyllum.
P. × Sedenii. P. × Faroultii.

5. **P. caudatum.**

P. × Ainsworthii. P. × Hardyanum.
P. × cardinale. P. × Finetianum.
P. caricinum. P. × Dominianum.
P. × conchiferum. P. × nitidissimum.
P. × grande. P. × giganteum.
P. Lindleyanum. P. × Geralda.
P. longifolium. P. × grande.
P. Schlimii. P. × Saundersianum.
P. × Sedenii. P. × Schrœderæ.

6. **P × conchiferum.**

P. caudatum. P. × nitidissimum.
P. × grande. P. × Elsteadianum.
P. longifolium P. × Mantinii.
P. Schlimii. P. × Baconis.
P. × Sedenii. P. × Coppinianum.

7. **P. × Dominianum.**

P. Schlimii. P. × albopurpureum.

8. **P. × grande.**

P. caudatum. P. × giganteum.
P. × conchiferum. P. × Elsteadianum.
P. Lindleyanum. P. × Uranus.
P. × Sedenii. P. × pulchellum.

9. **P. Klotzschianum.**

P. × Sedenii. P. × suave.

10. **P. Lindleyanum.**

P. × cardinale. P. × Cupid.
P. caudatum. P. × Geralda.
P. × grande. P. × Uranus.
P. longifolium. P. × Urgandiæ.
P. Schlimii. P. × Unique.
P. × Sedenii. P. × Perseus.

11. **P. longifolium.**

P. × cardinale. P. × Eva.
P. caricinum. P. × conchiferum.
P. caudatum. P. × grande.
P. × conchiferum. P. × Mantinii.
P. Lindleyanum. P. × Urgandiæ.

Phragmopedilum longifolium (*continued*).

P. Schlimii.	P. × Sedenii.
P. × Sedenii.	P. × Ainsworthii.

12. **P. Schlimii.**

P. Boissierianum.	P. × Cleola.
P. × cardinale.	P. × Ada.
P. caricinum.	P. × stenophyllum.
P. caudatum.	P. × Saundersianum.
P. × conchiferum.	P. × Baconis.
P. × Dominianum.	P. × albopurpureum.
P. Lindleyanum.	P. × Unique.
P. longifolium.	P. × Sedenii.
P. × Sedenii.	P. × cardinale.
P. vittatum.	P. × Stella.

13. **P. × Sedenii.**

P. × Ainsworthii.	P. × Lemoinierianum.
P. Boissierianum.	P. × Brysa.
P. × cardinale.	P. × Rosy-Gem.
P. caricinum.	P. × Faroultii.
P. caudatum.	P. × Schrœderæ.
P. × conchiferum.	P. × Coppinianum.
P × grande	P. × pulchellum.
P. Klotzschianum.	P. × suave.
P. Lindleyanum.	P. × Perseus.
P. longifolium.	P. × Ainsworthii.
P. Schlimii.	P. × cardinale.

14. **P. vittatum.**

P. Schlimii.	P. × Stella.

32. SCHOMBURGKIA.

1. **S. tibicinis.**

Cattleya Mossiæ.	Schombocattleya × spiralis.

33.—SOBRALIA.

1. **S. Holfordi.**

S. Wilsoni.	S. × luminosa.

2. **S. macrantha.**

S. rosea.	S. × Sedenii.
S. × Veitchii.	S. × mirabilis.
S. xantholeuca.	S. × Veitchii.

3. **S. rosea.**

S. macrantha.	S. × Sedenii.

Sobralia—(*continued*).

4. **S. × Veitchii.**

S. macrantha.	S. × mirabilis.

5. **S. Wilsoni.**

S. Holfordi.	S. × luminosa.
S. xantholeuca.	S. × Amesiana.

6. **S. xantholeuca.**

S. macrantha.	S. × Veitchii.
S. Wilsoni.	S. × Amesiana.

34. SOPHRONITIS.

1. **S. grandiflora.**

Cattleya Aclandiæ.	Sophrocattleya × Hardyana.
C. Bowringiana.	S.-c. × eximia.
C. × calummata.	S.-c. × Nydia.
C. Harrisoniana.	S.-c. × Chamberlainii.
C. intermedia.	S.-c. × Batemaniana.
C. Leopoldi.	S.-c. × Cleopatra.
C. Loddigesii.	S.-c. × Calypso.
C. Mossiæ.	S.-c. × Imperatrix.
C. Trianæ.	S.-c. × Saxa.
Epidendrum radicans.	Epiphronitis × Veitchii.
Lælia cinnabarina.	Sophrolælia × Psyche.
L. Dayana.	S.-l. × læta.
L. flava.	S.-l. × Marriottii.
L. harpophylla.	S.-l. × Valda.
L. pumila.	S.-l. × Opeti.
L. purpurata.	S.-l. × hertonensis
L. tenebrosa.	S.-l. × Gaatrixiæ.
Læliocattleya × elegans.	Sophrocattlælia × Eros.
L.-c × Schilleriana.	S.-c.-l. × Veitchii.

2. **S. violacea.**

Epidendrum × O'Brienianum.	Epiphronitis × Orpeti.

35. SPATHOGLOTTIS.

1. **S. aurea.**

S. Vieillardii.	S. × Veitchii.

2. **S. plicata.**

S. Vieillardii.	S. × kewensis.

3. **S. Vieillardii.**

S. aurea.	S. × Veitchii.
S. plicata.	S. × kewensis.

36. STANHOPEA.

1. S. insignis.

S. oculata.	S. × bellaerensis.

2. S. oculata.

S. insignis.	S. × bellaerensis.
S. tigrina.	S. × Spindleriana

3. S. tigrina.

S. oculata.	S. × Spindleriana.

37. THUNIA.

1. T. Bensonæ.

Thunia Marshalliana.	T × Veitchiana.

2. T. Marshalliana.

T. Bensonæ.	T. × Veitchiana.

38. VANDA.

1. V. Hookeriana.

V. teres.	V. × Joaquimiæ.

2. V. suavis.

V. teres.	V. × Maronæ.

3. V. teres.

V. Hookeriana.	V. × Joaquimiæ.
V. suavis.	V. × Maronæ.

39. ZYGOPETALUM.

1. Z. Burkei.

Z. intermedium.	Z. × leucochilum.

Zygopetalum—(*continued*).

2. Z. crinitum.

Batemannia Colleyi.	Zygobatemannia × Mastersii.
Colax jugosus.	Zygocolax × Veitchii.
Z. intermedium.	Z. × secundum.
Z. maxillare.	Z. × Clayi.

3. Z. intermedium.

Colax jugosus.	Zygocolax × Wiganianus.
Z. Burkei.	Z. × leucochilum.
Z. crinitum.	Z. × secundum.
Z. maxillare.	Z. × Sedenii.

4. Z. Mackayi.

Colax jugosus.	Zygocolax × Amesianus.
Z. × Perrenoudi.	Z. × Sanderi.

5. Z. maxillare.

Aganisia lepida.	Zygonisia × Rolfeana.
Colax jugosus.	Zygocolax × leopardinus.
Z. crinitum.	Z. × Clayi.
Z. intermedium.	Z. × Sedenii.
Z. rostratum.	Z. × Roeblingianum.

6. Z. × Perrenoudi.

Z. Mackayi.	Z. × Sanderi.

7. Z. rostratum.

Z. maxillare.	Z. × Roeblingianum.

NOMENCLATURE OF HYBRIDS.

A FEW suggestions for securing greater uniformity of practice than at present exists, and for securing something like a standard system of Nomenclature.

Plants of hybrid origin should if possible be distinguished from natural species, and this is secured by the use of the sign of hybridity " × " between the generic and specific names.

Hybrids between species should receive specific names, Latin or classical, consisting of a single word—the use, however, of two short words being permissible where they can be connected with a hyphen. Short names should be used for preference, those exceeding six syllables being considered inadmissible.

Hybrids raised between the same two species, even if of inverted parentage, should be considered as forms of one, any sufficiently distinct forms being distinguished by the addition of suitable varietal names.

Hybrids between genera should receive generic names formed by combining the names of the parent genera, or parts of them, to form a suitable word.

Secondary hybrids, *i.e.*, those in which one or both parents are themselves of hybrid origin, should as far as possible be dealt with under the preceding rules.

Existing names which do not conform to the above rules may be amended, the original idea, however, being conserved as far as possible.

In compiling these pages an attempt has been made to carry the above suggestions into practice.

PART II.

ALPHABETICAL enumeration of hybrids, with the names of the parents, raiser or exhibitor, date of first flowering, with references to the original record, description and figures, together with the synonyms. In some cases the exhibitor is not the original raiser, but if the latter is known his name is included within brackets before that of the exhibitor.

The hybrids are arranged alphabetically under their adopted names (see note under Nomenclature), and the synonyms as far as practicable in chronological sequence.

The parents are arranged alphabetically in Part I. of the work, followed by the names of the resulting hybrid.

1. AERIDES.

1. **A. × hybridum** (affine × Fieldingii), *G.C.* 1871, 44; *O.R.* 1893, 35.—Veitch, 1871.

A. × Dominyanum, *Will. O. Gr. Man.* ed 6, 100.

This hybrid seems to have been completely lost sight of.

2. ANGRÆCUM.

1. **A × Veitchii** (sesquipedale ♀ × superbum), *G.C.* 1891, i. 31, 35, f. 10; *J.H.* 1899, i. 48, 49, f. 10; *G.M.* 1899, 30, 31, f. 10; *O.R.* 1899, 63; 1901, 37.—Veitch, 1899.

A. eburneum was originally recorded as one of the parents, but this arose through confusion between that species and A. superbum.

3. ANGULOA.

1. **A. × Madouxiana** (Ruckeri × uniflora), *J.d.O.* v. 124; *Lind.* x. t. 434.—Linden, 1893.

Original record lost, but parentage no doubt correct. Said to have also appeared as a natural hybrid, in an importation of A. uniflora, received by Messrs. Linden (*Lind.* l.c.).

2. **A. × media** (Clowesii × Ruckeri), *G.C.* 1881, ii. 38; *O.R.* 1893, 40, 197.—Bowring, 1881.

A. × intermedia (Clowesii ♀), *G.C.* 1888, i. 798; *O.R.* 1893, 229.—Veitch.

Has also appeared as a natural hybrid, in the collection of R. H. Measures, Esq., Streatham (*O.R.* 1893, 40).

4. ANŒCTOMARIA.

A genus established to contain the following hybrid between Anœctochilus and Hæmaria.

1. **A.-m.** × **Dominyi** (Anœctochilus Roxburghii × Hæmaria discolor), *J.L. Soc.*, xxiv. 170.—Veitch, 1865.

Anœctochilus × Dominyi, *G.C.*, 1865, 462; *Proc. R.H.S.*, v. 139; *O.R.* 1893, 5.

This hybrid seems to have been completely lost sight of.

5. BRASSOCATTLÆLIA.

A genus established for the secondary hybrids derived from the three genera, Brassavola, Cattleya, and Lælia.

1. **B.-c.-l.** × **Lawrencei** (Brassocattleya × Lindleyana ♀ × Læliocattleya × elegans), *O.R.* 1902, 86.—Lawrence, 1897.

B.-c.-l. × Lindleyano-elegans, *G.C.* 1897, ii. 438; *O.R.* 1898, 30.

The parent Brassocattleya × Lindleyana is believed to be a natural hybrid between Brassavola tuberculata and Cattleya intermedia.

2. **B.-c.-l.** × **Mackayi** (B. Digbyana × L.-c. × elegans ♀), *O.R.* 1903, 174.—Chamberlain, 1903.

3. **B.-c.-l.** × **Wiganii** (B. Digbyana × L.-c. × Aphrodite ♀), *O.R.* 1902, 86.—Wigan, 1901.

Læliocattleya × Edgar Wigan, *G.C.* 1901, May 25, Suppl. 2: *O.R.* 1901, 184, 196: *G.M.* 1901, 317, 318, f.; *Gard.* 1902, ii. 219, f.

6. BRASSOCATTLEYA.

A genus established to contain the hybrids between Brassavola and Cattleya.

1. **B.-c.** × **belairensis** (Brassavola Perrinii ♀ × Cattleya Leopoldi) *Chron. O.* 150 (in note); *O.R.* 1902, 84.—Mantin, 1898.

Correvonia × bellaerensis, *Jard.* 1898, 240; *O.R.* 1899, 2.

The Cattleya parent was originally recorded as C. guttata, but we believe it to have been C. Leopoldi.

2. **B.-c.** × **Chamberlainæ** (B. Digbyana × C. quadricolor ♀). *O.R.* 1902, 326.—Chamberlain, 1902.

B.-c. × Mrs. Chamberlain, *O.R.* 1902, 340.

Læliocattleya × Mrs. Chamberlain, *G.C.* 1902, ii. 313; *O.R.* 1902, 340.

3. **B.-c.** × **conspicua** (B. glauca ♀ × C. Leopoldi), *G.M.* 1902, 440; *Gard.* 1902, ii. 50.—Sander, 1902.

L.-c. × conspicua, *G.C.* 1902, ii. 25; *O.R.* 1902, 243; *Sand. O. Guide*, 338.

Two of the above-mentioned works give Brassavola Digbyana as one of the parents, which appears to be erroneous.

4. **B.-c.** × **Fournieræ** (B. Digbyana × C. labiata ♀).—Fournier, 1902.

L.-c. × (unnamed), *J.S.H.Fr.* 1902, 142.

L.-c. × Marguerite Fournier, *J.S.H.Fr.* 1902, 229.

L.-c. × Madame Marguerite Fournier, *Dict. Ic. O.* L.-c. hyb. **t.** 21; *Rev. H.* 1902, 360, **t.**; *J.S.H.Fr.* 1902, 797.

Cogniaux differs from others in recording B. Digbyana as the seed parent.

5. **B.-c.** × **heatonensis** (B. Digbyana × C. × Hardyana), *G.C.* 1902, ii. 239; *O.R.* 1902, 310.—(Charlesworth) Hye, 1902.

6. **B.-c.** × **langleyensis** (B. Digbyana × C. Schrœderæ ♀).—Veitch, 1902.

L.-c. × Digbyano-Schrœderæ, *G.C.* 1902, i., 219, 235, 239, **f.** 75; *O.R.* 1902, 117.

B.-c. × Schrœderæ-Digbyana, *G.C.*, 1903, ii. 326; *O.R.* 1903, 366.

7. **B.-c.** × **Leemanniæ** (B. Digbyana × C. Dowiana ♀), *O.R.* 1902, 170; 1903, 57, **f.** 15.—Maron, 1902. **[See Fig. 1.]**

Fig. 1. Brassocattleya × Leemanniæ.

L.-c. × Mrs. J. Leemann, *G.C.* 1902, **i.** 280; *O.R.* 1902, 149; *Rev. H.* 1903, 68, 69, **f.** 28; *G.M.* 1903, 529, **f.**

L.-c. × Mistress J. Leemann, *J.S.H.Fr.* 1902, 798.

8. **B.-c.** × **Mariæ** (B. Digbyana × C. Warneri), *J.H.* 1902, ii. 535 (Marisæ).—Chamberlain, 1902.

L.-c. × Mariæ, *G.C.* 1902, ii., 384; *O.R.* 1902, 366.

9. **B.-c.** × **Maronæ** (B. Digbyana × C. Warscewiczii ♀), *O.R.* 1902, 85.—Maron, 1901. **[See Fig. 2.]**

L.-c. × Madame Chas. Maron, *J.S.H.Fr.* 1901, 1667; *G.C.* 1901, ii. 250; *O.R.* 1901, 317, 350.

L.-c. × Maronæ, *O.R.* 1901, 329, **f.** 48.

B.-c. × Madame Charles Maron, *J.S.H.Fr.* 1903, 650.—Garden.

10. B.-c. × Maroni (B. Digbyana × C. Mendelii ♀), *O.R.* 1902, 84, 129, 130.—Maron, 1899.

L.-c. × Imperatrice de Russie, *G.C.* 1899, i. 174; *O.R.* 1899, 127; *Rev. H.* 1900, 296, 516, **t.**; *Jard.* 1901, 120, **t.**; *Dict. Ic. O.* L.-c. hyb. **t.** 18.

L.-c. × Empress of Russia, *G.C.* 1900, i. 175; *O.R.* 1900, 109.

L.-c. × Digbyano-Mendelii, *G.C.* 1901, i. 306; ii. 204, 207, **f.** 63 (Veitch's

Fig. 2. Brassocattleya × Maronæ.

var.); *O.R.* 1901, 181, 182, 285, 365; *J.H.* 1901, ii. 237, 239, **f.** (Veitch's var.); *G.M.* 1901, 594, 597, **f.** (Veitch's var.).

B.-c. × Empress of Russia, *O.R.* 1903, 215.

Brassavola-cattleya × Empress of Russia, *G.C.* 1903, i. 367.—Sander.

11. B.-c. × Milton (B. glauca × C. Lueddemanniana ♀).—Holford, 1903.

L.-c. × Milton, *G.C.* 1903, ii. 309; *O.R.* 1903, 340.

12. B.-c. × nivalis (B. fragrans ♀ × C. intermedia).—*J.S.H.Fr.* 1900, 54; 1901, 371; *G.C.* 1901, i. 306; *O.R.* 1901, 182; 1902, 85; *J.H.* 1905, i. 484, 485, **f.**—Maron, 1900.

B.-c. × (Brassavola glauca × Cattleya intermedia), *J.S.H.Fr.* 1900, 670.—Maron.

The record "Brassavola glauca" evidently arose through some mistake.

13. B.-c. × **Orpheus** (B. glauca ♀ C. Trianæ alba) *O. R.*, 1902, 85.—Veitch, 1902.

L.-c. × Orpheus, *G. C.* 1902, i. 50; *O. R.* 1902, 51; *G. M.* 1902, 42.

14. B.-c. × **Pocahontas** (B. Digbyana × C. Eldorado ♀), O. *R.* 1903, 174. Chamberlain, 1903.

15. B.-c. × **Sanderi** (B. glauca × C. Schrœderæ ♀), *O. R.* 1905, 23, 49, f. 12.—Sander, 1903. [See Fig. 3.]

L.-c. × (unnamed) *G. C.* 1903, ii. 113.

16. B.-c. × **Sedeni** (B. Digbyana × C. Trianæ ♀), *O. R.* 1902, 84.—Veitch 1897.

Fig. 3. BRASSOCATTLEYA × SANDERI.

L.-c. × Digbyana-Trianæ, *G. C.*, 1897, i. 261; *O. R.* 1897, 132, 157; *G. M.* 1897, 254, 255, f.; *J. H.* 1897, ii. 244, 245, f. 34.

17. B.-c. × **striata** (B. fragrans × C. Mossiæ ♀), *G. C.* 1903, May 30, suppl. 1, 2; *O. R.* 1903, 184; *Rev. H.* 1903, 276, 277; *J. S. H. Fr.* 1903, 530.—(Maron) Charlesworth, 1903.

18. B.-c. × **Thorntoni** (B. Digbyana × C. Gaskelliana ♀), *O. R.* 1902, 84; *Wien. Ill. Gart.-Zeit.* 1904, 304, 307, f.—Thornton, 1897.

L.-c. × Thorntoni, *O. R.* 1897, 339; 1898, 159; 1902, 367; *G. C.*, 1898, i. 270; *J. H.* 1898, i. 390, 391, f. 74; *G. M.* 1898, 297, 298, f.

19. B.-c. × Veitchii (B. Digbyana × C. Mossiæ ♀), *O. R.* 1902, 83.—Veitch, 1889.

Lælia × Digbyano-Mossiæ, *G. C.* 1889, i. 630, 657, 658, f. 111; *Orchidoph.* 1889, 175, 176, f.; *G. W.* 1896, 598, f.

L.-c. × Digbyano-Mossiæ, *G. C.* 1889, i. 742; *O. A.* x. t. 449; *O. R.* 1893, 260; *Dict. Ic. O.* L.-c. hyb. t. 31 (v. splendens).

The first of the series of hybrids from Brassavola Digbyana.

7. BRASSOLÆLIA.

A genus established to contain the hybrids between Brassavola and Lælia.

1. B.-l. × Bouletii (B. glauca × L. harpophylla ♀.)—Maron, 1903.

B.-l. × Eugène Boulet, *J.S.H.Fr.* 1903, 766; *Jard.* 1903, 384.

Fig. 4. BRASSOLÆLIA × HELEN.

2. B.-l. × Clio (B. glauca × L. cinnabarina ♀), *O.R.* 1902, 86.—Veitch, 1902.

Lælia × Clio, *G.C.*, 1902, i. 50; *O.R.*, 1902, 51.

3. B.-l. × Gratrixiæ (B. Digbyana × L. cinnabarina ♀), *O.R*, 1902, 85.—Veitch, 1899.

L. × Mrs. Gratrix, *G.C.* 1899, ii. 334; 1900, ii. 466 (v. grandis); 1901, Jan. 5, Suppl. 11, f. 5 (v. grandis); *O.R.* 1899, 349 (L.-c.), 351; *J.H.* 1899, ii. 377, f. 71; *G.M.* 1899, 748, f.; 1901, 6, f. (v. grandis).

L. × Gratrixiæ, *Dict. Ic.O.* Lælia hyb. t. 10.

4. **B.-l. × Helen** (B. Digbyana × L. tenebrosa ♀), *Jard.* 1902, 149, f. 70; *O.R.* 1902, 169, f. 19; 1903, 185.—Maron, 1902. **[See Fig. 4.]**

L. × Helen, *G.C.* 1902, May 31, Suppl. 2; 1903, ii. 417, f. 165; *O.R.* 1902, 171; *Gard.* 1903, ii. 303, f.

L. Digbyana Helen, *J.S.H.Fr.* 1902, 461.

L. × Hebe, *G.C.* 1902, i. 380.—Maron.

L.-c. × Helène, *J.S.H.Fr.* 1902, 510.

5. **B.-l. × Rolfei** (B. Digbyana × L. crispa ♀), *O.R.* 1903, 135.—(Charlesworth) Chamberlain, 1903.

6. **B.-l. × Veitchii** (B. Digbyana × L. purpurata ♀) *O. R.* 1902, 85; 1903, 185; Veitch, 1898.

L. × Digbyano-purpurata, *G. C.*, 1898, ii. 446; *O. R.* 1899, 31.

L. × Edward VII., *G. C.* 1902, i. 413, suppl. f.

B.-l. × purpurato-Digbyana, *G. C.* 1903, i. 223; *O. R.* 1903, 154.—Charlesworth.

8. CALANTHE.

1. **C. × albata** (× Sedenii × veratrifolia ♀), *G. C.* 1896, ii. 602; *O. R.* 1896, 376; 1897, 10; 1899, 322.—Sander, 1896.

C. × Novelty, *G. C.* 1897, i. 16.

A remarkable hybrid between the deciduous and evergreen sections of the genus.

2. **C. × atrorubens** (× Darblayana ♀ × Ruby), *G. C.* 1900, i. 30; *O. R.* 1900, 58.—Cookson, 1900.

The form of the seed parent used was the one known as C. × William Murray.

3. **C. × Aurora** (Regnieri ♀ × rosea), *V. Man. O.* vi. 73.—Winn, 1889.

C. × (unnamed) *G. C.* 1890, i. 73.

4. **C. × Barberiana** (Turneri ♀ × vestita), *G. C.* 1881, i. 138; *O. R.* 1893, 70.—Barber, 1881.

C. × casta, *V. Man. O.* vi. 73.—Lawrence.

C. × Exquisite, *G. C.* 1894, ii. 670; *O. R.* 1895, 29.—Cowper.

5. **C. × bella** (Turneri ♀ × Veitchii), *G.C.* 1881, i. 234; *Reichenb.*, ser. 2, ii. 31, t. 63, f. 2; *V. Man. O.* vi. 73; *O.R.* 1893, 71.—Veitch, 1881.

C. × Oweniana, *O.R.* 1893, 32.—Williams.

C. vestita Oweniana, *O.A.* x. t. 464.

C. × Mylesii, *G.C.* 1893, ii. 692; *O.R.* 1894, 30; *O. A.* ix. t. 402; *Lind.* xvi. t. 759.—Williams.

C. × Harrisii, *G.C.* 1895, ii. 721; *O.R.* 1896. 32; 1898, 16; *G.M.* 1898, 49. f. —Harris.

C. × Phoebe, *Sand. O. Guide*, 258.

6. **C. × Darblayana** (Regnieri × vestita ♀), *J.S.H.Fr.* 1888, 635, 725; *Orchidoph.* 1889, 178, **t.**—Darblay, 1888.

C. × excellens (Regnieri ♀), *G.C.*, 1891, i. 87.—Veitch, 1888.

C. × Bryan, *O.R.* 1894, 62.—Cookson.

C. × William Murray, *O.R.* 1894, 62 - Cookson.

Messrs. Veitch's hybrid flowered as early as January, 1888, as shown by a flower preserved at Kew, but it was not named and recorded till afterwards.

7. **C. × Dominyi** (furcata × Masuca ♀), *G.C.* 1858, 4; *B.M.* **t.** 5042; *V. Man. O.* vi. 76; *O.R.* 1893, 3; 1902, 294; *Dict. Ic. O.* Cal. hyb. **t.** 2; *Day O. Draw.* lii. **t.** 81.—Veitch, 1856.

The earliest hybrid Orchid raised by hand.

8. **C. × Elwesii** (Regnieri × veratrifolia).—Elwes, 1903.

Calanthe × (unnamed). *G.C.* 1903, ii. 310; *O.R.* 1903, 341.

A hybrid between the deciduous and evergreen sections of the genus.

9. **C. × Florence** (× bella ♀ × Veitchii), *O.R.* 1894, 62.—Cowper, 189[illegible].

10. **C. × gigas** (grandiflora × Regnieri), *G.C.* 1893, i. 80; *O.R.* 1893, 61, 86; *J.H.* 1893, i. 129, **f.** 24; *Gard.* 1893, ii. 236, **t.** 926.—Veitch, 1893.

C. × Baron Schröder, *G.C.* 1894, i. 210; *O.R.* 1894, 95; *J.H.* 1894, i. 163, **f.** 25; *G.M.* 1897, 240, 241, **f.**—Veitch.

One of the most vigorous of Calanthe hybrids.

11. **C. × Harryana** (Masuca × tricarinata ♀).—Veitch, 1895.

C. × Masuco-tricarinata, *G.C.* 1895, ii. 210; *O.R.* 1895, 96.

12. **C. × Laucheana** (Sanderiana × veratrifolia ♀), *G.C.* 1894, ii. 194; *O.R.* 1894, 288.—Sander, 1894.

C. × Eclipse (Sanderiana ♀), *G.C.* 1897, ii. 243; *O.R.* 1897, 317.—H. H. Bolton.

"C. Regnieri Sanderiana," cited in the last-mentioned work, is believed to be a mistake. C. Sanderiana, Rolfe (*G.C.* 1892, ii. 396) is an East African species.

13. **C. × lentiginosa** (labrosa ♀ × Veitchii), *G. C.* 1883, i. 44; *V. Man. O.* vi. 74, **f.**; *O. R.* 1893, 100. -Veitch, 1883.

14. **C. × porphyrea** (labrosa × vestita ♀), *G. C.* 1884, i. 76; *V. Man. O.* vi. 74; *O. R.* 1893, 101.—Lawrence, 1884.

15. **C. × Rollissoni** (Masuca × veratrifolia ♀), *Hans. O. Hyb.* 82; *O. R.*, 1902, 294.—Rollisson, date uncertain.

C. × Mylami, *Day O. Draw.* lii. **t.** 71.

One of the early hybrids whose history is very imperfectly recorded.

16. **C × Ruby** (× Sedenii × vestita).—Cookson, 1898.

C. × Oakwood Ruby, *G. C.* 1899, i. 77; 1903, i. 125, 158; *O. R.* 1899, 92; 1901, 52; 1903, 83, 86, 116, 158.

C. × Sibyl, *G. C.* 1903, i. 125, 158; *O. R.* 1903, 83, 86, 116, 158.

The parentage of this hybrid is rather complex. It is described as C. × Sedenii Oakwood var. (vestita rubro-oculata × rosea) twice recrossed with C.

vestita rubro-oculata, and the progeny again seeded from for several years, the darkest form being selected on each occasion. A white form (C. × Sibyl) is said to have come out of the same capsule as the deep rose one.

17. **C. × Sedenii** (× Veitchii ♀ × vestita), *G.C.* 1878, i. 168; *V. Man. O.* vi. 75; *O.R.* 1893, 68.—Veitch, 1878.

C. × Alexandri, *G.C.* 1885, ii. 566; *O.R.* 1903, 116.—Cookson.

C. × Hallii, *G.C.* 1887, ii. 596; *V. Man. O.* vi. 74. - Hall.

C. × Cooksoni, *G.C.* 1885, ii. 566; *O.R.* 1903, 116.—Cookson.

C. × Eyermanii, *Gard. & For.* 1891, 16, 17, f. 3.—Lorillard.

C. vestita var. Cornelius Vanderbilt, *G.C.* 1893, i. 322.—Vanderbilt.

18. **C. × splendens** (× Darblayana × rosea ♀), *G.C.* 1898, i. 106; *O.R.* 1898, 94.—Cookson, 1898.

The form of the pollen parent used was C × Bryan.

19. **C. × Veitchii** (rosea ♀ × vestita), *G.C.* 1859, 1016; *B. Mag.* t. 5375; *Gtfl.* 1873, 65, t. 751, f. 1-4; *Fl. Mag.* 1866, t. 280; *O. A.* i. t. 31; *Gard.* 1887, ii. 12, t. 604; *Lind.* v. t. 217; *V. Man. O.* vi. 75, 76, f.; *O.R.* 1893, 4: *J.H.* 1902. i. 161, f.; *Dict. Ic. O.* Cal. hyb. t. 1 (and several other figures).—Veitch, 1859.

C. × Sandhurstiana, *G.C.* 1881, i. 395; *O.R.* 1893, 71.—Gosse.

C. × burfordiensis, *Gard.* 1892, ii. 398, t. 855, f.: *Reichenb.* ser. 2, ii. 31, t. 63, f. 3.—Lawrence.

C. × sanguinaria, *G.C.* 1886, i. 331; *O.R.* 1893, 132.—Lawrence.

C. × versicolor, *G.C.* 1891, ii. 712; *Gard.* 1892, i. 399, t. 855, f.—Lawrence.

Var. alba, *G.C.* 1889, i. 132.—Strickland. A very distinct, pure white variety.

C. × Veitchii has also been found as a wild plant, by Mr. Boxall, and flowered with Messrs. Hugh Low & Co. in 1893 (*O.R.* 1894, 19). The parentage of C. × versicolor was not recorded, but it is referred to C. × Veitchii as a variety in the R.H.S. List of Awards. The record of C. × burfordiensis requires confirmation, for it has been suggested that it is a form of C. × Sedenii.

20. **C × Victoria-Regina** (rosea ♀ × Veitchii), *Reichenb.*, ser. 2, ii. 31, t. 63, f. 1, *G. C.* 1893, ii. 692; *O. R.* 1894, 29.—Lawrence, 1890.

C. × rosea, *G. C.* 1890, i. 43; *Gard.* 1892, i. 399, t. 855, f. (not of Lindl.).

C. × Limatodes, *G. C.* 1900, i. 30; *O. R.* 1900, 57.

The original name of C. × rosea was changed to prevent confusion with the species, C. rosea, Benth., formerly known as Limatodes rosea, Lindl., which was one of the parents.

21. **C. × Winnii** (Regnieri ♀ × Veitchii).—Winn. 1889.

C. × (unnamed), *G.C.* 1890, i. 73.

A handsome hybrid, rather variable in colour, of which six different forms are preserved at Kew.

9. CATTLEYA.

1. **C. × Adela** (Percivaliana × Trianæ ♀), *G. C.* 1898, ii. 14; *O.R.* 1898, 223.—Veitch, 1898.

2. C. × **Adonis** (Mossiæ ♀ × Warscewiczii), *G. C.* 1897, ii. 316; *O.R.* 1897, 350; *J.S.H. Fr.* 1899, 46.—Mrs. Briggs-Bury, 1897.

C. × Enid, *G.C.* 1898, ii. 92; 1903, i. 174; *O.R.* 1898, 255; 1903, 115; *J.H.* 1903, i. 265, f.; *Gard.* 1903, i. 215, f.; *Dict. Ic. O.* Cat. hyb. t. 23.—Veitch.

3. C. × **Albertiana** (Loddigesii ♀ × Trianæ).—Vincke, 1900.

C. × Prince Albert, *Chron. O.* 1901, 331.

4. C. × **Apollo** (Aclandiæ × Mossiæ ♀), *G.C.* 1896, ii. 471; *O.R.* 1896, 348. —Veitch, 1890.

C. × Dortoly (Aclandiæ ♀), *R.H.* 1903, 507; *Jard.* 1903, 336; *J. S. H. Fr.* 1903, 649.—Maron.

First flowered in December, 1890, as proved by a flower preserved at Kew.

5. C. × **Ariel** (Bowringiana ♀ × Gaskelliana), *G.C.* 1898, ii. 446; *O.R.* 1899, 31; 1903, 335.—Veitch, 1898.

6. C. × **armainvillierensis** (Mendelii ♀ × Warscewiczii) *J. S. H. Fr.* 1896, 699; *G.C.* 1900, ii. 176; *O.R.* 1900, 285.—Baron E. Rothschild, 1896.

7. C. × **Arthuriana** (Dormaniana ♀ × luteola), *G.C.* 1894, i. 102; *O.R.* 1894, 143.—Dorman, 1894.

9. C. × **Astræa** (Loddigesii × Skinneri ♀), *Jard.* 1897, 309; *J. S. H. Fr*, 1897, 933; *O.R.* 1897, 359.—Maron, 1897.

10. C. × **Atalanta** (Leopoldi ♀ × Warscewiczii). *G.C.* 1894, ii. 194; 1899, ii. 182; *O.R.* 1894, 275, 287; 1896, 256; *Dict. Ic. O.* Cat. hyb. t. 11 (v. inversa), 11A (v. splendens); *J.H.* 1903, ii. 189, f. (v. superba).—Veitch, 1894.

11 C. × **aurantimedia** (aurantiaca × intermedia ♀), *Sand. O. Guide*, 333.—Thayer, 1902.

Epicattleya × auranti-media, *Amer. G.* 1902, 483.

12. C. × **Aurora** (Dowiana × luteola).—R. H. Measures, 1902.

C. × Golden Dawn.—*Gard.* 1903, i. 11.

13. C. × **Bactia** (Bowringiana ♀ × Leopoldi), *G.C.* 1901, ii. 330; *O.R.* 1901, 350.—Veitch, 1901.

14. C. × **Ballantiniana** (Trianæ ♀ × Warscewiczii), *G C.* 1889, i. 264; *Reichenb.* ser. 1, ii. 95, t. 91; *O.R.* 1893, 260.—Sander, 1889.

15. C. × **Barbara** (Bowringiana ♀ × Trianæ), *G.C.* 1902, ii. 445; *O.R.* 1903, 23.—Leon, 1902.

16. C. × **belairensis** (intermedia ♀ × Skinneri).—Mantin, 1897.

C. × intermedio-Skinneri, *J. S. H. Fr.* 1897, 609.

17. C. × **Bertheauana** (intermedia × Schilleriana ♀)—Duval, 1900.

C. × (unnamed), *J. S. H. Fr.* 1900, 391.—Duval.

C. × Bertheauana (intermedia ♀), *J. S. H. Fr.* 1903, 284; *Rev. H.* 1903, 269; *Jard.* 1903, 160.—Doin.

18. C. × **Bleui** (Aclandiæ × granulosa).—Bleu, 1900.

C. × memoria-Bleui, *Lind.* xvi. t. 764.

19. C. × **Brabantiæ** (Aclandiæ × Loddigesii ♀), *Fl. M.* 1867, t. 360; *O.R.* 1893, 5; 1903, 335, *Day O. Draw.* xlviii. t. 1.—Veitch, 1863

C. × Aclandi-Loddigesii, *G.C.* 1863, 602.

C. × hybrida, *G C.* 1863, 602.

20. **C. × Breauteana** (Loddigesii ♀ × superba). *Jard.* 1897, 310; *J.S.H. Fr.* 1897, 934; *O.R.* 1897, 360; 1899, 63; *G.C.* 1899, i. 31.—Maron, 1897.

C. × Alberta, *Nich. Dict.* 1900 Suppl. 208.—Van Imschoot.

C. × Lord Marsham, *Nich. Dict.* 1900 Suppl. 209. Charlesworth.

21. **C. × Browniæ** (Bowringiana × Harrisoniana ♀), *O.R.* 1894, 334, 351; 1901, 350; *J.H.* 1901, ii. 437, **f.** (Veitch's var.), *Rev. H.* 1895, 63.—Sander, 1904.

C. × Brownii, *G.C.* 1894, ii. 447.

The name was changed because of a species previously called C. Brownii (Rolfe in *Kew Bull.* 1894, 156).

22. **C. × brunoyensis** (intermedia ♀ × Percivaliana).—Maron, 1900.

C. × intermedio-Percivaliana, *Nich. Dict.* 1900 Suppl. 209.

23. **C. × Burberryana** (× intricata ♀ × superba), *G.C.* 1892, i. 535; *O.R.* 1893, 357.—Sander, 1892.

"C. imbricata," originally described as one parent, is believed to be a mistake for C. × intricata, the natural hybrid between C. Leopoldi and C. intermedia.

24. **C. × calummata** (Aclandiæ × intermedia ♀), *Rev. H.* 1881, 347 (unnamed); 1883, 564, **t.**; *O. A.* iv. **t.** 166: *G.C.* 1886, ii. 525, **f.** 104; *Gtfl.* 1887, 88, **f.** 31; *O.R.* 1893, 99; *Lind.* xvi. **t.** 749 (v. Grignani); *Day O. Draw.* xliii. **t.** 55, 56.—Bleu, 1881.

25. **C. × Cappei** (Schrœderæ × Trianæ).—Cappe, 1902.

C. × (unnamed), *J.S.H.Fr.* 1902, 229.

26. **C. × Ceciliæ** (Lawrenceana ♀ × Trianæ), *G.C.* 1895, ii. 588; *O.R.* 1895, 375; *Dict. Ic. O.* Cat. hyb. t. 9 (v. elata.)—Ingram, 1895.

C. × elata (Trianæ ♀) *G.C.* 1897, i. 177; *O.R.* 1897, 123.—Ingram.

C. × Louis Chaton, *Rev. H.* 1898, 136; *G.C.* 1898, i. 252; *O.R.* 1898, 141; *J. S. H. Fr.* 1899, 272.—Maron.

27. **C. × Chamberlainiana** (Dowiana × Leopoldi ♀); *G.C.* 1881, ii. 427; *O.R.* 1893, 71; *Dict. Ic. O.* Cat. hyb. **t.** 17; *Day O. Draw.* xxxvii. **t.** 11.—Veitch, 1881.

C. × Victor Hugo, *J. S. H. Fr.* 1900, 592; 1901, 906.—Maron.

28. **C. × Chapmanii** (Bowringiana × Warneri ♀).—R. I. Measures, 1900.

C. × Warnero-Bowringiana, *G.C.* 1900, ii. 137; *O.R.* 1900, 284.

29. **C. × Charlesworthii** (Bowringiana ♀ × superba).—Charlesworth, 1902.

C. × Bowringiano-superba, *G.C.* 1902, ii. 313; *O.R.* 1902, 341.

30. **C. × Chesnelliana** (bicolor ♀ × Bowringiana), *J. S. H. Fr.* 1897, 954. —Mantin, 1897.

C. × Chloe (Bowringiana ♀), *G.C.* 1899, ii. 267; *O.R.* 1899, 319; 1900, 315. —Veitch.

31. **C. × Chloris** (Bowringiana ♀ × maxima), *G.C.* 1893, ii. 470, 525, **f.** 88; *O.R.* 1893, 339.—Veitch, 1893.

32. **C. × Claesiana** (intermedia ♀ × Loddigesii), *O.R.* 1899, 72; 1900, 151. —Mead, 1899.

First appeared as a supposed natural hybrid between the species named, flowering in 1894 (see *O.R.* 1899, 72).

33. C. × Claridiana (intermedia × Lueddemanniana ♀), *Amer. G.* 1899, 367, f. 90 (right-hand figure), 788.—Lager & Hurrell, 1899.

34. C. × Clarissa (Loddigesi ♀ × Mendelii), *O.R.* 1903, 26.—Chamberlain, 1902.

35. C. × Clarkiæ (bicolor ♀ × labiata), *O.R.* 1901, 15.—(Charlesworth) Clark, 1900.

36. C. × Claudian (Lueddemanniana ♀ × Schilleriana), *O.R.* 1903, 175.—(Charlesworth) Chamberlain, 1902.

C. × Ceres, *G.C.* 1903, ii. 142 : *O.R.* 1903, 269.—Charlesworth.

37. C. × Clementinæ (Aclandiæ × Dowiana).—King of Belgium, 1902.

C. × Princesse Clémentine, *Rev. H. Belge*, 1902, 23.

38. C × Clymene (Rex × Warscewiczii ♀), *O.R.* 1901, 302; *Lind.* xvi, t. 761.—Linden, 1901.

39. C. × Clytie (Bowringiana ♀ × velutina), *G.C.* 1901, ii. 297; *O.R.* 1901, 349.—Miller, 1900.

C. × Bowringiano-velutina, *G.C.*, 1900, ii. 251 ; *O.R.* 1900, 315, 346.

40. C. × Comet (Dowiana × Warneri ♀), *G.C.* 1903, ii. 142; *O.R.* 1903, 268, 365.—Bradshaw, 1903.

41. C. × Cyane (Leopoldi × Mossiæ ♀), *Gard.* 1903, ii. 210.—Veitch, 1903.

42. C. × Cybele (Gaskelliana ♀ × Lueddemanniana), *G.C.* 1902, i. 18; *O.R.* 1902, 35, 36.—Veitch, 1901.

43. C. × Dallemagneæ (granulosa ♀ × Mossiæ).—Dallemagne, 1900.

C. × memoria Dallemagneæ, *J. S. H. Fr.* 1900, 567; 1901, 849.

44. C × Daphne (Harrisoniana × Schilleriana).—Duval, 1901.

C. × Schilleriano-Harrisoniæ, *J. S. H. Fr.* 1901, 599.—Duval.

45. C. × Doinii (Dormaniana ♀ × Dowiana).—Doin, 1902.

Lælio-cattleya × Dormaniano-aurea, *Rev. H.* 1902, 494; 1903, 507; *J. S. H. Fr.* 1902, 684.

46. C. × Dominiana (intermedia × maxima ♀), *G.C.* 1859, 948; *Fl. Mag.* 1867, t. 357 (v. alba); *O.R.* 1893, 4; *V. Man. O.* ii. 90; *Day. O. Draw.* ii. t. 37; viii. t. 39 (v. lutea),—Veitch, 1859.

C. × Pheidona (intermedia ♀), *G.C.* 1893, ii. 470 (Pheidinæ); *O.R.* 1893, 352, 363.—Veitch.

The second hybrid Cattleya raised by hand.

47. C. × Doris (Gaskelliana × Leopoldi).—R. H. Measures, 1903.

C. × (unnamed), *Gard.* 1903, ii. 168.

48. C. × Eclipse (maxima ♀ × Skinneri), *G.C.* 1896, ii. 471; *O.R.* 1896, 347.—Ingram, 1896.

49. C. × Edwardi (Schilleriana ♀ × Warscewiczii).—Sander, 1902.

C. × Prince Edward, *G.C.* 1902, i. 442; *O.R.* 1902, 213.—Wigan.

C. × Schilleriano-gigas, *J. S. H. Fr.* 1902, 500; *Rev. H.* 1902, 371.—Dallemagne.

50. C. × Ella (bicolor ♀ × Warscewiczii), *G.C.* 1898, ii. 202; *O.R.* 1898, 317; *J.S.H. Fr.* 1901, 907; *Dict. Ic. O.* Cat. hyb., **t.** 13—Veitch, 1898.

51. C. × Elvina (Schilleriana × Trianæ ♀), *G.C.* 1896, ii. 534; *O.R.* 1896, 351; 1903, 344.—Veitch, 1896.

C. × Schilleriano-Trianæ (Schilleriana ♀), *J. S. H. Fr.* 1898, 777.—Mantin.

C. Dione, *Sand. O. Guide*, 333.

52. C. × Eros (Mossiæ ♀ × Walkeriana), *G.C.* 1895, ii. 192; *O.R.* 1895, 259, 287.—Veitch, 1895.

53. C. × Eurydice (Aclandiæ × labiata ♀), *G.C.* 1895, ii. 527; *O.R.* 1895, 374.—Veitch, 1895.

54. C. × exquisita (luteola ♀ × Parthenia), *G.C.* 1903, ii. 181; *O.R.* 1903, 307.—Sander, 1903.

55. C. × Fabia (Dowiana × labiata ♀), *G.C.* 1894, ii. 604; *O.R.* 1894, 375; 1902, 367; *J.H.* 1897, ii. 499, **f.** 74; *J.S.H. Fr.* 1900, 118; *Dict. Ic. O.* Cat. hyb. **t.** 24 (v. Vigeriana).—Veitch, 1894.

C. × Lansbergei, *Lind.* xvi. t. 725.

C. × Vigeri, *J. S. H. Fr.* 1901, 1062.—Maron.

C. × Vigeriana, *J. S. H. Fr.* 1902, 777; *Gard.* 1902, ii. 372.—Maron.

56. C. × Fabiola (Bowringiana ♀ × Harrisii), *G.C.* 1896, ii. 601; *O.R.* 1896, 375.—Veitch, 1896.

57. C. × Faerie-Queene (Mossiæ × Rex), *G.C.* 1903, ii. 35.—Pitt, 1903.

58. C. × Fascelis (Aclandiæ × bicolor ♀), *G.C.* 1900, ii. 346; *O.R.* 1900, 371.—Veitch, 1900.

59. C. × Fernandi (Aclandiæ ♀ × Warscewiczii).—Maron. 1897.

C. × Fernand Denis, *Rev. H.* 1897, 255; *J. S. H. Fr.* 1897, 933; *O. R.* 1897, 359; 1898, 189; *G. M.* 1898, 339, 340, **f.**

60. C. × Feuillatii (Leopoldi ♀ × superba), *Jard.* 1897, 309; *O. R.* 1897, 360; *J. S. H. Fr.* 1897, 933; 1899, 486; *Rev. H.* 1897, 504.—Maron, 1897.

61. C. × Firebrand (Lawrenceana × Schilleriana ♀), *G. C.* 1899, ii. 58; *O. R.* 1899, 253.—Ingram, 1899.

62. C. × Firefly (Bowringiana × Dormaniana ♀), *O.R.* 1896, 347; 1903, 339; *G.C.* 1902, ii. 272.—Ingram, 1896.

Lælio-cattleya × Firefly, *G.C.* 1896, ii. 471.

63. C. × flavescens (luteola × Trianæ ♀), *J. S. H. Fr.* 1899, 47. —*Dict. Ic. O.* Cat. hyb. **t.** 19.—Maron, 1898.

C. × (unnamed), *J. S. H. Fr.* 1898, 1235 (parents wrongly recorded as "C. xanthina et Trianæ").

64. C. × Fowleri (× Hardyana × Leopoldi ♀), *G.C.* 1895, ii. 178, 192; *O.R.* 1895, 259, 286; *G.M.* 1895, 526, f.; *Dict. Ic. O.* Cat. hyb. **t.** 5.—Sander, 1895.

Lælio-cattleya × Fowleri, *G.C.* 1895, ii. 239, **f.** 47.

C. × Magneana, *J. S. H. Fr.* 1902, 631; *Jard.* 1902, 328, t.; *O.R.* 1902, 376. —Maron.

65. **C. × Frasquita** (bicolor ♀ × velutina), *Rev. H.* 1903, 507; *Jard.* 1903, 336; *J. S. H. Fr.* 1903, 650.—Maron.

C. × velutino-bicolor, *J. S. H. Fr.* 1900, 669.—Maron.

66. **C. × Frederickiæ** (Dowiana × Mossiæ ♀) (Veitch, 1888), Schröder, 1890.

C. × Mossiæ-Dowiana Empress Frederick, *G. World*, 1890, 716.

Fig. 5. CATTLEYA × GERMANIA.

"C. Mossiæ and C. Dowiana Emperor Frederick," *G. C.* 1890, ii. 51.

C. × Empress Frederick, *G. C.* 1892, i. 816; 1897, ii. 428, 429, **f. 127** (var. Leonata); *O. R.* 1893, 44.

First flowered in July, 1888, as proved by a flower preserved at Kew.

67. **C. × fulvescens** (Dowiana × Forbesii), *G. C.* 1901, ii. 250; *G. M.* 1901, 644, **f.**; *O. R.* 1904, 368.—Charlesworth, 1901.

C. × flavescens, *O. R.* 1901, 299, 303, 317.

68. **C. × Gautheriniana** (Leopoldi × Schrœderæ ♀), *J. S. H. Fr.* 1899, 940; *G.C.* 1903. ii. 378 (Gautheriana); *O.R.* 1903, 338, 339 (Gauthieriana).—Duval, 1899.

69. **C.** × **Geleniana** (bicolor × Lueddemanniana ♀), *Wien. Ill. G. Zeit.* 1901, 111, 112. **f.** 12 (lower fig.).—Hruby, 1901.

C. × Leander. *G.C.* 1902, ii. 105; *O.R.* 1902, 274.—Charlesworth.

C. Hyades, *G.M.* 1902, 517.—Charlesworth.

70. **C.** × **Germania** (granulosa ♀ × Hardyana), *G.C.* 1901, ii. 210; 1902, ii. 239; *O.R.* 1901, 315, 327; 1902, 297, **f.** 30 (v. burbagensis).—Charlesworth, 1901. **[See Fig. 5]**

71. **C.** × **Gertrude** (Mossiæ × superba ♀), *G.C.* 1898, i. 385; *O.R.*, 1898, 220, 223.—Veitch, 1898.

Fig. 6. CATTLEYA × GRANUGLOSSA.

72. **C.** × **Goossensiana** (Gaskelliana × Schilleriana ♀), *Dict. Ic. O.* Cat. hyb. **t.** 14; *O.R.* 1900, 119.—Peeters, 1900.

C. × Firmini, *Rev. H. Belge*, 1902, 238.—Lambeau.

C. × Bievreana (Gaskelliana ♀), *G.C.* 1903, ii. 209.—King of Belgium.

C. × De Bievreana, *Rev. H. Belge*, 1903, 283.

There appears to be a little doubt about the parentage of C. × Firmini.

73. **C.** × **granuglossa** (amethystoglossa × granulosa ♀), *Amer. Gard.* 1901, 61, **f.** 16; *O.R.* 1903, 345, **f.** 51.—Mead, 1901. **[See Fig 6]**

The cross was made by Mr. T. L. Mead, Oviedo, Florida, but the seedlings were raised by Mr. E. O. Orpet, S. Lancaster, Mass.

74. C. × Gratrixiæ (granulosa × Harrisoniana ♀).—Gratrix, 1897.

C. × Mary Gratrix, *G.C.* 1897, ii. 169; *O.R.*, 1897, 315; 1901, 287.

C. × Crashleyi, *G.C.* 1903, ii. 181; *O.R.* 1903, 307.—Stanley, Ashton & Co.

These two forms appear to be very nearly allied, but it is somewhat doubtful whether C. Harrisoniana was the second parent in both cases.

75. C. × Greavesiæ (Gaskelliana × Loddigesii ♀).—Leemann, 1899.

C. × Mrs. Herbert Greaves, *G.C.* 1899, ii. 426; *O.R.* 1899, 371; 1901, 349; 1902, 341.

C. × Mistress Herbert Greaves, *J. S. H. Fr.* 1901, 997.—Maron.

C. × (unnamed), *O.R.* 1901, 299.

This hybrid should be compared with C. × Williamsiæ, as the well-known confusion between C. Loddigesii and C. Harrisoniana is reflected in its hybrids.

76. C. × Greyæ (granulosa ♀ × velutina), *G.C.* 1900, i. 423; *O.R.* 1900, 214.—Wigan, 1900.

77. C. × Halevy (Mendelii ♀ × Rex), *J. S. H. Fr.* 1900, 536; *Jard.* 1900, 251.—Maron, 1900.

78. C. × Hardyana (Dowiana ♀ × Warscewiczii), *G.C.* 1896, ii. 310; *O.R.* 1896, 292, 298; 1897, 364; *Reichenb.* ser. 2, ii. 15, t. 55; *J.R.H.S.* xxiv. 192, f. 96. —Cookson, 1896.

C. × Semontiana, *J. S. H. Fr.* 1902, 400; *Rev. H.* 1902, 302.—Doin.

Originally appeared as a natural hybrid in 1883 (*G.C.* 1885, ii. 206; *O.A.* v. t. 231), and now fairly common in collections.

79. C. × Harold (Gaskelliana ♀ × Warscewiczii), *G.C.* 1893, i. 580; 1898, ii. 14; *O.R.* 1893, 188; 1898, 223.—Cookson, 1893.

80. C. × Harrisiæ (Mossiæ ♀ × Schilleriana), *O.R.* 1901, 226.—Harris, 1887.

C. × Miss Harris *G.C.* 1887, ii. 490; 1901, i. 242, 302, suppl. f. (v. E. Ashworth) *O.R.* 1893, 134; 1901, 153 (v. E. Ashworth); *G.M.* 1901, 481, f.

Catlælia × Miss Harris, *Hans. O. Hyb.* 96.

C. × (unnamed), *J. S. H. Fr.* 1897, 954.—Mantin.

C. × Mossi-Schilleriana, *J. S. H. Fr.* 1897, 1344.—Mantin.

C. × elatior (Schilleriana ♀), *G.C.* 1899, ii. 478: *O.R.* 1900, 28.—Ingram.

C. × Elisabethæ, *Lind.* xvi. t. 721.—Linden.

C. × Vulcain, *J. S. H. Fr.*, 1901, 1001; *Dict. Ic. O.* Cat. hyb. t. 16.—Dallemagne.

C. × Mme. Panzani, *J. S. H. Fr.* 1902, 145, 228, 247.—Maron.

81. C. × Harrisii (Leopoldi ♀ × Mendelii), *G.C.* 1887, i. 104; *O.R.* 1893, 133; 1897, 34.—Harris, 1887.

C. × (unnamed), *J. S. H. Fr.* 1895, 606.—Baron E. Rothschild.

C. × Lafontaine (Mendelii ♀), *J. S. H. Fr.* 1899, 271.—Maron.

C. guttata is recorded as the pollen parent of the last named, but we believe C. Leopoldi is intended.

82. C. × Heloisiæ (Forbesii × Mossiæ ♀), *J. S. H. Fr.* 1897, 608.—Mantin, 1897.

C. × Forbesi-Mossiæ, *J. S. H. Fr.* 1900, 669.—Bleu.

83. C. × highburiensis (Harrisoniana × Mossiæ).—Chamberlain, 1903.

C. × (unnamed), *G. World*, 1903, i. 383.

84. C. × hybrida (guttata × Loddigesii), *Proc. R. H. S.* ii. 619; *O.R.* 1893 4; 1897, 333; *Day O. Draw.* xlviii. t. 15.—Veitch, 1859.

C. × (unnamed), *G.C.* 1859, 672; *Proc. R. H. S.* i. 70.

C. × picta, *Proc. R. H. S.* iii. 369.

C. × hybrida picta, *Proc. R. H. S.* v. 173; *Fl. M.* 1881, t. 473.

C. × picturata, *G.C.* 1877, ii. 584; *O.R.* 1893, 36; *Amer. G.* 1902, 306, 307, f. 70.

The first hybrid Cattleya raised by hand, and one which has subsequently been much confused with allied hybrids.

85. C. × Imperator (granulosa ♀ × labiata), *G.C.* 1903, ii. 340; *O.R.* 1903, 364; *Dict. Ic. O.* Cat. hyb. t. 26.—Peeters, 1902.

First appeared as a natural hybrid, in 1896. See *O.R.* 1897, p. 365, where its history is fully detailed.

86. C. × Ingramiæ (Eldorado ♀ × Dowiana).—Ingram, 1895.

C. × Lady Ingram, *G.C.* 1895, ii. 588; *O.R.* 1895, 375; 1901, 338, 349.

C. × Suzannæ, *J. S. H. Fr.* 1900, 670.—Maron.

C. × Louis Fournier, *J. S. H. Fr.* 1900, 765; 1901, 371.—Maron.

87. C. × interglossa (amethystoglossa × intermedia), *Amer. G.* 1902, 578. —Thayer, 1902.

88. C. × intertexta (Mossiæ ♀ × Warneri), *G.C.* 1897, i. 177; *O.R.* 1897, 124; 1898, 319.—Veitch, 1897.

C. × Grace Moojen, *Sand. O. Guide*, 333.

89. C. × intricata (intermedia × Leopoldi ♀), *O.R.* 1897, p. 169; 1900, 229.—Sander, 1897.

C. × intricata v. Rossii, *O.R.* 1897, 169.

C. × Rossii, *G.C.* 1897, i. 354; *O.R.* 1897, 191.

C. × maculata, *Nich. Dict.* 1900 *Suppl.* 209.—Veitch.

First appeared as a natural hybrid in 1884, when it was described by Reichenbach (*G.C.* 1884, ii. 12), though its parentage was not understood till five years later (*G.C.* 1889, ii. 38).

90. C. × Iris (bicolor ♀ × Dowiana), *G.C.* 1901, ii. 249; 1901, ii. 297, 379; 1902, ii. 238; *O.R.* 1901, 317, 348, 367; 1902, 309, 369, f. 38 (v. oculata), 1903, 330, 343; *G. M.* 1901, 690, f. (v. aureo-marginata); 1902, 639, 651, f.; *J.H.* 1901, ii. 397, f. (v. aureo-marginata); 1905, ii. 320, 321, f. (v. magnifica); *Gard.* 1905, ii. 240, f. (v. His Majesty).—Charlesworth, 1901. **[See Fig. 7]**

One of the most variable and beautiful Cattleya hybrids yet raised.

91. C. × Isabella (Forbesii × intermedia ♀), Bleu, 1878.

C. × (unnamed), *J. S. H. Fr.* 1881, 239; 1889, 311.—Bleu.

C. × n. 1, *Rev. H.* 1881, 306; *Orchidoph.* i. 49.—Bleu.

C. × Krameriana, *O.R.* 1893, 2, 325.—Sander.

C. × Louryana, *G.C.* 1891, i. 683; *O.R.* 1893, 325.—Sander.

C. × fimbriata, *Bohnh. Dict. O. Hyb.* 6; *O.R.* 1893, 325; *J. S. H. Fr.* 1897, Suppl. ii. 68.—Bleu.

This has been somewhat confused with C. × calummata, owing to a record that C. Aclandiæ was one of the parents. It is believed to be identical with C. × Isabella, Rchb. f. (*Wochenschr.* 1859, 336), a rare natural hybrid.

92. C. × Juno (Forbesii × velutina), *G.C.* 1895, ii. 118.—Roebling, 1895.

Fig. 7. Cattleya × Iris.

93. C. × Jupiter (Lawrenceana ♀ × Warscewiczii), *G.C.* 1896, ii. 471; *O.R.* 1896, 347.—Ingram, 1896.

C. × Comfrey, *Nich. Dict.* 1900 *Suppl.* 209.

94. C. × Jussieu (Lawrenceana × Schrœderæ), *G.C.* 1902, i. 380.—Maron, 1902.

95. C. × Katherinæ (Schrœderæ × Warneri ♀), *Amer. G.* 1903, 134; *O.R.* 1903, 175.—Thayer, 1903.

96. C. × Kienastiana (Dowiana × Lueddemanniana ♀), *G.C.* 1894, ii. 257; 1899, ii. 232; *O.R.* 1894, 318; 1899, 317.—Sander, 1894.

97. C. × **Knightii** (quadricolor × Percivaliana).—King of Belgium, 1903.

C. × "Memoriæ Henry Knight," *Rev. H. Belge*, 1903, 96.

98. C. × **lamberhurstensis** (citrina × intermedia ♀).—Harris, 1888.

C. × citrino-intermedia, *G.C.* 1888, i. 73; *O.R.* 1893, 228.

99. C. × **Lawre-Mossiæ** (Lawrenceana ♀ × Mossiæ), *G.C.* 1896, i. 468; *O.R.* 1896, 157.—Brooman White, 1896.

C. × Duchesse Elisabeth, *J. S. H. Fr.* 1902, 461.—Maron.

C. × Grand Duchess Elizabeth, *G.C.* 1902, i. 314; *O.R.* 1902, 182.—Leemann.

C. × Milton, *G.C.* 1902. i. 380.—Maron.

C. × Fair Ellen, *Sand. O. Guide*, 330.

100. C. × **Leda** (Dowiana × Percivaliana ♀), *O.R.* 1901, 53.—Maron. 1900.

101. C. × **Leoni** (Schrœderæ ♀ × Warscewiczii).—Leon, 1900.

C. × H. S. Leon, *G.C.* 1900, ii. 384; *O.R.* 1900, 372; *J.H.* 1900, ii. 483, f. 125.

102. C. × **Leucothoe** (granulosa ♀ × Walkeriana), *Amer. G.* 1902, 513; *O.R.* 1902, 272.—Thayer, 1902.

103. C. × **Lloydiæ** (Rex × velutina).—R. H. Measures, 1901.

C. × Kitty Lloyd, *Gard.* 1901, ii. 54.

104. C. × **Lottie** (Aclandiæ ♀ × Trianæ), *G.C.* 1901, ii. 297; *O.R.* 1901, 349.—Charlesworth, 1901.

105. C. × **Lucieniana** (Harrisoniana ♀ × Leopoldi).—Sander, 1903.

C. × (unnamed), *O.R.* 1903, 263.

C. × Lucieniana originally appeared as a natural hybrid of somewhat doubtful parentage, in the establishment of Messrs. Linden, Brussels (See *G.C.* 1885, ii. 456; *O.R.* 1903, 282). It is only known from description, but the one cited above is suspected to be identical.

106.—C. × **Macænas** (superba × Warscewiczii ♀), *G.C.* 1896, i. 9; *O.R.* 1900, 319.—Veitch, 1895.

C. × Euphrasia, *G.C.* 1896, ii. 310; *O.R.* 1896, 297, 320; 1897, 318; 1900, 27.- Veitch.

107. C. × **Mackayi** (intermedia × Mossiæ).—Chamberlain, 1903.

C. × (unnamed), *G.W.* 1903, i. 383.

108. C. × **Mahleræ** (bicolor × Leopoldi).—R. H. Measures, 1901.

C. × Mrs. Mahler, *Boyle Woodl. O.* 13.

109. C. × **Manglesii** (Loddigesii × Lueddemanniana), *G.C.* 1880, ii. 556; *O.R.* 1893, 5.—Veitch, 1866.

110. C. × **Mantinii** (Bowringiana ♀ × Dowiana), *J. S. H. Fr.* 1894, 581; *O. R.* 1894, 365; 1895. 351, 374; 1902, 337, f. 36; *Rev. H.* 1894, 534, 558; 1895, 129, f. 35; 1897, 208, t.; *J. H.* 1895, ii. 503, f. 76; *G.M.* 1896, 82, 83, f.; *Amer. G.* xxi. 744, 745, 747, f. 158, 159; *Lind.* xi, t. 509; *Dict. Ic. O.* Cat. hyb. t. 7.—Mantin, 1894. [**See Fig. 8**]

C. × epicasta, *Sand. O. Guide*, 258.

111. C. × **Mariannæ** (dolosa ♀ × Trianæ), *J. S. H. Fr.* 1900, 60; 1901; 371.—Maron, 1900.

112. C. × **Maronæ** (Eldorado × labiata).—Maron, 1899.

C. × (unnamed), *J. S. H. Fr.* 1900, 84.

113. C. × **Maroni** (Dowiana × velutina ♀), *J. S. H. Fr.* 1898, 853; *G. C.* 1898, ii. 326, 332, f. 98; *O.R.* 1898, 336, 351; 1906, 25, f. 4 (Westfield var.); *G.M.* 1898, 718, 719, f.; *J. H.* 1898, ii. 360, 361, f. 62; 1903, i. 287, f.; *Dict. Ic. O.* Cat.

Fig. 8. Cattleya × Mantinii.

hyb. t. 10; *Jard.* 1899, 360, t. (v. violacea); *Amer. G.* 1902, 879, f. 180; *Gard.* 1901, ii. 347 (v. velutissima).—Maron, 1898. [See Fig. 9]

114. C × **Marriottiæ** (Eldorado ♀ × Warscewiczii), *G.C.* 1896, ii. 195; *O.R.* 1896, 286.—Marriott, 1896.

C. × Marriottiana, *G.C.* 1901, ii. 120; *O.R.* 1901, 283.

115. C. × **Mars** (labiata ♀ × Lawrenceana), *G.C.* 1897, ii. 277; *O.R.* 1897, 349.—Sander, 1897.

116. C. × Marstersoniæ (labiata × Loddigesii ♀), *G.C.* 1878. ii. 556; *O.A.* ix. t. 385; *Veitch. Man. O.* ii. 92: *O.R.* 1893, 68; *Day. O. Draw.* xxx. t. 43.—Veitch, 1878.

C. × (unnamed), *J. S. H. Fr.* 1901, 1062.—Bert.

The original record, "a hybrid between another seedling in the way of C. Loddigesii and of C. labiata," is not borne out by later statements.

Fig. 9. CATTLEYA × MARONI.

117. C. × Measuresiæ (Lueddemanniana ♀ × velutina).—Sander, 1895.

C. × Miss Measures, *G.C.* 1895, ii. 49; *O.R.* 1895, 243, 255.—Sander.

C. × velutino-Lueddemanniana, *J. S. H. Fr.* 1900, 536.—Maron.

118. C. × Melpomene (Forbesii ♀ × Mendelii), *G.C.* 1897, ii. 315; *O.R.* 1897, 318, 351.—Veitch, 1897.

119. C. × Milleri (Gaskelliana × maxima ♀).—Miller, 1900

C. × (unnamed), *G.C.* 1900, ii. 313; *O.R.* 1900, 348.

120. C. × Minerva (Bowringiana ♀ × Loddigesii), *G.C.* 1899. ii. 301; *O.R.* 1899, 350; 1903, 330.—Veitch, 1899.

121. C. × **Minucia** (Loddigesii ♀ × Warscewiczii), *G.C.* 1892, ii. 379; *O.R.* 1893, 357; 1895, 312; 1897, 291; 1899, 341.—Veitch, 1892.

C. × Johnsoniana, *G.C.* 1893, ii. 406; *O.R.* 1893, 350.—Lewis.

C. × Ashtoniana, *G.C.* 1893, ii. 406; *O.R.* 1893, 350.—Lewis.

C. × La Belle.—*G.C.* 1896, ii. 535; *O.R.* 1896, 350.—Marriott.

C. × Murruca, *Sand. O. Guide*, 1901, 259.

The above are suspected to be all forms of the same hybrid, and those that we have seen resemble C. Loddigesii rather than C. Harrisoniana, which is recorded as a parent in some cases.

122. C. × **mirabilis** (× Patrocinii ♀ × Warscewiczii), *Rev. H. Belge*, 1903, 307.—Wavrin, 1903.

123. C. × **Miranda** (amethystoglossa ♀ × Trianæ), *G.C.* 1897, i. 51; *O.R.* 1897, 62, 80, 124, 340; 1898, 125; *J.H.*, 1898, i. 257, f. 54.—Veitch, 1897.

124. C. × **Mitchellii** (Eldorado × Leopoldi ♀), *G.C.* 1876, ii. 386; *Fl.M.* 1879, t. 337; *O.R.* 1893, 40.—Ainsworth, 1876.

125. C. × **mollis** (Gaskelliana × superba ♀), *G.C.* 1899, ii. 198; 1901, ii. 360; *O.R.* 1899, 286; 1901, 365; 1902, 272; 1903, 330; *G.M.* 1902, 22, 23, f. (v. Lois); *Amer. G.* 1902, 513.—Wigan, 1899.

C. × Gaskelliano-superba, *J. S. H. Fr.* 1899, 834.—Maron.

126. C. × **Murrayi** (Lawrenceana × Mendelii ♀), *O.R.* 1896, 140.—Cookson, 1893.

C. × William Murray, *G.C.* 1893, i. 639; *O.R.* 1893, 167; 1896, 126.

C × William Murray fulgens (Lawrenceana ♀), *G.C.* 1896, i. 468; *O.R.* 1896, 156.—Ingram.

127. C. × **Nephthys** (granulosa ♀ × superba), *Amer. G.* 1902, 483.—Thayer, 1902.

128. C. × **Niobe** (Aclandiæ ♀ × Mendelii), *G.C.* 1900, ii. 18; *O.R.* 1900, 250; 1901, 284; *G.M.* 1902, 274. f.—Veitch, 1900.

129. C. × **Nymph** (Eldorado × Gaskelliana ♀).—Marriott, 1901.

C. × (unnamed), *G.C.* 1901, ii. 250; *O.R.* 1901, 316.

C. × La Nymph, *Sand. O. Guide*, 333.

130. C. × **Octavia** (Dowiana × Mendelii ♀).—Maron, 1899.

C. × Octave Doin, *J. S. H. Fr.* 1899, 57; *G.C.* 1899, i. 192; *O.R.* 1899, 121.

131. C. × **Œnone** (labiata × Mossiæ ♀), *G.C.* 1898, i. 385; *O.R.* 1898, 220.—Veitch, 1898.

C. × Juliet, *G.C.* 1899, ii. 17; *O.R.* 1899, 251.—Veitch.

132. C. × **olivetensis** (Loddigesii ♀ × maxima) *J. S. H. Fr.* 1897, 602, 954.—Mantin, 1897.

C. × Miss Endicott (maxima ♀), *G.C.* 1897, ii. 352; *O.R.* 1897, 375.—Chamberlain.

133. C. × **Olivia** (intermedia × Trianæ ♀), *G.C.* 1897, ii. 315; *O.R.* 1897, 351.—Veitch, 1897.

C. × dubiosa, *Jard.* 1897, 310; *O.R.* 1897, 360.—Maron.

C. × dubia, *J. S. H. Fr.* 1897, 934; 1898, 777.—Maron.

The parentage of C. × dubia was at first doubtful, but afterwards confirmed.

134. C. × Pandora (bicolor ♀ × Trianæ), *G.C.* 1900, ii. 384: *O.R.* 1900, 373; 1903, 335.—Veitch, 1900.

135. C. × Parthenia (× Isabella ♀ × Mossiæ), *J. S. H. Fr.* 1889, 311; 1897, 335; *Lind.* vi. **t.** 276; *Reichenb.* ser. 2, ii. 39, **t.** 67; *O.R.* 1893, 324; *Dict. Ic. O.* Cat. hyb. **t.** 4.—Bleu, 1889.

C. × Prince of Wales, *G.C.* 1891, i. 681, 683.—Sander.

C. × fimbriata, the recorded seed parent, is believed to be a form of the natural hybrid, C. × Isabella.

136. C. × Patrocinii (Leopoldi ♀ × Loddigesii), *O.R.* 1899, 254; *Dict. Ic. O.* Cat. hyb. **t.** 6.—Maron, 1897.

C. × Gaudii, *J. S. H. Fr.* 1897, 934; *Jard.* 1897, 310; *O.R.* 1897, 360; 1899, 254.

C. × Patrocinii first appeared as a natural hybrid in 1890. See *O.R.* 1893, p. 343.

137. C. × Paynteri (velutina × Warneri).—Paynter, 1899.

C. × (unnamed) *G.C.* 1899, ii. 156; *O.R.* 1899, 285.

There seems to be a slight doubt about the C. velutina parent, and we should like to see a flower.

138. C. × Pearl (Gaskelliana × Rex).—Sander, 1903.

C. × The Pearl, *G. World*, 1903, 686; *O.R.* 1903, 267.—Sander.

139. C. × peckaviensis (Aclandiæ × Schilleriana), *Wien Ill. G. Zeit.* 1901, 431, **f.** 52; *O.R.* 1902, 55.—Hruby, 1901.

The original record is C. Aclandiæ × Rex, but it is remarked that there is not the slightest trace of the latter in the flower. It looks most like a glorified C. Aclandiæ, but as C. Schilleriana is suggested as one parent we leave it as above. It, however, requires confirmation.

140. C. × Petersii (× Hardyana × labiata ♀), *G.C.* 1902, ii. 387; 1903, ii. 341; *O.R.* 1903, 364: *Dict. Ic. O.* Cat. hyb. **t.** 27.—Peeters, 1902.

141. C. × Philo (iricolor × Mossiæ ♀), *G.C.* 1892, i. 535; *O.R.* 1893, 357. —Veitch, 1892.

142. C. × Pittiæ (Dowiana × Harrisoniana ♀).—Pitt, 1902.

C. × Mrs. Pitt, *G.C.* 1902, ii. 344; *O.R.* 1902, 363; 1903, 267, 343, 352 *Amer. Flor.* 1903, 566, **f.**

C. × villenoyensis, *Rev. H.* 1903, 491, 511; *Jard.* 1903, 336; *J. S. H. Fr.* 1903, 650.—Ragot.

143. C. × Pittiana (Dowiana × granulosa), *G.C.* 1902, ii. 95; 1903, ii. 189, **f.** 74 (J. Wilson Potter's var.); *O.R.* 1903, 267, 269, 306; *J.H.* 1903, ii, 281, **f.** (J. Wilson Potter's var.); *Dict. Ic. O.* Cat. hyb. **t.** 28.—Pitt, 1902.

144. C. × porphyrophlebia (intermedia ♀ × superba), *G.C.* 1885, ii. 552; *O.R.* 1893, 103: 1900, 253; *Day O. Draw.* xlviii. **t.** 11.—Veitch, 1885.

C. × Alberti, *J. S. H. Fr.* 1890, 279; *Orchidoph.* 1890, 321, **t.**—Perrenoud.

145. C. × Portia (Bowringiana ♀ × labiata), *G.C.* 1897, ii. 352; *O.R.* 1897, 375; 1901, 366; 1902, 35, 44.—Veitch, 1897.

C. × (unnamed), *J. S. H. Fr.* 1897, 954.—Mantin.

C. × labiata-Bowringiana, *J. S. H. Fr.* 1897, 1344.—Mantin.

C. × Bowringiano-labiata, *J. S. H. Fr.* 1898. 1104 ; *Dict. Ic. O.* Cat. hyb. **t.** 15. —Mantin.

C. × Juliæ, *G.C.* 1901, ii. 423 ; *O.R.* 1901, 368.—Stanley, Ashton & Co.

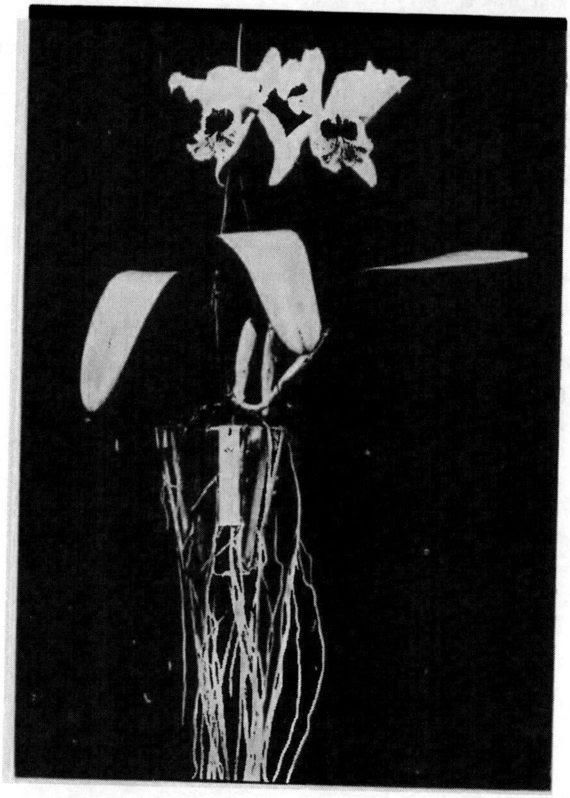

Fig. 10. CATTLEYA × ROTHSCHILDIANA.

146. C. × **Preciosa** (Lawrenceana × Lueddemanniana ♀), *G.C.* 1896, i. 593 ; *O.R.* 1896, 186 ; 1899, 92.—Ingram, 1896.

C. × Triumph, *G.C.* 1896, ii. 471 ; *O.R.* 1896, 347.—Ingram.

C. × Hislopi (Lawrenceana ♀), *G.C.* 1899, i. 77.—Leon.

147. C. × Princess (Lueddemaniana ♀ × Trianæ), *G.C.* 1899, ii. 334 ; *O.R.* 1899, 351.—Veitch, 1899.

148. C. × **quinquecolor** (Aclandiæ × Forbesii), *G.C.* 1865, 606 : *Fl. M.* 1870, **t.** 511 ; *Proc. H.S.* v. 145 (quincolor) ; *O.R.* 1893, 5.—Veitch, 1865.

149. C. × **Rafaeliæ** (Dowiana ♀ × Trianæ).—Leon, 1899.

C. × Maggie Rafael, *G.C.* 1899, ii. 441, 482, **f.** 158; *G.M.* 1899, 796, 797, **f**; *J.H.* 1899, ii. 515, **f.** 91; *O.R.* 1900, 27.

150. C. × **Rembrandt** (elongata × labiata ♀), *J. S. H. Fr.* 1901, 34, 1187; *G.C.* 1903, ii. 340; *O.R.* 1903, 364; *Dict. Ic. O.* Cat. hyb. t. 29.—Maron, 1901.

C × Sylvanus, *Gard.* 1903, ii. 408.—R. H. Measures.

151. C. × **resplendens** (granulosa ♀ × Schilleriana), *O.R.* 1900, 328; 1903, 131; *G.C.* 1902, ii. 387.—Peeters, 1900.

C. × Kerchoveana (Schilleriana ♀), *Chron. O.* i. 308.—Peeters.

C. × Kerchoveana is believed to be identical with the natural hybrid C. × resplendens, Rchb. f. (*G.C.* 1885, i. 692), which, however, is only known from description.

152. C. × **Roehrsiana** (× Hardyana × Mendelii ♀), *G.C.* 1903, i. 419; *O.R.* 1903, 213.—Sander, 1903.

153. C. × **Rooseveltiæ** (Aclandiæ × maxima).—Roebling, 1903.

C. × Mrs. Theodore Roosevelt, *Amer. G.* 1903, 107.

154. C. × **Rothschildiana** (Dowiana × Gaskelliana ♀).—Sander, 1893. [**See Fig. 10.**]

C. × Lord Rothschild, *G.C.* 1893, ii. 536; 1896, ii. 489, **f.** 86; *O.R.* 1893, 373; 1896, 337, **f.** 16: *J.H.* 1893, ii. 417, 425, **f.** 62; *Wien. Ill. G. Zeit.* 1894, 237, 238, **f.** 32.

155. C. × **Rothwelliæ** (Bowringiana × Eldorado), *Amer. G.* 1901, 879; *G.C.* 1902, i. 18; *O.R.* 1902, 35, 43.—Rothwell, 1901.

C. × Portia var. Rothwelliæ, *Amer. G.* 1901, 845, **f.** 174.

156. C. × **rubescens** (dolosa × labiata), *G.C.* 1903, i. 46; *Rev. H. Belge,* 1903, 47.—Peeters, 1903.

157. C. × **Saint-Benoit** (Aclandiæ × Schroederæ ♀), *G.C.* 1898, ii. 293; *O.R.* 1898, 348.—Lawrence, 1898.

158. C. × **Saint-Gilles** (Dowiana × Patrocinii ♀), *G.C.* 1903, ii. 340; *O.R.* 1903, 364; *Dict. Ic. O.* Cat. hyb. **t.** 30.—Peeters, 1902.

C. × Patrocinii × aurea, *G.C.* 1902, ii. 387.

159. C. × **Sedenii** (Lawrenceana ♀ × Percivaliana), *G.C.* 1896, i. 593; *O.R.* 1896, 186; 1898, 158.—Ingram, 1896.

160. C. × **Selfridgei** (Aclandiæ ♀ × superba).—Sander, 1902.

C. × H. G. Selfridge, *G.C.* 1902, i. 442; *O.R.* 1902, 213.

161. C. × **Shakespeare** (granulosa ♀ × Rex), *J. S. H. Fr.* 1901, 842; *G.C.* 1903, ii. 104; *O.R.* 1903, 267.—Dallemagne, 1901.

162. C. × **suavior** (intermedia ♀ × Mendelii), *V. Man. O.* ii. 92; *O.R.* 1893, 196; *Day O. Draw.* xlvi. **t.** 83; *Amer. G.* 1899, 367, **f.** 90 (left-hand figure).—Veitch, 1887.

163. C. × **superforbesii** (Forbesii × superba ♀), *G.C.* 1896, ii. 90: *O.R.* 1896, 265.—Cypher, 1896.

164. C. × **Tankervilleæ** (bicolor × Rex), *O.R.* 1903, 307.—Stanley, Ashton & Co., 1903.

C. × (unnamed), *O.R.* 1903, 268, 287.

C. × Tankerville, *G.C.* 1903, ii. 181.

165. C. × Thayeriana (intermedia ♀ × Schrœderæ), *Amer. Flor.* 1900, 1003; *O.R.* 1900, 147; 1903, 167; 1904, 49, f. 16; *Amer. G.* 1903, 138.—Thayer, 1900. [**See Fig. 11.**]

166. C. × Thorntoni (amethystoglossa × Lueddemanniana ♀), *O.R.* 1898, 359.—Thornton, 1898.

167. C. × Titus (granulosa ♀ × Leopoldi), *J. S. H. Fr.* 1901, 841.—Dallemagne, 1901.

Fig. 11. CATTLEYA × THAYERIANA.

C. Schofieldiana gigantea (*G.C.* 1897, ii. 246, suppl. fig. 75) is mentioned as a natural hybrid between the above two species, but we regard it as simply a fine spotted form of C. granulosa.

168. C. × vestalis (Dowiana × maxima ♀), *G.C.* 1899, ii. 402; *O.R.* 1899, 375; *G.M.* 1900, 555, f.—Veitch, 1899.

C. × Madame Chaumié, *J. S. H. Fr.* 1903, 766; *Jard.* 1903, 384.—Maron.

C. × Madame Malvina, *J. S. H. Fr.* 1901, 1187.—Maron.

169. C. × Viceroy (× Brymeriana × labiata), *O.R.* 1902, 30; *G.C.* 1902, i. 70.—(Sander) Miller, 1901.

170. C. × **Victoria-Regina** (labiata × Leopoldi), *J. S. H. Fr.* 1901, 906.—Dallemagne, 1901.

C. × Crethus, *J. S. H. Fr.* 1901, 906.—Dallemagne, 1901.

C. × Cogniauxii (Leopoldi ♀), *Dict. Ic. O.* Cat. hyb. t. 22.—Peeters.

C. × Victoria-Regina originally appeared among imported C. Leopoldi from Pernambuco, and was at first hopelessly confused with it (see *G.C.* 1892, i. 586, 808, 809, f. 115 (excl. f. 116); *O.R.* 1895, 17, f. 1; *Reichenb.* ser. 2, ii. 89, t. 85). It is believed to be a natural hybrid between C. Leopoldi and C. labiata. C. × Crethus, raised from these two species, is said to differ considerably, consequently it is suggested that C. amethystoglossa may have been one parent of the natural hybrid, but we do not know of its appearance in the same importation. In C. × Cogniauxii the influence of the Leopoldi ("guttata") parent is scarcely apparent, We should like to see flowers of both.

171. C. × **Wavriniana** (granulosa × Warscewiczii ♀), *G.C.* 1900, ii. 181; *J.H.* 1902, ii. 97, f. (Wigan's var.); *O.R.* 1902, 243; *Dict. Ic. O.* Cat. hyb. t. 18.—Peeters, 1900.

C. × Wiganiana, *Gard.* 1902, ii. 71.—Wigan.

172. C. × **weedoniensis** (granulosa × Mendelii ♀), *G.C.* 1899, ii. 268; *O.R.* 1899, 318; 1901, 348.—Thornton, 1899.

173. C. × **Wellsiæ** (× Parthenia ♀ × Warneri).—Sander, 1894.

C. × Mrs. M. Wells, *G.C.* 1894, ii. 194; *O.R.* 1894, 288.

174. C. × **Wendlandiana** (Bowringiana ♀ × Warscewiczii), *O.R.* 1894, 144, 351; 1902, 35, 44; *Dict. Ic. O.* Cat. hyb. t. 12.—Veitch, 1890.

C. × Wendlandii, *G.C.* 1894, ii. 447.

First flowered in October, 1891, as shown by flowers preserved at Kew.

175. C. × **Whitei** (Schilleriana × Warneri ♀), *O.R.* 1899, 292; 1901, 366; *B.M.* t. 7727; *Dict. Ic. O.* Cat. hyb. t. 20.—Mantin, 1897.

C. × Russelliana, *J. S. H. Fr.* 1897, 602, 608; *J. R. H. S.* xxiv. 192.—Mantin.

C. × gloriosa, *G.C.* 1901, i. 418; *O.R.* 1901, 255.—Peeters.

Originally described as a natural hybrid (Rchb. f. in *G.C.* 1882, ii. 586; *O. A.* iii. t. 115), at which time C. labiata and C. Schilleriana were given as the parents.

176. C. × **Whiteleyæ** (Bowringiana ♀ × Hardyana).—Miller, 1899.

C. × Mrs. J. W. Whiteley, *G.C.* 1899, ii. 402; *O.R.* 1899, 374.

C. × John Baguley (× Hardyana ♀), *G.C.* 1900, ii. 313; *O.R.* 1900, 348.—Charlesworth.

177. C. × **Wiganii** (Dowiana × Schilleriana ♀).—Wigan, 1900.

C. × F. W. Wigan, *G.C.* 1900, ii. 97; *O.R.* 1900, 228, 253 ("Sir F. Wigan"), 287; *J.H.* 1900, ii. 121, f. 33; 1904, ii. 109, f. (v. superba); *G.M.* 1900, 610, 611, f.; 1904, 510, f. (v. superba); *Dict. Ic. O.* Cat. hyb. t. 25.

178. C. × **Williamsiæ** (Gaskelliana × Harrisoniana ♀).—Temple, 1894.

C. × Miss Williams, *G.C.* 1894, ii. 603; *O.R.* 1894, 375.

C. × (unnamed), *G.C.* 1902, ii. 387.—Wavrin.

C. × Mary Measures, *Sand. O. Guide*, 333.

Owing to the unfortunate confusion between C. Loddigesii and C. Harrisoniana, it is possible that some of the above may not belong here. The hybrid should be compared with C. × Greavesiæ.

179. C. × Winniana (Forbesii × Gaskelliana ♀), *O.R.* 1902, 326; 1903, 310.—(Winn) Chamberlain, 1902.

180. C. × Zeo (Leopoldi ♀ × Trianæ), *O.R.* 1902, 55.—Charlesworth, 1902.

C. × Zeno, *Sand. O. Guide*, 334.

181. C. × Zephyra (Dowiana × Schrœderæ ♀), *G.C.* 1901, i. 146: *O.R.* 1901, 90.—Ingram, 1901.

10. CHYSIS.

1. C. × Chelsoni (lævis × Limminghei ♀), *G.C.* 1874, i. 385, 535; 1880, i. 717, 722, f. 122; *Fl. M.* 1878, t. 297; *Gartenfl.* 1880, 152, 153, f.; *Orchidoph.* 1882, 478, 479, f.; *V. Man. O.* vi. 27, f.; *O.R.* 1893, 38; *Day O. Draw.* xviii. t. 72; xl. t. 49.—Veitch, 1874.

The first hybrid Chysis. The parentage was originally given as C. Limminghei ♀ × bractescens ♂, but Reichenbach suggested that C. lævis was the second parent, which we believe to be correct, for we fail to trace C. bractescens in the plant, though Messrs. Veitch finally altered the record to C. bractescens × lævis.

2. C. × langleyensis (bractescens ♀ Chelsoni), *G.C.* 1896, i. 593; *O.R.* 1896, 187; 1897, 161.—Veitch, 1896.

C. × Sedeni was originally recorded as the second parent, but the record was afterwards amended by the raisers.

3. C. × Sedeni (bractescens × Limminghei ♀), *G.C.* 1880, i. 616; *V. Man. O.* vi. 27; *O.R.* 1893, 69; *Day O. Draw.* xli. t. 81.—Veitch, 1880.

11. CYMBIDIUM.

1. C. × Bennett-Poei (giganteum × Tracyanum).—Bennett-Pöe, 1903.

C. × Tracyano-giganteum, *G.C.* 1903, ii. 429; *O.R.* 1904, 19.

2. C. × Charlesworthii (Lowianum ♀ × Mastersii).—Charlesworth, 1902.

C. × Lowio-Mastersianum, *G.C.* 1902, i. 116; *O.R.* 1902, 90; *G.M.* 1902, 128, f.

3. C × Lowgrinum (Lowianum ♀ × tigrinum), *G.C.* 1903, i. 206; *O.R.* 1903, 118, 120.—R.I. Measures, 1903.

4. C. × Maroni (grandiflorum ♀ × Mastersii), *Chron. O.* 332; *J.S.H.Fr.* 1900, 766.—Maron, 1900.

5. C. × Sedeni (grandiflorum × Lowianum ♀).—Veitch, 1902.

C. × Lowio-grandiflorum, *G.C.* 1902, i. 116; *O.R.* 1902, 90, 100.

6. C. × Veitchii (eburneum × Lowianum ♀).—Veitch, 1889. [**See Fig. 12.**]

C. × eburneo-Lowianum, *G.C.* 1889, i. 363; 1903, i. 206; *V. Man. O.* ix. 23; *O.R.* 1893, 260; 1903, 118; 1904, 369, f. 50; *J.H.* 1895, i. 157, f. 29 (v. superbum); *Gard.* 1895, ii. 262, t. 1034; 1903, i. 250, 251, f. (v. concolor);

Lind. xiii. t. 578; *Dict. Ic. O.* Cymb. hyb. t. 1, 1a (v. armainvilliense); *G.M.* 1903, 219, 223, f. (v. concolor); *G. World*, 1904, 443, 449, f. (v. concolor).

Fig. 12. CYMBIDIUM × VEITCHII.

C. × armainvilliense, *J. S. H. Fr.* 1894, 78; 1895, 239; *J.d.O.*, v. 9.—Baron E. Rothschild.

C. × Lowio-eburneum, *G.C.* 1896, i. 337; *O.R.* 1896, 122; *G.M.* 1896, 190, f.—Lawrence, 1896.

C. Lowianum × eburneum, *G.C.* 1901, ii. 25, f. 10; *O.R.* 1901, 270.

7. **C. × Wiganianum** (eburneum ♀ × Tracyanum), *G.C.* 1902, i. 151; *O.R.* 1902, 92; *G.M.* 1903, 30.—Sander, 1902.

8. **C. × Winnianum** (giganteum ♀ × Mastersii), *G.C.* 1892, ii. 566; *O.R.* 1893, 22, 356, 361, f. 18; 1904, 313, f. 45; *V. Man. O.* ix. 24; *Reichenb.* ser. 2, ii. 61, t. 75; *G.M.* 1904, 562.—Winn, 1892. [**See Fig. 13.**]

Fig. 13. CYMBIDIUM × WINNIANUM.

C. × Mantinii, *Chron. O.* 150; *Rev. H.* 1898, 144; *O.R.* 1902, 343, 361, f. 37.—Mantin.

C. × Cæsaris Nicolai II, *Chron. O.* 290; *O.R.* 1902, 361.—Mantin.

C. × Holmesii (Mastersii ♀), *G.C.* 1902, ii. 314; *O.R.* 1902, 343, 361.—Holmes.

The parentage was at first recorded as C. eburneum and C. giganteum ♀, which has been shown to be erroneous.

12. CYNORCHIS.

1. **Cynorchis × kewensis** (Lowiana ♀ × purpurata), *O.R.* 1903, 219.—Kew, 1903.

13. DENDROBIUM.

1. D. × **Achilles** (× Ainsworthii × primulinum ♀), *O.R.* 1902, 101; 1903, 92.—Chamberlain, 1902.

2. D. × **Acis** (nobile × Schneiderianum), *O.R.* 1902, 157.—Hardy, 1902.

3. D. × **Adrastus** (Pierardi ♀ × superbum), *G.C.* 1892, i. 503; *O.R.* 1893, 358.—Veitch, 1892.

4. D. × **Æneas** (crystallinum × moniliforme ♀), *G.C.* 1893, i. 336; *O.R.* 1893, 128.—Veitch, 1893.

5. D. × **Ainsworthii** (aureum ♀ × nobile), *G.C.* 1874, i. 443, **f.** 93, 94; *Fl. M.* 1876, **t.** 196; *O.A.* i. **t.** 20 (v. roseum); *V. Man. O.* iii. 86, 87, **f.**; *Lind.* vii. **t.** 97; *Dict. Ic. O.* Dendr. hyb. **t.** 1, 1 A (v. Leechianum), 1 B (v. grandiflorum); *O.R.* 1893, 37; 1895, 103; 1900, 108; 1901, 38; *Gard.* 1897, i. 338, **f.**; *G.M.* 1901, 148, **f.** (v. splendidissimum); *Day O. Draw.* xxiii. **t.** 43; xxviii. **t.** 31, 67.—Ainsworth, 1874.

D. × Leechianum (nobile ♀), *G.C.* 1882, i. 256, **f.** 35; *V. Man. O.* iii. 89; *O.R.* 1893, 100; *J.H.* 1896, i. 229, **f.** 35; 1900, i. 323, 325, **f.** 89; 1902, ii. 215, **f.**; *Reichenb.* ser. 1, ii. 3, **t.** 50; *Rev. H.* 1904, 280, **t.**; *Day. O. Draw.* xlviii. **t.** 47.—Leech.

D. nobile aureum v. Leechianum, *Gard.* 1883, i. 6, **t.** 395.

D. × Sanderæ, *G.C.* 1893, i. 206; *O.R.* 1893, 96.—Sander.

D. × heterocarpo-nobile, *Bohnh. Dict. O. Hyb.* 37.—Lawrence.

D. × recurvum, *Gard.* 1896, i. 50.—Ingram.

D. × Robinsonianum, *Bohnh. Dict. O. Hyb.* 38.

D. × splendidissimum, *G.C.* 1879, i. 298; *V. Man. O.* iii. 91, **f.**; *J. S. H. Fr.* 1892, 435, 438, **f.** 8; *O.R.* 1893, 69; *Gard.* 1904, i. 140, **f.** (v. grandiflorum).—Veitch.

D. × Armstrongi, *O.R.* 1894, 93.—Armstrong.

D. × Edithæ, *O.R.* 1894, 126.—Lee.

D. × hetero-Cypheri, *O.R.* 1901, 55, 68.—Holmes.

D. × Germinyanum, *Sand. O. Guide*, 275.

6. D. × **Andromeda** (× Ainsworthii ♀ × Cassiope), *G.C.* 1896, i. 210; *O.R.* 1896, 94.—Chamberlain, 1896.

7. D. × **Ariel** (aureum × Rubens).—Chamberlain, 1903.

D. × (unnamed) *O.R.* 1903, 92.

8. D. × **Aspasia** (aureum ♀ × Wardianum), *G.C.* 1890, i. 336; 1892, i. 214; *O.R.* 1893, 137, **f.** 9.—Veitch, 1889. **[See Fig. 14.]**

D. × Wardiano-aureum, *G.C.* 1889, i. 490; *O.R.* 1893, 262.—Veitch.

D. × Ellerianum, *Gard.* 1896, i. 202, 280.—Hardy.

9. D. × **Astræa** (crassinode × luteolum ♀), *O.R.* 1895, 167; *G.C.* 1896, i. 391, 402.—Cookson, 1895.

10. D. × **Backhousei** (nobile ♀ × thyrsiflorum), *O.R.* 1897, 110; 1898, 121; 1904, 167.—(Backhouse) G. F. Moore, 1897.

D. × (unnamed), *O.R.* 1897, 76.

Although the parentage was very definitely recorded it requires confirmation.

for the hybrid resembles D. × Wiganiæ so closely as to have raised a suspicion that it is of similar origin.

11. D. × Benita (aureum ♀ × Falconeri), *G.C.* 1893, i. 355; *O.R.* 1893, 116.—Brymer, 1893.

Fig. 14. DENDROBIUM × ASPASIA.

12. D. × Berkeleyi (× Cassiope ♀ × Wardianum), *O.R.* 1899, 136.—Berkeley, 1899.

13. D. × Bryan (luteolum ♀ × Wardianum). *G.C.* 1893, i. 395; 1896, i. 391; *O.R.* 1893, 157.—Cookson, 1893.

14. D. × Burberryanum (× Dominyanum × Findlayanum ♀), *O.R.* 1897,

80, 93; 1901, 170; *G.C.* 1897, i. 115; *J.H.* 1900, i. 239, f. 64.—Chamberlain, 1897.

15. D. × Cassiope (moniliforme ♀ × nobile), *G.C.* 1890, ii. 620; *Orchidoph.* 1893, 105, 106, f.; *O.R.* 1893, 293; 1895, 126, 131; *Reichenb.* ser. 2, 5, t. 50, f. 2; *Dict. Ic. O.* Dendr. hyb. t. 2.—Cookson, 1890.

16. D. × cheltenhamense (aureum ♀ × luteolum), *Gard.* 1893, i. 347, 389; *O.R.* 1893, 125, 212.—Cypher, 1893.

17. D. × chlorostele (Linawianum ♀ × Wardianum), *G.C.* 1887, i. 477; *V. Man. O.* iii. 87; *O.R.* 1893, 16, 86, 197; 1903, 113, f. 25 (v. Owenianum);

Fig. 15. DENDROBIUM × ELLISII VAR. WIGANIANANUM.
Fig. 16. D. × SIBYL. Fig. 17. D. × WIGANIÆ.
Fig. 18. D. × CHLOROSTELE VAR. OWENIANUM. Fig. 19. D. × MELANODISCUS VAR. PALLENS.

G.M. 1901, 148, f. (v. Juno); *Dict. Ic. O.* Dendr. hyb. t. 4 (v. Juno).—Lawrence 1887. **[See Fig. 18.]**

D. × Juno, *G.C.* 1890, i. 87; *O.R.* 1893, 294; *G.C.* 1899, i. 114, f. 44.—Lawrence.

D. × Owenianum, *G.C.* 1893, i. 206; *O.R.* 1893, 95.—Cookson.

D. × xanthocentron, *G.C.* 1890, i. 87; *O.R.* 1893, 293.—Lawrence.

D. × Aurorea, *Sand. O. Guide*, 274.

18. D. × clarense (Findlayanum ♀ × signatum), *O.R.* 1903, 135.—Wigan 1903.

19. D. × Cordelia (aureum ♀ × euosmum), *O.R.* 1894, 172.—Veitch, 1894.

20. **D.** × **Corningianum** (lituiflorum × nobile ♀), *Hans. O. Hyb.* 196.—Corning, 1876.

According to Hansen, the reverse cross was afterwards raised by Messrs. Heath and Son.

21. **D.** × **Curtisii** (aureum × Cassiope ♀), *G.C.* 1896, i. 210; *O.R.* 1896, 96; 1906, 73, f. 9.—Sander, 1896. **[See Fig. 20.]**

Fig. 20. DENDROBIUM × CURTISII.

22. **D.** × **Cybele** (Findlayanum ♀ × nobile), *G.C.* 1887, ii. 778; 1899, i. 258. 259, f. 96 (Oakwood var.); 1903, i. 46; *V. Man. O.* iii. 87; *O.R.* 1893, 196; 1901, 170.—Veitch, 1887.

D. × Wrightæ, *Gard.* 1903, Jan. 17, Suppl. 7.—Wright.

D. × Aurora, *Sand. O. Guide*, 337.

23. **D.** × **Cypheri** (crassinode × Findlayanum ♀), *O.R.* 1902, 100.—Cypher, 1902.

24. D. × Dominyanum (Linawianum × nobile ♀), *G.C.* 1878, i. 202; *V. Man. O.* iii. 88; *O.R.* 1893, 36; *Day O. Draw.* xxxii. t. 45.—Veitch, 1864.

D. × (unnamed), *Proc. R. H. S.* iv. (1864), 73.

D. × Dormanianum, *Sand. O. Guide*, 275.

The earliest record, in 1864, states:—"Dendrobium moniliforme (seedling), a very interesting Orchid, as being a seedling raised at the Exeter Nursery, but with the appearance of an inferior D. nobile."

Fig. 21. DENDROBIUM × GEM. VAR. ARTEMIS

25. D. × Doris (× Ainsworthii ♀ × moniliforme), *O.R.* 1894, 142.—Cookson, 1894.

26. D. × dulce (aureum ♀ × Linawianum), *G.C.* 1892, i. 214; 1896, i. 402; *O R.* 1893, 358; *G.M.* 1901, 148, f.—Veitch, 1892.

D. × burfordiense, *G.C.* 1892, ii. 744; *O.R.* 1893, 29, 85.—Lawrence.

27. D. × Ellisii (Hildebrandii × nobile ♀), *O.R.* 1901, 37, 82, 87; 1903, 93, 113, f. 22 (v. Wiganianum).—Ellis, 1901. [See **Fig. 17** (p. 75)]

D. × Wiganianum (Hildebrandii ♀), *G.C.* 1901, i. 102, 114; 1903, i. 142; *O.R.* 1901, 87; 1903, 84; *G.M.* 1901, 167, f.—Wigan.

28 D. × Elwesii (aureum × Hildebrandii), *O.R.* 1900, 147.—Elwes, 1900.

29. D. × **endocharis** (aureum × moniliforme ♀), *G.C.* 1876, i. 298; *V. Man. O.* iii. 88, f.; *J. S. H. Fr.* 1892, 435, 436, f. 7; *O.R.* 1893, 39; *Day O. Draw.* xix. t. 76.—Veitch, 1876.

30. D. × **euosmum** (× endocharis ♀ × nobile), *G.C.* 1885, i. 174; *V. Man. O.* iii. 89; *O.R.* 1893, 102; 1894, 112; *Day O. Draw.* xliii. t. 89; xlviii. t. 39 (v. leucopterum).—Veitch, 1885.

D. × Snowflake, *O.R.* 1902, 125.—Statter.

31. D. × **Florence** (Bensonæ × nobile), *G.C.* 1903, i. 174; *O.R.* 1903, 116.—Douglas, 1903.

32. D. × **Galatea** (moniliforme ♀ × Pitcherianum), *G.C.* 1900, i. 62; *O.R.* 1900, 60.—Thwaites, 1900.

D. × Ethel, *G.C.* 1902, i. 314; *O.R.* 1900, 71; 1902, 179.—Berkeley, 1900.

33. D. × **Gem** (aureum ♀ × Ainsworthii),—Winn, 1894. [**See Fig. 21.**]

D. × The Gem, *Bohnh. Dict. O. Hyb.* 39; *Sand. O. Guide*, 275.—Winn.

D. × (unnamed), *G.C.* 1897, i. 115; *O.R.* 1897, 93.—Chamberlain, 1897.

D. × Artemis, *O.R.* 1906, 72, f. 8.—Colman.

34. D. × **Gemma** (aureum ♀ × superbum), *O.R.* 1895, 73.—Winn, 1895.

35. D. × **harefieldiense** (Findlayanum × Wardianum) —E. Ashworth, 1896.

D. × Findlayano-Wardianum, *G.C.* 1896, i. 337; *O.R.* 1896, 122.

36. D. × **Harold** (Findlayanum ♀ × Linawianum), *O.R.* 1896, 108.—Cookson, 1896.

37. D. × **Haywoodiæ** (Hildebrandii × Wardianum).—Haywood, 1902.

D. × Wardiano-Hildebrandii, *G.C.* 1902, i. 219; *O.R.* 1902, 117.

38. D. × **Holbrookii** (× Cassiope × Dominyanum), *O.R.* 1902, 56.—E. Ashworth, 1899.

D. × Domicassio, *G.C.* 1899, i. 108.

D. × (unnamed), *O.R.* 1899, 94.

39. D. × **Holmesianum** (× Dominyanum × Schneiderianum), *G.C.* 1896. i. 401.—Hardy, 1896.

40. D. × **Hunteri** (Brymerianum ♀ × nobile), *O.R.* 1902, 153.—Hunter, 1902.

Remarkable as the solitary hybrid from D. Brymerianum, yet the flowers have very largely the shape and colour of D. nobile, which is said to have been the pollen parent.

41. D. × **illustre** (chrysotoxum ♀ × pulchellum), *G.C.* 1895, i. 800; ii. 15, f. 4; *J.H.* 1895, i. 561, 566, f. 99; *G.M.* 1895, 385, f.; *O.R.* 1895, 243.—Veitch, 1895.

42. D. × **Imogen** (× euosmum ♀ × signatum), *G.C.* 1899, i. 255, *O.R.* 1899, 159.—Veitch, 1899.

43. D. × **Isis** (hercoglossum × moniliforme ♀), *O.R.* 1901, 16; 1903, 84; *G.C.* 1903, i. 142.—Berkeley, 1901.

44. D. × **Kenneth** (Bensonæ × Maccarthiæ ♀), *G.C.* 1896, i. 337; 1897, i. 134, 135, f. 37; *O.R.* 1896, 108; *Haus. O. Hyb.* 318.—Cookson, 1896.

D. Bensonæ was at first accidentally recorded as the pollen parent, but afterwards corrected. Mr. Cookson states that he has never been able to get a seed capsule on D. Bensonæ.

45. **D. × Lawrencei** (formosum ♀ × Lowii).—Lawrence, 1898.

D. × formoso-Lowii, *G.C.* 1898, ii. 391; *O.R.* 1898, 374.

46. **D. × Lotus** (nobile × suavissimum), *G.C.* 1901, i. 279.—Cookson, 1901.

47. **D. × Lutwycheanum** (× Ainsworthii × Wardianum), *O.R.* 1894, 202; 1901, 170 (v. Clio).—Lutwyche, 1894.

D. × Clio, *G.C.* 1896, i. 337; *O.R.* 1896, 122; *J.H.* 1896, i. 366, 367, f. 62 (Tyntesfield v.); *Gard.* 1900, i. 268, f. (v. superbum).—Lawrence.

48. **D. × Magda** (× melanodiscus × nobile ♀), *G.C.* 1902, i. 183; *O.R.* 1902, 114.—Rehder, 1902.

49. **D. × Mantinii** (nobile × fimbriatum) *Jard.* 1901, 7; *O.R.* 1901, 93.—Mantin, 1900.

This is said to be the first hybrid Dendrobium raised in France.

50. **D. × melanodiscus** (× Ainsworthii × Findlayanum ♀), *G.C.* 1887, i. 414; 1904, i. 219, f. 92 (v. gloriosum); *O.R.* 1893, 16, 197; 1899, 100; 1901, 170; 1903, 113, f. 26 (v. pallens), *Reichenb.* ser. 2, i. 27, t. 12; *J. H.* 1905, i. 25, f.; 1905, i. 25, f. (v. pallens).—Lawrence, 1877. [**See Fig. 19** (p. 75)]

D. × chrysodiscus, *G.C.* 1887, i. 414; *V. Man. O.* iii. 87; *O.R.* 1893, 16, 196.—Lawrence.

D. × Luna, *G.C.* 1890, i. 87; *O.R.* 1893, 294; *Amer. G.C.* 1905, 83, f.—Lawrence.

D. × Hebe, *G.C.* 1894, i. 84; *O.R.* 1894, 61.—Lawrence.

D. × Dido, *G.C.* 1894, i. 84; *O.R.* 1894, 61.—Lawrence.

D. × pallens, *G.C.* 1896, i. 210; *O.R.* 1896, 94; *J.H.* 1900, i. 239, 241, f. 65.—Lawrence.

D. × Rainbow, *Bohnh. Dict. O. Hyb.* 38; *O.R.* 1898, 92.—Lawrence.

D. × Clytie, *O.R.* 1899, 100.—Chamberlain.

D. × hessleense, *G.C.* 1899, i. 174; *O.R.* 1899, 126.—Burkinshaw.

D. × The Pearl, *Bohnh. Dict. O. Hyb.* 39; *O.R.* 1899, 100.—Lawrence.

D. × Salteri, *G.C.* 1903, i. 142; *O.R.* 1903, 84.—Haywood.

51. **D. × Melpomene** (× Ainsworthii × signatum), *G.C.* 1900, i. 207; *O.R.* 1900, 125; *J.H.* 1900, i. 281, f. 76; *G.M.* 1900, 206, f.; *Gard.* 1900, i. 28, f.—Lawrence, 1900.

52. **D. × Mentor** (primulinum ♀ × superbum), *G.C.* 1893, i. 580; *O.R.* 1893, 189.—Veitch, 1893.

53. **D. × micans** (lituiflorum × Wardianum ♀), *G.C.*, 1879, i. 332; *V. Man. O.* iii. 89; *O.R.* 1893, 69; *G.M.* 1899, 429, f.—Veitch, 1879.

D. × Euryclea (lituiflorum ♀), *G.C.* 1892, i. 503; *O.R.* 1893, 358.—Veitch.

D. × Alcippe (lituiflorum ♀), *G.C.* 1893, i. 396; *O.R.* 1893, 159; 1894, 173.—Veitch.

54. **D. × Minos** (× Cassiope × Findlayanum), *O.R.* 1901, 116.—Statter, 1901.

55. **D. Murrayi** (albosanguineum × nobile ♀), *O.R.* 1895, 166; *G.C.* 1896, i. 391, 401.—Cookson, 1895.

56. **D.** × **murrhiniacum** (nobile × Wardianum ♀), *G.C.* 1888, i. 554; *O.R.* 1893, 227.—R. H. Measures, 1888.

D. × Euterpe (nobile ♀), *G.C.* 1896, i. 431; 1899, i. 208; *O.R.* 1899, 131, 155.—Lawrence.

D. × nobile-Wardianum, *Sand. O. Guide*, 275.

D. × Wardiano-nobile, *Sand. O. Guide*, 276.

57. **D.** × **Nestor** (Parishii ♀ × superbum), *G.C.* 1892, i. 718; *O.R.* 1893, 358; 1894, 273, **f.** 28; 1901, 145, **f.** 24.—Winn, 1892. **[See Fig. 22.]**

Fig. 22. DENDROBIUM × NESTOR.

58. **D.** × **Niobe** (nobile × tortile ♀), *G.C.* 1893, i. 456; *O.R.* 1893, 146; 1901, 170.—Veitch, 1893.

59. **D.** × **Ophir** (aureum ♀ × signatum), *O.R.* 1902, 100; 1903, 84; *G.C.* 1903, i. 142.—Veitch, 1902.

60. **D.** × **Pitcherianum** (nobile × primulinum), *O.R.* 1901, 73, 74; **f.** 9 (v. Rolfeæ); **f.** 10.

D. × Rolfeæ (primulinum ♀), *G.C.* 1892, i. 522; *O.R.* 1893, 357; 1894, 113, 114, **f.** 9 type), 10 (v. roseum); 1896, 74 (v. candidulum).

Originally described by Reichenbach, in 1888, as a natural hybrid (*G.C.* 1888, i. p. 392), from a plant imported by Messrs. Sander.

61. D. × **porphyrogastrum** (Huttoni ♀ × pulchellum), *G.C.* 1888, i. 660; 1895, ii. 48; *V. Man. O.* iii. 90; *O.R.* 1895, 255.—Veitch, 1888.

The second *G.C.* record that D. superbum var. Huttoni was one parent is erroneous.

62. D. × **rhodostoma** (Huttoni ♀ × sanguinolentum), *G.C.* 1876, i. 795; 1885, i. 472, f. 84, C. (fruit); *V. Man. O.* iii. 90; *O.R.* 1893, 39; *Day O. Draw.* xxxv. t. 71.—Veitch, 1876.

63. D. × **Roeblingianum** (nobile × Ruckeri ♀), *O.R.* 1893, 211.—Pitcher and Manda, 1893.

64. D. × **Rubens** (Ainsworthii ♀ × nobile), *G.C.* 1893, i. 226; *O.R.* 1893, 148; 1895, 102 (v. grandiflorum).—Cypher, 1893.

D. × Euryalus, *G.C.* 1893, i. 336: *G.M.* 1901, 148, f.; *O.R.* 1893, 128; 1894, 142; *J. H.* 1894, i. 315, 322, f. 52.—Veitch.

D. × dellense, *G.C.* 1894, i. 602; *O.R.* 1894, 185; *J.H.* 1894, i. 379, 386, f. 61; *G.M.* 1894, 328, 329, t.—Schröder.

D. × Apollo (nobile ♀), *G.C.* 1895, i. 337; *O.R.* 1895, 102, 127; *J.H.* 1895, i. 245, f. 43 (v. grandiflorum), 1902, i. 201, f.; *G.M.* 1895, 188, 189, **suppl.** f. (v. grandiflorum).—Cypher.

D. × Thalia, *G.C.* 1896, i. 337; *O.R.* 1896, 122.—Lawrence.

D. × whitefieldense, *O.R.* 1899, 90.—Statter.

D. × Virgil, *G.C.* 1900, i. 143; *O.R.* 1900, 91; *G.M.* 1900, 235, f.—Haywood.

D. × splendidissimum illustre, *G.C.* 1895, i. 402.—Lee.

D. × splendidissimum nobilius, *G.C.* 1897, i. 177.—Veitch.

D. × Socius, *Sand. O. Guide*, 275.

D. × Desdemona, *Sand. O. Guide*, 337.

D. × Dorothy, *Sand. O. Guide*, 337.

D. × Flora, *Sand. O. Guide*, 338.

D. × Hector, *Sand. O. Guide*, 338.

D. × Joan, *Sand. O. Guide*, 338.

D. × Othello, *Sand. O. Guide*, 338.

D. × Souvenir de Queen Victoria, *Sand. O. Guide*, 338.

D. × Sylvia, *Sand. O. Guide*, 338.

65. D. × **Schneiderianum** (aureum × Findlayanum ♀), *G.C.* 1887, i. 209; 1897, i. 182; *V. Man. O.* iii. 90; *O.R.* 1893, 133; 1900, 169, f. 26 (with its parents); 1901, 137, f. 23.—Schneider, 1887. **[See Fig. 23.]**

66. D. × **Scylla** (× Cybele × moniliforme), *Gard.* 1903, i. 119; *O.R.* 1903, 366.—Veitch, 1903.

67. D. × **Sedeni** (crepidatum × nobile ♀).—Veitch, 1899.

D. × crepidato-nobile, *G.C.* 1899, i. 286; *O.R.* 1899, 189.

68. D. × **Sibyl** (bigibbum × Linawianum ♀), *G.C.* 1903, i. 395; 1896, i. 391; *O.R.* 1893, 157; 1894, 126; 1903, 113, f. 23; *G. World*, 1904, 319, f.—Cookson, 1893.

69. D. × **Spyersii** (Kingianum × speciosum ♀).—Lawrence, 1892.

D. speciosum × Kingianum, *G.C.* 1892, i. 409.

D. × specio-Kingianum, *Gard.* 1896, i. 201; *G.C.* 1896, i. 337.

D. × (unnamed), *O.R.* 1893, 16.

D. × Kingianum-speciosum, *Haus. O. Hyb.* 198.

D. × Kingiano-speciosum, *O.R.* 1896, 107.

70. D. × Staffordi (Bensonæ × Cassiope ♀), *O.R.* 1900, 147; 1901, 170.—Hardy, 1898.

D. × (unnamed), *O.R.* 1898, 131.

71. D. × Stratius (moniliforme ♀ × pulchellum), *G.C.* 1896, i. 593; *O.R.* 1896, 187.—Veitch, 1892.

D. × striatum, *G.C.* 1892, ii. 566; *O.R.* 1893, 358.

Originally flowered in February, 1892, as shown by flowers preserved at Kew. The first recorded name, D. × striatum, is said to have arisen through miscopying.

Fig. 23. DENDROBIUM × SCHNEIDERIANUM (with its parents).

72. D. × Thompsonianum (× cheltenhamense × nobile ♀), *O.R.* 1899 120, 136.—Thompson, 1899.

73. D. × Thwaitesiæ (× Ainsworthii ♀ × Wiganiæ), *G.C.* 1903, i. 174 1904, i. 274, f. 118 (Veitch's var.): *O.R.* 1903, 115, 120; *Gard.* 1903, i. 203, f.; *G.M.* 1904, 273, f.; *J. H.* 1904, i. 401, f. (Veitch's var.).—Thwaites, 1903.

D. × Pirene (× Wiganiæ ♀), *G.C.* 1903, i. 174; *O.R.* 1903, 115, 120.—Veitch.

74. D. × Vannerianum (Falconeri × moniliforme ♀), *G.C.* 1887, i. 72; *V. Man. O.* iii. 92; *O.R.* 1893, 133; 1895, 168.—Vanner, 1887.

75. D. × Veitchii (moniliforme ♀ × Wardianum).—Veitch, 1889.

D. × Wardiano-japonicum, *G.C.* 1890, i. 207; 1891, i. 38.

D. × Wardiano-moniliforme, *Haus. O. Hyb.* 201.

This hybrid first flowered a year before it was recorded, as shown by flowers preserved at Kew.

76. D. × Venus (Falconeri ♀ × nobile), *G.C.* 1890, i. 608; 1900, ii. 94, 95, f. 24; *Reichenb.* ser. 2, ii. 5, t. 50, f. 1; *O.R.* 1893, 293; *J.H.* 1899, i. 233, f. 58;

Sem. Hort. 1900, 233, 235, f. 79; *Dict. Ic. O.* Dendr. hyb. t. 3.—Cookson, 1890.

77. D. × **Virginia** (Bensonæ × moniliforme ♀), *G.C.* 1894, i. 343; *O.R.* 1894, 127, 171.—Veitch, 1894.

78. D. × **Vulcan** (× chlorostele ♀ × Wardianum), *O.R.* 1900, 71.—Chamberlain, 1900.

79. D. × **Waltoni** (crassinode × Wardianum ♀), *O.R.* 1900, 177, f. 29 (with its parents); 1901, 208.—Veitch, 1892. [**See Fig. 24.**]

Fig. 24. DENDROBIUM × WALTONI (with its parents).

D. × crassinode-Wardianum, *G.C.* 1892, i. 502.

Originally described as a natural hybrid in 1885 (*Gard.* 1885, i. 119), from a plant which flowered in the collection of Alfred Borwick, Esq., Higham Hill, Walthamstow (gr. Mr. Walton), but it is said to have appeared in the first importation of D. Wardianum Lowii received by Messrs. Hugh Low and Co. in 1885.

80. D. × **Whitei** (nobile × pulchellum ♀).—R. B. White, 1900.

D. × Dalhou-nobile, *G.C.* 1900, i. 371; *O.R.* 1900, 210; *J.H.* 1900, i. 523, f. 141; *G.M.* 1900, 364, f.

D. × Dalhousie-nobile, *G.C.* 1900, i. 379, f. 125.

81. D. × **Wiganiæ** (nobile ♀ × signatum), *O.R.* 1896, 107, 123, 160; 1903, 113, f. 24; *G.C.* 1896, i. 337, 553, f. 84; *J.H.* 1903, i. 245, f. (v. xanthochilum); *G. World*, 1903, 161, f. (v. xanthochilum).—Wigan, 1896. [**See Fig. 17** (p. 75).]

Also raised by Messrs. Veitch and Sir Trevor Lawrence, and flowered at about the same period.

82. D. × **Wilsoni** (nobile ♀ × chlorostele), *O.R.* 1901, 196.—Wilson, 1901.

14. DISA.

1. D. × **Diores** (grandiflora × Veitchii ♀), *O.R.* 1894, 238: 1898, 243.—Veitch, 1894.

Fig. 25. Disa × Premier. Fig. 26. D. × kewensis.
Fig. 27. D. × langleyensis. Fig. 28. D. × Veitchii.
(the upper centre and lower right-hand figures are D. grandiflora and D. tripetaloides, two of the parents).

D. × Clio (grandiflora ♀), *G.C.* 1898, ii. 168; *O.R.* 1898, 287; *J.H.* 1898, ii. 163, f. 29; *Gard.*, 1903, ii. 99, f.—Veitch.

2. **Disa** × **Elwesii** (× kewensis × Veitchii), *O.R.* 1903, 219. – Elwes, 1903. There is a slight doubt about the parentage of this hybrid.

3. D. × **kewensis** (grandiflora ♀ × tripetaloides), *G.C.* 1893, i. 625; 1895, ii. 273, f. 31; *O.R.* 1893, 193, 212; 1898, 241, 242, f. 10; *Gartenfl.* 1903, 57, t. 1510.—Kew, 1893. [**See Fig. 26.**]

4. D. × **langleyensis** (racemosa ♀ × tripetaloides), *G.C.* 1894, i. 602; ii. 35, f. 5; *O.R.* 1894, 186, 202, 203; 1898, 241, 242, f. 11; *Gartenfl.* 1902, 113, t. 1496, f. 1, 2.—Veitch, 1894. [**See Fig. 27.**]

Messrs. Veitch also made the reverse cross, and both were also made at Kew, and all flowered at about the same time.

5. D. × **Luna** (racemosa ♀ × Veitchii); *G.C.* 1902, i. 314; *O.R.* 1902, 179; *J.H.* 1902, i. 485, f.—Veitch, 1902.

6. D. × **Premier** (tripetaloides ♀ × Veitchii), *G.C.* 1893, ii. 470; *O.R.* 1893, 339, 351; 1898, 241, 242, f. 8; *G.M.* 1893, 658, f.—Kew, 1893. [**See Fig. 25.**]

7. D. × **Veitchii** (grandiflora × racemosa ♀), *G.C.* 1891, i. 741; 1894, ii. 93, f. 14; *O.R.* 1893, 194, 323; 1898, 241, 242, f. 12; *J.H.* 1901, ii. 145, f.; *Gartenfl.* 1902, 113, t. 1496, f. 3, 4; *Dict. Ic. O.* Disa hyb. t. 1.—Veitch, 1891. [**See Fig. 28.**]

8. D. × **Watsoni** (grandiflora × kewensis ♀), *O.R.* 1900, 247.—Kew, 1900.

D. × kewensis superba, *G.C.* 1900, ii. 54; *O.R.* 1900, 247.

15. DOSSINIMARIA.

A genus established to contain the following hybrid between Dossinia and Hæmaria.

1. **Dossinimaria** × **Dominyi** (Dossinia marmorata × Hæmaria discolor), *J. L. Soc.* xxiv. 170.—Veitch, 1861.

Anœctochilus × Dominii, *G.C.* 1861, 531; *O.R.* 1893, 5.

16. EPICATTLEYA.

A genus established to contain the hybrids between Cattleya and Epidendrum.

1. **Epicattleya** × **Lilianæ** (C. Gaskelliana ♀ × E. costaricense), *J. S. H. Fr.* 1903, 766; *Jard.* 1903, 384.—Maron, 1903.

2. E.-c. × **matutina** (C. Bowringiana ♀ × E. radicans), *G.C.* 1897, i. 210, 232, 233, f. 77; *O.R.* 1897, 110, 127.—Veitch, 1897.

3. E.-c. × **Nebo** (C. × Claesiana × E. × O'Brienianum ♀), *Amer. G.* 1902, 483.—Thayer, 1902.

4. E.-c. × **O'Brieniæ** (C. Bowringiana ♀ × E. × O'Brienianum).—Veitch, 1899.

E.-c. × Mrs. James O'Brien *G.C.* 1899, i. 31, 37, f. 11; *O.R.* 1899, 63.

5. E.-c. × **Orpeti** (C. amethystoglossa ♀ × E. × O'Brienianum), *O.R.* 1901, 114, 288. Thayer, 1901.

E.-c. × Orpetiana, *Amer. G.* 1901, 251, 272.

6. E.-c. × **Sedeni** (C. Bowringiana ♀ × E. radiatum).—Veitch, 1898.

E.-c. × radiato-Bowringiana, *G.C.* 1898, i. 385, 391, f. 146; *O.R.* 1898, 198, 220; *G.M.* 1898, 385, f.

17. EPIDENDRUM.

1. **E.** × **Acis** (cinnabarinum × O'Brienianum ♀).—Thayer, 1901.

E. × (unnamed), *O.R.* 1901, 103.

2. **E.** × **Berkeleyi** (× O'Brienianum × Stamfordianum ♀), *O.R.* 1899, 10.—Berkeley, 1898.

3. **E.** × **Boundii** (× Burtoni × radicans ♀), *O.R.* 1903, 175.—Colman, 1903.

4. **E.** × **Burtoni** (ibaguense ♀ × O'Brienianum), *O.R.* 1899, 73, 94, 135; 1903, 134.—Burton, 1899.

The reverse cross was made at the same time, but was rather later in flowering.

5. **E.** × **Cassiope** (radicans × vitellinum ♀).—Veitch, 1897.

E × radico-vitellinum, *G.C.* 1897, ii. 16; *O.R.* 1897, 301, 314; 1898, 225.

6. **E.** × **Charlesworthii** (Frederici-Gulielmi ♀ × radicans).—Charlesworth, 1899.

E. × (unnamed), *O.R.* 1899, 333.

7. **E.** × **Clarissa** (× elegantulum × Wallisii ♀), *G.C.* 1900, i. 239; *O.R.* 1900, 155; 1901, 154 (v. superbum); *J.H.* 1901, i. 341, **f.** (v. superbum).—Veitch, 1900.

E. Wallisii has been used as a parent three times over in the production of this hybrid, its composition being seven-eighths E. Wallisii and one-eighth E. Endresii.

8. **E.** × **Cuco** (cochleatum × cucullatum), *Amer. G.* 1902, 670, **f.** 138.—Mead, 1902.

9. **E.** × **dellense** (radicans × xanthinum ♀), *G.C.* 1891, i. 502; *O.R.* 1893, 44, 324; 1896, 189.—Schröder, 1891.

E. × xantho-radicans, *G.C.* 1897, i. 210; *O.R.* 1897, 126.—Lawrence.

10. **E.** × **Delphi** (× O'Brienianum × pristes), *G.C.* 1903, i. 142; *O.R.* 1903, 85.—Veitch, 1903.

11. **E.** × **elegantulum** (× Veitchii × Wallisii ♀), *G.C.* 1896, i. 337, 361, **f.** 49; *O.R.* 1896, 108, 124; *J.H.* 1896, i. 251, **f.** 46; 1899, i. 381, **f.** 85 (v. luteum); *G.M.* 1899, 276, 277, **f.** (v. luteum); *Dict. Ic. O.* Epidend. hyb. **t.** 1, 1 a (v. leucochilum).—Veitch, 1896.

12. **E.** × **Galatea** (cinnabarinum × radicans).—Thayer, 1901.

E. × (unnamed), *Amer. G.* 1901, 331, **f.** 7, n. 2; *O.R.* 1901, 179.

13. **E.** × **heatonense** (Cooperianum ♀ × O'Brienianum).—Charlesworth, 1899.

E. × (unnamed), *O.R.* 1899, 333.

E. × Tennyson, *Sand. O. Guide*, 338.

14. **E.** × **kewense** (evectum ♀ × xanthinum), *O.R.* 1903, 6.—Kew, 1902.

The reverse cross was also made, and the seedlings flowered a few months later than the original.

15. **E.** × **langleyense** (pseudepidendrum × Wallisii ♀), *G.C.* 1899, i. 402; *O.R.* 1899, 223.—Veitch, 1899.

16. E. × **O'Brienianum** (evectum ♀ × radicans), *G.C.* 1888, i. 770, 771, f. 103 (and parents); *V. Man. O.* vi. 128, 129, f. (and parents); *O.R.* 1893, 227; *Dict. Ic. O.* Epidend. hyb. t. 2.—Veitch, 1888.

17. E. × **Olenus** (radicans × Stamfordianum ♀).—Veitch, 1898.

E. × radicanti-Stamfordianum, *O.R.* 1898, 198, 220, 287; *G.C.* 1898, ii. 168.

18. E. × **Orpeti** (elongatum × O'Brienianum ♀).—Thayer, 1901.

E. × (unnamed), *Amer. G.* 1901, 331, f. 71, n. 1 and 4; *O.R.* 1901, 179.

19. E. × **Phœbus** (O'Brienianum × vitellinum ♀), *O.R.* 1898, 169.—Veitch, 1898.

20. E. × **Sedeni** (ciliare ♀ × Wallisii).—Veitch, 1894.

E. × Wallisio-ciliare, *G.C.* 1894, ii. 730; *O.R.* 1895, 14, 32; *J.H.* 1900, i. 89, f. 20 (v. superbum); *Gard.* 1900, i. 422. f.

21. E. × **Thayeri** (× O'Brienianum ♀ × radicans).—Thayer, 1901.

E. × (unnamed), *O.R.* 1901, 103.

22. E. × **Veitchii** (Endresii × Wallisii ♀).—Veitch, 1892.

E. × Endresio-Wallisii, *G.C.* 1892, i. 88; *O.R.* 1893, 104, 356.

E. × Armstrongii, *Sand. O. Guide*, 276.

18. EPILÆLIA.

A genus established to contain the hybrids between Epidendrum and Lælia.

1. E.-l. × **belairensis** (E. ciliare × L. autumnalis ♀).—Mantin, 1897.

Læliodendron × bellaerense, *J. S. H. Fr.* 1897, 602.

2. E.-l. × **Charlesworthii** (E. radicans × L. cinnabarina ♀), *G.C.* 1898, i. 334; *O.R.* 1898, 169, 189; 1899, 254.—Charlesworth, 1898.

3. E.-l. × **Eros** (E. ciliare × L. Dayana ♀), *G.C.* 1901, ii. 297; *O.R.* 1901, 349.—Veitch, 1901.

4. E.-l. × **Hardyana** (E. ciliare ♀ × L. anceps), *G.C.* 1894, ii. 605, 629, f. 80; *O.R.* 1894, 364, 376; 1895, 99.—Baron N. Rothschild, 1894.

The Epilælia × Hardyana of the *Dict. Icon. des Orch.* is quite different. See Læliocattleya × Amelia.

5. E.-l. × **heatonensis** (E. × O'Brienianum × L. cinnabarina ♀), *G.C.* 1899, i. 361; *O.R.* 1899, 219; 1900, 92, 118.—Charlesworth, 1899.

6. E.-l. × **Lawrencei** (E. vitellinum × L. tenebrosa).—Lawrence, 1902,

E.-l. × (unnamed), *G.C.* 1902, ii. 112; *O.R.* 1902, 272.

7. E.-l. × **Margaritæ** (E. Parkinsonianum × L. grandis ♀)—Mantin, 1897.

Læliodendron × Margaritæ, *J. S. H. Fr.* 1897, 1245.

The pollen parent is recorded as E. falcatum or Parkinsonianum, but we believe it was the latter.

8. E.-l. × **Sylvia** (L. cinnabarina × E. Cooperianum ♀), *G.C.* 1902, i. 218; *O.R.* 1902, 118, 157; 1904, 169.—Charlesworth, 1902.

E.-l. × Aspasia (L. cinnabarina ♀), *G.C.* 1903, i. 302; *O.R.* 1903, 179.—Charlesworth.

9. **E.-l. × Veitchii** (Epidendrum radicans × Lælia purpurata ♀).—Veitch, 1897. [**See Fig. 29.**]

E.-l. × radico-purpurata, *G.C.* 1897. ii. 61, 78, 83, f. 23; *O.R.* 1897, 229, 232, 256, 273, f. 12 (with Epidendrum parent).

10. **E.-l. × Whitei** (E. fucatum × L. cinnabarina).—Lawrence, 1902.

E.-l. × (unnamed). *G.C.* 1902, ii. 112; *O.R.* 1902, 272.

19. EPIPHRONITIS.

A genus established to contain the hybrids between Epidendrum and Sophronitis.

1. **E.-ph. × Orpeti** (E. × O'Brienianum × S. violacea).—Thayer, 1901.

Sophronitis violacea × Epidendrum × O'Brienianum, *Amer. G.* 1901, 331, f. 71, n. 3; *O.R.* 1901, 179.

Fig. 29. EPILÆLIA × VEITCHII (with Epidendrum parent).

2. **E.-ph. × Veitchii** (E. radicans × S. grandiflora ♀), *G.C.* 1890, i. 799; *O.R.* 1893, 116, 291; 1896, 48; 1898, 296; 1903, 314; *Rev. H.* 1896, 480, t.; *Gtfl.* 1897, 553, 555 f. 74; *Wien Ill. G. Zeit.* 1897, 160, 161, f. 24; *J.H.* 1899, i. 514, f. 112; *J. R. H. S.* xxiv. 16, 17, f.; *Dict. Ic. O. Epiphr. hyb.* t. 1.—Veitch, 1890.

A remarkable hybrid, most resembling a dwarfed edition of the pollen parent in habit.

20. LÆLIA.

1. **L. × amœna** (anceps × pumila ♀), *G. C.* 1894, ii. 447; *O.R.* 1894, 334, 351; 1904, 372.—Ingram, 1894.

2. **L. × Briseis** (harpophylla ♀ × purpurata), *G.C.* 1897, ii. 438; *G.M.* 1898, 68, f.; *O.R.* 1898, 31, 351.—Douglas, 1897.

L.-c. × (unnamed), *J. S. H. Fr.* 1902, 229.—Fournier.

3. **L × cinnabrosa** (cinnabarina ♀ × tenebrosa), *O.R.* 1898, 189; *Dict. Ic. O.* Læl. hyb. t. 9.—Charlesworth, 1898.

L. × Halévy (tenebrosa ♀), *J. S. H. Fr.* 1902, 651.—Maron.

4. **L. × Coronet** (cinnabarina ♀ × harpophylla), *G.C.* 1902, i. 151; *O.R.* 1902, 157.—Charlesworth, 1902.

5. **L. × crispabrosa** (crispa × tenebrosa), *G.C.* 1903, ii. 64; *O.R.* 1903, 243; 1904, 244.—Sander, 1903.

6. **L. × Diana** (Dayana × purpurata ♀), *G.C.* 1901, i. 413; *O.R.* 1901, 197, 219, 249, f. 34.—(Winn) Hurst, 1900. [**See Fig. 30.**]

Fig. 30. LÆLIA × DIANA.

Lælio-cattleya × Hurstii, *O.R.* 1900, 287.

The earliest record that Cattleya Skinneri was one of the parents is believed to be erroneous.

7. **L. × Dutremblayi** (cinnabarina ♀ × grandiflora).—Dutremblay, 1902.

L. × Monsieur Dutremblay, *J. S. H. Fr.* 1902, 632.

8. **L. × Edissa** (anceps ♀ × purpurata), *G. C.* 1900, i. 143; *J. H.* 1900, i. 194, 195, f. 51; *G. M.* 1900, 193, 195, f.; *Gard.* 1900, i. 175, f.; *O. R.* 1900, 92.—Veitch, 1900.

9. **L. × Euterpe** (crispa × Dayana ♀), *G.C.* 1888, ii. 533; 1893, ii. 536;

1899, ii. 301; *O.R.* 1893, 259, 373; 1895, 31; 1899, 350 (Tyntesfield var.).—Veitch, 1888.

L. × Gemma, *G.C.* 1900, ii. 346; *O.R.* 1900, 371.—Sander.

10. L. × Exquisite (Dayana × Perrinii ♀), *G.C.* 1897, i. 51; *O.R.* 1897, 62.—Ingram, 1897.

11. L. × flammea (cinnabarina ♀ × Pilcheri), *G.C.* 1874, i. 599; 1876, i. 394; *Fl. and Pom.* 1874, 116, 133, t.; *O.A.* v. t. 217; *Day O. Draw.* xxxi. t. 57.—Veitch, 1874.

Fig. 31. LÆLIA × IONA VAR. NIGRESCENS.

L. × Veitchii, *Nich. Dict.* ii. 229.

12. L. × Flavina (flava × pumila ♀), *G.C.* 1902, i. 251; *O.R.* 1902, 147.—Veitch, 1902.

13. L. × Gravesiæ (crispa × pumila ♀), *Bohnh. Dict. O. Hyb.* 41; *Hans. O. Hyb.* 323; *Boyle Woodl. O.* 1901, 88.—Sander, 1895.

There is a slight doubt about the parentage. We have followed the original record, but Messrs. Sander, who raised it, give the parentage as L. pumila

Dayana × crispa Buchaniana (*O. Guide*, pp. 99, 276), which would make it a form of L. × Euterpe.

14. L. × **Icarius** (cinnabarina ♀ × flava), *G.C.* 1902, i. 50; *O.R.* 1902, 51; (Icarus).—Veitch, 1902.

15. L. × **Ingramiæ** (Perrinii × purpurata ♀).—Ingram, 1897.

L. × Lucy Ingram, *G.C.* 1897, i. 51; 1902, i. 70; *O.R.* 1897, 62; *G.M.* 1897, 92, 93, f.

16. L. × **Iona** (Dayana × tenebrosa ♀), *G.C.* 1899, ii. 233; *O.R.* 1899, 315; 1901, 327; 1905, 166, 168, f. 36 (v. nigrescens); *Gard.* 1903, ii. 168, f. (Southgate var.).—Charlesworth, 1899. [See Fig. 31.]

17. L. × **juvenilis** (Perrinii ♀ × pumila), *Orchidoph.* 1890, 240, t.; *J. S. H. Fr.* 1890, 636; *Lind.* ix. t. 415; *O.R.* 1893, 293; 1897, 28; 1901, 30; *Dict Ic. O.* Læl. hyb. t. 8 (v. Fournieri).—Bleu, 1890.

L. × (unnamed) (pumila ♀), *J. S. H. Fr.* 1893, 721.—Perrenoud.

L. × Clarinda, *G.C.* 1896, ii. 471; *O.R.* 1896, 348, 359.

Læliocattleya × juvenilis, *J. S. H. Fr.* 1896, 1063; *Sand. O. Guide*, 278.—Bleu.

18. L. × **Latona** (cinnabarina ♀ × purpurata), *G.C.* 1892, i. 598; *J. H.* 1892, i. 353, f. 61; 1902, i. 379, f.; *O.R.* 1893, 10, 357; 1896, 150; 1897, 99; *Dict. Ic. O.* Læl. hyb. t. 3; *J. S. H. Fr.* 1899, 375; *Chron. O.* 196, 296 (v. inversa).—Veitch, 1892.

L. × Yula, *Sand. O. Guide*, 276.

L. × purpurato-cinnabarina, *Sand. O. Guide*, 338.

L. × Zula, *Amer. G.* 1903, 107.—Rothwell.

19. L. × **Mantinii** (grandis × purpurata ♀).—Mantin, 1898.

L. × purpurato-grandis, *J. S. H. Fr.* 1898, 440; *Dict. Ic. O.* Læl. hyb. t. 5; *O.R.* 1903, 179.

20. L. × **Minerva** (× Latona × tenebrosa), *Gard.* 1903, i. 380; *O.R.* 1903, 182.—Keeling.

21. L. × **Mozart** (Boothiana × tenebrosa), *G.C.* 1901, i. 305; *O.R.* 1901, 181.—Leemann, 1901.

There is some confusion in the records of "L. × Mozart," both L. tenebrosa and purpurata having been recorded as the second parent. We have followed the original, for otherwise it would be a synonym of L. × pulcherrima, which see.

22. L. × **Nemesis** (anceps × superbiens ♀), *G.C.* 1902, i. 85; *O.R.* 1902, 52, 56.—Crawshay, 1901.

23 L. × **nigrescens** (pumila ♀ × tenebrosa), *J. S. H. Fr.* 1899, 46; *G.C.* 1899, ii. 58; *O.R.* 1899, 254, 291, 337, f. 17; 1901, 30; *Amer. G.* 1900, 709, f.—Maron, 1898. [See Fig. 32.]

L. × Alpha, *O.R.* 1899, 337.—Thayer.

L. × Eveline, *G.C.* 1900, i. 409; *O.R.* 1900, 212.—Miller.

Two hybrids may have been confused here, for the original record of L. × nigrescens was L. Dayana × tenebrosa, though it was subsequently altered. The figures cited represent L. × Alpha, whose origin is clear. We should like to see the point cleared up.

24. L. × **Olivia** (crispa ♀ × xanthina), *G.C.* 1897, ii. 387; *O.R.* 1898, 29; 1901, 349.—Veitch, 1897.

25. L. × **Omen** (autumnalis × purpurata ♀), *G.C.* 1896, ii. 667; *O.R.* 1897, 29: 1899, 31; *G.M.* 1902, 9, f.—Veitch, 1896.

26. L. × **Oweniana** (Dayana ♀ × xanthina), *G.C.* 1892, ii. 191; 1893, i. 682; *O.R.* 1893, 11, 212, 357.—Sander, 1892.

27. L. × **Pacavia** (purpurata ♀ × tenebrosa), *G.C.* 1901, ii. 172: *O.R.* 1901, 285.—Veitch, 1901.

28. L. × **Pilcheri** (crispa × Perrinii ♀), *Fl. M.* 1867, t. 340; *G.C.* 1867, 239; 1870, 315 (v. alba); *O.R.* 1893, 5.—Veitch, 1865.

Cattleya × Pilcheri, *G.C.* 1865, 222; *J. R. H. S.* 1865, 66.

Fig. 32. LÆLIA × NIGRESCENS.

L. × Pilcheriana, *G.C.* 1868, 815; 1886, i. 617 (in note); *V. Man. O.* ii. 97; *Day O. Draw.* xli. t. 33.

L. × lilacina (*G.C.* 1868, 342, 617; *O.R.* 1893, 132) is believed to be a natural hybrid with the same parentage. It appeared in the collection of F. A. Philbrick, Esq., of Oldfield.

29. L. × **pulcherrima** (Boothiana × purpurata), *G.C.* 1899, ii. 198; *O.R.* 1900, 287; 1901, 224.—Sander, 1899.

L. × Baden-Powell, *Sand. O. Guide*, 338.

L. × Mozart, *G.C.* May 25, 1901, Suppl. 1; *O.R.* 1901, 187.—Charlesworth.

30 **L. × Ragotiana** (cinnabarina × grandis ♀), *J. S. H. Fr.* 1898, 438; 1902, 475; *Chron. O.* 114; *G.C.* 1899, i. 362; *O.R.* 1899, 219.—Ragot, 1898.

31. **L. × splendens** (crispa ♀ × purpurata), *G.C.* 1897, ii. 188; *O.R.* 1897, 318.—Ingram, 1897.

32. **L. × Stanislaus** (autumnalis × cinnabarina ♀), *Charlesw. Cat.* 1903, 68. —Charlesworth, 1902.

L. × autumno-cinnabarina (autumnalis ♀), *Dict. Ic. O.* Læl. hyb. **t.** 7; *O.R.* 1903, 30.—Lawrence.

L. autumnalis cinnabarina, *G.C.* 1903, i. 19.—Clark.

33. **L × stellata** (harpophylla ♀ × tenebrosa), *O.R.* 1898, 218.—Statter, 1898.

L. × stilata, *G.C.* 1898, ii. 36.

21. LÆLIOCATTLEYA.

1. **L.-c. × Acis** (C. Mendelii × L. tenebrosa ♀), *O.R.* 1902, 220; 1903, 341. —(Sander) Miller, 1902.

L.-c. × Eugène Coutin (C. Mendelii ♀), *J. S. H. Fr.* 1902, 747.—Truffaut.

L.-c. × Gladiator, *G.C.* 1903, ii. 28; *O.R.* 1903, 243.—Sander.

2. **L.-c. × Ada** (C. Lueddemanniana × L.-c. × Schilleriana ♀), *G.C.* 1899, ii. 350; *O.R.* 1899, 348.—Leemann, 1899.

3. **L.-c. × Adolphus** (C. Aclandiæ × L. cinnabarina ♀), *G.C.* 1898, ii. 110; 1902, ii. 111, **f.** 37 (v. superba); *O.R.* 1898, 253; 1899, 252; *G.M.* 1899, 580, **f.**; 1902, 666, **f.** (v. superbus); *J.H.* 1902, ii. 169, **f.** (v. superbus).—Charlesworth, 1898.

L.-c. × Donizetti (Aclandiæ ♀), *J. S. H. Fr.* 1901, 908.—Maron.

4. **L.-c. × Agnes** (L.-c. × callistoglossa × L.-c. × Schilleriana ♀), *O.R.* 1901, 302.—Keeling, 1901.

5. **L.-c. × albanensis** (C. Warneri × L. grandis ♀), *O.R.* 1895, 164; *Dict. Ic. O.* L.-c. hyb. **t.** 6.—Linden, 1895.

L.-c. × Varjenevskyana, *Lind.* x. **t.** 466.

This appeared first as a natural hybrid, in the establishment of Messrs. Sander. See *O.R.* 1893, 339.

6. **L.-c. × Alberti** (C. velutina × L. purpurata), *Lind.* xvi. **t.** 723; *O.R.* 1901, 15; *J. R. H. S.* xxvi. 946.—Linden, 1900.

This hybrid most resembles the Lælia parent, being cream-white with purple radiating veins on the lip's disc, but the smaller size, and the shape of the lip, including its small side lobes, show the influence of the other parent.

7. **L.-c. × Alexandræ** (C. Trianæ × L.-c. × bella ♀).—Veitch, 1902.

L.-c. × Queen Alexandra, *G.C.* 1902, i. 116, 340, **Suppl. f.**; 413, **col. t.**; *O.R.* 1902, 89; *J.H.* 1902, i. 181, **f.**

8. **L.-c. × Amazone** (C. maxima × L. purpurata), *G.C.* 1899, i. 362; *O.R.* 1899, 219; 1903, 213.—Ingram, 1899.

L.-c. × Dante, *G.C.* 1903, i. 419.—Charlesworth.

9. **L.-c. × Amelia** (C. intermedia ♀ × L. cinnabarina), *G.C.* 1898, ii. 375, 411; *O.R.* 1898, 370, 372 (unnamed).—Gratrix, 1898.

L.-c. × intermedio-cinnabarina, *O.R.* 1899, 316; *G.C.* 1900, ii. 270.—Charlesworth.

L.-c. × elegantissima, *J. S. H. Fr.* 1900, 795.—Cappe.

Epilælia × Hardyana, *Dict. Ic. O.* Epilæl. hyb. t. 1 (not the original plant).—De Lairesse.

10. L.-c. × Amesiana (C. maxima × L. crispa ♀), *J.L.Soc.* xxiv. 169.—Veitch, 1884.

L. × Amesiana, *G.C.* 1884, i. 109; *O.A.* vi. t. 253; *O.R.* 1893, 101; *Day O. Draw.* xxxix. t. 67.

Cattleya × Amesiana, *Will. O. Gr. Man.* ed. 6, 173.

11. L.-c. × amœna (C. Loddigesii ♀ × L. Perrinii), *J.d.O.* iii. 281; *Lind.* viii. t. 367 (v. delicata).—Bleu, 1887.

L. c. × (unnamed), *J. S. H. Fr.* 1887, 678.

C. × amœna, *Orchidoph.* 1891, 273, t.; *O.R.* 1893, 323.

12. L.-c. × Andreana (C. bicolor ♀ × L.-c. × Schilleriana), *Rev. H.* 1895, 401; 1896, 328, t.; *J. S. H. Fr.* 1895, 558; *O.R.* 1895, 293.—Maron, 1895.

L.-c. × elegans-bicolor, (Schilleriana ♀), *J. S. H. Fr.* 1898, 440; *Chron. O.* 183.—Mantin.

From the description and figure we believe that L.-c. × Schilleriana (not L.-c. × elegans, as recorded) was the second parent of this hybrid.

13. L.-c. × Antigone (C. Schilleriana × L. purpurata ♀), *J. S. H. Fr.* 1901, 212; *Chron. O.* 297; *O.R.* 1901, 338.—Maron, 1900; Peeters, 1901.

L.-c. × purpurato-Schilleriana, *J. S. H. Fr.* 1900, 60; *G.C.* 1902, i. 183; *O.R.* 1902, 124.—Maron.

L.-c. × Aspasia, *J. S. H. Fr.* 1901, 1062.—Dallemagne.

L.-c. × Aleschiana, *Lind.* xvi. t. 754.—Linden.

L.-c. × Duchesnei, Lind. xvii. t. 777.—Linden.

L.-c. × Pauli, Lind. xvii. t. 784.—Linden.

L.-c. × Hermann Holmes, *O.R.* 1900, 247.—Holmes.

14. L.-c. × Antimachus (C. Warscewiczii ♀ × L.-c. × Dominiana), *G.C.* 1899, ii. 318; *O.R.* 1899, 347.—Veitch, 1899.

15. L.-c. × Aphrodite (C. Mendelii ♀ × L. purpurata), *G.C.* 1895, i. 721; *O.R.* 1895, 199, 219; *G.M.* 1899, 345, 348, f. (v. Ruth); 1902, 531, f. (v. King Edward VII.); *J.H.* 1899, ii. 34, f. 9 (v. Ruth).—Baron E. Rothschild, 1894.

L.-c. × (unnamed), *J. S. H. Fr.* 1894, 314; *Rev. H.* 1894, 334.—Baron E. Rothschild.

L.-c. × Eudora (purpurata ♀), *G.C.* 1896, i. 593; *O.R.* 1896, 186, 224; *J.H.* 1899, ii. 406, 407, f. 75 (v. Madame Albert Hye).—Ingram.

L.-c. × regalis, *G.C.* 1896, i. 740; *O.R.* 1896, 221, 224.—Ingram.

L.-c. × Jacobiana, *J. S. H. Fr.* 1896, 699; *Monit d'Hort.* 1896, 185, t.—Baron E. Rothschild.

L.-c. × armainvillierensis, *J.S.H.Fr.* 1896, 790.—Baron E. Rothschild.

The name L.-c. × Jacobiana was not recorded when the hybrid was first exhibited in 1894, or it must have superseded L.-c. × Aphrodite. The latter was exhibited in 1895 by W. R. Lee, Esq., but the actual raiser is not recorded.

16 L.-c. × Ascania (C. Trianæ ♀ × L. xanthina), *G.C.* 1893, i. 518; *O.R.* 1893, 167; *J.H.* 1893, i. 351, f. 65.—Veitch, 1893.

17. L.-c. × Astoriæ (C. Gaskelliana ♀ × L. xanthina).—Sander, 1894.

L.-c. × The Hon. Mrs. Astor, *G.C.* 1894, i. 230, 231, f. 24; *O.R.* 1894, 94, 111; *J.H.* 1894, i. 141, f. 22; *Reichenb.* ser. 2, ii. 97, t. 89; *G.M.* 1894, 103, f.; *Amer. G.* 1894, 240, f.

L.-c. × Prince Yellow (xanthina ♀), *J. S. H. Fr.* 1901, 211.—Maron.

L.-c. × Ascania, *O.R.* 1902, 317, 351.

L.-c. × Yellow Prince, *G.C.* 1899, ii. 426; *O.R.* 1899, 371; *Rev. H.* 1903, 12, t.—Maron.

18. L.-c. × Astræa (C. Dowiana × L × Euterpe ♀).—Sander, 1902.

L.-c. × Euterpe-aurea, *G.C.* 1902, ii. 313; *Gard.* 1902, ii. 295: *Sand. O. Guide*, 339.

19. L.-c. × aurelianensis (C. Leopoldi × L.-c. × Schilleriana ♀), *J. S. H. Fr.* 1895, 799.—Mantin, 1895.

L.-c. × bellaerensis, *J. S. H. Fr.* 1895, 671, 680.

The parents are recorded as "Lælia elegans × G. guttata," but the hybrid is said to most resemble C. intermedia, and it is believed that the above represents its origin.

20. L.-c. × Aurora (C. Loddigesii × L. Dayana ♀), *G.C.* 1889, ii. 380; *O.R.* 1893, 261.—Veitch, 1892.

21. L.-c. × Baden-Powellii (C. Lawrenceana × L. tenebrosa ♀).—Hye, 1900.

L.-c. × General Baden-Powell, *G.C.* 1900, March 26, Suppl. 1.

L.-c. × Major-General Baden-Powell, *O.R.* 1900, 174.

22. L.-c. × Ballii (C. Schrœderæ × L. cinnabarina ♀), *O.R.* 1902, 156.—Veitch, 1900.

L.-c. × G. S. Ball, *G.C.* 1900, i. 302; *O.R.* 1900, 171, 176.—Veitch, 1900.

L.-c. × cinnabarino-Schrœderæ, *O.R.* 1903, 147.—De Smet-Duvivier.

L.-c. × flaveola, *J. S. H. Fr.* 1901, 97, 212.—Doin.

23 L.-c. × Behrensiana (C. Loddigesii × L.-c. × Schilleriana ♀), *G.C.* 1891, ii. 254; *O.R.* 1893, 325; *Reichenb.* ser. 2, ii. 29, t. 62.—Sander, 1891.

C. × Behrensiana (Loddigesii ♀), *J.S.H.Fr.* 1895, 671.—Mantin.

L.-c. × Behrensiana inversa (Loddigesii ♀), *J. S. H. Fr.* 1895, 681; 1897, 609.—Mantin.

We are not certain that M. Mantin's hybrid belongs here. In one case L. elegans colorata was recorded as the pollen parent, and if that means elegans typical the hybrid would be a form of L.-c. × Zenobia, but we do not find a description to settle the point. L.-c. × elegans was originally recorded as the seed parent of Messrs. Sander's hybrid, but it was afterwards amended to L.-c. × Schilleriana.

24. L.-c. × belairensis (C. Bowringiana ♀ × L. autumnalis), *G.C.* 1896, ii. 534; *O.R.* 1896, 325, 350.—Mantin, 1896.

L.-c. × bellaerensis, *J. S. H. Fr.* 1897, 954.

25. **L.-c. × bella** (C. labiata × L. purpurata ♀), *J. L. Soc.* xxiv. 169.—Veitch, 1884.

L.-c. × bella, *G.C.* 1884, i. 174; *O.R.* 1893, 101.

L.-c. × Wellsiæ, *G.C.* 1894, ii. 378; *O.R.* 1904, 349.—Wells.

L.-c. × T. W. Bond (C. labiata ♀), *G.C.* 1896, ii. 471; *O.R.* 1896, 347, 359.—Ingram.

L.-c. × illuminata, *J. S. H. Fr.* 1895, 991.—Cahuzac.

26. **L.-c. × Beranekii** (C. Mossiæ × L. Perrinii ♀).—Beranek, 1902.

L.-c. × Perrino-Mossiæ, *J. S. H. Fr.* 1902, 747; *Rev. H.* 1902, 582.

27. **L.-c. × Bertha** (C. Schrœderæ × L. grandis ♀), *Gard.* 1901, i. 369; *O.R.* 1901, 255.—R. H. Measures, 1901.

L.-c. × Sheila, *Sand. O. Guide*, 340.

28. **L.-c. × Bievreana** (C. Rex × L. crispa ♀), *O.R.* 1903, 150; *Rev. H. Belge*, 1903, 104.—King of the Belgians, 1903.

29. **L.-c. × Binoti** (C. bicolor × L. pumila), *O.R.* 1901, 304, 326; *Dict. Ic. O.* L.-c. hyb. **t.** 30.—(Lewis) Chamberlain, 1901.

L.-c. × præstans-bicolor (pumila ♀), *G.C.* 1901, ii. 250; *O.R.* 1901, 316.—Lawrence.

This originally appeared as a natural hybrid in the establishment of Messrs. Peeters, of Brussels. See *G.C.* 1900, ii. 370; *O.R.* 1900, 357.

30. **L.-c. × Birkbeckiæ** (L. purpurata × L.-c. × callistoglossa ♀).—Wigan, 1900.

L.-c. × Mrs. Birkbeck, *G.C.* 1900, ii. 384; *O.R.* 1900, 372; *Gard.* 1900, ii. 406.

L.-c. × bletchleyensis (C. Warscewiczii × L. tenebrosa ♀), *G.C.* 1899, ii. 198; 1904, i. 88, **Suppl. f.**; *O.R.* 1899, 286; 1900, 63; *Amer. G.* 1900. 709, **f.**; 1902, 578, 579, **f.** 128; *J.H.* 1902, ii. 489, **f.** (Fowler's var.); *Dict. Ic. O.* L.-c. hyb. **t.** 27.—Leon, 1899.

L.-c. × Minerva (C. Warscewiczii ♀), *J. S. H. Fr.* 1899, 833.—Maron.

Cattleya × Minerva, *J.S.H.Fr.* 1900, 673.

L.-c. × Hettie, *O.R.* 1901, 368.—Stanley, Ashton and Co.

L.-c. × Godiniana, *J. S. H. Fr.* 1902, 253; *Rev. H.* 1902, 218.—Dallemagne.

L.-c. × loochristiensis (C. Warscewiczii ♀), *Sand. O. Guide*, 339.

32 **L.-c. × Bowrialbida** (C. Bowringiana × L. albida), *Amer. G.* 1902, 12.—Thayer, 1901.

33. **L.-c. × Boylei** (C. Trianæ ♀ × L. anceps), *O.R.* 1895, 260, 261.—Sander, 1894.

L.-c. × Frederick Boyle, *G.C.* 1894, i. 809, **f.** 105; *G.M.* 1894, 312, 316, **f.**; *O.R.* 1894, 189, 239; 1899, 31; *Dict. Ic. O.* L.-c. hyb. **t.** 29 (v. Kerchoveæ).

L.-c. × Kerchoveæ, *G.C.* 1903, i. 267; *O.R.* 1903, 146, 149; *Jard.* 1904, 20, **f.** Peeters.

34. **L.-c. × Britannia** (C. Warscewiczii × L.-c. × Canhamiana), *G.C.* 1903, ii. 181; *O.R.* 1903, 307.—Sander, 1903.

35. L.-c. × Bryan (C. Gaskelliana ♀ × L. crispa), *G.C.* 1896, ii. 310; *O.R.* 1896, 296, 319.—Cookson, 1896.

L.-c. × Duchess of York (crispa ♀), *G.C.* 1899, ii. 334; *O.R.* 1899, 351. Veitch.

36. L.-c. × Brymeriana (C. Warscewiczii × L.-c. × amanda ♀), *O.R.* 1893, 21.—Brymer, 1893.

37. L.-c. × burbagensis (C. granulosa × L. purpurata), *O.R.* 1902, 271.—Hurst, 1901.

38. L.-c × callistoglossa (C. Warscewiczii × L. purpurata ♀), *J. L. Soc.* xxiv. 169; *Garden*, 1900, i. 231, f. (v. splendens); *Dict. Ic. O.* L.-c. hyb. t. 8, 8a (v. inversa).—Veitch, 1882.

Lælia × callistoglossa, *G.C.* 1882, i. 76; *O. A. v.* t. 235; *V. Man. O.* ii. 94, f.; *Gard.* 1897, 310.

L. × Arnoldiana, *G.C.* 1891, i. 740, 742; *J.H.* 1891, i. 491, f. 93.—Sander.

L.-c. × Arnoldiana, *J. d. O.* ii. 134; *Lind.* vii. t. 299; *Reichenb.* ser. 2, i. 103, t. 48; *O.R.* 1893, 323.—Sander.

L.-c. × Hardyana, *G.C.* 1895, ii. 248.—Hardy.

L.-c. × Bleuana, *J. S. H. Fr.* 1897, 844.—Bleu.

L.-c. × purpurato-gigas, *Chron. O.* 173.—Mantin.

L.-c. × Princess of Wales, *O.R.* 1899, 4.—Wigan.

L.-c × excellens, *Boyle Woodl. O.* 91.—R. H. Measures.

L.-c. × Mme. Georges Halphem, *Chron. O.* 356.—Maron.

39. L.-c. × Canhamiana (C. Mossiæ × L. purpurata ♀), *J. L. Soc.* xxiv. 169; *J.H.* 1894, ii. 12, 13, f. 2 (v. alba); 1900, ii. 97, f. 26 (v. alba); *G.M.* 1894, 502, 507, f. (v. alba); *Dict. Ic. O.* L.-c. hyb. t. 18 (v. alba).

Lælia × Canhamiana, *G.C.* 1885, ii. 6; *O.R.* 1893, 102.

L.-c. × Canhamiæ (C. Mossiæ ♀), *G.C.* 1890, i. 800; *O.R.* 1893, 292.—Veitch.

Cattleya × Elsteadiana, *G.C.* 1890, i. 747.—Ingram.

L.-c. × Marriottii, *G.C.* 1890, i. 747.—Marriott.

L.-c. × Ridolfiana, *Bull. Soc. Tosc. Ort.* 1893, 72, t. 3; *Lind.* xiii. t. 597 (v. armainvillierensis).—School of Horticulture, Florence.

Cattleya × Dallemagnei, *Rev. H.* 1894, 334.—Dallemagne.

L.-c. × Aylingii, *O.R.* 1894, 189.—Sander.

L.-c. × fastuosa, *J. S. H. Fr.* 1896, 420.—Bleu.

L.-c. × Lady Wigan, *G.C.* 1897, i. 354.—Charlesworth.

L.-c. × purpurato-Mossiæ, *Jard.* 1897, 310; *Chron. O.* 78; *J. S. H. Fr.* 1897, 934.—Maron.

L.-c. × Captain Law-Schofield, *J. S. H. Fr.* 1898, 538; *Chron. O.* 168.—Maron.

L.-c. × President Viger, *J. S. H. Fr.* 1898, 536, 705.—Maron.

L.-c. × Edouard André, *J. S. H. Fr.* 1898, 537.—Maron.

L.-c. × Bertie Warburton, *G.C.* 1898, i. 398, 399.—Warburton.

L.-c. × G. Galpin, *Jard.* 1899, 208.—Maron.

L.-c. × Madame Wallet, *J. S. H. Fr.* 1901, 637.—Maron.

L.-c. × Comtesse de Bassetière, *Chron. O.* 355.—Maron.

L.-c. × Marguerite, *J. S. H. Fr.* 1902, 510.—Maron.

L.-c. × Rex, *G.M.* 1902, 328.—Sander.

40. **L.-c. × Cappei** (C. Warscewiczii × L. cinnabarina ♀), *O.R.* 1899, 46; 1901, 38; 1902, 44; *J. S. H. Fr.* 1899, 45, 1129; 1904, ii. 452, 453, f. (Charlesworth's var.); *G.C.* 1902, i. 86; *G.M.* 1904, 841, f. (Charlesworth's var.).—Cappe, 1899.

41. **L.-c. × Cassiope** (L. pumila ♀ × L.-c. × exoniensis), *G.C.* 1889, ii. 620; *O.R.* 1893, 261; 1903, 364; *J.H.* 1904, i. 26, 27, f. (Westonbirt var.).—Veitch, 1889.

L.-c. × Thetis, *G.C.* 1896, i. 337; *O.R.* 1896, 122.—Lawrence.

42. **L.-c. × Celestinæ** (L. tenebrosa × L.-c. × Schilleriana ♀), *Rev. H.* 1903, 218,—Fournier, 1903.

Lælia × Celestinæ, *Jard.* 1903, 128.

43. **L.-c. × Ceres** (C. Mossiæ ♀ × L.-c. × Hippolyta), *G.C.* 1900, May 28, Suppl. 1; *O.R.* 1900, 176, 183.—Peeters, 1900.

44. **L.-c. × Chantinii** (C. × Hardyana × L.-c. × elegans).—Maron, 1900.

Cattleya × Monsieur A. Chantin, *J. S. H. Fr.* 1900, 592.

L.-c. × (unnamed), *G.C.* 1903, ii. 340; *O.R.* 1903, 364.

These should be compared with L.-c. × Greenwoodii. We have not been able to compare them.

45. **L.-c. × Charlesworthii** (C. Dowiana × L. cinnabarina ♀), *G.C.* 1900, i. 62; 1902, i. 67, 85; *O.R.* 1900, 61; 1902, 53, 54; 1905, 168, f. 37 (v. magnifica); *G.M.* 1904, 169, 170, f.—Charlesworth, 1900. **[See Fig. 33.**

46. **L.-c. × Choletiana** (C. Mossiæ ♀ × L. superbiens), *J. S. H. Fr.* 1902, 138, 139; *G.C.* 1902, i. 151; *G.M.* 1902, 133, 215, f.; *J.H.* 1902, i. 249, f.; *O.R.* 1902, 92, 99.—Dallemagne, 1902.

47. **L.-c. × Cicero** (C. intermedia ♀ × L.-c. × elegans), *G.C.* 1896, i. 88; *O.R.* 1896, 63; 1899, 310.—Ingram, 1896.

L.-c. × Regina, *G.C.* 1897, i. 51; *O.R.* 1897, 62, 112,—Ingram.

L.-c. × inter-elegans, *Sand. O. Guide*, 278.

48. **L.-c. × claptonensis** (C. Dormaniana × L.-c. × Schilleriana ♀), *G.C.* 1892, ii. 566; *O.R.* 1893, 96, 357.—Low, 1892.

L.-c. × elegans was recorded as the seed parent of this hybrid, but the note that the flower "nearly approached" L.-c. × Schilleriana induces us to alter the record.

49. **L.-c. × Clementineæ** (C. Trianæ × L.-c. × Sallieri).—Fournier, 1903.

L.-c. × Mdlle. Clémentine, *Jard.* 1903, 80; *Rev. H.* 1903, 140.

50. **L.-c. × Clive** (C. Dowiana ♀ × L. pumila), *O.R.* 1893, 318; 1896, 304; *G.C.* 1897, ii. 388, 426, 427, f. 126; *G.M.* 1896, 637, f.; *Dict. Ic. O.* L.-c. hyb. t. 28.—Cookson, 1896.

L.-c. × (unnamed), *G.C.* 1893, ii. 342.

C. × (unnamed), *J. S. H. Fr.* 1897, 839.—Cappe.

C. × Pineli-aurea (L. pumila ♀), *J. S. H. Fr.* 1897, 1344; 1898, 770.—Cappe.

L.-c. × broomfieldensis (pumila ♀), *G.C.* 1894, ii. 194, 223, f. 33: *J.H.* 1894, ii. 170, 171, f. 25; *G.M.* 1894, 519, f.—Wells.

L.-c. × Ingrami v. broomfieldensis, *O.R.* 1894, 287.

L.-c. × Normani, *Sand. O. Guide*, 278.

51. L.-c. × Clonia (C. Warscewiczii ♀ × L.-c. × elegans), *G.C.* 1894, ii. 511; *O.R.* 1894, 373 (Chlonia); *G.M.* 1895, 591, f. (v. superba).—Veitch, 1894.

The hybrid L.-c. × Marguerite has been confused with this.

Fig. 33. LÆLIOCATTLEYA × CHARLESWORTHII MAGNIFICA.

L.-c. × Atalanta, *G.C.* 1901, ii. 142; *O.R.* 1901, 284.—Thornton.

L.-c. × Lord Roberts, *Sand. O. Guide*, 339.

52. L.-c. × Clytie (C. Dowiana ♀ × L. × Gravesiæ), *O.R.* 1901, 338.—Wigan, 1901.

53. L.-c. × Colmaniana (C. Dowiana ♀ × L.-c. × callistoglossa), *G.C.* 1900, ii. 240.—Sander, 1900.

54. L.-c. × confusa (C. Harrisoniana × L. pumila).—Low.

L.-c. × Harrisoni-præstans, *G.C.* 1897, ii. 150; *O.R.* 1897, 287.—Low.

L. pumila × C. Harrisoniana, *G.C.* 1897, ii. 150; *O.R.* 1897, 287.—Sander.

This should be compared with L.-c. × Leeana, as the unfortunate confusion between Cattleya Harrisoniana and C. Loddigesii renders the parentage uncertain.

55. L.-c. × **Constance** (C. Rex × L. xanthina ♀).—Wigan, 1902.

L.-c. × Constance Wigan, *G.C.* 1902, ii. 272; *O.R.* 1902, 325.

56. L.-c. × **Cooksonæ** (C. labiata × L.-c. × Clive), *G.C.* 1902, ii. 183; *O.R.* 1902, 307; *J.H.* 1902, ii. 375, f.—Cookson, 1902.

57. L.-c. × **Cora** (C. Mendelii × L. × Latona ♀), *G.C.* 1902, May 31, Suppl. 1; *Sand. O. Guide*, 339.—Veitch, 1902.

58. L.-c. × **Cornelia** (C. labiata × L. pumila ♀), *G.C.* 1893, ii. 692; *O.R.* 1894, 30.—Veitch, 1893.

L.-c. × (unnamed), *J. S. H. Fr.* 1902, 140.—Duval.

Cattleya × Cornelia, *J. S. H. Fr.* 1900, 670; *Rev. H.* 1900, 463.—Maron.

59. L.-c. × **cornuta** (C. labiata ♀ × L. autumnalis), *J. S. H. Fr.* 1900, 848.—Maron, 1900.

60. L.-c. × **Coronis** (C. labiata × L. cinnabarina), *G.C.* 1900, ii. 466; *O.R.* 1901, 23.—Veitch, 1900.

61. L.-c. × **Cowperi** (C. Warneri ♀ × L. crispa).—Cowper, 1894.

L.-c. × Mauve Queen, *G.C.* 1894, ii. 605; *O.R.* 1894, 374.

62. L.-c. × **Cranstounæ** (C. Harrisoniana ♀ × L. tenebrosa), *O.R.* 1900, 19, 119; 1901, 15; *G.C.* 1901, ii. 462.—(Berkeley) Cranstoun, 1899.

63. L.-c. × **Cybele** (C. Trianæ × L.-c. × Schilleriana ♀), *G.C.* 1901, i. 272; *O.R.* 1901, 156.—Veitch, 1901.

L.-c. × D. S. Brown, *G.C.* 1895, ii. 49; *O.R.* 1895, 244, 255.—Sander.

64. L.-c. × **Dallemagnei** (C. Aclandiæ × L. pumila).—Dallemagne, 1901.

Cattleya Aclandiæ × præstans, *J. S. H. Fr.* 1901, 1001.—Dallemagne.

L.-c. × Wm. Pitt, *G.C.* 1903, ii. 104; *O.R.* 1903, 267.—Pitt.

65. L.-c. × **Darwiniana** (C. maxima × L.-c. × elegans ♀), *O.R.* 1895, 293.—Ingram, 1895.

L.-c. × Charles Darwin, *G.C.* 1895, ii. 248; *O.R.* 1895, 319; *J.H.* 1895, ii. 197, 206, f. 28; 1896, ii. 377, f. 69.

L.-c. × Othello (maxima ♀), *G.C.* 1895, ii. 588; *O.R.* 1895, 375.—Ingram.

66. L.-c. × **Decia** (C. Dowiana × L. Perrinii ♀), *G.C.* 1894, ii. 670, 699, f. 89; 1897, i. 120, 121, f. 34 (v. alba); *O.R.* 1895, 30; *J.H.* 1895, i. 130, 131, f. 21; *G.M.* 1894, 746, f.—Veitch, 1894.

67. L.-c. × **decora** (C. Bowringiana ♀ × L.-c. × Clive.—Sander, 1902.

L.-c. × Bowringiano-Clive, *G.C.* 1902, ii. 384; *O.R.* 1902, 367; *Gard.* 1902, ii. 295.

L.-c. Bowring-Clive, *Gard.* 1903, ii. 387.

68. L.-c. × **dellensis** (C. × Hardyana × L.-c. × albanensis).—Sander, 1902.

L.-c. × memoria Baroness Schröder, *G.C.* 1902, i. 442; *Sand. O. Guide*, 340.

69. L.-c. × **devoniensis** (C. Leopoldi × L. crispa ♀), *O.R.* 1902, 270.—Veitch, 1863.

Cattleya × Devonia, *Proc. R. H. S.* 1863, 372.

C. × devoniensis, *G.C.* 1877, ii. 424 (in note); *O.R.* 1893, 5.

Lælia × Mylamiana, *G.C.* 1876, ii. 740, 741, **f.** 138.—Rollisson.

L. × devoniensis, *G.C.* 1877, ii. 424 (in note).

L.-c. × Mylamiana, *J. L. Soc.* xxiv. 169.

L.-c. × Watellieriana, *J. S. H. Fr.* 1901, 1002.—Belin.

L.-c. × Wylamiana, *G.C.* 1902, ii. 183 (misprint).

70. L.-c. × **Deweyi** (C. Warneri ♀ × L.-c. × elegans).—Charlesworth, 1898.

L.-c. × Admiral Dewey, *G.C.* 1898, i. 334, 350; 1901, ii. 270; *O.R.* 1898, 189; *G.M.* 1898, 508, 509, **f.**; *Dict. Ic. O.* L.-c. hyb. **t.** 34.

71. L.-c. × **Diarmid** (L. Perrinii ♀ × L.-c. × elegans), *G.C.* 1897, ii. 316; *O.R.* 1897, 351.—Ingram, 1897.

72. L.-c. × **Dido** (C. Skinneri × L. cinnabarina), *G.C.* 1901, May 25, Suppl. 1, *O.R.* 1901, 186.—Hon. W. Rothschild, 1901.

L. c. × Macnabiana, *Gard.* 1903, i. 133.—Fowler.

73. L.-c. × **Diogenes** (C. Leopoldi × L. cinnabarina ♀), *G.C.* 1901, i. 53; *O.R.* 1901, 37.—Charlesworth, 1900.

L.-c. × Vacuna (Leopoldi ♀), *G.C.* 1901, i. 179; *O.R.* 1901, 119.—Veitch.

74. L.-c. × **Doinii** (C. Rex × L. tenebrosa ♀).—Doin, 1902.

L.-c. × Gaston Doin, *J. S. H. Fr.* 1902, 553.

75. L.-c. × **Dominiana** (C. Dowiana × L. purpurata ♀), *G.C.* 1889, ii, 78; *J.H.* 1898, ii. 317, **f.** 56 (v. langleyensis); *O.R.* 1899, 50, 69, 228; *Gard.* 1898, ii. 465, f. (v. langleyensis); 1899, ii. 142, 143, f. and t. 1256 (langleyensis).

Lælia × Dominiana, *G.C.* 1878, ii. 332; 1881, ii. 53, 108 (v. rosea); *Fl. M.* 1878, **t.** 325.

L.-c. × Fire King, *O.R.* 1898, 217; 1899, 228, 247, 250.—Mrs. Briggs-Bury.

L.-c. × Sir William Ingram, *G.C.* 1896, i. 468; *O.R.* 1896, 156.—Ingram.

L. × Apollonia, *G.C.* 1896, ii. 667; *O.R.* 1897, 29.—Douglas.

L. × Empress of India, *G.C.* 1897, i. 410; *O.R.* 1897, 222.—Sander.

L. × Radiance, *G.C.* 1897, ii. 150; *O.R.* 1897, 287.—Ingram.

L. × tyntesfieldensis, *G.C.* 1897, i. 354, 359; *O.R.* 1897, 169, 189, 222.—Hardy.

76. L.-c. × **Dora** (C. Schrœderæ × L.-c × Hippolyta ♀), *G.C.* 1902, i. 251; 1903, i. 239; *O.R.* 1902, 147; *Gard.* 1903, i. 321, **f.** (v. magnifica).—Charlesworth, 1902.

L.-c. × Thyra (Schrœderæ ♀) *G.C.* 1903, i. 206; *O.R.* 1903, 119.—Veitch.

77. L.-c. × **Doris** (C. Trianæ × L. harpophylla ♀), *O.R.* 1894, 79, 111; 1896, 124, 133 (v. Xantho); *Dict. Ic. O.* L.-c. hyb. **t.** 22 (v. Marquis de Colbert); *G.C.* 1896, i. 337 (v. Xantho).—Cookson, 1894.

Lælia × vitellina, *G.C.* 1893, i. 365, **f.** 53; *O.R.* 1896, 149.—Schröder.

L.-c. × Noel, *G.C.* 1903, i. 223: *O.R.* 1903, 154.—Hodgkinson.

78. L.-c. × **Duvaliana** (C. Lueddemanniana × L. purpurata), *J. S. H. Fr.* 1898, 536; *Chron. O.* 172; *O.R.* 1899, 253; *G.M.* 1899, 467, **f.**; *G.C.* 1899, ii. 58. —Maron, 1899.

Cattleya × Duvaliana, *J. S. H. Fr.* 1900, 592.

79. **L.-c. × Edwardi** (C. × Hardyana × L. cinnabarina ♀), *G.C.* 1902, i. 183; *O.R.* 1902, 116.—Sander, 1902.

80. **L.-c. × Electra** (C. Percivaliana ♀ × L. purpurata), *G.C.* 1896, i. 741; *O.R.* 1896, 221.—Ingram, 1896.

81. **L.-c. × Ella** (C. intermedia × L. grandis ♀), *O.R.* 1900, 324.—Thornton, 1900.

L.-c. × Stella, *O.R.* 1900, 319.—Thornton, 1900.

82. **L.-c. × elsteadensis** (C. bicolor ♀ × L. xanthina), *O.R.* 1895, 293.—Ingram, 1895.

L.-c. × Elstead Gem, *G.C.* 1895, ii. 192; *O.R.* 1895, 287.

83. **L.-c. × Emiliæ** (C. Aclandiæ ♀ × L. purpurata), *Dict. Ic. O.* L.-c. hyb. t. 24.—Duval, 1900.

L.-c. × (unnamed), *J. S. H. Fr.* 1900, 840; 1901, 411.—Duval.

L.-c. × purpurato-Aclandiæ (L. purpurata ♀), *J. S. H. Fr.* 1901, 842; *O.R.* 1901, 338; 1902, 318.—Duval.

Cattleya × (unnamed), *J. S. H. Fr.* 1902, 140.—Duval.

84. **L.-c. × epicasta** (C. Warscewiczii × L. pumila ♀), *G.C.* 1893, ii. 342; *O.R.* 1893, 320; *J.H.* 1895, i. 353, 364, f. 60; *G.M.* 1895, 261, f.—Veitch, 1893.

85. **L.-c. × Ernesti** (C. Percivaliana ♀ × L. flava), *J. S. H. Fr.* 1899, 262, 263; *Rev. H.* 1899, 476, t. (v. Van Dyck); *G.C.* 1899, i. 149, f. 54 (v. Princess Olga); *G.M.* 1899, 144, f. (id.); *J.H.* 1899, 251, f. 61 (id.); *O.R.* 1899, 125.—Maron, 1899.

86. **L.-c. × Ethelwald** (C. Gaskelliana ♀ × L. Boothiana), *G.C.* 1899, ii. 273; *O.R.* 1899, 336.—Paynter, 1899.

87. **L.-c. × Eumæa** (C. Trianæ ♀ × L. grandiflora), *G.C.* 1893, ii. 536; *O.R.* 1893, 374; 1894, 21.—Veitch, 1893.

88. **L.-c. × Eunomia** (C. Gaskelliana × L. Dayana ♀), *G.C.* 1895, ii. 307; *O.R.* 1895, 292, 320.—Veitch, 1895.

89. **L.-c. × Euphrosyne** (C. Warscewiczii × L. Dayana ♀), *G.C.* 1895, ii. 527; *O.R.* 1895, 374.—Veitch, 1895.

L.-c. × illustris, *G.C.* 1897, ii. 278; *O.R.* 1897, 348.—Ingram.

L.-c. × (unnamed), *O.R.* 1899, 219.—Cypher.

L.-c. × Iona, *G.C.* 1903, i. 366.—Cypher.

90. **L.-c. × Eva** (C. Gaskelliana × L. tenebrosa), *G.C.* 1902, ii. 313; *O.R.* 1902, 341.—Veitch, 1902.

L.-c. × Gladys, *Amer. G.* 1902, 574; *O.R.* 1903, 26, 255.—Thayer.

L.-c. × Orpetiana, *G.C.* 1903, i. 165; *Dict. Ic. O.* L.-c. hyb. t. 26 (v. massiliensis).—Thayer.

L.-c. × Endymion, *Sand. O. Guide*, 339.

91. **L.-c. × eximia** (C. Warneri ♀ × L. purpurata), *G.C.* 1890, i. 800; *O.R.* 1893, 292; *Lind.* ix. t. 386.—Veitch, 1890.

L.-c. × parisiensis, *G.C.* 1895, ii. 467; *J. S. H. Fr.* 1897, 335.—(Bleu) Statter.

L.-c. × Valvassorii, *G.C.* 1894, i. 762; *O.R.* 1894, 221.—Linden.

92. **L.-c. × exoniensis** (C. Mossiæ × L. crispa), *J. L. Soc.* xxiv. 169; *G.C.* 1903, i. 419; *O.R.* 1903, 213; *Amer. Flor.* 1903, 527, f.—Veitch, 1863.

C. × exoniensis, *Proc. R. H. S.* 1863, 368; 1864, 177; *Fl. M.* 1866, t. 269; *G.C.* 1863, 870; 1867, 1144; *Warn. Sel. O.* ii. t. 36; *Jenn. O.* t. 1; *O.R.* 1893, 5.

L. × exoniensis, *Warn. Sel. O.* ii. sub. t. 36; *G.C.* 1887, ii. 716; *V. Man. O.* ii. 95; *O.A.* x. t. 443; *Amer. G.* 1901, 861, f. 176.

There was much uncertainty as to the parentage of this hybrid, but the supposed cross has since been repeated, and set the matter at rest.

93. **L.-c. × Fascinator** (C. Schrœderæ ♀ × L. purpurata), *G.C.* 1898, i. 302; *O.R.* 1898, 184; *Gard.* 1903, i. 396, f. (v. splendens).—Ingram, 1898.

L.-c. × Isabella (L. purpurata ♀), *G.C.* 1899, ii. 82; *O.R.* 1899, 240.—(Maron) Leemann, 1899.

94. **L.-c. × fausta** (C. Loddigesii ♀ × L.-c. × exoniensis), *G.C.* 1889, i. 619; ii. 155.—Veitch, 1873.

C. × fausta, *G.C.* 1873, 289, 290, f. 57 A (type), 57 B (v. radicans); *Fl. M.* 1875, t. 189; *O.R.* 1893, 37.

95. **L.-c. × felix** (C. Schilleriana × L. crispa ♀), *J. L. Soc.* xxiv. 169.—Veitch, 1876.

Cattleya × felix, *G.C.* 1876, ii. 68; *O.R.* 1893, 35.

Lælia × felix, *V. Man. O.* ii. 96.

Catlælia × felix, *Hans. O. Hyb.* 96 (excl. syn.).

L.-c. × crispo-Schilleriana, *J. S. H. Fr.* 1898, 961; *Chron. O.* 168.—Mantin.

96. **L.-c. × Fortuna** (C. Mossiæ ♀ × L.-c. × Schilleriana), *G.C.* 1895, ii. 467; *O.R.* 1895, 351.—Veitch, 1895.

L.-c. × Daphne, *G.C.* 1897, ii. 352; *O.R.* 1897, 375.—Veitch.

L.-c. × Harrisii, *G.C.* 1895, i. 748; *O.R.* 1895, 222.—Miss Harris.

There is a slight doubt about the parentage of L.-c. × Harrisii.

97. **L.-c. × Fournieræ** (C. Dowiana × L.-c. × elegans ♀).—Maron, 1898.

L.-c. × Berthe Fournier, *O.R.* 1898, 141; *G.M.* 1900, 108, 109, f. (v. splendida); *J.H.* 1905, ii. 266, 267, f. (Westonbirt var.).—Maron.

L.-c. × Alcides (C. Dowiana ♀), *O.R.* 1900, 319.—Thornton.

L.-c. × Baron C. Goffinet, *G.C.* 1903, ii. 359.—King of the Belgians.

L.-c. × aureo-elegans, *Sand. O. Guide*, 338.

98. **L.-c. × Fournieri** (C. intermedia ♀ × L. flava).—Fournier, 1896.

L.-c. × intermedio-flava, *Rev. H.* 1896, 549; *J. d. O.* vii. 290; *J. S. H. Fr.* 1897, 843; *O.R.* 1898, 141, 169; *J. H.* 1898, i. 499, f. 94 (v. Golden Queen, "Golden Gem" by error); *Dict. Ic. O.* L.-c. hyb. t. 3.

Cattleya × Mozart, *J. S. H. Fr.* 1902, 462.—Maron.

99. **L.-c. × Galatea** (C. granulosa ♀ × L. Dayana), *O.R.* 1900, 319; 1901, 317; *G.C.* 1901, ii. 50.—Charlesworth, 1900.

L.-c. × Phalaris, *Sand. O. Guide*, 340.

100. **L.-c. × Gazelle** (C. bicolor × L.-c. elegans ♀), *G.C.* 1896 ii. 535; *O.R.* 1896, 350.—Ingram, 1896.

101. L.-c. × **Gemma** (C. Schilleriana ♀ × L. xanthina), *J. S. H. Fr.* 1899, 931; *Chron. O.* 298.—Duval, 1900.

L.-c. × xanthino-Schilleriana (xanthina ♀), *J. S. H. Fr.* 1900, 256, 391.—Duval

102. L.-c. × **Ghislainæ** (C. amethystoglossa × L. harpophylla ♀), *O.R.* 1896, 39; *J. S. H. Fr.* 1896, 102.—Van Imschoot, 1896.

This is said to have been the first Læliocattleya raised in Belgium.

103. L.-c. × **Gladys** (C. Harrisoniana ♀ × L. cinnabarina), *G.C.* 1902, i. 238; *Dict. Ic. O.* L.-c. hyb. **t.** 20.—Fournier, 1901.

L.-c. × H. J. Harris, *Sand. O. Guide*, 339.

104. L.-c. × **Gottoiana** (C. Warneri ♀ × L. tenebrosa), *G.C.* 1900, ii. 346; *O.R.* 1900, 358, 372; 1901, 6; 1902, 343; *Lind.* xiv. **t.** 658.—Douglas, 1900.

This originally appeared as a natural hybrid in the collection of E. Gotto, Esq., The Logs, Hampstead Heath, in 1891. See *O.R.* 1903, 338.

105. L.-c. × **Greenwoodii** (C. × Hardyana × L.-c. × Schilleriana ♀). —Maron, 1897.

L.-c. × Stelzneriano-Hardyana, *Jard.* 1897, 310; *O.R.* 1897, 360.—Maron.

L.-c. × Henry Greenwood, *G.C.* 1898, i. 252; 1900, ii. 47, **f.** 8 (excl. name and text); *O.R.* 1898, 140, 350, 351; 1899, 316; *G.M.* 1898, 686, 687, **f.**; *J.H.* 1900, ii. 53, **f.** 12 (v. superba); *G.M.* 1904, 524, 525 (v. Imperator).

L.-c. × Duc de Massa, *J.S.H.Fr.* 1900. 419.—Maron.

L.-c. × Madame Martin Cahuzac, *J.S.H.Fr.* 1900, 350.—Maron.

L.-c. × Madame Debac, *J.S.H.Fr.* 1901, 637.—Maron.

L.-c. × Marquis de Wavrin, *G.C.* 1903, i. 267.—Peeters.

106. L.-c. × **Groganiæ** (C. Harrisoniana × L. Dayana), *O.R.* 1902, 30, 64, 316.—Grogan, 1901.

107. L.-c. × **Hamiltoni** (C. bicolor ♀ × L. Dayana), *O.R.* 1900, 348 (unnamed); 1901, 363; *G.C.* 1902, ii. 344.—Miller, 1900.

108. L.-c. × **Haroldiana** (C. × Hardyana × L. tenebrosa ♀), *G.C.* 1901, ii. 172, 297; *O.R.* 1901, 284, 317, 348; *G.M.* 1902, 832, 833, **f.** (v. superba); 1903, 741, **f.** (v. John Bradshaw); *Gard.* 1904, i. 25, **f.** (id.).—(Charlesworth) Tunstill, 1901.

109. L.-c. × **Hebe** (C. Mossiæ ♀ × L. grandis), *G.C.* 1902, i. 313; *O.R.* 1903, 179; *Sand. O. Guide*, 339.—Wigan, 1902.

The parentage was not originally recorded, and has been added from Messrs. Sander's work, which we suppose refers to the same hybrid. We have not seen it.

110. L.-c. × **Helena** (C. Schilleriana × L. cinnabarina ♀), *G.C.* 1901, ii. 360; 1903, i. 46; *O.R.* 1901, 366.—Charlesworth, 1901.

L.-c. × Miss Laura Webb, *G.M.* 1903, 45.—Wellesley.

The reverse cross has also been raised.

111. L.-c. × **Henri** (L. c. × callistoglossa × L.-c. × Canhamiana).—Maron, 1900.

L.-c. × Henri Maron, *J. S. H. Fr.* 1903, 604.—Maron.

112. **L.-c. × Hera** (C. Bowringiana × L.-c. × Leeana).—Maron, 1897.

C. × Bowringiano-blesensis, *J. S. H. Fr.* 1907, 954: *Jard.* 1897, 310; *O.R.* 1897, 360.

113. **L. c. × Herga** (C. Gaskelliana × L.-c. × elegans ♀), *G.C.* 1901, i. 374; *O.R.* 1901, 218.—Low, 1901.

114. **L.-c. × Hermione** (C. Lueddemanniana × L. Perrinii ♀), *Gard.* 1900, ii. 134; *G.C.* 1900, ii. 137.—Baron N. Rothschild, 1900.

115. **L.-c. × Herode** (C. × O'Brieniana ♀ × L.-c. × elegans), *G.C.* 1900, May 26, Suppl. 1; *O.R.* 1900, 176, 183; *G.M.* 1900, 348, f.; *Dict. Ic. O.* L.-c. hyb. t. 17.—Peters, 1900.

116. **L.-c × highburiensis** (C. Lawrenceana ♀ × L. cinnabarina), *G.C.* 1896, i. 468; *O.R.* 1896, 157, 187; *Dict. Ic. O.* L.-c. hyb. t. 15 (type), 15a (v. Fournieri); *Wien Ill. G. Zeit.* 1904, 201, t. 2, f. 45.—Chamberlain, 1896.

117. **L.-c. × Hilda** (C. Lawrenceana × L. Boothiana), *O.R.* 1903, 175; *J.H.* 1903, i. 397.—Chamberlain, 1902.

Cattleya × Mozart, *Gard.* 1903, i. 287.—Peeters.

118. **L.-c. × Hippolyta** (C. Mossiæ × L. cinnabarina ♀), *G.C.* 1890, i. 398, 431; *O.R.* 1893, 292; *Lind.* xiii. t. 592; *G.M.* 1898, 390, 391, f.; *Dict. Ic. O.* L.-c. hyb. t. 14.—Veitch, 1890.

Cattleya × Hippolyta, *J.S.H.Fr.* 1899, 376. –Duval.

L.-c. × Phœbe (C. Mossiæ ♀), *G.C.* 1892, i. 598, 791, f. 114; *O.R.* 1893, 357; *Reichenb.* ser. 2, ii. 107, t. 93.—Cookson.

119. **L.-c. × Hodgkinsonæ** (C. Mossiæ × L. harpophylla ♀), *O.R.* 1902, 219.—Hodgkinson, 1902.

L.-c. × Phœbe superba, *G.C.* 1902, ii. 25; *O.R.* 1902, 215, 226.

120.—**L.-c. × Homere** (C. Percivaliana × L. Perrinii ♀), *G.C.* 1896, ii. 602; *O.R.* 1896, 375. Ingram, 1896.

121. **L.-c. × Horniana** (L. purpurata ♀ × L.-c. × Schilleriana), *G.C.* 1889, ii. 155; *O.R.* 1902, 317.—Baron N. Rothschild, 1888.

Lælia × Horniana, *G.C.* 1888, i. 770; *O.R.* 1893, 228.

L.-c. × purpurato-Schilleriana, *J.S.H.Fr.* 1900, 60.—Maron.

L. × elegans Beatrice, *Boyle Woodl. O.* 13.—R. H. Measures.

122. **L.-c. × Humberti** (C. Aclandiæ × L. superbiens ♀), *J.S.H.Fr.* 1902, 337; *Rev. H.* 1902, 297.—Dallemagne., 1902.

The *Revue Horticole* records Lælia majalis as one of the parents, which appears to be a mistake.

123. **L.-c. × hybrida** (C. Warneri × L. pumila), *G.C.* 1903, ii. 209; *Rev. H. Belge*, 1903, 284. Wavrin, 1903.

The second reference speaks of this as a natural hybrid, a point which we should like to see confirmed.

124. **L. c. × Hyeana** (C. Lawrenceana × L. purpurata ♀), *O.R.* 1899, 191: 1900, 171; *Chron. O.* 34; *Dict. Ic. O.* L.-c. hyb. t. 13.—Hye, 1897.

L.-c. × Hyeana (*Rev. H. Belge*, 1895, 22, 95).

L.-c. × Myersiana, *Sand. O. Guide*, 340.

Catlælia × Hyeana, *Hans. O. Hyb.* p. 95, may be a form of L.-c. × Gottoiana or L.-c. × albanensis.

125. **L.-c.** × **Iberia** (L. cinnabarina × L.-c. × bella), *G.C.* 1902, i. 280; *O.R.* 1902, 149; *G.M.* 1902, 265 (Ibera).—Veitch, 1902.

126. **L.-c.** × **Ida** (C. Lawrenceana × L. harpophylla ♀), *O.R.* 1902, 101.—Chamberlain, 1902.

127. **L.-c.** × **Illione** (C. Bowringiana ♀ × L.-c. × Dominiana), *G.C.* 1901, ii. 401; *O.R.* 1901, 367.—Veitch, 1901.

128. **L.-c.** × **Ingrami** (C. Dowiana × L. Dayana ♀), *G.C.* 1892, ii. 191;

Fig. 34. LÆLIOCATTLEYA × INGRAMI.

O.R. 1893, 357; 1896, 49, f. 4; *J.H.* 1892, ii. 141, f. 20; 1898, ii. 108, 109, f. 20 (v. gigantea).

L.-c. × Stanleyensis, *G.C.* 1896, ii. 534.—Statter. **[See Fig. 34.**

129. **L.-c.** × **Ira** (L. longipes ♀ × L.-c. × Schilleriana), *G.C.* 1902, ii. 272 ("Iva"); *O.R.* 1902, 325, 329.—Wigan, 1902.

L.-c. × Catherinæ, *G.C.* 1903. i. 419; *O.R.* 1903, 212.—Sander.

130. **L.-c.** × **Irene** (C. Bowringiana × L. tenebrosa), *G.C.* 1903, ii. 377; *O.R.* 1903, 365.—Charlesworth, 1900.

L.-c. × (unnamed), *O.R.* 1900, 317; *G.C.* 1900, ii. 282.—Statter.

131. **L.-c. × Isis** (C. × Marstersoniæ × L. pumila ♀), *G.C.* 1895, ii. 467; *O.R.* 1895, 351.—Veitch, 1895.

132. **L.-c. × Issy** (C. Leopoldi × L. tenebrosa ♀), *O.R.* 1901, 299, 303.—Charlesworth, 1901.

133. **L.-c. × Ivernia** (L. tenebrosa × L.-c. × callistoglossa ♀), *G.C.* 1901, May 25, Suppl. 2; *O.R.* 1901, 162, 187.—Charlesworth, 1901.

L.-c. × Coustoni, *J. S. H. Fr.* 1901, 1186.—Maron.

134. **L.-c. × Jeanette** (C. labiata × L.-c. × Gottoiana), *G.C.* 1903, i. 143; *O.R.* 1903, 88.—Gratrix, 1903.

135. **L.-c. × Juno** (C. Mossiæ × L. grandiflora ♀), *G.M.* 1897, 539; *G.C.* 1897, ii. 150; *O.R.* 1897, 281.—Cookson, 1897.

136. **L.-c. × Kathleen** (L. tenebrosa × L.-c. × Canhamiana), *G.C.* 1903, ii. 104; *O.R.* 1903, 267.—Pitt, 1903.

137 **L.-c. × Krænzlinii** (C. Mossiæ ♀ × L.-c. × elegans), *O.R.* 1893, 350; *Dict. Ic. O.* L.-c. hyb. **t.** 11 (v. Clementinæ).—Sander, 1893.

Cattleya × Krænzlinii, *G.C.* 1893, ii. 470.

L.-c. × (unnamed), *J. S. H. Fr.* 1900, 513.—Gibez.

L.-c. × Ludovicii, *Bohnh. Dict. O. Hybr.* 44.—Perrenoud.

L.-c. × Thiebauxii, *J. S. H. Fr.* 1903, 591; *Rev. H.* 1903, 463.—Beranek.

L.-c. × Pommeryæ, *J. S. H. Fr.* 1903, 604; *Jard.* 1903, 208.—Beranek.

L.-c. × Mossiæ-elegans, *Wien. Ill. G.Zeit.* 1904, 445, **t.** 4.

138. **L.-c. × La-France** (C. bicolor × L. tenebrosa), *Chron. O.* 173; *G.C.* 1902, ii. 272; *O.R.* 1902, 339.—Mantin, 1898.

L.-c. × Wilmer, *Sand. O. Guide*, 340.

139. **L.-c. × La-Fresnaie** (C. Leopoldi ♀ × L.-c. × elegans), *J. S. H. Fr.* 1901, 907; *O.R.* 1901, 338; *Rev. H.* 1903, 395.—Doin, 1901.

The last record gives L.-c. × Schilleriana as the second parent, which may be correct, but this record was overlooked until Part I. was printed off.

140. **L.-c. × Leeana** (C. Loddigesii × L. pumila), *O.R.* 1901, 311.—Perrenoud, 1889.

Lælia × Leeana, *G.C.* 1882, i. 492.

Cattleya × (unnamed), *Orchidoph.* 1890, 289, **t.**; *J. S. H. Fr.* 1892, 477.—Darblay.

C. × Vedasti, *Orchidoph.* 1891, 48, **t**; *O.R.* 1893, 323.—Perrenoud.

C. × blesensis, *J. S. H. Fr.* 1892, 540; *Rev. H.* 1892, 416; 1893, 424, **t.**; *O.R.* 1893, 315.—Darblay.

L.-c. × blesensis, *O.R.* 1893, 287; *O.A.* xi. **t.** 519.

L.-c. × Vedasti, *O.R.* 1898, 290, 331.

L.-c. × corbeillana, *J. S. H. Fr.* 1898, 484.—Darblay.

L.-c. × corbeilensis, *J. S. H. Fr.* 1895, 240; *Dict. Ic. O.* L.-c. **t.** 5.

There has been some uncertainty about the parentage of L.-c. × corbeillana, but, according to M. Maron, it came out of the same seed pod as L.-c. × Vedasti. All the above are believed to be forms of L.-c. × Leeana, which originally appeared as a natural hybrid, under the name of Lælia × Leeana, Rchb. f., in 1882.

141. L.-c. × **Leoniæ** (C. labiata × L.-c. × exoniensis ♀).—Leon, 1900.

L.-c. × Fanny Leon, *G.C.* 1900, i. 62; *O.R.* 1900, 60; *Gard.* 1900, i 95, f.

142. L.-c. × **Leopoldi** (C. quadricolor × L. cinnabarina ♀).—King of Belgium, 1903.

L.-c. × Prince Leopold, *G.C.* 1903, i. 267; *O.R.* 1903, 148; *Gard.* 1903, i. 288.

143. L.-c. × **leucasta** (C. bicolor ♀ × L. harpophylla), *G.C.* 1897, ii. 438 (Loucousta); *O.R.* 1898, 31 (Loucousta), 41 (Locusta); 1901, 23; *G.M.* 1901, 775, f.

144. L.-c. × **leucoglossa** (C. Loddigesii ♀ × L.-c × fausta), *O.R.* 1894, 43.—Veitch, 1892.

Cattleya × leucoglossa, *G.C.* 1892, ii. 566; *J.H.* 1892, ii. 413, f. 56; *O.R.* 1893, 357.

145. L.-c. × **Lily** (L.-c. × callistoglossa ♀ × L.-c. × Gottoiana).—Sander, 1898.

L.-c. × Lily Measures, *O.R.* 1898, 220.

L.-c. × Miss Lily Measures, *Boyle Woodl. O.* 94.

146. L.-c. × **Liptoni** (C. labiata × L. anceps ♀), *O.R.* 1902, 29; *G.M.* 1902, 101.—(Maron, 1901) Peeters.

L.-c. × labiato-anceps, *J. S. H. Fr.* 1901, 29; *O.R.* 1901, 338.—Maron.

147. L.-c. × **Lowii** (L. cinnabarina × L.-c. × callistoglossa), *Gard.* 1903, June 27, Suppl. (unpaged).—Low, 1902.

L.-c. × (unnamed), *Gard.* 1902, ii. 50.—Low.

148. L.-c. × **Lucasiana** (C. labiata ♀ × L. tenebrosa), *J. S. H. Fr.* 1900, 54; *O.R.* 1901, 23; *G.C.* 1900, ii. 466; *Dict. Ic. O.* L.-c. t. 25.—Maron, 1900.

L.-c. × tenebroso-labiata (tenebrosa ♀), *J. S. H. Fr.* 1901, 212.—Peeters.

149. L.-c. × **Lucia** (C. Mendelii ♀ × L. cinnabarina), *O.R.* 1899, 166; 1902, 116; *G.C.* 1902, i. 183.—(Winn) Clark, 1899.

L.-c. × Lutèce, *J. S. H. Fr.* 1902, 462.—Balme.

L.-c. × Panope, *G.C.* 1903, i. 419; *O.R.* 1903, 213.—Veitch.

150. L.-c. × **Lucilia** (C. Dowiana × L.-c. × Schilleriana ♀), *G.C.* 1897, ii. 277; 1898, ii. 92; *O.R.* 1897, 348; 1898, 255.—Veitch, 1897.

The earliest record gave L.-c. × elegans as the seed parent, but this was afterwards corrected.

151. L.-c. × **Luna** (C. Harrisoniana ♀ × L. harpophylla), *G.C.* 1901, ii. 360; *O.R.* 1901, 365; 1903, 365.—Charlesworth, 1901.

152. L.-c. × **Lutetia** (C. velutina ♀ L.-c. × elegans), *G.C.* 1902, ii. 238; *O.R.* 1902, 309.—(Fournier, 1896) Beranek.

L.-c. × velutino-elegans, *J. S. H. Fr.* 1896, 725; *G.C.* 1896, ii. 360; *O.R.* 1896, 325.—Fournier.

L.-c. × New Century, *G.C.* 1901, ii. 232; *O.R.* 1901, 318.—Gratrix.

153. L.-c. × **Lycidas** (C. Schrœderæ × L. tenebrosa), *G.M.* 1902, 374.—Veitch, 1902.

L.-c. × Lycias, *G.C.* 1902, ii. 398; *O.R.* 1902, 212.

154. L.-c. × Mabel (C. Trianæ ♀ × L. tenebrosa), *G.C.* 1902, i. 398; *O.R.* 1902, 211.—Leon, 1902.

L.-c. × Fanyauana, *O.R.* 1903, 131, 146.—Peeters.

155 L.-c. × Magnei (C. granulosa × L. tenebrosa ♀), *Chron. O.* 308.—Peeters, 1900.

L.-c. × (unnamed) *G.C.* 1901, ii. 142; *O.R* 1901, 283.—Miller.

L.-c. × Donna Roma, *Sand. O. Guide*, 339.

L.-c. × Mrs. E. Rogerson, *Sand. O. Guide*, 340.

L.-c. × tene-Schofieldiana, *Sand. O. Guide*, 340.

156. L.-c. × Mardelli (C. Lueddemanniana ♀ × L.-c. × devoniensis), *G.C.* 1889, i. 746; ii. 155; *O.R.* 1896, 222.—Veitch, 1879.

Cattleya × Mardelli, *G.C.* 1879, i. 234; *Fl. Mag.* 1881, t. 437; *O.A.* vi. t. 287; *V. Man. O.* ii. 91; *O.R.* 1893, 68; *Day Orch. Draw.* xxx. t. 65.

157. L.-c. × Marguerite (C. Warscewiczii × L.-c. × Schilleriana).—Maron, 1898.

L.-c. × Clonia var. Marguerite Maron, Cogn. in *Dict. Ic. O.* L.-c. t. 12 A.—Maron.

L.-c. × Clonia var. Amy Leemann, Cogn. in *Dict. Ic. O.* L.-c. t. 12.—Maron.

L.-c. × Clonia, with which this has been confused, is a hybrid between C. Warscewiczii and L.-c. × elegans.

158. L.-c. × Marica (C. amethystoglossa × L. cinnabarina ♀), *O.R.* 1903, 58.—(Clark, 1902) R. Young.

L.-c. × (unnamed), *O.R.* 1902, 373; 1903, 93.—Clark.

L.-c. × Edmund Rothwell, *Amer. G.* 1902, 564.—Rothwell.

159. L.-c. × Maroni (C. Eldorado × L. harpophylla ♀).—Maron, 1902.

L.-c. × amoena, *J. S. H. Fr.* 1902, 747; *Rev. H.* 1902, 582.

160. L.-c. × Marriottiana (C. Skinneri × L. flava ♀), *G.C.* 1892, i. 503; *O.R.* 1893, 357.—Marriott, 1892.

161. L.-c. × Martinetii (C. Mossiæ × L. tenebrosa), *J. S. H. Fr.* 1899, 496; *Chron. O.* 238; *O.R.* 1899, 195, 253; *G.M.* 1903, 511, f.—Maron, 1899.

L.-c. × tenebrosa-Mossiæ, *J. S. H. Fr.* 1902, 400.—Page.

L.-c. × Mossiæ × grandis, *G.C.* 1902, i. 380; *Rev. H.* 1902, 261.—Dallemagne.

L.-c. × The Coronation, *J.H.* 1902, ii. 4; *G.M.* 1902, 409.—Peeters.

L.-c. × (unnamed), *J. S. H. Fr.* 1902, 463.—Dallemagne.

162. L.-c. × Massangeana (C. Schilleriana × L. tenebrosa ♀), *Chron. O* 269; *G.C.* 1900, May 26, Suppl. 1; *O.R.* 1900, 176, 182; *Dict. Ic O. L.-c.* t. 16.—Peeters, 1900.

163. L.-c. × massiliensis (C. Trianæ × L. crispa ♀), *O.R.* 1897, 358.—Fournier, 1897.

Cattleya × massiliensis, *Rev. H.* 1897, 12, t.; *O.R.* 1897, 357.

L.-c. × Josephine, *O.R.* 1899, 354.—Chamberlain.

L.-c. × Labiena, *G.C.* 1900, ii. 384; *O.R.* 1900, 373.—Veitch.

164. L. c. × **Maynardi** (C. dolosa × L. Dayana ♀), *G.C.* 1893, i. 715, 724, f. 108; *O.R.* 1893, 96, 213.—Sander, 1893.

165. L.-c. × **Measuresii** (C. maxima × L. pumila).—R. H. Measures, 1902.

L.-c. × (unnamed) *Gard.* 1902, ii. 55.

166. L.-c. × **Mercia** (C. Schroderæ × L. flava ♀), *G.C.* 1903, i. 239; *O.R.* 1903, 152.—Charlesworth, 1903.

167. L.-c. × **Meteor** (C. Bowringiana × L. Dayana ♀), *G.C.* 1896, ii. 602; *O.R.* 1896, 375.—Ingram, 1896.

168. L.-c. × **Milleræ** (C. granulosa × L. cinnabarina ♀).—Miller, 1900.

L.-c. × Lady Miller, *G.C.* 1900, April 28, Suppl. 4; May 26, Suppl. 1; *O.R.* 1900, 156, 175.

L.-c. × Rosamond Taylor, *Sand. O. Guide*, 340.

169. L.-c. × **Milleri** (C. × Brymeriana × L. tenebrosa).—Miller, 1900.

L.-c. × (unnamed), *G.C.* 1900, ii. 424; *O.R.* 1901, 21.

170. L.-c. × **Minerva** (C. Lawrenceana × L. Perrinii ♀), *G.C.* 1896, ii. 602; *O.R.* 1896, 375.—Ingram, 1896.

171. L.-c. × **mollis** (C. Mossiæ ♀ × L. Boothiana), *O.R.* 1902, 342; *Sand. O. Guide*, 340.—Sander, 1902.

172. L.-c. × **Morrisii** (Cattleya Schilleriana ♀ × L.-c. × Schilleriana).—Sander, 1900.

L.-c. × Harold Morris, *G.C.* 1900, i. 302; *O.R.* 1900, 171.

173. L.-c. × **Mylamiana** (C. granulosa ♀ × L. crispa), *J.L.S.* xxiv. 169.

Lælia × Mylamiana, *G.C.* 1876, ii. 740, 741, f. 138.

L.-c. × Sidneana, *Bohnh. Dict. O. Hyb.* 45.

L.-c. × Mandarin, *O.R.* 1902, 270, 294.—Miller.

L.-c. × Wylamiana, *G.C.* 1902, ii. 183; *O.R.* 1902, 307.—Moss.

174. L.-c. × **Myra** (C. Trianæ ♀ × L. flava), *G.C.* 1895, i. 337; 1898, i. 106; 1902, i. 219; *O.R.* 1895, 103, 127; *Dict. Ic. O.* L.-c. t. 10; *J.H.* 1904, i. 157, f. (v. Charlesworthii).—Veitch, 1895.

L.-c. × Etoile d' Or, *Jard.* 1898, 80; *J. S. H. Fr.* 1898, 173, 287; *Chron. O.* 102.—Fournier.

175. L.-c. × **Nephelia** (C. Mossiæ × L.-c. × Amesiana), *G.C.* 1900, ii. 18; *O.R.* 1900, 250.—Veitch, 1900.

176. L.-c. × **Noel** (C. granulosa × L.-c. × Schilleriana ♀), *G.C.* 1903, ii. 132.—Hardy, 1903.

177. L.-c. × **Norba** (C. Mossiæ ♀ × L. xanthina), *G.C.* 1902, ii. 63; *O.R.* 1902, 244; 1903, 339, 352; *G.M.* 1903, 725, f. (v. superba); *Gard.* 1903, ii. 321, f. (v. superba); *J.H.* 1903, ii. 437, f. (v. superba).—Veitch, 1902.

L.-c. × (unnamed), *O.R.* 1903, 214.—Tracy.

178. L.-c. × **Novelty** (L. pumila ♀ × L.-c. × elegans), *G.C.* 1889, ii. 155; 1890, ii. 354.—Veitch, 1887.

Lælia × Novelty, *G.C.* 1887, ii. 490; *O.R.* 1893, 134.

L.-c. × trentonensis (× elegans ♀) *O.R.* 1895, 15.—Roebling.

179. L.-c. × novissima (C. Gaskelliana ♀ × L. anceps), *G.C.* 1903, i. 78; *O.R.* 1903, 53.—Sander, 1903.

180. L.-c. × Nysa (C. Warscewiczii × L. crispa ♀), *G.C.* 1891, ii. 254; 1893, ii. 343; *J.H.* 1894, i. 31, f. 5; 1897, i. 118, 119, f. 28 (v. superba); 1900, ii. 329, f. 91; *O.R.* 1893, 307, 325; *Dict. Ic. O.* L.-c. t. 1.—Veitch, 1891.

181. L.-c. × ochracea (L. harpophylla ♀ × L.-c. × Sallieri) *J. S. H. Fr.*, 1900, 841; *O.R.* 1901, 53.—Maron, 1900.

L.-c. × leucasta, *O.R.* 1901, 24 (not elsewhere).

182. L.-c. × odorata (C. Eldorado ♀ × L. xanthina), *G.C.* 1897, ii. 278; *O.R.* 1897, 348.—Ingram, 1897.

183. L.-c. × olivetensis (C. Leopoldi × L. pumila ♀), *J. S. H. Fr.* 1897, 608; *Chron. O.* 44, 55, 57.—Mantin, 1897.

184. L.-c. × Ophir (C. Dowiana × L. xanthina ♀), *G.C.* 1901, ii. 330; *O.R.* 1901, 350.—Veitch, 1901.

185. L.-c. × Osyana (C. Leopoldi × L. harpophylla ♀), *Chron. O.* 198.—Peeters, 1899.

L.-c. × Oxyana, *Sand. O. Guide*, 340.

L.-c. × "Oxyana" is probably a misprint for Osyana, which is omitted from the work cited. "L. cinnabarina" there also appears to be a mistake for L. harpophylla.

186. L.-c. × Pallas (C. Dowiana × L. crispa ♀), *G.C.* 1889, ii. 701; *O.R.* 1894, 21; *Lind.* xiii. t. 608 (v. inversa); *G.W.* 1897, 553, f.; *Rev. H. Belge*, 1897, 130, 131, f. 22; *Gtfl.* 1897, 553, 557, f. 75; *Dict. Ic. O.* L.-c. t. 9.—Veitch, 1889.

187. L.-c. × Parysatis (C. Bowringiana ♀ × L. pumila), *O.R.* 1894, 310. —Veitch. 1893.

188. L.-c. × Percibarina (C. Percivaliana ♀ × L. cinnabarina), *Sand. O. Guide*, 340.—Sander, 1902 or 1903.

Messrs. Sander inform us that this has not been elsewhere recorded.

189. L.-c × Pharos (C. superba × L. tenebrosa ♀), *G.C.* 1902, ii. 105.—Holford, 1902.

190. L.-c. × Philbrickiana (C. Aclandiæ ♀ × L.-c. × elegans), *J.L.S.* xxiv. 169; *O.R.* 1893, 69; *J. S. H. Fr.* 1901, 599; *Day Orch. Draw.* xxx. t. 41; xliv. t. 5.—Veitch, 1879.

Lælia × Philbrickiana, *G.C.* 1879, ii. 102.

L.-c. × tigrina (elegans ♀) *J. S. H. Fr.* 1901, 97.—Doin.

191. L.-c. × Phryne (C. Warscewiczii ♀ × L. xanthina), *G.C.* 1899, ii. 197; *O.R.* 1899, 287.—Veitch, 1897.

192. L.-c. × Picanus (L. cinnabarina × L.-c. × Pallas), *G.C.* 1902, i. 218; *O.R.* 1902, 117.—Veitch, 1902.

193. L.-c. × Pisandra (C. Eldorado × L. crispa ♀), *G.C.* 1893, ii. 536; *J.H.* 1893, ii. 394, 407, f. 60; *O.R.* 1893, 374; 1901, 39.—Veitch, 1893.

194. L.-c. × porphyrea (C. Lueddemanniana × L. pumila ♀).— Thayer, 1903.

L.-c. × Timora var. porphyrea, *Amer. G.* 1903, 134

Formerly considered as a variety of L.-c. × Timora, which has L. Dayana for the second parent.

195. L.-c. × **Powelli** (C. Mendelii ♀ × L.-c. × Schilleriana), *G.C.* 1901, ii. 330; *O.R.* 1901, 350.—Brymer, 1901.

196. L.-c. × **Praetii** (C. dolosa × L. Boothiana), *G.C.* 1903, i, 401; *R. H. Belge*, 1903, 205. -Praet, 1903.

197. L.-c. × **princeps** (C. × Brymeriana × L.-c. × elegans ♀).—Sander, 1898.

L.-c. × Duke of York, *G.C.* 1898, i. 398; *O.R.* 1898, 217, 220.

198. L.-c. × **Pringiersi** (L. purpurata × L.-c. × elegans), *Lind.* xvi. t. 750. —Linden, 1901.

L.-c. × dellensis, *Sand. O. Guide*, 277.

199. L.-c. × **Proserpine** (C. velutina × L. Dayana ♀), *G.C.* 1890, ii. 352; *O.R.* 1893, 292; *Dict. Ic. O.* L.-c. t. 2.—Veitch, 1890.

200. L.-c. × **radiata** (C. dolosa × L. purpurata ♀), *G.C.* 1898, i. 334; 1899, ii. 58, 99; *O.R.* 1898, 189; 1399, 249, 253; *Rev. H.* 1898, 335.—(Maron) Charlesworth, 1898.

The pollen parent of this hybrid has been variously stated as C. dolosa, C. nobilior and C. Walkeriana. We have followed the original record.

201. L.-c. × **Reginæ** (C. Forbesii × L. purpurata ♀), *Chron. O.* 55; *O.R.* 1899, 310.—Mantin, 1897.

C. × Reginæ, *J. S. H. Fr.* 1897, 609.—Mantin.

L.-c. × Cypheri, *O.R.* 1897, 313.—Cypher.

L. c. × Mariæ Piæ, *Chron. O.* 173; *J. S. H. Fr.* 1898, 699.—Mantin.

202. L.-c. × **Remula** (C. Aclandiæ ♀ × L. tenebrosa), *G.C.* 1900, ii. 97; 1902, i. 50; *O.R.* 1900, 228, 253; 1902, 51.—Veitch, 1900.

203. L.-c. × **Robinii** (C. granulosa × L. xanthina ♀).—Sander, 1897.

L.-c. × Robin Measures, *G.C.* 1897, ii. 150; *O.R.* 1897, 277, 287.

204. L.-c. × **Robsonæ** (C. Bowringiana × L.-c. × Ingrami), *G.C.* 1903, ii. 411; *O.R.* 1904, 21.—Robson, 1903.

205. L.-c. × **Robsoni** (C. superba × L.-c. × elegans ♀).—Robson, 1899

L.-c. × superbo-elegans, *O.R.* 1899, 317; 1902, 172.—Robson.

L.-c. × Harold Measures, *Boyle Woodl. O.* 11.—R. H. Measures.

206. L.-c. × **Roeblingii** (C. Gaskelliana ♀ × L. purpurata), *J. R. H. S.* xxvi. 692.—Sander, 1895.

L.-c. × C. G. Roebling, *G.C.* 1895, i. 800; *O.R.* 1895, 243, 253; *G.M.* 1895, 492, 493, f.; *Amer. G.* xxi. 709, f.

L.-c. × Violetta, *G.C.* 1897, i. 115; *O.R.* 1897, 94, 117.—Veitch.

L.-c. × Boreli, *J. S. H. Fr.*, 1898, 846; *Chron. O.* 167.—Maron.

207. L.-c. × **Rosalind** (C. Trianæ ♀ × L.-c. × Dominiana), *G.C.* 1896, ii. 766; 1897, i. 2, 3, f. 1; 1902, i. 219 (v. Prince of Wales); *O.R.* 1897, 31; 1902, 117; *J.H.* 1897, i. 54, 55, f. 16; *G.M.* 1897, 20, 21, f.—Veitch, 1896.

208. L.-c. × **Rothschildiæ** (C. Warscewiczii × L. Perrinii ♀).—Veitch, 1895.

L.-c. × Lady Rothschild, *O.R.* 1895, 353; 1896, 32, 375; *G.C.* 1895, ii. 721.

209. L.-c. × rubens (C. × Hardyana ♀ × L. pumila), *G.C.* 1903, ii. 278; *Sand. O. Guide*, 340.—Sander, 1903.

210. L.-c. × Ruby (C. Lawrenceana ♀ × L.-c. × elegans). Ingram, 1897.

L.-c. × Ruby Gem, *G.C.* 1897, ii. 150; *O.R.* 1897, 287. Ingram.

L.-c. × eleganti-Lawrenceana, *O.R.* 1898, 315.—Keeling.

L.-c. × elegans-Lawrenceana, *G.C.* 1898, ii. 279.—Keeling.

211. L.-c. × Sallieri (C. Loddigesii × L. purpurata ♀), *Rev. H.* 1895, 511; *J.d.O.* vii. 290; *O.R.* 1898, 354; *Dict. Ic. O.* L.-c. t. 4.—Fournier, 1895.

Cattleya × Sallieri, *J. S. H. Fr.* 1895, 671.—Fournier.

L.-c. × weedoniensis (C. Loddigesii ♀), *O.R.* 1898, 5, 192, 354.- Thornton.

212. L.-c. × Sanderæ (C. Dormaniana × L. xanthina ♀), *G.C.* 1893, ii. 406; *O.R.* 1893, 350, 363.—Sander, 1893.

Lælia × Sanderæ, *Sand. O. Guide*, 276.

213. L.-c. × Santiago (C. intermedia × L.-c. × Hippolyta ♀), *Amer. G.* 1899, 700; *Chron. O.* 299.—Roebling, 1899.

214. L. c. × Schilleriana (C. intermedia × L. purpurata ♀), *O.R* 1898, 168, 259; 1901, 221, 222 (intermedia ♀).—Charlesworth, 1898.

L.-c. × elegans, *Rev. H.* 1898, 335.—Maron.

This was originally described as a species, under the name of Lælia Schilleriana (Rchb. f. in *Allg. Gartenz.* 1855, 322), when it appeared in the collection of Consul Schiller, of Hamburg. Its hybrid origin was afterwards recognised, and the plant was referred to Lælio-cattleya. It has been much confused with L.-c. × elegans, the natural hybrid between C. Leopoldi and L. purpurata. For its history and synonymy see *O.R.* 1893, 237, 238.

215. L.-c. × Schrœderæ (C. Trianæ ♀ × L. Jongheana).—Schröder, 1892.

L.-c. × Baroness Schröder, *G.C.* 1892, ii. 249; *O.R.* 1893, 357.

Cattleya × Baroness Schröder, *Sand. O. Guide*, 258.

216. L.-c. × Schulzeana (C. labiata × L.-c. × elegans ♀), *Lind.* xi. t. 489. —Linden, 1895.

L.-c. × Wilhelmina, *G.C.* 1903, ii. 377; *O.R.* 1903, 365.—Charlesworth.

217. L.-c. × Scottiana (C. labiata × L.-c. × Schilleriana).—(Maron) Leemann, 1899.

L.-c. × Captain Scott, *G.C.* 1899, ii. 426; *O.R.* 1899, 371.—Leemann.

L.-c. × Captain Percy Scott, *J. S. H. Fr.* 1900, 766; *G.C.* 1901, i. 171: *O.R.* 1901, 119.—Maron.

218. L.-c. × Scylla (C. Warscewiczii × L.-c. Sallieri ♀).—Maron, 1902.

L.c. × Salliero-gigas, *J. S. H Fr.* 1902, 693, 777; *Rev. H.* 1902, 538.

219. L.-c. × Sedeni (C. superba ♀ × L. c. × devoniensis), *G.C.* 1889, ii. 155.—Veitch, 1877.

Lælia × Sedeni, *G.C.* 1877, ii. 424, 1881, ii. 281; *Day Orch. Draw.* xxxviii. t. 17.

220. L.-c. × Semiramis (C. Gaskelliana × L. Perrinii ♀), *G.C.* 1895, ii. 588; *O.R.* 1895, 376.—Veitch, 1895.

221. L.-c. × **Senarti** (L.-c. × callistoglossa × L.-c. × elegans ♀), *J. S. H. Fr.* 1901, 211; *O.R.* 1901, 338.—Maron, 1900.

222. L.-c. × **Seraph** (C. citrina × L.-c. × elegans ♀), *G.C.* 1896, ii. 195; *O.R.* 1896, 286.—Ingram, 1896.

223. L.-c. × **Speranskyæ** (C. Skinneri × L. purpurata ♀).—Leemann, 1900.

L.-c. × Marie Speransky, *O.R.* 1900, 165.

224. L.-c. × **Statteriana** (C. labiata × L. Perrinii ♀), *G.C.* 1893, ii. 630; *J.H.* 1893, ii. 462, 463, f. 67; *O.R.* 1893, 375; 1894, 21; 1902, 367 (v. superba). —Veitch, 1893.

L.-c. × Clodoald, *J. S. H. Fr.* 1900, 841.—Lesuer.

225. L.-c. × **Stella** (L. crispa ♀ × L.-c. × Schilleriana), *G.C.* 1889, ii. 222; *O.R.* 1893, 261.—Veitch, 1889.

226. L.-c. × **Stepmani** (C. Warscewiczii × L.-c. × Leeana ♀).—Peeters, 1902. Cattleya × Stepmani, *G.C.* 1902, ii. 387; *Rev. H. Belge*, 1902, 280.

227. L.-c. × **Sunray** (C. superba × L. cinnabarina ♀), *G.C.* 1900, i. 62, 1902, i. 151; *O.R.* 1900, 61; 1902, 58.—Charlesworth, 1900.

L.-c. × (unnamed), *Rev. H. Belge*, 1903, 96.—De Smet-Duvivier.

228. L.-c. × **Terentia** (C. bicolor × L. crispa), *G.C.* 1900, ii. 466; *O.R.* 1901, 22.—Veitch, 1900.

229. L.-c. × **Timora** (C. Lueddemanniana × L. Dayana ♀), *G.C.* 1889, ii. 155; *G.M.* 1894, 405, f.; *O.R.* 1894, 255.—Veitch, 1887.

Lælia × Timora, *G.C.* 1887, ii. 428.

230. L.-c. × **Tiresias** (C. Bowringiana ♀ × L.-c. × elegans), *O.R.* 1896, 15.—Veitch, 1895.

L.-c. × Ophelia, *G.C.* 1898, ii. 342; *O.R.* 1898, 347; 1902, 94.—Leemann.

231. L.-c. × **Topaz** (C. Warneri × L. cinnabarina), *O.R.* 1902, 58.—(Charlesworth), Chamberlain, 1902.

232. L.-c. × **Tresederiana** (C. Loddigesii ♀ × L. crispa), *G.C.* 1889, ii. 155.—Heath, 1888.

Lælia × Tresederiana, *G.C.* 1888, i. 136; *O.R.* 1893, 227.

233. L.-c. × **triophthalma** (C. superba ♀ × L.-c. × exoniensis), *G.C.* 1889, i. 802; ii. 155; *O.R.* 1894, 40.—Veitch, 1883.

Cattleya × triophthalma, *G.C.* 1883, ii. 526; *O.R.* 1893, 101; *Day Orch. Draw.* xlvii. t. 83.

Lælia × triophthalma, *V. Man. O.* ii. 97.

234. L.-c. × **Truffautiana** (C. Dowiana × L. tenebrosa ♀), *O.R.* 1901, 338; *J. S. H. Fr.* 1901, 996, 1002; 1902, 228; *Jard.* 1902, 103; *Dict. Ic. O.* L.-c. t. 23, 23a (v. Fournieri).—Maron, 1901. [**See Fig. 35.**

L.-c. × luminosa, *G.C.* 1901, ii. 360; 1902, i. 85; *O.R.* 1901, 366; 1902, 53, 152, 153, f. 18; *G.M.* 1904, 405, 408, f. (v. The Mikado).—Charlesworth.

L.-c. × (unnamed), *J. S. H. Fr.* 1896, 929.—Treyeran.

235. L.-c. × **Tydea** (C. Trianæ × L. pumila ♀), *G.C.* 1894, i. 210; *O.R.* 1894, 95; 1902, 94; *J.H.* 1894, i. 181, f. 30.—Veitch, 1894.

236. L.-c. × Tyro (C. Gaskelliana × L.-c. × Proserpine), *G.C.* 1902, ii. 272; *O.R.* 1902, 339.—Veitch, 1902.

237. L.-c. × Veitchiana (C. labiata ♀ × L. crispa) *J.L.S.* xxiv. 169; *Jard.* 1903, 48.—Veitch, 1874.

Lælia × Veitchiana, *G.C.* 1874, i. 566; 1876, i. 567; 1883, ii. 142, 144, **Suppl. f.**; *Fl. M.* 1878, t. 305.

Cattleya × Veitchiana, *G.C.* 1874, i. 385.

Lælia × caloglossa, *G.C.* 1877, i. 202; *O.R.* 1893, 35; *Bohnh. Dict. O. Hyb.* 41.—Veitch.

L.-c. × caloglossa, *G.C.* 1889, ii. 79.

Fig. 35. LÆLIOCATTLEYA × TRUFFAUTIANA.

L.-c. × Veitchii, *Rev. H.* 1903, 70; *J. S. H. Fr.* 1903, 45.—Ragot.

Lælia × caloglossa is a mysterious plant. Reichenbach thought the parents were Cattleya labiata and either Lælia crispa or L. Boothiana. Bohnhof gives L. crispa and L. Perrinii, which would make it a form of L. × Pilcheri, but this seems erroneous. The plant has been lost sight of.

238. L.-c. × Venus (C. Percivaliana × L.-c. × elegans ♀), *G.C.* 1897, i. 51; *O.R.* 1897, 62.—Ingram, 1897.

239. L.-c. × Vesta (C. superba × L.-c. × Doris ♀), *G.C.* 1902, i. 5.—Veitch, 1902.

240. L.-c. × Victoria (L. crispa ♀ × L.-c. × Dominiana), *G.C.* 1889, ii. 156. Veitch, 1888.

Lælia × Victoria, *G.C.* 1888, ii. 578; *Gard. and For.* 1888, 495.

241. L.-c. × Vinesiæ (L. tenebrosa ♀ × L.-c. × Hippolyta), *O.R.* 1901, 197; *G.C.* 1902, ii. 25.—(Charlesworth) Clark, 1901.

L.-c. × Eclipse, *Sand. O. Guide*, 339.

242. L.-c. × warnhamensis (C. Trianæ × L. cinnabarina ♀), *G.C.* 1898, i. 15; *O.R.* 1898, 124; 1899, 66; *J. S. H. Fr.* 1900, 113, 180 (v. Cappei).—Lucas, 1898.

Fig. 36. LÆLIOCATTLEYA × WIGANIÆ.

L.-c. × Onyx, *J. S. H. Fr.* 1901, 454, 635; *Rev. H.* 1903, 213.—Fanyau.

L.-c. × General French, *Sand. O. Guide*, 339.

243. L.-c. × Wavrinii (C. superba × L. pumila).—Wavrin, 1903.

L.-c. × (unnamed), *O.R.* 1903, 149.

244. L.-c. × Wellsiana (C. Trianæ ♀ × L. purpurata), *G.C.* 1894, i. 762; *O.R.* 1894, 224; 1903, 82; *J.H.* 1898, i. 459, f. 86 (v. langleyensis); *J. S. H. Fr.* 1903, 194; *G. World*, 1903, 183, f. (v. magnifica).—Sander, 1894.

L.-c. × (unnamed), *J. S. H. Fr.* 1902, 462.—Duval.

L.-c. × Cythera, *Sand. O. Guide*, 339.

245. L.-c. × **Whitiniæ** (C. Harrisoniana × L. purpurata ♀).—Whitin. 1899.

L.-c. × Sallieri, *Amer. G.* 1899, 700. Whitin.

L.-c. × Catherine L. Whitin, *Amer. G.* 1899, 700 (in note). Whitin.

L.-c. × Ancona (Harrisoniana ♀), *Boyle Woodl. O.* 88. R. H. Measures.

This hybrid was classed as a form of L.-c. × Sallieri, but if C. Harrisoniana was one parent, as recorded, it should be considered as distinct.

Fig. 37. LÆLIOCATTLEYA × WILSONÆ.

246. L.-c. × **Wiganiæ** (C. Mossiæ × L.-c. × Gottoiana ♀), *G.C.* 1900, ii. 18, 47, f. 8 (v. aurea); *O.R.* 1900, 214, 249; 1903, 233, f. 39.—Wigan, 1900.

L.-c. × Adrastus, *Gard.* 1903, i. 380. Keeling. [**See Fig. 36.**

247. L.-c. × **Wiganiana** (L. purpurata ♀ × L.-c. Dominiana) *G.C.* 1899, ii. 156; *O.R.* 1899, 285.—Wigan, 1899.

L.-c. × Wiganiæ, *J.H.* 1899, ii. 192, 193, f. 39.

248. L.-c. × **Wilsonæ** (C. labiata ♀ × L. Dayana), *G.C.* 1899, ii. 441; *O.R.* 1900, 28; 1901, 324, 371, f. 53.—Sander, 1899. **See Fig. 37.**

249. L.-c. × **wisetonensis** (C. Warneri × L.-c. × callistoglossa ♀), *Sand. O. Guide*, 340.—Sander, 1901 or 1902.

We only know of the above record, but Messrs. Sander write that it is one of their hybrids, which flowered in 1901 or 1902.

250 **L.-c.** × **Wrigleyi** (C. Bowringiana × L. anceps ♀), *O.R.* 1899, 359; 1900, 145, f.; 1902, 29; *G.M.* 1903, 795, f.; *Dict. Ic. O.* L.-c. t. 33.—Wrigley, 1899. [**See Fig. 38**.

L.-c. × gracilis, *G.C.* 1902, ii. 387; *Rev. H. Belge* 1902, 280.—Peeters.

251. **L.-c.** × **Zampa** (C. intermedia × L.-c. × Schilleriana ♀).—Fournier, 1903.

Fig. 38. LÆLIOCATTLEYA × WRIGLEYI.

L.-c. × (unnamed) *Rev. H.* 1903, 47; *J. S. H. Fr.* 1903, 37.

252. **L. c.** × **Zenobia** (C. Loddigesii ♀ × L.-c. × elegans), *G.C.* 1889, i. 802; ii. 156. Veitch, 1887.

Cattleya × Zenobia, *G.C.* 1887, ii. 552; *O.R.* 1893, 196.

C. × Cassandra, *G.C.* 1888, ii. 596; *O.R.* 1893, 259.—Veitch.

L.-c. × Cassandra, *G.C.* 1889, i. 491; ii. 78.

L.-c. × Ino, *Sand. O Guide*, 278.

L.-c. × Pytho, *G.C.* 1896, i. 740; *O.R.* 1896, 221; *J. H.* 1896, i. 535, 579, 588, f. 102.—Ingram.

253. L.-c. × Zephyra (C. Mendelii ♀ × L. xanthina), *G.C.* 1894, ii. 103; *O.R.* 1894, 285.—Veitch, 1894.

20. LEPTOLÆLIA.

A genus established to contain the following hybrid between Leptotes and Lælia.

1. Leptolælia × Veitchii (Lælia cinnabarina × Leptotes bicolor ♀), *G.C.* 1902, i. 280; 1903, i. 50, **ff.** 23, 24; *O.R.* 1902, 149, 157.—Veitch, 1902.

21. LYCASTE.

1. L. × Balliæ (macrophylla × Skinneri), *O.R.* 1898, 371; 1903, 80, **f.** 19; *G.M.* 1903, 356, f.—Ball, 1896.

L. × schœnbrunnensis, *O.R.* 1896, 40 (not earlier).—Ball.

L. × Charlesworthii, *G.C*, 1902, i. 135; *O.R.* 1902, 94, 118.—Charlesworth.

L. × Cappei, *J. S. H. Fr.* 1900, 58; 1901, 371; 1902, 139.—Cappe.

L. × (unnamed), *O.R.* 1900, 95.—Cappe.

L. × Mary Gratrix, *G.C.* 1898, i. 255; *O.R.* 1898, 153; 1903, 81.—Gratrix.

2. L. × Groganii (aromatica × Deppei), *O.R.* 1904, 158.—Grogan, 1902.

3. L. × hybrida (Deppei × Skinneri), *V. Man. O.* ix. 97; *O.R.* 1893, 197; 1901, 100.—Marshall, 1878.

L. × (unnamed) *G.C.* 1878. ii. 535.—Marshall.

L. × Mantini (Deppei ♀), *J. S. H. Fr.* 1897, 242.—Mantin.

Lycaste Deppei punctatissima, *G.C.* 1881, ii. 717; *O.A.* vi. **t.** 262, is believed to be a natural hybrid with the same origin.

4. L. × Imschootiana (cruenta × Skinneri ♀), *G.C.* 1893, ii. 756, 775, f. 119; *J.H.* 1893, ii. 549, **f.** 79; *G.M.* 1894, 151, **f.**; *O.R.* 1894, 8, 30; 1896, 78.—Van Imschoot, 1893.

Originally recorded as possibly a natural hybrid from Peru, and then as derived from Lycaste Skinneri × Maxillaria nigrescens, both of which are certainly erroneous.—See *O.R.* 1898, 78.

5. L. × Janetæ (Rossiana × Skinneri ♀), *O.R.* 1899, 360; 1901, 95; 1903, 63.—Ross, 1899.

6. L. × schœnbrunnensis (Schilleriana × Skinneri), *O.R.* 1893, 51.—Emperor of Austria, 1893.

22. MACOMARIA.

A genus established to contain the following hybrid between Macodes and Hæmaria.

1. **Macomaria × Veitchii** (Hæmaria discolor ♀ × Macodes Petola), *J. L. Soc.* xxiv. 170.—Veitch, 1862.

Goodyera × Veitchii, *Proc. R. H. S.*, ii. 546; v. 139; *G.C.* 1865, 462; *O.R.* 1893, 4.

23. MASDEVALLIA.

1. **M. × Acis** (abbreviata × Veitchiana), *O.R.* 1896, 82.—Hincks, 1896.

2. **M. × Ajax** (Chelsoni ♀ × peristeria), *G.C.* 1896, ii. 137; *O.R.* 1896, 228, 256.—Veitch, 1896.

3. **M. × Alceste** (Asmodia ♀ × Veitchiana), *G.C.* 1901, i. 242; *O.R.* 1901, 154.—Veitch, 1901.

4. **M. × Amesiana** (tovarensis × Veitchiana ♀), *G.C.* 1890, ii. 197; *O.R.* 1893, 293; *Dict. Ic. O.* Masd. hyb. t. 2 (v. McVittiæ).—Sander, 1890.

5. **M. × Asmodia** (× Chelsoni ♀ × Reichenbachiana), *G.C* 1894, i. 762; *O.R.* 1894, 202, 224.—Veitch, 1894.

6. **M. × bockingensis** (cucullata × Veitchiana).—(Courtauld) Lawrence, 1900.

M. × Bocking Hybrid, *G.C.* 1900, ii. 346; *O.R.* 1900, 370.

7. **M. × Cassiope** (coccinea × triangularis ♀), *G.C.* 1892, i. 749; *O.R.* 1893, 356.—Hincks, 1892.

By some mistake the original description is credited to "J. O'Brien." It should have been "R. A. Rolfe."

8. **M. × Chelsoni** (amabilis ♀ × Veitchiana), *G.C.* 1880, i. 554; 1889, i. 619 (var. splendens); *O.R.* 1893, 69.—Veitch, 1880.

The variety splendens was raised from the reverse cross.

9. **M. × Circe** (Schrœderiana × Veitchiana ♀), *G.C.* 1898, ii. 168; *O.R.* 1898, 287.—Veitch, 1898.

10. **M. × Courtauldiana** (caudata × rosea), *G.C.* 1889, i. 200; *O.R.* 1893, 261; *Reichenb.* ser. 2, ii. 63, t. 76, f. 1; *Dict. Ic. O.* Masd. hyb. t. 1.—Cookson, 1889.

11. **M. × Curlei** (Macrura ♀ × tovarensis), *G.C.* 1896, i. 40; *O.R.* 1896, 83.—Curle, 1896.

12. **M. × Doris** (racemosa × triangularis ♀), *O.R.* 1894, 22.—Hincks, 1894.

13. **M. × Eric** (Chimæra × tovarensis).—Veitch, 1902.

M. × Circe, *G.C.* 1902, i. 251; *O.R.* 1902, 147.

The first hybrid from M. Chimæra, which unfortunately received a name already in use. Mr. Seden informs us that the record is quite correct, hence we have re-named the plant as above, using an anagram of the original name

14. **M. × falcata** (coccinea ♀ × Veitchiana), *G.C.* 1899, i. 109: *O.R.*, 1899, 93.—Lawrence, 1899.

15. **M. × Fraseri** (coccinea × ignea ♀), *G.C.* 1882, i. 143; *O.R.* 1893, 100. Fraser, 1882.

M. × Ellisiana (coccinea ♀), *G.C.* 1889. ii. 154; *O.R.* 1893, 262.—Veitch, 1889.

M. × Parksii, *Sand. O. Guide*, 280.

M. × Weathersiana, *Sand. O. Guide*, 280.

16. **M.** × **Gairiana** (Davisii × Veitchiana ♀), *G.C.* 1884, ii. 38; *O.R.* 1893, 101.—Veitch, 1884.

17. **M.** × **Geleniana** (caudata ♀ × xanthina), *G.C.* 1887, ii. 586; *O.R* 1893, 133, 186; *J.H.* 1893, ii. 119, f. 18; 1899, i. 293, f. 70; *Reichenb.* ser. 2, ii. 63, t. 76, f. 2.—Sander, 1887.

18. **M.** × **glaphyrantha** (Barlæana × infracta ♀), *G.C.* 1886, ii. 648; *O.R.* 1893, 132.—Veitch, 1886.

19. **M.** × **Heathii** (ignea × Veitchiana) *G.C.* 1889, i. 342; *Hans. O. Hyb.* 210.—Heath, 1889.

M. × Mundyana, *G.C.* 1891, i. 682, 683; *O.R.* 1893, 324.—Sander.

20. **M.** × **Hebe** (coriacea ♀ × Veitchiana), *O.R.* 1899, 101.—Hincks, 1899.

M. × ferrieriensis (Veitchiana ♀), *G.C.* 1902, ii. 112.—Lawrence.

21. **M.** × **Henrietta** (caudata × ignea ♀), *G.C.* 1893, i. 740; *O.R.* 1893, 246; 1894, 203; *Lind.* xii. t. 557.—Ames, 1893.

22. **M.** × **Hincksiæ** (caudata ♀ × Gairiana), *O.R.* 1903, 7.—Hincks, 1902.

23. **M.** × **Hincksiana** (ignea × tovarensis ♀), *G.C.* 1887, ii. 214; *O.R.*, 1893, 78, 133.—Hincks, 1887.

24. **M.** × **Imogen** (Schlimii ♀ × Veitchiana), *G.C.* 1898, ii. 56; *O.R.* 1898, 255.—Veitch, 1898.

25. **M.** × **Kimballiana** (caudata × Veitchiana ♀), *O.R.* 1893, 61.—Sander, 1893.

M. × Pourbaixii, *Lind.* ix. t. 387.—Pourbaix.

26. **M.** × **langleyensis** (Estradæ ♀ × Veitchiana).—Hincks, 1893.

M. × Veitchiano-Estradæ, *G.C.* 1893, i. 724; *O.R.* 1893, 193, 211.

27. **M.** × **Lawrencei** (Veitchiana × xanthina).—Lawrence, 1902.

M. × xanthino-Veitchiana, *G.C.* 1902, i. 183; *O.R.* 1902, 114.

28. **M.** × **Leda** (Arminii × Estradæ ♀), *O.R.* 1895, 203.—Hincks, 1895.

29. **M.** × **McVittiæ** (coccinea × tovarensis ♀), *G.C.* 1892, ii. 744; *O.R.* 1893, 22, 356; *Thompson Sale Cat.* t. 5.—Thompson, 1892.

M. Veitchiana was first recorded as the pollen parent of this hybrid, which would make it a form of M. × Amesiana, but it was afterwards said to agree better with M. coccinea.

30. **M.** × **Measuresiana** (amabilis × tovarensis ♀), *G.C.* 1890, ii. 379; *O.R.* 1893, 293; *Reichenb.* ser. 2, ii. 63, t. 76, f. 3; *Dict. Ic. O.* Masd. hyb. t. 3.—Sander, 1890.

31. **M.** × **Pluto** (coccinea × Gairiana ♀), *O.R.* 1899, 240.—Hincks, 1899.

32. **M.** × **Rebecca** (amabilis × ignea ♀), *G.C.* 1893, i. 740; *O.R.* 1893, 245.—Ames, 1893.

33. **M.** × **Rushtoni** (ignea ♀ × racemosa), *O.R.* 1893, 210.—Hincks, 1893.

34. M. × Sanderi (Veitchiana ♀ × Wageneriana).—Sander, 1898.

M. × (unnamed), *O.R.* 1898, 296; 1900, 251, 255.—Sander.

M. × Veitchiano-Wageneri, *G.C.* 1903, i. 239; *O.R.* 1903, 151.—Lawrence.

35. M. × Sedenii (caudata × Estradæ ♀).—Veitch, 1889.

M. × caudato-Estradæ, *G.C.* 1889, i. 714; *O.R.* 1893, 261.—Veitch.

M. × Estradæ-Shuttleworthii, *Sand. O. Guide*, 279.

36. M. × Shuttryana (caudata ♀ × coccinea), *G.C.* 1892, i. 764; 1896, i. 210, 262, 263, f. 36 (Chamberlain's var.); *O.R.* 1893, 356; 1896, 83 (v. Chamberlainii); *G.M.* 1895, 341, f.—Lawrence, 1892.

M. × Chamberlainiana (coccinea ♀), *O.R.* 1896, 133.—Chamberlain.

37. M. × splendida (Barlæana × Veitchiana ♀), *G.C.* 1878, i. 493; *V. Man. O.* v. 73.—Veitch, 1888.

Fig. 39. Miltonia × Bleuana var. Stevensii.

M. × Parlatoreana, *G.C.* 1879, i. 172; 1889, i. 680; *O.R.* 1893, 261.—Veitch.

M. × splendida and M. × Parlatoreana were both described by Reichenbach as natural hybrids, but they are forms of one, since raised by Messrs. Veitch.

38. M. × Stella (coccinea × Estradæ ♀), *G.C.* 1890, ii. 325; *O.R.* 1893, 293.—Hincks, 1890.

39 M. × Whitei (Estradæ ♀ × ignea).—Lawrence, 1902.

M. × igneo-Estradæ, *O.R.* 1902, 171; 1904, 117.

40. M. × Winniæ (Davisii × tovarensis ♀).—Winn, 1894.

M. × Jessie Winn, *O.R.* 1894, 365.

24. MILTONIA.

1. **M.** × **Bleuana** (Roezlii × vexillaria ♀), *J. S. H. Fr.* 1889, 29, 30; *Orchidoph*, 1889, 45; *G.C.* 1889, i. 203: *Lind.* iv. **t.** 176; *Reichenb.* ser. **2**, i. 67, **t.** 32; *O.A.* ix. **t.** 412 (v. splendens); *V. Man. O.* viii. 118, 119. **f.**; *O.R.* 1893, 260; 1894, 355, **Frontispiece**: 1905, 313, **f.** 67 (v. Stevensii); *G.M.* 1894, 637, **f.** (v. rosea); *Dict. Ic. O.* Milt. hyb. **t.** 1., 1 A. (v. nobilior). Bleu, 1889. [**See Fig. 39.**

Fig. 40. Odontoglossum × Armainvilliérense var. ardentissimum.

Odontoglossum × Bleuanum, *J. S. H. Fr.* 1889, 29, 30, 36.
Miltoniopsis × Bleui, *Orchidoph.* 1889, 145, **t.** (v. aurea and splendens).
Miltoniopsis × (unnamed), *J. S. H. Fr.* 1890, 196.

25. ODONTOGLOSSUM.

1. **O.** × **amœnum** (nobile × sceptrum), *O.R.* 1903, 183; 1905, 82.—(De Smet Duvivier) Hye, 1903.

O. × (unnamed), *G.C.* 1903, i. 267.—De Smet Duvivier.

2. **O. × armainvillierense** (crispum × nobile ♀), *J.S.H. Fr.* 1898, 1240; *O.R.* 1902, 209, f. 22 (v. ardentissimum), 210 (type), 240; 1903, 188; 1904, 14, f. 6 (v. ardentissimum); 1906, 240, 241, f. 28 (v. Apollo), f. 29 (v. eximium) *Dict. Ic. O. Od. hyb.* t. 12 (v. ardentissimum).—Baron E. Rothschild, 1898. [**See Fig. 40.**

O. × ardentissimum, *O.R.* 1902, 175; *G.C.* 1902, ii. 50, f. 19; *G.M.* 1903, 374, f. (v. exquisitum); 1906, 366, 368, f. (v. Venus); *G. Alb.* 1906, 27, f. (v. Theodora).—Vuylsteke.

O. crispum v. ardentissimum, *G.C.* 1902, i. May 31, Suppl. 2; *Gard.* 1902, ii. 44. f: *G.M.* 1902, 349, f: *J.H.* 1902, i. 507, f.

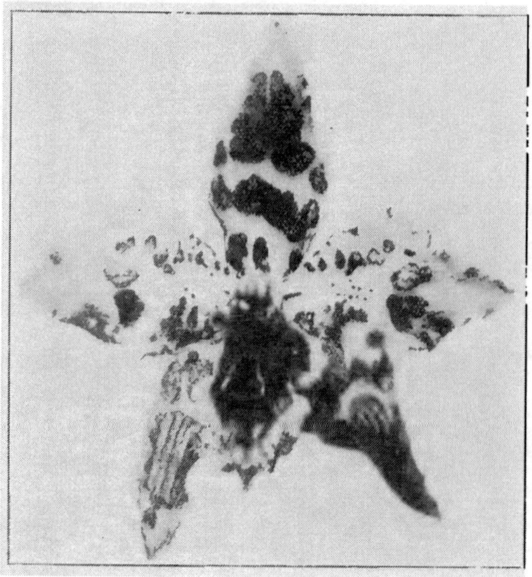

Fig. 41. ODONTOGLOSSUM × BELLATULUM.

O. × concinnum, *O.R.* 1902, 175.—Vuylsteke.

O. crispum v. concinnum, *G.C.* 1902, i. May 31, Suppl. 2.

O. × dulce, *O.R.* 1902, 175.—Vuylsteke.

O. crispum v. dulce, *G.C.* 1902, i. May 31, Suppl. 2.

O. × venificum, *O.R.* 1902, 175.—Vuylsteke.

O. crispum v. venificum, *G.C.* 1902, i. May 31, Suppl. 2.

O. × Rochfordianum, *Sand. O. Guide*, 341.

The original O. × armainvillierense appears to have been lost sight of, and its parentage has been doubted, but the details were fully recorded when the plant originally appeared, and received a First-class Certificate from the Société Nationale de Horticulture de France. All the others were out of a single capsule.

3. O. × **beardwoodiense** (elegans × nobile ♀), *G.C.* 1903, i. 206: *O.R.* 1903, 118, 121.—Rutherford, 1903.

4. O. × **bellatulum** (crispum × tripudians), *O.R.* 1902, 99: 1903, 183; 1904, 80, f. 19.—Vuylsteke, 1902. **See Fig. 41.**

Originally described as a hybrid between O. Pescatorei and O. sceptrum, but a year later from O. crispum and O. tripudians, which latter agrees best with the characters of the hybrid.

5. O. × **Bradshawiae** (× Andersonianum × Harryanum), *G.C.* 1903, i. 78, 82, f. 35: *J.H.* 1903, i. 113, f.: *G.M.* 1903, 86, 87, f.; *O.R.* 1903, 52, 58; *Gard.* 1903, i. 184, f.—Bradshaw, 1903.

6. O. × **Charlesworthii** (Harryanum × triumphans).—Charlesworth, 1902.

O. × Harryano-triumphans, *G.C* 1902, i. 442; 1903, i. 108, 223; *O.R.* 1902, 214; 1903, 82, 154.—Charlesworth.

O. × Queen Alexandra, *O.R.* 1902, 173, 195; 1903, 179, 182; *G.M.* 1902, 473, f.—Rutherford.

O. × Harryano-excellens, *G.M.* 1902, 328.—Rutherford.

The two latter were at first recorded as hybrids of O. × excellens, which is now believed to be erroneous.

7. O. × **Cooksoni** (crispum × Hallii ♀), *O.R.* 1899, 240, 253; 1900, 314, 318.—Cookson, 1896.

O. × crispo Hallii, *G.C.* 1896, ii. 66; 1899, i. 349: *O.R.* 1897, 10, 28.—Cookson.

O. × Hallio-crispum, *G.M.* 1896, 808; 1897, 138, f.: *O.R.* 1900. 253; 1902. 339; 1903, 235.—Cookson.

O. × Dickensianum, *J. S. H. Fr.* 1902, 253.—Dallemagne.

8. O. × Crawshayanum (Hallii ♀ × Harryanum), *G.C.* 1901, ii. 60, 77, f. 27; *O.R.* 1903, 218.—Crawshay, 1901.

O. × Braeckmani v Crawshayanum, *O.R.* 1901, 232.

O. × Braeckmanii, at first supposed to have the above parentage, proves to be a form of O. × spectabile (see *O.R.* 1903, 218).

9. O. × **Denisonæ** (crispum ♀ × luteopurpureum), *O.R.* 1897, 10 (in note); 1903, 188; *J. R. H. S.* xxiv. 190, f. 94. —Baron E. Rothschild, 1890.

O. × Wilckeanum, *Reichenb.* ser. 2, i. 47, 77, t. 37 (v. Leroyanum); *J. S. H. Fr.* 1900, 390; 1902, 797; *O.R.* 1903, 182; *Gard.* 1903, i. 397, f. (v. venerandum).—Baron E. Rothschild.

O. × Leroyanum, *G.C.* 1890, i. 704: *Orchidoph.* 1891, 112, t.; *O.R.* 1893, 204, 205.—Baron E. Rothschild.

O. × Jacobeanum, *J. S. H. Fr.* 1893, 452.—Baron E. Rothschild.

O. × luteopurpureo-crispum, *O.R.* 1893, 201.—Baron E. Rothschild.

O. × hystrix-crispum, *J. S. H. Fr.* 1900, 180; 1901, 371.—Baron E. Rothschild.

O. × Denisonæ originally appeared in the collection of Lord Londesborough, in 1872 (*Fl. Mag.* 1872, t. 26), and was thought to be a natural hybrid between O.

crispum and O. luteopurpureum. O. × Wilckeanum was described by Reichenbach, in 1880, as a natural hybrid with the same parentage (*G.C.* 1880, i. 298), which had appeared in the collection of M. Massange de Louvrex, of Baillonville, near Marche, Belgium. It is now known to be common, remarkably variable, and to have numerous other synonyms (see *O.R.* 1893, 201-206).

10. **O × elegans** (cirrhosum ♀ × Hallii), *J. R. H. S.* xxiv. 193, f. 97; *Dict. Ic. O.* Od. hyb. t. 5.—Linden, 1897.

O. × cirrhoso-Hallii, *O.R.* 1895, 326.—Linden.

O. × cirrho-Hallii, *Sem. H.* 1897, 109: *Lind.* xii. t. 569.—Linden.

O. × Marriottianum, Rchb. f. (*G.C.* 1881, i. 168), may possibly be an earlier name for this hybrid, but it is known only from description. There is an earlier O. × elegans, Rchb. f. (*G.C.* 1879, i. 462), which, however, is supposed to be a form of O. × hinnus, Rchb. f., and a natural hybrid between O. cirrhosum and O. cristatum. The present hybrid appeared in the collection of H. M. Pollett, Esq., Fernside, Bickley, in 1883, and was described by Reichenbach as O. × elegans, Mr. Pollett's var. (*G.C.* 1883, i. 720, 721, f. 118; *O.A.* iii. t. 111). Its history is detailed in *O.R.* 1895, 326-327.

11. **O. × excellens** (nobile (Pescatorei) ♀ × triumphans), *G.C.* 1891, i. 754; 1893, i. 396; *Reichenb.* ser. 2, i. 41, t. 19; *J. S. H. Fr.* 1893, 478; *J. R. H. S.* xxiv. 190; *O.R.* 1894, 200; 1897, 111; 1903, 42—Veitch, 1891.

O. × Tresederianum, *O.R.* 1893, 158.—Heath.

O. × nobili-triumphans, *O.R.* 1894, 200, 201.—Veitch.

Originally described by Reichenbach as probably a natural hybrid between O. Pescatorei and O. tripudians, but the second parent afterwards amended to O. triumphans, from which parents the hybrid was afterwards raised artificially by Messrs. Veitch.

12. **O. × harvengtense** (crispum × triumphans), *O.R.* 1904, 198; *Dict. Ic. O.* Od. hyb. t. 4.—Vuylsteke, 1898.

O. × loochristiense (crispum ♀), *O.R.* 1898, 41, 107; 1899, 355; 1900, 95; 1903, 250; 1904, 61.—Vuylsteke.

O. × nobilius, *Sand. O. Guide*, 341.

O. × harvengtense was originally described in 1894 as a [natural] hybrid between O. crispum and O. sceptrum (L. Lind. in *J. d. O.* v. p. 7), and also figured (*Lind.* x. t. 478), but the hybrid afterwards raised by M. Ch. Vuylsteke from O. crispum and O. triumphans, and called O. × loochristiense, which ultimately appeared also as a wild plant, has since proved identical.

13. **O. × Hyeanum** (Harryanum ♀ × luteopurpureum),—Hye, 1900.

O. × Souvenir de Victor Hye Lebrun, *G.C.* 1900, i. May 26, Suppl. 1; *O.R.* 1900, 174.

14. **O. × Juno** (cirrhosum × sceptrum), *G.C.* 1903, ii. 214; *O.R.* 1903, 308.—Thompson, 1903.

15. **O. × mirificum** (crispum × sceptrum), *O.R.* 1903, 183; 1904, 81, f. 20 (merificum); 1905, 52.—Vuylsteke, 1902. **[See Fig. 42.**

O. × (unnamed), *O.R.* 1902, 170 (the second hybrid mentioned).

16. O. × mirum (crispum ♀ × Denisonæ), Crawshay, 1900.

O. × (unnamed), *G.C.* 1903, ii. 253; *O.R.* 1903, 326.

Mr. Crawshay's first hybrid Odontoglossum, and remarkable for its close resemblance to O. crispum, though this peculiarity is not likely to extend to all hybrids derived from the same parentage.

17. O. × Rolfeæ (Harryanum × nobile ♀), *O.R.* 1898, 270; 1899, 4, 163; 1900, 216; 1902, 57, **f.** 6; 1904, 253; *G.C.* 1900, i. 410, 415, **f.** 136 (Walton Grange v.); ii. 451, **f.** 116 (v. meleagris): *G.M.* 1900, 818, **f.** (id.); *J.H.* 1900, i. 475, **f.** 127 (v. optimum), 547, **f.** 147 (Walton Grange v.); ii. 527, **f.** 134 (v. meleagris); *Gard.* 1900, ii. 55, **f.** (Walton Grange v.); *Dict. Ic. O.* Od. hyb. **t.** 7.—Vuylsteke, 1898. **[See Fig. 43.**

Fig. 42. ODONTOGLOSSUM × MIRIFICUM.

A variable and very beautiful hybrid.

18. O. × spectabile (crispum ♀ × Harryanum), *Jard.* 1899, 151; *O.R.* 1899, 135; 1900, 28, 47; *G.M.* 1903, 683, **f.**—Vuylsteke, 1898.

O. × crispo-Harryanum, *G.C.* 1898, i. 334; 1903, ii. 282; *O.R.* 1898, 170, 191; *J.H.* 1902, ii. 421, **f.** (v. delicatum); *Dict. Ic. O.* Od. hyb. **t.** 8 (v. amœnum), **t.** 8 A. (v. spectabile).—Vuylsteke.

O. × vivicans, *Jard.* 1899, 151.—Vuylsteke.

O. × Harryano-crispum (Harryanum ♀), *O.R.* 1898, 259 (unnamed); 1899, 250; *G.C.* 1899, ii. 17, 66, 67, **f.** 29.—Sander.

O. × Braeckmani, *Lind.* xvi. **t.** 744; *O.R.* 1901, 232; 1903, 218.—Metdepenningen.

Not to be confounded with O. × spectabile, L. Lind. (*Lind.* xi. t. 523), which is believed to be a form of O. × excellens.

19. **O. × Vuylstekei** (× Denisonæ × triumphans), *O.R.* 1902, 99, 170; 1903, 183; 1904, 54.—Vuylsteke, 1902.

First recorded as a doubtful hybrid between O. triumphans and O. tripudians, but afterwards O. × Denisonæ was suggested as the second parent, though the matter requires confirmation.

20. **O. × waltonense** (crispum ♀ × Kegeljani,, *G.C.* 1903, i. 46, 51, f. 25; *J.H.* 1903, i. 71, f.; *G.M.* 1903, 73, f.; *Gard.* 1903, i. 78, f.; *O.R.* 1903, 49, f. 14; 1904, 15, f. 7; 1905, 168, f. 27 (v rosefieldiense).—Thompson, 1902.

[See Fig. 44.

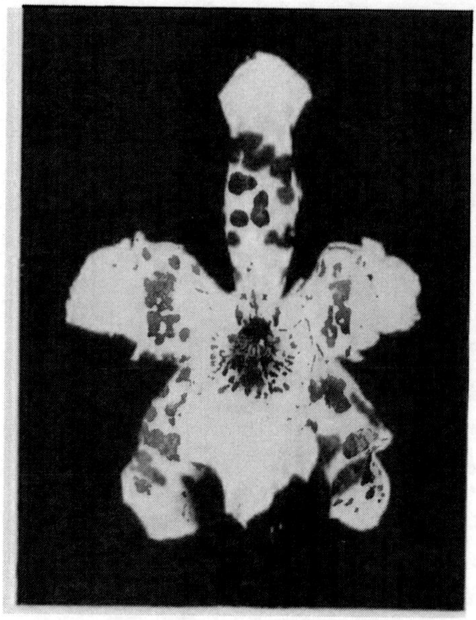

Fig. 43. ODONTOGLOSSUM × ROLFEÆ.

21. **O. × Wattianum** (Harryanum × Lindleyanum), *O.R.* 1900, 299, 314, 323; 1904, 235; *G.C.* 1900, ii. 214, 286, f. 83 (v. Crawshayanum).—Crawshay, 1900.

Originally described in 1890 as possibly a natural hybrid between O. Lindleyanum and O. luteo-purpureum (Rolfe in *G.C.* 1890, i. 354), and afterwards, in deference to the opinion of the collector, as possibly a distinct species (*Reichenb.* ser. 2, i. 19, t. 9), though intermediate in habit between O. Lindleyanum and Harryanum. Its real origin, then suspected, has since been proved by Mr. Crawshay.

26. PAPHIOPEDILUM.

1. **P. × Aasenii** (Fairrieanum × Swanianum ♀).—Ames, 1900.
Cypripedium × Aasenii, *Amer. G.* 1900, 795; *Rev. H.* 1903, 257; *O.R.* 1903, 41.
2. **P. × Abas** (Stonei ♀ × villosum).—Veitch, 1900.
C. × Abas, *G.C.* 1900, i. 143; *O.R.* 1900, 92.
3. **P. × Abessa** (barbatum × Euryale).—Ames, 1900.
C. × Abessa, *Amer. G.* 1900, 489, 507, f. 101; *G.C.* 1900, ii. 102.
4. **P. × Adamsii** (× Calypso × regale).—Roebling, 1903.
C. × John Quincy Adams, *Amer. G.* 1903, 107.
5. **P. × Adela** (Boxallii ♀ × superbiens).—Duval, 1899.
C. × Boxalli-superbiens, *J. S. H. Fr.* 1900, 84.—Duval.

Fig. 44. Odontoglossum × waltonense.

6. **P. × Adonis** (Curtisii × hirsutissimum ♀).—*Kerch. Liv. d. O.* 475.—Ingram, 1893.
C. × Adonis, *G.C.* 1893, ii. 342; *O.R.* 1893, 318; 1896, 11.
C. × refulgens, *G.C.* 1895, i. 338; *O.R.* 1895, 127.—Ingram.
7. **P. × Adrien** (Rothschildianum × Swanianum ♀).—Sander, 1899.
C. × Comte Adrien de Germiny, *G.C.* 1899, ii. 58; *O.R.* 1899, 254.
8. **P. × Æneas** (Haynaldianum ♀ × Hookeræ).—Sander, 1900.
C. × Haynaldo-Hookeræ, *G.C.* 1900, ii. 57.
C. × Haynaldiano-Hookeræ, *O.R.* 1900, 252.

9. **P. × Æson** (Druryi × insigne ♀), *Kerch. Liv. d. O.* 475.—Veitch, 1893.

C. × Æson, *G.C.* 1893, i. 80; 1897, ii. 438; *O.R.* 1893, 61; 1898, 31.

10. **P. × Ajax** (Chamberlainianum × Germinyanum ♀).—Pitt, 1901.

C. × Ajax, *G.C.* 1901, i. 310; *O.R.* 1903, 81.

11. **P. × albanense** (insigne × Mastersianum ♀).—Sander, 1903.

C. × Masters-insigne, *G.C.* 1903, ii. 377; *O.R.* 1903, 365.

12. **P. × Alcides** (hirsutissimum × insigne ♀), *Stein O.* 452.—Sander, 1891.

C. × Alcides, *G.C.* 1891, i. 40; *O.R.* 1893, 326.

C. × Etienne Jolibois, *Jard.* 1895, 53.—Jolibois.

C. × n. 174, *J. S. H. Fr.* 1891, 45.—Jolibois.

C. × Pheres, *G.C.* 1892, ii. 744; *O.R.* 1893, 32.—Veitch.

C. × Roberti, *G.C.* 1894, ii. 605; *O.R.* 1894, 374.—Gillett.

13. **P. × Alcippe** (callosum × Chamberlainianum).—Cappe, 1898.

C. × (unnamed), *J. S. H. Fr.* 1898, 709.

14. **P. × Alexandræ** (Godefroyæ × nitens).—Sander, 1903.

C. × Empress Alexandra, *G.C.* 1903, i. 46; *O.R.* 1903, 51.

C. × Mrs. Pitt, *G.C.* 1903, i. 239; *O.R.* 1903, 152; *J.H.* 1903, i. 377, f.—Pitt.

15. **P. × Alfred** (philippinense × venustum ♀), *Kerch. Liv. d. O.* 475.—Drewett, 1890.

C. × Alfred, *G.C.* 1890, ii. 294; *J.H.* 1891, ii. 153, f. 23; *O.R.* 1893, 294.

C. × Arthur, *G.C.* 1890, ii. 252.—Drewett.

C. × triangularis, *R. H. Meas. Cyp.* ed. 3, 165.—Sander.

C. × Euterpe, *Sand. O. Guide*, 335.

C. × latiflorum, *Sand. O. Guide*, 336.

16. **P. × Alfredianum** (× Bleui ♀ × superciliare).—Bleu, 1900.

C. × Chantino-ciliolare-barbato-Veitchianum, *J. S. H. Fr.* 1900, 457.

17. **P. × Alice** (Spicerianum × Stonei ♀), *Stein O.* 453.—Drewett, 1890.

C. × Alice, *G.C.* 1890, ii. 294; 1899. i. 351, f. 125 (abnormal); *J.H.* 1892, i. 469; 481, f. 82; *O.R.* 1893, 294.

C. × Hebe (Spicerianum ♀), *Gard. & For.* 1893, 105; *O.R.* 1893, 119.—Graves.

C. × Masonii, *G.C.* 1895, i. 800; *O.R.* 1895, 253.—Low.

C. × Stonei-Spicerianum, *Rev. H. Belge*, 1896, 49, t. (v. gandavense).

18. **P. × Allanianum** (Curtisii × Spicerianum ♀), *Kerch. Liv. d. O.* 475.—Pitcher & Manda, 1894.

C. × Allanianum, *O.R.* 1894, 22; *G.C.* 1895, ii. 527; *G.M.* 1896, 33, f., (v. superbum).

C. × Uihleinianum, *G.C.* 1895, i. 201; *Desb. Cyp.* ed. 2, 456.—Sander.

19. **P. × allertonense** (bellatulum × villosum ♀).—Tate, 1897.

C. × allertonense, *G.C.* 1897, ii. 352; *O.R.* 1897, 375.

C. × auriferum, *Sand. O. Guide*, 334.

C. × Duncan, *Sand. O. Guide*, 335.

C. × Lansbergeæ, *Sand. O. Guide*, 336.

20. **P.** × **almum** (barbatum × Lawrenceanum), *Stein. O.* 453.—Cookson, 1887.

C. × almum, *G.C.* 1887, i. 512; *V. Man. O.* iv. 76; *O.R.* 1893, 196.

C. × hephæstus, *G.C.* 1888, i. 425; *O.R.* 1893, 227.—R. H. Measures.

C. × Cooksonianum, *V. Man. O.* iv. 76 (in syn.); *Hans. O. Hyb.* 133.—Cookson.

C. × Cooksoni, *R. H. Meas. Cyp.* ed. 3, 43.—Cookson.

21. **P.** × **amabile** (Hookeræ × Sementa ♀), *Kerch. Liv. d. O.* 475.—Bleu, 1890.

C. × amabile, *J. S. H. Fr.* 1890, 637; *Rev. H.* 1891, 496, t.; *O.R.* 1893, 328.

22. **P.** × **Ameliæ** (bellatulum × Mabeliæ).—Gratrix, 1902.

C. × Mary Amelia, *G.C.* 1902, ii. 314; *O.R.* 1902, 343.

23. **P.** × **Amesiæ** (Fairrieanum × tonsum ♀), *O.R.* 1900, 10.—Mrs. F. L. Ames, 1895.

C. × Mrs. F. L. Ames, *Amer. G.* March 23, 1895, ex *Hans. O. Hyb.* 164.

C. × Amesiæ, *O.R.* 1896, 15; 1899, 330; *Desb. Cyp.* ed. 2. 47.

24. **P.** × **Amesii** (ciliolare × Rothschildianum).—Sander, 1897.

C. × Oakes Ames, *O.R.* 1897, 153.

C. × ciliolare-Rothschildianum, *Sand. O. Guide*, 335.

C. × Imperator, *G.C.* 1903, ii. 411.—Cowan.

25. **P.** × **amethystinum** (Hookeræ × superciliare ♀), *Kerch. Liv. d. O.* 475.—Bleu, 1904.

C. × amethystinum, *J. d. O.* v. 8; *J. S. H. Fr.* 1894, 68; 1895, 239; *Desb. Cyp.* ed. 2, 49.

26. **P.** × **Andromeda** (Sanderianum ♀ × superbiens).—Cookson, 1893.

C. × Sandero-superbiens, *G.C.* 1893, ii. 278; *J.H.* 1893, ii. 215, f. 31 (Sander-superbiens); *O.R.* 1893, 307 (Sanderiano-superbiens), 317.

27. **P.** × **Angeliæ** (callosum ♀ × Leeanum).—Mantin, 1893.

C. × Angelæ, *J. S. H. Fr.* 1893, 812, 813; *Hans. O. Hyb.* 286.—Mantin.

C. × Angelianum, *J. S. H. Fr.* 1893, 819.—Mantin.

C. × Heloisæ, *J. S. H. Fr.* 1893, 812.—Mantin.

C. × Gautieri, *J. S. H. Fr.* 1898, 1104.—Gautier.

28. **P.** × **Annærtii** (× Ashburtonæ × insigne).—Moens, 1892.

C. × Annærti, *Rev. H. Belge*, 1892, 263; *Desb. Cyp.* ed. 2. 50.

C. × placidum, *R. H. Meas. Cyp.* ed. 3, 138.—Bull.

29. **P.** × **Annie** (bellatulum ♀ × Dayanum).—Sander, 1894.

C. × Annie Measures, *G.C.* 1894, i. 539, 657, f. 81; *J.H.* 1894, i. 337, f. 55. *G.M.* 1894, 278, f.; *O.R.* 1894, 159; *Dict. Ic. O.* Cyp. hyb. t. 16.

C. × Coronis, *J.H.* 1902, ii. 526.—Statter.

30. **P.** × **Aphrodite** (Lawrenceanum × niveum ♀), *Stein O.* 453.—Veitch, 1889.

C. × Aphrodite, *V. Man. O.* iv. 76; *O.R.* 1893, 262; *G.M.* 1894, 76. f.—Veitch.

C. × Antigone (Lawrenceanum ♀), *G.C.* 1890, ii. 716; *O.R.* 1893, 295; *J.H.* 1891, ii. 262, 263, f. 49.—Veitch.

C. × Telemachus, *G.C.* 1892, i. 816; *O.R.* 1893, 359.—Veitch.

C. × Madame Harry Veitch, *Lind.* iv. 98.—Veitch.

C. × Mrs. Harry Veitch, *Bohnh. Dict. O. Hyb.* 27; *Desb. Cyp.* ed. 2, 352.—Veitch.

C. × Prince of Wales, *G.C.* 1902, i. 235; *O.R.* 1902, 119.—*Gratrix.*

31. P. × apiculatum (barbatum ♀ × Boxallii), *Stein O.* 453; *J.R.H.S.* xxiv. 101, f. 18.—Drewett, 1886.

C. × apiculatum, *G.C.* 1886, i. 617; *V. Man. O.* iv. 77; *O.R.* 1893, 131; *Day O. Draw.* ii. t. 95.

C. × n. 239, *J.S. H. Fr.* 1891, 67.—Jolibois.

C. × Harrisianum v. lineatum, *G.C.* 1895, i. 550.—Pitcher & Manda.

Fig. 45. PAPHIOPEDILUM × ARTHURIANUM.

C. × Boxalli-barbatum, *Rev. H. Belge*, 1902, 70.—Pynaert.

32. P. × Apollo (Stonei × vexillarium ♀), *O.R.* 1900, 39.—R. I. Measures, 1890.

C. × Apollo, *G.C.* 1890, i. 526; *O.R.* 1893, 295.

33. P. × Appletonæ (ciliolare × Harrisianum ♀), *O.R.* 1898, 112.—Appleton, 1898.

C. × Appletonæ, *R. H. Meas. Cyp.* ed. 3, 9.

34. P. × Arete (concolor ♀ × Spicerianum), *Kerch. Liv. d. O.* 476.—Veitch, 1892.

C. × Arete, *G.C.* 1892, ii. 744; *O.R.* 1893, 32.

35. P. × Argo-Morganiæ (Argus ♀ × Morganiæ).—Lawrence, 1898.

C. × Argo-Morganiæ, *G.C.* 1898, ii. 391 ; *O.R.* 1898, 374 ; *G.M.* 1898, 766, **f.** ; *J.R.H.S.* xxii. Proc. 220, 221, **f.** 141.

36. P. × Argutus (Argus × Arthurianum), *O.R.* 1903, 56.—R. I. Measures, 1898.

C. × Argo-Arthurianum, *Gard.* 1898, i. 334 ; *Chron. O.* 150 ; *O.R.* 1902, 91.—R. I. Measures.

37. P. × Ariel (bellatulum × Haynaldianum ♀).—W. C. Clarke, 1899.

C. × Haynaldo-bellatulum, *G.C.* 1899, i. 50.

38. P. × Arnoldiæ (bellatulum ♀ × superciliare).—Sander, 1894.

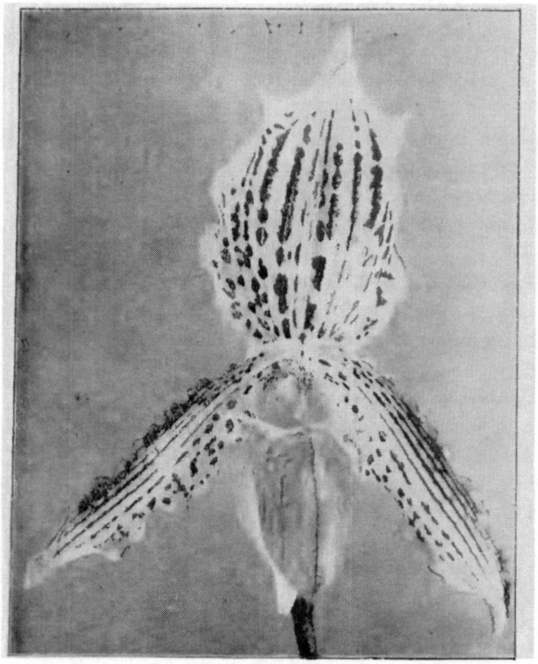

Fig. 46. PAPHIOPEDILUM × ARTHURIANUM VAR. PULCHELLUM.

C. × Arnoldiæ, *G.C.* 1894, ii. 378 ; *Gar. & For.* 1894, 425, **f.** 67 : *O.R.* 1894, 349.

C. × (unnamed), *J. S. H. Fr.* 1895, 671, 799 ; 1896, 793.—Bleu.

C. × Madame A. Bleu, *O.R.*, 1903, 54 ; *Dict. Ic. O.* Cyp. hyb. **t.** 70.—Peeters.

39. P. × Arnoldianum (concolor × superbiens), *Kerch. Liv. d. O.* 476.—Pitcher & Manda, 1890.

C. × Arnoldianum, *G.C.* 1890, ii. 632, 633, **f.** 123 ; *O.R.* 1893, 294.

40. P. × Artemis (Dayanum × Swanianum).—Veitch, 1895.

C. × Artemis, *G.C.* 1895, i. 199 ; *O.R.* 1895, 253.

C. × (unnamed), *J. S. H. Fr.* 1896, 699.—Opoix.

C. × Dayano-Swanianum, *J. S. H. Fr.* 1900, 84.—Opoix.

41. P. × Arthurianum (Fairrieanum × insigne ♀), *Stein. O.* 454; *O.R.* 1897, 17, **f.** 5; 1900, 7, 8, **f.** 2.—Veitch, 1874. [**See Fig. 45, 46.**

C. × Arthurianum, *G.C.* 1874, ii. 676; 1893, ii. 470; *V. Man. O.* iv. 77, 78, **f.**; *O.A.* ix. **t.** 389; *Lind.* iii. **t.** 121 (v. pallidum); *Orchidoph.* 1887, 209, **t.**; *J.H.* 1892, ii. 499, **f.** 66 (v. pulchellum); *O.R.* 1893, 38, 305, **f.** 16; 1894, 44; 1905, 40, **f.** 8 (v. pulchellum); *Dict. Ic. O.* Cyp. hyb. **t.** 12; *Nich. Dict.* 1900 suppl. 285, **f.** 298; *Day. O. Draw.* xxx. **t.** 37.

42. P. × Ashburtonæ (barbatum ♀ × insigne), *Stein. O.* 454; *J. R. H. S.* xxiv. 101, **f.** 20 (v. Laforcadei,)—Ashburton, 1871.

C. × Ashburtoniæ, *G.C.* 1871, 1647, **f.** 348; 1884, ii. 552 (v. expansum); *Gtfl.* 1879, **t.** 976; *O.A.* ix. **t.** 400 (v. superbum); *Ill. H.* 1888, 71, **t.** 61; *V. Man. O.* iv. 78, 79 (v. majus); *O.R.* 1893, 37; *Dict. Ic. O.* Cyp. hyb. **t.** 14 (v. Bartetii); Reichenb. ser. 2, i. 79, **t.** 38, **f.** 1 (v. Laforcadei); *Rev. H. Belge*, 1904, 97, **t.** 8, **f.** 2 (v. expansum); *Day O. Draw.* xxix. **t.** 75.

C. × Laforcadei (insigne ♀), *J. S. H. Fr.* 1884, 649; *Orchidoph.* 1886, 121, **t.**; *O.R.* 1893, 102.—Bauer.

C. × Barteti, *J.S.H.Fr.* 1885, 640; *Orchidoph.* 1886, 121, **t.**; *G.C.* 1886, i. 532.—Bauer.

C. × obscurum, *G.C.* 1887, i. 8.—Veitch.

C. × Edgard Jolibois, *J. S. H. Fr.* 1889, 725, 735, 787.—Jolibois.

C. × Laucheanum, *G.C.* 1890, ii. 570.—Sander.

C. × Chantino-barbatum, *J. S. H. Fr.* 1899, 1129.—Opoix.

C. × Gardnerianum, *Sand. O. Guide*, 335.

43. P. × Ashtoni (ciliolare ♀ × selligerum).—Lewis, 1895.

C. × Ashtoni, *G.C.* 1895, ii. 721; *O.R.* 1896, 32.

44. P. × Ashworthiæ (× Leeanum ♀ × venustum).—E. Ashworth, 1895.

C. × Beatrice Ashworth, *R.H. Meas. Cyp.* ed. 2, 16; *G.C.* 1895, i. 200.

45. P. × Ashworthii (× Measuresianum ♀ × Spicerianum), *Kerch. Liv. d. O.* 476.—Sander, 1892.

C. × E. Ashworth, *G.C.* 1892, ii. 622.—Sander.

C. × Ashworthii, *O.R.* 1893, 359.—Sander.

C. × Vesta, *G.C.* 1895, i. 201; *O.R.* 1896, 38.—Sander.

46. P. × Asmodia (bellatulum × Bleui).—Bleu, 1898.

C. × Chantino-ciliolare × bellatulum, *Sem. Hort.* 1898, 316.

C. × (unnamed), *J. S. H. Fr.* 1898, 707.

47. P. × Aspasia (× selligerum ♀ × tonsum).—Sander, 1895.

C. × Aspasia, *O.R.* 1895, 15; *Desb. Cyp.* ed. 2, 65.

48. P. × aspasioides (Argus × selligerum).—Rothwell, 1900.

C. × Aspasia, *Amer. G.* 1900, 200.

C. × aspasioides, *Amer. G.* 1902, 137.

49. P. × Astræa (philippinense × Spicerianum ♀), *Stein. O.* 454.—Veitch, 1892.

C. × Astræa, *G.C.* 1892, ii. 191; *O.R.* 1894, 349.

50. P. × **Atropos** (× Ashburtoniæ ♀ × purpuratum).—Young, 1895.

C. × Atropos, *O.R.* 1895, 292; 1896, 309; *G.C.* 1896, ii. 251.

51. P. × **Atys** (Hookeræ ♀ × venustum), *Kerch. Liv. d. O.* 476.—Harris, 1888.

C. × Atys, *G.C.* 1888, ii. 6; *O.R.* 1893, 259; 1896, 53.

C. × Cassiope (venustum ♀), *G.C.* 1889, i. 200; *O.R.* 1893, 263.—Seeger & Tropp.

C. × rubrum, *G.C.* 1893, ii. 747; *Gard.* 1894, i. 206; *O.R.* 1896, 53.—Burton.

C. × Burtoni, *Gard.* 1894, i. 181, 206; *O.A.* xi. sub. t. 481; *O.R.* 1894, 144.—Burton.

52. P. × **augustum** (Lawrenceanum × superciliare),—Bleu, 1895.

C. × augustum, *J. S. H. Fr.* 1895, 163; 1903, 71; *Jard.* 1903, 64.

53. P. × **aurelianense** (callosum × Sementa).—Mantin, 1896.

C. × aurelianense, *J. S. H. Fr.* 1897, 602; 1898, 289; *Chron. O.* 53.

54. P. × **aureum** (× nitens × Spicerianum ♀), *J. R. H. S.* xxiv. 111-113 (and 21 vars.); *O.R.* 1901, 16.—Hye, 1894.

C. × aureum, *Rev. H. Belge*, 1894, 70; *O.R.* 1894, 92; *Dict. Ic. O.* Cyp. hyb. t. 24 (type); 24 A. (v. virginale); 24 B. (v. Hebe); 24 C. (v. Œdipe); 24 D. (v. Cyrus); 24 E. (v. Marie Closon); *J.H.* 1904, i. 179, f.

C. × Mme. Margaret Hye, *G.C.* 1894, ii. 670; *O.R.* 1895, 29.—Hye.

C. × Augusta, C. × delicatum, C. × Hebe, C. × Nicias, *G.C.* 1894, ii. 728; *O.R.* 1895, 27.—Hye.

C. × Surprise, *Ill. H.* 1895, 62; *Rev. H. Belge*, 1895, 83.

C. × Pomone, *Ill. H.* 1895, 63; *Rev. H. Belge*, 1895, 83.—Hye.

C. × Eteocle, C. × Vertumne, *Ill. H.* 1895, 63; *Rev. H. Belge*, 1895, 83.—Hye.

C. × Mellona, *Ill. H.* 1895, 63; *Rev. H. Belge*, 1895, 84.—Hye.

C. × Hermione, C. × Hermode, C. × Ixion, C. × Œdipe, C. × Olympia, C. × Polynice, C. × Zephire, *Rev. H. Belge*, 1895, 84.—Hye.

C. × Bellona, C. × Ixion, C. × Zephyra, *G.C.* 1895, i. 207.—Hye.

C. × Jeanne Voortman, *Rev. H. Belge*, 1896, 69; *J. d. O.* vii. 40.—Hye.

C. × amœnum, *Desb. Cyp.* ed. 2, 47.—Hye.

C. × Cyrus, *Desb. l.c.* 150.—Hye.

C. × Hero, *Desb. l.c.* 227.—Hye.

C. × Osiris, *Desb. l.c.* 380.—Hye.

C. × tigrinum. *Desb. l c.* 452.—Hye.

C. × roseum, *J. S. H. Fr.* 1898, 43.—Peeters.

C. × Terpsichore, *J. S. H. Fr.* 1898, 44.—Peeters.

C. × Madame Mary Hye, *R. H. Meas. Cyp.* ed. 3, 114.—Hye.

C. × Hector, *R. H. Meas. l.c.* 189.—Hye.

C. × virginale, *Dict. Ic. O.* Cyb. hyb. sub. t. 24 A.

C. × Hyeanum, *G.C.* 1899, i. 288; *O.R.* 1899, 155.—Charlesworth.

C. × lacteum, *J. S. H. Fr.* 1900, 113.—Duval.

C. × Sallieri-Spicerianum, *J. S. H. Fr.* 1900, 118.—Duval.

C. × Spicero-nitens, *O.R.* 1901, 24.—Wrigley.

C. × belgicum, *O.R.* 1902, 28.—Tunstill.

C. × Rialto, *G.C.* 1903, i. 267 ; *Gard.* 1903, i. 287.—Janssens & Putzeys.

C. × Carmen, *Gard.* 1903, i. 287.—Janssens & Putzeys.

55. P. × auroreum (Lawrenceanum ♀ × venustum), *Stein. O.* 454.—Cookson, 1887.

C. × auroreum, *G.C.* 1887, i. 179 ; *V. Man. O.* iv. 79 : *O.R.* 1893, 196.

C. × Lawre-venustum, *Hans. O. Hyb.* 136.—Cappe.

56. P. × Aylingii (ciliolare × niveum ♀), *Stein O.* 455.—Hollington, 1890.

C. × Aylingii, *J.H.* 1890, i. 480, 481, f. 74 ; *G.C.* 1890, i. 792, 797, f. 131 ; *O.R.* 1893, 185, 294 ; *Lind.* xi. t. 497 (Stand. Hall v.).

C. × Winifred Hollington, *G.C.* 1894, i. 475, 495, f. 60 ; *O.R.* 1894, 157 ; *J.H.* 1894, i. 295, f. 48 ; *G.M.* 1894, 218, 220, f.—Hollington.

C. × niveo-ciliolare, *Gard.* 1894, i. 492 ; *G.C.* 1895, i. 200 ; *O.R.* 1898, 363. —R. H. Measures.

C. × Hollingtoniæ, *O.R.* 1899, 330.—Hollington.

The record of C. callosum as one parent of C. × Winifred Hollington is clearly erroneous.

57. P. × Bagshaweæ (callosum × œnanthum ♀).—Le Doux, 1899.

P. × Olga Bagshawe, *O.R.* 1899, 73.

58. P. × Bala (Boxallii × Lathamianum) Duval, 1899.

C. × Lathamiano-Boxallii, *J. S. H. Fr.* 1899, 1131.

59. P. × Balfouriæ (× Chapmanii × Cycnides).—Gratrix, 1902.

C. × Miss Balfour, *G.C.* 1902, ii. 314 ; *O.R.* 1902, 343.

60. P. × Ballantinei (Fairricanum × purpuratum ♀), *Kerch. Liv. d. O.* 476 ; *O.R.* 1900, 8 ; 1905, 18, f. 5 (Westfield v.).—Veitch, 1890. **[See Fig.**

C. × H. Ballantine, *G.C.* 1890, ii. 408 ; *O.R.* 1893, 295.

61. P. × barbato-præstans (barbatum × præstans).—Beranek, 1903.

C. × barbato-praestans, *J. S. H. Fr.* 1903, 604.

62. P. × Barbeyæ (Lawrenceanum × tonsum ♀) ; *O.R.* 1901, 93.—Jolibois, 1891.

C. × n. 260, *J. S. H. Fr.* 1891, 67.—Jolibois.

C. × Madame Barbey, *Orchidoph.* 1892, 337, t. f. 3 : *O.R.* 1893, 154.—Jolibois.

C. × tonso-Lawrenceanum, *J. S. H. Fr.* 1900, 391—Opoix.

63. P. × Bartelsii (Boxallii ♀ × callosum), *O R.* 1902, 94.—Sander, 1894.

C. × J. Bartels, *G.C.* 1894, ii. 670 ; 1903, i. 130 ; *O.R.* 1895, 30.—Sander.

C. × (unnamed) (callosum ♀), *J. S. H. Fr.* 1897, 745.—Gibez.

64. P. × Batalinii (Argus × purpuratum ♀).—Sander, 1894.

C. × Batalinii, *G.C.* 1894, ii. 378 ; *O.R.* 1894, 349.

65. P. × Beatrice (Boxallii ♀ × Lowii), *Kerch. Liv. d. O.* 476.—Drewett, 1889.

C. × Beatrice, *G.C.* 1889, ii. 266 ; *O.R.* 1893, 263.

C. × lucidum v. Beatrice, *Hans. O. Hyb.* 159.—Drewett.

66. P. × Behrensianum (Boxallii ♀ × Io), *Kerch. Liv. d. O.* 476.—Sander, 1894.

C. × Behrensianum, *O.R.* 1894, 111; *J. S. H. Fr.* 1896, 929.

C. × Roeblingianum, *Bohnh. Dict. O. Hyb.* 31.

C. × Ionodes, *R. H. Meas. Cyp.* ed. 2, 60.—Sander.

C. × Ionides, *G.C.* 1895, i. 500.—Sander.

67. P. × bellinum (× Harrisianum × vernixium ♀), *Kerch. Liv. d. O.* 476.—Sander, 1894.

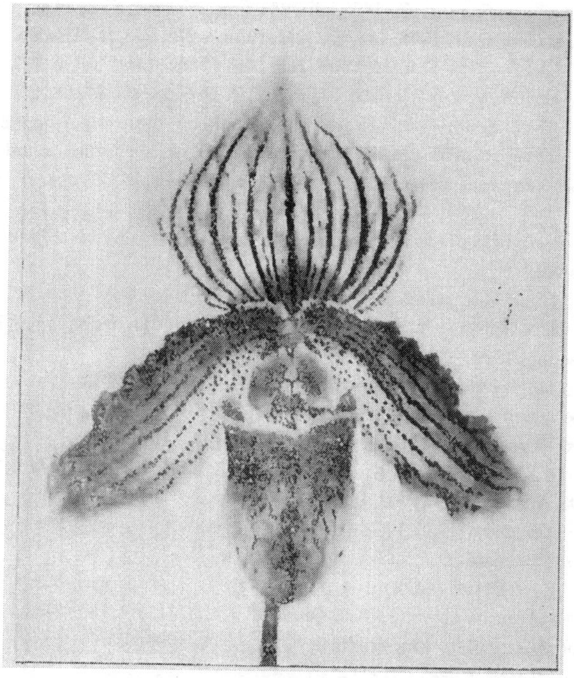

Fig. 47. Paphiopedilum × Ballantinei, Westfield var.

C. × bellinum, *O.R.* 1894, 42.

C. × Wendlandianum, *R. H. Meas. Cyp.* ed. 2, 111; *Bohnh. Dict. O. Hyb.* 35; *O.R.* 1896, 39.—Sander.

Not to be confounded with P. × Wendlandianum, Kerch. (× œnanthum × venustum).

68. P. × Belus (× Harrisianum ♀ × Mastersianum), *O.R.* 1900, 100.—Young, 1898.

C. × Belus, *G.C.* 1898, i. 302; *O.R.* 1898, 185; *Dict. Ic. O.* Cyp. hyb. t. 31.

69. P. × Beranekii (bellatulum ♀ × Youngianum).—Beranek, 1902.

C. × Jeanette, *G.C.* 1902, i. 380; *J. S. H. Fr.* 1902, 463.

The specific name is changed because of an earlier hybrid with the same name.

70. **P × Berenice** (Lowii × philippinense ♀), *Kerch. Liv. d. O.* 476.—Vipan, 1891.

C. × Berenice, *G.C.* 1891, i. 136; *O.R.* 1893, 328.

71. **P. × Berkeleyanum** (bellatulum × Boxallii).—Lawrence, 1902.

C. × Berkeleyanum, *G.C.* 1902, i. 151; *O.R.* 1902, 90.

C. × Berkeleyi, *G.C.* 1902, i. 217; *O.R.* 1902, 118.—Charlesworth.

C. × Beeckmani, *G.C.* 1897, ii. 388; *Sem. H.* 1897, 458; 1898, 165, **f.** 269; *Lind.* xiii. **t.** 600; *G.M.* 1898, 145, **f.**; *J.H.* 1904, i. 272, 273, **f.**—Linden.

C. × Lansbergeæ, *Sem. H.* 1900, 555, 556, **f.** 179; *Lind.* xvi. **t.** 727.—Linden.

C. × auriferum, *Lind.* xvii. **t.** 771; *Rev. H. Belge*, 1905, 97, 99, **t.** 8, **f.** 1.

There is a doubt about the parentage of the three preceding synonyms, though we have followed the original records. C. × auriferum is said to have come from the same cross as C. × Beeckmani, but all three are remarkably diverse.

72. **P. × Bijou** (Lawrenceanum × oenanthum ♀), *Kerch. Liv. d. O.* 476.—Ingram, 1892.

C. × Bijou, *G.C.* 1892, ii. 138; *O.R.* 1893, 359.

73. **P. × bingleyense** (Charlesworthii ♀ × Harrisianum); *O.R.* 1900, 350.—Keeling, 1899.

C. × bingleyense, *G.C.* 1899, ii. 198; *O.R.* 1899, 287, 291.

C. × rubens, *O.R.* 1899, 285, 291 (rubrum by error).—Keeling.

C. × Dryope, *G.C.* 1903, i. 46, 80; *O.R.* 1903, 51.—Veitch.

C. × J. Wilson Potter, *G.C.* 1903, i. 46, 78, 83, **f.** 36; *G. World*, 1903, i. 113; *O.R.* 1903, 51, 52; *J.H.* 1903, i. 177, **f.**—Potter.

C. × Chorltoni, *G.C.* 1903, ii. 230.—Gratrix.

C. × Charltoni, *O.R.* 1903, 310.—Gratrix.

74. **P. × Bleui** (ciliolare ♀ × insigne), *J. R. H. S.* xxvi. 692.—Bleu, 1891.

C. × Chantino-ciliolare, *J. d. O.* ii. 343; *J. S. H. Fr.* 1893, 452.

C. × Alfred Bleu, *Rev. H.* 1893, 84, **t.**; *O.R.* 1893, 93.

C. × Alfredi, *Bohnh. Dict. O. Hyb.* 10.

75. **P. × Bollerillæ** (× Lathamianum ♀ × Savageanum).—McMeekin, 1897.

C. × Mrs. Geo. Bollerill, *G.C.* 1897, ii. 438; *O.R.* 1898, 31.

76. **P. × Boltonianum** (× calophyllum ♀ × Leeanum).—Sander, 1895.

C. × Boltonianum, *O.R.* 1896, 362; *R. H. Meas. Cyp.* ed. 3, 22.

77. **P. × Bondii** (hirsutissimum × Swanianum ♀).—Ingram, 1893.

C. × T. W. Bond, *G.C.* 1893, i. 396; 1901, i. 114, 127, **f.** 51 (Coundon Court v.); *O.R.* 1893, 158; *Dict. Ic. O.* Cyp. hyb. **t.** 25; *J. H.* 1901, i. 169, **f.**

78. **P. × Bookeri** (ciliolare × Spicerianum).—Marwood, 1893.

C. × Bookeri, *G.C.* 1894, ii. 447; *O.R.* 1894, 352.

79. **P. × Boyleanum** (× Crossianum (?) × Harrisianum ♀), *Kerch. Liv. d. O.* 476; *O.R.* 1903, 69.—Sander, 1893.

C. × Boyleanum, *R. H. Meas. Cyp.* ed. 2, 17; *Hans. O. Hyb.* 1895, 137.—Sander.

C. × Haumonti, *Lind.* xiv. t. 668; *O.R.* 1899, 352.—Linden.

80. P. × Bræckmanii (Charlesworthii × Savageanum (Moensii).—Maes. Bræckman, 1903.

C. × (unnamed), *G.C.* 1903. ii. 359.

The second parent is given as C. × Moensii, which we have taken to represent a form of P. × Savageanum, but if it is P. Argus Moensii this hybrid would be a form of P. × Ian.

81. P. × Brandtiæ (× Io ♀ × Youngianum).—Sander, 1895.

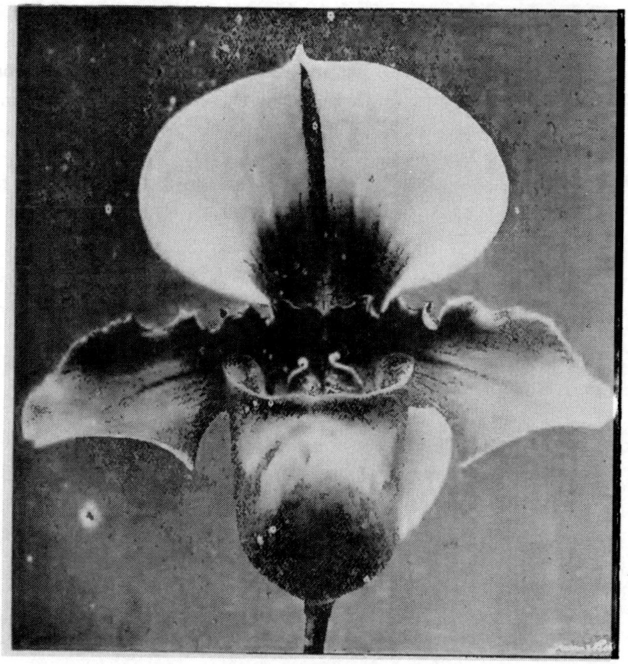

Fig. 48. PAPHIOPEDILUM × BUCHANIANUM.

C. × Frau Ida Brandt, *G.C.* 1895, i. 748; *O.R.* 1895, 223; *Amer. G.* 1900, 375, f. 78.

82. P. × Brunhild (× Lathamianum × Victoria-Mariæ.)—Sander, 1902.

C. × Brunhild, *G.C.* 1902, i. 350, f. 118.

83. P. × Brunianum (× Leeanum ♀ × œnanthum).—Sander, 1892.

C. × Brunianum, *G.C.* 1892, ii. 443.—Sander.

C. × A. J. Herrington, *G.C.* 1895, ii. 588; *O.R.* 1896, 361.—Sander.

C. × Leeanum-Galatea, *R. H. Meas. Cyp.* ed. 3, 107.—Sander.

C. × Madonna, *Sand. O. Guide*, 336.—Charlesworth.

84. P. × Bruno (× Leeanum × Spicerianum ♀).—Veitch, 1895.

C. × Bruno, *Gard.* 1895, ii. 347; *O.R.* 1896, 375; *Desh. Cyp.* ed. 2, 94.

C. × (unnamed), *J. S. H. Fr.* 1901, 1137.—Bultel.

C. × Tagus, *O.R.* 1903, 365.—Cypher.

C. × nobile, *G.C.* 1901, i. 408.—Smet-Duvivier.

85. P. × bruxellense (Rothschildianum × venustum), *J. R. H. S.* xxvi. 692.—Linden, 1901.

C. × bruxellense, *Lind.* xvi. t. 751.

86. P. × Bryan (philippinense × tonsum ♀).—Drewett, 1901.

C. × Bryan, *G.C.* 1901, ii. 172; *O.R.* 1901, 285.

87. P. × Buchanianum (Druryi ♀ × Spicerianum) *Kerch. Liv. d. O.* 476.—Buchan, 1887. **[See Fig. 48.**

C × Buchanianum, *Garden*, 1889, i. 8; *G.C.* 1890, i. 73 (Buchananianum), 142; *O.R.* 1893, 291; 1895, 36, 81, f. 4 (v. magnificum).—Buchan.

C. × excelsum, *Desb. Cyp.* ed. 2, 181.—Hye.

C. × Excelsior, *O.R.* 1894, 92.—Hye.

88. P. × Buckinghami (bellatulum × enfieldense ♀).—Hollington, 1896.

C. × James Buckingham, *G.C.* 1896, i. 210: *J.H.* 1896, i. 159, f. 23; *O.R.* 1896, 95.—Hollington.

C. × Gratrixianum, *O. A.* xi. t. 524.—Gratrix.

89. P. × Bullieri (tonsum × villosum).—Opoix, 1894.

C. × Théodore Bullier, *J. S. H. Fr.* 1894, 134; 1895, 238.—Opoix.

C. × tonso-villosum, *Gard. and For.* 1893, 117.—Pitcher and Manda.

90. P. × Bullii (Chamberlainianum × exul).—Bull, 1903.

P. × (unnamed), *O.R.* 1903, 346.

91. P. × burbagense (insigne ♀ × selligerum), *O.R.* 1902, 220.—Hurst, 1898.

92. P. × Burberryanum (Boxallii ♀ × chloroneurum (plunerum), *Kerch. Liv. d. O.* 476.—Sander, 1893.

C × Burberryanum, *G.C.* 1893, i. 395; *O.R.* 1893, 159.—Sander.

P. × Nemesis, *O.R.* 1902, 100.—Young.

93. P. × Burbidgeanum (concolor × Dayanum ♀), *Kerch. Liv. d. O.* 476. —R. H. Measures, 1889.

C. × Burbidgeanum, *Lind.* iii. 86; *Orchidoph.* 1889, 11; *Hans. O. Hyb.* 137.

C. × Salus, *G.C.* 1897, ii. 10; *O.R.* 1897, 223.—R. I. Measures.

C × Salis, *Chron. O.* 158.—R. I. Measures.

94. P. × burfordiense (Argus × philippinense), *Kerch. Liv. d. O.* 476.—Lawrence, 1888.

C. × burfordiense, *G.C.* 1888, ii. 724; *O.R.* 1893, 259; 1896, 340.—Lawrence.

C. × Bryani, *G.C.* 1892, ii. 138; *O.R.* 1893, 359; 1896, 340.—Cookson.

C. × pendulum, *G.C.* 1895, ii. 192; 1899, ii. 99, *O.R.* 1895, 288; 1899, 249. —Heath.

On the second occasion that this plant was exhibited the second parent was recorded as C. Haynaldianum, but the point requires confirmation.

95. P. × **buryense** (× Swinburnei × venustum).—Wrigley, 1902.
P. × (unnamed), *O.R.* 1902, 124.
96. P. × **Cahuzacii** (× pavoninum × villosum).—Cahuzac, 1899.
C. × villoso-pavoninum, *J. S. H. Fr.* 1899, 262.
97. P. × **calanthum** (barbatum ♀ × Lowii), *Stein. O.* 457.—Veitch, 1878.
C. × calanthum, *G.C.* 1880, ii. 652; *V. Man. O.* iv. 79; *O.R.* 1893, 70.
C. × chelseense, *G.C.* 1888, ii. 406; *O.R.* 1893, 228.—Bull.
C. × Sappho, *R. H. Meas. Cyp.* ed. 2, 98; *G.C.* 1895, i. 200.—Veitch.
C. × Sirius, *R. H. Meas. Cyp.* ed. 3, 155.—Charlesworth.
98. P. × **caligare** (Dayanum × venustum ♀), *Stein. O.* 457.—Drewett, 1888.
C. × caligare, *G.C.* 1888, i. 264; *O.R.* 1893, 259; *Orchidoph.* 1888, 130.
99. P. × **Calliope** (callosum × Lathamianum).—W. C. Clarke, 1899.
C. × Calliope, *G.C.* 1899, i. 98.
C. × Apuleus, *R. H. Meas. Cyp.* ed. 3, 9.—Charlesworth.
100. P. × **calloso-Argus** (Argus ♀ × callosum).—Graves, 1894.
C. × calloso-argus, *O.R.* 1894, 110.
101. P. × **calloso-barbatum** (barbatum × callosum ♀).—Jolibois, 1890.
C. Crossi × callosum, *J. S. H. Fr.* 1890, 201.—Jolibois.
C. × calloso-barbatum, *O.R.* 1898, 371; 1899, 48.—Charlesworth.
C. × calloso-Warneri, *G.C.* 1902, ii. 445; *O.R.* 1903, 22.—Wrigley.
102. P. × **calloso-niveum** (callosum × niveum ♀).—Sander, 1895.
C. × calloso-niveum, *O.R.* 1895, 359.—Sander.
C. × Mrs. Edgar Cohen, *G.C.* 1898, ii. 203; *O.R.* 1898, 317.—Sander.
C. × niveo-callosum, *G.C.* 1903, ii. 343; *O.R.* 1903, 367.—Ardern.

103. P. × **calophyllum** (barbatum ♀ × venustum), *Stein. O.* 458.—Veitch, 1881.

C. × calophyllum, *G.C.* 1881, i. 169; *V. Man. O.* iv. 80; *O.R.* 1893, 71.—Veitch.

C. × politum, *G.C.* 1880, ii. 525; 1887, i. 764, 765, f. 143; *O.A.* i. t. 36; *V. Man. O.* iv. 96; *O.R.* 1893, 70; 1905, 291; *Dict. Ic. O.* Cyp. hyb. t. 20; *Day. O. Draw.* xliv. t. 17.—Warner.

C. × venusto-Crossii, *Bohnh. Dict. O. Hyb.* 35; *Desb. Cyp.* ed. 2, 460.—Drieger.

C. × Thetis, *R. H. Meas. Cyp.* ed. 2, 102; *Bohnh. Dict. O. Hyb.* 33.—Harris.

104. P. × **Calypso** (Boxallii ♀ × Spicerianum), *Stein. O.* 458.—Veitch, 1890.

C. × Calypso, *G.C.* 1890, i. 207; 1891, i. 86; *J.H.* 1891, ii. 559. f. 101; *O.R.* 1893, 327; 1896, 15; *Reichenb.* ser. 2, ii. 69, t. 77 (Oakwood var.); *Dict. Ic. O.* Cyp. hyb. t. 26 (type), 26 A. (Oakwood var.), 26 B. (v. Flamingo).

C. × Denisianum, *G.C.* 1893, i. 486; *Haus. O. Hyb.* 156.—Vervaet.

C. × Vanderwielianum, *G.C.* 1893, i. 286.—Vervaet.

C. × Leo, *G.C.* 1894, i. 84; *O.R.* 1894, 62.—W. R. Lee.

C. × Flamingo, *Rev. H. Belge,* 1895, 84; *Ill. H.* 1895, 63; *Desb. Cyp.* ed. 2, 190.—Hye.

C. × Eurydice, *G.C.* 1895, i. 199 ; *O.R.* 1896, 12.—" Continental."

C. × Flora, *R. H. Meas. Cyp.* ed. 2, 39 ; ed. 3, 60.—R. I. Measures.

C. × Boutemyæ, *G.C.* 1897, i. 227.—Linden.

C. × hybridum, *Bohnh. O. Hyb.* 21 ; *O.R.* 1896, 14.

105. P. × **calypsoides** (× Calypso × Rothschildianum).—Drewett, 1903.

C. × calypsoides, *G.C.* 1903, ii. 214 ; *O.R.* 1903, 308.—Drewett.

C. × Lamonteanum, *G.C.* 1903, ii. 278 ; *O.R.* 1903, 339.—Sander.

106. P. × **Canhami** (superbiens ♀ × villosum), *Stein O.* 458.—(Douglas) Veitch, 1887.

C. × Charles Canham, *G.C.* 1887, ii. 490 ; *V. Man. O.* iv. 81 ; *O.R.* 1893, 133 ; *Dict. Ic. O.* Cyp. hyb. **t.** 9.

C. × Mrs. Canham (villosum ♀), *G.C.* 1887, ii. 746 ; *V. Man. O.* iv. 93, **f.** ; *O.R.* 1893, 134.

C. × Canhami, *Wien Ill. G. Zeit.* 1888, 32 ; 1899, 413, **t.** 4.

C. × Canhamiæ, *G.C.* 1894, ii. 667, **f.** 86 (abnormal).

C. × inversum, *Bohnh. O. Hyb.* 21.

C. × (unnamed), *J. S. H. Fr.* 1897, 844.—Ferrier.

107. P. × **Carderi** (hirsutissimum × selligerum).—Sander, 1898.

C. × John Carder, *O.R.* 1898, 372.

108. P. × **Cardosoæ** (Charlesworthii × macropterum).—Cardoso.

C. × Madame Elise Cardoso, *J. S. H. Fr.* 1896, 741.

109. P. × **Cardosoanum** (barbatum ♀ × Leeanum), *O.R.* 1901, 14 ; 1903, 54, 119.—Peeters, 1900.

C. × Cardosoanum, *Dict. Ic. O.* Cyp. hyb. **t.** 46.

110. P. × **Carnusianum** (Haynaldianum × Spicerianum), *Stein O.* 460.—Carnus, 1890.

C. × (unnamed), *G.C.* 1890, ii. 754.

C. × Carnusianum, *G.C.* 1891, i. 87 ; 1895, ii. 102 ; *O.R.* 1893, 328 ; *G.M.* 1896, 250, **f.**—(Carnus) Parr.

C. × hybridum, *J.H.* 1891, i. 50.—(Carnus) Parr.

C. × Cahuzac, *Bohnh. Dict. O. Hyb.* 13 ; *O.R.* 1896, 320.—Sander.

C. × Peruzzianum, *Bull Soc. Tosc. Ort.* 1903, 5.—Recenti.

111. P. × **Carrierei** (superbiens ♀ × venustum), *Stein O.* 460.—Bauer, 1887.

C. × Carrierei, *Monit. H.* 1887, 54 ; *O.R.* 1893, 374 ; *Bull. Soc. Tosc. Ort.* 1887, 152, **t.** 7 ; *V. Man. O.* iv. 80.

112. P. × **Cassandra** (× Goweri × Sanderianum).—Parker, 1903.

C. × Cassandra, *G.C.* 1903, ii. 65 ; *O.R.* 1903, 244.

113. P. × **Castalia** (Druryi × Godseffianum).—Dallemagne, 1902.

C. × Castalia, *J. S. H. Fr.* 1902, 139.—Dallemagne.

C. × A. Dimmock, *G.C.* 1902, i. 151, 157, **f.** 48 ; *O.R.* 1902, 92.—Sander.

114. P. × **Castleanum** (hirsutissimum ♀ × superbiens).—*Stein O.* 460.—Sander, 1890.

C. × Castleanum, *G.C.* 1890, ii. 702; 1891, i. 39; *J.H.* 1890, ii. 513; 1891, i. 101, f. 19; *Reichenb. ser.* 2, i. t. 45; *O.R.* 1893, 28, 326.—Sander.

C. × Captain Holford (superbiens ♀), *G.C.* 1899, ii. 198; *O.R.* 1899, 287; *G.M.* 1899, 561, f.—Veitch.

C. × Thoorisianum, *Bohnh. Dict. O. Hyb.* 34; *Desb, Cyp.* ed. 2, 452.—Moens.

C. × Bellonc, *Chron. O.* 56; *R. H. Meas. Cyp.* ed. 3, 21 ("Bellune").—Vuylsteke.

115. **P. × Celia** (Spicerianum × tonsum), *Kerch. Liv. d. O.* 477.—Kimball, 1890.

C. × Celia, *G.C.* 1891, i. 104; *O.R.* 1893, 327.—Kimball.

C. × Cecilia, *O.R.* 1893, 350.—Sander.

C. × Madame Jules Hye, *G.C.* 1894, i. 198; 1895, i. 103, f. 14; *O.R.* 1894, 92, 144; *Dict. Ic. O.* Cyp. hyb. t. 8.—Hye.

C. × Inspirator, *Rev. H. Belge*, 1894, 25; *O.R.* 1894, 82.—Hye.

C. × Spicero-tonsum, *G.C.* 1895, i. 201; *R. H. Meas. Cyp.* ed. 3, 158.—Ingram.

C. × Spico-tonsum, *Haus. O. Hyb.* 139.—Pitcher and Manda.

C. × Imperator, *Desb. Cyp.* ed. 2, 237.—Hye.

C. × Jules Hye, *J. S. H. Fr.* 1899, 53.—Peeters.

116. **P. × Chamber-Leeanum** (Chamberlainianum × Leeanum), *O.R.* 1898, 168; 1899, 68.—Lebaudy, 1898.

C. × Chamber-Leeanum, *O.R.* 1898, 207; *Dict. Ic. O.* Cyp. hyb. t. 66.—Pynaert.

C. × Leeano-Chamberlainianum, *J. S. H. Fr.* 1898, 50.—Lebaudy.

C. × Mariæ, *J. S. H. Fr.* 1899, 152; *Jard.* 1899, 64 (Maria).—Lebaudy.

C. × Morteni, *G.C.* 1899, ii. 478; *O.R.* 1900, 28.—Appleton.

P. × Maria, *O.R.* 1903, 56.—Hardy.

117. **P. × Chapmanii** (bellatulum × Curtisii ♀), *J. S. H. Fr.* xxvi. 692.—Cookson, 1896.

C. × Chapmanii, *Gard.* 1896, ii. 262; *G.C.* 1896, ii. 667; *G.M.* 1896, 794, f.; *O.R.* 1897, 28, 170; *G.C.* 1897, i. 365, f. 134 (v. magnificum); *J.H.* 1897, ii. 21, f. 4 (id.); *Nich. Dict.* 1900 Suppl. 287, f. 300 (id.); *Dict. Ic. O.* Cyp. hyb. t. 57 (type), 57 A (v. superbum).

118. **P. × Charlesianum** (× Leeanum × nitens ♀), *O.R.* 1898, 359 1902, 38, 39.—Madoux, 1894.

P. × variabile, *O.R.* 1902, 38.—Cappe.

C. × Charlesianum, *G.C.* 1894, i. 430.—Madoux.

C. × nitens-Leeanum, *G.C.* 1897, i. 115.—Sander.

C. × Mrs. C. Maynard, *O.R.* 1898, 26.—Ball.

C. × Samuel Gratrix, *G.C.* 1899, ii. 426; 1903, i. 46, 78; *Gard. World*, 1903, 73, f. (v. Minnie); *O.R.* 1899, 371; 1903, 50, 63.—Gratrix.

C. × Angelæ, *J. S. H. Fr.* 1899, 375.—Cappe.

C. × Hector, *Woodlands O.* 179.—R. H. Measures.

C. × lacteum, *J. S. H. Fr.* 1900, 113.—Duval.

C. × Minnie, *G.C.* 1901, ii. 462, *O.R.* 1902, 27.—Wellesley.

C. × variabile, *J. S. H. Fr.* 1899, 538; 1900, 181.

C. × Loyensi, *J. S. H. Fr.* 1900, 53.—Peeters.

C. × Dr. Picard, *J. S. H. Fr.* 1900, 349.—Cappe.

C. × Sybil, *Sand. O. Guide*, 337.

C. × Leeanum superbum S. Gratrix, *Gard.* 1903, i. Jan. 17, Suppl. 7.—Gratrix.

119. P. × **Charpinianum** (× Morganiae × Spicerianum ♀).—Mantin, 1897.

C. × Charpinianum, *J. S. H. Fr.* 1897, 608; *Sem. Hort.* 300; *Desb. Cyp.* ed. 2, 119.

C. × Spiceriano-Morganiæ, *J. S. H. Fr.* 1898, 285.—Mantin.

120. P. × **chloroneurum** (× Harrisianum × venustum), *Stein O.* 462.—Warner, 1880.

C. × chloroneurum, *G.C.* 1880, ii. 525; *V. Man. O.* iv. 81; *O.A.* i. t. 37; *O.R.* 1893, 71; 1905, 291; *Dict. Ic. O.* Cyp. hyb. t. 30; *Day O. Draw.* xxxii. t. 69.—Warner.

C. × melanophthalmum, *G.C.* 1880, ii. 525; *O.A.* iii. t. 109: *V. Man. O.* iv. 92; *O.R.* 1893, 70: 1905, 292; *Day O. Draw.* xl. t. 57.—Warner.

C. × discolor, *G.C.* 1882, i. 218; *O.R.* 1905, 292; 1906, 350.—Warner.

C. × Williamsianum, *G.C.* 1882, i. 218; *V. Man. O.* iv. 100; *O.A.* viii. t. 365; *O.R.* 1893, 100; 1905, 292; *Dict. Ic. O.* Cyp. hyb. t. 29; *Day O. Draw.* xliv. t. 29.—Warner.

C. × plunerum, *G.C.* 1887, i. 40; *O.R.* 1893, 196; 1905, 293.—Cookson.

C. × doliare, *G.C.* 1887, i. 447; *O.R.* 1893, 196; 1905, 293.—Cookson.

C. × lineolare, *G.C.* 1887, i. 447; *O.R.* 1893, 196: 1905, 293.—Cookson.

C. × Ianthe, *G.C.* 1892, i. 343; *O.R.* 1893, 358; *Amer. G.* 1899, 737, f. 191 (abnormal).—Veitch.

C. × Minerva, *G.C.* 1889, ii. 464; *O.R.* 1893, 263; 1905, 293.—R. H. Measures.

C. × Leda, *G.C.* 1892, i. 202; *O.R.* 1893, 114; 1905, 293.—Bowring.

121. P. × **Chouvetii** (× Germinyanum × insigne).—Cappe, 1899.

C. × Souvenir de Emile Chouvet, *J. S. H. Fr.* 1899, 56.

122. P. × **Christopher** (× Leeanum × Simonii).—Thompson, 1902.

C. × Christopher, *G.C.* 1902, i. 67; *O.R.* 1902, 54.

C. × Diadem, *R. H. Meas. Cyp.* ed. 2, 32; Sand. O. Guide, 335.

123. P. × **chrysotoxum** (× Lathamianum ♀ × villosum).—Duval, 1900.

C. × chrysotoxum, *J. S. H. Fr.* 1900, 60; *Chron. O.* 332.—Duval.

C. × villoso-Lathamianum, *J. S. H. Fr.* 1902, 140.—Lebaudy.

124. P. × **Clarkiæ** (× Ashburtonæ × Stonei).—W. C. Clark, 1898.

C. × Mrs. Walter Clark, *G.C.* 1898, ii. 92; *O.R.* 1898, 255.

125. P. × **Claudii** (Spicerianum × vernixium ♀), *Kerch. Liv. d. O.* 477.—Moens, 1892.

C. × Claudii, *J. d. O.* 1892, 382; *Lind.* ix t. 397.

C. × Anton Joly, *G.C.* 1894, i. 198; *O.R.* 1894, 144.—Moens.

C. × Odette, *R.H. Meas. Cyp.* ed. 3, 197; *Desb. Cyp.* ed. 2, 369.—Moens.

126. P. × Cleopatra (Hookeræ ♀ × œnanthum), *Kerch. Liv. d. O.* 477.—Winn, 1892.

C. × Cleopatra, *G.C.* 1892, i. 458; *O.R.* 1893, 359.

127. P × Clinkaberryanum (Curtisii × philippinense ♀), *Kerch. Liv. d. O.* 477. Pitcher and Manda, 1893.

C. × Clinkaberryanum, *G.C.* 1893, ii. 86, f. 18; 756; *O.R.* 1893, 246; *Amer. G.* 1900. 536, 537, f. 112.

C. × warnhamense, *O.R.* 1894, 31; *G.C.* 1895, ii. 248.—Lucas.

128. P. × Clotilde (Haynaldianum × Leeanum ♀).—Moens, 1893.

C. × Clotilde Moens, *O.R.* 1893, 284; *G.M.* 1894, 34, f.

129. P × Clusia (× Crossianum ♀ × Leeanum).—Lebaudy, 1897.

C. × (unnamed), *J. S. H. Fr.* 1897, 844.

C. × Crossi-Leeanum, *J. S. H. Fr.* 1898, 286.

130. P. × Clytie (× Godseffianum ♀ × hirsutissium).—Holford, 1900.

C. × (unnamed), *G.C.* 1900, i. 30; *O.R.* 1900, 58.

131. P. × Cobbiæ (× Canhami × Colossus (J. Howes).—Cobb, 1900.

C. × Cobbiæ, *G.C.* 1900, ii. 384; *O.R.* 1900, 372.

132. P. × Coffigniezii (Lawrenceanum × vernixium ♀).—Jolibois, 1892.

C. × Julien Coffigniez, *J. S H. Fr.* 1894, 314; 1895, 238.—Opoix.

C. × Mme. Élysée Descombes, *Jard.* 1895, 53; *G.C.* 1895, i 370.

There is a doubt about the correctness of the last-named.

133. P. × Coffinetii (Dayanum × superciliare ♀).—Jolibois, 1889.

C. × (unnamed), *J. S. H. Fr.* 1889, 25, 725; 1890, 390; 1900, 391.

C × Monsieur Coffinet, *J. S. H. Fr.* 1894, 314.—Opoix.

134. P. × Colesii (Dayanum × Godefroyæ (v. leucochilum, ♀).—R. H. Measures, 1898.

P. × J. Coles, *O.R.* 1898, 335.

135. P. × Colmanii (× Harrisianum × javanicum ♀).—*Kerch Liv. d. O.* 477.—Sander, 1893.

C. × Colmanni, *R. H. Meas. Cyp.* ed. 2. 28; *Bohnh. Dict. O. Hyb.* 15; *G.C.* 1895, i. 200.

136. P. × colombense (Curtisii × nitens ♀).—Bert, 1898.

C. × colombense, *J. S. H. Fr.* 1898, 1235.

137. P. × Colossus (× nitens × villosum).—Cobb, 1894.

C. × J. Howes, *G.C.* 1894, ii. 731; *O.R.* 1895, 31.

C. × Colossus, *G.C.* 1902, i. 250, 314; *O.R.* 1902, 147.—Charlesworth

C. × Mahlerianum, *R. H. Meas. Cyp.*, ed. 3, 195.—R. H. Measures.

C. × Amy Robsart, *G C.* 1903, ii. 377; *O.R.* 1903, 365.—Whateley.

138. P. × Comet (Stonei × superciliare).—Sander, 1899.

C. × Comet, *G.C.* 1899, i. 108; *R. H. Meas. Cyp.* ed. 3, 183.

139. P. × Comus (insigne × Swanianum).—Graves, 1895.

C. × Comus, *Amer. G.* March 23, 1895 : *Hans. O. Hyb.* 141 ; *G.C.* 1895, i. 550.

140. P. × concinnum (purpuratum × Harrisianum), *Stein O.* 463.—Bowring, 1887.

C. × concinnum, *Bull Cat.* 1887, 10 ; *V. Man. O.* iv. 81 ; *Amer. G.* March, 23, 1895 ; *G.C.* 1895, i. 550.

In some of the records P. villosum is given as the second parent, but we have followed the original record, which seems to agree best with a dried flower and drawing preserved at Kew.

Fig. 49. PAPHIOPEDILUM × CONCO-BELLATULUM VAR. WALKERIANUM.

141. P. × conco-bellatulum (bellatulum × concolor).—Heath, 1891.

[See Fig. 49.

C. concolor × bellatulum, *G.C.* 1895, i. 627 ; 1896, i. 741 ; *O.R.* 1895, 187, 1896, 221, 222.—Strickland.

C. × conco-bellatulum, *G.C.* 1897, i. 354, 359 ; *O.R.* 1897, 169, 189.—Statter.

C. × Walkerianum, *G.M.* 1898, 386 ; *O.R.* 1898, 233.—Druce.

P. × Walkerianum, *O.R.* 1903, 360, f. 53.—Druce.

142. P. × conco-callosum (callosum × concolor ♀).—R. H. Measures, 1895.

C. × conco-callosum, *O.R.* 1895, 14; 1900, 28.

C. × McNabianum (callosum ♀), *G.C* 1896, ii. 471; *O.R.* 1896, 349: *Desb. Cyp.* ed. 2, 322.—Sander.

143. P × concolawre (concolor ♀ × Lawrenceanum).—Lawrence, 1893.

C. × conco-Lawre, *G C.* 1893, i. 206; 1896, i. 337; *O.R.* 1893, 15, 94; 1896, 122: *J. H.* 1893, i. 193, **f.** 41; *O. Alb.* xi. **t.** 506; *O.R.* 1894, 337, **f.** 33; *Lind.* ix. **t.** 408.

C. × "concolor inversum" (Lawrenceanum ♀), *J. S. H. Fr.* 1894, 582.—Mantin.

C. × Lawre-conco, *O.K.* 1893, 286.—Sander.

C. × Lawre-concolor, *R. H. Meas. Cyp.* ed. 2, 69.—Sander.

C. × Lawrenceo-Regnieri, *Lind.* xi. t. 504.—Bleu.

C. × (unnamed), *J. S. H. Fr.* 1895, 178, 799.—Mantin.

144. P. × conco-villosum (concolor × villosum), *J. R. H. S.* xxiv. 100. —Sander, 1898.

C. × conco-villosum, *G.C.* 1897, i. 210, 390; *O.R.* 1897, 127; 1899, 155, 185; *Dict. Ic. O.* Cyp. hyb. **t.** 40.

145. P. × conspicuum (Harrisianum × villosum) *Kerch. Liv. d. O.* 477.—Swan, 1888.

C. × conspicuum, *G.C.* 1888, i. 521; *O.R.* 1893, 227; *R. H. Meas. Cyp.* ed, 2, 23.

C. × claptonense, *G.C.* 1889, i. 168; *O.R.* 1893, 262.—Low.

C. ×. Wallaertii, *G.C.* 1892, ii. 249.—Pitcher and Manda.

C. × Wallaertianum, *R. H. Meas. Cyp.* ed. 2, 109, 110; *G.C.* 1895, ii. 655.—Peeters.

C. × ornatum, *G.C.* 1892, i. 428; *Desb. Cyp.* ed. 2, 377.—Hye.

C. × Masonianum, *R. H. Meas. Cyp.* ed. 2, 75.—Sander.

C. × villoso-Harrisianum, *O.R.* 1894, 28; *Desb. Cyp.* ed. 2, 467.—Pourbaïx.

C. × Gautieri, *J. S. H. Fr.* 1896, 24.—(Moreau) Cardoso.

C. × Harrisianum v. Wallaertianum, *Desb. Cyp.* ed. 2, 219.

C. × W. A. Allen, *R. H. Meas. Cyp.* ed. 3, 174.—McArthur.

C. × Harrisi-villosum, *J. S. H. Fr.* 1899, 133; *G.C.* 1902, ii. 344; *O.R.* 1902, 362.—Lebaudy.

C. × (unnamed). *J. S. H. Fr.* 1900, 113.—Mantin.

C. × Alfred Thierrard, *J. S. H. Fr.* 1901, 1062.—Cappe.

C. × Rex, *G.C.* 1903, i. 126; *O.R.* 1903, 87.—Gratrix.

146. P. × Constableanum (Dayanum × Fairrieanum), *Kerch Liv. d. O.* 477: *O.R.* 1900, 10; 1905, 38.—Pitcher and Manda, 1893.

C. × Constableanum, *Gard.* 1893, i. 75; *O.R.* 1893, 118.

147. P. × Constance (Curtisii × Stonei ♀), *Stein. O.* 464.—Drewett, 1890.

C. × Constance, *G.C.* 1890, ii. 294; *O.R.* 1893, 294; *J.H.* 1890, ii. 353. **f.** 40; 1903, ii. 259, **f.**; *J. S. H. Fr.* 1897, 944.

C. × James H. Veitch (Curtisii ♀), *G.C.* 1894, ii. 258, 287, **f.** 40: *O.R.* 1894, 309: *J.H.* 1894, ii. 227, **f.** 33.—Veitch.

148. **P.** × **Conwayi** (callosum × exul).—Wellesley, 1902.

C. × Dr. Conway, *G.C.* 1902, i. 85; *O.R.* 1902, 53.

149. **P.** × **Cooksonæ** (Curtisii ♀ × Sanderianum).—Cookson, 1900.

C. × Sanderiano-Curtisii, *G.C.* 1900, i. 62, 75, f. 23; *O.R.* 1900, 59; *Gard.* 1900, i. 74, f.

150. **P.** × **corbeillense** (Bullenianum × insigne), *Kerch. Liv. d. O.* 477.—Darblay, 1892.

C. × corbeillense, *J. S. H. Fr.* 1892, 611; *Rev. H.* 1893, 250; *O.R.* 1893, 212.

151. **P.** × **Coronis** (× Leeanum × Lynchianum).—Sander, 1902.

C. × Coronis, *G.C.* 1902, ii. 344; *O.R.* 1902, 364.

152. **P.** × **Cowleyanum** (Curtisii ♀ × niveum), *Kerch. Liv. d. O.* 477.—Tautz, 1892.

C. × Cowleyanum, *G.C.* 1892, i. 72; 1896, i. 656; *J. d. O.* 1892, ii. 357; *O.R.* 1893, 359; 1896, 190.

C. × F. S. Roberts, *G.C.* 1898, i. 47; *O.R.* 1898, 62, 63, 75; *G.M.* 1898, 249, f. ("F. S. Ames" by error), 256; *J.H.* 1898, i. 77, f. 12.—Low.

C. × Non Plus Ultra, *O.R.* 1898, 364.

153. **P.** × **crassifolium** (Lawrenceanum × Sementa ♀).

C. × crassifolium, *Jard.* 1903, 64; *J. S. H. Fr.* 1903, 71.—Ferrier.

154. **P.** × **Creon** (Harrisianum ♀ × œnanthum), *Stein O.* 464.—Veitch, 1891.

C. × Creon, *G.C.* 1891, i. 214; *J. d. O.* ii. 6; *J.H.* 1892, i. 197, 205, f. 31; *O.R.* 1893, 61, 327.

C. × La Nymphe, *G.C.* 1892, i. 214.—Ingram.

C. × Mrs. Warren Hook, *O.R.* 1893, 117.—Pitcher and Manda.

C. × Brennus, *R. H. Meas. Cyp.* ed. 2, 94.—R. H. Measures.

C. × Brunius, *R. H. Meas. Cyp.* ed. 3, 26.—R. H. Measures.

155. **P.** × **Crethus** (Argus × Spicerianum ♀).—*Kerch. Liv. d. O.* 477.—Veitch, 1892.

C. × Crethus, *G.C.* 1892, ii. 622; *O.R.* 1893, 359.

C. × Argus-Spicerianum, *G.C.* 1894, ii. 731; *O.R.* 1895, 32.—Low.

C. × Memoire d'Edouard Pynaert, *Rev. H. Belge*, 1905, 95.—De Smet Duvivier.

156. **P.** × **Crossianum** (insigne ♀ × venustum), *Stein O.* 464.—Ashburton, 1873.

C. × Crossianum, *G.C.* 1873, 877; 1889, i. 9, 43; *Ill. H.* 1888, 97, t. 72; *V.Man.O.* iv. 82; *O.R.* 1893, 37; *Desb. Cyp.* ed. 2, 144.

C. × amandum, *G.C.* 1887, i. 174; *O.R.* 1893, 196.—Bowring.

C. × aurantiacum, *R. H. Meas. Cyp.* ed. 2, 9; *Boyle Woodl. O.* 197.—Sander.

C. × Francis Heygate, *G.C.* 1902, ii. 313; *O.R.* 1902, 324.—Heygate.

157. **P.** × **Curtia** (Curtisii × Dayanum)—Oakes Ames, 1900.

C. × Dayano-Curtisii, *Amer. G.* 1900, 151.

158. **P.** × **Cybele** (Druryi × Lawrenceanum), *Kerch. Liv. d. O.* 477.—Pitcher and Manda, 1892.

C. × Cybele, *Gard. & For.* 1892, 562; *G.C.* 1895, i. 199.

C. × basileum, *R. H. Meas. Cyp.* ed. 2, 16.—R. H. Measures.

C. × highfieldense, *G.C.* 1896, i. 530; *O.R.* 1896, 159; *Gard.* 1896, i. 316 (" highfieldianum ").—Burton.

C. × Drurio-Lawrenceanum, *O.R.* 1897, 349; *G.C.* 1897, ii. 277.—Veitch.

C. × Lawrenceo-Druryi, *G.C.* 1897, ii. 113.—Sander.

159. P. × Cycnides (bellatulum ♀ × Swanianum).—Hollington, 1894.

[See Fig 50.

Fig. 50. PAPHIOPEDILUM × CYCNIDES VAR. WILLIAM LLOYD.

C. × William Lloyd, *G.C.* 1894, ii. 731, 757, **f.** 97; *J.H.* 1894, ii. 557, **f.** 91; *O.R.* 1895, 32, 177, **f.** 7; 304; 1896, 99; *Boyle Woodl. O.* 182, 191, **t.**; *G.M.* 1894, 794, **f.**—Hollington.

C. × Cycnides, *O.R.* 1895, 304; 1896, 99; *Boyle Woodl. O.* 180 ("Cyanides"). —R. H. Measures.

C. × General French, *G.C.* 1900, ii. 18; *O.R.* 1900, 250.—Hollington.

160. P. × Cymatodes (Curtisii ♀ × superbiens), *O.R.* 1900, 184, **f.** 32. —Tautz, 1893.

[See. Fig. 51.

C. × Cymatodes, *R. H. Meas. Cyp.* 1893, ed. 2, 29 : *G.C*, ii. 684 (unnamed). —R. H. Measures.

C. × beechense, *G.C.* 1894, i. 762 : *O.R.* 1894, 223.—W. R. Lee.

161. P. × Cythera (purpuratum × Spicerianum ♀). *Kerch. Liv. d. O.* 478.—R. H. Measures, 1890.

C. × Cythera, *G.C.* 1890, i. 73 ; *O.R.* 1893, 295.

C. × Maynardii, *G.C.* 1890, ii. 702 ; *Reichenb.* ser. 2, i. 93, **t.** 43, **f.** 2 ; *J.H.* 1891, i. 281, **f.** 51 ; *O.R.* 1893, 326.—Sander.

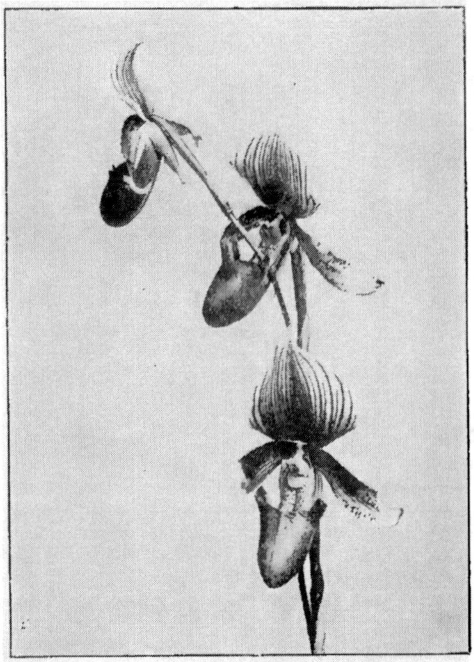

Fig. 51. PAPHIOPEDILUM × CYMATODES.

C. × Cecilia, *R. H. Meas. Cyp.* ed. 2, 25.—Sander.

C. × Rodigasianum, *R. H. Meas. Cyp.* ed. 2, 90 ; *G.C.* 1895, i. 200.—Capart.

162. P. × Dacia (purpuratum ♀ × superbiens).—Sander, 1903.

C. × purpurato-Veitchii, *Gard.* 1903, ii. 210.—Sander.

163. P. × Dædalus (insigne ♀ × vexillarium). *O.R.* 1898, 360 ; 1900, 104, 1905, 71.—Young, 1898.

164. P. × Daisyæ (Lowii ♀ × œnanthum), *Kerch. Liv. d. O.* 478.—Graves, 1892.

C. × Daisyæ, *G.C.* 1892, ii. 301 ; *Gard. & For.* 1892, 460, 463, **f.** 79 : *J. d. O.* iii. 249 ; *O.R.* 1893, 12, 360.

165. **P.** × **Dakini** (barbatum ♀ × Lathamianum).—Hurst, 1900.

C. × Lilian, *G.C.* 1898, ii. 375; *Sand. O. Guide*, 336.—Charlesworth.

166 **P.** × **Dallemagnei** (Druryi ♀ × hirsutissimum).—Dallemagne, 1900.

P. × Druryi-hirsutissimum, *J. S. H. Fr.* 1900, 840.

167. **P.** × **Danervaliæ** (philippinense × selligerum).—Opoix, 1897.

C. × Madame N. Danerval, *J. S. H. Fr.* 1897, 945.

C. × Monsieur Danerval, *J. S. H. Fr.* 1898, 283.

168. **P.** × **Daphne** (Charlesworthii × exul), *O.R.* 1903, 59.—Appleton, 1903.

C. × Daphne, *G.C.* 1903, ii. 326; *O.R.* 1903, 367.—Keeling.

169. **P.** × **Deception** (hirsutissimum × venustum). Carnus, 1895.

C. × Deception, *Bohnh. Dict. O. Hyb.* 16.

Fig. 52. Paphiopedilum × Deedmanianum.

170. **P.** × **Decia** (Charlesworthii ♀ × superciliare).—Bull, 1902.

C. × Decia, *G.C.* 1902, ii. 106; *O.R.* 1902, 275.

171. **P.** × **decipiens** (Charlesworthii × Lawrenceanum).—Duval, 1899.

C. × decipiens, *J. S. H. Fr.* 1899, 832.—Duval.

C. × Lawrenceano-Charlesworthii, *G.C.* 1901, ii. 59; 1903, i. 78; *O.R.* 1901, 252.—Low.

C. × Lawrenworthii, *O.R.* 1901, 351.—Peeters.

172. **P.** × **decorum** (Lawrenceanum × nitens), *Kerch. Liv. d. O.* 478.—Hye, 1891.

C. × decorum, *Rev. H. Belge*, 1892, 6; *O.R.* 1893, 12, 360.

C. × Ganesa, *O.R.* 1893, 308; *G.C.* 1893, ii. 342.—R. I. Measures.

C. × Johnsonianum, *G.C.* 1892, ii. 714; *O.R.* 1893, 31; *J.H.* 1893, i. 171, **f.** 30.—Sander.

C. × Cobbianum, *G.C.* 1893, ii. 692; *O.R.* 1894, 29.—Cobb.

C. × giganteum, *G.C.* 1902, i. 67; *O.R.* 1902, 54.—Statter.

173. P. × Deedmanianum (Chamberlainianum × Spicerianum ♀), *O.R.* 1898, 49, **f.** 2; 70.—Latham, 1897. **[See Fig. 52.**

C. × Deedmanianum, *G.C.* 1897, ii. 388; *O.R.* 1898, 29; *Amer. G.* 1900, 874, f. 218.

C. × scitulum, *J. S H. Fr.* 1898, 351; *Cogn. Chron. O.* 158; *O.R.* 1899, 132.—Cappe.

C. × Spicero-Chamberlainianum, *Le Jard.* 1899, 39; *O.R.* 1899, 132.—Cappe.

C. × Dr. Ryan, *Boyle Woodl. O.* 219, **t.**; *O.R.* 1902, 7.—R. H. Measures.

C. × Watteau, *J. S. H. Fr.* 1898, 1236; 1902, 140.—Doin.

C. × Chamberlaini-Spicerianum, *J. S. H. Fr.* 1900, 112.—Opoix.

174. P. × Descombesiæ (Argus × œnanthum ♀).—Opoix, 1894.

C. × Madamoiselle Josée Descombes, *J. S. H. Fr.* 1894, 139; 1895, 238.

C. × Madame Josci Descombes, *G.C.* 1895, i. 200.

175. P. × Descombesii (barbatum ♀ × ciliolare).—Opoix, 1894.

C. × Mons. Elysée Descombes, *J. S. H. Fr.* 1894, 583.

C. × Descombesii, *O.R.* 1899, 330.

176. P. × Dido (Sanderianum × selligerum ♀).—Lawrence, 1895.

C. × (unnamed), *G.C.* 1895, ii. 49; *O.R.* 1895, 254.

C. × Sanderi-selligerum, *G.C.* 1895, ii. 192; *O.R.* 1895, 286.

177. P. × Donatii (× Ashburtonæ ♀ × Spicerianum).—Sander, 1893.

C. × Joseph Donat, *G.C.* 1893, ii. 630; *O.R.* 1893, 374.

178. P. × **Doncasterianum** (callosum × hirsutissimum ♀), *J.R.H.S.* xxiv. 102.—Sander, 1894.

C. × Doncasterianum, *G.C.* 1894, ii. 670; *O.R.* 1895, 30.

C. × Furzeanum, *R. H. Meas. Cyp.* ed. 3, 187.—Sander.

179. P. × **Dora** (bellatulum ♀ × Charlesworthii).—Charlesworth, 1900.

C. × Dora Crawshaw, *G.C.* 1900, ii. 346, 375, **f.** 117; *O.R.* 1900, 371, 374; *J.H.* 1900, ii. 437, **f.** 117; *Gard.* 1900, ii. 406, **f.**

C. × Edithæ, *Sand. O. Guide*, 335.

C. × Para, *G.C.* 1903, ii. 230; *O.R.* 1903, 310.—Rogerson.

180. P. × **Doris** (Stonei × venustum ♀), *Stein O.* 465.—Cookson, 1890.

C. × Doris, *G.C.* 1890, ii. 716; *O.R.* 1893, 295.

181. P. × **Drewettii** (Lowii × niveum).—Drewett, 1892.

C. niveum × Lowii, *G.C.* 1892, i. 470.—Lewis.

C. × niveo-Lowii, *R. H. Meas. Cyp.* ed. 2, 78.—Drewett.

182. P. × **Druryo-Hookeræ** (Druryi × Hookeræ).—Veitch, 1896.

C. × Druryo-Hookeræ, *G.C.* 1896, i. 530; *O.R.* 1896, 160, 187; *Dict. Ic. O.* Cyp. hyb. **t.** 39.

183. P. × **Durbar** (hirsutissimum × Morganiæ).—Sander, 1903.

C. × "The Durbar," *G.C.* 1903, i. 46; *O.R.* 1903, 51.

184. **P.** × **Duvalii** (ciliolare × nitens ♀).—Duval, 1900.

C. × Sallieri-ciliolare, *J. S. H. Fr.* 1900, 118; *Jard.* 1902, 79.—Duval.

C. × Pleides, *Charlesw. Cat.* Feb. 1900; *Sand. O. Guide*, 336.—Charlesworth

Fig. 53. PAPHIOPEDILUM × EDMUNDII (on the left), with its two parents.
Fig. 54. P. × NITENS VAR. HYEANUM (on the right).

185. **P.** × **Echo** (Hookeræ ♀ × insigne), *Kerch. Liv. d. O* 478.—Graves, 1894.

C. × Echo, *O.R.* 1894, 111.

186. **P.** × **Edith** (Boxallii × Rothschildianum).—(Cookson) R. I. Measures, 1900.

C. × Boxallo-Rothschildianum, *G.C.* 1900, i. 174; *O.R.* 1900, 125.—R. I. Measures.

C. × Rothschildiano-Boxallii, *Sand. O. Guide*, 337.

C. × Edith, *G.C.* 1903, ii. 343; *O.R.* 1903. 367.—Rogerson.

187. P. × Edmundii (Hookeræ × nitens).—Rothwell, 1902. **[See Fig. 53.**

C. × Edmund Rothwell, *Amer. G.* 1902, 137, 138, **f.** 33; *O.R.* 1902, 144, **f.** 16.

188. P × Edwardii (Fairrieanum × superbiens ♀), *Kerch. Liv. d. O.* 478; *O.R.* 1900, 9, **f.** 4; 1905, 39, **f.** 7.—Graves, 1892. **[See Fig. 55.**

C. × Edwardii, *O.R.* 1893, 23, **f.** 2; *G.C.* 1893, ii. 133; *G. World*, 1903, 682, **f.**

189. P. × Eira (Chamberlainianum × concolor).—Wigan, 1903.

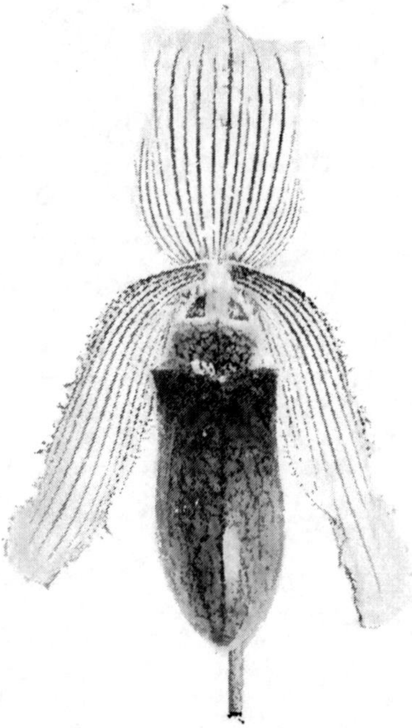

Fig. 55. Paphiopedilum × Edwardii.

C. × Eira, *G.C.* 1903, i. 108; *O.R.* 1903, 82.

190. P. × Eismannianum (Boxallii × Harrisianum), *Kerch. Liv. d. O.* 478.—Seeger and Tropp, 1890.

C. × Eismannianum, *Garden*, 1890, ii. 608.

C. × tenebrosum, *G.C.* 1894, i. 211; *O.R.* 1894, 95; *Desb. Cyp.* ed. 2, 447.—Tate.

C. × Lobengula, *G.C.* 1894, i. 343; *O.R.* 1894, 126.—Ingram.

C. × (unnamed), *J. S. H. Fr.* 1895, 25.—Lebaudy.

C. × amabile, *Jard.* 1895, 53; *J. S. H. Fr.* 1896, 298; *G.C.* 1895, i. 370; *O.R.* 1896, 11.—Lebaudy.

C. × Suzanne Cayeux, *J. S. H. Fr.* 1899, 58 —Cayeux.

C. × Alfred Thierrard, *J. S. H. Fr.* 1901, 1062.—Cappe.

191. P. × Elinor (× selligerum ♀ × superbiens), *Kerch. Liv. d. O.* 478. —Drewett, 1890.

C. × Elinor, *G.C.* 1890, ii. 38; *O.R.* 1893, 294.

C. × Denisianum, *G.C.* 1894, ii. 118; *G.M.* 1896, 216, f.; *O.R.* 1894, 276 *Lind.* x. t. 437.—Linden.

192. P. × Elise (× Pallas × Rothschildianum).—Feiling, 1903.

C. × Elise, *G.C.* 1903, ii. 214; *O R.* 1903, 308.

193. P. × Elizabethæ (Lawrenceanum × Parishii).—R. H. Measures, 1893.

C. × Elizabethæ, R. H. Meas. Cyp. ed. 2, 35; *Hans. O. Hyb.* 145.—R. I. Measures.

C. × (unnamed), *O.R.* 1894, 106.—R. I. Measures.

194. P. × Elsie (Boxallii × Charlesworthii).—Appleton, 1903.

C. × Elsie, *G.C.* 1903, ii. 429.

195. P. × Endymion (barbatum ♀ × Mastersianum), *O.R.* 1899, 47.—Young, 1899.

C. × Endymion, *Dict. Ic. O.* Cyp. hyb. t. 33.

196. P. × enfieldense (Hookeræ × Lawrenceanum ♀), *Kerch. Liv. d. O.* 478.—Hollington, 1891.

C × enfieldense, *G.C.* 1891, ii. 546; *O.R.* 1893, 309, 327: 1896, 40.

C. × Hebe, *G.C.* 1893, ii. 342; *O.R.* 1893, 309, 319.—R. I. Measures.

C. × Richardsoni, *G.C.* 1893, ii. 470; *Will. O. Gr. Man.* 1894, 295.—Hollington.

C. × suffusum, *G.C* 1895, i. 210; *O.R.* 1896, 40.—Burton.

C. × Lawrenceano-Hookeræ, *J. S. H. Fr.* 1895, 163.—Bleu.

197. P. × Enid (bellatulum ♀ × Spicerianum).—Veitch, 1897.

C. × Enid, *G.C.* 1897, i. 115; *O.R.* 1897, 93, 161; *J. S. H. Fr.* 1901, 90; *Dict. Ic. O.* Cyp. hyb. t. 68.

198. P. × Ensign (barbatum × Harrisianum ♀), *Kerch. Liv. d. O.* 478.—Winn, 1892.

C. × Ensign, *G.C.* 1892, i. 73; *O.R.* 1893, 12, 359.

199. P. × Eos (Charlesworthii × niveum ♀), *O.R.* 1901, 14.—Appleton, 1900.

C. × Eos, *G.C.* 1902, ii. 143..

200. P. × Ephialtes (× auroreum × insigne), *Kerch. Liv. d. O.* 478.—Pitcher & Manda, 1892.

C. × Ephialtes, *Gard. & For.* 1892, 562.

201. P. × Erato (hirsutissimum × nitens ♀), *Kerch. Liv. d. O.* 478.—Vuylsteke, 1892.

C. × (unnamed), *Rev. H. Belge*, 1892, 238.—Vuylsteke.

C. × Erato, *O.R.* 1893, 118; *Dict. Ic. O.* Cyp. hyb. t. 5.

C. × hirsuto-Sallieri, *G.C.* 1897, i. 177; *O.R.* 1897, 124; *J.H.* 1897, ii. 389, f. 58.—Lawrence.

C. × Leopoldianum, *Desb. Cyp.* ed. 2, 310; *R. H. Meas. Cyp.* ed. 3, 194.—Vuylsteke.

C. × (unnamed), *J. S. H. Fr.* 1903, 130.—Garden.

202. P. × Eros (barbatum ♀ × Canhami), *O.R.* 1898, 335.—Wills, 1898.

203. P. × erubescens (Charlesworthii × hirsutissimum), *O.R.* 1903, 68.—Ross.

204 P. × Ettyi (Godefroyæ × insigne).—Drewett, 1901. **[See Fig. 56.**

C. × Robert Etty, *G.C.* 1901, i. 209; *O.R.* 1901, 121.

P. × Dowlingianum, *O.R.* 1902, 101; *G.M.* 1902, 134.—Appleton.

Fig. 56. Paphiopedilum × Ettyi var. Queen of Italy.

C. × Dowlerianum, *G.C.* 1902, i. 152; *O.R.* 1902, 91.—Appleton.

C. × Hindeanum, *G.C.* 1903, i. 46, 53, **f.** 26; *O.R.* 1903, 51.—Sander.

C. × Queen of Italy, *G.C.* 1903, ii. 377; *O.R.* 1903, 366.—Charlesworth.

P. × Queen of Italy, *O.R.* 1904, 17, **f.** 8.—Charlesworth.

205. P. × Eucharis (insigne ♀ × Lawrenceanum), *Kerch. Liv. d. O.* 478.—Vuylsteke, 1893.

C. × Eucharis, *G.C.* 1893, i. 195; *O.R.* 1893, 87; *Dict. Ic. O.* Cyp. Hyb. **t.** 53 (v. Fournierianum).

C. × Umlauftianum, *G.C.* 1893, ii. 70; *O.R.* 1893, 286.—Sander.

C. × Acis, *R. H. Meas. Cyp.* ed. 2, 3; *J. S. H. Fr.* 1894, 582; *Bohnh. Dict. O. Hyb.* 9.

C. × Fournierianum, *R. H. Meas. Cyp.* ed. 2, 39.—Sander.

C. × Eylesianum, *G.C.* 1896, i. 655.—Lewis.

C. × Lawrenceano-Chantini, *J. S. H. Fr.* 1897, 465; 1899, 55.—Bleu.

C. × (unnamed), *J. S. H. Fr.* 1896, 742.—Cardoso.

206. P. × **Euryale** (Lawrenceanum × superbiens), *Stein O.* 466.—Veitch, 1887.

C. × Euryale, *V. Man. O.* iv. 83: *O.R.* 1893, 262.

C × Vervaetianum, *G.C.* 1888, i. 712; *O.R.* 1893, 228; *V. Man. O.* iv. 83.

C. × Siemonii, *Pucci Cyp.* 187; *Desb. Cyp.* ed. 2. 426.—Pucci.

C. × Robinsonianum. *R. H. Meas. Cyp.* ed. 2, 90.—Sander.

C. × Lawrenceano-superbiens, *J. S. H. Fr.* 1894, 414.—Bleu.

C. × Roch Jolibois, *J. S. H. Fr.* 1897, 686.—Opoix.

207. P. × **euryandrum** (barbatum ♀ × Stonei), *Stein O.* 466.—Veitch, 1875.

C. × euryandrum, *G.C.* 1875, ii. 772; *Fl. d. Ser.* t. 2278; *O. Alb.* vii. t. 301; *V. Man. O.* iv. 83, f.; *Gard.* 1881, ii. 636, 637, f.; *Orchidoph.* 1883, 764, f.; *O.R.* 1893, 38; *Will. O. Gr. Man.* ed. 6, 244, f.; *Day O. Draw.* xxx. t. 61.

C. × hybridum, *Fl. M.* 1875, t. 187.

C. × The Duke, *G.C.* 1893, i. 206; *O.R.* 1893, 95.

C. × Duke, *Bohnh. Dict. O. Hyb.* 17.

C. × intermedium, *Hans. O. Hyb.* 146; *Desb. Cyp.* ed. 2, 270.

208. P. × **Eurydice** (Hookeræ × Spicerianum ♀).—Graves, 1894.

C. × Eurydice, *Hans. O. Hyb.* 146.

209. P. × **Eurylochus** (ciliolare ♀ × hirsutissimum), *Kerch. Liv. d. O.* 478.—Veitch, 1892.

C. × Eurylochus, *G.C.* 1892, i. 664; *O.R.* 1893, 359.

210. P. × **Evadne** (Charlesworthii ♀ × superbiens).—Charlesworth, 1901.

C. × General Knox, *Charlesw. Cat.* 1901; *Sand. O. Guide*, 335.—Charlesworth.

P. × (unnamed), *O.R.* 1903, 91.—Young.

C. × Evadne, *G.C.* 1904, ii. 156; *Sand. O. Guide*, 335.—Goodson.

P. × General Knox, *O.R.* 1905, 281.—Young.

211. P. × **Evelyn** (× Calypso × Leeanum).—Oakes Ames, 1900.

C. × Evelyn Ames, *Amer. G.* 1900, 112, 113, f. 20; *O.R.* 1900, 95; *Amer. Florist*, 1903, 567, f. (v. superbum).—Oakes Ames.

C. × The Gem, *G.C.* 1900, i 110; *O R.* 1900, 89.—Ingram.

C. × Mrs. W. Mostyn, *G.C.* 1902, i 50, 75, f. 28; *O.R.* 1902, 51; *J.H.* 1902, i. 101, f.

212. P. × **Evenor** (Argus ♀ × concolor), *Kerch. Liv. d. O.* 478.—Veitch, 1892.

C. × Evenor, *G.C.* 1892, i. 661; 1895, i. 199; *O.R.* 1893, 11, 188, 359; *Lind.* ii. t. 497 (v. grandiflorum); *G. World*, 1898, 635, f. (Southgate var.).

The original record of parentage was C. Argus × bellatulum, but this was afterwards amended as above.

213. P. × Excelsior (× Harrisianum × Rothschildianum ♀).—Statter, 1894.

C. × Excelsior, *G.C.* 1894, ii. 194; *O.R.* 1894, 286; *Desb. Cyp.* ed. 2, 119, 180, f. (v. Mars.)

C. × excellens, *O.R.* 1884, 275.—Statter.

214. P. × eximium (Boxallii × Germinyanum).—Veitch, 1902.

C. × eximium, *O.R.* 1902, 115; 1905, 118; *Sand. O. Guide*, 335.

215. P. × exoptatum (ciliolare × superciliare ♀).—Bleu. 1898.

C. × exoptatum, *J. S. H. Fr.* 1899, 707.

216. P × Eyermanianum (barbatum ♀ × Spicerianum). *Stein O.* 467.—Sander, 1890.

C. × Eyermanianum, *G.C.* 1890, ii. 746; *O.R.* 1893, 295, 309; 1894, 22; *Reichenb.* ser. 2, i. 81, t. 38, f. 2; *Dict. Ic. O.* Cyp. hyb. t. 34 (v. Hermione).

C. × Hermione (Spicerianum ♀), *G.C.* 1893, ii. 682.—Young.

C. × Diana, *G.C.* 1893, ii. 342; *O.R.* 1893, 319.—Sander.

C. × De Bosscherianum, *Rev. H. Belge*, 1892, 6.—Vuylsteke.

C. × Bosscherianum, *G.C.* 1892, i. ii.—Vuylsteke.

C. × Alector, *G.C.* 1895, i. 199.—Veitch.

C. × Zephyr, *Sand. O. Guide* 274.

217. P. × Fabia (Lawrenceanum × Pollettianum).—Charlesworth, 1900.

C. × Ajax, *Charlesw. Cat.* 1900; *G.C.* 1902, ii. 370; *Sand. O. Guide*, 334.

218.—P. × Fairy-Queen (Curtisii ♀ × Druryi).—Sander, 1896.

C. × Fairy-Queen, *G.C.* 1896, ii. 471; *O.R.* 1896, 349; *Desb. Cyp.* ed. 2. 187; *Amer. G.* 1903, 335, f.

219. P. × Faroultii (Rothschildianum × Spicerianum ♀).—Faroult, 1893.

C. × (unnamed), *J. S. H. Fr.* 1893, 756.

220. C. × Fausianum (× calophyllum × Harrisianum ♀), *Kerch. Liv. d. O.* 478.—Sander, 1893.

C. × Fausianum, *G.C.* 1893, ii. 133; *O.R.* 1893, 286.

221. P. × Favarger (Charlesworthii × concinnum).—Rehder, 1900.

C. × Favarger, *G.C.* 1900, i. 110; *O.R.* 1900, 89.

222. P. × Felicity (callosum × tonsum).—Pitt, 1902.

C. × Felicity, *G.C.* 1902, i. 152; *O.R.* 1902, 91, 308.

There appears to be a slight doubt about the parentage of this hybrid.

223. P. × festum (barbatum × chloroneurum).—Seeger, 1902.

C. × festum, *Gard.* 1892, i. 26; *G.C.* 1895, i. 199.

224. P. × Figaro (× œnanthum × Spicerianum ♀) *Kerch. Liv. d. O.* 478. Seeger and Tropp, 1889.

C. × Figaro, *G.C.* 1889, ii. 750; *O.R.* 1893, 263.

C. × Tityus, *G.C.* 1892, ii. 622; *O.R.* 1893, 13, 358; 1899, 17, f. 4.—Veitch.

C. × Chas. Reffold (œnanthum ♀) *G.C.* 1892, ii. 745; *O.R.* 1896, 361.—Ingram.

C. × Clarence, *G.C.* 1894, ii. 605; *O.R.* 1894, 375.—Wigan.

C. × œno-Spicerianum, *G.C.* 1895, ii. 200; *O.R.* 1896, 361; *J. S. H. Fr.* 1902, 35. R. I Measures.

225. **P. × Finetianum** (ciliolare ♀ × philippinense).—Seeger, 1893.

C. × Finetianum, *R. H. Meas. Cyp.* ed. 2, 37.—Seeger.

C. × Alfred Hollington, *G.C.* 1895, ii. 467; *O.R.* 1895, 351.—Hollington.

C. × Hollingtoni, *O.R.* 1899, 330.—Hollington.

226. **P. × Finetii** (callosum ♀ × Godefroyæ).—Regnier, 1891.

C. × Mons. Finet, *Orchidoph.* 1891, 321, 5, **ff**; *Desb. Cyp.* ed. 2, 346.

C. × Felix Faure (Godefroyæ) *J. d. O.* v. 372; *J. S. H. Fr.* 1895, 477; *G.C.* 1895, i. 228; *Lind.* X. **t.** 469; *O.R.* 1895, 216.—Dallemagne.

C. × Fournieri, *J. S. H. Fr.* 1893, 185.—Regnier.

C. Madame Regnier, *J. S. H. Fr.* 1897, 684. -Regnier.

227. **P. × Fitchianum** (Bullenianum × venustum), *Stein O.* 467; *O.R.* 1899, 52.—Williams, 1888.

C, × Fitchianum, *O. Alb.* vii. **t.** 350; *O.R.* 1899, 52.

Originally described as a hybrid between C. Hookeræ and C. barbatum, which is clearly erroneous.

228. **P. × Florence** (Druryi × Harrisianum).—Ross, 1901.

P. × (unnamed), *O.R.* 1901, 223.

229. **P. × Fordianum** (callosum × Stonei ♀).—Sander, 1895.

C. × Fordianum, *G.C.* 1895, i. 210; *O.R.* 1895, 96.

230. **P. × Fortuna** (callosum × Hookeræ), *O.R.* 1899, 100.—(Charlesworth) Young, 1896.

231. **P. × Fowleræ** (Chamberlainianum × insigne).—Sander, 1899.

C. × Gertrude, *R. H. Meas. Cyp.* ed. 3, 63, *Boyle Woodl. O.* 194.—Sander.

C. × Miss Louisa Fowler, *G.C.* 1899, i. 77; *O.R.* 1899, 92; *G.M.* 1899, 88, **f.**—Fowler.

C. × Rogeri, *J. S. H. Fr.* 1900, 179; 1901, 90.—Page.

C. Chamberlaino-insigne, *G.C.* 1900, i. 143; *O.R.* 1900, 90.—Lawrence.

C. × hybridum Frau Geheimrat Borsig, *Gtfl.* 1902, 393, **t.** 1501; *O.R.* 1902, 288.—Borsig.

C. × bingleyense superbum, *G.C.* 1900, ii. 424; *Sand. O. Guide*, 334.—Hayward.

C. × Alexandræ, *J. S. H. Fr.* 1903, 190; *Jard.* 1903, 128; *Rev. H.* 1903, 218.—Fournier.

C. × Chamber-insigne, *J.H.* 1901, i. 311, *Sand. O. Guide*, 334.

232. **P. × Fowleri** (callosum × Rothschildionum).—Fowler, 1897.

C. × callo-Rothschildianum, *G.C.* 1897, ii. 113; *O.R.* 1897. 286.

233. **P. × Frederico-nobile** (Boxallii × Morganiæ).—Seeger and Trapp, 1891.

C. × Frederico-nobile, *Garden*, 1891, i. 345; *R.H. Meas. Cyp.* ed. 2, 39.

C. × Fredericus nobilis, *G.C.* 1895, i. 199.

234. P. × **fulgens** (Hookeræ × marmorophyllum).—Sander, 1893.

C. × fulgens, *R. H. Meas. Cyp.* ed. 2, 39 : *G.C.* 1895, i. 200.

235. P. × **Gabrieli** (Harrisianum × orphanum).—Gabriel, 1899.

C. × Gabrieli, *R. H. Meas. Cyp.* ed. 3, 61.

236. P. × **gandavense** (barbatum × Swanianum, *Kerch. Liv. d. O.* 479.—Pitcher and Manda, 1888.

C. × gandavense, *Lind.* iii. 100; *Desb. Cyp.* ed. 2, 196.

C. × Olivet, *Hans. O. Hyb.* 169; *Jard.* 1895, 53; *G.C.* 1895, i. 370.—Mantin.

237. P. × **Ganymedes** (× œnanthum × tonsum ♀), *O.R.* 1900, 20.—Young, 1899.

238. P. × **Garfieldii** (× regale × tonsum).—Oakes Ames, 1900.

C. × James Garfield, *Amer. G.* 1900, 277.

239. P. × **Gaudianum** (Curtisii ♀ × Harrisianum).—Fournier, 1903.

C. × Gaudianum, *Dict. Ic. O.* Cyp. hyb. **t.** 56.

C. × (unnamed), *J. S. H. Fr.* 1903, 37; *Rev. H.* 1903, 47.—Fournier.

240. P. × **Gayotiæ** (Dayanum ♀ × insigne).—Jolibois, 1889.

C. × n. 180, *J. S. H. Fr.* 1889, 735, 787; 1891, 45.—Jolibois.

C. × (unnamed), *J. S. H. Fr.* 1890, 390.—Jolibois.

C. × Madamoiselle Madeleine Gayot, *J. S. H. Fr.* 1891, 67; *Hans. O. Hyb.* 162: *Desb. Cyp.* ed. 2, 327.—Jolibois.

C. × pellucidum, *Fl. Exch.* Jan. 9, 1892; *Hans. O. Hyb.* 162; *Desb. Cyp.* ed. 2, 338.—Pitcher and Manda.

241. P. × **Gem** (insigne × marmorophyllum ♀).—Ingram, 1892.

C. × The Gem, *G.C.* 1892, ii. 138; *O.R.* 1893, 359.

242. P. × **gemmiferum** (Hookeræ ♀ × purpuratum), *Stein O.* 467.—Bowring, 1881.

C. × gemmiferum, *G.C.* 1181, i. 814; *O.R.* 1893, 71; *V. Man. O.* iv. 85.

243. P. × **Georgeanum** (niveum × superbeins ♀).—Graves, 1894.

C. × Georgeanum, *O.R.* 1894, 164.

C. × The Bard, *G.C.* 1894, ii. 257; *O.R.* 1894, 317.—Lawrence.

244. P. × **Georgei** (Boxalli × Stonei).—Keeling, 1900.

C. × Sir George White, *O.R.* 1900, 142.

245. P. × **Germinyanum** (hirsutissimum × villosum ♀); *Stein. O.* 468.—Veitch, 1886.

C. × Germinyanum, *G.C.* 1886, i. 200; *J.H.* 1890, ii. 89, **f.** 12; 1893, i. 67, 74, **f.** 10; *V. Man. O.* iv. 85; *O.R.* 1893, 147; *Dict. Ic. O.* Cyp. hyb. **t.** 52.

C. × (unnamed), *J. S. H. Fr.* 1891, 46.—Cappe.

C. villosum violaceum, *G.C.* 1893, i. 195. Vuylsteke.

C. × violaceum, *R. H. Meas. Cyp.* ed. 3, 173.—Vuylsteke.

C. × villoso-violaceum, *Desb. Cyp.* ed. 2, 467.—Vuylsteke.

C. × hirsuto-villosum, *J. S. H. Fr.* 1896, 111.—Cappe.

C. × Roberti, *O.R.* 1894, 93: 1896, 38.—Cowper.

C. × (unnamed), *G.C.* 1894, i. 211.—Cowper.

246. P. × **giganteum** (× Harrisianum × nitens ♀), *Kerch. Liv. d. O.* 479.—Hye, 1893.

C. × giganteum, *O.R.* 1893, 316; *Desb. Cyp.* ed. 2, 200.

C. × Talisman, *G.C.* 1899, i. 174; *O.R.* 1899, 126.—Hye.

C. × Harrisiano-nitens, *J. S. H. Fr.* 1895, 606.—Garden.

C. × Dauthieri-nitens, *J. S. H. Fr.* 1896, 110.—Opoix.

C. × Docteur Allix, *J. S. H. Fr.* 1902, 139.—Cappe.

C. × René, *J. S. H. Fr.* 1899, 1130.—Duval.

C. × President Krüger, *J. S. H. Fr.* 1902, 778.—Beranek.

247. P. × **gigas** (× Harrisianum × Lawrenceanum ♀), *Kerch. Liv. d. O.* 479.—Opoix, 1888.

C. × gigas, *G.C.* 1892, i. 136; *J.H.* 1892, i. 257, f. 42; *O.R.* 1893, 359.

C. × Amphion, *R. H. Meas. Cyp.* ed. 2, 113; *Boyle Woodl. O.* 181.—R. H. Measures.

C. × gloriosum, *R. H. Meas. Cyp.* ed. 2, 42.—Hye.

C. × The Hendre, *G.C.* 1894, ii. 103; *O.R.* 1894, 285.—Lord Llangattock.

C. × Monsieur Paul Descombes, *J. S. H. Fr.* 1894, 314.—Opoix.

C. × Paul Descombes, *J. S. H. Fr.* 1895, 238.—Opoix.

C. × Corndeani, *G.C.* 1895, i. 627; *O.R.* 1895, 187, 215; 1896, 190.—Swinburne.

C. × Flambeau, *G.C.* 1900, ii. 482; *O.R.* 1901, 26.—Sander.

C. × Monsieur Scellier de Gisors, *J. S. H. Fr.* 1897, 602.—Opoix.

C. × Prewettii, *G.C.* 1897, i. 210; *O.R.* 1897, 128; *Dict. Ic. O.* Cyp. hyb. t. 23.—Hollington.—The parentage of this hybrid is doubtful.

C. × Esculapias, *R. H. Meas. Cyp.* ed. 3, 56.—R. I. Measures.

C. × Emperor of India, *G.C.* 1902, i. 281, 322, 413, 415, f. 153; *J.H.* 1902, i. 423, f.; *O.R.* 1902, 149; *G.M.* 1902, 274, 275, f.; *Rev. H.* 1902, 333, f. 139.—Sander.

248. P. × **Glonerianum** (× Leeanum × Victoria-Mariæ)—Linden, 1901.

C. × Glonerianum, *Lind.* xvi. t. 753; *O.R.* 1902, 63, 383.

249. P. × **Godseffianum** (Boxallii ♀ × hirsutissimum), *Stein O.* 469.—Cookson, 1888.

C. × Godseffianum, *G.C.* 1888, i. 296; *Orchidoph.* 1888, 133; *Rev. H. Belge*, 1892, 85, t. 8; *O.R.* 1893, 259; *J.H.* 1895, i. 223, f. 40; *Dict. Ic. O.* Cyp. hyb. t. 7 (type), 7 A. (v. Jupiter).

C. × Bragaianum, *J. d. O.* ii. 55; *G.C.* 1891, i. 406; *Lind.* vi. t. 279.—Linden.

C. × Jupiter, *Rev. H.* 1894, 89; *O.R.* 1894, 60; *Chron. O.* 6; *J. S. H. Fr.* 1897, 132; *Desb. Cyp.* ed. 2, 280.—Vuylsteke.

C. × Othello, *G.C.* 1890, i. 336; *O.R.* 1893, 295.—Veitch.

C. × hirsutissimo-Boxallii, *J. S. H. Fr.* 1899, 153.—Opoix.

250. P. × **Goodsoni** (× Haywoodianum × Swinburnei).—Goodson, 1903

C. × H. S. Goodson, *G.C.* 1903, ii. 246; *O.R.* 1903, 309.

C. × Kitty, *G.C.* 1903, ii. 262; *O.R.* 1903, 342.—Crook.

251. P. × Gordoni (Boxallii × Druryi).—Gordon, 1903.

C. × (unnamed), *G.C.* 1903, i. 46; *O.R.* 1903, 51.

252. P. × Goultenianum (callosum × Curtisii ♀), *Kerch. Liv. d. O.* 479.—Goulten, 1894.

C. × Goultenianum, *G.C.* 1894, i. 84; *O.R.* 1894, 62; 1895, 144.

C. × Francesiæ, *G.C.* 1900, ii. 424; *O.R.* 1901, 22, 60.—Statter.

C. × calloso-Curtisii, *J. S. H. Fr.* 1901, 193.—Mantin.

C. × Mme. Alfred Janssens, *G.C.* 1903, i 46; *Rev. H. Belge*, 1903, 47.—Janssens and Putzeys.

253. P. × Gowerianum (Curtisii × Lawrenceanum) *Kerch. Liv. d. O.* 479.—Sander, 1893.

Fig. 57. PAPHIOPEDILUM × GRAVESIÆ.

C. × Gowerianum, *G.C.* 1893, i. 682 (in note); *O.R.* 1893, 212; *Will. O. Gr. Man.* ed. 7, 262; *G.M.* 1900, 78, f. (v. formosum).

C. × Goweri, *R. H. Meas. Cyp.* ed. 2, 43; *G.C.* 1895, i. 529.—Sander.

C. × Sylvia, *G.C.* 1893, i. 682; *O.R.* 1893, 212.—Winn.

C. × Lawrenceo-Curtisii, *J. S. H. Fr.* 1894, 414; 1895, 239.—Bleu.

C. × Curtisii-Lawrenceanum, *Desb. Cyp.* ed. 2, 149.—Bleu.

254. P. × Graceæ (Boxallii × niveum).—Keeling, 1902.

C. × Graceæ, *G.C.* 1902, ii. 294; *O.R.* 1902, 343.

255. P × gracile (Haynaldianum ♀ × Swanianum).—Ingram, 1897.

C. × gracile, *G.C.* 1897, ii. 150; *O.R.* 1897, 287.

256. P. × **grandiflorum** (× auroreum × Harrisianum).—Pitcher and Manda, 1899.

C. × luridum grandiflorum, *R. H. Meas. Cyp.* ed. 3, 111.—Pitcher and Manda.

257. P. × **Gratrixiæ** (bellatulum ♀ × vexillarium), *O.R.* 1900, 39.—Briggs-Bury, 1897.

C. × bellatulo-vexillarium, *G.C.* 1897, i. 326; *O.R.* 1897, 184; 1905, 71.—Briggs-Bury.

C. × Gratrixiæ, *O.R.* 1898, 183.—Gratrix.

C. × vexillario-bellatulum, *Sand. O. Guide*, 337.

258. P. × **Gratrixii** (bellatulum × Godefroyæ).—Gratrix, 1898.

C. × S. Gratrix, *O.R.* 1898, 183.

259. P. × **Gravesiæ** (Argus ♀ × niveum), *Kerch. Liv. d. O.* 479.—Graves, 1894. **[See Fig. 57.**

C. × Gravesiæ, *O.R.* 1894, 81, f. 8; *G.C.* 1894, i. 298, f. 34.

C. × Madamoiselle Nancy Descombes, *J. S. H. Fr.* 1894, 139; 1895, 238.—Opoix.

C. × Ruth Ayling (niveum ♀), *G.C.* 1895, i. 337; *O.R.* 1895, 127.—Hollington.

260. P. × **Gravesii** (Lawrenceanum ♀ × Marshallianum).—Graves, 1894.

C. × Henry Graves, *O.R.* 1895, 50.

261. P. × **Greyanum** (ciliolare ♀ × Druryi), *J. R. H. S.* xxvi. 692.—Pitcher and Manda, 1892.

C. × Greyanum, *Fl. Exch.* May 21, 1892; *G.C.* 1893, i. 396; *O.R.* 1893, 159.

C. × Merops, *G.C.* 1894, i. 475; *O.R.* 1894, 159; *G.M.* 1896, 302, f.—Veitch.

262. P. × **Greyi** (× Godefroyæ ♀ × niveum).—Corning, 1888.

C. × (unnamed), *O.R.* 1894, 227.

263. P. × **Grovesianum** (× Lathamianum × Leeanum).—Sander, 1896.

C. × Grovesianum, *G.C.* 1897, i. 16; *O.R.* 1898, 370; *Chron. O.* 283.

C. × Mrs. Herbert Measures, *G. World*, 1899, 499, f.; *O.R.* 1899, 289; *Boyle Woodl. O.* 199.—R. H. Measures.

C. × nanum, *R. H. Meas. Cyp.* ed. 3, 196; *O.R.* 1902, 367.—R. H. Measures.

C. × Zenobia, *Amer. G.* 1903, 107.—Rothwell.

264. P. × **Hanningtoni** (× Medeia × villosum).—R. H. Measures, 1900.

C. × H. Hannington, *Gard.* 1900, ii. 107, f.

265. P. × **Hanseni** (Haynaldianum × villosum).—Pitcher & Manda, 1895.

C. × augustum, *Hans. O. Hyb.* 135.—Pitcher & Manda.

266. P. × **Harri-exul** (exul × Harrisianum).—R. I. Measures, 1903.

C. × Harri-exul, *G.C.* 1903, i. 270; *O.R.* 1903, 153.

267. P. × **Harri-Leeanum** (× Harrisianum × Leeanum).—W. C. Clarke, 1893.

C. × Harri-Leeanum, *G.C.* 1893, ii. 630; *O.R.* 1893, 375.

C. × Clement Moore, *Gard.* 1895, i. 48; *G.C.* 1896, i. 10; *Desb. Cyp.* ed. 2, 127.—Sander.

268. P. × Harrisander (× Harrisianum ♀ × Sanderianum).—Winn, 1896.

C. × Harrisander, *G.C.* 1896, ii. 137; *O.R.* 1896, 228; 273, **f.** 14. **[See Fig. 58.**

269. P. × Harrisianum (barbatum × villosum ♀), *Stein O.* 469.—Veitch, 1869.

C. × Harrisianum, *G.C.* 1869, 108; *Fl. & Pomol.* 1871, 56, 57, **f.**; *Fl. d. Ser.* **t.** 2289; *V. Man. O.* iv. 85, **ff.** (type and v. superbum); *G. World*, 1891, 393, **f.**; *Lind.* iii. **t.** 118 (v. superbum); iv. **t.** 166 (v. polychromum); *O.R.* 1893, 6; 1894, 235 (v. virescens); *Dict. Ic. O.* Cyp. hyb. **t.** 11 (v. superbum).

Fig. 58. PAPHIOPEDILUM × HARRISANDER.

C. × Dauthieri, *Orchidoph.* 1882, 218; *G.C.* i. 576, **f.** 109 (v. marmoratum); 1888, i. 425 (v. Rossianum); 1891, i. 426 (v. Poggio Gherardo); 1895. i. 335, **f.** 45 (v. dimidiate); *Rev. H. Belge*, 1889, 241, **t.** (v. marmoratum); *Rev. H.* 1890, 143; *Bull. Soc. Tosc. Ort.* 1891, 336, **t.** 11 (v. Poggio Gherardo); *O.R.* 1894, 20, 147 (v. Albino).—(Veitch) Van Houtte.

C. × Van Houtteanum, *Lind.* iii. **t.** 130; *O.R.* 1893, 259; 1899, 71; *Desb. Cyp.* ed. 2, 456.—(Veitch) Van Houtte.

C. × Houtteanum, *G.C.* 1888, i. 561.—(Veitch) Van Houtte.

C. × Carnianum, *Rev. H.* 1888, 274; *Desb. Cyp.* ed. 2, 215 (in note).—Sander.

C. × Madame Van Houtte, *V. Man. O.* iv. 90; *Desb. Cyp.* ed. 2, 326.—(Veitch) Van Houtte.

C. × Van Houttei, *Orchidoph.* 1889, 111.—(Veitch) Van Houtte.

C. × elegans, *R. H. Meas. Cyp.* ed. 2, 33.—R. H. Measures.

C. × hybridum, *R. H. Meas. Cyp.* ed. 2, 47.—Bull.

C. × Botelaerianum, *G.C.* 1895, ii. 391; 1896, i 369.—Pauwels. Reproduced from seed.

C. × Vervaetianum, *Hans. O. Hyb.* 151.—Vervaet.

C. × Madame Vincke, *Desb. Cyp.* ed 2, 326.—Vincke.

C. × intermedium, *R. H. Meas. Cyp.* ed. 3, 91.—Pitcher & Manda.

C. × virescens, *Charlesw. Cat.* 1900; *Sand. O. Guide*, 337.—Charlesworth. The first hybrid in the genus.

270. P. × Harrisifroyæ (× Godefroyae × Harrisianum ♀).—Lawrence, 1893.

C. × Harrisifroyæ, *G.C.* 1893, ii. 192; *O.R.* 1893, 287.

271. P. × Harveyanum (× Leeanum × Stonei).—Backhouse, 1893.

C. × Harveyanum, *R. H. Meas. Cyp.* ed. 2, 49; *Hans. O. Hyb.* 151.

C. × (unnamed), *G.C.* 1895, i. 264.—W. C. Clarke.

272. P. × Haywoodianum (Druryi × superbiens ♀), *Kerch. Liv. d. O* 479.—Veitch, 1889.

C. × T. B. Haywood, *G.C.* 1889, i. 428; *J.H.* 1889, i. 174, f. 26; *O.R.* 1893, 262.—Veitch.

C. × Haywoodianum, *Bohnh. O. Hyb.* 20.—Veitch.

C. × Hay-wood, *J. S. H. Fr.* 1896, 1063.—Veitch.

C. × Druryi-superbiens, *J. S. H. Fr.* 1900, 59.—Opoix.

273. P. × Hecla (superbiens ♀ × Swanianum).—Ingram, 1892.

C. × Hecla, *G.C.* 1892, ii. 138; *O.R.* 1893, 12, 359.

The *O.R.* reference to C. × superciliare as one parent is an error.

274. P. × Helen (Charlesworthii × Dayanum ♀), *O.R.* 1900, 324.—Wigan, 1900.

C. × Helen, *G.C.* 1900, ii. 313; *O.R.* 1900, 324, 347.

275. P. × Helena (bellatulum × insigne), *O.R.* 1902, 30, 64.—Tunstill, 1901.

C. × Helena, *J.H.* 1901, ii. 555, f.; *O.R.* 1902, 64.

C. × Helen, *G.C.* 1901, ii. 401; *O.R.* 1902, 30.

C. × Helen II., *Dict. Ic. O.* Cyp. hyb. t. 29; *J. R. H. S.* xxvi. Proc. 248, f. 357.—Tunstill.

276. P. × Helios (Curtisii ♀ × villosum), *O.R.* 1900, 72.—Hurst, 1898.

277. P. × Heloisianum (Boxallii × gemmiferum).—Mantin, 1893.

C. × Heloisianum, *J. S. H. Fr.* 1893, 819.

C. × Heloisiæ, *J. S. H. Fr.* 1894, 582.—Mantin.

278. P. × Helvetia (Chamberlainianum × philippinense), *O.R.* 1899, 336.—Froebel, 1899.

C. × Helvetia, *G.C.* 1899, ii. 273; *Dict. Ic. O.* Cyp. hyb. t. 43; *Gartenz.* 1901, 361, f.

279. P. × **Hera** (Boxallii × Leeanum ♀), *Kerch. Liv. d. O.* 479; *O.R.* 1901, 64; 1902, 74; 1903, 71, f. 16 (12 vars. incl. Cæsar, Dakini, Hurstii, maculatum, punctatum, and Stormberg), 72, f. 17 (12 vars. incl. burbagense), 73, f. 18 (6 vars.)—Veitch, 1892.

C. × Hera, *G.C.* 1892, i. 214; 1899, ii. 483, f. 159 (v. Euryades); *J.H.* 1899, ii. 562, 563, f. 98 (v. Euryades); *Dict. Ic. O.* Cyp. hyb. t. 61 A (v. Gillianum).

C. × Adrastus *G.C.* 1892, i. 343; *O.R.* 1893, 358; *J.H.* 1894, i. 103, f. 16; *G.M.* 1894, 232, f.; *Amer. G.* 1900, 150, 151, f. 33; *Dict. Ic. O.* Cyp. hyb. t. 44 (v. Mariæ), 44 A (v. Hurstii).—Veitch.

Fig. 59. Paphiopedilum × Hitchinsiæ.

C. × Euryades, *G.C.* 1893, ii. 630; *O.R.* 1893, 375; *J.H.* 1896, i. 47, 59 f. 7.—Veitch.

C. × Magdalena, *G.C.* 1895, i. 228.—Madoux. Precise parentage doubtful.

C. × Leonis, *J.S.H.Fr.* 1898, 961.—Cappe.

C. × Boxalli-Leeanum, *J.S.H.Fr.* 1899, 45.—Cappe.

C. × Brunnianum, *J.S.H.Fr.* 1899, 152.—Poirier.

C. × Gillianum, *G.C.* 1899, i. 46; *O.R.*, 1899, 61.—Greenwood.

C. × M. Galpin, *J.S.H.Fr.* 1900, 53.—Peeters.

C. × Neron, *J.S.H.Fr.* 1900, 53.—Peeters.

C. × Mariæ, *Dict. Ic. O.* Cyp. hyb. sub t. 44.—Peeters.

C. × Leeano-Boxallii, *J.S.H.Fr.* 1901, 90.—Cappe.

C. × Jean Magne, *J.S.H.Fr.* 1901, 97, 212.—Magne.

C. × robustum, *Gard.* 1903, i. 289—Peeters.

A remarkably variable hybrid.

280. P. × **Hiawatha** (× Godseffianum × Leeanum).—Sander, 1902.

C. × Hiawatha, *J.H* 1902, ii. 434; *Sand. O. Guide*, 335.

281. P. × **Hiero** (Chamberlainianum × Lawrenceanum ♀).—Veitch, 1900.

C. × Hiero, *G.C.* 1900, i. 239; *O.R.* 1900, 155.

282 P. × **Hitchinsiæ** (Charlesworthii × insigne), *O.R.* 1899, 335; 1900, 49, f. 7; 1901, 15.—Duval, 1899. **[See Fig. 59.**

C. × Elmireanum, *Jard.* 1899, 303; *J. S. H. Fr.* 1899, 833.—Duval.

C. × Hitchinsiæ, *G.C.* 1901, ii. 401; *O.R.* 1901, 366.—Hitchins.

C. × bingleyense, *O.R.* 1900, 373.—Keeling.

C. × Zethus, *G.C.* 1900, ii. 384; *O.R.* 1900, 373.—Veitch.

C. × Henriette Duval, *J. S. H. Fr.* 1901, 996.—Duval.

C. × (unnamed), *J. S. H. Fr.* 1902, 631.—Duval.

283. P. × **Hobartii** (insigne × Lathamianum).—Roebling, 1899.

C. × Garret A. Hobart, *R. H. Meas. Cyp.* ed. 3, 62; *G.C.* 1903, ii. 429; *O.R.* 1904, 20.—Roebling.

C. × dellense, *G.C.* 1903, ii. 429.—Schröder.

C. × Alexandre Debille, *Jard.* 1903, 384; *Rev. H.* 1904, 7.—Debille.

284. P. × **Hobsoni** (Lawrenceanum ♀ × philippinense).—Hollington, 1894.

C. × Hobsoni, *G.C.* 1894, ii. 103; *O.R.* 1894, 285.

C. × Hodgsoni, *G.C.* 1894, ii. 194.—Hollington.

C. × Burtoni, *G.C.* 1895, i. 801; 1896, i. 20, 40.—Burton.

C. × Chas. Steinmetz, *G.C.* 1896, ii. 137; *O.R.* 1896, 255.—Lawrence.

The records of this plant have been hopelessly confused with those of P. × Millmanii, but at least some of the above have P. Lawrenceanum for one parent.

285. P. × **Hollidayanum** (× almum × concolor ♀).—Sander, 1894.

C. × Hollidayanum, *G.C.* 1894, ii. 731; *O.R.* 1895, 32.

286. P. × **Holtii** (Curtisii × præstans).—Sander, 1897.

C. × E. Holt, *G.C.* 1897, i. 390; *O.R.* 1897, 219.—Sander.

C. × (unnamed), *J. S. H. Fr.* 1900, 513.—Gibez.

C. × Curtiso-praestans, *G.C.* 1900, ii. 18; *O.R.* 1900, 250; *J. S. H. Fr.* 1902, 778.—Fowler.

287. P. × **Hornianum** (Spicerianum × superbiens), *Stein O.* 471.—Baron N. Rothschild, 1887.

C. × Hornianum, *G.C.* 1887, ii. 428; *O.R.* 1893, 133.

C. × picturatum, *G.C.* 1889, ii. 420; 1891, i. 680; 1895, ii. 326; *G. World*, 1889, 92; *Gard.* 1889, ii. 350; *O.R.* 1893, 319.—Lawrence.

C. × multicolor, *G.C.* 1892, ii. 744.—Sander.

288. P. × **Hunteri** (bellatulum × tonsum ♀), *O.R.* 1902, 100.—Steel, 1902.

289. P. × **Hurrellianum** (Argus ♀ × Curtisii).—Roebling, 1894.

C. × Hurrellianum, *O.R.* 1894, 324; 1895, 15.

290. P. × Huttiæ (× Fitchianum × insigne). Swinburne, 1895.

C. × Lady Hutt, *G.C.* 1895, ii. 721; *O.R.* 1896, 32.—Swinburne.

291. P. × Iago (Dayanum ♀ × villosum), *O.R.* 1899, 48.—Wrigley, 1899.

292. P. × Ian (Argus × Charlesworthii).—Charlesworth, 1902.

C. × Ian Hamilton, *G.C.* 1902, ii. 105; *O.R.* 1902, 274.

293. P. × I'Ansoni (× Morganiæ × Rothschildianum), *O.R.* 1902, 373.—Low, 1898.

Fig. 60. PAPHIOPEDILUM × IO VAR. GRANDE.

C. × I'Ansoni, *G.C.* 1898, ii. 14; *O.R.* 1898, 223; *G.M.* 1898, 458, 459, f. 2; *J.H.* 1900, i. 475, f. 126; 1903, i. 397, f.

C. × L'Ansoni, *Desb. Cyp.* ed. 2, 286.—Low.

C. × Mrs. Leemann, *O.R.* 1900, 144.—Sander.

P. × (unnamed), *O.R.* 1902, 319.—Statter, 1902.

There is a slight doubt about this record.

294. P. × Ilione (insigne × Lynchianum).—Sander, 1903.

C. × Ilione, *G.C.* 1903, i. 108; *O. R.* 1903, 82.

295. P. × illustre (× Lathamianum × nitens).—Sander, 1903.

C. × illustre, *G.C.* 1903, i. 108; *O.R.* 1903, 82.

C. × (unnamed), *Amer. G.* 1903, 59.—Loveless.

296. P. × **Imperatrix** (× Ashburtonæ ♀ × calophyllum), *Kerch. Liv. d. O.* 479.—Sander, 1893.

C. × Imperatrix, *R. H. Meas. Cyp.* ed. 2, 57 ; *Hans. O. Hyb.* 152.

297. P. × **Indra** (callosum ♀ × villosum), *Kerch. Liv. d. O.* 479.—R. I. Measures, 1893.

C. × Indra, *G.C.* 1893, ii. 630 ; *O.R.* 1893, 374.

C. × villoso-callosum, *J. S. H. Fr.* 1894, 414 ; 1895, 239.—Bleu.

298. P. × **Ino** (Canhami × Haynaldianum ♀).—Grey, 1895.

C. × Ino, *Amer. G.* March 23, 1895 ; *Hans. O. Hyb.* 153.

299. P. × **Io** (Argus ♀ × Lawrenceanum), *Stein O.* 473.—Cookson, 1886.
[See Fig. 60.

C. × Io, *G.C.* 1886, i. 488 ; *Reichenb.* ser. 1, i. 51, t. 23 ; *Rev. H. Belge*, 1888, 13, t. ; *Veitch Man. O.* iv. 87 ; *O.R.* 1893, 131 ; 1894, 49, f. 6 (v. grande).

C. × Eldorado, *Bohnh. Dict. O. Hyb.* 16 ; *Hans. O. Hyb.* 297.

300. P. × **Iphis** (Argus × tonsum ♀), *O.R.* 1900, 118, 119 ; *G.C.* 1901, i. 102.—Young, 1900.

301. P. × **Ira** (superbiens × Youngianum).—Cookson, 1903.

C. × Youngiano-superbiens, *G.C.* 1903, ii. 429 ; *O.R.* 1904, 18.—Cookson.

302. P × **Irene** (Boxallii ♀ × exul), *O.R.* 1904, 102.—Fournier, 1903.

C. × (unnamed), *J. S. H. Fr.* 1903, 37 ; *Rev. H.* 1903, 48.—Fournier.

C. × Boxalli-exul, *Bull. Soc. Tosc. Ort.* 1903, 181.—Fournier.

C. × memoria-Fournieri, *Dict. Ic. O.* Cyp. hyb. t. 60.—Fournier.

303. P. × **Iris** (ciliolare × Sementa ♀), *Kerch. Liv. d. O.* 480.—Williams, 1892.

C. × Iris, *G.C.* 1892, ii. 566 ; *R. H. Meas. Cyp.* ed. 2, 115 ; *Jard.* 1894, 44 ; *J. d. O.* v. 8 ; *J. S. H. Fr.* 1894, 68 ; 1895, 163, 239.—Bleu.

It is not quite clear whether the plant originally exhibited by Messrs. B. S. Williams & Son is identical with that raised by M. Alfred Bleu, to which the later records refer, as the parentage was not originally stated.

304. P. × **Jacobianum** (bellatulum × Crossianum).—Baron E. Rothschild, 1894.

C. × Jacobianum, *Hans. O. Hyb.* 153.

305. P. × **Janet** (præstans ♀ × Spicerianum).—Veitch, 1899.

C. × Janet, *G.C.* 1899, ii. 197 ; *O.R.* 1899, 287.

There is a slight doubt about the parentage of this hybrid.

306. P. × **Jean** (Argus × Harrisianum).—Lesueur, 1899.

C. × Jean, *J. S. H. Fr.* 1899, 751.—Lesueur.

C. × Harrisiano-Argus, *J. S. H. Fr.* 1902, 501.—Beranek.

307. P. × **Jeanette** (× Leeanum ♀ × niveum).—Charlesworth, 1897.

C. × Jeanette, *G.C.* 1897, i. 278 ; *O.R.* 1898, 365.

308. P. × **Jensenianum** (hirsutissimum × vexillarium), *O.R.* 1900, 39 ; 1905, 71.—Sander, 1898.

C. × Jensenianum, *G.C.* 1898, ii. 357 ; *O.R.* 1898, 374.

309. P. × **Johnsoni** (philippinense × Rothschildianum).—Statter, 1901.

C × (unnamed), *O.R.* 1901, 318

310. P. × Joiceyi (barbatum ♀ × selligerum).—Joicey, 1893.

C. × selligero-barbatum, *G.C.* 1893, ii. 278.—Joicey.

311. P. × Joliboisii (Curtisii × Lowii ♀), *J. R. H. S.* xxvi. 692.—Opoix. 1893.

C. × Souvenir de Roch Jolibois, *J. S. H. Fr.* 1893, 661; *Dict. Ic. O.* Cyp. hyb. t. 36.—Opoix.

C. × Svend Brun, *G.C.* 1895, i. 749; *G.M.* 1895, 315; *O.R.* 1900, 126 *Amer. G.* 1902, 385, f. 89.

C. × Svend Brunson, *G.C.* 1896, i. 10.—Sander.

Fig. 61. Paphiopedilum × Juno.

312. P. × Josephianum (Druryi × Sementa), *Kerch. Liv. d. O.* 480.—Pitcher and Manda, 1891.

C. × Josephianum, *Fl. Exch.* Oct. 17, 1891; *Desb. Cyp.* ed. 2, 277.

313. P. × Julia (exul × Lawrenceanum).—Appleton, 1899.

C. × Julia, *G.C.* 1899, ii. 268; *O.R.* 1899, 318; 1902, 276.

314. P. × Juno (callosum ♀ × Fairrieanum) *Kerch. Liv. d. O.* 480; *O.R.* 1900, 8; 1905, 17, f. 4.—Drewett, 1891. **[See Fig. 61.**

C. × Juno, *G.C.* 1891, 360; *O.R.* 1893, 327; *G. World*, 1903, 682, f.

C. × calloso-Fairrieanum, *G.C.* 1896, ii. 534; *O.R.* 1896, 349.—Statter.

315. P × Jupiter (Hookeræ × Rothschildianum).—R. I. Measures, 1895.

C. × Jupiter, *R. H. Meas. Cyp.* ed. 3, 95 (second entry).

C. × Y'Mir, *G.C* 1895, i. 200; *R. H. Meas. Cyp.* ed. 3, 178; *Amer. G.* 1900, 680, 681, f. 144 (v. Hallii)—R. I. Measures.

C. × Symonsianum, *Boyle Woodl. O.* 200.—R H. Measures.

316. P. × Juturna (Boxallii × Orpheus), *O.R.* 1900, 118.—Young, 1900.

317. P. × Kamilii (Boxallii × Chamberlainianum ♀).—Froebel, 1900.

C. × Prince Hussein Kamil, *G.C.* 1900, ii. 424; *O.R.* 1901, 22; *Gartenz.* 1901, 361.—Froebel.

C. × Chamberlaino-Boxallii, *J. S. H. Fr.* 1900, 256; 1901, 212.—Duval.

318. P. × Keelingii (Chamberlainianum × Parishii).—Keeling, 1903.

C. × (unnamed), *G.C.* 1903, ii. 411; *O.R.* 1904, 21.

319. P. × Kerchoveanum (barbatum × Curtisii), *Kerch. Liv. d. O.* 480.—Brussels Bot. Garden, 1892.

C. × Kerchovianum, *G.C.* 1893, i. 132.

C. × W. H. Young (barbatum ♀), *G.C.* 1900, i. 371.—Wigan.

320. P. × Kittelii (Dayanum ♀ × superbiens).—Kittel, 1890.

C. × George Kittel, *Gartenfl.* 1890, 311.—Kittel.

C. × (unnamed), *J. S. H. Fr.* 1896, 699.—Opoix.

C. × Dayano-Veitchii, *J. S. H. Fr.* 1900, 84.—Opoix.

This is said to be the first hybrid of the genus raised in Germany.

321. P. × Kohinoor (× Haywoodii × œnanthum ♀), *O.R.* 1903, 247.—Young.

322. P. × Kramerianum (× œnanthum ♀ × villosum), *Stein O.* 473.—Sander, 1891.

C. × Kramerianum, *G.C.* 1891, i. 86; *J.H.* 1891, i. 50: *O.R.* 1893, 326.

C. × villoso-œnanthum, *G.C.* 1899, i. 108; *O.R.* 1899, 94.—E. Ashworth.

C. × Mrs. Caroline Allen, *R. H. Meas. Cyp.* ed. 3, 195.—McArthur.

C. × Ernesto, *G.C.* 1903, i. 179; *O. R.* 1901, 119; 1903, 364.—Rehder.

323. P. × Krishna (insigne × tonsum).—Graves, 1895.

C. × Krishna, *Amer. G.* March 23, 1895; *G.C.* 1895, i. 550; *R. H. Meas. Cyp.* ed. 3, 97; *O.R.* 1904, 351.

C. × insigne-tonsum, *R. H. Meas. Cyp.* ed. 3, 90; *Sand. O. Guide*, 266.—Sander.

324. P. × Kubele (× œnanthum ♀ × Youngianum); *O.R.* 1901, 271.—Young, 1901.

C. × Kubele, *G.C.* 1901, ii. 172; *O.R.* 1901, 285; 1903. 282; *Dict. Ic. O.* Cyp. hyb. t. 50.

325. P. × Lachesis (× Crossianum ♀ × marmorophyllum).—Young, 1896.

C. × Lachesis, *O.R.* 1896, 104; *Dict. Ic. O.* Cyp. hyb. t. 21.

326. P. × Lachmee (ciliolare ♀ × superbiens).—Bleu, 1894.

C. × Curtisii, *Jard.* 1894, 171 (not of Rchb. f.); *O.R.* 1894, 307.—Bleu.

C. × (unnamed), *J. S. H. Fr.* 1894, 414; 1895, 239.—Bleu.

C. × Lachmee, *G.C.* 1895, i. 199; *O.R.* 1895, 319.—R. I. Measures.

327. P. × La-France (× nitens × niveum).—Seeger & Tropp, 1892.

C. × La-France, *Gard.* 1892, i. 48; *Monit. H.* 1892, 54, t.; *Orchidoph.* 1892, 2; *O.R.* 1898, 365; *Desb. Cyp.* ed. 2, 286.

328. P. × Lairessei (Curtisii ♀ × Rothschildianum), *J. R. H. S.* xxvi. 692. —Sander, 1895.

Fig. 62. Paphiopedilum × Lathamianum.

C. × A. de Lairesse, *G.C.* 1895, i. 748; *O.R.* 1895, 223; *Dict, Ic. O.* Cyp. hyb. t. 41; *Chron. O.* 362; *Desb. Cyp.* ed. 2, 158. —Sander.

C. × M. Georges Magne, *J. S. H. Fr.* 1899, 497.—Peeters.

329. P. × Lasellei (× Leeanum × Schlesingerianum).—Whitin, 1903.

C. × Hildegard Laselle, *Amer. G.* 1903, 27.—Whitin.

330. P. × Lathamianum (Spicerianum ♀ × villosum), *Stein O.* 473; *J. R. H. S.* xxiv. 101, f. 19; 107, f. 27; *O.R.* 1901, 105, f. 18.—Latham, 1888.

[See Fig. 62.

C. × Lathamianum, *G.C.* 1888, i. 360; *J. H.* 1889, i. 175, f. 27; *Gtfl.* 1889, 528, f. 79; *V. Man. O.* iv. 88; *Lind.* ix. t. 397, f. 2; xvi. t. 732 (v. latisepulum); *Reichenb.* ser. 2, i. 21, t. 10; *Orchidoph* 1892, 209, t.; *O.R.* 1893, 227; *Desb. Cyp.* ed. 2, 287; *Wien. Ill. Gart. Zeit.* 1898, 237, t. 2, f. 1; *Dict. Ic. O.* Cyp. hyb. t. 28.

C. × Hera, *G.C.* 1890, i. 105; *O.R.* 1893, 295.—R. H. Measures.

C. × Spicero-villosum, *J. S. H. Fr.* 1891, 198; 1894, 68.—Bleu.

C. × Bellona, *G.C.* 1893, ii. 630; *O.R.* 1893, 374.—R. I. Measures.

C. × Rex, *G.C.* 1894, i. 343; *O.R.* 1894, 124, 126; *Desb. Cyp.* ed. 2, 406. —Hye.

C. × Leo, *G.C.* 1894, i. 84; *O.R.* 1906, 37.—W. R. Lee.

C. × Cellini (villosum ♀), *Chron. O.* 5; *Desb. Cyp.* ed. 2, 114.—Vuylsteke.

C. × Madame Elysée Descombes, *J. S. H. Fr.* 1895, 239; *Rev. H.* 1895, 48; *J. d. O.* vi. 44.—Jolibois.

C. × signatum, *Bull. Cat.* 1895, 7; *Kew Bull.* 1896, App. ii. 9.—Bull.

C. × Bellina, *Bohnh. Dict. O. Hyb.* 12 —R. I. Measures.

C. × nobilius, *J. S. H. Fr.* 1896, 111.—Bleu.

C. × Margueritæ, *J. S. H. Fr.* 1897, 132; *Chron. O.* 157.—Opoix.

C. × Thompsoni, *G.C.* 1898, i. 191; *Sand. O. Guide*, 337.—Gratrix.

C. × Albert Hye, *G.C.* 1898, ii. 446; *R. H. Meas. Cyp.* ed. 3, 179.—Sander.

C. × villoso-Spicerianum, *J. S. H. Fr.* 1900, 118.—Peeters.

C. × Œdipe, *J. S. H. Fr.* 1901, 212.—Magne.

C. × Rosa Bonheur, *Rev. H. Belge*, 1901, 95.—Smet-Duvivier.

C. × (unnamed), *Gartenz.* 1902, 205, f.

C. × Felix Putzeys, *Rev. H. Belge*, 1903, 71; *G. World*, 1903, 174.—Janssens & Putzeys.

C. × antwerpiense, *Gard.* 1903, i. 288.—Janssens & Putzeys.

331. P. × **Lauræ** (× superciliare ♀ × villosum), *Kerch. Liv. d. O.* 480.—Sander, 1892.

C. × Mrs. C. D. Owen, *G.C.* 1892, ii. 312; *O.R.* 1893, 11. 359.—Sander.

C. × Lauræ, *O. R.* 1894, 80.—R. le Doux.

332. P. × **Lawrebel** (bellatulum × Lawrenceanum ♀), *Kerch. Liv. d. O.* 480.—Lawrence, 1892.

C. × Lawrebellum, *G.C.* 1892, i. 502, 503.—Lawrence.

C. × Lawrebel, *G.C.* 1892, i. 560, 561, f. 82; *J. H.* 1892, i. 295, f. 50; *Lind.* x. t. 407; *O. Alb.* xi. t. 498; *O.R.* 1893, 15, 359; *Desb. Cyp.* ed. 2, 290.—Lawrence.

C. × Lansbergeæ, *Lind.* xvi. t. 727; *J. R. H. S.* xxvi. 923.—Linden. C. Boxallii is given as the second parent, but there is no evidence of this, either in leaf or flower.

333. P. × **Leander** (× Leeanum ♀ × villosum), *J.R.H.S.* xxvi. 923.—R. H. Measures.

C. × Leander, *R.H. Meas. Cyp.* ed. 2, 69; *G.M.* 1902, 42, 68, f. (Cambridge Lodge v.); *O.R.* 1902, 50.

C. × Janus, *Gard. & For.* 1895, 64; *Haus. O. Hyb.* 299.—Pitcher & Manda.

C. × Leonidas (villosum ♀), *G.C.* 1897, i. 115; *O.R.* 1897, 94.—Veitch.

C. × Mrs. E. G. Uihlein, *G.C.* 1897, i. 51; *Boyle Woodl. O.* 195.—Sander.

C. × Bessie K. Pitcher, *Hans. O. Hyb.* 298 — Pitcher & Manda.

C. × Lady Wimborne, *G.C.* 1896, ii. 766; *Desb. Cyp.* ed. 2, 284.—Sander.

C. × St. Mark, *G.M.* 1895, 769; *Sand. O. Guide*, 357.—Palmer.

C. × Saturn, *Desb. Cyp.* ed. 2, 419.—Sander.

C. × Dreherianum, *R. H. Mens Cyp.* ed. 3, 52.—Sander.

C × villoso-Leeanum, *J. S. H. Fr.* 1899, 45.—Cappe.

C. × Leeanum var. Simonei, *J. S. H. Fr.* 1899, 45.—Cardoso.

C. × Leeano-villosum, *J. S. H. Fr.* 1900, 112.—Opoix.

C. × Borchgraveanum, *Lind.* xv. t. 715.—Linden.

C. × Drapsianum, *Lind.* xvi. t. 724.—Draps-Dom.

C. × Stepmaniæ, *Lind.* xvi. t. 765; *O.R.* 1902, 159.—Stepman.

Fig. 63. PAPHIOPEDILUM × LEEANUM.

C. × Exselsior, *Rev. H. Belge*, 1901, 71.—Stepman.

C. × Mme. Stepman, *Rev. H. Belge*, 1901, 71.—Stepman.

C. × Mons Galpin, *Sand. O. Guide*, 336.

C. × Neron, *Sand. O. Guide*, 336.

C. × Hoogendyckeanum, *G.C.* 1902, i. 118.—Stepman.

C. × Ridolfianum, *J. S. H. Fr.* 1902, 140; *Jard.* 1902, 63.—Duval.

C. × De Mesmaeckerianum, *Rev. H. Belge*, 1903, 71; *G. World*, 1903, 174.—Stepman.

334. P. × Lebaudyanum (Haynaldianum × philippinense ♀).—Lebaudy, 1895.

C. × Lebaudyanum, *J. S. H. Fr.* 1895, 338, 345; *Rev. H.* 1895, 360; *Lind.* xii. t. 529; *O.R.* 1897, 63; *Amer. G.* 1902, 385, 387, f. 90.

335. P. × **Ledouxiæ** (callosum × Harrisianum), *Kerch. Liv. d. O.* 480.—G. Ledoux, 1893.

C. × Ledouxiæ, *G.C.* 1893, i. 336; *O.R.* 1893, 117.

C. × Hayetti, *R. H. Meas. Cyp.* ed. 2, 49.—Shuttleworth.

C. × Titanes, *R. H. Meas. Cyp.* ed, 2, 116.—R. H. Measures.

C. × Savoyanum, *J. S. H. Fr.* 1893, 185.—Regnier.

C. × Triomphe de Watermael, *Dict. Ic. O.* Cyp. hyb. t. 28.—Duchesne and Lanthoine Parentage not recorded, but apparently belongs here.

336. **P.** × **Leeæ** (× Arthurianum × Leeanum ♀).—Lee, 1893.

C. × Mary Lee, *G.C.* 1893, ii. 692; *O.R.* 1894, 29.—Lee.

C. × Jamesonianum *G.C.* 1896, i. 210; *O.R.* 1896, 96.—Statter.

337. **P.** × **Leeanum** (insigne ♀ × Spicerianum), *Stein. O.* 474; *O.R.* 1899, 17, f. 1 (v. giganteum); 1902, 25, f. 3; *J. R. H. S.* xxiv. 108, f. 29 (v. superbum).—Veitch, 1884. **[See Fig. 63.**

C. × Leeanum, *G.C.* 1884, i. 50, 140; *Orchidoph.* 1885, 238, 240, t. (v. superbum); *O. Alb.* v. t. 223; *Lind*, iii. t. 125; *J.H.* 1885, 83, f. 14; *Rev. H. Belge*, 1885, 232, f. (v. superbum); *Ill. H.* 1889, 23, t. 77; *Reichenb.* ser. 2. ii. 19, t. 57 (v. giganteum); V. Man. O. iv. 88, 89, f. (v. superbum); *G.M.* 1892, 48, f. (v. giganteum); *O.R.* 1893, 101; *Dict. Ic. O.* Cyp. hyb. t. 3 (type), 3 A. (v. Albertianum); *Lind.* xvii. t. 776 (v. Alexandræ); Desb. Cyp. ed. 2, 300-307 (many vars.).

C. × Masereelianum, *Ill. H.* 1889, 23, t. 77.—Vervaet.

C. × Albertianum (Spicerianum ♀), *G.C.* 1892, ii. 672; *Rev. H. Belge*, 1892, 279; 1893, 3, t. 1; *O.R.* 1893, 58; *Lind.* xvi. 81, 93, t. 734 (v. rotundiflorum).—Hye.

C. × Ashworthiæ, *G.C.* 1893, ii. 630; *O.R.* 1893, 375; *J.H.* 1894, i. 197, f. 33; *G.M.* 1893, 705, f.—E. Ashworth.

Parentage recorded as C. × Leeanum × selligerum, but we cannot trace the latter in the flower.

C. × Engelhardtiæ, *Lind.* vi. t. 285; *Boyle Woodl. O.* 193.—Linden.

C. × Yvonnæ, *Ill. H.* 1895, 23, t. 26; *O.R.* 1895, 93.—Linden.

C. × Robertianum, *Desb. Cyp.* ed. 2, 408.—Hye.

C. × Valerandi, *Lind.* v. 100.—Vallerand.

C. × trentonense, *Hans. O. Hyb.* 158.—Pitcher & Manda.

C. × Vervaeti, *Charlesw. Cat.* ex. *Hans. O. Hyb.* 299.—Charlesworth.

C. × Claudi, *Bohnh. Dict. O. Hyb.* 14; *Sand. O Guide*, 263.

C. × Prospero, *G.C.* 1897, i. 51.—Veitch.

C. × Ansorge Klein Flotbeck, *Gartenwelt*, 1902.

C. × (unnamed), *Gartenz.* 1902, 205, f.

C. × (unnamed), *Wien. Ill. Gart. Zeit.* 1898, 237, t. 2, f. 2.

C. × Philomene, *G.M.* 1903, 272.—Janssens & Putzeys. Parentage somewhat uncertain.

338. **P.** × **Leemanni** (× Bruno × Leeanum).—Leemann, 1900.

C. × (unnamed), *O.R.* 1900, 79; 1901, 26.

Intermediate between P. × Leeanum and P. × Bruno, being composed of ten parts P. Spicerianum and six parts P. insigne.

339. P. × **Lendyanum** (Boxallii ♀ × Canhami).—Ingram, 1894.

C. × Captain Lendy, *G.C.* 1894, i. 211; *O.R.* 1894, 93.—Ingram.

340. P. × **Leonæ** (callosum × insigne), *Kerch. Liv. d. O.* 480.—Linden, 1892.

C. × Leonæ, *Lind.* viii. t. 360; *G.C.* 1893, ii. 342; *O.R.* 1893, 57, 318.

C. × Van Imschootianum, *Rev. H. Belge*, 1892, 262; *Amer. G.* 1902, 103, f. 25.—Moens.

C. × Robertsianum, *G.C.* 1894, ii. 605; *O.R.* 1894, 375.—Lewis.

C. × Gautieri, *J. S. H. Fr.* 1897, 844.—Lebaudy.

C. × Reynaldianum, *Sand. Cat.* 1896, 24, ex. *Hans. O Hyb.* 296; *Desb. Cyp.* ed. 2, 407 ("Reynoldianum").—Sander.

341. P. × **leopardinum** (Argus × nitens).—Paynter, 1899.

C. × leopardinum, *G.C.* 1899, i. 98; *O.R.* 1902, 174.

The name C. × leopardinum originated in 1895 (*Bohnh. Dict. O. Hyb.* 23), but as neither parentage nor raiser were given the plant remains doubtful.

342. P. × **Lewisii** (Dayanum × Harrisianum).—Lewis, 1893.

C. × (unnamed), *G.C.* 1893, ii. 747.—Lewis.

343. P. × **liegense** (× calophyllum ♀ × vexillarium).—Lairesse, 1896.

C. × Phœbe, *Lairesse Cat.* ex. *O.R.* 1896, 38.—Lairesse.

344. P. × **Lily** (Dayanum ♀ × niveum).—R. H. Measures, 1898.

C. × Lily Measures, *O.R.* 1898, 293.—R. H. Measures.

C. × William Pitt, *G.C.* 1902, i. 219; *O.R.* 1902, 116.—The parentage of this is doubtful, and has been suspected to be P. Dayanum and P. Tautzianum.

345. P. × **Lincolnii** (× Niobe × orphanum).—Oakes Ames, 1900.

C. × Abraham Lincoln, *Amer. G.* 1900, 210.—Oakes Ames.

346. P. × **Little-Gem** (× Harrisianum ♀ × Schröderi), *O.R.* 1905, 108, f. 25.—Veitch, 1903. **[See Fig. 64.**

C. × Little-Gem, *G.C.* 1903, i. 270; ii. 310; *O.R.* 1903, 154, 341.

347. P. × **Llangattockiæ** (Lawrenceanum × selligerum ♀).—Llangattock, 1901.

C. × Lady Llangattock, *G.C.* 1901, i. 272; *O.R.* 1901, 155.—Llangattock.

C. × Kelpie, *G.C.* 1902. i. 357.—Wellesley.

348. P. × **Lloydiæ** (× Godefroyæ ♀ × venustum).—Sander, 1896.

C. × Said Lloyd, *G.C.* 1896, i. 83; *O.R.* 1896, 64; *Boyle Woodl. O.* 1901, 191.—Sander.

C. × Lloydiæ, *O.R.* 1896, 83.—Sander.

349. P. × **Lœwegrenianum** (× Io × Spicerianum), *Kerch. Liv. d. O.* 480, —Sander, 1893.

C. × Lœwegrenianum, *Hans. O. Hyb.* 158; *Desb. Cyp.* ed. 2, 315; *O.R.* 1897, 317.

C. × Io-Spicerianum, *G.C.* 1893, ii. 756; *O.R.* 1894, 31, 143.—Vanner.

350. P. × **longwoodense** (Charlesworthii × Leeanum).—Duval, 1900.

C. × Leeano-Charlesworthii, *J. S. H. Fr.* 1900, 118.—Duval.

C. × longwoodense, *Amer. G.* 1901, 350, f. 76; 366.—Rothwell.

C. × Charlesworthii-Leeanum, *J. S. H. Fr.* 1901, 1062.—Cappe.

C. × optimum, *G.C.* 1902, ii. 430.—Tunstill.

C. × Holbrook Gaskell, *G.C.* 1903, i. 210.—Gaskell.

351. P. × loochristiense (× Harrisianum ♀ × Hookeræ).—Vuylsteke, 1895.

C. × loochristianum, *G.C.* 1895, i. 100; *Rev. H. Belge*, 1895, 40; *Desb. Cyp.* ed. 2, 313; *O.R.* 1895, 94.

C. × Mira, *Desb. Cyp.* ed. 2, 343.—Vuylsteke.

C. × Harrisianum v. robustum, *Desb. Cyp.* ed. 2, 216.—Vuylsteke.

C. × H. E. Moojen, *R. H. Meas. Cyp.* ed. 3, 190.—R. H. Measures.

C. × loochristiense, *J. S. H. Fr.* 1899, 45.—Duval.

Fig. 64. PAPHIOPEDILUM × LITTLE GEM, WESTFIELD VAR.

352. P. × Louisæ (× Ashburtonæ × Leeanum), Le Doux, 1895.

C. × Louisæ, *O.R.* 1895, 50.

There is a slight doubt about the parentage.

353. P. × Lowryanum (× Ashburtonæ × vernixium), *Kerch. Liv. d. O.* 480.—Sander, 1892.

C. × Lowryanum, *G.C.* 1892, i. 88; *Hans. O. Hyb.* 159; *O.R.* 1896, 361.

The date is wrongly given by Hansen.

354. P. × lucidum (Lowii ♀ × villosum). *Kerch. Liv. d. O.* 480.—Veitch, 1877.

C. × lucidum, *G.C.* 1877, ii. 521; *O.R.* 1893, 68.

C. × Prince di Venose, *Gard.* 1895, i. 296.—Prince di Venose.

C. × senonense (villosum ♀), *J. S. H. Fr.* 1896, 111.—Gibez.

C. × Lowii-villosum, *Desb. Cyp.* ed. 2, 316.—Madoux.

355. P. × **Lucie** (ciliolare × Lawrenceanum ♀), *Kerch. Liv. d. O.* 480; *O.R.* 1904, 345, f. 48 (v. Smithii).—Moreau, 1892. [See Fig. 65.

C. × Lucie, *Orchidoph.* 1892, 17, t.

C. × Smithii, *G.C.* 1893, ii. 756; *O.R.* 1894, 31.—Low.

C. × (unnamed), *J. S. H. Fr.* 1895, 163.—Opoix.

356. P. × **Lumsdenii** (barbatum ♀ × Charlesworthii).—Lumsden, 1899.

C. × barbato-Charlesworthii, *G.C.* 1899, i. 3; *O.R.* 1899, 48.—Lumsden.

Fig. 65. PAPHIOPEDILUM × LUCIE VAR. SMITHII.

357. P. × **luridum** (Lawrenceanum × villosum), *Kerch. Liv. d. O.* 480.—Garden, 1890.

C. × grande, *J. S. H. Fr.* 1890, 202.—Garden.

C. × luridum, *Fl. Exch.* Jan. 9, 1892; *Desb. Cyp.* ed. 2, 318.—Pitcher & Manda.

C. × (unnamed), *J. S. H. Fr.* 1898, 169.—Cappe.

358. P. × **lutescens** (javanicum × Spicerianum ♀), *Kerch. Liv. d. O.* 480.—Lebaudy, 1890.

C. × javanico-Spicerianum, *Orchidoph.* 1891, 287; *Desb. Cyp.* ed. 2, 274.—Lebaudy.

C. × lutescens, *Gard. & Forest*, 1892, 598; *O.R.* 1893, 51.—Lebaudy.

359. P. × **Lynchianum** (× selligerum × Spicerianum ♀), *Kerch. Liv. d. O.* 480—Sander, 1892.

C. × Lynchianum, *G.C.* 1892, ii. 744; *O.R.* 1893, 31.

C. × Ariadne, *G.C.* 1893, ii. 630; *O.R.* 1893, 375.—Statter.

C. × Euphrosyne, *G.C.* 1895, i. 82; *O.R.* 1895, 63.—Statter.

P. × Ariadne, *O.R.* 1898, 243.—Statter.

P. × Euphrosyne, *O.R.* 1898, 243.—Statter.

360. P. × **Mabeliæ** (Rothschildianum × superbiens ♀), *O.R.* 1902, 349.—Lee, 1894.

C. × Mabelianum, *G.C.* 1894, ii. 194; *O.R.* 1894, 287; 1895, 294.—W. C. Clarke.

C. × W. R. Lee, *G.C.* 1894, ii. 194; *O.R.* 1894, 287, 309; 1895, 294; *G.M.* 1901, 194, 195, f. (Sander's var.); *Amer. G.* 1900, 617, f. 132 (v. Oakes Ames).—Lee.

C. × Lord Derby, *G.C.* 1895, ii. 192, 357, 358, f. 66; *O.R.* 1895, 287, 293; *J.H.* 1901, i. 255, f. (Sander's var).—Statter.

C. × Andronicus, *Gard.* 1895, ii. 51; *O.R.* 1895, 294.—R. H. Measures.

C. × Mabeliæ, *O.R.* 1895, 293, 294.—W. C. Clarke.

C. × Mrs. Harry Smith, *G.C.* 1899, ii. 233.—Charlesworth.

C. × Rothschildiano-superbiens, *G.C.* 1900, i. 143; *O.R.* 1900, 251.—Lawrence.

361. P. × **Macfarlaneanum** (Lawrenceanum × Lowii ♀).—Lewis, 1892.

C. × Macfarlaneanum, *G.C.* 1892, ii. 75; *O.R.* 1894, 37.—Lewis.

C. × Patersonii, *R. H. Meas. Cyp.* ed. 2, 85; *G.C.* 1894, ii. 49; *O.R.* 1894, 255.—Lewis.

362. P. × **Macfarlanei** (× calophyllum ♀ × Spicerianum), *Kerch. Liv. d. O.* 480.—Sander, 1891.

C. × Macfarlanei, *G.C.* 1891, ii. 300; *O.R.* 1893, 326.

C. × Amandinæ, *J. S. H. Rhone*, March 30, 1897, f.; *J. S. H. Fr.* 1897, 493. Combet et Bierry.

363. P. × **macropterum** (Lowii ♀ × superbiens), *Stein O.* 476.—Veitch, 1882.

C. × macropterum, *G.C.* 1882, ii. 552; *O.R.* 1893, 100; *O.A.* ix. t. 391; *V. Man. O.* iv. 90; *Day O. Draw.* xxxvii. t. 3.

C. × Lowii-superbiens, *R. H. Meas. Cyp.* ed. 2, 70.—Lawrence.

364. P. × **maculatum** (× Leeanum × tonsum ♀).—Sander, 1892.

C. × maculatum, *G.C.* 1892, ii. 744; *J. S. H. Fr.* 1896, 1003.—Cardoso.

365. P. × **Madeline** (Argus × bellatulum).—Palmer, 1895.

C. × Madeline, *G.C.* 1895, ii. 655; *O.R.* 1896, 30.

366. P. × **Madiotianum** (Chamberlanianum × villosum ♀), *O.R.* 1899, 47, 132.—Cappe, 1898.

C. × villoso-Chamberlanianum, *J. S. H. Fr.* 1898, 168, 352; 1900, 83; *Chron. O.* 159.—Duval.

C. × Madiotianum, *R. H. Meas. Cyp.* ed. 3, 195.—Cappe.

C. × Madioti, *J. S. H. Fr.* 1899, 374; 1900, 591; *Dict. Ic. O.* Cyp. hyb, t. 58. —Cappe.

C. × Mansellii, *G.C.* 1899, i. 288; *O.R.* 1899, 132, 155; 1902, 124.—Charlesworth.

367. P. × Magnei (Lawrenceanum ♀ × Leeanum).—Magne, 1900.

C. × Paul Magne, *J. S. H. Fr.* 1900, 765.—Magne.

368. P. × magnificum (insigne × Pollettianum), *O.R.* 1900, 30.—Keeling, 1899.

C. × magnificum, *O.R.* 1899, 370.

369 P. × Mahleræ (Lawrenceanum × Rothschildianum ♀), *O.R.* 1898, 271; 1901, 345.—R. H. Measures, 1898.

C. × Wiertzianum, *Sem. H.* 1898, 425; *G.C.* 1899, i. 77; *O.R.* 1899, 92; 1900, 254; *Lind.* xiv. t. 644.—Linden.

P. × Wiertzianum, *O.R.* 1898, 335.—Linden.

C. × Mahleræ, *Desb. Cyp.* ed. 2, 329; *Dict. Ic. O.* Cyp. hyb. t. 42 (v. Dr. Clinge Doorenbos).—R. H. Measures.

C. × Gabari, *G.C.* 1899, ii. 58; *O.R.* 1899, 249, 254.—Sander.

C. × Alport, *O.R.* 1899, 284.—Gratrix.

C. × tixallense, *O.R.* 1900, 112.—Bostock.

C. × Docteur Clinge Doorenbos, *J. S. H. Fr.* 1900, 118, 413; 1902, 229.—Peeters.

C. × Rothschildiano-Lawrenceanum, *G.C.* 1900, ii. 58; *O.R.* 1900, 251, 254. —Lawrence.

370. P. × Malyanum (× Crossianum × Spicerianum ♀), *Kerch. Liv. d. O.* 481.—Sander, 1891.

C. × Malyanum, *G.C.* 1891, ii. 591; *O.R.* 1893, 327.

C. × Ashworthianum, *R. H. Meas. Cyp.* ed. 2, 9.—Sander.

C. × Krouseanum, *R. H. Meas. Cyp.* ed. 2, 63.—Pitcher.

371. P. × Mandæ (insigne × javanicum ♀).—Pitcher & Manda, 1893.

C. × javanico-insigne, *Haus. O. Hyb.* 1895, 255.—Pitcher & Manda.

372. P. × Mantinii (× almum × Swanianum).—Mantin, 1897.

C. × (unnamed), *Rev. H.* 1897, 282—Mantin.

373. P. × Manto (Chamberlainianum × Harrisianum), *O.R.* 1900, 183.—Cappe, 1899.

C. × Harrisiano-Chamberlainianum, *J. S. H. Fr.* 1899, 56.—Cappe.

C. × Harri-Chamber, *Chron. O.* 292.—Cappe.

C. × Manto, *Dict. Ic. O.* Cyp. hyb. t. 64.—Young.

374. P. × Mapleæ (× Gowerianum × Youngianum ♀).—Sander, 1899.

C. × Lady Maple, *G.C.* 1899, ii. 58; *O.R.* 1899, 254.—Sander.

375. P × Marchandii (concolor × superciliare).—Duval, 1900.

C. × Colonel Marchand, *J. S. H. Fr.* 1900, 264.—Duval.

376. P. × Margaritæ (barbatum × Crossianum).—Mantin, 1894.

C. × Margaritæ, *J. S. H. Fr.* 1894, 582; 1895, 178, 240.

C. × Marguerite Mantin, *Jard.* 1895, 52; *G.C.* 1895, i. 370; *Hans. O. Hyb.* 1895, 160.—Mantin.

C. × Dauthieri violaceum purpureum, *J. S. H. Fr.* 1894, 68; *Jard.* 1895, 52; *G.C.* 1895, i. 370.—Opoix.

377. P. × **marmorophyllum** (barbatum × Hookeræ ♀), *Stein. O.* 476.—Veitch, 1876.

C. × marmorophyllum, *G.C.* 1876, ii. 130; *O.R.* 1893, 40; *V. Man. O* iv. 90; *Day O. Draw.* xxxii. **t.** 9.

C. × patens, *G.C.* 1877, ii. 456; *O.R.* 1893, 68.—Veitch.

378. P. × **Marshallianum** (concolor × venustum ♀) *Stein. O.* 476.—Veitch, 1875.

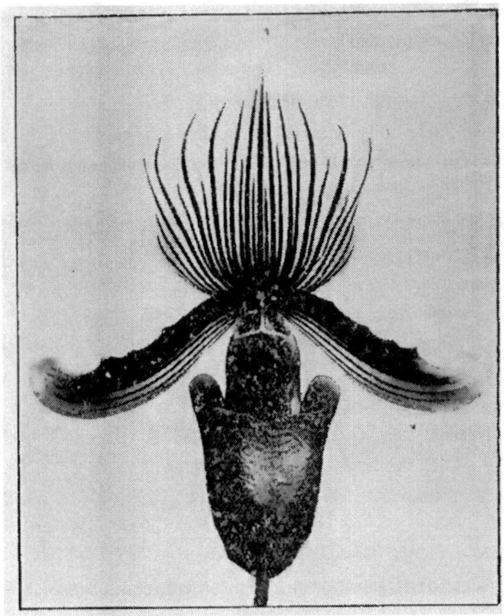

Fig. 66. PAPHIOPEDILUM × MAUDIÆ.

C. × Marshallianum, *G.C.* 1875, ii. 804; 1887, i. 513, **f.** 99; *O. A.* ix. **t.** 418; *O.R.* 1893, 39; *V. Man. O.* iv. 91; *Hans. O. Hyb.* 161.

379. P. × **Marwoodii** (× Harrisianum × niveum ♀), *Stein O.* 477.—Marwood, 1890.

C. × Marwoodii, *G.C.* 1890, ii. 252.

C. × Lady Roberts, *G.C.* 1900, ii. 313; *O.R.* 1900, 348.—Appleton.

C. × (unnamed), *Jard.* 1903, 64; *Rev. H.* 1903, 118.—Debille.

C. × Harrisiano-superbum × niveum v. Leon Duval, *J. S. H. Fr.* 1903, 71.—Duval.

380. P. × **Mary-Beatrice** (bellatulum × Gowerianum ♀).—Charlesworth, 1900.

C. × Mary Beatrice, *G.C.* 1900, i. May 26, suppl. 1; *O.R.* 1900, 174, 175.—Charlesworth.

381. P. × Massaianum (Rothschildianum × superciliare ♀), *Kerch. Liv. d. O.* 481.—Sander, 1893.

C. × Massaianum, *G.C.* 1893, ii. 70, 267, f. 48; *O.R.* 1893, 225, 245, 255; *Gard.* 1896, ii. 89 ("Masseanum").

382. P. × Matthewsii (Lawrenceanum × Mastersianum).—Charlesworth, 1899.

C. × Eros, *O.R.* 1899, 155.—Charlesworth.

C. × Lawreaceano-Mastersianum, *O.R.* 1899, 254.—Low.

C. × William Matthews, *G.C.* 1902, ii. 143; *O.R.* 1902, 276.—Sander.

383. P. × Maudiæ (callosum × Lawrenceanum ♀), *O.R.* 1901, 17, f. 4; 1906, 207.—Charlesworth, 1900. **[See Fig. 66.**

C. × Maudiæ, *O.R.* 1900, 308; 1906, 125; *G.M.* 1900, 771, f.; *G.C*, 1901, ii. 129, f. 41 (v. magnificum); *J.H.* 1901, ii. 121, f. (id.).

P. Maudiæ was originally derived from the albino forms, P. Lawrenceanum Hyeanum and P. callosum Sanderæ. The normal coloured form did not appear until 1906.

384. P. × May (callosum ♀ × Sanderianum).—Sander, 1895.

C. × Princess Mary, *Gard.* 1895, ii. 52.—Sander.

C. × Princess May, *Boyle. Woodl. O.* 201.—Sander.

C, × Sanderiano-callosum, *Sand. O. Guide*, 337.

385. P. × Measuresiæ (bellatulum × superbiens ♀), *Kerch. Liv. d. O.* 481.—Sander, 1893.

C. × Measuresiæ, *R. H. Meas. Cyp.* ed. 2, 75; *Hans. O. Hyb.* 1895, 162.

C. × Mrs. Fred Hardy, *G.C.* 1895, i. 81, 111, f. 16; *G.M.* 1895, 27, f.; *J.H.* 1895, i. 111, f. 18; *O.R.* 1895, 64; *Dict. Ic. O.* Cyp. hyb. t. 67.

C × Cravenianum, *G.C.* 1897, i. 451; *O.R.* 1898, 26; *Desb. Cyp.* ed. 2, 143.—Law-Schofield.

C. × (unnamed), *G.C.* 1894, i. 654.—Prewett.

386. P. × Measuresianum (venustum × villosum), Stein O. 477.—Williams, 1887.

C. × Measuresianum, *O.A.* vii. t. 304; *J.H.* 1888, ii. 47, f. 5; *Rev. H. Belge*, 1888, 266, 267, f. 26; *V. Man. O.* iv. 91; *J. S. H. Fr.* 1893, 812; *Will O. Gr. Man.* ed. 6, 281, f.

C. × Rowallianum, *G.C.* 1891, i. 21; 1895, i. 201.—Fraser.

C. × Madame Gibez, *Orchidoph.* 1893, 67; *O.R.* 1893, 211.—Gibez.

C. × Amesianum, *O.A.* viii. t. 340; *Will. O. Gr. Man.* ed. 6, 229; *Desb. Cyp.* ed. 2, 49.—Williams.

C. × Julien Coffigniez, *J. S. H. Fr.* 1894, 314; *Jard.* 1895, 53; *G.C.* 1895, i. 370.—Opoix.

C. × Thetis, *R. H. Meas. Cyp.* ed. 2, 102; *Bohnh. Dict. O. Hyb.* 32; *Hans. O. Hyb.* 162.—Harris.

C. × refulgens, *G.C.* 1895, i. 210; *O.R.* 1896, 35.—Burton.

C. × Gibezianum, *J. S. H. Fr.* 1896, 111; *Lind.* ix. t. 425.—Gibez.

C. × venusto-villosum, *Sem. H.* 1897, 459; *Desb. Cyp.* ed. 2. 461.—Sallier.

387. P. × Medeia (hirsutissimum × Spicerianum ♀), *Stein. O.* 477. Latham, 1889.

C. × Medeia, *J. R. H. S.* xii. *Proc.* 171; *G.C.* 1892, ii. 712 (v. monstrosa); 1896, ii. 686 (id.); *O.R.* 1896, 360 (id.); *Hans. O. Hyb.* 70 (id). —Veitch.

C. × Ceres, *G.C.* 1891, i. 360; *J. d. O.* ii. 37; *O.R.* 1893, 327.—Drewett.

C. × Van Molianum, *J. d. O.* i. 251; *G.C.* 1892, i. 502.—Miteau.

C. × Huybrechtianum, *Rev. H. Belge*, 1892, 117; *G.C.* 1892, i. 554.—Vervaet.

C. × fascinatum, *G.C.* 1893, ii. 756; *Rev. H. Belge*, 1894, 25, t.; *O.R.* 1894, 28, 30.—Hye.

C. × Sirius, *R. H. Meas. Cyp.* ed. 2, 99.—Sander.

C. × Spicero-hirsutissimum, *Bohnh. Dict. O. Hyb.* 32.

C. × Steurbauti, *Desb. Cyp.* ed. 2, 439.—Vervaet.

P. × Ceres, *J.R.H.S.* xxiv. 100, f. 17 (v. medea).—Drewett.

The first seedling, raised by Mr. Latham, had a constantly abnormal flower.

388. P. × medium (Druryi × nitens).—Hye, 1898.

C. × medium, *Desb. Cyp.* ed. 2, 335.

389. P. × Melanthus (Hookeræ × Stonei), *Kerch. Liv. d. O.* 481.—Veitch, 1893.

C. × Melanthus, *O.R.* 1893, 147.

390. P. × Melia (× Calypso × insigne), *O.R.* 1902, 61.—Wrigley, 1902.

C. × (unnamed), *Gard.* 1903, i. Jan. 17, *Suppl.* vii.—Joicey.

391. P. × Memnon (Charlesworthii × Spicerianum ♀).—Veitch, 1900.

C. × Memnon, *G.C.* 1900, ii. 384; *O.R.* 1900, 373.

C. × radians, *G.C.* 1901, ii. 401; *O.R.* 1901, 367; 1902, 14, 15.—Keeling.

P. × radians, *O.R.* 1903, 30.—Keeling.

392. P. × Menelik (Boxallii × Calypso), *O.R.* 1903, 92; 1904, 120.—Keeling, 1901.

C. × Menelik, *G.C.* 1901, ii. 401; *O.R.* 1901, 367.

P. × (unnamed), *O.R.* 1902, 124.—Vanner.

393. P. × Merope (Chamberlainianum × hirsutissimum), *O.R.* 1903, 59. —Appleton, 1903.

394. P. × Metis (Boxallii ♀ × philippinense).—Veitch, 1895.

C. × Metis, *G.C.* 1895, ii. 307; *O.R.* 1895, 320.

395. P. × microchilum (Druryi × niveum ♀) *Stein O.* 477.—Veitch, 1882.

C. × microchilum, *G.C.* 1882, i. 77; *V. Man. O.* iv. 92, f.; *Lind.* ii. t. 50; *O.R.* 1893, 100; *Dict. Ic. O.* Cyp. hyb. t. 17; *Day O. Draw.* xli. t. 59; xlvi t. 21.

C. × niveo-Druryi, *Sand. O. Guide*, 336.

396. P. × Millmanii (callosum ♀ × philippinense).—Hollington, 1894.

C. × Millmanii, *G.C.* 1894, ii. 103; 1895, i. 800; *O.R.* 1894, 285.

C. × calloso-laevigatum, *Hans. O. Hyb.* 163.—Hollington.

397. P. × Milo (insigne ♀ × œnanthum).—Veitch, 1894.

C. × Milo, *G.C.* 1894, ii. 70; *O.R.* 1895, 30; *J.H.* 1899, ii. 503, f. 89 (Westonbirt var.); *G.C.* 1899, ii. 413, f. 131 (id.).

398. P. × miniatum (Curtisii ♀ × insigne).—Sander, 1895.

C. × miniatum, *Gard.* 1895, i. 50; *G.C.* 1895, i. 199; *O.R.* 1896, 38; 1900, 351.

C. × Atalanta, *Charlesworth Cat.* March, 1901; *Sand. O. Guide*, 334 (second entry).—Charlesworth.

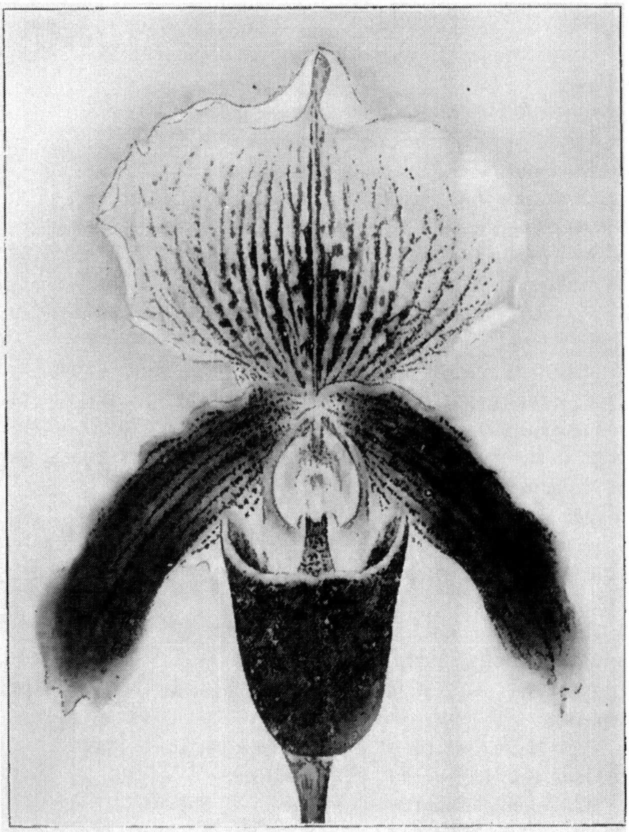

Fig. 67. PAPHIOPEDILUM × MINOS VAR. YOUNGII.

399. P. × Minnie (concolor × Curtisii ♀).—Sander, 1896.

C. × Minnie Ames, *G.C.* 1896, i. 83; *O.R.* 1896, 64; *Desb. Cyp.* ed. 2, 343 (Miss Minnie Ames).—Sander.

C. × Annie Ayling, *G.C.* 1896, i. 210; *O.R.* 1896, 95.—Hollington.

C. × conco-Curtisii, *Boyle Woodl. O.* 181.—R. H. Measures.

C. × Cydonia, *Boyle Woodl. O.* 200.—R. H. Measures.

400. P. × Minos (× Arthurianum × Spicerianum ♀), *Kerch. Liv. d. O.* 481; *O.R.* 1900, 40; 1902, 41, f. 4 (v. Youngii); 1905, 71, 72, f. 18 (v. Youngii), 73, f. 19 (Westfield var.).—Veitch, 1893. **[See Fig. 67.**

C. × Minos, *G.C.* 1893, ii. 692; 1903, i. 108 (v. Youngii); *O.R.* 1894, 30; 1899, 17, f. 6; 1903, 82 (v. Youngii); *Dict. Ic. O.* Cyp. hyb. t. 4 (id.).

C. × Minosa, *G.C.* 1894, ii. 730.—Veitch.

P. × Alonzo, *G.C.* 1897, ii. 387; *O.R.* 1898, 29.—Veitch.

C. × Alonzo, *O.R.* 1900, 40.—Veitch.

401. P. × Miranda (× augustum × Rothschildianum ♀).—Bleu, 1901.

C. × Rothschildianum-augustum, *Rev. H.* 1901, 515; *J. S. H. Fr.* 1901, 996.

402. P. × modestum (× Io × purpuratum ♀).—Sander, 1894.

C. × modestum, *G.C.* 1894, ii. 103; *O.R.* 1894, 286.

C. × molestum, *Hans. O. Hyb.* 163.—Sander.

Re-named by Hansen, but this is the first recorded C. × modestum.

403. P. × Moensiæ (callosum × Spicerianum), *O.R.* 1901, 38.—Moens, 1892.

C. × Mdlle. Gabrielle Moens, *Bohnh. Dict. O. Hyb.* 25; *Desb. Cyp.* ed. 2, 328.—Moens.

C. × Moensiæ, *O.R.* 1899, 330.—Moens.

404. P. × Moreauanum (callosum × superciliare ♀).—*Kerch. Liv. d. O.* 481.—Regnier, 1892.

C × Moreauanum, Hans. O. Hyb. 164; Desb. Cyp. ed. 2, 348.

405. P. × Morganiæ (Stonei × superbiens ♀), Stein. O. 478.—Veitch, 1880.

C. × Morganianum, *G.C.* 1880, ii. 134.—Veitch. **[See Fig. 68.**

C. × Morganiæ, *G.C.* 1886, ii. 241, 243, f. 49; 1890, i. 264, suppl. f., 545, 552, f. 85; 1892, ii. 217, 218, f. 37; *J.H.* 1887, i. 232, 233, f. 42; *O. A.* vii. t. 313; *V. Man. O.* iv. 92, f.; *Gard.* 1883, i. 58, t. 372; 1902, i. 75, t. f.; *Reichenb.* ser. 2, i. 1, t. 1 (v. burfordiense); *Ill. H.* 1887, 16, t. 5; *Rev. H. Belge*, 1885, 217, f.; *O.R.* 1893, 41, f. 3, 70; 1894, 79; *Nich. Dict. G.* 1900 Suppl. 290, f. 303; *Dict. Ic. O.* Cyp. hyb. t. 27; *Day. O. Draw.* xliv. t. 13.

406. P. × Moussetianum (callosum × superbiens).—Mantin, 1894.

C. × Moussetianum, *J. S. H. Fr.* 1894, 582.

C. × Memoria Mousseti, *J. S. H. Fr.* 1895, 240.—Mantin.

C. × purum, *Amer. G.* 1902, 189, f. 43; *G.C.* 1902, ii. 294.—Parker.

C. × Katherine, *G.C.* 1902, ii. 445; *O.R.* 1903, 23.—Veitch.

C. × Mme. Osterrieth, *Rev. H. Belge*, 1903, 3.

C. × calloso-Veitchii, *G.C.* 1903, ii. 343; *O.R.* 1903, 367.—Statter.

C. × Cassandra, *G.C.* 1903, ii. 340; *O.R.* 1903, 364.—Sander.

407. P. × mulus (hirsutissimum ♀ × Lawrenceanum), *Kerch. Liv. d. O.* 481.—Vuylsteke, 1892.

C. × mulus, *G.C.* 1893, i. 752; *O.R.* 1893, 244; *Hans. O. Hyb.* 165 (excl. var.).—Sander.

The variety cited by Hansen belongs to P. × Erato, the error arising from a confusion of C. × Sallieri Hyeanum with C. Lawrenceanum Hyeanum.

408. P. × Murillo (Argus × Boxallii ♀), *Kerch. Liv. d. O.* 481.—Vuylsteke, 1892.

C. × Murillo, *G.C.* 1893, i. 162; *O.R.* 1893, 147.

C. × Dibdin (Argus ♀), *G.C.* 1893, i. 162; *O.R.* 1893, 118.—Tautz.

C. × Cyris, *G.C.* 1894, ii. 605; *O.R.* 1894, 374; *G.M.* 1894, 701, f.; *J.H.* 1895, ii. 363, f. 58.—Cookson.

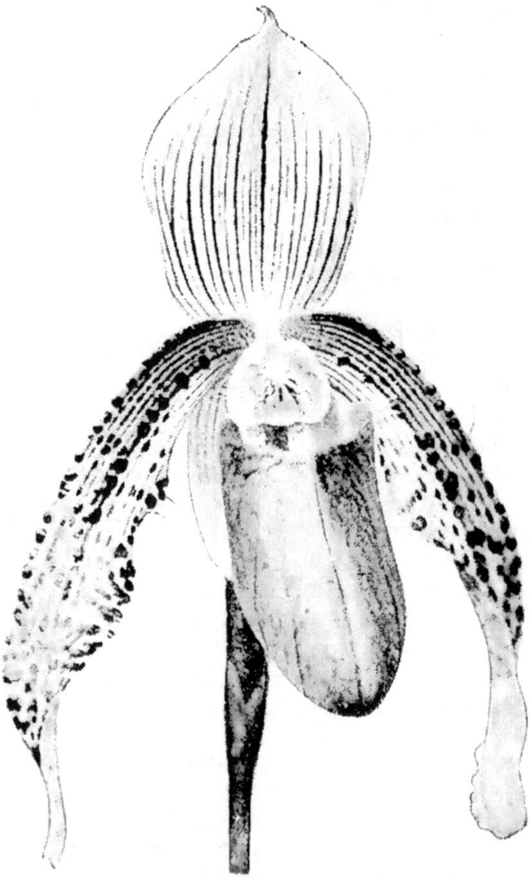

Fig. 68. Paphiopedilum × Morganiæ var. burfordiense.

C. × Horneri, *O.R.* 1894, 80.—Marwood.

C. × Daviesianum, *G.C.* 1893, i. 206; *O.R.* 1893, 95.—Statter.

C. × (un-named), *J. S. H. Fr.* 1896, 110.—Opoix.

C. × Sphinx, *R. H. Meas. Cyp.* ed. 3, 156; *Desb. Cyp.* ed. 2, 428.—Vuylsteke.

409. P. × Myra (Chamberlainianum × Haynaldianum).—E. Ashworth, 1897.

C. × Haynaldo Chamberlaini), *G.C.* 1897, ii. 316.—E. Ashworth.

C. × Haynaldo-Chamberlainianum, *O.R.* 1897, 350.—E. Ashworth.

C. × Myra, *Boyle Woodl. O.* 179.—R. H. Measures.

410. P. × Nandii (callosum ♀ Tautzianum).—R. I. Measures, 1894.

C. × Nandii, *G.C.* 1894, ii. 318; *O.R.* 1894, 310, 319; *G.M.* 1895, 403, **f.**

411. P. × Nansen (× Morganiæ × selligerum ♀).—Cookson, 1897.

C. × Nansen, *G.C.* 1897, i. 246; *Chron. O.* 39.

412. P × Nebula (Rothschildianum × selligerum ♀).—Sander, 1898.

C. × selligero-Rothschildianum, *O.R.* 1898, 252.—Sander.

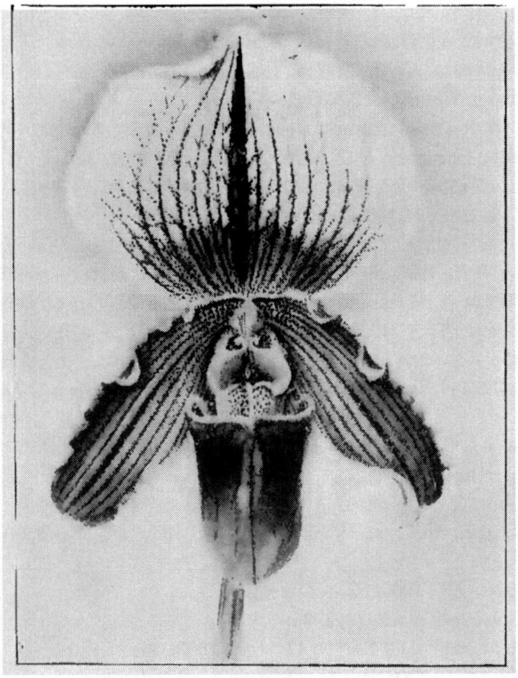

Fig. 69. PAPHIOPEDILUM × NIOBE.

C. × Orion, *G.C.* 1898, ii. 92; 1902, ii. 191, 211 (v. Mrs. Arthur Wells); *O.R.* 1898, 256.—Sander.

C. × Mrs. Arthur Wells, *G.C.* 1902, ii. 243.—Wellesley.

413. P. × Nellie (Charlesworthii × tonsum).—Law-Schofield, 1899.

C. × (unnamed), *G.C.* 1899, ii. 478; *O.R.* 1900, 25.—Law-Schofield

C. × tonso-Charlesworthii, *Amer. G.* 1900, 795; *Chron. O.* 342.—Mrs. F. L. Ames.

C. × Nellie, *G.C.* 1901, ii. 172; *O.R.* 1901, 284.—Pitt.

414. P. × Neptune (× Io ♀ × Rothschildianum).—Sander, 1896.

C. × Neptune, *G.C.* 1896, i. 792; *O.R.* 1896, 224; *Desb. Cyp.* ed. 2, 358.

C. × Mars, *G.C.* 1902, ii. 143; *O.R.* 1902, 276.—Sander.

415. **P. × Niobe** (Fairrieanum × Spicerianum ♀), *Stein O.* 478; *O.R.* 1900, 9, f. 3; 1905, 41, f. 9.—Veitch, 1889. [**See Fig. 69.**

C. × Niobe, *J.H.* 1889, ii. 527, f. 67; *G.C.* 1889, ii. 701; 1890, i. 9; *Wien Ill. G. Zeit.* 1890, 342, 343, f. 69; *O.A.* x. t. 438; *Orchidoph.* 1892, 81, f.; *O.R.* 1893, 7, f. 1; 1894, 80, 172; *Gard.* 1891, ii. 482, t. 806; *Will. O. Gr. Man.* ed 7, 285; *Dict. Ic. O.* Cyp. hyb. t. 13.

C. × Gaskelliana, *Gard.* 1890, ii. 150; *O.R.* 1893, 8; *Desb. Cyp.* ed. 2, 197.—Gaskell.

C. × miniatum, *Rev. H. Belge*, 1893, 290; *O.R.* 1893, 371.—Hye.

C. × oliganthum, *Hans. O. Hyb.* 165.—Graves.

C. × purpureum, *Hans. O. Hyb.* 165.—Graves.

C. × luteum, *Hans. O. Hyb.* 165.—Graves.

416. **P. × Niobe-Leeanum** (Leeanum × Niobe).—Sander, 1902.

C. × Niobe-Leeanum, *G.C.* 1902, ii. 383; *O.R.* 1902, 367.

417. **P. × nitens** (insigne × villosum ♀), *Stein O.* 478; *J.R.H.S.* xxiv. 109, f. 31; *O.R.* 1901, 16.—Veitch, 1878.

C. × nitens, *G.C.* 1878, i. 398; *Lind.* v. t. 223; *V. Man. O.* iv. 93; *Monit. H.* 1889, 127, t.; *O.R.* 1893, 68; *Dict. Ic. O. Cyp. hyb.* t. 22 (v. superbum), t. 22A (v. Sallieri), t. 22B (v. Hyeanum); *Desb. Cyp.* ed. 2, 363; *Day O. Draw.* xl. t. 3.

C. × Sallieri, *J. S. H. Fr.* 1884, 164; *Rev. H.* 1885, 476; *Orchidoph.* 1884, 147; 1887, 33; *V. Man. O.* iv. 97; *Godefr. and Br., Cyp.* t.; *Lind.* ii. t. 84; *O.R.* 1893, 102; 1902, 144, f. 17 (v. Hyeanum); *Day. O. Draw.* xlvii. t. 77.—Godefroy-Lebeuf.

C. × Celeus, *G.C.* 1893, ii. 630; *O.R.* 1893, 374; *Will. O. Gr. Man.* ed. 6, 241.—R. I. Measures.

C. × Almos, *R. H. Meas. Cyp.* ed. 2, 7.—Ebner.

C. × Chantino-villosum, *J.S.H.Fr.* 1897, 133; *G. World*, 1903, i. 89.—Lebaudy.

C. × Colin, *O.R.* 1900, 62.—Bostock.

C. × Laflacheri, *Jard.* 1902, 86.

C. × Great Rex, *G.C.* 1903, i. 47; *O.R.* 1903, 54.—Gratrix.

C. × Dido, *G.C.* 1903, ii. 340.—Sander.

C. × Souvenir du Dr. Weber, *J.S.H.Fr.* 1903, 708.—Magne.

C. × Souvenir du Presdtt. Weber, *Rev. H.* 1903, 575; *Jard.* 1903, 368.—Magne.

C. × Mrs. Cary Batten, *G.C.* 1903, ii. 429.—Cary Batten.

418. **P. × nitidum** (× nitens × selligerum).—R. H. Measures, 1901.

C. × nitidum, *Boyle Woodl. O.* 1901, 204.

419. **P. × nobilior** (Haynaldianum ♀ × Lathamianum).—Sander, 1894.

C. × nobilior, *Hans. O. Hyb.* 167.

C. × nobilius, *G.C.* 1895, i. 200; *J. S. H. Fr.* 1896, 649.—Sander.

420. **P. × Norma** (× Niobe × Spicerianum ♀), *O.R.* 1900, 40; 1905, 104 f. 22; 105, f. 23 (Westfield var.).—Veitch, 1895. [**See Fig. 70.**

C. × Norma, *G.C.* 1895, i. 82 ; *O.R.* 1895, 64.

421. P. × Norrisianum (Leeanum × purpuratum ♀).—Rehder, 1897.

C. × Norrisianum, *G. World*, 1897, ii. 148 ; *O.R.* 1897, 360.

422. P. × Northumbrian (× calophyllum ♀ × insigne), *Kerch. Liv. d. O.* 481.—Drewett, 1890.

C. × Northumbrian, *G.C.* 1890, i. 160 ; *O.R.* 1893, 294.

C. × Artemis, *R. H. Meas. Cyp.* ed. 2, 8.

C. × Thora, *Gard.* 1895, ii. 347.—Veitch.

C. × calophyllum-Chantini, *J. S. H. Fr.* 1900, 84.—Opoix.

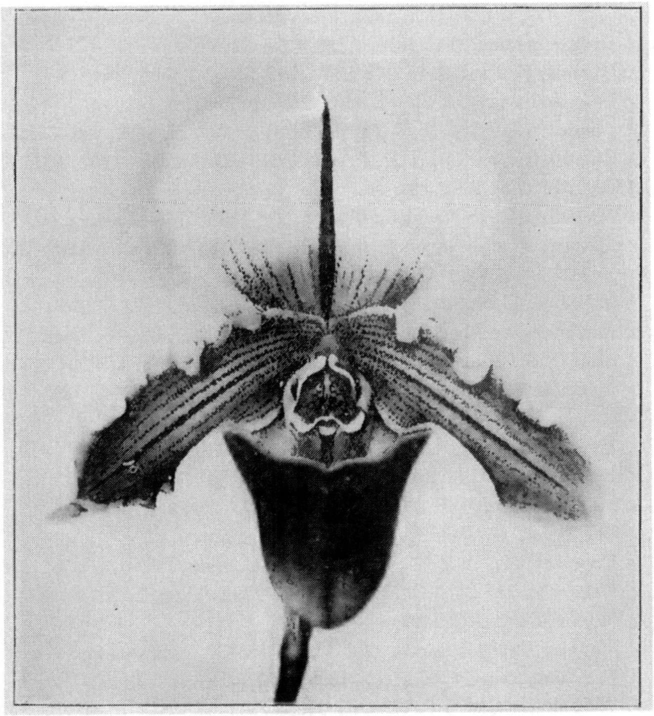

Fig. 59. Paphiopedilum × Norma, Westfield var.

423. P. × Numa (Lawrenceanum ♀ × Stonei), *Kerch. Liv. d. O.* 481.—Veitch, 1890.

C. × Numa, *G.C.* 1890, i. 608 ; *O.R.* 1893, 295.

424. P. × Oakesii (Curtisii × purpuratum).—Mrs. F. L. Ames, 1899.

C. × purpurato-Curtisii, *Amer. G.* 1899, 753 ; *G.C.* 1899, ii. 430.—Mrs. F. L. Ames.

425. P. × œnanthum (× Harrisianum ♀ × insigne), *Stein O.* 479.—Veitch, 1876.

C. × œnanthum, *G.C.* 1876, i. 297; *Lind.* i. t. 33 (v. superbum); *Rev. H. Belge*, 1885, 231, 233, f. 39 (id.); *J.H.* 1886, i. 62, f. 11 (id.); *O.A.* viii. t. 379; ix. t. 420 (id.); *Reichenb.* ser. 1, i. 85, t. 38 (id); *V. Man. O.* iv. 93, f. (id.); *O.R.* 1893, 39; 1894, 334; *Day O. Draw.* xxx. t 71; xxxiv. t. 79.

C. × Thibautianum, *G.C.* 1886, i. 104; *V. Man. O.* iv. 99.—Veitch.

C. × Cambridgeanum, *J.H.* 1887, i. 376, f. 66.—R. I. Measures.

C. × Galatea, *G.C.* 1888, i. 168; *V. Man. O.* iv. 84; *O.R.* 1893, 259; *G.M.* March 4, 1893, suppl. t.; *J.H.* 1896, ii. 627, f. 108 (v. majus).—Veitch.

C. × Electra, *G.C.* 1888, i. 297; *V. Man. O.* iv. 83; *O.R.* 1893, 259.—Veitch.

C. × Josephine Jolibois, *J. S. H. Fr.* 1888, 296; *Rev. H.* 1888, 236; *Orchidoph.* 1892, 337, t. f. 2; *O.R.* 1893, 154.—Jolibois.

C. × Berggrenianum, *G.C.* 1888, i. 798.—Sander.

C. × Orestes, *V. Man. O.* iv. 94; *O.R.* 1893, 259.—Veitch.

C. × Felix Jolibois, *J. S. H. Fr.* 1889, 25.—Jolibois.

C. × Clement Loury, *J. S. H. Fr.* 1889, 231; *Rev. H.* 1889, 206.—Jolibois.

C. × Charles Gondoin, *J. S. H. Fr.* 1889, 310; *Orchidoph.* 1892, 237, f. 1; *Rev. H.* 1889, 251; *O.R.* 1893, 154—Jolibois.

C. × Madame Charles Gondoin, *J. S. H. Fr.* 1889, 377.—Jolibois.

C. × Madame Emilie Gayot, *J. S. H. Fr.* 1889, 377; *Rev. H.* 1889, 303.—Jolibois.

C. × n. 192, *J. S. H. Fr.* 1891, 45.—Jolibois.

C. × Mademoiselle Alice Gayot, *J. S. H. Fr.* 1891, 67, 68.—Jolibois.

C. × Mme. Roch Jolibois, *Jard.* 1895, 53; *G.C.* 1895, i. 370.

C. × Mademoiselle Germaine Scellier de Gisors, *J. S. H. Fr.* 1893, 652.—Opoix.

C. × Madame Coffinet, *J. S. H. Fr.* 1893, 652.—Opoix.

C. × Donatianum, *R. H. Meas. Cyp.* ed. 2, 33.—Sander.

C. × pulcherrimum, *R. H. Meas. Cyp.* ed. 2, 87.—Drewett.

C. × Themis, *R. H. Meas. Cyp.* ed. 2, 103.—Veitch.

C. × René Jolibois, *J. S. H. Fr.* 1894, 726.—Jolibois.

C. × Louryi, *Bohnh. Dict. O. Hyb.* 24; *G.C.* 1895, i. 200.

C. × Morrisianum, *G.C.* 1897, i. 51.—Sander.

C. × Madame Georges Boucher, *J. S. H. Fr.* 1897, 1242.—Opoix.

C. × President Kruger, *J.S.H.Fr.* 1899, 1131.—Duval.

C. × Wilmslowianum, *G.C.* 1899, ii. 366.—E. Ashworth.

C. × Madeleine Thiebaux, *J. S. H. Fr.* 1903, 765.—Opoix.

C. × Madeleine Thiebaut, *Jard.* 1903, 384.—Opoix.

426. P. × Œnomaus (× Calypso × tonsum ♀).—Oakes Ames, 1898.

C. × Œnomaus, *Amer. G.* 1898, 792; *Chron. O.* 299.

427. P. × œno-superbiens (× œnanthum ♀ × superbiens).—Lawrence, 1893.

C. × œno-superbiens, *G.C.* 1893, ii. 192; *O.R.* 1893, 287; *J.H.* 1893, ii. 269, f. 38.

428. P. Olbia (× Leeanum ♀ × Romulus).—Peeters, 1900.

C. × Norma, *J. S. H. Fr.* 1900, 53.—Peeters.

Re-named because of an earlier C. × Norma.

429. P. × **Olenus** (bellatulum ♀ × ciliolare), *J.R.H.S.* xxvi. 692.—R. I. Measures, 1895.

C. × Olenus, *G.C.* 1895, i. 402, 613, f. 86; *O R.* 1895, 157; *Gard.* 1902, i. 355, f.

C. × Gertrude Hollington, *G.C.* 1895, i. 626, 644, f. 90; *O.R.* 1895, 188; *Monit. H.* Oct. 10, 1895, f.; *J.H.* 1896, i. 3, f. 1; *G. World*, 1898, i. 616, f. (Southgate var.).

C. × Sir Thomas Lipton, *G.C.* 1898, i. 385.—Stanley & Ashton.

430. P. × **Olivia** (niveum × tonsum ♀), *O.R.* 1900, 358.—Oakes Ames, 1898.

C. × Olivia, *G.C.* 1898, ii. 128; 1899, ii. 339, f. 113; *O.R.* 1898, 285, 286; 1899, 28, 350; *J.H.* 1898, ii. 142, 143, f. 26.

The parentage was first recorded as C. tonsum and C. concolor, but afterwards amended as above.

431. P. × **Ollendorffii** (× Harrisianum × hirsutissimum), *O.R.* 1899, 135. —Ollendorff, 1899.

432. P. × **Omphale** (× Lucie × tonsum ♀),*O.R.* 1903, 26.—Young, 1902.

433. P. × **Opoixiæ** (niveum × superciliare ♀).—Opoix, 1893.

C. × Madame Octave Opoix, *J.S.H.Fr.* 1893, 500; *Jard.* 1895, 53; *Lind.* x. t. 462; *Journ. d. O.* v. 310.—Opoix.

434. P. × **Opoixii** (Lowii ♀ × vexillarium).—Opoix, 1895.

C. × (unnamed), *J. S. H. Fr.* 1895, 602; 1896, 792.—Opoix.

435. P. × **orangense** (× Harrisianum ♀ × tonsum).—Graves, 1894.

C. × modestum, *Amer. G.* March 23, 1895; *Hans. O. Hyb.* 163.—Graves.

Re-named because of an earlier C. × modestum.

436. P. × **Orion** (concolor × insigne ♀). *Kerch. Liv. d. O.* 482.—Veitch, 1893.

C. × Orion, *G.C.* 1893, i. 80; *O.R.* 1893, 61; *J.H.* 1899, i. 151, f. 31; *G.M.* 1899, 104, f.; *Dict. Ic. O.* Cyp. hyb. t. 62.

C. × Chantino-Regnieri, *Sem. H.* 1897, 468; *Desb. Cyp.* ed. 2, 118.—Bleu.

437. P. × **Orissa** (barbatum ♀ × Haynaldianum).—Jolibois, 1890.

P. × (unnamed), *J. S. H. Fr.* 1890, 200.—Jolibois.

438. P. × **orphanum**, (barbatum × Druryi), *Stein O.* 479.—Veitch, 1886.

C. × orphanum, *G.C.* 1886, ii. 166; *V. Man. O.* iv. 94; *O.A.* x. t. 455; *O.R.* 1893, 27, 131; *Lind.* v. t. 206; *J.H.* 1887, ii. 135, f. 16; *Day O. Draw.* l. t. 85.

The name refers to the fact that the parents were unknown when the hybrid originally appeared.

439. P. × **Orpheus** (callosum × venustum ♀), *Stein O.* 479.—Sander, 1891.

C. × Orpheus, *G.C.* 1891, i. 39; *O.R.* 1893, 326; 1896, 39.

440. P. × **Osyanum** (× Arthurianum × Harrisianum).—Craen-Longhé, 1901.

C. × Souv. du Baron Osy, *R. H. Belge*, 1901, 71.—Craen-Longhé.

441. P. × **Pageanum** (Hookeræ × superbiens), *Kerch. Liv. d. O.* 482.—Lebaudy, 1888.

C. × Pageanum, *G.C.* 1888, ii. 264; *O.R.* 1893, 228; *Orchidoph.* 1888, 257.

C. × Œnone, (Hookeræ ♀), *G.C.* 1890, i. 260; *O.R.* 1893, 295.—Sander.

C. × Cydippe, *R. H. Meas. Cyp.* ed. 2, 29.—Veitch.

C. × Hookero-Veitchii, *Journ. d. O.* iii. 281.—Bleu.

C. × superbiens-Hookeræ, *J. S. H. Fr.* 1899, 1059.—Dallemagne.

442. P. × **Pallas** (callosum × calophyllum ♀), *Kerch. Liv. d. O.* 482.—Drewett, 1891.

C. × Pallas, *G.C.* 1891, i. 360; *O.R.* 1893, 327.

443. P. × **pallens** (Dayanum × Spicerianum ♀).—Pitcher & Manda, 1892.

C. × pallens, *Fl. Exch.* Jan. 9, 1892.

444. P. × **Pandora** (Argus × Dayanum), *Kerch. Liv. d. O.* 482.—Baron N. Rothschild, 1894.

C. × Pandora, *G.C.* 1894, i. 230; *O.R.* 1894, 111.

445. P × **Parkerianum** (Boxallii × nitens), *O.R.* 1900, 94.—Parker, 1898.

C. × Parkerianum, *G.C.* 1898, ii. 463; 1899, i. 31; *O.R.* 1899, 27, 63.

C. × Sirdar, *G.C.* 1899, i. 31; *O.R.* 1899, 63.—Tate.

C. × Cromer, *G.C.* 1899, i. 31; *O.R.* 1899, 63.—Tate.

C. × Mrs. Plummer, *R. H. Meas. Cyp.* ed. 3, 122.--Mc. Arthur.

C. × Boxallii-Sallieri, *J. S. H. Fr.* 1899, 56.—Cappe.

C. × Coloris-nova, *Rev. H. Belge*, 1901, 95.—Smet-Duvivier.

C. × Geneviène Opoix, *Jard.* 1903, 384; *Rev. H.* 1904, 26.—Opoix.

446. P. × **Parksianum** (× marmorophyllum × Spicerianum), *Kerch. Liv. d. O.* 482.—Pollett, 1892.

C. × Parksianum, *G.C.* 1892, i. 88; *O.R.* 1893, 359; *Dict. Ic. O. Cyp. hyb.* t. 15.

C. × Senateur Montefiore, *G.C.* 1892, i. 211; *J. S. H. Fr.* 1896, 929.—Peeters.

C. × marmorophyllum v. superbum, *G.C.* 1892, ii. 745.—Ingram.

447. P. × **Patersoni** (Dayanum × Lowii).—Cardoso, 1896.

C. × Patersoni, *J. S. H. Fr.* 1896, 929.

448. P. × **Patria** (× nitens × calophyllum (politum).—Young, 1903.

C. × polito-Sallieri, *G.C.* 1903, i. 302; *O.R.* 1903, 69, 179.

449. P. × **Paulii** (× Harrisianum × selligerum ♀), *Kerch. Liv. d. O.* 482.—Bowring, 1893.

C. × Paulii, *O.R.* 1893, 147.

C. × selligero-Harrisianum, *Rev. H. Belge*, 1894, 48; *Desb. Cyp.* ed. 2, 422.—Van Imschoot.

450. P. × **pavoninum** (Boxallii ♀ × venustum), *Stein. O.* 480.—Drewett, 1888.

C. × pavoninum, *G.C.* 1888, i. 264; *O.R.* 1893, 259; *Orchidoph.* 1888, 132; *Desb. Cyp.* ed. 2, 386; *V. Man. O.* iv. 95.

C. × Desboisianum, *G.C.* ii. 1890, 747; *Rev. H. Belge*, 1891, i. 48; *Lind.* vi. t. 277; *O.R.* 1893, 295.—Vervaet.

C. × dubium, *R. H. Meas. Cyp.* ed. 3, 52.

C. × maculosum, *Gard.* 1895, i. 123, 170.—Burton.

451. P. × Pegasus (× Leeanum ♀ × Morganiæ).—R. I. Measures, 1896.

C. × Pegasus, *G.C.* 1896, i. 210; *O.R.* 1896, 95; *Gard.* 1896, i. 89.

C. × Leeanum-Morganiæ, *R. H. Meas. Cyp.* ed. 3, 107.—R. I. Measures.

452. P. × Pelias (Haynaldianum ♀ × insigne), *Kerch. Liv. d. O.* 482.—Graves, 1894.

C. × Pelias, *O.R.* 1894, 144.

C. × Iocasta, *G.C.* 1900, i. April 28, Suppl. 4.—Veitch.

C. × jocasta, *O.R.* 1900, 157.—Veitch.

453. P. × Pelops (× Niobe × Sementa ♀).—Oakes Ames, 1898.

C. × Pelops, *Amer. G.* 1898, 792; *Chron. O.* 229; *O.R.* 1905, 106.

454. P. × Penelope (× Morganiæ × superbiens)—Law-Schofield, 1899.

C. × Veitchii-Morganiæ, *G.C.* 1899, ii. 198; *O.R.* 1899, 287.—Law-Schofield.

C. × Penelope, *G.C.* 1905, ii. 74; *O.R.* 1905, 247.—Fowler.

455. P. × Persephone (exul × Lathamianum), *O.R.* 1903, 58.—Young, 1903.

456. P. × Petri (Dayanum ♀ × virens), *O.R.* 1896, 366.—Sander, 1895.

C. × Petri, *G.C.* 1880, i. 680; Wien. Ill. *G. Zeit.* 1894, 213, t. 2; *O.R.* 1896, 247.

C. × woodlandense, *R. H. Meas. Cyp.* ed. 2, 111; *G.C.* 1895, i. 199; *O.R.* 1896, 262; *Boyle Woodl. O.* 195.—Sander.

We have not seen C. × woodlandense, but from the parentage given it should be a form of the natural hybrid P. × Petri.

457. P. × Petri-insigne (insigne × Petri ♀).—Opoix, 1896.

C. × (unnamed), *J.S.H.Fr.* 1896, 110.—Opoix.

C. × Petri-insigne, *J.S.H.Fr.* 1897, 1006.—Opoix.

458. P. × Philene (× Ashburtonæ ♀ × barbatum).—Opoix, 1896.

C. × Ashburtoniæ-barbatum, *J.S.H.Fr.* 1896, 649.—Opoix.

459. P. × Philo (philippinense × purpuratum ♀).—Lawrence, 1900.

C. × lævigato-purpuratum, *G.C.* 1900, ii. 57; *O.R.* 1900, 251.—Lawrence.

460. P. × Phœbe (bellatulum × philippinense).—Statter, 1895.

C. × Phœbe, *G.C.* 1895, i. 337; *O.R.* 1895, 127; *Dict. Ic. O.* Cyp. hyb. t. 71.

461. P. × Picardianum (Pageanum × Spicerianum).—Mantin, 1894.

C. × Picardianum, *J.S.H.Fr.* 1894, 582; 1895, 240; *Bohnh. Dict. O. Hyb.* 29; *R. H. Meas. Cyp.* ed. 3, 137.

462. P. × Piercei (Druryi × tonsum).—Oakes Ames, 1900.

C. × Franklin Pierce, *Amer. G.* 1900, 362.—Oakes Ames.

463. P. × Pitcheri (barbatum × purpuratum).—Pitcher and Manda, 1894.

C. × barbato-purpuratum, *Hans. O. Hyb.* 136.— Pitcher and Manda.

464. P. × platycolor (concolor ♀ × Stonei).—Lawrence, 1895.

C. × platycolor, *G.C.* 1895, ii. 655; *O.R.* 1896, 29.

465. P. × pleistochlorum (barbatum ♀ × virens), *Stein O.* 480.—Drewett, 1887.

C. × pleistochlorum, *G.C.* 1887, ii. 552; *O.R.* 1893, 196; *V. Man. O.* iv. 95; *Day O. Draw.* li. **t.** 1.

466. P. × plumosum (barbatum × œnanthum).—Statter, 1895.

C. × plumosum, *G.C.* 1895, ii. 655; *O.R.* 1896, 30.

Fig. 71. PAPHIOPEDILUM × PORPHYROCHLAMYS.

467. P. × Pluto (Boxallii ♀ × calophyllum), *Kerch. Liv. d. O.* 482; *J.R.H.S.* xxiv. 114, 116. **f.** 39; *O.R.* 1902, 263.—Low, 1893.

C. × Pluto, *G.C.* 1893, ii. 692; *O.R.* 1894, 29.

C. × Clotho, *G.C.* 1895, ii. 527; *O.R.* 1895, 374; *Dict. Ic. O.* Cyp. hyb. **t.** 32.—Young.

468. P. × Polkii (Chamberlainianum × nitens).—Roebling, 1900.

C. × James K. Polk, *Amer. G.* 1900, 200; *Rep. Miss. Bot. G.* 1900, 201. **t.**—Roebling.

C. × edgbastonense, *G.C.* 1902, i. 219; *O.R.* 1902, 117.— Latham.

P. × elgbastonense, *O.R.* 1903, 95.—Latham.

C. × Violetta, *G.C.* 1903, i. 302: *O.R.* 1903, 179.—Charlesworth.

469. P. × Pollettianum (× calophyllum ♀ × œnanthum) *Stein. O.* 481.—Sander, 1890.

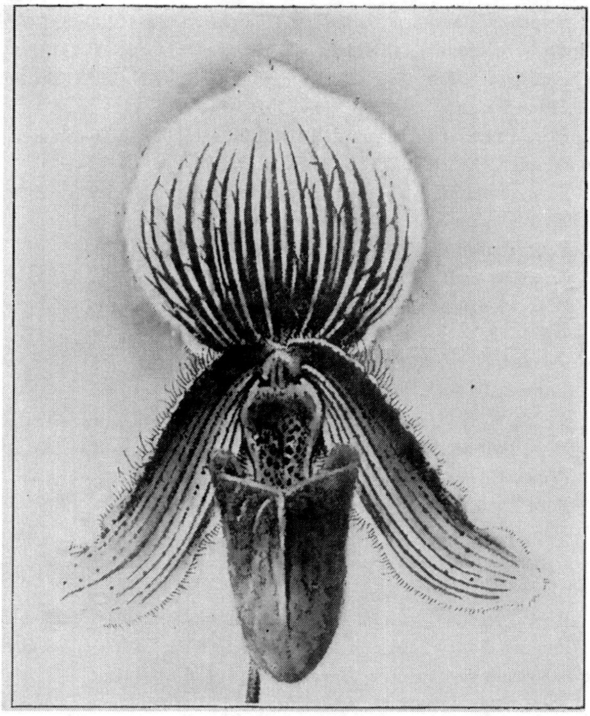

Fig. 72. PAPHIOPEDILUM × PRINCESS.

C. × Pollettianum, *G.C.* 1890, ii. 702; *J.H.* 1891, i. 559, **f.** 101; *Reichenb.* ser. 2, i. 93, **t.** 43, **f.** 1; *O.R.* 1893, 326; *Dict. Ic. O. Cyp.* hyb. **t.** 35.

470. P. × polychromum (× calophyllum ♀ × superbiens).—W. C. Clark, 1896.

C. × polychromum, *G.C.* 1896, ii. 668; *O.R.* 1897, 28.

471. P. × Polyphemus (tonsum × venustum ♀).—Graves, 1894.

C. × tonso-venustum, *Amer. G.* March 23, 1895; *G.C.* 1895, i. 550.—Pitcher and Manda.

C. × Polyphemus, *Hans. O. Hyb.* 171.—Graves.

472. P. × polystigmaticum (Spicerianum × venustum), *Stein. O.* 481.—R. H. Measures, 1888.

C. × polystigmaticum, *G.C.* 1888, ii. 407; *O.R.* 1893, 59, 227.

C. × venusto- Spicerianum, *G.C.* 1889, i. 394 ; *O.R.* 1893, 59, 263.—Drewett.

C. × Yperianum, *Desb. Cyp.* ed. 2, 488.—Moens.

C. × Florentiæ, *Bull. Soc. Tosc. Ort.* 1903, 5.—Recenti.

473. P. × porphyrochlamys (barbatum ♀ × hirsutissimum), *Stein. O.* 481.—Veitch, 1884. **[See Fig. 71.**

C. × porphyrochlamys, *G.C.* 1884, i. 476; *O.R.* 1893, 101, 105, **f.** 7; *V. Man. O.* iv. 96 (porphyrochlamis); *O.A.* ix. **t.** 426; *Day. O. Draw.* xli. **t.** 13.

C. × Fraseri, *V. Man. O.* iv. 84; *Lind.* vi. **t.** 253; *O.R.* 1893, 106, 262; *Desb. Cyp.* ed. 2, 191.—Fraser.

474. P. × Premier (× Cymatodes × Rothschildianum).—Sander, 1899.

C. × Premier, *G.C.* 1899 ii. 58; *O.R.* 1899, 254.

475. P. × prestonense (Argus × marmorophyllum ♀), *O R.* 1902, 101.—Parker, 1902.

476. P. × Priam (insigne ♀ × Niobe).—Veitch, 1900.

C. × Priam, *G.C.* 1900, ii. 384; *O.R.* 1900, 373; *J.H.* 1900, ii. 505, **f.** 129.

477. P. × Priapus (philippinense ♀ × villosum), *Kerch. Liv. d. O.* 482.—Veitch, 1890.

C. × Priapus, *Gard.* 1890, i. 402; *Hans. O. Hyb.* 172.

C. × (unnamed), *G.C.* 1890, i. 526.—Veitch.

C. × Æolus, *R. H. Meas. Cyp.* ed. 2, 6 ; *Desb. Cyp.* ed. 2, 42. –Veitch.

478. P. × Prince (Rothschildianum × Sanderianum).—Gratrix, 1899.

C. × Prince Edward of York, *O.R.* 1899, 249.—Gratrix.

479. P. × Princess (× Coffinetii × Fairrieanum), *O.R.* 1905, 43; 1906, 113, **f.** 13.—Opoix, 1902. **[See Fig. 72.**

C. × Princess, *G.C.* 1902, ii. 272; *O.R.* 1902, 339; 1905, 277.—(Opoix) Charlesworth.

480. P. × Prœtus (Boxallii × Haynaldianum).—Graves, 1895.

C. × Prœtus, *Amer. G.* March 23, 1895; *G.C.* 1895, i. 550; *Hans. O. Hyb.* 307.

C. × augustum var. Prœtus, *Hans. O. Hyb.* 135.—Graves.

481. P. × Pryorianum (× Harrisianum × Lathamianum ♀), *Kerch. Liv. d. O.* 482.—Sander, 1893.

C. × Pryorianum, *G.C.* 1893, ii. 692; *O.R.* 1894, 29; *Dict. Ic. O.* Cyp. hyb. **t.** 45 (v. inversum).

482. P. × Psyche (bellatulum × niveum).—Winn, 1893. **[See Fig. 73.**

C. × Psyche, *G.C.* 1893, i. 751; *O.R.* 1893, 223; 1894, 262; 1898, 232, 363.

C. × Mrs. Herbert Druce, *G.C.* 1897, i. 411; *O.R.* 1898, 232, 363.—Druce.

C. × Lily, *O.R.* 1899, 27.—Keeling.

P. × Mrs. H. Druce, *O.R.* 1903, 359, **f.** 52.—Druce.

This has sometimes been thought to agree with P. Godefroyæ leucochilum, but careful comparison fails to confirm this.

483. P. × punctatissimum (Argus × hirsutissimum).—Rehder, 1899.

C. × Miss Rehder, *G.C.* 1899, ii. 96; *O.R.* 1899, 255.—Rehder.

484. P. × **pycnopterum** (Lowii × venustum ♀).—*Stein O.* 481.—Veitch, 1876.

C. × pycnopterum, *G.C.* 1876, i. 622; *O.R.* 1893, 39; *V. Man. O.* iv. 96, 97.

C. × porphyrospilum, *G.C.* 1879, ii. 489; *O.R.* 1893, 69 --Veitch.

485. P. × **Pygmalion** (ciliolare × villosum) – Graves, 1895.

C. × Pygmalion, *Amer. G.* March 23, 1895; *Hans. O. Hyb.* 172.

C. × cilio-villosum, *G.C.* 1895, i. 401; *O.R.* 1895, 158.—Lewis.

486. P. × **Pynaertii** (× Lathamianum × Lawrenceanum).—Pynaert, 1903.

Fig. 73. PAPHIOPEDILUM × PSYCHE VAR. MRS. H. DRUCE.

C. × (unnamed), *O.R.* 1903, 149.—Pynaert.

487. P. × **Pytho** (callosum × Mastersianum).—R. I. Measures, 1897.

C. × calloso-Mastersianum, *G.C.* 1897, ii. 277; *O.R.* 1897, 347.—R. I. Measures.

488. P. × **Quies** (Curtisii × Hookeræ ♀), *J.R.H.S.* xxiv. 102.—R. I. Measures, 1896.

C. × Quies, *G.C.* 1896, i. 468; *O.R.* 1896, 157.

489. P. × **Quirinus** (Appletonianum × Spicerianum ♀), *O.R.* 1900, 72, 119.—Young, 1900.

C. × Quirinus, *G.C.* 1900, ii. 479.

490. P. × Rachel (Charlesworthii × Curtisii ♀).—Rogerson, 1903.

C. × Rachel, *G.C.* 1903, ii. 147; *O.R.* 1903, 269.

491. P. × radiosum (Lawrenceanum ♀ × Spicerianum), *Stein. O.* 482.—Veitch, 1885.

C. × radiosum, *G.C.* 1885, ii. 424 (radissum); *V. Man. O.* iv. 97; *O.R.* 1893, 102; *Amer. G.* 1901, 669; *Desb. Cyp.* ed. 2, 403; *Day O. Draw.* xlvii. **t.** 3.

C. × variopictum, *G.C.* 1888, ii. 407; *O.R.* 1893, 227.—R. H. Measures.

C. × shorthillense, *Hans. O. Hyb.* 173.—Pitcher & Manda.

C. × G. S. Ball, *G.C.* 1892, ii. 622; *O.R.* 1893, 11.—Sander.

C. × Bradshawianum, *G.C.* 1893, ii. 70; *O.R.* 1893, 255.—Lewis.

C. × Ballianum, *R. H. Meas. Cyp.* ed. 3, 15.—Sander.

C. × Pirbright, *R. H. Meas. Cyp.* ed. 3, 137.—McArthur.

C. × Lawre-Spicer, *G.C.* 1901, i. 98; *O.R.* 1901, 68.—Holmes.

492. P. × Rafaeli (× Crossianum ♀ insigne).—Rafael, 1893.

C. × Crossianum, Castle Hill var., *G.C.* 1893, ii. 648; *O.R.* 1894, 42.—Rafael.

C. × Castle Hill, *Hans. O. Hyb.* 139.—Rafael.

493. P. × Rappartii (Charlesworthii × Lathamianum), *O.R.* 1901, 272.—Duval, 1899.

C. × Ami Paul, *Sem. H.* 1899, 474; *J. S. H. Fr.* 1900, 83.—Duval.

C. × Ami Jean, *Chron. O.* 290.—Duval.

C. × Mrs. Alfred Fowler, *G.C.* 1901, ii. 401; *O.R.* 1901, 366; *G.M.* 1901, 823, **f.**—Fowler.

C. × Lathamiano-Charlesworthii, *J. S. H. Fr.* 1901, 28; *Jard.* 1902, 48.—Cappe.

C. × Charlesworthii-Lathamianum, *J. S. H. Fr.* 1901, 28; 1902, 35.—Cappe.

C. × Rappartianum, *G.C.* 1903, ii. 214; *O.R.* 1903, 308; *G.M.* 1903, 723, **f.**—Crook.

494. P. × Redversii (insigne × Lucie).—Appleton, 1900.

C. × Sir Redvers Buller, *G.C.* 1900, i. 30, 35, 43, **f.** 13; *O.R.* 1900, 58, 94; *J.H.* 1900, i. 45, **f.** 9; *G.M.* 1900, 37, **f.**—Appleton.

495. P. × regale (insigne × purpuratum), *Stein. O.* 482.—Bowring, 1887.

C. × regale, *Bull. Cat.* 1887, 10; *G.C.* 1891, i. 21; *J. S. H. Fr.* 1892, 426; *O.R.* 1896, 324, 353.

C. × Madame Leoni Doin, *Hans. O. Hyb.* 173; *J. S. H. Fr.* 1897, 1006.—Opoix.

496. P. × Reginæ (Farrieanum × Leeanum ♀), *O.R.* 1900, 39.—Veitch, 1896.

C. × Reginæ, *G.C.* 1896, ii. 534; *O.R.* 1896, 351; *G. World*, 1897, 537, **f.**; *Nich. Dict.* 1900 Suppl. 291, 292, **f.** 305.—Veitch.

497. P. × Reginaldiæ (Lowii ♀ × Sanderianum).—Low, 1898.

C. × Mrs. Reginald Young, *G.C.* 1898, ii. 14; *O.R.* 1898, 223; *G.M.* 1898, 458, 459, **f.** 1.—Low.

498. P. × Reginaldianum (insigne × siamense).—Heath, 1893.

C. × (unnamed), *G.C.* 1893, ii. 536.—Heath.

C. × Reginaldianum, *G.C.* 1893, ii. 630.—Moseley.

499. P. × Rehderæ (Argus ♀ × Rothschildianum).—Rehder, 1899.

C. × Mrs. Rehder, *G.C.* 1899, i. 286; 1901, ii. 102; *O.R.* 1899, 189.—Rehder.

C. × Argo-Rothschildianum, *G.C.* 1901, ii. 102 (in syn.); *O.R.* 1901, 252.—Cookson.

500. P. × Rehderianum (purpuratum × Savageanum ♀).—Rehder, 1898.

C. × Rehderianum, *G.C* 1898, i. 47; *O.R.* 1898, 63.

501. P × Remus (Bullenianum × purpuratum ♀).—Grey, 1895.

C. × Remus, *Amer. G.* March 23, 1895; ex *Hans. O. Hyb.* 173.—Grey.

C. × Romulus, *Amer. G.* March 23, 1895, ex *Hans. O. Hyb.* 173.—Grey.

502. P. × resplendens (× Cleopatra × Lawrenceanum).—Charlesworth, 1903.

C. × resplendens, *G.C.* 1903, i. 126; *O.R.* 1903, 87.

503. P. × Reynaldi (Boxallii × villosum ♀).—Heath, 1894.

C. × (unnamed), *G.C.* 1894, i. 211.—Heath.

C. × Reynaldi, *R. H. Meas. Cyp.* ed. 3, 143.

C. × Hero, *G.C.* 1895, i. 201; *R. H. Meas. Cyp.* ed. 3, 73; *Hans. O. Hyb.* 296.

C. × Mme. Petrick, *G.C.* 1896, i. 207.—Maenhout.

C. × (unnamed), *J. S. H. Fr.* 1895, 430.—Cappe.

C. × Boxo-villosum, *G.C.* 1903, i. 267.—Janssens & Putzeys.

C. × Boxvillo, *O.R.* 1903, 149.—Pynaert.

504. P. × Rhodopsis (Charlesworthii ♀ × enfieldiense).—Young, 1902.

C. × Rhodopsis, *Dict. Ic. O.* Cyp. hyb. t. 51.

505. P. × Richmanii (barbatum ♀ × bellatulum), *O.R.* 1899, 161.—Palmer, 1893.

C. × Charles Richman, *G.C.* 1893, i. 580; *O R.* 1893, 188; 1894, 303; 1897, 41; *J.H.* 1893, i. 517, f. 92; *G.M.* 1894, 549, f.; *Dict. Ic. O.* Cyp. hyb. t. 19.—Palmer.

C. × Météore, *G.C.* 1894, ii. 318; *O.R.* 1894, 303; *J.H.* 1894, ii. 535, f. 84; *Desb. Cyp.* ed. 2, 338.—Hye.

C. × Leysenianum, *G.C.* 1894, i. 817; *O.R.* 1894, 253; *Rev. H. Belge,* 1894, 169, t.; *Dict. Ic. O.* Cyp. hyb. t. 1.—Hye.

C. × Marchioness of Salisbury, *J.H.* 1895, ii. 526, 527, f. 79.—Sander.

C. × Countess of Salisbury, *G.C.* 1895, ii. 588; *O.R.* 1895, 376.—Sander.

C. × François Peeters, *O.R.* 1895, 352, 354.—Peeters.

C. × barbato-bellatulum, *Gard.* 1896, i. 201; *G.C.* 1896, i. 337; *O.R.* 1897, 41.—Lawrence.

C. × barbato-bellum, *O.R.* 1896, 122.—Lawrence.

C. × Lilian Greenwood, *G.C.* 1897, i. 35; *O.R.* 1897, 61, 67.—Greenwood.

C. × Carl Peeters, *Nich. Dict.* 1900 Suppl. 286.

C. × Charles Richmond, *R. H. Meas. Cyp.* ed. 2, 26; *Boyle Woodl. O.* 202.—Palmer.

C. × Miss Clara Measures, *Boyle Woodl. O.*—203.

506. **P. × Ridolfianum** (insigne × conspicuum), *Kerch. Liv. d. O.* 483.—Sander, 1893.

C. × Ridolfianum, *R. H. Meas. Cyp.* ed. 2, 90; *G.C.* 1893, ii. 756; *O.R.* 1894, 31; *Bull. Soc. Tosc. Ort.* 1896, 144, t. 4.

C. × Boegnerianum, *J. S. H. Fr.* 1894, 582; 1895, 178, 240.—Mantin.

C. × Préfet Boegner, *Haus. O. Hyb.* 173.—Mantin.

C. × Leo, *Proth. & Mor. Sale Cat.* Sept. 24, 1895; *R. H. Meas. Cyp.* ed. 3, 107 (second entry).

507. **P. × Rimbertianum** (ciliolare ♀ × Hookeræ).—Mantin, 1898.

C × Rimbertianum *J. S. H. Fr.* 1898, 440.

508. **P. × Robertsii** (Charlesworthii × Creon).—Charlesworth, 1899.

C. × Lord Roberts, *G.C.* 1899, ii. 478; *O.R.* 1900, 29; *G.M.* 1900, 20, f.—Charlesworth.

509. **P. × Robinianum** (Lowii × Parishii ♀), *Kerch. Liv. d. O.* 483.—Linden, 1893.

C. × Robinsianum, *G.C.* 1893, ii. 756.—Linden.

C. × Robinianum, *O.R.* 1894, 79.—Linden.

C. × Parishii-Lowianum, *R. H. Meas. Cyp.* ed. 3, 134; *Desb. Cyp.* ed. 2, 384.—Linden.

Named after Robin Measures, a son of Mr. R. H. Measures, hence "Robinsianum" is incorrect, and should be corrected in Part 1.

510. **P. × Rogersii** (Lawrenceanum × Swanianum ♀).—Wrigley, 1902.

P. × (unnamed), *O.R.* 1902, 221.—Wrigley.

511. **P. × Rogersoni** (Charlesworthii × Druryi).—Rogerson, 1902.

C. × E. Rogerson, *O.R.* 1902, 310.—Rogerson.

C. × T. Rogerson, *G.C.* 1902, ii. 239.—Rogerson.

There is a slight doubt about the parentage, and C. × orphanum (barbatum × Druryi) has been suggested as the second parent, but the influence of barbatum is not apparent.

512. **P. × Rolfei** (bellatulum × Rothschildianum), *O.R.* 1901, 287, 305, f. 46; 1903, 287; 1904, 264, 349.—Appleton, 1901. [See Fig. 74.

C. × Rolfei, *G.C.* 1901, ii. 172; 1904, ii. 395, 399, f. 171 (v. superbum); *O.R.* 1901, 284; 1905, 19; *G. World*, 1903, 732, f.

C. × W. E. Dickson, *G.C.* 1902, i. 251, 257; *O.R.* 1902, 146.—Wellesley.

There is a slight doubt about the parentage of the last-mentioned plant, which we have not seen.

513. **P. × Romulus** (insigne × nitens).—Hye, 1894.

C. × Romulus, *G.C.* 1894, ii. 728; *Haus. O. Hyb.* 173; *J. S. H. Fr.* 1898, 43; *Rev. H.* 1898, 71; *Desb. Cyp.* ed. 2, 411; *Dict. Ic. O.* Cyp. hyb. t. 59.—Hye.

C. × Zeno, *G.C.* 1894, ii. 731; *O.R.* 1895, 32.—Veitch.

C. × Hebe, *J. S. H. Fr.* 1898, 288.—Peeters.

C. × Troilus, *G.C.* 1901, ii. 462; *O.R.* 1902, 26.—Fowler.

C. × Sampaianum, *J. S. H. Fr.* 1899, 44.—Cardoso.

C. × nitens Cleverley's variety, *G.C.* 1902, ii. 430.—Fournier.

C. × W. H. Cannon, *Proth. & Mor. Sale Cat.* Jan. 14, 1898; *Sand. O. Guide,* 337.—Sander.

C. × Ville de Paris, *G.C.* 1903, i. 174, ii. 340; *O.R.* 1903, 115, 363; *G.M.* 1903, 839, f.—Wellesley.

514. **P.** × **roseum** (× Leeanum × Lowii ♀).—Corning, 1895.

C. × roseum, *Hans. O. Hyb.* 308.

515. **P.** × **Rosita** (callosum ♀ × Charlesworthii).—Low, 1902.

Fig. 74. Paphiopedilum × Rolfei.

C. × (unnamed), *G.C.* 1902, i. 67; *O.R.* 1902, 54; *Dict. Ic. O.* Cyp. hyb. t., 65.—Low.

C. × (unnamed). *J. S. H. Fr.* 1902, 631; 1903, 37.—Duval.

C. × Rosita, *O.R.* 1903, 54.—Charlesworth.

C. × calloso-Charlesworthii, *Rev. H.* 1903, 47, 101.—Fournier.

C. × Stanley Rogerson, *G.C.* 1903, ii. 411.—Rogerson.

516. **P.** × **Rossiæ** (× Harrisianum × Swanianum ♀).—Ross, 1894.

C. × Janet Ross, *O.R.* 1894, 311.—Ross.

517. **P.** × **Rossianum** (barbatum × tonsum), *O.R.* 1899, 35.—Ross, 1895.

C. × Rossianum, *O.R.* 1895, 359; 1896, 312.—Ross.

518. P. × **Rossii** (insigne × Lowii).—Lewis, 1896.

C. × Rossii, *Hans. O. Hyb.* 308.—Lewis.

C. × Rossianum, *G.C.* 1896, i. 655.—Lewis.

519. P. × **Rothwelliæ** (× almum × niveum).—Rothwell, 1903.

C. × Mrs. James E. Rothwell, *Amer. G.* 1903, 462, f.—Rothwell.

520. P. × **Rothwellianum** (Argus ♀ × Stonei).—Sander, 1896.

C. × Rothwellianum, *G.C.* 1896, ii. 310; *Boyle. Woodl. O.* 190, t.; *O.R.* 1896. 296, 320.

C. × Argo-Stonei, *G.C.* 1896, ii. 554.—Cookson.

C. × Bothwillianum. *Desb. Cyp.* ed. 2, 93 (a mistake for Rothwellianum).

521. P. × **rotundum** (× Lathamianum × purpuratum).—Keeling, 1899.

C. × rotundum, *O.R.* 1899, 154.

522. P. × **Rowena** (bellatulum × Chamberlainianum ♀), *O.R.* 1898, 168.—R. H. Measures, 1898.

C. × Rowena, *Boyle Woodl. O.* 201.

C. × Edithæ, *G.C.* 1902, i. 281; *O.R.* 1902, 182.—Tunstill.

523. P. × **rubescens** (Boxallii × œnanthum ♀), *J. R. H. S.* xxiv. 101, f. 22.—Statter, 1893.

C. × rubescens, *G.C.* 1893, ii. 630; *O.R.* 1893, 375.

C. × Lucienianum, *J. d. O.* iii. 314; *Lind.* viii. t. 362; *G.C.* 1894, i. 199; *O.R.* 1894, 155; *Desb. Cyp.* ed. 2, 318.—Linden.

C. × Madouxianum, *Bohnh. Dict. O. Hyb.* 25; *Desb. Cyp.* ed. 2, 328.—Linden.

C. × Ranjitsinghi, *G.C.* 1897, ii. 58; *O.R.* 1897, 254.—Charlesworth.

There is a doubt about the precise origin of C. × Lucienianum.

524. P. × **Saint-Hilda** (Boxallii ♀ × Curtisii).—Marwood, 1895.

C. × St. Hilda, *O.R.* 1895, 144.

525. P. × **Salomonæ** (× Lathamianum ♀ × Spicerianum).— Bleu, 1891.

C. × Spicero-Lathamianum, *J. S. H. Fr.* 1891, 139.—Bleu.

C. × Mrs. D. Solomon, *G.C.* 1897, i. 51; *O.R.* 1897, 62.—Sander.

C. × Mrs. D. Salomon, *Sand. O. Guide*, 57, 269.—Sander.

C. × Monarch, *Gard.* 1900, i. 164, f.—Law-Schofield.

526. P. × **Sanderi** (× Calypso × nitens).—Sander, 1903.

C. × Louis Sander, *G.C.* 1903, i. 46; ii. 340; *O.R.* 1903, 51, 364.—Sander.

527. P. × **Saron** (niveum × venustum).—R. I. Measures, 1897.

C. × Saron, *G.C.* 1897, ii. 388; *O.R.* 1898, 28.

C. × Lord Roberts, *G.C.* 1899, ii. 478; *O.R.* 1900, 29.—Charlesworth.

528. P. × **Savageæ** (× Canhami × Curtisii).—Kimball, 1899.

C. × Anna Savage, *R. H. Meas. Cyp.* ed. 3, 8.—Kimball.

529. P. × **Savageanum** (× Harrisianum ♀ × Spicerianum), *Kerch. Liv. d. O.* 483.—Seeger and Tropp.

C. × Savageanum, *G.C.* 1888, ii. 407; *O.R.* 1893, 228.

C. × Seegerianum (Spicerianum ♀), *G.C.* 1888, ii. 407 (in note); *G. World*, 1888, 822; *Gard.* 1889, ii. 494; *O.R.* 1893, 228.—Seeger and Tropp.

C. × Pitcherianum, *G.C.* 1889, i. 73, f. 10; *O.A.* x. t. 453 (Williams' var.); *J.H.* 1892, i. 101, f. 15 (id.); *Will. O. Gr. Man.* ed. 7, 290, 291, f. (id.); *O.R.* 1893, 27, 262.—Cookson.

C. × Osbornei, *G.C.* 1890, ii. 702; *G. World*, 1890, 238.—Buchan.

C. × Adonis, *G.C.* 1891, ii. 591; *O.A.* xi. t. 500; *O.R.* 1893, 328; *Will. O. Gr. Man.* ed. 7, 226.—Williams.

C. × Erycina, *R. H. Meas. Cyp.* ed. 1, 21.—R. H. Measures.

C. × Kirckhoffianum, *R. H. Meas. Cyp.* ed. 1, 38.—Seeger.

C. × Spicerio-Harrisi, *J. S. H. Fr.* 1892, 611; *Desb. Cyp.* ed. 2, 432.—Moens.

C. × Madame Cappe, *Jard.* 1889, 265; *Gard.* 1889, ii. 397.—Cappe.

C. × (unnamed), *J. S. H. Fr.* 1889, 587; 1890, 116.—Cappe.

C. × memoria Moensii, *Lind.* viii. t. 361.—Moens.

C. × Moensii, *O.R.* 1893, 98; 1894, 335; *Desb. Cyp.* ed. 2, 344.—Moens.

C. × Fiveanum, *G.C.* 1894, ii. 755.—Moens.

C. × Mauriceanum, *O.R.* 1893, 118; *R. H. Meas. Cyp.* ed. 2, 77.—Block.

C. × ashburtonioides, *R. H. Meas. Cyp.* ed 2, 8.—Thompson.

C. × Albert Truffaut, *G.C.* 1894, ii. 731; *O.R.* 1895, 32.—Sander.

C. × (unnamed), *J. S. H. Fr.* 1893, 652.—Opoix.

C. × Souvenir de Madame Jules Dupré, *J. S. H. Fr.* 1894, 583.—Opoix.

C. × Mdlle. Louise Scellier de Gisors, *J. S. H. Fr.* 1894, 694.—Opoix.

C. × Souvenir de Jules Dupré, *J. S. H. Fr.* 1895, 238.—Opoix

C. × Harrisiano-Spicerianum, *J. S. H. Fr.* 1896, 29.—Garden.

C. × palatinum, *Wien. Ill. G. Zeit.* 1896, 105; 1897, 3, 115, t. 1.—Lauche.

C. × Madame Emile Cappe, *J. S. H. Fr.* 1897, 34.—Cappe.

C. × ledeense, *Desb. Cyp.* ed. 2, 298; *R. H. Meas Cyp.* ed. 3, 193.—Moens.

C. × Gaetano, *G.C.* 1901, i. 146; *O.R.* 1901, 90.—Bennett-Pöe.

530. P. × Schlesingerianum (Boxallii × insigne), *Kerch. Liv. d. O.* 483.—Seeger & Tropp, 1891.

C. × Schlesingerianum, *Gard.* 1891, i. 86; *O.R.* 1895, 74; *Desb. Cyp.* ed. 2, 420.—Seeger & Tropp.

C. × sibyrolense, *Journ. d. O.* iii. 383; *Ill. H.* xl. 69, t. 179; *O.R.* 1893, 314.—Cahuzac.

C. × Mons. de Curte, *G.C.* 1893, i. 486; *O.R.* 1895, 71; *Gard.* 1900, i. 164 f.—Vervaet.

C. × Mme. de Curte, *G.C.* 1893, i. 486.—Vervaet.

C. × Mrs. Tautz, *G.C.* 1893, ii. 798; *O.R.* 1894, 44.—Tautz.

C. × W. W. Lunt, *Hans. O. Hyb.* 166.—Pitcher & Manda.

C. × Nilssoni, *J. S. H. Fr.* 1895, 178; 1896, 24.—Lebaudy.

C. × Hoffmannianum, *G.C.* 1897, i 51.—Sander.

C. × René Vervaet, *G.C.* 1896, i. 84.—Vervaet.

C. × Monsieur Henri Berthier, *J. S. H. Fr.* 1898, 267. Dutremblay.

C. × Magnet, *G.C.* 1898, i. 47.—Ingram.

C. × hybridum, *Bohnh. Dict. O. Hyb.* 21; *O.R.* 1896, 13, 14.

C. × Paulii, *Lind* xii. t. 571.—Miteau.

C × Caroline, *G.C.* 1903, i. 46; *Rev. H. Belge*, 1903, 47.—Janssens & Putzeys.

C. × Chantino-Boxallii, *J. S. H. Fr.* 1899, 55.—Bleu.

C. × fulshawense, *G.C.* 1903, ii. 340; *O.R.* 1903, 363.—E. Ashworth.

531. P. × Schofieldianum (bellatulum ♀ × hirsutissimum).—Law-Schofield, 1896.

C. × Schofieldianum, *G.C.* 1896, i. 530; *O.R.* 1896, 159; *J.H*, 1896, ii. 101, f. 19: *G.M.* 1896, 283, f.

Fig. 75. PAPHIOPEDILUM × SCHRŒDERI.

532. P. × Schrœderi (Fairrieanum × œnanthum ♀).—Veitch, 1896. **[See Fig. 75.**

C. × Baron Schröder, *G.C.* 1896, ii. 667; *J.H.* 1896, ii. 533, f. 92; *G.M.* 1896, 890, f.; *O.R.* 1897, 29.—Veitch.

P. × Baron Schröder, *O.R.* 1900, 39; 1901, 81, f. 16; 1905, 42, f. 10; 136, f. 30 (v. Germaine Opoix), 137, f. 31 (v. Gaston Bultel).—Veitch.

C. × Germaine Opoix, *Jard.* 1899, 303; *J. S. H. Fr.* 1899, 831.—Opoix.

C. × Gaston Bultel, *J. S. H. Fr.* 1900, 59; 1901, 372; *Rev. H.* 1904, 160, t.—Opoix.

C. × Schrœderæ, *J.H.* 1902, ii. 526.—Charlesworth.

533. P × Schusterianum (Hookeræ × villosum).—Linden, 1900.

C. × Schusterianum, *G.C.* 1900, i. 110; *O.R.* 1900, 90.

534. P. × Scylla (Boxallii × Dayanum), *O.R.* 1899, 55.—Graves, 1895.

C. × Scylla, *Amer. G.* March 23, 1895; *G.C.* 1895, i. 500.

535. P. × selligerum (barbatum ♀ × philippinense), *Stein O.* 485; *J.R.H.S.* xxiv. 100, f. 15 (with its parents).—Veitch, 1878.

C. × selligerum, *G.C.* 1880, i. 776, 780, f. 133; *Fl. & Pom.* 1878, 85, f.; *O.A.* vi. t. 255; xi. t. 483 (v. majus); *O.R* 1893, 99; *Dict. Ic. O. Cyp. hyb.* t. 37; *V.*

Fig. 76. PAPHIOPEDILUM × SIAMENSE (with its parents).
(P. callosum in the centre and P. Appletonianum on the right).

Man. O. iv. 97, f.; *Lind.* i. t 22 (v. majus); *Reichenb.* ser. 1, ii. 11, t. 54 (id.); *Orchidoph.* 1890, 272, t. (id.); *Day O. Draw.* xxv. t. i; xxxv. t. 63.

C. × Peetersianum (philippinense ♀), *G.C.* 1888, i. 331; *O.R.* 1893, 227.—Peeters.

C. × Monica, *G.C.* 1896, i. 40.—Burton.

536. P. × Sementa (superbiens × virens ♀), *Kerch. Liv. d. O.* 483.—Bleu 1883.

C. × (unnamed), *J. S. H. Fr.* 1883, 443; 1884, 465.—Bleu.

C. × n. 1, *Rev. H.* 1885, 476.—Bleu.

C. × javanico-superbiens, *V. Man. O.* iv. 87; *O.R.* 1893, 102; *Desb. Cyp.* ed. 2, 275; *Day O. Draw.* lii. t. 5.—Bleu.

C. × Sementa, Bergm. ex. *Hans. O. Hyb.* 154.—Bleu.

There is a slight doubt about the parentage of this hybrid. It was first exhibited as a hybrid from C. javanicum, which was afterwards corrected to C. javanicum virens, with the statement that the latter was the seed parent. Hansen cites *Bergm. O. des Semis* as the authority for the name C. × Sementa, but it is not in the copy accessible to us (*J. S. H. Fr.* 1892), except as C. × javanico-superbiens (p. 280).

537. P. × **Shillianum** (× Gowerianum × Rothschildianum), *O.R.* 1902, 287.—Law-Schofield, 1899.

C. × Shillianum, *G.C.* 1899, ii. 37; *O.R.* 1899, 247, 253, 311; *G. World*, 1899, ii. 57, f.

538. P. × **siamense** (Appletonianum ♀ × callosum), *O.R.* 1903, 44, f. 11 (with its two parents).—Young, 1903. **[See Fig. 76.**

Originally described as a species, C. siamense (Rolfe in *G.C.* 1889, i. 192), but afterwards (*O.R.* iii 20) considered to be a natural hybrid, with the parentage above indicated, which was afterwards proved by the late Mr. Reginald Young.

539. P. × **simile** (ciliolare × Curtisii).—Sander, 1897.

C. × (unnamed), *O.R.* 1897, 199.—Sander.

C. × Curtiso-ciliolare, *G.C.* 1903, ii. 429; *O.R.* 1904, 19.—Wrigley.

540. P. × **simonii** (insigne × Leeanum ♀), *Kerch. Liv. d. O.* 483; *O.R.* 1899, 11.—Fournier, 1890.

C. × Simonii, *J. S. H. Fr.* 1890, 138; *Rev. H.* 1890, 190; *Orchidoph.* 1891, 62 ("Simonis"); *J. S. H. Fr.* 1897, 944 ("Simonei").

C. × Leopoldianum, *G.C.* 1895, i. 333; *Desb. Cyp.* ed. 2, 309.—Hye.

C. × Acteus, *G.C.* 1897, ii. 352; *O.R.* 1897, 375; 1901, 368.—Veitch.

C. × Leeano-superbo-Chantini, *J. S. H. Fr.* 1899, 53.—Page.

C. × Marjorie, *G.C.* 1900, i. 30; *O.R.* 1900, 58.—Wigan.

C. × Hilda Davis, *G.C.* 1900, ii. 466; *O.R.* 1901, 23.—C. S. Harris.

C. × Putzeysii, *G.C.* 1903, i. 46; *Rev. H. Belge*, 1903, 47.—Janssens and Putzeys.

541. P. × **Singletonianum** (barbatum × vexillarium ♀), *O.R.* 1900, 39; 1905, 68.—Singleton, 1896.

C. × Singletonianum, *G.C.* 1896, ii. 195; *O.R.* 1896, 286; *Gard.* 1896, ii. 130 ("Singtonianum"). **[See Fig. 77.**

542. P. × **Sirius** (barbatum × Godefroyæ).—Low, 1894.

C. × J. Gurney Fowler (Godefroyæ ♀), *G.C.* 1894, i. 410; *O.R.* 1894, 156, 361, f. 34 ("18.")—Low.

C. × Sirius, *G.C.* 1894, ii, 730; *O.R.* 1895, 32.—Veitch.

C. × Rhenia, *G.C.* 1897, i. 354; *R. H. Meas. Cyp.* ed. 3, 144.—R. I. Measures.

543. P. × **Smithianum** (callosum ♀ × Druryi).—Sander, 1896.

C. × A. R. Smith, *G.C.* 1896, i. 88; *O.R.* 1896, 64; *Desb. Cyp.* ed. 2, 427.—Sander.

544. P. × **Solon** (Rothchildianum × tonsum ♀).—Lawrence, 1900.

C. × Rothschildiano-tonsum, *G.C.* 1900, ii. 57; *O.R.* 1900, 251.—Lawrence.

545. P. × **Sophie** (× Gowerianum × niveum).—Rehder, 1902.

C. × Sophie, *G.C.* 1902, ii. 106; *O.R.* 1902, 274; 1903, 63.

C. × Desdemona, *Gard.* 1903, ii. Oct. 31, Suppl. vii.—Low.

546. P. × **Spicero-niveum** (niveum × Spicerianum).—Sander, 1893.

C. × Spicero-niveum, *R. H. Meas. Cyp.* ed. 2, 100.

C. × Isabellæ, *Amer. G.* March 23, 1895; *Hans. O. Hyb.* 153; *G.C.* 1885, i. 550; *O.R.* 1899, 28.—Williams.

C. × Marriottianum, *O.R.* 1895, 322, 351.—Marriott.

The parentage of the last-mentioned is somewhat doubtful.

547. P. × **southgatense** (bellatulum × Harrisianum), *Kerch. Liv. d. O.* 483.—Lewis, 1892.

C. × southgatense, *G.C.* 1892, i. 698; 1893, ii. 630; *J.H.* 1892, ii. 39, **f.** 6; *O.R.* 1893, 11.

Fig. 77. PAPHIOPEDILUM × SIRIUS VAR. J. GURNEY FOWLER.

C. × Fowlerianum, *G.C.* 1895, i. 337; *O.R.* 1895, 128.—Sander.

C. × Macfarlanei, *O.R.* 1901, 350.—Statter.

548. P. × **stamfordiense** (× Chapmanii × Harrisianum).—Pitt, 1901.

C. × (unnamed) *G C.* 1901, ii. 172; *O.R.* 1901, 284.—Pitt.

549. P. × **standense** (Lawrenceanum × Numa).—Statter, 1902.

C. × (unnamed), *G.C.* 1902, ii. 293; *O.R.* 1902, 342.—Statter.

550. P. × **Statterianum** (Spicerianum ♀ × vexillarium), *Kerch. Liv. d. O.* 483; *O.R.* 1900, 39; 1905, 68; 1906, 89, **f.** 11.—Statter, 1893. **[See Fig. 78.**

C. × Statterianum, *G.C.* 1893, ii. 536; *O.R.* 1893, 373; *J.H.* 1893, ii. 417, **f.** 61.

C. × Janus, *R. H. Meas. Cyp.* ed. 2, 61; *G.C.* 1895, i. 501.—R. H. Measures.

551. P. × **Stevensii** (× Calypso × Lathamianum).—Thompson, 1902.

C. × Stevensii, *G.C.* 1902, i. 50, 67; *O.R.* 1902, 51, 54.

552. **P.** × **Stottianum** (Charlesworthii × œnanthum).—Law-Schofield, 1901.

C. × Stottianum, *G.C.* 1901, ii. 102.

553 **P.** × **Straeteni** (× Canhami × Leeanum).—Sander, 1896.

C. × Henri Van der Straeten, *G.C.* 1896, i. 88; *O.R.* 1896, 64.—Sander.

554. **P.** × **streathamense** (Fairrieanum × Lawrenceanum ♀).—R. H. Measures, 1893.

Fig. 78. PAPHIOPEDILUM × STATTERIANUM.

C. × Fairrieano-Lawrenceanum, *O.R.* 1893, 307; 1894, 29; *G.M.* 1893, 728, f.; *J.H.* 1894, i. 45, f. 7.

C. × Lawrenceo-Fairrieanum, *R. H. Meas. Cyp.* ed. 3, 103; *Rev.H.* 1903, 257.—R. H. Measures.

P. × Fairrieano-Lawrenceanum, *O.R.* 1900, 10; 1905, 17.—R. H. Measures.

555. **P.** × **superciliare** (barbatum ♀ × superbiens), *Stein O* 488.—Veitch, 1876.

C. × superciliare, *G.C.* 1876, i. 795; *O.R.* 1893, 39; *V. Man. O.* iv. 98; *Dict. Ic. O.* Cyp. hyb. **t.** 38; *Desb. Cyp.* ed. 2, 443; *Day O. Draw.* xxxiv. **t.** 77; *Berl. Gart. Zeit.* 1885, 450, 451, **f.** 107.

C. × barbato-Veitchianum, *J. S. H. Fr.* 1887, 709; *Orchidoph.* 1889, 10; *Lind.* v. **t.** 228.—Bleu.

C × Warnero-superbiens, *G.C.* 1892, ii. 301; *Gard. & For.* 1892, 510, 511, **f.** 87.—Graves.

C. × barbato-superbiens, *G.C.* 1891, i. 682.—Sander.

Fig. 79. Paphiopedilum × Tautzianum var. Youngii.

C. × Boucardi, *G.C.* 1896, ii. 534; *O.R.* 1896, 350 (unnamed).—Mantin.

C. × Cappei, *R. H. Meas. Cyp.* ed. 2, 20; ed. 3, 32.—Cappe.

556. P. × Sutherlandiæ (Rothschildianum × Youngianum ♀).—Sander, 1899.

C. × Duchess of Sutherland, *G.C.* 1899, ii. 58; *O.R.* 1899, 254.—Sander.

557. P. × Suttonæ (Chamberlainianum × niveum).—Sutton, 1902.

C. × Mrs. A. W. Sutton, *G.C.* 1902, i. 50; *O.R.* 1902, 51.—Sutton.

C. × Godiva, *G.C.* 1902, i. 218; *O.R.* 1902, 118.—Charlesworth.

558. P × Swanianum (barbatum × Dayanum ♀), *Stein. O.* 488. Leech, 1876.

C. × Swanianum, *G.C.* 1876, ii. 36; *O. R.* 1893, 39; *V. Man. O.* iv. 98; *J. S. H. Fr.* 1900, 391; *Day O. Draw.* xl. t. 11.

C. × delicatulum, *G.C.* 1887, ii. 552; *O.R.* 1893, 196.—Drewett.

C. × Wiganiæ, *R. H. Meas. Cyp.* ed. 3, 203; *Desb. Cyp.* ed. 2, 482.—Wigan.

C. × Crossi-Dayanum, *J. S. H. Fr.* 1896, 110.—Opoix.

559. P. × Swinburnei (Argus × insigne ♀), *Kerch. Liv. d. O* 483; *J.R.H.S.* xxiv. 100, f. 16 (with its parents). – Heath, 1892.

C. × Swinburnei, *G.C.* 1892, i. 88, 136; *O.R.* 1893, 11; *Dict. Ic. O. Cyp.* hyb. t. 48.

C. × Argus-Chantini, *J. S. H. Fr.* 1901, 34; 1903, 37.—Doin.

560. P. × Symondsiæ (purpuratum × venustum).—Ross, 1896.

C. × Symondsiæ, *O.R.* 1896, 16, 34.

C. × meirax, *G.C.* 1880, ii. 524; *O.A.* ii. t. 95; *V. Man. O.* iv. 91; *O.R.* 1893, 70; 1905, 291, 295; *Day O. Draw.* xxxix. t. 65.—Warner.

The second parent of C. meirax is doubtful, but the absence of warts on the petals long ago suggested C. purpuratum to Mr. Day, and if this is correct the name Symondsiæ will have to be superseded.

561. P. × Syrinx (tonsum ♀ × Youngianum).—Young, 1902.

C. × Syrinx, *Dict. Ic. O.* Cyp. hyb. t. 55.

562. P. × Tacita (tonsum × Measuresianum ♀), *Kerch. Liv. d. O.* 483.—Graves, 1893.

C. × Tacita, *Gard. & For.* 1893, 105; *O.R.* 1893, 119.

563. P. × Tantalus (Mastersianum × tonsum ♀).—Young, 1901.

C. × Tantalus, *G.C.* 1901, i. 197.

564. P. × Tautzianum (barbatum × niveum ♀), *Stein O.* 488; *O.R.* 1901, 241, f. 33 (v. Youngii).—Veitch, 1886. [See Fig. 79.

C. × Tautzianum, *G.C.* 1886, ii. 681; 1888, ii. 756 (v. lepidum); 1889, i. 237 (id.); *V. Man. O.* iv. 98; *O.R.* 1893, 132; 1897, 364 (v. lepidum); *Reichenb.* ser. 1, ii. 35, t. 65; *Gard.* 1899, i. 86.

C. × lepidum, *R. H. Meas. Cyp.* ed. 2, 67.—Bull.

565. P. × Tennyson (Dayanum × œnanthum ♀), *Kerch. Liv. d. O.* 483. McArthur, 1893.

C. × Tennyson, *G.C.* 1893, ii. 490; *O.R.* 1893, 364.

566. P. × tessellatum (barbatum × concolor), *Stein. O.* 488; *J. R. H. S.* xxvi. 693. Veitch, 1875.

C. × tessellatum, *G.C.* 1875, ii. 614; *G.C.* 1881, i. 41 (v. porphyreum); *O.R.* 1893, 38; *Lind.* i. t. 18; *J. H.* 1888, i. 382, f. 43; *Dict. Ic. O.* Cyp. hyb. t. 14; *G.M.* 1894, 732, f.; *J. S. H. Fr.* 1902, 35; *Day O. Draw.* xxx. t. 35 (v. porphyreum).

C. × Lavinia, *Boyle Woodl. O.* 209.—R. H. Measures.

567. P × Thalia (insigne × Schrœderi), *O.R.* 1905, 107, f. 24. (v. punctatum). -Veitch, 1902. [See Fig. 80.

C. × Thalia, *G.C.* 1902, ii. 344; *O.R.* 1902, 363.

568. P. × Thayerianum (Boxallii × Lawrenceanum), *Kerch. Liv. d. O.* 484.—Sander, 1893.

C. × Thayerianum, *G.C.* 1893, ii. 192; *O.R.* 1893, 288.

C × Whitelyanum, *G.C.* 1895, ii. 307. Shaw.

C. × Diomede, *Desb. Cyp.* ed. 2, 162. Vuylsteke.

The parentage of the last-named is somewhat doubtful.

569. P. × Thomyris (× Hera (robustum) × superciliare). Dallemagne, 1901.

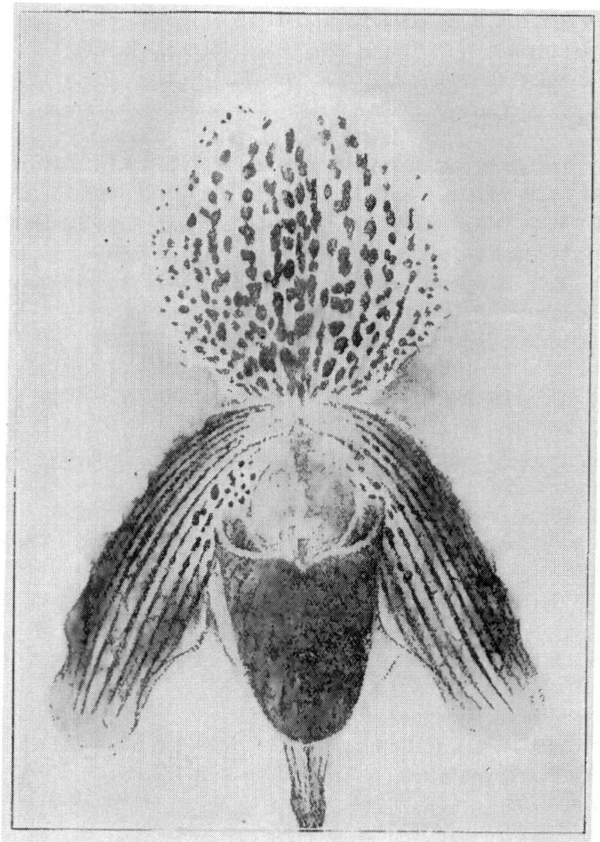

Fig. 80. PAPHIOPEDILUM × THALIA VAR. PUNCTATUM.

C. × Thomyris, *J.S.H.Fr.* 1901, 841.

570. P. × Thorntoni (insigne × superbiens ♀), *Kerch. Liv. d. O.* 484. Thornton, 1887.

C. × (unnamed), *G.C.* 1887, ii. 398.—Thornton.

C. × Thorntoni, *Hans. O. Hyb.* 178; *Amer. G.* 1898, 792 (v. Blonbergi). Thornton.

C. × G. H. Rogers (insigne ♀), *G.C.* 1895, ii. 192; *O.R.* 1895, 288.—Williams.

571. P. × Thyades (Chamberlainianum × superbiens ♀).—R. I. Measures, 1899.

C. × Thyades, *G.C.* 1899, i. 286; *O.R.* 1899, 189; *Gard.* 1899, i. 351.

572. P. × Tia (exul × chloroneuron (Ianthe).—Rehder, 1903.

C. × Tia, *G.C.* 1903, i. 108; *O.R.* 1903, 82.

C. × ex-Ianthe, *G.C.* 1903, ii. 377; *O.R.* 1903, 365.—Rehder.

C. × Zia, *G.C.* 1903, ii. 429; *O.R.* 1904, 19.—Rehder.

573. P. × Transvaal (Chamberlainianum × Rothschildianum).—Appleton, 1901.

C. × Transvaal, *G.C.* 1901, ii. 172; 1902, ii. 361, **f.** 123 (v. superbum); *O.R.* 1901, 284; *J.H.* 1902, ii. 445, **f.** (v. superbum); *G. World*, 1903, 731, **f.**

574. P. × Treleasei (Parishii × Rothschildianum ♀).—Sander, 1898.

C. × William Trelease, *G.C.* 1898, ii. 203; *O.R.* 1898, 317.—Sander.

575. P. × tringiense (barbatum ♀ × Rothschildianum).—Sander, 1897.

C. × (unnamed), *G.C.* 1897, ii. 188.—Sander.

C. × barbato-Rothschildianum, *O.R.* 1897, 319; 1903, 243; *G.C.* 1903, i. 78. —Sander.

576. P. × triumphans (× nitens × œnanthum), *Kerch. Liv. d. O.* 484; *J.R.H.S.* xxiv. 97.—Hye, 1893.

C. × triumphans, *Rev. H. Belge.* 1893, 228; *O.R.* 1893, 316; *Dict. Ic. O.* Cyp. hyb. **t.** 6; *G.C.* 1894, i. 198.

577. P. × Truffautiæ (ciliolare ♀ × Stonei).—Sander, 1895.

C. × Madame Georges Truffaut, *G.C.* 1895, i. 82; *O.R.* 1895, 64, 73.—Sander.

C. × Georges Truffaut, *R. H. Meas. Cyp.* ed. 3, 62; *Boyle Woodl. O.* 194.—Mantin.

578. P. × Tryanowskyanum (insigne ♀ × Io), *Kerch. Liv. d. O.* 484.—Sander, 1894.

C. × Tryanowskyanum, *O.R.* 1894, 43.

C. × gloriosum, *G.C.* 1894, ii. 447; *O.R.* 1894, 350, 365.—Statter.

579. P × Tryonianum (× Harrisianum ♀ × superbiens), *Kerch. Liv. d. O.* 484.—Tate, 1893.

C. × Tryonianum, *G.C.* 1893, ii. 134; *O.R.* 1893, 285.

C. × Veitchi-Dauthieri, *J. S. H. Fr.* 1894, 577.—Opoix.

C. × Madame Silva Freire, *J. S. H. Fr.* 1897, 752; 1898, 286.—Cardoso.

C. × grossum, *Wien. Ill. G. Zeit.* 1902, 109, **t.** 1; *O.R.* 1902, 159.—Hruby.

There is a slight doubt about the origin of the last-named.

581. P. × Ultor (Lawrenceanum ♀ × Sanderianum).—Young, 1903.

C. × Ultor, *G.C.* 1903, ii. 28, 64; *O.R.* 1903, 242; *Gard.* 1903, ii. 155, **f.**

582. P. × Una (Godefroyæ (v. leucochilum) × villosum ♀), *O.R.* 1903, 59.—Appleton, 1903.

583. P. × Unixia (× Harrisianum ♀ × Lawrebel).—R. I. Measures, 1900.

C. × Unixia, *G.C.* 1900, ii. 214 ; *O.R.* 1900, 314.

584. P. × Urania (Charlesworthii × Io ♀).—Cappe, 1900.

C. × (unnamed), *J.S.H.Fr.* 1900, 537.—Cappe.

C. × Urania, *G.C.* 1901, i. 374 ; *O R.* 1901, 218.—Cappe.

Fig. 81. PAPHIOPEDILUM × VENETIA.

C. × Martin-Cahuzac, *J.S.H.Fr.* 1901, 410 ; 1902, 500 ; *Rev. H.* 1901, 419. —Cappe.

585. P. × Uriel (javanicum × Leeanum).—Oakes Ames, 1900.

C. × Uriel, *Amer. G.* 1900, 151 ; *Chron. O.* i. 342.

586. P. × **Vacuna** (Rothschildianum × villosum ♀). Veitch, 1898.

C. × Rothschildiano-villosum, *G.C.* 1898, ii. 168 ; *O.R.* 1898, 287.—Veitch.

587. P. × **Vanneræ** (Curtisii ♀ × selligerum), *O.R.* 1902, 316, 317.—Vanner, 1895.

C. × Vanneræ, *G.C.* 1895, i. 402 ; *O.R.* 1895, 144, 157.

588. P. × **Vanneri** (× Calypso ♀ × Chamberlainianum), *O.R.* 1901, 190.—Vanner, 1901.

C. × Chamber-Calypso, *G.M.* 1903, 141.—Sander.

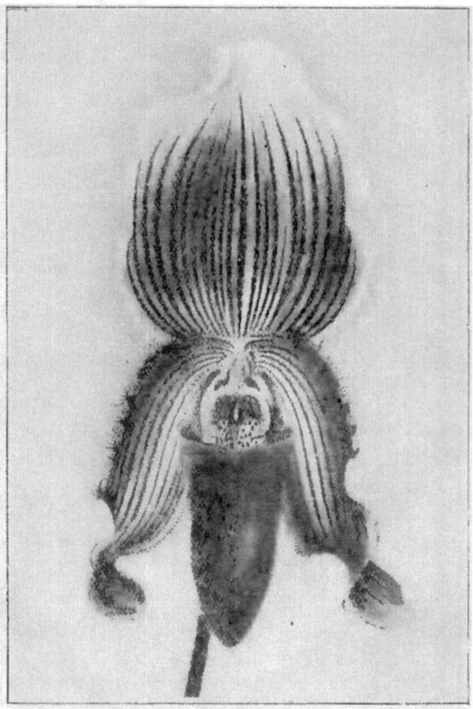

Fig. 82. PAPHIOPEDILUM VEXILLARIUM VAR REX.

589. P. × **Vanninii** (× Io × Lawrenceanum).—Ross, 1897.

C. × Vanninii, *O.R.* 1897, 132, 196.

590. P. × **Venetia** (Lawrenceanum × Morganiæ), *O.R.* 1902, 241, **f.** 25.—Ross, 1902. **[See Fig. 81.**

591. P. venubel (bellatulum × venustum).—Bennett, 1895.

C. × bellatulo-venustum, *G.C.* 1895, i. 402 ; *O.R.* 1895, 157.—Bennett.

C. × venubel, *J.H.* 1899, i. 315, **f.** 73.—Bennett.

592. P. × **Venus** (insigne × niveum).—Hollington, 1890.

C. × Muriel Hollington, *G.C.* 1890, ii. 570; *O.R.* 1893, 327; 1897, 37 (in note).—Hollington.

C. × Venus, *R. H. Meas. Cyp.* ed. 2, 107 (second entry); ed. 3, 169 (first entry); *O.R.* 1902, 62; *G.C.* 1895, i. 200; 1902, i. 86, [91, f 31 (Oakwood var.); *J.H.* 1902, i. 123, f. (id.); *G. World*, 1903, 315, 316, f.—R. H. Measures.

P. × niveo-insigne, *O.R.* 1897, 37.—Sander.

C. × Mrs. E. V. Low, *G.C.* 1897, ii. 10; *O.R.* 1897, 223, 253.—Low.

The parentage of C. × Muriel Hollington has been doubted, but we are convinced that it belongs here.

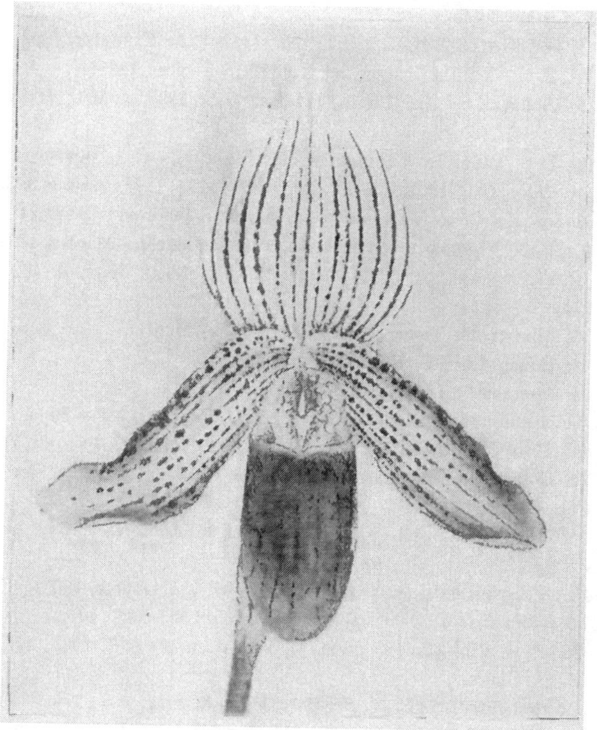

Fig. 83. PAPHIOPEDILUM × VEXILL-IO.

593. P. × **vernixioides** (Boxallii × javanicum).—Graves, 1895.

C. × vernixioides, *Amer. G.* March 23 1895; *G.C.* 1895, i. 550; *Hans. O. Hyb.* 180.

594. P. × **vernixium** (Argus ♀ × villosum), *Stein. O.* 489.—Veitch, 1878.

C. × vernixium, *G.C.* 1879, i. 398; *O.R.* 1893, 69; *Veitch Man. O.* iv. 99; *Desb. Cyp.* ed. 2, 464; *Day. O. Draw.* xxxii. t. 97.

C. × Smeeanum, *G.C.* 1894, ii. 670; *O.R.* 1895, 29.—Smee.

C. × auricularum, *R. H. Meas. Cyp.* ed. 2, 6.—De Cock.

595. P. × vexillarium (barbatum ♀ × Fairrieanum), *Stein. O.* 489; *O.R.* 1900, 7, f. 1: 1905, 16, f. 3 (v. Rex).—Veitch, 1870. [**See Fig. 82.**

C. × vexillarium, *G.C.* 1870, 1373; 1880, i. 780, 781, f. 135 (selligerum, by error); 1887, i. 456, f. 87; *Fl. & Pom.* 1880, 13, f.; *O.A.* x. t. 447; *Lind.* vii. t. 309; *V. Man. O.* iv. 100, f.; *O R.* 1893, 35, 297, f. 15; *Desb. Cyp.* ed. 2, 466; *Day O. Draw.* xxviii. t. 9; *G. World*, 1903, 682, f.

C. × Warocqueanum, *Rev. H. Belge*, 1892, 263; *Desb. Cyp.* ed. 2, 479.—Warocque.

596. P. × vexill-Io (× Io × vexillarium ♀), *Kerch. Liv. d. O.* 484; *O.R.* 1905, 69, f. 16.—Cookson, 1893. [**See Fig. 83.**

C. × vexill-Io, *G.C.* 1893, i. 752; *O.R.* 1893, 223; *G. World*, 1903, 682, f.

597. P. × Vibilia (insigne × Sementa).—Graves, 1895.

C. × Vibilia, *Amer. G.* March 23, 1895; *G.C.* 1895, i. 550; *Hans. O. Hyb.* 181.

598. P. × Vidor (× Canhami × Harrisianum).—R. I. Measures, 1900.

C. × Vidor, *G.C.* 1900, ii. 313; *O.R.* 1900, 347; *J. H.* 1900, ii. 393, f. 108.

The record of C. × Leeanum as one parent is believed to be erroneous.

599. P. × Vigerianum (barbatum × superciliare).—Mantin, 1892.

C. × Vigerianum, *J. S. H. Fr.* 1895, 502; *G.C.* 1895, ii. 100; *Rev. H.* 1895, 359.

C. × Ministre A. Viger, *Hans. O. Hyb.* 163.—Mantin.

C. × Boucardii, *G.C.* 1896, ii. 534.—Mantin.

C. × (unnamed), *O.R.* 1896, 350.—Mantin.

C. bellatulum × barbato-Veitchii, *J. S. H. Fr.* 1898, 288.—Bleu.

600. P. × Villeboisii (Charlesworthii ♀ × ciliolare).—Cappe, 1900,

C. × Colonel de Villebois-Mareuil, *J. S. H. Fr.* 1901, 29; *Rev. H.* 1901, 131.—Cappe.

C. × Villebois-Mareuil, *J. S. H. Fr.* 1902, 35; *Dict. Ic. O.* Cyp. hyb. t. 63.—Cappe.

601. P. × villexul (exul × villosum).—R. I. Measures, 1903.

C. × villexul, *G.C.* 1903, i. 174; *O.R.* 1903, 115; 1904, 101.

602. P. × Violettæ (× nitens × venustum ♀), *O.R.* 1903, 176.—Mantin, 1900; E. F. Clark.

C. × (unnamed), *J. S. H. Fr.* 1900, 113.—Mantin.

603. P. × Vipani (niveum × philippinense ♀), *Kerch. Liv. d. O.* 484; *J.R.H.S.* xxvi. 693.—Vipan, 1890. **See Fig. 84.**

C. × Vipani, *G.C.* 1890, i. 792; *J.H.* 1892, i. 420, 421, f. 73; *G.M.* 1892, 306, f.; *O.R.* 1893, 245, 294; 1897, 241, f. 11 (v. Corningii); *Amer. G.* 1899, 428, 429, f. 111 (Corning's var.).

C. × Corningii, *O.R.* 1897, 241 (in note).—Corning.

C. × striatum, *J.R.H.S.* xvi. Proc. 103; *O.R.* 1898, 365.—Ingram.

604. P. × Vitazo (Charlesworthii ♀ × Gowerianum).—Loveless, 1901.

C. × Vitazo, *Amer. G.* 1901, 731.

C. × Belinda, *Charlesw. Cat.* Jan. 1902; *Sand. O. Guide*, 334.—Charlesworth.

605. P. × **Warburtoni** (Curtisii × Morganiæ).—Warburton, 1901.

C. × (unnamed), *O.R.* 1901, 253.—Warburton.

606. P. × **Watsonianum** (concolor × Harrisianum ♀), *Kerch. Liv. d. O.* 484.—Sander, 1893.

C. × Watsonianum, *O.R.* 1893, 244; 1898, 85.

C. × J. H. Berry, *G.C.* 1895, i. 82; *O.R.* 1895, 64.—Sander.

607. P. × **Wendlandianum** (× œnanthum ♀ × venustum), *Kerch. Liv. d. O.* 484.—Sander, 1895.

C. × Wendlandianum, *Hans. O. Hyb.* 181; *O.R.* 1896, 38; *Sand. O. Guide* 1901, 274 (first entry).

A second C. × Wendlandianum is considered to be a form of P. × bellinum.

608. P. × **westoniense** (Appletonianum ♀ × barbatum), *O.R.* 1898, 112.—Appleton, 1898.

Fig. 84. PAPHIOPEDILUM × VIPANI VAR. CORNINGII.

609. P. × **whalleyense** (× nitens × Stonei).—Gratrix, 1899.

C. × Stoneo-Sallieri, *O.R.* 1899, 370.—Gratrix.

610. P. × **whitefieldiense** (× Ashburtonæ ♀ × Numa).—Statter, 1895.

C. × annamense, *G.C.* 1895, i. 468; *O.R.* 1896, 63.—Statter.

The specific name is changed, annamense being misleading for a hybrid of garden origin.

611. P. × **Whitei** (concolor × Leeanum).—Law-Schofield, 1899.

C. × Sir George White, *O.R.* 1899, 371.—Law-Schofield.

612. P. × **Wiganianum** (× Ashburtonæ × Harrisianum), *Kerch. Liv. d. O.* 484.—Wigan, 1893.

C. × Wiganianum, *O.R.* 1894, 143.

The parentage is somewhat doubtful.

613. P. × Wilsonæ (Argus × Sanderianum ♀).—Drewett, 1901.

C. × Miss Fanny Wilson, *G.C.* 1901, ii. 172; 1902, i. 50; *O.R* 1901, 285; 1902, 50.—Drewett.

614. P. × Wincqzianum (× Harrisianum × Haynaldianum).—Opoix, 1896.

C. × (unnamed) *J. S. H. Fr.* 1896, 132.—Opoix.

C. × Wincqzianum, *Sem. H.* 1898. 295; *Lind.* xiii. t. 620; *O.R.* 1898, 256; *Chron. O.* 159.—Linden.

C. × Luxemburgianum, *J. S. H. Fr.* 1899, 153.—Opoix.

C. × Dauthieri-Haynaldianum, *J. S. H. Fr.* 1900, 840.—Dallemagne.

615. P. × Winniæ (purpuratum × Stonei ♀).—Winn, 1892.

C. × Edith Winn, *G.C.* 1892, ii. 138; *O.R.* 1893, 308.—Winn.

616. P. Winnianum (Druryi × villosum ♀), *Stein O.* 491; *J. R. H. S.* xxiv. 99.—Veitch, 1886.

C. × Winnianum, *G.C.* 1886, i. 362; *V. Man. O.* iv. 100; *J. H.* 1893, ii 71, f. 12; *O.R.* 1893, 131; *Dict. Ic. O.* Cyp. hyb. t. 18.

C. × Druryo-villosum, *J. S. H. Fr.* 1891, 198.—(Veitch) Finet.

C. × senonense, *J. S. H. Fr.* 1897, 745.—Gibez.

617. P. × Wittii (Lowii × Spicerianum ♀).—Low, 1889.

C. × De Witt Smith, *G.C.* 1889, ii. 6; *O.R.* 1893, 262.—Low.

C. × Spicero-Lowianum, *G.C.* 1893, ii. 470; *O.R.* 1893, 351; *Desb. Cyp.* ed. 2, 433.—Linden.

C. × Spicero-Lowii, *R. H. Meas. Cyp.* ed. 3, 158.—Linden.

C. × Dallemagnei, *Lind.* ix. t. 411; *O.R.* 1894, 219.—Linden.

C. × Smithii v. pretiosa, *Amer. G.* March 23, 1895; *G.C.* 1895, i. 550.—Corning.

C. × (unnamed), *J. S. H. Fr.* 1897, 42.—Lebaudy.

618. P. × Woden (× Leeanum × superbiens).—R. I. Measures, 1902.

C. × Woden, *G.C.* 1902, i 50; *O.R.* 1902, 50.

619. P. × woodfordiense (Charlesworthii × Cymatodes).—Fowler, 1900.

C. × woodfordiense, *G.C.* 1900, i. 110; *O.R.* 1900, 89.

620. P. × Wottoni (bellatulum × callosum ♀), *O.R.* 1902, 313.—R. I Measures, 1896. **[See Fig. 85.**

C. × Wottoni, *G.C.* 1896, i. 337; *O.R.* 1896, 124; *J.H.* 1899, i. 61, f. 12.

C. × rubens, *G.C.* 1897, i. 115. Statter.

C. × calloso-bellum, *G.C.* 1896, i. 337; *O.R.* 1896, 122. Lawrence.

C. × callo-bellum, *O.R.* 1898, 45. Lawrence.

C. × Paris, *O.R.* 1893, 87, 88, f. 6; 288; *G.C.* 1893, i. 444 (Hall ?) R. H. Measures.

P. × Paris, *Kerch. Liv. d. O.* 482; *O.R.* 1902, 313, f. 34; *J. R. H. S.* xxvi 692.—R. H. Measures.

C. × Paris was originally described as a hybrid between C bellatulum and

C. Stonei, but it shows no trace of the latter. Since then C. callosum has been suggested as the second parent, but the precise origin remains doubtful.

621. **P.** × **Wrightiæ** (Chamberlainianum × Lathamianum).—Sutton, 1902.

C. × Jessie Wright, *G.C.* 1902, i. 50; *O.R.* 1902, 51.—Sutton.

C. × Menas, *G.C.* 1902, i. 346; *O.R.* 1902, 181.—Veitch.

C. × Lath-Chamber, *Hans. O. Hyb.* 298.—McMeeking. This record apparently applies to some unflowered seedlings, and we find no confirmation.

Fig. 85. Paphiopedilum × Wottoni var. Paris.

622. **P.** × **Wrigleyi** (Charlesworthii × villosum).—Wrigley, 1902.

P. × (unnamed), *O.R.* 1902, 124.—Wrigley.

623. **P.** × **wyndhurstense** (Charlesworthii × Euryale).—Loveless, 1901.

C. × wyndhurstense, *Amer. G.* 1901, 731.

624 **P.** × **xanthophyllum** (Hookeræ × Mastersianum), *Kerch. Liv. d. O.* 485.—R. H. Measures, 1893.

C. × xanthophyllum, *R. H. Meas. Cyp.* ed. 2, 111.

The parentage of this hybrid is doubtful.

625. **P.** × **Xuthus** (Appletonianum × chloroneurum ♀), *O.R.* 1902, 56.—Young, 1901.

626. **P.** × **Youngiæ** (bellatulum ♀ × Hookeræ), *O.R.* 1901, 186, 196.—Young, 1901.

C. × Youngiæ, *G.C.* 1901, May 25, suppl. 1; *Dict. Ic. O.* Cyp. hyb. t. 49.

627. **P.** × **Youngianum** (philippinense × superbiens ♀), *Stein. O.* 491; *J.R.H.S.* xxvi. 693.—Sander, 1890.

C. × Youngianum, *G.C.* 1890, ii. 183; 1892, ii. 138; *Reichenb.* ser. 2, i. 65, t. 31; *O.R.* 1893, 295; *Dict. Ic. O.* Cyp. hyb. t. 10; *J. H.* 1891, ii. 405, f. 78; *J. S. H. Fr.* 1895, 241.

C. × Corningianum, *G.C.* 1891, ii. 199.—Veitch.

C. × Clovenford's, *G.C.* 1892, i. 502; *J.R.H.S.* xv. Proc. 158; *Haus. O. Hyb.* 183.—(Thompson) Lawrence.

628. **P.** × **Zalmoxis** (× vexillarium × chloroneurum ♀), *O.R.* 1900, 119.—Young, 1900.

629. **P.** × **Zampa** (hirsutissimum × Leeanum ♀), *Kerch. Liv. d. O.* 485.—Vuylsteke, 1892.

C. × Zampa, *O.R.* 1893, 118; *Rev. H.* 1894, 90; *G.C.* 1894, i. 110; *Dict. Ic. O.* Cyp. hyb. t. 4 A (v. Phidias), t. 4 B (v. Eurydice), t. 4 C (v. Steriope); *J. S. H. Fr.* 1896, 132.

C. × (unnamed), *Rev. H. Belge*, 1893, 70.—Vulysteke.

C. × Weathersianum, *Lind.* ix. t. 397; *O.R.* 1894. 59.—Linden.

C. × Eurydice, *G.C.* 1894, i. 110; *O.R.* 1894, 61; *Rev. H.* 1894, 90; *Desb. Cyp.* ed. 2, 177.—Vulysteke.

C. × Phidias, *Chron. O.* i. 6.—Vuylsteke.

C. × Steriope, *Chron. O.* i. 6.—Vuylsteke.

C. × Proserpine, *J. S. H. Fr.* 1899, 1131; *Chron. O.* i. 294.—Duval.

C. × Hector MacDonald, *Gard.* 1901, i. 53.—R. H. Measures.

630. **P.** × **Zeno** (Boxallii × tonsum ♀), *O.R.* 1899, 48.—Wrigley, 1899.

C. × Zeus, *Boyle Woodl. O.* 196.—R. H. Measures.

631. **P.** × **Zenobia** (× Ashburtonæ × callosum ♀).—Sander, 1902.

C. × Zenobia, *G.C.* 1902, ii. 344; *O.R.* 1902, 364.

632. **P.** × **Zeus** (callosum ♀ × ciliolare).—R. I. Measures, 1894.

C. × Zeus, *G.C.* 1894, ii. 670; *O.R.* 1895, 29.

C. × calloso-ciliolare, *J. S. H. Fr.* 1900, 113.—Gautier.

632. **P.** × **Zollingeri** (Spicerianum × Victoria-Mariæ).—Zollinger-Jenny, 1903.

C. × (unnamed), *G.C.* 1903, ii. 279; *O.R.* 1903, 338.—Zollinger-Jenny.

633. **P.** × **Zurigo** (Chamberlainianum × œnanthum ♀).—Frœbel, 1899.

C. × Zurigo, *O.R.* 1899, 348; *Die. Gart.* 1901, 361; *J. R. H. S.* xxvi, 212.—(Frœbel) Leemann.

C. × Gordoni, *G.C.* 1903, i. 302; *O.R.* 1903, 179.—Linden.

27. PHAIOCALANTHE.

A genus established to contain the hybrids between Phaius and Calanthe.

1. **P.-c. × Arnoldiæ** (Calanthe Regnieri ♀ × Phaius grandifolius, *G.C.* 1894, i. 84; *O.R.* 1894, 63; *J. S. H. Fr.* 1897, 1245.—Sander, 1894.

P.-c. × (unnamed), *J. S. H. Fr.* 1896, 794.—Sallier.

2. **P.-c. × Berryana** (C. Masuca × P. Humblotii ♀), *G.C.* 1895, ii. 655; *O.R.* 1896, 30. Sander, 1896.

Phalanthe × Berryana, *Hans. O. Hyb.* 331.

3. **P.-c. × Brandtiæ** (C. × Veitchii × P. Wallichii ♀), *G.C.* 1897, i. 115; *O.R.* 1897, 95.—Sander, 1897.

Phalanthe × Brandtiæ, *Hans. O. Hyb.* 331.

4. **P.-c. × grandis** (C. × Darblayana × P. grandifolius ♀), *G.C.* 1898, i. 106; *O.R.* 1898, 94—Cookson, 1898.

5. **P.-c. × inspirata** (C. Masuca × P. grandifolius ♀), *G.C.* 1897, ii. 315; *O.R.* 1897, 351.—Veitch, 1897.

Phalanthe × inspirata, *Hans. O. Hyb.* 233.

6. **P.-c. × irrorata** (C. vestita × P. grandifolius ♀), *J. L. Soc.* xxiv. 168; *V. Man. O.* vi. 17; *J.H.* 1885, i. 331, **f.** 56 (v. rosea).—Veitch, 1867.

Phaius × irroratus, *G.C.* 1867, 264, **f.**; 1882, ii. 565, 566, **f.** 100; *Fl. M.* 1869, **t.** 426; *O.R.* 1893, 6; *Day O. Draw.* xii. **t.** 57.

P. × inquilinus, *G.C.* 1867, 544; *O.R.* 1893, 6.—Veitch.

Phalanthe × irrorata, *Hans. O. Hyb.* 233.

Phalanthe × inquilina, *Hans. O. Hyb.* 233.

Phaius × inquilinus is suspected to have been a seedling out of the same batch.

7. **P.-c. × Niobe** (C. × gigas × P. grandifolius ♀), *G.C.* 1899, i. 109; *O.R.* 1899, 95.—Veitch, 1899.

8. **P.-c. × Ruby** (C. × Ruby × P. Wallichii ♀). *G.C.* 1902, i. 151; *O.R.* 1902, 91.—Cookson, 1902.

9. **P.-c. × Schrœderiana** (C. × gigas × P. Wallichii ♀), *G.C.* 1901, i. 146; *J.H.* 1901, i. 181, 189, **f.**; *G.M.* 1901, 387, **f.**—Veitch, 1901.

10. **P.-c. × Sedeniana** (C. × Veitchii × P. grandifolius ♀), *G.C.* 1888, i. 136; *V. Man. O.* vi. 17, **f.**; *Wien Ill. G. Z.* 1891, 257, 258, **f.** 60; *O.R.* 1893, 85; *J.H.* 1894, ii. 512, 513, **f.** 80; *J.R.H.S.* xvii. 254, 255, **f.** 33.—Veitch, 1887.

Phaius × Sedenianus, *G.C.* 1887, i. 174; *O.R.* 1893, 195.

P.-c. × Sedeni, *G.C.* 1896, i. 88; *O.R.* 1896, 64; *J. H.* 1896, i. 99, **f.** 15 (v. albiflora).—Veitch.

Phalanthe × Sedeniana, *Hans. O. Hyb.* 234, 331.

28. PHAIOCYMBIDIUM.

A genus established to contain a hybrid recorded as derived from Phaius and Cymbidium, which requires confirmation.

1. **Phaiocymbidium × chardwarense** (Cymbidium giganteum × Phaius Wallichii ♀), *G.C.* 1902, i. 219, 322; *O.R.* 1902, 117, 190; 1903, 325; *G.M.* 1903, 740; *J.H.* 1903, ii. 507, **f.**—G. F. Moore, 1902.

29 PHAIUS.

1. P × **amabilis** (grandifolius ♀ × simulans), *G.C.* 1893, i 206, 226, 229, f. 32; *J.H.* 1893, i. 453, f. 82: *O.R.* 1893, 87: 1895. 86; *Reichenb.* ser. 2, ii. 99, t. 90, f. 1. Veitch, 1893.

2. P. × **Ashworthianus** (maculatus × Wallichii ♀), *G.C.* 1896, ii. 534; *O.R.* 1896, 351; *G.M.* 1897. 551, f.; *Neub. G. M.* 1897, 385; *Sand. Cat. New O.* 1897, 14, 15, f. Sander, 1896.

Fig. 86. PHAIUS × CLIVE.

3. P. × **Brownii** (P. × amabilis × P. grandifolius).—Sander, 1899.
P. × D. S. Brown, *G.C.* 1899, i. 108; *O.R.* 1899, 95. -Sander.

4. P × **Chapmanii** (Humblotii × Phœbe), *G.C.* 1903, i. May 30, Suppl. I.; 411, 412, f. 159, n. 2 (type), n. 5 (v. superbus); *G.M.* 1903, 593, f. (v. superbus); *J.H.* 1903, ii. 47, f (id.); *O.R.* 1903, 182. Cookson, 1903.

5. P. × **Clive** (× Cooksoni (Norman) × simulans), *G.C.* 1903, i. 142; *O.R.* 1903, 84, 137, 138, f 33; 174. Cookson, 1903. **[See Fig. 86**

6. P. × **Cooksonæ** (grandifolius ♀ × Humblotii), *G.C.* 1895, i. 748; 1903, i. 411, 412, f. 159, n. 6; *O.R.* 1895, 199, 220; *J.H.* 1895, i. 512, 513, f. 92; 1900, i, 323, 325, f. 90; 1903, i 353, f.; *G.M.* 1895, 353, f. Cookson, 1895.

7. P. × **Cooksoni** (simulans × Wallichii ♀), *G.C.* 1890, i. 336, 388, 389, f.

57; *V. Man. O.* vi. 16; *O.R.* 1893, 292; 1895, 36; 1903, 136, 138, **f.** 31; *J. R. H. S.* xii. Proc. 62, 63, **f.** 40; *O. A.* x. **t.** 478; *Reichenb.* ser. 2, i. 31, **t.** 14; *Neub. G.M.* 1895, 587, 596, **f.** Cookson, 1890.

P. × Norman, *G.C.* 1897, i. 245; 1898, i. 159; 1899, i. 108, 115, **f.** 45 (unnamed);

Fig. 87. PHAIUS × HYBRIDUS VAR. GRAVESII.

O.R. 1898, 126; 1903, 136, 138, **ff.** 27, 28A; *G.M.* 1898, 185, 186, **f.**; *Gard.* 1898, i. 278, 369 **f.**—Charlesworth.

P. × Normani, *G.C.* 1900, i. 174; *O.R.* 1900, 124; *Lind.* xiii. **t.** 618.—Charlesworth.

8. P. × Crawshawianus (Humblotii × Blumei ♀). *O.R.* 1903, 215.—Charlesworth, 1903.

P. × Phoebe, *G.C.* 1903, i. 367 (not elsewhere).—Charlesworth.

9. P. × **Harold** (× Cooksoni (Norman) × Wallichii ♀), *G.C.* 1903, i 206; *O.R.* 1903, 121; 136, 138, f. 29; 174.—Cookson, 1903.

10. P. × **hybridus** (grandifolius ♀ × Wallichii), *G.C.* 1892, i. 619; *O.R.* 1893, 241, f. 13 (v. Gravesii); 356.—Drewett, 1892. [**See Fig. 87**.

P. × Gravesii, *G.C.* 1893, i. 357; *O.R.* 1893, 167.—Graves.

11. P. × **Joiceyanus** (× amabilis × Blumei), *G.C.* 1899, i. 174; *O.R.* 1899, 127.—Sander, 1899.

12. P. × **Marthæ** (Blumei ♀ × simulans), *G.C.* 1894, i. 343; *O.R.* 1894, 127; 1895, 86; *J.H.* 1894, i. 219, f. 36; *Reichenb.* ser. 2, ii. 99, t. 90, f. 2; *Neub. G. M.* 1895, 593, 596, f.: *Lind.* xii. t. 561; *Rev. H. Belge*, 1903, 73, t.; *Gtfl.* 1904, 449, t. 1580.—Sander, 1894.

13. P. × **oakwoodiensis** (× Cooksoni ♀ × Humblotii), *G.C.* 1900, ii, 58, 92, 93, f. 23; 1903, i. 411, 412, f. 159, n, 3; *O.R.* 1900, 227, 252; *G.M.* 1900, 491, f.—Cookson, 1900.

14. P. × **orphanus** (grandifolius ♀ × Marthæ), *G.C.* 1899, i. 108; *O.R.* 1899, 95.—Sander, 1899.

15. P.× **Owenianus** (bicolor ♀ × Humblotii ♀), *G.C.* 1894, i, 663, 783; 787, f. 102: *O.R.* 1894, 189, 193; 1895, 86; *J.H.* 1894, i. 445, f. 72.—Sander, 1894.

16. P. × **Phœbe** (Humblotii × Wallichii ♀), *G.C.* 1899, i. 325; 1903, i. 411, 412, f. 159, n. 1; *O.R.* 1899, 166, 190; *J.H.* 1899, i. 445, 450, f. 97.—Cookson, 1899.

P. × Opoix ii., *J.S.H.Fr.* 1900, 256; 1901, 371; *O.R.* 1903, 146; *Rev. H. Belge*, 1903, 105.—Opoix.

17. **Phaius × Ruby** (× Cooksonæ × Humblotii), *G.C.* 1902, i. 347; 1903, i. 411, 412, f. 159, n. 4; *O.R.* 1902, 180.—Cookson, 1902.

18. P. × **Veitchii** (grandifolius ♀ × maculatus).—Veitch, 1891.

P. × maculato-grandifolius, *G.C.* 1891, ii. 591; *O.R.* 1893, 324.—Veitch.

19. P. × **Wiganianus** (× Owenianus × Humblotii), *O.R.* 1903, 181; *G.M.* 1903, 357.—Wigan, 1903.

30. PHALÆNOPSIS.

1. P. × **Amesii** (amabilis ♀ × intermedia).—Veitch, 1888.

P. × F. L. Ames, *G.C.* 1888, i. 200, 201, f. 32; *Gard. & For.* 1890, 28, 29, f. 5; *V. Man. O.* vii. 48, f.; *O.R.* 1893, 229; 1894, 106.—Veitch.

2. P. × **Amphitrite** (Sanderiana ♀ × Stuartiana), *G.C.* 1892, i. 618; *O.R.* 1893, 356.—Sander, 1892.

3. P. × **Ariadne** (Aphrodite ♀ × Stuartiana), *O.R.* 1896, 147.—Veitch, 1896.

4. P. × **Artemis** (amabilis ♀ × rosea), *G.C.* 1892, ii. 75; *O.R.* 1893, 356.—Veitch, 1892.

5. P. × **Cassandra** (rosea ♀ × Stuartiana), *G.C.* 1898, i. 106; 1899, i. 174; *O.R.* 1898, 95. Veitch, 1898.

6. P. × **Harriettæ** (amabilis ♀ × violacea), *G.C.* 1887, ii. 8, 9, f. 1; *Orchidoph.* 1887, 247, 249, f.; 1888, 208, f.; *O.R.* 1893, 195; *J.H.* 1901, ii. 236,

237, **f.**: *Gard.* 1890, ii. 158, **t.** 766; *V. Man. O.* vii. 44, 45, **f.**; *Day O. Draw.* iii. **t.** 35.—Veitch, 1887.

7. **P. × Hebe** (not of Rchb. **f.**) (rosea × Sanderiana ♀), *G.C.* 1897, i. 115; 1898, i. 106: *O.R.* 1897, 79, 94.—Veitch, 1897.

P. Hebe, Rchb. f. in *Hamb. Gartenz.* 1862, p. 35, is a species, a native of Java.

8. **P. × Hermione** (Lueddemanniana × Stuartiana ♀), *G.C.* 1899, i. 174; *O.R.* 1899, 99, 127.—Veitch, 1899.

9. **P. × Hymen** (Lueddemanniana × Mannii ♀), *G.C.* 1900, i. 62; *O.R.* 1900, 60.—Veitch, 1900.

10. **P. × intermedia** (Aphrodite ♀ × rosea), *G.C.* 1886, i. 427; ii. 169, 212; *V. Man. O.* vii. 44, 45, **f.**; *O.R.* 1893, 52, 132; *J. R. H. S.* xxiv. 189, **f**; *Day O. Draw.* xlviii. **t.** 59.—Veitch, 1886.

P. × Vesta (rosea ♀), *G.C.* 1893, i. 80; 1894, i. 343; *O.R.* 1893, 61; 1894, 128.—Veitch.

Originally described as a natural hybrid, by Lindley, in 1853 (*Paxt. Fl. Gard.* iii. 163, **f.** 110), from a plant introduced by Messrs. James Veitch & Sons, from the Philippines, through their collector, Thomas Lobb. The parentage was subsequently proved by Seden.

11. **P. × langleyensis** (Mannii × Stuartiana).—Veitch, 1898.

P. × Stuartiano-Mannii, *G.C.* 1898, i. 238; *O.R.* 1898, 157.—Veitch.

12. **P. × Leda** (amabilis × Stuartiana), *G.C.* 1888, i. 457; *O.R.* 1893, 229, —Veitch, 1888.

The parentage is somewhat doubtful. Hansen includes it as a synonym of P. × leucorrhoda, but its characters are quite distinct.

13. **P. × leucorrhoda** (Aphrodite × Schilleriana).—A natural hybrid between the species mentioned, described by Reichenbach in 1875 (*Gard. Chron.* 1875, i. 301; *Fl. Mag.* 1875, **t.** 166), from a plant imported from the Philippines by Messrs Hugh Low & Co., in 1874, with its supposed parents. It was inserted in Part I. under an impression that it had also been raised artificially, but the record by Hansen breaks down on investigation.

14. **P. × Lueddeviolacea** (Lueddemanniana × violacea ♀), *G.C.* 1895, ii. 102; 1898, ii. 43, **f.** 11; *O.R.* 1895, 259, 285; *J.H.* 1895, ii. 77, 87, **f.** 11; 1899, ii. 3, **f.** 1; *G. World*, 1899, 746, **f.**—Veitch, 1895.

15. **P. × Rothschildiæ** (intermedia × Sanderiana ♀).—Low, 1900.

P. × Lady Rothschild, *G.C.* 1900, i. 239; *O.R.* 1900, 155.—Low.

16. **P. × Rothschildiana** (amabilis × Schilleriana), *G.C.* 1887, i. 606; *V. Man. O.* vii. 51, **f.**; *O.R.* 1893, 195.—Veitch, 1887.

17. **P. × Schrœderæ** (× intermedia × leucorrhoda ♀), *G.C.* 1898, i. 238, 259, **f.** 99; *O.R.* 1898, 157; *Gard.* 1899, i. 449, **f.** and **t.** 1228.—Low, 1898.

18. **P. × Sedeni** (amabilis ♀ × Lueddemanniana).—Veitch, 1888.

P. × John Seden, *G.C.* 1888, i. 331, 332, **f.** 50; 1898, i. 171, **f.** 68; *V. Man. O.* vii. 50, **f.**; *O.R.* 1893, 228; *Gard.* 1898, i. 297, **f.**; 1899, i. 448, **f.**; *J.H.* 1898, i. 321, **f.** 63.—Veitch, 1888.

19. **P. × Veitchiæ** (Lueddemanniana ♀ × Sanderiana).—Veitch, 1899.

P. × Mrs. J. H. Veitch, *G.C.* 1899, i. 109, 114, f. 43; *O.R.* 1899, 68, 95. *J.H.* 1899, i. 195, f. 47; 1901, i. 226, 227, f.—Veitch.

20. P. × **Veitchiana** (rosea × Schilleriana), *G.C.* 1896, i. 210; *J. R. H. S;* xx. Proc. 100; xxiv. 193.—Heath, 1896.

Originally described as a natural hybrid, from the species indicated, by Reichenbach (*Gard. Chron.* 1872, 935), from a plant which flowered with Messrs. James Veitch & Sons, in 1872, and subsequently figured (*Fl. Mag.* 1876, t. 213). The parentage was proved by Messrs. Heath & Son, in 1896.

21. P. × **Wiganiæ** (Schilleriana × Stuartiana), *G.C.* 1899, i. 77; *O.R.* 1899, 92.—Low, 1899.

P. × Schilleriano-Stuartiana, *G.C.* 1900, i. 62, 83, 84, f. 26; *O.R.* 1900, 61, 113, f. 18; 136; *G.M.* 1900, 63, f. ; *J. H.* 1900, i. 89, f. 21.—Low.

This is probably a natural hybrid, though the original record is not quite clear.

31. PHRAGMOPEDILUM.

1. P. × **Ada** (× cardinale × Schlimii).—R. I. Measures, 1900.

Cypripedium × Cardinal Schlim, *Nich. Dict.* 1900 Suppl. 286.—R. I. Measures.

P. × (unnamed), *O.R.* 1904, 89.—R. I. Measures.

A curious hybrid in which P. Schlimii is represented three times over, thus giving seven-eights of that species and one-eighth P. longifolium.

2. P. × **Ainsworthii** (longifolium ♀ × Sedenii).—Ainsworth, 1879.

Cypripedium × Ainsworthii, *G.C.* 1879, i. 748; *V. Man. O.* iv. 101, 102.

Selenipedium × Ainsworthii, *G.C.* 1879, i. 748 (in note); *O.R.* 1893, 244; 1895, 77, 79.

C. × calurum, *G.C.* 1881, i. 41; *Fl. & Pomol,* 1884, 145, t. 619; *O.A.* iii. t. 136; *O.R.* 1893, 70; *Day O. Draw.* xxx. t. 55.—Veitch.

S. × Ainsworthianum, *Desb. Cyp.* ed. i. 143.

C. × robustius (Sedenii ♀), *G.C.* 1889, i. 394.—Baron N. Rothschild.

C. × Brownii, *G.C.* 1891, ii. 49; *O.R.* 1893, 326.—Pitcher and Manda.

S. × Sedeni v. Pellizzarianum, *Bull. Soc. Tosc. Ort.* 1897, 207.—Linari.

S. × calurum, *Nich. Dict.* iii. 413; *Lind.* vii. t. 304; *O.R.* 1893, 70.

P. × calurum, *O.R.* 1902, 237.

3. P. × **albopurpureum** (× Dominianum × Schlimii ♀).—Veitch, 1877.

C. × albopurpureum, *G.C.* 1877, ii. 38; *J.H.* 1883, i. 472, 473, f. 105; *Orchidoph.* 1883, 508, 509, f. ; *Gard.* 1882, i. 332, 333, f.; *V. Man. O.* iv. 101, 102, f.

S. × albopurpureum, *G.C.* 1877, ii. 38 (in note); *O.R.* 1893, 67; 1895, 77. 80; *Day O. Draw.* xlii. t. 21.

4. P. × **Baconis** (× conchiferum ♀ × Schlimii).—Sander, 1892.

C. × Baconis, *G.C.* 1892, i. 171.

C. × Edithæ, *G.C.* 1892, ii. 458.—Sander.

S. × Baconis, *O.R.* 1893, 358; 1895, 77, 80.—Sander.

S. × Edithæ, *O.R.* 1893, 358.—Sander.

5. **P. × Brysa** (Boissierianum × Sedenii ♀), *O.R.* 1903, 249.—Veitch 1892.

C. × Brysa, *G.C.* 1892, ii. 343.

S. × Brysa, *O.R.* 1893, 358 ; 1895, 77, 80.

C. × John Ashworth, *G.C.* 1894, ii. 605. -E. Ashworth.

S. × John Ashworth, *O.R.* 1894, 374.

6. **P. × cardinale** (Schlimii × Sedenii ♀), *O.R.* 1899, 98; 1903, 248, **f.** 41.—Veitch, 1882. **[See Fig. 88.**

C. × cardinale, *G.C.* 1882, ii. 488 ; 1890, i. 208 ; *Gard.* 1885, i. 520, **t.** 495 *V. Man. O.* iv. 102, 103, f. : *O.A.* viii. **t.** 370.

Fig. 88. PHRAGMOPEDILUM × CARDINALE.

S. × cardinale, *G.C.* 1882, ii. 488 (in note) ; *O.R.* 1893, 81, **f.** 5 ; 1895, 77, 79; *Day O. Draw.* xxxviii. **t.** 91.

C. × Sedenii v. albanense, *V. Man. O.* iv. 105.—Sander.

S. × albanense, *Desb. Cyp.* ed. 1, 143.—Sander.

C. × albanense, *R. I. Meas. Cyp.* ed. 2, 4 ; ed. 3, 3 ; *Sand. O. Guide*, 260.

C. × rubicundum, *R. I. Meas. Cyp.* ed. 2, 21 ; ed. 3, 50.—R. I. Measures.

C. × album, *G.C.* 1895, ii. 192.—Ingram.

S. × album, *O.R.* 1895, 287.

7. **P. × Cleola** (Boissierianum × Schlimii ♀), *O.R.* 1897, 86.—Veitch, 1891.

C. × Cleola, *G.C.* 1890, ii. 570.

S. × Cleola, *O.R.* 1893, 326; 1895, 77, 79; *Dict. Ic. O.* Sel. hyb. t. 2.

8. P. × **conchiferum** (caricinum ♀ × longifolium), *O.R.* 1897, 86.—Bowring, 1881.

C. × conchiferum, *G.C.* 1881, i. 330; *V. Man. O.* iv. 102.

S. × conchiferum, *Nich. Dict.* iii. 414; *O.R.* 1895, 77, 79; *Day O. Draw.* xlvi. t. 69.

C. × chlorops, *G.C.* 1888, i. 584.—Baron N. Rothschild.

S. × chlorops, *G.C.* 1888, i. 584 (in note).

The parentage of the last-mentioned is somewhat doubtful.

9. P. × **Coppinianum** (× conchiferum × Sedenii ♀).—Sander, 1891.

C. × Coppinianum, *G.C.* 1891, i. 502; R. H. Meas. Cyp. ed. 2, 28.

S. × Coppinianum, *O.R.* 1893, 325; 1895, 78, 80.

10. P. × **Cupid** (× cardinale × Lindleyanum).—Veitch, 1903

C. × Cupid, *G.M.* 1903, 45; *O.R.* 1903, 51.

11. P. × **Dominianum** (caricinum ♀ × caudatum), *O.R.* 1897, 86.—Veitch, 1870.

C. × Dominianum, *G.C.* 1870, 1151; *Fl. M.* 1870, t. 499; *Fl. & Pomol.* 1874, 57, f.; *Gard.* 1873, i. 490, 491, f.; 1891, i. 412, t. 803; *V. Man. O.* iv. 103, f.

S. × Dominianum, *G.C.* 1870, 1151 (in note); *O.R.* 1893, 35, 160; 1895, 77, 79.

C. × Dominii, *Orchidoph.* 1882, 452, 453, f.—Veitch.

C. × Clymene, *G.C.* 1893, i. 456.—Veitch.

S. × Clymene, *O.R.* 1893, 160.

The pale-coloured P. caudatum var. Wallisii was the pollen parent of the last-mentioned form.

12. P. × **Elsteadianum** (× conchiferum ♀ × grande).—Ingram, 1892.

C. × Elsteadianum, *G.C.* 1892, ii. 191; *R. H. Meas. Cyp.* ed. 2, 35.

S. × Elsteadianum, *O.R.* 1893, 358; 1895, 78, 80.

13. P. × **Eva** (× cardinale ♀ × longifolium).—R. I. Measures, 1893.

S. × (unnamed), *O.R.* 1893, 319, 320.—R. I. Measures.

S. × longifolio-cardinale, *Hans. O. Hyb.* 239.—R. I. Measures.

A hybrid in the third degree (P. × Schlimii $\frac{5}{8}$, P. longifolium $\frac{3}{8}$), and very near to the original P. × Sedenii.

14. P. × **Faroultii** (caricinum × Sedenii ♀).—Faroult, 1893.

C. × Raymond Faroult, *J. S. H. Fr.* 1893, 508; *Rev. H.* 1893, 435.—Faroult.

S. × Raymond Faroult, *Hans. O. Hyb.* 333; *Desb. Cyp.* ed. 2, 528.—Faroult.

15. P. × **Finetianum** (× cardinale ♀ × caudatum).—Finet, 1895.

S. × Finetianum, *O.R.* 1895, 102.—Finet.

16. P. × **Geralda** (caudatum × Lindleyanum ♀), *O.R.* 1899, 336.—Rockefeller, 1899.

S. × Geralda, *Amer. G.* 1899, 654.

S. × Mauriceanum, *Gard.* 1902, 303; *J. S. H. Fr.* 1902, 722.—Lemoinier.

17. P × **giganteum** (caudatum ♀ × grande).—Veitch, 1894.

C. × macrochilum v. giganteum, *G.C.* 1894, i. 602; *J.H.* 1894, i. 386, 387, f. 62 *G.M.* 1894, 265, f.; 1899, 307, f. (abnormal).—Veitch.

S. × macrochilum v. giganteum, *O.R.* 1894, 186; *G.C.* 1899, i. 360, suppl. **f.** (v. grande).

S. × giganteum, *O.R.* 1895, 77, 80.—Veitch.

18. P. × grande (caudatum × longifolium ♀), *O.R.* 1897, 86 : *J. R. H. S.* xxiv. 99, f. 14 (v. macrochilum).—Veitch, 1881.

C. × grande, *G.C.* 1881, i. 462 : 1882, ii. 488; 1894, i. 692, **f.** (v. atratum); *Warn. Sel. O.* iii. **t.** 33; *Berl. Gart. Zeit.* 1884, 498, **f.** 146; *V. Man. O.* iv. 104, **f.**; *Rev. H. Belge*, 1898, 27, **f.**

S. × grande, *G.C.* 1882, ii. 488; *Desb. Cyb.* ed. i. 147, **f.**; ed. 2, 512; *Lind.* vi. **t.** 242; *Reichenb.* ser. 2, i. 35, **t.** 16; *O.R.* 1895, 77, 79.

C. × macrochilum, *G.C.* 1891, ii. 199, 343, **f.** 146.—Veitch.

S. × macrochilum. *O.R.* 1893, 326; *Amer. G.* 1901, 763, **f.** 160.

P. × macrochilum, *Amer. G.* 1901, 763.

S. × Verdieri, *J. S. H. Fr.* 1896, 373.—Verdier.

C. × caudatum-Roezlii, *Rev. H. Belge*, 1898, 25, **t.**; *O.R.* 1898, 96.—Vervaet.

19. P. × Hanischianum (Boissierianum × cardinale ♀).—Sander, 1893.

C. × Hanischianum, *J. d. O.* v. 61.—Sander.

C. × Venus, *J. d. O.* v. 69.—Sander.

S. × (unnamed), *O.R.* 1893, 286.—Sander.

S. × Brysa v. Venus, *O.R.* 1895, 80.—Sander.

20. P. × Hardyanum (× Ainsworthii (calurum) × caudatum ♀), *J.R.H.S.* xxiv. 97, **f.** 13 (v. Penelaus).—Hardy, 1892.

C. × Penelaus, *O.R.* 1893, 61; *G.C.* 1893, i. 80; *J.H.* 1893, i. 219, **f.** 45.—Veitch.

C. × Hardyanum, *G.C.* 1893, i. 636.—Hardy.

S. × Hardyanum, *O.R.* 1893, 358; 1895, 77, 80.

21. P. × Lemcinierianum (× Ainsworthii (calurum) × Sedenii), *O.R.* 1903, 239.—Lemoinier, 1888.

C. × Lemoinierianum, *G.C.* 1888, i. 712; *Reichenb.* ser. 1, ii. 89, **t.** 89.

C. × Lemoinieri, *J.S.H.Fr.* 1888, 322.—Lemoinier.

C. × calurum v. Rougieri, *Orchidoph.* 1892, 175, **t.**—Chauvière.

C. × compactum, *G.C.* 1893, i. 396; *O.R.* 1893, 157.—Ingram.

22. P. × Mantinii (× conchiferum × longifolium ♀).—Mantin, 1900.

C. × (unnamed), *J.S.H.Fr.* 1900, 113.—Mantin.

23. P. × nitidissimum (caudatum ♀ × conchiferum).—Cookson, 1888.

C. × nididissimum, *G.C.* 1888, ii. 6.—Cookson.

S. × nitidissimum, *G.C.* 1888, ii. 6 (in note); *Reichenb.* ser. 2, i. 57, **t.** 27; *O.R.* 1895, 77, 80; *Dict. Ic. O.* Sel. hyb. **t.** 3.

C. × hybridum, *G.C.* 1891, i. 502.—Sander.

S. × hybridum, *O.R.* 1893, 326.

C. × chrysocomes, *G.C.* 1892, i. 781.—R. H. Measures.

C. × Clonius (conchiferum ♀), *G.C.* 1893, ii. 536; *J.H.* 1893, ii. 394, 395, **f.** 59; *G.M.* 1894, 535, **f.**—Veitch.

S × Clonius, *O.R.* 1893, 374.

In the last-mentioned the pale P. caudatum Wallisii was the pollen parent.

24. P. × Perseus (Lindleyanum × Sedenii ♀).—Veitch, 1892.

C. × Phædra, *G.C.* 1893, i. 80; *O.R.* 1893, 61.—Veitch.

S. × Phædra, *O.R.* 1893, 52.

C. × Perseus, *G.C.* 1892, ii. 622.

S. × Perseus, *O.R.* 1893, 358; 1895. 77, 80.

C. × Thersites, *G.C.* 1893, ii. 756; *O.R.* 1894, 32.—Veitch.

25. P. × pulchellum (× grande ♀ × Sedenii).—Vanner, 1893.

S. × pulchellum, *O.R.* 1893, 166; 1895, 78, 80.

C. × pulchellum, *R. H. Meas. Cyp.* ed. 2, 87.

Fig. 89. PHRAGMOPEDILUM × SCHRŒDERÆ.

26. P. × Rosy-Gem (× cardinale × Sedenii).—Ingram, 1894.

C. × Rosy Gem, *R. I. Meas. Cyp.* ed. 3, 51; *R. H. Meas. Cyp.* ed. 3, 145.

S. × Rosy Gem, *O.R.* 1895, 77, 80.

C. × Pylæus *Bohnh. Dict. O. Hyb.* 30; *R. H Meas. Cyp.* ed. 3, 141; *Hans. O. Hyb.* 333.—Veitch.

C. × Empress, *R. H. Meas. Cyp.* ed. 3, 54.—Bull.

27. P. × Saundersianum (caudatum ♀ × Schlimii), *O.R.* 1897, 86.—Marshall, 1886.

C. × Saundersianum, *G.C.* 1886, ii. 654.—(Marshall) Bull.

S. × Saundersianum, *O.R.* 1893, 16, 131; 1895, 77, 79.

28. P. × Schrœderæ (caudatum ♀ × Sedenii), *O.R.* 1898, 361, **f.** 17.—Veitch, 1883. **[See Fig. 89.**

C. × Schrœderæ, *G.C.* 1883, i. 432; *O.A.* v. **t.** 196; *Lind.* ii. **t.** 69 (v. splendens); *V. Man. O.* iv. 105, **f.**, *J.H.* 1890, i. 405, **f.** 60; *G. World*, 1890, 200, **f.**

S. × Schröderæ, *Nich. Dict.* iii. 414; *O.R.* 1895, 77, 80; 1896, 64; *G.C.* 1896, i. 88; *Day O. Draw.* xxxix. **t.** 23.

S. × Dallei, *J. S. H. Fr.* 1895, 179.—Dallé.

S. × Dalleanum, *Rev. H.* 1895, 164, 180, **t.**—Dallé.

Fig. 90. PHRAGMOPEDILUM × SENDENII VAR. LEUCORRHODUM.

C. × Helenæ, *R. H. Meas. Cyp.* ed. 3, 189.—Ames.

S. × Hylas, *G.C.* 1902, i. 250; *O.R.* 1902, 147.—Veitch.

C. × Mrs. W. A. Roebling, *Hans. O. Hyb.* 240; *R. I. Meas. Cyp.* ed. 3, 42.—Roebling.

C. × Comicea, *G.C.* 1901, i. 146.—Veitch.

C. × splendens, *Sand. O. Guide*, 337.

29. P. × Sedenii (longifolium × Schlimii), *O.R.* 1897, 86.—Veitch, 1873.

C. × Sedenii, *G.C.* 1873, 1431; 1884, ii. 489 (v. candidulum); *Fl. M.* 1876, **t.** 206; 1878, **t.** 302; *Gtfl.* 1875, 149, 150, **f.**; *Jenn. O.* **t.** 4; *Puydt. O.* 265, **t.** 13; *Orchidoph.* 1882, 179, **f.**; *O. A.* xi. **t.** 481 (v. candidulum); *Bull. Soc. Tosc. Ort.* 1882, 81, **f.**; *V. Man. O.* iv. 105, 106, **f.**; *Will. O. Gr. Man.* ed. 6, 299. **f.** **[See Fig. 90.**

S. × Sedenii, *G.C.* 1873, 1431; 1886, ii. 596, 597, **f.** 117, 118 (peloria): *Lind.* vi. **t.** 245 (v. candidulum); *Reichenb.* ser. 2, ii. 7, **t.** 51 (v. Weidlichianum); *Rev. H.* 1879, 470, **t.**; *Dict. Ic. O.* Sel. hyb. **t.** 1 (type), 1 A. (v. candidulum); *O.R.* 1895, 77, 79; *Day O. Draw.* xviii. **t.** 9; xxviii. **t.** 15; xliv. **t.** 23 (v. candidulum).

C. × porphyreum, *G.C.* 1878, i. 366.—Veitch.

S. × porphyreum, *G.C.* 1878, i. 366; *Day O. Draw.* xxx. **t.** 45; lii. **t.** 3 (Mr. Drewett's var).

C. × leucorrhodum, *G.C.* 1885, i. 270; *J.H.* 1886, i. 129, **f.** 21; *V. Man. O.* iv. 104.—Veitch.

S. × leucorrhodum, *Desb. Cyp.* ed. i. 48; *O.R.* 1893, 169, **f.** 11; *Day O. Draw.* xliv. **t.** 25.

P. × leucorrhodum, *O.R.* 1903, 249, **f.** 42.

S. × Weidlichianum, *G.C.* 1890, ii. 702.—Sander.

C. × Weidlichianum, *R. H. Meas. Cyp.* ed. 2, 111.

S. × tenellum, *Hans. O. Hyb.* 241.—Pitcher and Manda.

30. P. × Stella (Schlimii ♀ × vittatum), *O.R.* 1897, 86.—Sander, 1894.

S. × Stella, *O.R.* 1894, 110; 1895, 77, 79.

C. × Stella, *R. H. Meas. Cyp.* ed. 3, 158.

31. P. × stenophyllum (caricinum × Schlimii ♀), *O.R.* 1897, 86.—Bowring, 1876.

S. × stenophyllum, *G.C.* 1876, i. 461; *O.R.* 1895, 77, 79; *Day O. Draw* xlvi. **t.** 67.

C. × stenophyllum, *G.C.* 1876, i. 461; *V. Man. O.* iv. 107.

32. P. × suave (Klotzschianum × Sedenii ♀), *O.R.* 1901, 93.—Veitch, 1901.

S. × suave, *G.C.* 1901, i. 146.—Veitch.

C. × suave, *Sand. O. Guide*, 337.

33. P. × Unique (Lindleyanum ♀ × Schlimii).—Ingram, 1893.

C. × L'Unique, *G.C.* 1893, ii. 342; *O.R.* 1893, 318.

S. × L'Unique, *O.R.* 1895, 77, 78.

P. × unicum, *O.R.* 1897, 86.—Ingram.

The original records are contradictory, one recording the peloriate Uropedium Lindeni as the first parent, which would make the present hybrid a form of P. × Saundersianum. We have not seen it.

34. P. × Uranus (× grande × Lindleyanum ♀).—Sander, 1896.

C. × Uranus, *G.C.* 1896, i. 792.

S. × Uranus, *O.R.* 1896, 224.

35. P. × Urgandæ (Lindleyanum ♀ × longifolium).—Mantin, 1896.

S. × Duvali, *J.S.H.Fr.* 1896, 792.—Mantin.

S. × Urgandæ, *Amer. G.* 1901, 192, **f.** 46; *J.R.H.S.* xxvi. 242.—Ames.

S. × Titanum, *G.C.* 1900, i. 143; *O.R.* 1900, 93.—Sander.

32. SCHOMBOCATTLEYA.

A genus established to contain the following hybrid between Cattleya and Schomburgkia.

1. **Schombocattleya × spiralis** (Cattleya Mossiæ × Schomburgkia tibicinis ♀), *O.R.* 1905, 245, 249, f. 61.—Dallemagne, 1903. [See Fig. 91.

Schomburgkio-Cattleya × spiralis, *J. S. H. Fr.* 1903, 534; *Rev. H.* 1903, 438; *Jard.* 1903, 272.

Schom-Cattleya × spiralis, *G.C.* 1905, ii. 53.

Fig. 91. SCHOMBOCATTLEYA × SPIRALIS.

33. SOBRALIA.

1. **S. Amesiana** (× Wilsoni × xantholeuca ♀), *O.R.* 1895, 203; 1903, 222; *Hans. O. Hyb.* 242.—Sander, 1895.

S. × Amesiæ, *G.C.* 1895, i. 721; 1906, ii. 149, suppl. t.; *O.R.* 1895, 219.—Sander.

2. **S. × luminosa** (Holfordi × Wilsoni), *G.C.* 1903, i. 302; *O.R.* 1903, 179.—Sander.

The parent S. Holfordi (*Sand. Cat. N. Orch* 1899, p. 17, with fig.) is suspected to be a fine form of S. macrantha.

3. **S. × mirabilis** (macrantha × Veitchii), *G.C.* 1903, i. 302; *O.R.* 1903, 179.—Sander.

4. S. × **Sedeni** (macrantha × rosea).—Veitch, 1897.

S. × roseo-macrantha, *G.C.* 1897, ii. 277; *O.R.* 1897, 348.—Veitch.

5. S × **Veitchii** (macrantha ♀ × xantholeuca), *G.C.* 1894, ii. 103; *O.R.* 1894, 226, 239, 285; *J.H.* 1894, ii. 98, 99, f. 15; *Lind.* xvi. t. 740; *Dict. Ic. O.* Sobral. hyb. t. 1.—Veitch, 1894.

S. × Wiganiæ, *G.C.* 1892, ii. 14; *O.R.* 1898, 222, 259, 297; 1902, 213; 1903, 242; *G.M.* 1902, 441, f.

S. Wiganiæ is believed to be a natural hybrid with the same parentage.

34. SOPHROCATLÆLIA.

A genus established for the secondary hybrids derived from the three genera, Cattleya, Lælia and Sophronitis.

1. **Sophrocatlælia** × **Eros** (Lælio-cattleya × elegans ♀ × Sophronitis grandiflora), *O.R.* 1900, 354.—Charlesworth, 1900.

Sophrolælia × Eros, *G.C.* 1900, ii. 314; *O.R.* 1900, 348, 354; *G.M.* 1900, 706, f.

2. **Sophrocatlælia** × **Veitchii** (L.-c. × Schilleriana × Sophronitis grandiflora ♀), *O.R.* 1900, 354.—Veitch, 1892.

Sophrocattleya × Veitchii, *G.C.* 1892, ii. 312; 1896, ii. 310; *O.R.* 1896, 319; *J.H.* 1892, ii. 240, 245, f.

Sophrocattleya × Veitchiana, *O.R.* 1893, 356.

Catlænitis × Veitchiana, *Hans. O. Hybr.* 100.

35. SOPHROCATTLEYA.

A genus established to contain the hybrids between Cattleya and Sophronitis.

1. **S.-c.** × **Batemaniana** (C. intermedia × S. grandiflora ♀), *J. L. Soc.* xxiv. 169; *V. Man. O.* ii. 92, 93, f.; *Rev. H. Belge*, 1888, 208, 209, f. 18, 19; *O.R.* 1893, 44, 131.—Veitch, 1886.

Lælia × Batemaniana, *G.C.* 1886, ii. 263; *J. H.* 1887, ii. 54, 55, f. 6; *G IV.* 1888, 809, f.; *Day O. Draw.* li. t. 33, 45.

Sophroleya × Batemaniana, *Hans. O. Hyb.* 242.

2. **S.-c.** × **Calypso** (C. Loddigesii × S. grandiflora ♀), *G.C.* 1890, ii. 588; 1896, ii. 695, f. 122; *O.R.* 1893, 31; 1897, 3; 1898, 270; *J.H.* 1892, ii. 568, f. 76; 1900, i. 15, f. 3.—Veitch, 1890.

Sophroleya × Calypso, *Hans. O. Hyb.* 242.

3. **S.-c.** × **Chamberlainii** (C. Harrisoniana ♀ × S. grandiflora), *O.R.* 1898, 270; 1900, 27; 1902, 294; *G.C.* 1899, ii. 446, f. 141 (v. triumphans).—Chamberlain, 1898.

Sophronitis × Chamberlainiana, *O.R.* 1903, 271 (by error).

4. **S.-c.** × **Cleopatra** (C. Leopoldi × S. grandiflora ♀), *G.C.* 1898, ii. 293; 1899, ii. 318; *O.R.* 1898, 349; 1899, 347.—Charlesworth, 1898.

S.-c. × Cleopatra inversa (C. Leopoldi ♀), *J. S. H. Fr.* 1903, 37; *Rev. H.* 1903, 75.—Beranek.

5. **S-c. × eximia** (C. Bowringiana ♀ × S. grandiflora), *G.C.* 1894, ii. 378; *J.H.* 1894, ii. 321, f. 48; 1900, ii. 373, f. 103; 1903, i. 3, f; *O.R.* 1894, 333, 349; *G.M.* 1895, 83, f.—Veitch, 1894.

Sophroleya × eximia, *Hans. O. Hyb.* 242.

6. **S.-c. × Hardyana** (C. Aclandiæ × S. grandiflora ♀), *O.R.* 1899, 209, f. 13; 1902, 248.—Hardy, 1898. **[See Fig. 92.**

S.-c. × George Hardy, *G.C.* 1898, i. 302; *O.R.* 1898, 185, 270.—Hardy.

7. **S.-c. × Imperatrix** (C. Mossiæ ♀ × S. grandiflora).—Veitch, 1899.

S.-c. × Queen Empress, *G.C.* 1899, ii. 96; 112, 113, f. 43; *O.R.* 1899, 255, 258; *G.M.* 1899, 484, f.; *J.H.* 1899, ii. 73, 83, f. 18.—Veitch.

Fig. 92. Sophrocattleya × Hardyana.

8. **S.-c. × Nydia** (C. × calummata × S. grandiflora ♀), *G.C.* 1901, ii. 360; *J.H.* 1901, ii. 530, 531, f.; *O.R.* 1901, 366; *Dict. Ic. O.*. S.-c. t. 1; *Jard.* 1903, 184, t.—Charlesworth, 1901.

9. **S.-c. × Saxa** (C. Trianæ × S. grandiflora), *G.C.* 1903, ii. 104; *O.R.* 1903, 267—Veitch, 1903.

36. SOPHROLÆLIA.

A genus established for the hybrids between Lælia and Sophronitis.

1. **S.-l. × Gratrixiæ** (L. tenebrosa × Sophronitis grandiflora), *G.C.* 1901, ii. 210; *O.R.* 1901, 315; 1903, 306.—Charlesworth, 1901.

2 **S.-l. × heatonensis** (L. purpurata × S. grandiflora), *G.C.* 1902, ii. 239;

O.R. 1902, 311, 339 ; *G.M.* 1902, 694, 698, f. ; *J.H.* 1902, ii. 397, f.—Charlesworth, 1902.

3. **S.-l. × læta** (L. Dayana ♀ × S. grandiflora), *O.R.* 1894, 333 ; 1896, 33 ; 1898, 323.—Veitch, 1894.

Sophrocattleya × læta, *G.C.* 1894, ii. 447, 476, 477, f. 63 ; *O.R.* 1894, 351.

4. **S.-l. × Marriottii** (L. flava × S. grandiflora ♀), *G.C.* 1896, ii. 667 ; *O.R.* 1897, 28.—Marriott, 1896.

S.-l. × Marriottiana, *G.C.* 1900, i. 30, 66, f. 20 ; *O.R.* 1900, 58 ; 1903, 271.

Sophrocattleya × Marriottiana, *Gard.* 1902, i. 248.

5. **S.-l. × Orpeti** (Lælia pumila ♀ × Sophronitis grandiflora), *O.R.* 1901, 288 ; 1902, 116 ; 1904, 22.—Orpet, 1901.

S.-l. × læta var. Orpetiana, *G.C.* 1901, i. 306 ; *O.R.* 1901, 182 ; 1904, 22 ; *J.H.* 1905, ii. 99, f.—Orpet.

6. **S.-l. × Psyche** (Lælia cinnabarina ♀ × Sophronitis grandiflora), *O.R.* 1902, 55 ; *Dict. Ic. O.* S.-l. t. 1.—Charlesworth, 1902.

7. **S.-l. × Yalda** (L. harpophylla × Sophronitis grandiflora ♀), *G.C.* 1901, i. 54 ; *O.R.* 1901, 37.—Veitch, 1901.

37. SPATHOGLOTTIS.

1. **S. × kewensis** (plicata ♀ × Vieillardii), *O.R.* 1903, 218.—Kew, 1903.

2. **S. × Veitchii** (aurea ♀ × Vieillardii).—Veitch, 1897.

S. × aureo-Vieillardii, *G.C.* 1897, i. 354 ; 1898, i, 309, f. 115 ; *O.R.* 1897, 192 ; *G.M.* 1898, 308, f. ; *J.H.* 1898, i. 439, 445, f. 82 ; 1900, i. 434, f. 117 ; *Dict. Ic. O.* Spath. hyb. t. 1.—Veitch.

38. STANHOPEA.

1. **S. × bellaerensis** (insignis ♀ × oculata), *J. S. H. Fr.* 1895, 502 ; 1897, 602 ; *Rev. H.* 1896, 231, 232, t.—Mantin, 1894.

2. **S. × Spindleriana** (oculata ♀ × tigrina), *Gtfl.* 1890, 625, t. 1335 (with parents) ; *O.R.* 1893, 323.—Spindler, 1890.

39. THUNIA.

1. **T. × Veitchiana** (Bensonæ × Marshalliana ♀), *G.C.* 1885, i. 818 ; *O.A.* vii. t. 326 ; *V. Man. O.* vi. 20 ; *O.R.* 1893, 291 ; 1905, 204 ; *Day O. Draw.* xlvi. t. 45.—Veitch, 1885.

T. × Wrigleyana, *O.A.* vii. sub t. 326 ; *O.R.* 1893, 291 ; 1905, 204.—Wrigley.

40. VANDA.

1. **Vanda × Joaquimiæ** (Hookeriana × teres).—Joaquim, 1893.

V. × Miss Joaquim, *G.C.* 1893, i. 740 ; 1897, i. 427, f. 165 ; 1898, ii, 123, f. ; *O.R.* 1893, 245 ; 1897, 211 ; 1903, 271.—Joaquim.

2. **V. × Maronæ** (suavis × teres ♀), *O.R.* 1903, 209, f. 38.—Maron, 1903.

V. × Marguerite Maron, *J. S. H. Fr.* 1903, 406 ; *Rev. H.* 1903, 254, 574, t. ; *G.C.* 1903, i. May 30, suppl 2 ; *O.R.* 1903, 183.—Maron.

41. ZYGOBATEMANNIA.

A genus established to contain a hybrid between Batemannia and Zygopetalum.

1. Z. × **Mastersii** (Batemannia Colleyi × Zygopetalum crinitum ♀), *Sem. Hort.* 1899, 76; *G.C.* 1899, i. 77, 99, f. 40; *O.R.* 1899, 46; *Lind.* xiv. t. 657.—Linden, 1899.

42. ZYGOCOLAX.

A genus established to contain the hybrids between Colax and Zygopetalum.

1. Z.-c. × **Amesianus** (Colax jugosus × Zygopetalum Mackayi (brachypetalum) ♀), *G.C.* 1899, ii. 478; *O.R.* 1900, 29.—Sander, 1899.

Z.-c. × Amesiæ, *O.R.* 1900, 13.—Sander.

2. Z.-c. × **leopardinus** (C. jugosus × Z. maxillare ♀), *V. Man. O.* ix. 66; *O.R.* 1900, 12; *G.M.* 1900, 121, f. (Wigan's var.).—Veitch, 1886.

Zygopetalum × leopardinum, *G.C.* 1886, ii. 199; *O.R.* 1893, 132.

3. Z.-c. × **Veitchii** (C. jugosus × Z. crinitum ♀), *G.C.* 1887, i. 765; *J. L. Soc.* xxiv. 156, 170, t. 4, f. 3 (with parents); *V. Man. O.* ix. 66, 67, f. (with parents); *J.H.* 1893, i. 87, 94, f. 13; *O.R.* 1893, 61, 195; 1900, 12; 1904, 93, 343; *J. R. H. S.* xxi. 479, f. 110; *Dict. Ic. O.* Z.-c. t. 1; *G. World*, 1903, 89, f.; *Bot. Mag.* t. 7980.—Veitch, 1887.

4. Z.-c. × **Wiganianus** (C. jugosus × Z. intermedium ♀), *G.C.* 1900, i. 30; 1902, i. 156, f. 47 (v. superbus); *J.H.* 1902, i. 313, f. (id.); *O.R.* 1900, 58; 1902, 92; *G.M.* 1900, 121, f.—Wigan, 1900.

43. ZYGONISIA.

A genus established to contain the hybrid between Aganisia and Zygopetalum.

1. Z. × **Rolfeana** (Aganisia lepida × Zygopetalum maxillare ♀), *G.C.* 1902, i. 443; ii. 30, f. 11; *O.R.* 1902, 214, 220, 374; *Fl. & Sylva*, 1905, 176, t.—Sander, 1902.

44. ZYGOPETALUM.

1. Z. × **Clayi** (crinitum × maxillare ♀), *G.C.* 1877, i. 684; *Fl. M.* 1877, t. 267; *O.A.* ii. t. 50; *Orchidoph.* 1884, 213, 214, f.; 1886, 326, 327, f.; *O.R.* 1893, 67; 1904, 315; *Lind.* xvi. t. 741; *V. Man. O.* ix. 66; *Day O. Draw.* xlix. t. 85.—Clay, 1877.

Z. × crinito-maxillare, *G.C.* 1890, ii. 51; *O.R.* 1893, 293; *G.W.* 1890, 733.—Lord Rothschild.

Z. × crinito-Gautieri, *G.C.* 1902, i. 151; 1903, i. 205; *O.R.* 1902, 92; 1903. 118.—Sander.

2. Z. × **leucochilum** (Burkei × intermedium ♀), *G.C.* 1902, i. 214; *O.R.* 1893, 356; 1896, 62; *G.W.* 1903, 90, 91, f.—Veitch, 1892.

3. **Z. × Perrenoudi** (intermedium ♀ × maxillare), *J. S. H. Fr.* 1894, 137, 138; 1895, 239; *O.R.* 1896, 107; 1897, 157; *G.C.* 1896, i. 337, 367, f. 50; *Dict. Ic. O*, Zygopet. hyb. t. 1.—Perrenoud, 1894.

Owing to confusion between Z. intermedium and Z. Mackayi (see *Orch, Rev.* 1904, p. 325) there is some confusion in the records, and some alterations to the list on p. 41 were overlooked until too late. That should read "Z. intermedium × maxillare = Z. × Perrenoudi," while "Z. Mackayi × maxillare = Z. × Sedeni" should be added. The entries should also be made under the second parent. Z. × Perrenoudi was included as a parent.

4. **Z. × Roeblingianum** (maxillare (Gautieri) × rostratum ♀), *Amer. G.* 1902, 324; *O.R.* 1902, 220; 1903, 308, 311; *G.C.* 1903, ii. 214, 227, f. 93.—Roebling, 1902.

5. **Z. × Sanderi** (Mackayi × Perrenoudi ♀), *G.C.* 1903, i. 78; *G. World*, 1903, 113; *O.R.* 1903, 53.—Sander, 1903.

Z. Mackayi is recorded as one of the parents, but we think it must have been Z. intermedium.

6. **Z. × secundum** (crinitum × intermedium), *J. S. H. Fr.* 1899, 154; *Sem. Hort.* 1899, 76.—Maron, 1899.

The second parent is recorded as Z. Mackayi, which may be correct, though the name often stands for the finer Z. intermedium in gardens.

7. **Z. × Sedeni** (Mackayi × maxillare ♀), *G.C.* 1874, ii. 290; *Fl. M.* 1880. t. 417; *Gtfl.* 1883, 279, 280, f.; *O.R.* 1893, 38; *J.H.* 1893, i. 377, f. 69; *V. Man. O* ix. 66, f.; *Day O. Draw.* xxxiv. t. 89.—Veitch, 1874.

Z. × pentachromum (Mackayi ♀), *G.C.* 1885, i. 532; *O.R.* 1893, 102.—Veitch.

The first hybrid Zygopetalum. The parentage given on p. 41 should be amended as above.

SUPPLEMENT TO PART I.

Containing additions up to the end of 1907 (the numbers and pages indicate the position in the body of the work).

7. BRASSAVOLA (p. 1).

1. B. Digbyana (p. 1).

Cattleya citrina.	Brassocattleya × Alexanderi.
C. Forbesii.	B.-c. × Holfordii.
C. granulosa.	B.-c. × Pluto.
C. Harrisoniana.	B.-c. × Hyeæ.
C. intermedia.	B.-c. × Cordelia.
C. Lawrenceana.	B.-c. × Ena.
C. Leopoldi.	B.-c. × Praetii.
C. Lueddemanniana.	B.-c. × Wellesleyæ.
C. × Patrocinii.	B.-c. × brunoyensis.
C. × Rothschildiana.	B.-c. × Baron.
Lælia anceps.	Brassolælia × Lelieuxii.
L. Boothiana.	B.-l. × Louis-Bel.
L. grandiflora.	B.-l. × Thwaitesii.
L. xanthina.	B.-l. × Jessopi.
Læliocattleya × callistoglossa.	Brassocatlælia × tringiensis.
L.-c. × Doris.	B.-c.-l. × Rowena.
L.-c. × Greenwoodii.	B.-c.-l. × Lido.
L.-c. × Hippolyta.	B.-c.-l. × Hippocrates.
L.-c. × Schilleriana.	B.-c.-l. × balarucensis.

2. B. fragrans (p. 1).

Cattleya Mendelii.	Brassocattleya × Seguinii.

3. B. glauca (p. 2).

Cattleya labiata.	Brassocattleya × Pyrrha.
C. Lawrenceana.	B.-c. × Peetersii.
C. Walkeriana.	B.-c. × Erotion.
Epidendrum Parkinsonianum.	Brassoepidendrum × stamfordiense.
Lælia flava.	Brassolælia × westfieldiensis.

3a. B. nodosa.

Cattleya Lawrenceana.	Brassocattleya × Mary.
Lælia flava.	Brassolælia × fladosa.

8. BRASSOCATTLEYA (p. 2).

1a. B.-c. × Maronæ.

C. Lueddemanniana.	B.-c. × Bayard.

1b. B.-c. × Veitchii.

Lælia purpurata.	Brassocatlælia × Veitchii.

8a. BRASSOLÆLIA.

1. B.-l. × Gratrixiæ

Cattleya Schrœderæ.	Brassocatlælia × Fowleri.

2. B.-l. × Helen.

Lælia × cinnabrosa.	Brassolælia × Gipsy.

9. CALANTHE (p. 2).

8. C. Regnieri (p. 2).

Phaius × Norman.	Phaiocalanthe × Colmanii.

10. C. × Ruby (p. 2).

C. × Veitchii.	C. × Chapmanii.

15. C. × Veitchii (p. 2).

C. × Ruby.	C. × Chapmanii.

10. CATTLEYA (p. 3).

1. C. Aclandiæ (p. 3).

C. citrina.	C. × Shakersii.
C. Gaskelliana.	C. × Madouxiæ.
C. Harrisoniana.	C. × Olenus.

2. C. amethystoglossa (p. 3).

C. Dowiana.	C. × Rosa.
C. Gaskelliana.	C. × Adolphinæ.
C. Lawrenceana.	C. × Lawreglossa.
Lælia flava.	Læliocattleya × Merciana.
Sophronitis grandiflora.	Sophrocattleya × warnhamensis.

4. C. bicolor (p. 3).

C. × Hardyana.	C. × Adula.
C. × Iris.	C. × Farquharsoniana.
Sophrolælia × Orpeti.	Sophrocatlælia × Medea.

5. C. Bowringiana (p. 3).

C. Forbesii.	C. × Meadii.
C. granulosa.	C. × Hopkinsii.
C. Schilleriana.	C. × lucida.
Læliocattleya × Nysa.	Læliocattleya × Tenos.

6. C. × Brymeriana (p. 3).

L. xanthina.	L.-c. × ilsingtonensis.

7. C. citrina (p. 4).

Brassavola Digbyana.	Brassocattleya × Alexanderi.
C. Aclandiæ.	C. × Shakersii.

10. C. dolosa (p. 4).

Lælia cinnabarina.	Læliocattleya × chardwarensis.
L. tenebrosa.	L.-c. × dolotene.
Læliocattleya × elegans.	L.-c. × Lambeaui.

11. C. Dormaniana (p. 4).

C. labiata.	C. × Lambeaui.

12. C. Dowiana (p. 4).

C. amethystoglossa.	C. × Rosa.
C. elongata.	C. × Appletoni.
C. × flavescens.	C. × Loubetii.
C. × Frasquita.	C. × Milano.
C. Loddigesii.	C. × Sapho.
C. × O'Brieniana.	C. × Ethelreda.
C. Rex.	C. × triumphans.
C. superba.	C. × Cleopatra.
C. × Whitei.	C. × Waldemar.
Lælia Cowanii.	Læliocattleya × Ariel.
L. flava.	L.-c. × Andromeda.
L. harpophylla.	L.-c. × harpo-aurea.
L. × Latona.	L.-c. × illustris.
Læliocattleya × Amelia.	L.-c. × Schneideri.
L.-c. × Charlesworthii.	L.-c. × Golden-Oriole.
L.-c. × Cranstonnæ.	L.-c. × Kelpie.
L.-c. × Ernestii.	L.-c. × Golden-Beauty.
L.-c. × Leeana.	L.-c. × Georgina.
Sophronitis grandiflora.	Sophrocattleya × Doris.

13. C. Eldorado (p. 4).

Lælia Perrinii.	Læliocattleya × Soulageana.
Læliocattleya × elegans.	L.-c. × vivicans.

14. C. elongata (p. 4).

C. Dowiana.	C. × Appletoni.

14a. C. × Enid.

Sophrocattleya × Calypso.	Sophrocattleya × Marcus.

14b. C. × flavescens.

C. Dowiana.	C. × Loubetii.
Læliocattleya × Ernesti	L.-c. × Mount-Ophir.
L.-c. × Fournieri.	L.-c. × Kronprinz.

15. C. Forbesii (p. 4).

Brassavola Digbyana.	Brassocattleya × Holfordii.
C. Bowringiana.	C. × Meadii.
Lælia cinnabarina.	Læliocattleya × ronselensis.

15a. Cattleya × Frasquita.

C. Dowiana.	C. × Milano.

16. C. Gaskelliana (p. 4).

C. Aclandiæ.	C. × Madouxiæ.
C. amethystoglossa.	C. × Adolphinæ.
C. granulosa.	C. × Caduceus.
C. × Gratrixiæ.	C. × Nyeæ.
C. intermedia.	C. × Vulcan.
C. Mossiæ.	C. × Hyeæ.
C. velutina.	C. × Casca.
C. Warneri.	C. × Peetersiæ.
Epidendrum Parkinsonianum.	Epicattleya × Lawrencei.
E. vitellinum.	E.-c. × magdeburgensis.
Lælia Cowanii.	Læliocattleya × Lydia.
Læliocattleya × Schilleriana.	L.-c. × Blountiæ.
L.-c. × Wellsiana.	L.-c. × Dicksoniæ.

17. C. granulosa (p. 5).

Brassavola Digbyana.	Brassocattleya × Pluto.
C. Bowringiana.	C. × Hopkinsii.
C. Gaskelliana.	C. × Caduceus.
C. Lueddemanniana.	C. × Minnie.
C. Trianæ.	C. × Alfredi.
Lælia Perrinii.	Lælio-cattleya × Perrilosa.
Læliocattleya × elegans.	L.-c. × Alexanderi.

17a. C. × Gratrixiæ.

C. Gaskelliana.	C. × Nyeæ.

19. C. × Hardyana (p. 5).

C. bicolor.	C. × Adula.
C. Harrisoniana.	C. × Cypheri.
C. Loddigesii.	C. × Armstrongiæ.
C. Lueddemanniana.	C. × Thurgoodiana.
C. Mossiæ.	C. × Knollysiæ.
C. Trianæ.	C. × Cooksoni.
C. velutina.	C. × Davisii.
Lælia crispa.	Læliocattleya × crispo-Hardyana.
L. × Latona.	L.-c. × Jason.
L. Perrinii.	L.-c. × Ægina.
L. purpurata.	L.-c. × Capartii.
Læliocattleya × callistoglossa.	L.-c. × Whiteleggei.
L.-c. × Gottoiana.	L.-c. × Duncanii.
L.-c. × Hippolyta.	L.-c. × Duchess.

21. C. Harrisoniana (p. 5).

Brassavola Digbyana.	Brassocattleya × Hyeæ.

Cattleya Harrisoniana (*contd.*)

C. Aclandiæ.	C. × Olenus.
C. × Hardyana.	C. × Cypheri.
C. labiata.	C. × Bertii.
C. maxima.	C. × Hester.
C. Walkeriana.	C. × Heathii.
Lælia flava.	Læliocattleya × Amarylloso.
Læliocattleya × callistoglossa.	L.-c. × Priam.
L.-c. × exoniensis.	L.-c. × Arethusa.
L.-c. × Nysa.	L.-c. × Thetis.

22. C. intermedia (p. 5).

Brassavola Digbyana.	Brassocattleya × Cordelia.
C. Gaskelliana.	C. × Vulcan.
Epidendrum falcatum.	Epicattleya × Figaro.
Lælia xanthina.	Læliocattleya × stellata.
Læliocattleya × warmhamensis.	L.-c. × Orestes.

22a. C. × intertexta.

Lælia tenebrosa.	Læliocattleya × Gouldiæ.

24a. C. × Iris.

C. bicolor.	C. × Farquharsoniana.
C. labiata.	C. × Aliciæ.
C. Warscewiczii.	C. × bellatula.
Læliocattleya × Phryne.	L.-c. × Lusitania.
L.-c. Truffautiana.	L.-c. × Aureole.

26. C. labiata (p. 6).

Brassavola glauca.	Brassocattleya × Pyrrha.
C. Dormaniana.	C. × Lambeaui.
C. Harrisoniana.	C. × Bertii.
C. × Iris.	C. × Aliciæ.
C. × Rothschildiana.	C. × Law-Schofieldii.
C. Schilleriana.	C. × Neptune.
C. velutina.	C. × Lesueri.
C. Warscewiczii.	C. × amabilis.
Epidendrum eburneum.	Epicattleya × balarucensis.

27. C. Lawrenceana. (p. 6).

Brassavola Digbyana.	Brassocattleya × Ena.
B. glauca.	B.-c. × Peetersii.
B. nodosa.	B.-c. × Mary.
C. amethystoglossa.	C. × Lawreglossa.

Cattleya Lawrenceana—(*continued*).

Læliocattleya × callistoglossa. Læliocattleya × Peetersii.
L.-c. × Schilleriana. L.-c. × gattonensis.
L.-c. × warnhamensis. L.-c. × Lawrie.
Sophronitis grandiflora. Sophrocattleya × Atreus.
Sophrolælia × læta. Sophrocatlælia × Phyllis.

28. **C. Leopoldi** (p. 6).

Brassavola Digbyana. Brassocattleya × Praetii.

29. **C. Loddigesii** (p. 7).

C. Dowiana. C. × Sapho.
C. × Hardyana. C. × Armstrongiæ.
C. Rex. C. × Wavriniæ.
Epidendrum vitellinum. Epicattleya × Wolteri.
Lælia anceps. Læliocattleya × Wolteræ.

30. **C. Lueddemanniana** (p. 7).

Brassavola Digbyana. Brassocattleya × Wellesleyæ.
Brassocattleya × Maroni. B.-c. × Bayard.
C. granulosa. C. × Minnie.
C. × Hardyana. C. × Thurgoodiana.
C. Warscewiczii. C. × Carmen.
Lælia superbiens. Læliocattleya × Denisii.
Læliocattleya × callistoglossa. L.-c. × Lustre.
L.-c. × elegans. L.-c. × Templeana.
L.-c. × Myra L.-c. × Ixion.

31a. **C. × Mantinii.**

Læliocattleya × Ingramii. Læliocattleya × Gilberta.

33. **C. maxima** (p. 7).

C. Harrisoniana. C. × Hester.
C. Schilleriana. C. × Oviedo.
C. Warscewiczii. C. × Adrienne.

34. **C. Mendelii** (p. 7).

Brassavola fragrans Brassocattleya × Seguinii.
C. × Murrayi. C. × oakwoodiensis.
C. Schilleriana. C. × McMastersiæ.
C. Schrœderæ. C. × Unique.
Lælia × cinnabrosa. Læliocattleya × Veronique.
L. flava. L.-c. × Paradise.

Cattleya Mendelii—(*continued*).

Læliocattleya × bella. L.-c. × Zixa.
L.-c. × callistoglossa. L.-c. × Schiffmanii.
L.-c. × elegans. L.-c. × Memnon.
L.-c. × Greenwoodii. L.-c. × Birkbeckii.
L.-c. × Hippolyta. L.-c. × Goodsoni.

34a. **C. × Minerva.**

Læliocattleya × Clive. Læliocattleya × Perseus.

35. **C. Mossiæ** (p. 8).

C, Gaskelliana. C. × Hyeæ.
C. × Hardyana. C. × Knollysiæ.
Læliocattleya × highburiensis. L.-c. × Sirius.
L.-c. × Hyeana. L.-c. × Milo.
L.-c. × Zephyra. L.-c. × Golden-Glory.

35a. **C. × Murrayi.**

C. Mendelii. C. × oakwoodiensis.
Lælia tenebrosa. Læliocattleya × Leeseæ.

36. **C. × O'Brieniana** (p. 8).

C. Dowiana. C. × Ethelreda.

38. **C. × Patrocinii** (p. 8).

Brassavola Digbyana. Brassocattleya × brunoyensis.

39. **C. Percivaliana** (p. 8).

C. Schilleriana. C. × Evadne.
Lælia harpophylla. Læliocattleya × Adelina.
L. Jongheana. L.-c. × Sunset.
L. pumila. L.-c. × Sheila.

40. **C. quadricolor** (p. 8.)

Lælia harpophylla. Læliocattleya × chocophylla.

41. **C. Rex** (p. 8.)

C. Dowiana. C. × triumphans.
C. Loddigesii. C. × Wavriniæ.
C. Trianæ. C. × Fallieri.
Lælia crispa. Læliocattleya × Bievreana.

41a. **C. × Rothschildiana.**

Brassavola Digbyana. Brassocattleya × Baron.
C. labiata. C. × Law-Schofieldii.
Læliocattleya × callistoglossa. L.-c. × Beta.

42. **Cattleya Schilleriana** (p. 8).

C. Bowringiana. C. × lucida.
C. labiata. C. × Neptune.
C. maxima. C. × Oviedo.
C. Mendelii. C. × McMastersiæ.
C. Percivaliana. C. × Evadne.
C. Schrœderæ. C. × Robertii.
Lælia flava. Læliocattleya × Alcyone.
Læliocattleya × elegans. L.-c. × Kitcheneri.

43. **C. Schrœderæ** (p. 9).

Brassolælia × Gratrixiæ. Brassocatlælia × Fowleri.
C. Mendelii. C. × Unique.
C. Schilleriana. C. × Robertii.
C. Skinneri. C. × suavis.
Lælia Jongheana. Læliocattleya × Olivia.
L. × Latona. L.-c. × Ganymede.
L. Perrinii. L.-c. × Goodsonæ.
Læliocattleya × Aphrodite. L.-c. × Bradeæ.
L.-c. × Ernestii. L.-c. × Alpha.
L.-c. × Hippolyta. L.-c. × Lesueri.
Sophronitis grandiflora. Sophrocattleya × Heathii.

44. **C. Skinneri** (p. 9).

C. Schrœderæ. C. × suavis.
C. Warneri. C. × Susannæ.
Epidendrum nocturnum. Epicattleya × Lesueri.

45. **C. superba** (p. 9).

C. Dowiana. C. × Cleopatra.
Lælia crispa. Læliocattleya × Salus.

46. **C. Trianæ** (p. 9).

C. granulosa. C. × Alfredi.
C. × Hardyana. C. × Cooksoni.
C. Rex. C. × Fallieri.
C. velutina. C. × Wildemanii.
Lælia Cowanii. Læliocattleya × Oriens.
L. rupestris. L.-c × Glycera.
L. superbiens. L.-c. × Pujeti.
Læliocattleya × callistoglossa. L.-c. × Barbarossa.
L.-c. × Ingramii. L.-c. × Beauclerkiæ.
L.-c. × warnhamensis. L.-c. × Veisenpachii.

47. **Cattleya velutina** (p. 9).

C. Gaskelliana. C. × Casca.
C. × Hardyana. C. × Davisii.
C. labiata. C. × Lesueri.
C. Trianæ. C. × Wildemanii.
C. Warscewiczii. C. × Wincqxiana.

48. **C. Walkeriana** (p. 10).

Brassavola glauca. Brassocattleya × Erotion.
C. Harrisoniana. C × Heathii.

49. **C. Warneri** (p. 10).

C. Gaskelliana. C. × Peetersiæ.
C. Skinneri. C. × Susannæ.
C. Warscewiczii. C. × Dupreana.
Læliocattleya × Gottoiana. L.-c. × Linnæus.
L.-c. × Hippolyta. L.-c. × Firmin.

50. **C. Warscewiczii** (p. 10).

C. × Iris. C. × bellatula.
C. labiata. C. × amabilis.
C. Lueddemanniana. C. × Carmen.
C. maxima. C. × Adrienne.
C. velutina. C. × Wincqxiana.
C. Warneri. C. × Dupreana.
Epidendrum ciliare. Epicattleya × decipiens.
Lælia × cinnabrosa. Læliocattleya × Tunis.
L. × Iona. L.-c. × Lucasii.
L. × juvenilis. L.-c. × Hardieri.
L. longipes. L.-c. × Geoffrey.
Lælio-cattleya × callistoglossa. L.-c. × Purple-Emperor.
L.-c. × Decia. L.-c. × Hildegard.
L.-c. × Ingramii. L.-c. × Elba.
L.-c. × Martinetii. L.-c. × Wellesleyi.
Sophrocattleya × Cleopatra. Sophrocattleya × Antiochus.

50a. **C. × Wendlandiana.**

Læliocattleya × Clive. Læliocattleya × Goodyii.

50b. **C. × Whitei.**

C. Dowiana. C. × Waldemar.

11a. COCHLIODA.

1. **C. Nœtzliana.**

Odontoglossum crispum. Odontioda × Bradshawiæ.
O. Edwardii. O. × Devossiana.
O. nobile. O. × Vuylstekeæ.

2. **C. sanguinea.**

O. cirrhousm. O. × heatonensis.

3. **Cochlioda vulcanica.**
O. cirrhosum. O. × Bohnhoffiæ.

11b. CŒLOGYNE.

1. **C. asperata.**
C. Dayana. C. × Brymeriana.

2. **C. cristata.**
C. speciosa. C. × Colmanii.

3. **C. Dayana.**
C. asperata. C. × Brymeriana.

4. **C. speciosa.**
C. cristata. C. × Colmanii.

13. CYMBIDIUM.

1. **C. eburneum** (p. 11).
C. giganteum. C. × heatonense.
C. grandiflorum. C. × Holfordianum.
C. × Veitchii. C. × Colmaniæ.

2. **C. giganteum** (p. 11).
C. eburneum. C. × heatonene.

3. **C. grandiflorum** (p. 11).
C. eburneum. C. × Holfordianum.

4. **C. Lowianum** (p. 11).
C. Tracyanum. C. × Cravenianum.
C. × Veitchii. C. × Woodhamsianum.

5. **C. Mastersii** (p. 11).
C. Tracyanum. C. × woodlandense.

7. **C. Tracyanum** (p. 11).
C. Lowianum. C. × Cravenianum.
C. Mastersii. C. × woodlandense.

7a. **C. × Veitchii.**
C. eburneum. C. × Colmaniæ.
C. Lowianum. C. × Woodhamsianum.

15. DENDROBIUM (p. 11).

1. **D. × Ainsworthii** (p. 11).
D. Hildebrandii. D. × Rallianum.

3. **D. aureum** (p. 11).
D. × Curtisii. D. × Nancy.
D. × Wiganiæ. D. × chessingtonense.

6. **D. Brymerianum** (p. 11).
D. pulchellum. D. × Ashworthii.

7. **D. × Cassiope** (p. 11).
D. nobile. D. × Snowflake.

13a. **Dendrobium × Curtisii.**
D. aureum. D. × Nancy.
D. Findlayanum. D. × gattonense.

15. **D. × Dominyanum** (p. 12).
D. × Wiganiæ. D. × Brodiei.

15a. **D. × Ellisii.**
D. nobile. D. × streathamense.

20. **D. Findlayanum** (p. 12).
D. × Curtisii. D. × gattonense.
D. Hildebrandii. D. × Boundii.
D. × Wiganiæ. D. × Blackianum.

23. **D. Hildebrandii** (p. 12).
D. × Ainsworthii. D. × Rallianum.
D. Findlayanum. D. × Boundii.

26. **D. Linawianum** (p. 12).
D. signatum. D. × Myra.

30. **D. Maccarthiæ** (p. 12).
D. moniliforme. D. × Macjap.

32. **D. moniliforme** (p. 12).
D. Maccarthiæ. D. × Macjap.

33. **D. nobile** (p. 12).
D. × Cassiope. D. × Snowflake.
D. × Ellisii. D. × streathamense.
D. × Wiganiæ. D. × Cooksoni.

38. **D. pulchellum** (p. 13).
D. Brymerianum. D. × Ashworthii.

43. **D. signatum** (p. 13).
D. Linawianum. D. × Myra.

50. **D. × Wiganiæ** (p. 13).
D. aureum. D. × chessingtonense.
D. × Dominyanum. D. × Brodiei.
D. Findlayanum. D. × Blackianum.
D. nobile. D. × Cooksoni.

15a. DIACRIUM.

1. **D. bicornutum.**
Epidendrum Ellisii. Epidiacrium × Boundii.
E. radicans. E.-d. × gattonense.
Lælia cinnabarina. Dialælia × Veitchii.

18. EPIDENDRUM (p. 14).

Oa. **E. atropurpureum.**
Lælia cinnabarina. Epilælia × Thalia.
L. harpophylla. E.-l. × Fletcheriana.
L. purpurata. E.-l. × Laucheana.

Ob. **Epidendrum aurantiacum.**

Lælia cinnabarina.	Epilælia × Eva.

Oc. **E. × Boundii.**

E. xanthinum.	E. × gattonense.

2. **E. ciliare** (p. 14).

Cattleya Warscewiczii.	Epicattleya × decipiens.
Lælia longipes.	Epilælia × longiciliare.

7a. **E. eburneum.**

Cattleya labiata.	Epicattleya × balarucensis.

8a. **E. Ellisii.**

Diacrium bicornutum.	Epidiacrium × Boundii.

11a. **E. falcatum.**

Cattleya intermedia.	Epicattleya × Figaro.

14a. **E. nocturnum.**

Cattleya Skinneri.	Epicattleya × Lesueri.

16. **E. Parkinsonianum** (p. 14).

Brassavola glauca.	Brassoepidendrum × stamfordiense.
Cattleya Gaskelliana.	Epicattleya × Lawrencei.

16a. **E. prismatocarpum.**

Lælia tenebrosa.	Epilælia × bradfordiensis.

18. **E. pseudepidendrum** (p. 14).

E. radicans.	E. × Cleon.

20. **E. radicans** (p. 14).

Diacrium bicornutum.	Epidiacrium × gattonense.
E. pseudepidendrum.	E. × Cleon.

23. **E. vitellinum** (p. 15).

Cattleya Gaskelliana.	Epicattleya × magdeburgensis.
C. Loddigesii.	E.-c. × Wolteri.

25. **E. xanthimum** (p. 15).

E. × Boundii.	E. × gattonense.

20. LÆLIA (p. 15).

Oa. L. acuminata.

L. anceps.	L. × Maroni.

2. **Lælia anceps** (p. 15.)

Brassavola Digbyana	Brassolælia × Lelieuxii.
Cattleya Loddigesii.	Læliocattleya × Wolteræ.
L. acuminata.	L. × Maroni.
L. harpophylla.	L × canariensis.

4. **L. Boothiana** (p. 15).

Brassavola Digbyana.	Brassolælia × Louis-Bel.

5. **L. cinnabarina** (p. 15).

Cattleya dolosa.	Læliocattleya × chardwarensis.
C. Forbesii.	L.-c. × ronselensis.
Diacrium bicornutum.	Dialælia × Veitchii.
Epidendrum atropurpureum.	Epilælia × Thalia.
E. aurantiacum.	E.-l. × Eva.
L. Jongheana.	L. × Sidneana.
L. xanthina.	L. × Nora.

5a. **L. × cinnabrosa.**

Brassolælia × Helen.	Brassolælia × Gipsy.
Cattleya Mendelii.	Læliocattleya × Veronique.
C. Warscewiczii.	L.-c. × Tunis.

5b. **L. Cowanii.**

Cattleya Dowiana.	Læliocattleya × Ariel.
C. Gaskelliana.	L.-c. × Lydia.
C. Trianæ.	L.-c. × Oriens.
L. Jongheana.	L. × Gwennie.

6. **L. crispa** (p. 16).

Cattleya × Hardyana.	Læliocattleya × crispo-Hardyana.
C. Rex.	L.-c. × Bievreana.
C. superba.	L.-c. × Salus.
Læliocattleya × Leeana.	L.-c. × Ursula.
L.-c. × Roeblingii.	L.-c. × woodfordiensis.

7. **L. Dayana** (p. 16).

Læliocattleya × bella.	Læliocattleya × Cordelia.

9. **L. flava** (p. 16).

Brassavola glauca.	Brassolælia × westfieldiensis.
B. nodosa.	B.-l. × fladosa.
Cattleya amethystoglossa.	Læliocattleya × Merciana.
C. Dowiana.	L.-c. × Andromeda.
C. Harrisoniana.	L.-c. × Amarylloso.
C. Mendelii.	L.-c. × Paradise.

Lælia flava—(*continued*).

C. Schilleriana.	L.-c. × Alcyone.
L. Jongheana.	L. × Degeestiana.
L. purpurata.	L. × Statheræ.
Læliocattleya × Cappei.	Læliocattleya × vesinetensis.

10. **L. grandiflora** (p. 16).

Brassavola Digbyana.	Brassolælia × Thwaitesii.
L. purpurata.	L. × Lawrencei.
L. tenebrosa.	L. × Bertii.

11. **L. grandis** (p. 16).

Læliocattleya × Ascania.	Læliocattleya × Martiniæ.

13. **L. harpophylla** (p. 17).

C. Dowiana.	Læliocattleya × harpo-aurea.
C. Percivaliana.	L.-c. × Adelina.
C. quadricolor.	L.-c. × chocophylla.
Epidendrum atropurpureum.	Epilælia × Fletcheriana.
L. anceps.	L. × canariensis.

13a. **L × Iona.**

Cattleya Warscewiczii.	Læliocattleya × Lucasii.

14. **L. Jongheana** (p. 17).

Cattleya Percivaliana.	Læliocattleya × Sunset.
C. Schrœderæ.	L.-c × Olivia.
L. cinnabarina.	L. × Sidneana.
L. Cowanii	L. × Gwennie.
L. flava.	L. × Degeestiana.
L. tenebrosa.	L. × Daphne.
Læliocattleya × Ernestii.	Læliocattleya × Gamma.
Sophrolælia × læta.	Sophrolælia × Phroso.

14a. **L. × juvenilis.**

Cattleya Warscewiczii.	L.-c. × Hardieri.
L. tenebrosa.	L. × Dellacii.

15. **L. × Latona** (p. 17).

Cattleya Dowiana.	Læliocattleya × illustris.
C. × Hardyana.	L.-c. × Jason.
C. Schrœderæ.	L.-c. × Ganymede.
L. purpurata.	L. × Ithone.
Læliocattleya × Canhamiana.	Læliocattleya × Zoroaster.
L.-c. × Gottoiana.	L.-c. × Mazharata.

16. **Lælia longipes** (p. 17).

Cattleya Warscewiczii.	Læliocattleya × Geoffrey.
Epidendrum ciliare.	Epilælia × longiciliare.

17. **L. Perrinii** (p. 17).

Cattleya Eldorado.	Læliocattleya × Soulageana.
C. granulosa.	L.-c. × Perrilosa.
C. × Hardyana.	L.-c. × Ægina.
C. Schrœderæ.	L.-c. × Goodsonæ.
Læliocattleya × Gottoiana.	L.-c. × Perrigottoi.

19. **L. pumila** (p. 17).

Cattleya Percivaliana.	Læliocattleya × Sheila.
Læliocattleya × Schilleriana.	L.-c. × Oracle.
Sophrolælia × Gratrixiæ.	Sophrolælia × Leda.

20. **L. purpurata** (p. 17).

Brassocattleya × Veitchii.	Brassocatlælia × Veitchii
Cattleya × Hardyana.	Læliocattleya × Capartii.
Epidendrum atropurpureum.	Epilælia × Laucheana.
L. flava.	L. × Statheræ.
L. grandiflora.	L. × Lawrencei.
L. × Latona.	L. × Ithone.
Læliocattleya × warnhamensis.	Læliocattleya × Duquesnei.

20a. **L. rupestris.**

Cattleya Trianæ.	Læliocattleya × Glycera.

21. **L. superbiens** (p. 18).

Cattleya Lueddemanniana.	Læliocattleya × Denisii.
C. Trianæ.	L.-c. × Pujeti.

22. **L. tenebrosa** (p. 18)

Cattleya dolosa.	Læliocattleya × dolotene.
C. × intertexta.	L.-c. × Gouldiæ.
C. × Murrayi.	L.-c. × Leeseæ.
Epidendrum prismatocarpum.	Epilælia × bradfordiensis.
L. grandiflora.	L. × Bertii.
L. × juvenilis.	L. × Dellacii.
L. Jongheana.	L. × Daphne.
Læliocattleya × elegans.	Læliocattleya × Dumatii.
L.-c. × Gottoiana.	L.-c. × tenegottoi.
L.-c. × Pallas.	L.-c. × Hopkinsii.

23. **Lælia xanthina** (p. 18).

Brassavola Digbyana.	Brassolælia × Jessopi.
Cattleya × Brymeriana.	Læliocattleya × ilsingtonensis.
C. intermedia.	L.-c. × stellata.
L. cinnabarina.	L. × Nora.
Læliocattleya × callistoglossa.	Læliocattleya × Wellesleyæ.
L.-c. × elegans.	L.-c. × Measuresiæ.

21. LÆLIOCATTLEYA (p. 19).

2a. **L.-c. × Amelia.**

Cattleya Dowiana.	L.-c. × Schneideri.

4. **L.-c. × Aphrodite** (p. 19).

Cattleya Schrœderæ.	L.-c. × Bradeæ.
L.-c. × callistoglossa.	L.-c. × Marnhami.

4a. **L.-c. × Ascania.**

Lælia grandis.	L.-c. × Martiniæ.

5. **L.-c. × bella** (p. 19).

Cattleya Mendelii.	L.-c. × Zixa.
Lælia Dayana.	L.-c. × Cordelia.

6. **L.-c. × callistoglossa** (p. 19).

Brassavola Digbyana.	Brassocatlælia × tringiensis.
Cattleya × Hardyana.	L.-c. × Whiteleggei.
C. Harrisoniana.	L.-c. × Priam.
C. Lawrenceana.	L.-c. × Peetersii.
C. Lueddemanniana.	L.-c. × Lustre.
C. Mendelii.	L.-c. × Schiffmanii.
C. × Rothschildiana.	L.-c. × Beta.
C. Trianæ.	L.-c. × Barbarossa.
C. Warscewiczii.	L.-c. × Purple-Emperor.
Lælia xanthina.	L.-c. × Wellesleyæ.
L.-c. × Aphrodite.	L.-c. × Marnhami.

7. **L.-c. × Canhamiana** (p. 19).

Lælia × Latona.	L.-c. × Zoroaster.

7a. **L.-c. × Cappei.**

Lælia flava.	L.-c × vesinetensis.

7b. **L.-c. × Charlesworthii.**

Cattleya Dowiana.	L.-c. × Golden-Oriole.

8. **L.-c. × Clive** (p. 19).

Cattleya × Minerva.	L.-c. × Perseus.
C. × Wendlandiana.	L.-c. × Goodyi.

8a. **L.-c. × Cranstounæ.**

Cattleya Dowiana.	L.-c. × Kelpie.

8b. **L.-c. × Decia.**

C. Warscewiczii.	L.-c. × Hildegard.

11. **L.-c. × Doris** (p. 19).

Brassavola Digbyana.	Brassocatlælia × Rowena.

12. **L.-c. × elegans** (p. 19).

Cattleya dolosa.	L.-c. × Lambeaui.
C. Eldorado.	L.-c. × vivicans.
C. granulosa.	L.-c. × Alexanderi.
C. Lueddemanniana.	L.-c. × Templeana.
C. Mendelii.	L.-c. × Memnon.
C. Schilleriana.	L.-c. × Kitcheneri.
Lælia tenebrosa.	L.-c. × Dumatii.
L. xanthina.	L.-c. × Measuresiæ.
L.-c. × Martinetii.	L.-c. × Laura.

12a. **L-c. × Ernestii** (p. 19).

Cattleya Dowiana.	L.-c. × Golden-Belle.
C. × flavescens.	L.-c. × Mount-Ophir.
C. Schrœderæ.	L.-c. × Alpha.
Lælia Jongheana.	L.-c. × Gamma.
L.-c. × Greenwoodii.	L. c. × Golden-Beauty.
L.-c. × Lucasiana.	L.-c. × Melina.

13. **L.-c. × exoniensis** (19).

Cattleya Harrisoniana.	L.-c. × Arethusa.

14a. **L.-c. × Fournieri.**

Cattleya × flavescens.	L.-c. × Kronprinz.

15. **L.-c. × Gottoiana** (p. 19).

Cattleya × Hardyana.	L.-c. × Duncanii
C Warneri.	L -c. × Linnæus.
Lælia × Latona.	L.-c. × Mazharata.
L. Perrinii.	L.-c. × Perrigottoi.
L. tenebrosa.	L.-c. × tenegottoi.

15a. **L.-c. × Greenwoodii.**

Brassavola Digbyana.	Brassocatlælia × Lido.
Cattleya Mendelii.	L.-c. × Birkbeckii.
L.-c. × Ernestii.	L -c. × Golden-Beauty.

Læliocattleya—(*continued*).

15b. **L.-c. × highburiensis.**

C. Mossiæ.	L.-c. × Sirius.

16. **L.-c. × Hippolyta** (p. 20).

Brassavola Digbyana.	Brassocatlælia × Hippocrates.
Cattleya × Hardyana.	L.-c. × Duchess.
C. Mendelii.	L.-c. × Goodsoni.
C. Schrœderæ.	L.-c. × Lesueri.
C. Warneri.	L.-c. × Firmin.

16a. **L.-c. × Hyeana.**

C. Mossiæ.	L.-c. × Milo.

17. **L.-c. × Ingrami** (p. 20).

Cattleya × Mantinii.	L.-c. × Gilberta.
C. Trianæ.	L.-c. × Beauclerkiæ.
C. Warscewiczii.	L.-c. × Elba.

18. **L.-c. × Leeana** (p. 20).

Cattleya Dowiana.	L.-c. × Georgina.
Lælia crispa.	L.-c. × Ursula.

18a. **L.-c. × Lucasiana.**

L.-c. × Ernestii.	L.-c. × Melina.

18a. **L. c. × Martinetii.**

Cattleya Warscewiczii.	L.-c. × Mitchelliæ.
L.-c. × elegans.	L.-c. × Laura.

18b. **L.-c. × Myra.**

C. Lueddemanniana.	L.-c. × Ixion.

18b. **L.-c. × Nysa.**

Cattleya Bowringiana.	L.-c. × Tenos.
C. Harrisoniana.	L.-c. × Thetis.

19. **L.-c. × Pallas** (p. 20.).

Lælia tenebrosa.	L.-c. × Hopkinsii.

19a. **L.-c. × Phryne.**

Cattleya × Iris.	L.-c. × Lusitania.

20a. **L.-c. × Roeblingii.**

Lælia crispa.	L.-c. × woodfordiensis.

22. **L.-c. × Schilleriana** (p. 20).

Brassavola Digbyana.	Brassocatlælia × balarucensis.
Cattleya Gaskelliana.	L.-c. × Blountiæ.
C. Lawrenceana.	L.-c. × gattonensis.
Lælia pumila.	L.-c. × Oracle.

Læliocattleya—(*continued*).

23. **L.-c. × Truffautiana.**

Cattleya × Iris.	L.-c. × Aureole.

24. **L.-c. × warnhamensis.**

Cattleya intermedia.	L.-c. × Orestes.
C. Lawrenceana.	L.-c. × Lawrie.
C. Trianæ.	L.-c. × Veisenpachii.
Lælia purpurata.	L.-c. × Duquesnei.

25. **L.-c. × Wellsiana.**

Cattleya Gaskelliana.	L.-c. × Dicksonæ.

26. **L.-c. × Zephyra.**

Cattleya Mossiæ.	L.-c. × Golden-Glory.

25. MASDEVALLIA (p. 20).

13a. **M. fragrans.**

M. Veitchiana.	M. × Veitchio-fragrans.

26. **M. Veitchiana** (p. 21).

M. fragrans.	M. × Veitchio-fragrans.

26. MILTONIA (p. 22).

0a. **M. × Bleuana.**

M. vexillaria.	M. × Hyeana.

1. **M. Roezlii** (p. 22).

Odontoglossum cirrhosum.	Odontonia × Ellwoodii.

2. **M. vexillaria** (p. 22.)

M. × Bleuana.	M. × Hyeana.

3. **M. Warscewiczii.**

Odontoglossum crispum.	Odontonia × Lairesseæ.
O. nobile.	Odontonia × culiginosa.

27. ODONTOGLOSSUM (p. 22).

0a. **O. × Adrianæ.**

O. crispum.	O. × Fascinator.
O. Hallii.	O. × Hallio-Adrianæ.
O. Harryanum.	O. × Othello.
O. × harvengtense.	O. × Oberthuri.
O. Kegeljani.	O. × ashlandense.
O. Rossii.	O. × Bertii.
O. triumphans.	O. × Ernestii.

0b. **O. × amabile.**

O. nobile.	O. × Lobbii.

Odontoglossum—(*continued*).

1. **O. × Andersonianum** (p. 22).

O. crispum.	O. × Stewartianum.
O. luteopurpureum.	O. × Nesta.

1a. **O. × armainvillierense.**

O. crispum.	O. × Beaute-Celeste.
O. × Denisonæ.	O. × Albertii.
O. Hallii.	O. × altum.
O. nobile.	O. × splendidissimum.
O. × percultum.	O. × Cooksonæ.
O. × Rolfeæ.	O. × percultum.
O. × spectabile.	O. × venustulum.
O. × Vuylstekeæ.	O. × gandavense.

1b. **O. blandum.**

O. nobile.	O. × blando-nobile.

1c. **O. Cervantesii.**

O. Edwardii.	O. × Lairessei.

2. **O. cirrhosum** (p. 22).

Cochlioda sanguinea.	Odontioda × heatonensis.
Cochlioda vulcanica.	Odontioda × Bohnhoffiæ.
Miltonia Roezlii.	Odontonia × Ellwoodii.
Odontoglossum crispum.	Odontoglossum × Phœbe.
O. Edwardii.	O. × Fletcherianum.
O. Harryanum.	O. × Elaine.
O. hastilabium.	O. × Eurydice.
O. × Rolfeæ.	O. × Sylvia.
O. Rossii.	O. × Fowlerianum.
O. × spectabile.	O. × Gladys.

2a. **O. × Coradinei.**

O. crispum.	O. × crispodinei.
O. triumphans.	O. × Nemesis.

2b. **O. cordatum.**

O. nobile.	O. × Gardneri.

2c. **O. × Crawshayanum.**

O. × cristatellum.	O. × Amneris.

3. **O. crispum** (p. 22).

Cochlioda Nœtzliana.	Odontioda × Bradshawiæ.
Miltonia Warscewiczii.	Odontonia × Lairesseæ.
Odontoglossum × Adrianæ	Odontoglossum × Fascinator.

Odontoglossum crispum—(*contd.*)

O. × Andersonianum.	O. × Stewartianum.
O. × armainvillierense.	O. × Beauté-Celeste.
O. cirrhosum.	O. × Phœbe.
O. × Coradinei.	O. × crispodinei.
O. × cristatellum.	O. × Urania.
O. Edwardii.	O × Thompsonianum.
O. × excellens.	O. × exultans.
O. × Hallixanthum.	O. × auriferum.
O. × harvengtense.	O. × hellemense.
O. Hunnewellianum.	O. × Adrianæ.
O. nevadense.	O. × Una.
O. × Rolfeæ.	O. × Japonais.
O. × spectabile.	O. × amabile.
O. × Vuylstekeæ.	O. × caloglossum.

3a. **O. × cristatellum.**

O. × Crawshayanum.	O. × Amneris.
O. crispum.	O. × Urania.
O. Hallii.	O. × Lucasianum.
O. Harryanum.	O. × Amonasro.

4. **O. × Denisonæ** (p. 22).

O. × armainvillierense.	O. × Albertii.
O. × harvengtense.	O. × moortebeekiense.
O. Kegeljani.	O. × Mossiæ.
O. nobile.	O. × amandum.
O. sceptrum.	O. × fuscum.
O. × spectabile.	O. × nitidum.

4a. **O. Edwardii.**

Cochlioda Nœtzliana.	Odontioda × Devossiana.
O. Cervantesii.	O. × Lairessei.
O. cirrhosum.	O × Fletcherianum.
O. crispum.	O. × Thompsonianum.
O. × spectabile.	O. × Aliceæ.

5a. **O. × excellens.**

O. crispum.	O. × exultans.

5b. **O. × Fascinator.**

O. Harryanum.	O. × tigrinum.
O. × Wattianum.	O. × Astræa.

6. **O. Hallii** (p. 22).

O. × Adrianæ.	O. × Hallio-Adrianæ.
O. × armainvillierense.	O. × altum.
O. × cristatellum.	O. × Lucasianum.
O. hastilabium.	O. × heatonense.
O. Kegeljani.	O. × Hallixanthum.

Odontoglossum Hallii—(*contd.*)

O. nobile. O. × warnhamense.
O. × Rolfeæ. O. × lapidense.
O. triumphans. O. × Leo.

6a. **O. × Hallixanthum.**

O. crispum. O. × auriferum.

7. **O. Harryanum** (p. 22).

O. × Adrianæ. O. × Othello.
O. cirrhosum. O. × Elaine.
O × cristatellum. O × Amonasro.
O. × Fascinator. O. × tigrinum.
O. Hunnewellianum. O. × Iago.
O. sceptrum. O. × Lambeauiæ.
O. tripudians. O. × Astarte.

7a. **O. × harvengtense.**

O. × Adrianæ. O. × Oberthuri.
O. crispum. O. × hellemense.
O. × Denisonæ. O. × moortebeekiense.
O. × Rolfeæ. O. × Wiganianum.

7b **O. hastilabium.**

O. cirrhosum. O. × Eurydice.
O. Hallii. O. × heatonense.

7c. **Hunnewellianum.**

O. crispum. O. × Adrianæ.
O. Harryanum. O. × Iago.

8. **O. Kegeljani** (p. 22).

O. × Adrianæ O. × ashlandense.
O. × Denisonæ. O. × Mossiæ.
O. Hallii. O. × Hallixanthum
O. nobile. O. × Terpsichore.

10. **O. luteopurpureum** (p. 22).

O. × Andersonianum. O. × Nesta.
O. nobile. O. × Brandtiæ.
O. triumphans. O. × Jorisianum.

10a. **O. nevadense.**

O. crispum. O. × Una.

11. **O. nobile** (p. 22).

Cochlioda Noetzliana. Odontioda × Vuylstekeæ.
Miltonia Roezlii. Odontonia × culiginosa.
Odontoglossum × amabile. Odontoglossum × Lobbii.
O. × armainvillierense. O. × splendidissimum.
O. blandum. O. × blando-nobile.
O. cordatum. O. × Gardneri.
O. × Denisonæ. O. × amandum.
O. Hallii. O. × warnhamense.

Odontoglossum nobile—(*contd.*)

O. Kegeljani. O. × Terpsichore.
O. luteopurpureum. O. × Brandtiæ.
O. × Rolfeæ. O × formosum.
O. × spectabile. O × Ossultoni.
O. × Wattianum. O × Ariadne.

11a. **O. × percultum.**

O. × armainvillierense. O. × Cooksonæ.

11b. **O. × Rolfeæ.**

O. × armainvillierense. O. × percultum.
O. cirrhosum. O. × Sylvia.
O. crispum. O. × Japonais.
O. Hallii. O. × lapidense.
O. × harvengtense. O. × Wiganianum.
O. nobile. O. × formosum.
O. × spectabile. O. × Cambria.
O. triumphans. O. × Lawrenceanum.

11c. **O. Rossii.**

O. × Adrianæ. O. × Bertii.
O. cirrhosum. O. × Fowlerianum.
O. × spectabile. O. × Smithii.

12. **O. sceptrum** (p. 22).

O. × Denisonæ. O. × fuscum.
O. Harryanum. O. × Lambeauiæ.
O. × spectabile. O. × Euphrosyne.
O. triumphans. O. × Stella.

12a. **O × spectabile.**

O. × armainvillierense. O. × venustulum.
O. cirrhosum. O. × Gladys.
O. crispum. O. × amabile.
O × Denisonæ. O. × nitidum.
O. Edwardii. O. × Aliceæ.
O. nobile. O. × Ossultoni.
O. × Rolfeæ. O. × Cambria.
O. Rossii. O. × Smithii.
O. sceptrum. O. × Euphrosyne.

13. **O. tripudians** (p. 22).

O. Harryanum. O. × Astarte.

14. **O. triumphans** (p. 22).

O. × Adrianæ. O. × Ernestii.
O. × Coradinei. O. × Nemesis.
O. Hallii. O. × Leo.
O. luteopurpureum. O. × Jorisianum.
O. × Rolfeæ. O. × Lawrenceanum.
O. sceptrum. O. × Stella.

Odontoglossum -(*continued*).

15. **O. × Vuylstekeæ.**

O. × armainvilliierense. O. × gandavense.
O. crispum. O. × caloglossum.

16. **O. × Wattianum.**

O. × Fascinator. O. × Astræa.
O. nobile. O. × Ariadne.

28. PAPHIOPEDILUM (p. 22).

1a. **P. × Andromeda.**

P. Rothschildianum. P. × Pelican.

1b. **P. × Annie.**

P. bellatulum. P. × Fred.

1c. **P. × Aphrodite.**

P. × Harrisianum. P. × St.-Albans.

3. **P. Argus** (p. 22).

P. exul. P. × Phryne.
P. Fairrieanum. P. × luxemburgense.
P. Godefroyæ. P. × exquisitum.
P. × Godseffianum. P. × Bridgei.
P. × Io. P. × Io-Argus.
P. Mastersianum. P. × Upcheri.
P. × Schlesingerianum. P. × bridgense.
P. × Swinburnei. P. × nigratum.
P. × Youngianum. P. × Argo-Youngii.

4. **P. × Arthurianum** (p. 23).

P. ciliolare. P. × Imogene.
P. insigne. P. × Sanarthur.
P × Lathamianum. P. × Lonsdaleæ.
P. × œnanthum. P. × Laura.
P. × nitens. P. × keigleyense.

5a. **P. × Atys.**

P. × calloso-barbatum. P. × Riddifordii.

5b. **P. × augustum.**

P. Rothschildianum. P. × fastuosum.

5c. **P. × aureum.**

P. callosum. P. × altrinchamense.
P. Charlesworthii. P. × De-Vere.
P. insigne. P. × Duchess.
P. × Leeanum. P. × Tracyanum.

Paphiopedilum—(*continued*).

7. **P. barbatum** (p. 23).

P. × calophyllum. P. × Lubbersii
P. exul. P. × Yolande.
P. × nitens. P. × Sally.

8. **P. bellatulum** (p. 23).

P. × Annie. P. × Fred.
P. × Euryale. P. × Whiteleggei.
P. × Haywoodianum. P. × Haywoodiæ.
P. × Io. P. × dourdaniense.
P. Mastersianum. P. × Hopkinsianum.

8a. **P. × Berkeleyanum.**

P. × Swinburnei. P. × Lucasii.

11a. **P. × Buchanianum.**

P. × Calypso. P. × Brilliant.

12a. **P. × calloso-barbatum.**

P. × Atys. P. × Riddifordii.

13. **P. callosum** (p. 24).

P. × aureum. P. × altrinchamense.
P. × Matthewsii. P. × Readii.
P. × nitens. P. × Wendigo.
P. × gigas ? (Prewettii). P. × Seymouri.
P. × triumphans. P. × Rajah.

14. **P. × calophyllum** (p. 25).

P. barbatum. P. × Lubbersii.

15. **P. × Calypso** (p. 25).

P. × Buchanianum. P. × Brilliant.
P. × Figaro. P. × Madame.
P. × Godseffianum. P. × Robbinsii.

17. **P. Chamberlainianum** (p. 25).

P. Charlesworthii. P. × Willoughbyæ
P. ciliolare. P. × claptonense.
P. Mastersianum. P. × Statherianum.
P. Stonei. P. × Ethel.
P. tonsum. P. × Muriel.

19. **P. Charlesworthii** (p. 25).

P. × aureum. P. × De-Vere.
P. Chamberlainianum. P. × Willoughbyæ.
P. × Haywoodianum. P. × leyburnense.
P. × Hera. P. × Moloch.
P. × Lucie. P. × Aitchisonæ.
P. × Niobe. P. × Blanche.
P. × nitens. P. × Thornianum.
P. purpuratum. P. × Faunus.
P. × Swanianum. P. × Clarkii.

Paphiopedilum—(*continued*).

20. **P. × chloroneurum** (p. 26).

P × nitens. P. × Chameleon.

21. **P. ciliolare** (p. 26).

P. × Arthurianum. P. × Imogene.
P. Chamberlainianum. P. × claptonense.
P. Fairrieanum. P. × Beauclerkiæ.

22a. **P. × Clinkaberryanum.**

P. insigne. P. × Lucasiæ.

25a. **P. × conco-bellatulum.**

P. insigne. P. × Singeri.

26. **P. concolor** (p. 26).

P. exul. P. × exul-concolor.
P. tonsum. P. × conco-tonsum.

30. **P. Curtisii** (p. 26).

P. Mastersianum. P. × Cypheri.
P. tonsum. P. × Frankeanum.

33. **P. Dayanum** (p. 27).

P. × Gowerianum. P. × Iacchus.

34. **P. Druryi** (p. 27).

P. Godefroyæ. P. × Honnoriæ.
P. Rothschildianum. P. × Cooksoni.
P. × Youngianum. P. × Healei.

34a. **P. × Eismannianum.**

P. insigne. P. × Hackenschmidtii.

36. **P. × Euryale** (p. 27).

P. bellatulum. P. × Whiteleggei.
P. × triumphans. P. × Victory.

36a. **P. × Evelyn** (p. 27).

P. × nitens. P. × Mooreanum.

37. **P. exul** (p. 27).

P. Argus. P. × Phryne.
P. barbatum. P. × Yolande.
P. concolor. P. × exul-concolor.
P. insigne. P. × Robsoni.
P. Mastersianum. P. × Mastersio-exul.
P. × nitens. P. × Tankervillei.
P. superbiens. P. × Minerva.
P. tonsum. P. × Margery.

38. **P. Fairrieanum** (p. 27).

P. Argus. P. × luxembergense.
P. ciliolare. P. × Beauclerkiæ.
P. × Io. P. × Fairrieano-Io.

Paphiopedilum—(*continued*).

38a. **P. × Figaro.**

P. × Calypso. P. × Madame.

41a. **P. × gigas ? (Prewettii).**

P. callosum. P. × Seymouri.
P. × Leeanum. P. × Leon.

42. **P. Godefroyæ** (p. 28).

P. Argus. P. × exquisitum.
P. Druryi. P. × Honnoriæ.
P. Hookeræ. P. × Pharos.
P. Lawrenceanum. P. × Dom-Carlos.
P. × Mabeliæ. P. × Fletcherianum.
P. Rothschildianum. P. × Barclayæ.
P. Spicerianum. P. × Vera.
P. tonsum. P. × Moorei.

43. **P. × Godseffianum** (p. 28).

P. Argus. P. × Bridgei.
P. × Calypso. P. × Robbinsii.

44. **P. × Gowerianum** (p. 28).

P. Dayanum. P. × Iacchus.
P. Lawrenceanum. P. × Lawregower.
P. Sanderianum. P. × Wellesleyæ.

46. **P. × Harrisianum** (p. 28).

P. × Aphrodite. P. × St.-Albans.
P. × Hera. P. × Trippiæ.
P. triumphans. P. × Sheila.
P. × Winnianum. P. × Rhesus.

48. **P. × Haywoodianum** (p. 29).

P. bellatulum. P. × Haywoodiæ.
P. Charlesworthii. P. × leyburnense.
P. Spicerianum. P. × Rose.

49. **P. × Hera** (p. 29).

P. Charlesworthii. P. × Moloch.
P. × Harrisianum. P. × Trippiæ.
P. insigne. P. × Draco.
P. × Lathamianum. P. × Emile.
P. Rothschildianum. P. × Black-Prince
P. Spicerianum. P. × Cravenianum
P. villosum. P. × Dicksonianum.

50a. **P. × Hitchinsiæ.**

P. × nitens. P. × Baron.

51. **P. Hookeræ** (p. 29).

P. Godefroyæ. P. × Pharos.

52. **P. insigne** (p. 29).

P. Arthurianum. P. × Sanarthur.
P. × aureum. P. × Duchess.

Paphiopedilum insigne (*contd.*)

P. × Clinkaberry-anum. P. × Lucasiæ.
P. × conco-bellatulum. P. × Singeri.
P. × Eismann-ianum. P. × Hacken-schmidtii.
P. exul. P. × Robsoni.
P. × Hera. P. × Draco.
P. × Orpheus. P. × Thais.
P. Rothschild-ianum. P. × ingens.
P. × Sanacteus. P. × Sanacderæ.
P. × Simonii. P. × Sanacteus.
P. Victoria-Mariæ. P. × Dorothy.

53. **P.** × **Io** (p. 30).

P. Argus. P. × Io-Argus.
P. bellatulum. P. × dourdaniense.
P. Fairrieanum. P. × Fairrieano-Io.

55. **P.** × **Lathamianum** (p. 30).

P. × Arthurianum. P. × Lonsdaleæ.
P. × Hera. P. × Emile.
P. × Wottoni. P. × Brunette.

57. **P. Lawrenceanum** (p. 30).

P. Godefroyæ. P. × Dom Carlos.
P. × Gowerianum. P. × Lawregower.
P. × Niobe. P. × Wellesleyi.

58. **P.** × **Leeanum** (p. 31).

P. × aureum. P. × Tracyanum.
P. × Medeia. P. × Shaferi.
P. × Pollettianum. P. × westfield-iense.
P. × gigas? (Prewettii). P. × Leon.
P. Rothschild-ianum. P. × Williamson-ianum.
P. × Simonii. P. × Marjorie.

59. **P. Lowii** (p. 31).

P. Stonei. P. × Mercatellii.

60. **P.** × **Lucie** (p. 32).

P. Charlesworthii. P. × Aitchisonæ.

62. **P.** × **Mabeliæ** (p. 32).

P. Godefroyæ. P. × Fletcherianum.
P. superbiens. P. × Braceyanum.

66. **P. Mastersianum** (p. 32).

P. Argus. P. × Upcheri.
P. bellatulum. P. × Hopkinsianum.
P. Chamberlain-ianum. P. × Statherianum.
P. Curtisii. P. × Cypheri.

Paphiopedilum Mastersianum (*contd.*)

P. exul. P. × Mastersio-exul.
P. niveum. P. × Humbertii.
P. Rothschild-ianum. P. × dellense.
P. villosum. P. × Mastersio-villosum.

66a. **P.** × **Matthewsii.**

P. callosum. P. × Readii.

68. **P.** × **Medeia** (p. 32).

P. × Leeanum. P. × Shaferi.

68a. **P.** × **Minos.**

P. × nitens. P. × Webbiæ.

70. **P.** × **Niobe** (p. 32.)

P. Charlesworthii. P. × Blanche.
P. Lawrenceanum. P. × Wellesleyi.
P. villosum. P. × Fabiola.

71. **P.** × **nitens** (p. 32).

P. × Arthurianum. P. × keighleyense.
P. barbatum. P. × Sally.
P. callosum. P. × Wendigo.
P. Charlesworthii. P. × Thornianum.
P. × chloroneurum. P. × Chameleon.
P. × Evelyn. P. × Mooreanum.
P. exul. P. × Tankervillei.
P. × Hitchinsiæ. P. × Baron.
P. × Minos. P. × Webbiæ.
P. Rothschild-ianum. P. × Edwardianum.
P. × Schlesinger-ianum. P. × Scipio.
P. × triumphans. P. × bowdonense.

72. **P. niveum** (p. 32).

P. Mastersianum. P. × Humbertii.

72a. **P.** × **Norma.**

P. villosum. P. × villma.

74. **P.** × **œnanthum** (p. 33).

P. × Arthurianum. P. × Laura.
P. × Orpheus. P. × Seraphis.
P. × Pollettianum. P. × Stephanos.
P. × selligerum. P. × Earl.
P. × vexillarium. P. × epicasta.

76. **P.** × **Orpheus** (p. 33).

P. insigne. P. × Thais.
P. × œnanthum. P. × Seraphis.

82. **P. philippinense** (p. 33).

P. × vexillarium. P. × Bella.

Paphiopedilum—(*continued*).

83. **P. × Pollettianum** (p. 33).

P. × Leeanum. P. × westfieldiense.
P. × œnanthum. P. × Stephanos.

84. **P. præstans** (p. 83).

P. villosum. P. × Vanessa.

85. **P. purpuratum** (p. 33).

P. Charlesworthii. P. × Faunus.

88. **P. Rothschildianum** (p. 34).

P. × Andromeda. P. × Pelican.
P. × augustum. P. × fastuosum.
P. Druryi. P. × Cooksoni.
P. Godefroyæ. P. × Barclayæ.
P. × Hera. P. × Black-Prince.
P. insigne. P. × ingens.
P. × Leeanum. P. × Williamsonianum.
P. Mastersianum. P. × dellense.
P. × nitens. P. × Edwardianum.
P. Stonei. P. × imperiale.

88a. **P. × Sanacteus.**

P. insigne. P. × Sanacderæ.

89. **P Sanderianum** (p. 34).

P. × Gowerianum. P. × Wellesleyæ.
P. × Youngianum. P. × Herbert.

91. **P. × Schlesingerianum** (p. 34).

P. Argus. P. × bridgense.
P. × nitens. P. × Scipio.

93. **P. × selligerum** (p 34).

P. × œnanthum. P. × Earl.

96. **P. × Simonii** (p. 35).

P. insigne. P × Sanacteus.
P. × Leeanum. P. × Marjorie.

97. **P. Spicerianum** (p. 35).

P. Godefroyæ. P. × Vera.
P. × Haywoodianum. P. × Rose.
P. × Hera. P. × Cravenianum.
P. × Winnianum. P. × Jermınghamiæ.

98. **P. Stonei** (p. 35).

P. Chamberlainianum. P. × Ethel.
P. Lowii. P. × Mercatellii.
P. Rothschildianum. P. × imperiale.

Paphiopedilum—(*continued*).

99. **P. superbiens** (p. 35).

P. exul. P. × Minerva.
P. × Mabeliæ. P. × Braceyanum.
P. tonsum. P. × tonso-superbiens.

101. **P. × Swanianum** (p. 36).

P. Charlesworthii. P. × Clarkii.

102. **P. × Swinburnei** (p. 36).

P. Argus. P. × nigratum.
P. × Berkeleyanum. P. × Lucasii.

104. **P. tonsum** (p. 36).

P. Chamberlainianum. P. × Muriel.
P. concolor. P. × conco-tonsum.
P. Curtisii. P × Frankeanum.
P. exul. P. × Margery.
P. Godefroyæ. P. × Moorei.
P. superbiens. P. × tonso-superbiens.

104a. **P. × triumphans.**

P. callosum P. × Rajah.
P. × Euryale. P. × Victory.
P. × Harrisianum. P. × Sheila.
P. × nitens P. × bowdonense.

107. **P. × vexillarium** (p. 37).

P. × œnanthum. P. × epicasta.
P. philippinense. P. × Bella.

108. **P. Victoria-Mariæ** (p. 37).

P. insigne. P. × Dorothy.
P. villosum. P. × Venilla.

109. **P. villosum** (p. 37).

P. × Hera. P. × Dicksonianum.
P. Mastersianum. P. × Mastersio-villosum.
P. × Niobe. P. × Fabiola.
P. × Norma. P. × villma.
P. præstans. P. × Vanessa.
P. Victoria-Mariæ. P. × Venilla.

110a. **P. × Winnianum.**

P. × Harrisianum. P. × Rhesus.
P. Spicerianum. P. × Jerninghamiæ.

110b. **P. × Wottoni.**

P. × Lathamianum. P. × Brunette.

111. **P. × Youngianum** (37).

P. Argus. P. × Argo-Youngii.
P. Druryi. P. × Healei.
P. Sanderianum. P. × Herbert.

29. PHAIUS (p. 37).

4. **P. × Cooksonæ** (p. 38).

P. × oakwoodiensis. P. × Doris.

5. **P. × Cooksoni (Norman).**

Calanthe Regnieri. Phaiocalanthe × Colmanii.

9a. **P. × oakwoodiensis.**

P. × Cooksonæ. P. × Doris.

31. PHRAGMOPEDILUM (p. 39).

4. **P. caricinum** (p. 39).

P. × Lemoinierianum. P. × turconiense.

9a. **P. × Lemoinierianum.**

P. caricinum. P. × turconiense.

31a. PROMENÆA.

1. **P. stapelioides.**

P. xanthina. P. × Rollisoni.

2. **P. xanthina.**

P. stapelioides. P. × Rollissoni.

33. SOBRALIA (p. 40).

1a. **S. leucoxantha.**

S. Lowii. S. × dellensis.

1b. **S. Lowii.**

S. leucoxantha. S. × dellensis.

33a. SOPHROCATTLEYA.

1. **S.-c. × Calypso.**

Cattleya × Enid. S.-c. × Marcus.

2. **S.-c. × Cleopatra.**

C. Warscewiczii. S.-c. × Antiochus.

33b. SOPHROLÆLIA.

1. **S.-l. × Gratrixiæ.**

L. pumila. S.-l. × Leda.

2. **S.-l. × læta.**

Cattleya Lawrenceana. Sophrocatlælia × Phyllis.
Lælia Jongheana. S.-l. × Phroso.

2. **S.-l. × Orpeti.**

Cattleya bicolor. Sophrocatlælia × Medea.

34. SOPHRONITIS (p. 40).

1. **S. grandiflora** (p. 40).

Cattleya amethystoglossa. Sophrocattleya × warnhamensis.
C. Dowiana. S.-c. × Doris.
C. Lawrenceana. S.-c. × Atreus.
C. Schrœderæ. S.-c. × Heathii.

35. SPATHOGLOTTIS (p. 40).

1. **S. aurea** (p. 40).

S. × Veitchii. S. × Colmanii.

2a. **S. × Veitchii.**

S. aurea. S. × Colmanii.

36. STANHOPEA (p. 41).

1a. **S. Martiana.**

S. tigrina. S. × Wolteriana.

3. **S. tigrina** (p. 41.)

S. Martiana. S. × Wolteriana.

39. ZYGOPETALUM (p. 41).

3a. **Z. Jorisianum.**

Z. maxillare. Z. × maxjorisii.

5. **Z. maxillare** (p. 41).

Z. Jorisianum. Z. × maxjorisii.
Z. × Perrenoudi. Z. × Gottianum.

6. **Z. × Perrenoudi** (p. 41).

Z. maxillare. Z. × Gottianum.

SUPPLEMENT TO PART II.

Containing additions up to the end of 1907 (the numbers and pages indicate the position in the body of the work).

5. BRASSOCATLÆLIA (p. 44).

0a. **B.-c.-l. × balarucensis** (Brassavola Digbyana × Læliocattleya × Schilleriana ♀), *O.R.* 1906, 135.—Denis, 1906.

0b. **B.-c.-l. × Fowleri** (Brassolælia × Gratrixiæ × Cattleya Schrœderæ ♀), *O.R.* 1907, 151 ; *J.H.* 1907, i. 455, f.—Fowler, 1907.

Brasso-Lælia-Cattleya × Fowleri, *G.C.* 1907, i. 290, 303, f 125.

0c. **B.-c.-l. × Hippocrates** (Brassavola Digbyana × Læliocattleya × Hippolyta ♀).—Holford, 1907.

Brasso-Lælio-Cattleya × Hippocrates, *G.C.* 1907, ii. 221 ; *O.R.* 1907, 308.

1a. **B.-c.-l. × Lido** (Brassavola Digbyana ♀ × Læliocattleya × Green woodii), *O.R.* 1907, 63, 179.—Maron, 1906.

Læliocattleya × Lido, *J. S. H. Fr.* 1906, 753.

Brasso-Lælio-Cattleya × Lido, *G.C.* 1907, i. 354.

2. **B.-c.-l. × Mackayi** (p. 44).

Brasso-Lælio-Cattleya × elegans-Digbyana, *G.C.* 1906, ii. 201.—Charlesworth.

B.-c.-l. × elegans-Digbyana, *O.R.* 1906, 309.

2a. **B.-c.-l. × Rowena** (Brassavola Digbyana × Læliocattleya × Doris), *O.R.* 1907, 315.—Holford, 1907.

Brasso-Lælio-Cattleya × Rowena, *G.C.* 1907, ii. 190 ; *O.R.* 1907, 306 ; *G.M.* 1907, 661, f.

Brasso-catt-lælia × Rowena, *J.H.* 1907, ii. 267, f.

Brassocattleya × Rowena, *O.R.* 1907, 341 (v. rubella).

2b. **B.-c.-l. × tringiensis** (Brassavola Digbyana × Læliocattleya × callistoglossa ♀).—Hon. W. Rothschild, 1904.

Læliocattleya × Digbyano-Arnoldi, *G.C.* 1904, i. June 4, suppl. 2.—Hon. W. Rothschild.

L.-c. × Arderniæ, *G.C.* 1904, ii. 346; *O.R.* 1904, 368.—Ardern.

B.-c.-l. × Tring Park Hybrid, *O.R.* 1906, 180.—Hon. W. Rothschild.

2c. **B.-c.-l. × Veitchii** (Brassocattleya × Veitchii × Lælia purpurata ♀), *O.R.* 1907, 149. -Veitch, 1906.

Lælio-Brasso-Cattleya × Veitchii, *G.C.* 1906, i. 254 ; *O.R.* 1906, 150.

Brasso-Cattleya-Lælia × Veitchii, *G.C.* 1907, i. 259.

Brasso-Catt-Lælia × Veitchii, *G.C.* 1907, i. 259 ; *J.H.* 1907, i. 479, f.

6. BRASSOCATTLEYA (p. 44).

0a. **B.-c. × Alexanderi** (Brassavola Digbyana × Cattleya citrina ♀), *O.R.* 1907, 125.—Holford, 1907.

B.-c. × H. G. Alexander, *G.C.* 1907, i. 161; *O.R.* 1907, 115.—Holford.

0b. **B.-c. × Baron** (B. Digbyana × C. × Rothschildiana).—Sander, 1906.

B.-c. × The Baron, *G.C.* 1906, i. 223, 281, suppl. **f.**; *O.R.* 1906, 147.—Sander.

Lælioocattleya × The Baron, *G.M.* 1906, 239, **f.**

0c. **B.-c. × Bayard** (B.-c. × Maroni × C. Lueddemanniana ♀). Maron, 1906.

Fig. 93. Brassocattleya × Erotion.

Lælio-cattleya × Bayard, *J. S. H. Fr.* 1906, 510.

1a. **B.-c. × brunoyensis** (B. Digbyana × C. × Patrocinii ♀).—Maron, 1906.

Lælio-cattleya × Gaudi-Digbyana, *J. S. H. Fr.* 1906, 505.—Maron.

3a. **B.-c. × Cordelia** (B. Digbyana × C. intermedia ♀), *O.R.* 1906, 287.—Holford, 1906.

3b. **B.-c. × Ena** (B. Digbyana × C. Lawrenceana ♀), *G.C.* 1907, ii. 190; *O.R.* 1907, 307.—Veitch, 1907.

3c. **B.-c. × Erotion** (B. glauca ♀ × C. Walkeriana), *O.R.* 1906, 49, **f.** 6.—Thayer, 1906. **[See Fig. 93.**

5a. **B.-c. × Holfordii** (B. Digbyana × C. Forbesii ♀).—Holford, 1906.

Lælioattleya × Digbyano-Forbesii, *J. S. H. Fr.* 1907, 467.—Maron.

B.-c. × Digbyano-Forbesii, *G.C.* 1906, ii. 265; *O.R.* 1906, 339, 350.—Holford.

5b. **B.-c. × Hyeæ** (B. Digbyana × C. Harrisoniana ♀), *O.R.* 1907, 113, f. 12.—Hye, 1905.

See Fig. 94

B.-c. × Madame Jules Hye, *Rev. H. Belge*, 1906, 23, 281; *G.C.* 1906, ii. 36; *O.R.* 1906, 243, 255.—Hye.

6. **B.-c. × langleyensis** (p. 45).

B.-c. × Warburtoni, *G.C.* 1907, i. 31; *O.R.* 1907, 55.—Warburton.

Fig. 94. Brassocattleya × Hyeæ.

7. **B.-c. × Leemanniæ** (p. 45).

B.-c. × Mrs. J. Leemann, *Gard.* 1906, ii. 311, f. (v. inversa); *G.C.* 1907, i. 351, f. 148 (v. Rajah).

8. **B.-c. × Mariæ** (p. 45).

B.-c. × Warneri-Digbyana, *Gard.* 1904, ii. 216.—Charlesworth.

Læliocattleya × Eric Lucas, *Gard.* 1904, ii. 320.—Lucas.

10a. **B.-c. × Mary** (B. nodosa ♀ × C. Lawrenceana), *G.C.* 1907, ii. 37; *O.R.* 1907, 242; *J.H.* 1907, ii. 99, f. Colman, 1907.

13. **B.-c. × Orpheus** (p. 47).

B.-c. × Juliette Wallet, *J.S.H.Fr.* 1906, 758.—Maron.

13a. B.-c. × Peetersii (B. glauca ♀ × C. Lawrenceana), *O.R.* 1905, 119; *Dict. Ic. O.* B.-c. t. 1.—Peeters, 1905.

13b. **B.-c. × Pluto** (B. Digbyana × C. granulosa ♀), *G.C.* 1907, i. 31; *O.R.* 1907, 39, 49.—Holford, 1907.

14a. **B.-c. × Praetii** (B. Digbyana × C. Leopoldi).—Praet, 1904.

B.-c. × (unnamed), *Rev. H. Belge*, 1904, 240.—Praet.

14b. **B.-c. × Pyrrha** (B. glauca ♀ × C. labiata), *G.C.* 1906, i. 30; *O.R.* 1906, 51.—Veitch, 1906.

16a. **B.-c. × Seguinii** (B. fragrans ♀ × C. Mendelii), *J. S. H. Fr.* 1904, 761. —Lesueur, 1904.

19. **B.-c. × Veitchii** (p. 48)

B.-c. × Princess Victoria, *Gard.* 1904. ii. 283; *G. World*, 1904, 852. Charlesworth.

B.-c. × Queen Alexandra, *G.C.* 1905, ii. 190.—Charlesworth.

20. **B.-c. × Wellesleyæ** (B. Digbyana × C. Lueddemanniana ♀). Wellesley, 1906.

B.-c. × Mrs Francis Wellesley, *G.C.* 1906, i. 254, 422, suppl. t.; *O.R.* 1906, 135, 149; *G.M.* 1906, 269, f.—Wellesley.

6a. BRASSOEPIDENDRUM.

1. **B.-e. × stamfordiense** (Brassavola glauca × Epidendrum Parkinsonianum ♀), *O.R.* 1906, 342.—Pitt, 1906.

B.-e. × Stamfordianum, *G.C.* 1906, ii. 298.—Pitt.

7. BRASSOLÆLIA (p. 48).

1. **B.-l. × Bouletii** (p. 48).

Lælia × Eug. Boulet, *Dict. Ic. O.* Læl. hyb. t. 11.

2. **B.-l. × Clio** (p. 48).

B.-l. × Etoile de Marseilles, *J. S. H. Fr.* 1905, 106.—Gaud.

2a. **B.-l. × fladosa** (Brassavola nodosa ♀ × Lælia flava), *G.C.* 1906, ii. 169; *O.R.* 1906, 277, 286, 287; 1907, 306.—Colman, 1906.

2b. **B.-l. × Gipsy** (B.-l. × Helen × L. × cinnabrosa), *G.C.* 1907, i. 290; *O.R.* 1907, 151; *G.M.* 1907, 331, f.—Holford, 1907.

4a. **B.-l. × Jessopi** (Brassavola Digbyana × L. xanthina ♀), *O.R.* 1907, 191.—Jessop, 1907.

4b. B.-l. × Lellieuxii (B. Digbyana × L. anceps ♀), *J. S. H. Fr.* 1906, 30; *O.R.* 1906, 60.—Denis, 1905.

B.-l. × (unnamed), *O.R.* 1906, 28.—Denis.

The specific name was inadvertently misspelt on p. 239.

4c. **B.-l. × Louis-Bel** (B. Digbyana × L. Boothiana ♀), *O.R.* 1907, 39.—Denis, 1907.

5a. **B.-l. × Thwaitesii** (B. Digbyana × L. grandiflora), *G.C.* 1907, ii. 116; *O.R.* 1907, 264, 275.—Thwaites, 1907.

6. **B.-l. × Veitchii** (p. 49).

B.-l. × Edward VII., *Orchis*, i. 37, t. 5.

B.-l. × Digbyana-purpurata, *J.H.* 1907, ii. 27, f. (v. King Edward).

7. **B.-l. × westfieldiensis** (B. glauca × L. flava), *G.C.* 1907, i. 61, 62; *O.R.* 1907, 52.—Wellesley, 1907.

8. CALANTHE (p. 49).

5. **C. × bella** (p. 49).

C. × Phœbe, *G.C.* 1905, i. 60; *O.R.* 1905, 52.—Cookson.

5a. **C. × Chapmanii** (× Ruby × Veitchii), *G.C.* 1905, i. 61; *O.R.* 1905, 52; *G.M.* 1905, 87, f.—Cookson.

6. **C. × Darblayana** (p. 50).

C. × Bryan, *Gard.* 1906, i. 172, f.

9. CATTLEYA (p. 51).

1a. **C. × Adolphinæ** (amethystoglossa × Gaskelliana), *Rev. H. Belge*, 1906, 21; *Dict. Ic. O.* Cat. hyb. t. 36.—Peeters, 1903.

2a. **C. × Adrienne** (maxima × Warscewiczii).—Wavrin, 1906.

C. × Adrienne de Wavrin, *G.C.* 1906, ii. Nov. 10, Suppl. 4; *O.R.* 1906, 364.—Wavrin.

2b. **C. × Adula** (bicolor × Hardyana), *G.C.* 1905, ii. 254; *O.R.* 1905, 308.—Charlesworth.

3a. **C. × Alfredi** (granulosa × Trianæ).—Fowler, 1904.

C. × Alfred Fowler, *G.C.* 1904, i. 302; *O.R.* 1904, 171.—Fowler.

3b. **C. × Aliciæ** (× Iris × labiata).—Goodson, 1907.

C. × Aliciæ, *G.C.* 1907, ii. 318; *O.R.* 1907, 363.—Goodson.

3c. **C. × amabilis** (labiata × Warscewiczii), *G.C.* 1904, ii. 293; *O.R.* 1904, 339.—Sander, 1904.

4a. **C. × Appletoni** (Dowiana × elongata ♀), *O.R.* 1905, 350.—Appleton, 1905.

C. × (unnamed), *J. S. H. Fr.* 1905, 477.—Maron.

C. × Appletonæ, *G.C.* 1906, ii. 234; *O.R.* 1906, 310.—Appleton.

6a. **C. × Armstrongiæ** (× Hardyana × Loddigesii), *G.C.* 1907, ii. 190; *O.R.* 1907, 307.—Armstrong & Brown, 1907.

C. × Castræana, *G.C.* 1907, ii. 221; *O.R.* 1907, 309.—Sander.

12. **C. × Aurora** (p. 52); *O.R.* 1905, 350.—Appleton.

16a. **C. × bellatula** (Iris × Warscewiczii), *G.C.* 1906, ii. 265; *O.R.* 1906, 340.—Sander, 1906.

17a. **C. × Bertii** (Harrisoniana × labiata).—Bert, 1904.

C. × (unnamed) *J. S. H. Fr.* 1904, 595.—Bert.

21. **C. × Browniæ** (p. 53): *O.R.* 1906, 345, f. 45.

23a. **C. × Caduceus** (Gaskelliana × granulosa), *G.C.* 1905, ii. 115; *O.R.* 1905, 275.—Charlesworth.

C. × Thalia, *Rev. H. Belge*, 1906, 219.—Hye.

25a. **C. × Carmen** (Lueddemanniana × Warscewiczii), *G.C.* 1905, ii. 74; *O.R.* 1905, 247.—Veitch.

25b. **C. × Casca** (Gaskelliana × velutina), *G.C.* 1904, ii. 230; *O.R.* 1904, 309.—Veitch.

31. **C. × Chloris** (p. 53).

C. × schonbrunnensis, *G.C.* 1907, ii. 170; *O.R.* 1907, 318.—Emperor of Austria.

36. **C. × Claudian** (p. 54).

C. × Nestor, *O.R.* 1905, 245.—Charlesworth.

37a. **C. × Cleopatra** (Dowiana × superba), *G.C.* 1906, ii. 357; *O.R.* 1907, 349.—Charlesworth, 1906.

C. × Leda, *G.C.* 1906, ii. 234, Nov. 10, Suppl. 4; *O.R.* 1906, 311, 363, 374.—Charlesworth.

38. **C. × Clymene** (p. 54).

C. × Ethel, *G.C.* 1905, ii. 254; *O.R.* 1905, 308.—Marriott.

C. × Capartiana, *G.C.* 1906, ii. 234; *O.R.* 1906, 312.—Schuster.

40a. **C. × Cooksoni** (× Hardyana × Trianæ).—Cookson, 1906.

C. × Chapmanii, *G.C.* 1906, i. 30; *O.R.* 1906, 51.—Cookson.

42a. **C. × Cypheri** (× Hardyana × Harrisoniana).—Cypher, 1907.

C. × (unnamed), *O.R.* 1907, 366.—Cypher.

44. **C. × Daphne** (p. 54).

C. × Pittiæ, *G.C.* 1905, i. 333; *O.R.* 1905, 171; *G.M.* 1905, 515, 517, f.—Pitt.

C. × Lucieniana, *O.R.* 1906, 251, 344; *Rep. R. H. S. Genet. Conf.* 226, 239.

It is now suspected that C. × Daphne may have the same parentage as the earlier C. × Lucieniana, *Rchb. f.* (p. 61), but the materials which would clear the matter up are wanting.

44a. **C. × Davisii** (× Hardyana × velutina), *G.C.* 1906, ii. 224; 1907, ii. 190; *O.R.* 1907, 307, 342.—(Sander) Fowler, 1906.

47a. **C. × Dupreana** (Warneri × Warscewiczii), *Chron. O.* ii. 75.—Lambeau, 1906.

52a. **C. × Ethelreda** (Dowiana × O'Brieniana), *G.C.* 1907, ii. 190; *O.R.* 1907, 307.—Sander, 1907.

53. **C. × Eurydice** (p. 55).

C. × Vincius, *J. S. H. Fr.* 1904, 23.—Doin.

53a. **C. × Evadne** (Percivaliana × Schilleriana).—Armstrong & Brown, 1907.

C. × (unnamed), *O.R.* 1907, 308.—Armstrong & Brown.

55. **C. × Fabia** (p. 55); *Dict. Ic. O.* Cat. hyb. t. 24a (v. Mary de Wavrin).

57. **C. × Faerie-Queene** (p. 55).

C. × Goodsonæ, *Gard.* 1904, i. 440.—Tracy.

57a. **C. × Fallieri** (Rex × Trianæ), *G.C.* 1906, ii. 234; *O.R.* 1906, 312.—Schuster, 1906.

57b. **C. × Farquharsoniana** (bicolor × Iris), *G.C.* 1906, ii. 201; *O.R.* 1906, 309, 316.—Colman, 1906.

61. **C. × Firebrand** (p. 61).

C. × Herodia, *J. S. H. Fr.* 1905, 105.—Maron.

62. **C. × Firefly** (p. 55).

C. × Gem, *O.R.* 1906, 29.—Chamberlain.

67. **C. × fulvescens** (p. 56); *G.M.* 1907, 802, **f.** (Westonbirt var.); *J. H.* 1907, ii. 505, **f.** (id.).

80. **C. × Harrisiæ** (p. 58).

C. × Petrone, *J. S. H. Fr.* 1904, 27.—Doin.

C. × Miss Harris, *J.H.* 1907, ii. 243, **f.**

81a. **C. × Heathii** (Harrisoniana × Walkeriana).—Heath, 1907.

C. × (unnamed), *G.C.* 1907, i. 30; *O R.* 1907, 51.—Heath.

82a. **C. × Hester** (Harrisoniana ♀ × maxima), *O.R.* 1904, 92.—(Charlesworth) Craven, 1904.

83. **C. × highburiensis** (p. 59).

C. × Lord Nelson, *G.C.* 1905, ii. 316; *O.R.* 1905, 339.—Fowler.

83a. **C. × Hopkinsii** (Bowringiana × granulosa).—Wellesley, 1906.

C. × Mrs. Frederick Knollys, *G.C.* 1906, ii. 265; *O.R.* 1906, 339, 340; 1907, 308.—Wellesley.

84a. **C. × Hyeæ** (Gaskelliana × Mossiæ ♀).—Hye, 1906.

C. × Suzanne Hye de Crom, *Rev. H. Belge*, 1906, 72.—Hye.

A beautiful albino, raised from albino forms of the two parents.

85. **C. × Imperator** (p. 59).

C. × Madame Galpin, *J. S. H. Fr.* 1906, 672—Lesueur.

90. **C. × Iris** (p. 59); *G.M.* 1907, 653, **f.** (v. His Majesty); *Gard.* 1907, ii. 481, **f.** (id.).

C. × La France, *Rev. H. Belge*, 1905, 271.—Beranek.

97a. **C. × Knollysiæ** (× Hardyana × Mossiæ).—Wellesley, 1906.

C. × (unnamed), *G.C.* 1906, i. 191.—Wellesley.

C. × Mrs. Frederick Knollys, *O.R.* 1906, 110.—Wellesley.

97b. **C. × Lambeaui** (Dormaniana × labiata).—Lambeau, 1906.

Læliocattleya × (unnamed), *Rev. H. Belge*, 1906, 23.—Lambeau.

98a. **C. × Lawreglossa** (amethystoglossa ♀ × Lawrenceana), *O.R.* 1905, 119; 1907, 102.—Chamberlain.

99a. **C. × Law-Schofieldii** (labiata × Rothschildiana).—Sander, 1904.

C. × G. W. Law-Schofield, *G.C.* 1904, ii. 324; *O.R.* 1904, 364.—Sander.

101a. **C. × Lesueuri** (labiata × velutina ♀).—Lesueur, 1906.

C. × velutino-labiata, *J. S. H. Fr.* 1906, 672.—Lesueur.

104a. C. × Loubetii (Dowiana × flavescens).—Maron, 1905.

C. × President Loubet, *Rev. H. Belge*, 1905, 271; *J. S. H. Fr.* 1906, 35, 160.—Maron.

104b. **C. × lucida** (Bowringiana × Schilleriana), *Dict. Ic. O.* Cat. hyb. t 37.—Peeters, 1903.

C. × Bowringiano-Schilleriana, *G.C.* 1905, ii. 269; *O. R.* 1905, 343.—Lambeau.

Læliocattleya × Saxa, *O.R.* 1906, 252.—Grogan.

C. × Saxa, *O.R.* 1906, 287.

107. **C. × Mackayi** p. 61).

C. × Dusseldorfii, *J. S. H. Fr.* 1904, 564: *G.C.* 1906, ii. 414 (v. Undine); *J.H.* 1907, i. 3. f. (id.): *O.R.* 1906. 19. –Maron.

107a. **C. × Madouxiæ** (Aclandiæ × Gaskelliana).—Mme. Madoux, 1905.

C. × (unnamed). *G.C.* 1905. ii. 269; *O.R.* 1905, 344: *Rev. H. Belge,* 1905, 239.—Madame Madoux, 1905.

112. **C. × Maronæ** (p. 62).

C. × Marguerite Maron. *J. S. H. Fr.* 1906, 753.—Maron.

116a. **C. × McMastersiæ** (Mendelii × Schilleriana), *G.C.* 1906, ii. 265; *O.R.* 1906, 339.—Colman. 1906.

116b. **C. × Meadii** (Bowringiana × Forbesii).—Mead, 1904.

C. × (unnamed). *O.R.* 1904. 72.—Mead.

118a. **C. × Milano** (Dowiana × Frasquita), *J. S. H. Fr.* 1907, 546.—Maron, 1907.

120a. **C. × Minnie** (granulosa × Lueddemanniana), *G.C.* 1907, ii. 116; *O.R.* 1907, 275.—Wellesley, 1907.

121. **C. × Minucia** (p. 64): *Gart. Welt.* 1906, 199, f.

126a. **C. × Peetersiæ** (Gaskelliana ♀ × Warneri).—Peeters, 1904.

C. × Mrs. Myra Peeters, *G.C.* 1904, June 4, suppl. 1; *O.R.* 1904, 181.—(Peeters) Sander.

C. × Madame Myra Peeters. *O.R.* 1904, 229.—Peeters.

A beautiful albino, raised from the albino forms of the parent species.

127a. **C. × Neptune** (labiata × Schilleriana), *G.C.* 1904, ii. 323; *O.R.* 1904. 364.—Sander, 1904.

128a. **C. × Nyeæ** (Gaskelliana ♀ × Gratrixiæ)—Nye, 1904.

C. × Mrs. Kate Nye. *G.C.* 1904. ii. 267.—Nye.

129a. **C. × oakwoodiensis** (Mendelii × Murrayi). *G.C.* 1904, i. 301: *O.R.* 1904, 170.—Cookson, 1904.

130. **C. × Octavia** (p. 64).

C. × Octave Doin, *J.H.* 1906. i. 201, f.: *G.M.* 1906, 724, 725, f (Herbert Goodson's var.).

131a. **C. × Olenus** (Aclandiæ × Harrisoniana).—Doin, 1904.

C. × (unnamed). *J. S. H. Fr.* 1904, 595.—Doin.

133a. **C. × Oviedo** (maxima × Schilleriana).—Mead, 1904.

C. × (unnamed), *O.R.* 1904. 72.—Mead.

140. **C. × Peetersii** (p. 65); *G.M.* 1905, 791. 792, f. (v. Mrs. Francis Wellesley).

142. **C. × Pittiæ** (p. 65).

C. × Kitty Measures, *Gard.* 1906, ii. 246.—*R. H. Measures.*

151a. **C. × Robertii** (Schilleriana × Schrœderæ).—Wavrin. 1906.

C. × Robert de Wavrin, *G.C.* 1906, ii. 298; *O.R.* 1906, 342.—Wavrin.

153a. **C. × Rosa** (amethystoglossa × Dowiana).—Charlesworth. 1904.

C. × Rosa Leemann. *G.C.* 1904, ii. 293; *O.R.* 1904, 339.—Charlesworth.

156. **C. × rubescens** (p. 67).

C. × Ariadne, *G.C.* 1906, ii. 234; *O.R.* 1906, 311.—Low.

158a. **C. × Sapho** (Dowiana ♀ × Loddigesii), *Rev. H. Belge*, 1904, 23; *Dict. Ic. O.* Cat. hyb. **t.** 31.—Peeters, 1903.

160a. **C. × Shakersii** (Aclandiæ × citrina ♀), *J. S. H. Fr.* 1904, 210.—Fanyau, 1904.

162a. **C. × suavis** (Schrœderæ × Skinneri), *G.C.* 1904, i. 302; *O.R.* 1904, 172.—Sander, 1904.

163a. **C. × Susannæ** (Skinneri × Warneri), *J.H.* 1905, i. 252.—Orpet, 1905.

Fig. 95. CATTLEYA × TRIUMPHANS.

165. **C. × Thayeriana** (p. 68, fig. 11).

C. × nivea. *J. S. H. Fr.* 1907, 423.—Lambeau.

166a. **C. × Thurgoodiana** (× Hardyana × Lueddemanniana), *G.C.* 1904, ii. 82; *O.R.* 1904, 246.—Pitt, 1904.

167a. **C. × triumphans** (Dowiana × Rex), *G.C.* 1904, ii. 43; *O.R.* 1904, 244; 1905, 264, 305, **f.** 66 (Maron's var.); *J. S. H. Fr.* 1905, 575, 576, fig. 38 (id.); *Dict. Ic. O.* Cat. hyb. **t.** 33 (v. Ch. Maron).—Sander, 1904. **See Fig. 95.**

167b. **C.** × **Unique** (Mendelii × Schrœderæ), *G.C.* 1906, i. 286; *O.R.* 1906, 170.—Ingram, 1906.

170a. **C.** × **Vulcan** (Gaskelliana × intermedia), *G.C.* 1905, ii. 118; *O.R.* 1905, 280.—Vincke-Dujardin.

170b. **C.** × **Waldemar** (Dowiana × Whitei), *G.C.* 1907, ii. 77; *O.R.* 1907 245.—Holford, 1907.

170c. **C.** × **Wavriniæ** (Loddigesii ♀ × Rex).—Wavrin, 1905.

C. × Marie Henriette de Wavrin, *G.C.* 1905, ii. 316.—Wavrin.

C. × Mdlle. Marie Henriette de Wavrin, *Rev. H. Belge*, 1905, 272; *Dict. Ic O.* Cat. hyb. **t.** 34.—Wavrin.

172. **C.** × **weedoniensis** (p. 69); *Gart. Welt.* x. 199, **f.**

176. **C.** × **Whiteleyæ** (p. 69).

Fig. 96. CŒLOGYNE × COLMANII.

C. × J. W. Whiteley, *J.H.* 1906, ii. 451, **f.** (Rosslyn var.).

177a. **C.** × **Wildemanii** (Trianæ × velutina), *G.C.* 1906, ii. 298; *O.R.* 1906, 342.—Wavrin, 1906.

178a. **C.** × **Wincqxiana** (velutina × Warscewiczii), *Dict. Ic. O* Cat. hyb. **t.** 35 (29 in text, by error); *Chron. O.* ii. 72—Peeters 1906.

10a. CŒLOGYNE.

1. **C.** × **Brymeriana** (asperata × Dayana), *G.C.* 1906, i. 317; *O.R.* 1906, 173.—Brymer, 1906.

2. **C.** × **Colmanii** (cristata × speciosa), *G.C.* 1907, i. 108, 109, **f.** 48; *O.R.* 1907, 73, **f.** 8; 82, 90 (v. magdeburgensis).—Colman, 1907. **[See Fig. 96.**

11. CYMBIDIUM (p. 70).

2a. **C. × Colmaniæ** (eburneum × Veitchii), *G.C.* 1906, i. 286; *O.R.* 1906, 170; *G.M.* 1907, 212, f. (Edenside var.).—Colman, 1906.

2b. **C. × Cravenianum** (Lowianum × Tracyanum), *G.C.* 1906, ii. 413; *O.R* 1907, 20.—J. W. Moore, 1906.

2c. **C. × heatonense** (eburneum × giganteum).—Charlesworth, 1906.

C. × eburneo-giganteum, *G.C.* 1906, i. 110; *O.R.* 1906, 85.—Charlesworth.

2d. **C. × Holfordianum** (eburneum × grandiflorum ♀), *G.C.* 1906, i. 110; *O.R.* 1906, 85; 1907, 83; *G.M.* 1906, 130, f.—Sander, 1906.

8. **C. × Winnianum** (p. 72).

C. × Steppeanum, *Rev. H. Belge*, 1906, 278; *Chron. O.* ii. 74.—De Ceuninck.

9. **C. × Woodhamsianum** (Lowianum × Veitchii), *G.C.* 1907, i. 116; *O.R.* 1907, 116.—Armstrong & Brown, 1907.

C. × (unnamed), *O.R.* 1907, 252.—Colman.

10. **C. × woodlandense** (Mastersii × Tracyanum), *G.C.* 1904, ii. 293; *O.R.* 1904, 339.—Sander, 1904.

13. DENDROBIUM (p. 73).

7a. **D. × Ashworthii** (Brymerianum × pulchellum).—E. Ashworth, 1906.

D. × Arthur Ashworth, *G.C.* 1906, ii. 234; *O.R.* 1906, 215, 310.—E. Ashworth.

12a. **D. × Blackianum** (Findlayanum × Wiganiæ), *G.C.* 1904, i. 173; *O.R.* 1904, 104, 114; 1905, 100.—Thwaites, 1904.

12b. **D. × Boundii** (Findlayanum × Hildebrandii), *O.R.* 1907, 104.—Colman, 1907.

12c. **D. × Brodiei** (× Dominyanum × Wiganiæ), *G.C.* 1906, i. 110; *O.R.* 1906, 80, 83.—Colman, 1906.

16a. **D. × chessingtonense** (aureum × Wiganiæ), *G.C.* 1905, i. 141; *O.R.* 1905, 78, 101.—Thwaites, 1905.

18a. **D. × Cooksoni** (nobile × Wiganiæ).—Cookson, 1904.

D. × nobile-Wiganiæ, *G.C.* 1904, i. 174; *O.R.* 1904, 115; 1907, 104.—Cookson.

27. **D. × Ellisii** (p. 77).

D. × Wiganianum, *G.C.* 1906, i. 219, f. 85 (Gatton Park var.).

32a. **D × gattonense** (Curtisii × Findlayanum).—Colman, 1907.

D. × (unnamed), *O.R.* 1907, 104.—Colman.

47a. **D. × Macjap** (Maccarthiæ × moniliforme), *G.C.* 1904, i. 174; *O.R.* 1904, 115.—Cookson, 1904.

50. **D. × melanodiscus** (p. 79).

D. × Haywoodiæ, *G.C.* 1905, i. 205; *O.R.* 1905, 117.—Mrs. Haywood.

D. × Luna, *Amer. G.C.* 1906, 106, f.

56a. **D. × Myra** (Linawianum × signatum), *G.C.* 1904, i. 205: *O.R.* 1904, 111, 118.—Lawrence, 1904.

56b. **D. × Nancy** (aureum × Curtisii), *G.C.* 1904, i. 205; *O.R.* 1904, 117, 120 —Bilney, 1904.

61a. **D. × Rallianum** (× Ainsworthii × Hildebrandii), *O.R.* 1905, 158.—Ralli, 1904.

68a. **D × Snowflake** (× Cassiope × nobile), *G.C.* 1904, i. 76; *O.R.* 1904, 51, 55.—Colman, 1904.

71a. **D. × streathamense** (× Ellisii × nobile).—Thwaites, 1907.

D. × (unnamed), *O.R.* 1907, 101.—Thwaites.

72. **D. × Thompsonianum** (p. 82).

D. × Mary McCartney, *J.H.* 1907, i. 340.—Holmes.

81. **D. × Wiganiæ** (p. 83) ; *O.R*, 1907, 100, 101.

13a. DIALÆLIA.

A genus established to contain the hybrids between Diacrium and Lælia.

Dialælia × Veitchii (Diacrium bicornutum × Lælia cinnabarina), *G.C.* 1905. i. 174; *O.R.* 1905, 115.—Veitch, 1905.

16. EPICATTLEYA (p. 85).

0a. **Epicattleya × balarucensis** (Cattleya labiata ♀ × Epidendrum eburneum), *O.R.* 1907, 90. – Denis, 1907.

0b. **E.-c. × decipiens** (C. Warscewiczii × E. ciliare), *J. S. H. Fr.* 1905, 803, —Gaud, 1905.

0c. **E.-c. × Figaro** (C. intermedia × E. falcatum), *G C.* 1906, ii. 234 ; *O.R.* 1906, 310.—Wellesley, 1906.

0d. **E.-c. × Lawrencei** (C. Gaskelliana ♀ × Epidendrum Parkinsonianum). — Lawrence, 1905.

E.-c. × Gaskello-Parkinsoni, *G.C.* 1905, i. 74 ; *O.R.* 1905, 115.—Lawrence.

0e. **E.-c. × Lesueuri** (C. Skinneri × E. nocturnum).—Lesueur, 1907.

E.-c. × (unnamed), *J.S.H.Fr.* 1907, 343.—Lesueur.

1a. **E.-c. × magdeburgensis** (C. Gaskelliana ♀ × E. vitellinum), *O.R.* 1905, 375 ; *Gart. Welt.* x. 200, f.—Wolter, 1905.

7. **E.-c. × Wolteri** (C. Loddigesii × E. vitellinum).—Wolter, 1906.

E.-c. × (unnamed), *O.R.* 1906, 318.—Wolter.

17. EPIDENDRUM (p. 86).

7a. **Epidendrum × Cleon** (pseudepidendrum × radicans), *O.R.* 1906, 149. —Schröder, 1906.

9. **E. × dellense** (p. 86).

E. × radico-xanthinum, *G.C.* 1905, i. 237 ("radico-xanthina") ; *O.R.* 1905, 146. —Lawrence.

12a. **E. × gattonense** (× Boundii × xanthinum).—Colman, 1907.

E. × (unnamed), *O.R.* 1907, 251.—Colman.

14. E. × **kewense** (p. 86) : *O.R.* 1907, 58, 122, 123.

17a. EPIDIACRIUM.

A genus established to contain the hybrids between Diacrium and Epidendrum.

1. E.-d. × **Boundii** (Diacrium bicornutum × Epidendrum Ellisii).—Colman, 1907.

E.-d. × (unnamed), *G.C.* 1907, i. 272; *O.R.* 1907, 150.—Colman.

2. E.-d. × **gattonense** (D. bicornutum × E. radicans ♀).—Colman, 1905.

E.-d. × (unnamed), *G.C.* 1905, i. 301; *O.R.* 1905, 170; 1907, 251.—Colman.

18. EPILÆLIA (p. 87).

1a. E.-l. × **bradfordiensis** (Epidendrum prismatocarpum × Lælia tenebrosa).—Charlesworth, 1906.

E.-l. × (unnamed), *G.C.* 1906, i. 285; *O.R.* 1906, 170.—Charlesworth.

3a. E.-l. × **Eva** (E. aurantiacum × L. cinnabarina), *G.C.* 1907, i. 226; *O.R.* 1907, 147.—Veitch, 1907.

3b. E.-l. × **Fletcheriana** (E. atropurpureum × L. harpophylla), *G.C.* 1905, i. 60; *O.R.* 1905, 53.—Sander, 1905.

5a. E.-l. × **Laucheana** (E. atropurpureum × L. purpurata), *G.C.* 1906, i. 285; *O.R.* 1906, 170.—Charlesworth, 1906.

6. E.-l. × **Lawrencei** (p. 87).

E.-l. × vitell-brosa, *G.C.* 1905, i. 398; *O.R.* 1905, 210.—Lawrence.

6a. E.-l. × **longiciliare** (E. ciliare × L. longipes ♀), *G.C.* 1907, ii. 116; *O.R.* 1907, 275.—Colman, 1907.

8a. E.-l. × **Thalia** (E. atropurpureum × L. cinnabarina), *O.R.* 1905, 117.—Charlesworth, 1905.

20. LÆLIA (p. 88).

1a. L. × **Bertii** (grandiflora ♀ × tenebrosa).—Bert, 1906.

L. × majalis-tenebrosa, *J. S. H. Fr.* 1906, 616.—Bert.

L. × (unnamed), *Chron. O.* ii. 76.—Bert.

2a. L. × **canariensis** (anceps × harpophylla), *G.C.* 1906, i. 109: *O.R.* 1906, 84.—Ingram, 1906.

5a. L. × **Daphne** (Jongheana × tenebrosa), *O.R.* 1906, 253.—Holford, 1906.

L. × (unnamed), *G.C.* 1906, ii. 97; *O.R.* 1906, 247.—Holford.

5b. L. × **Degeestiana** (flava × Jongheana ♀), *Rev. H. Belge*, 1904, 191; *G.C.* 1904, ii. 122; 1905, ii. 348; *O.R.* 1905, 364; *Dict. Ic. O.* Læl. hyb. t. 12.—Wavrin.

L. × La Perle (flava ♀), *J.S.H.Fr.* 1905, 168, 229.—Maron.

L. × Mary Colman, *O.R.* 1906, 80.—Colman.

5c. L. × **Dellacii** (× juvenilis × tenebrosa)—Marcoz.

L. × Docteur Marcel Dellac, *J. S. H. Fr.*, 1907, 405.—Marcoz.

13a. L. × **Gwennie** (Cowanii × Jongheana ♀), *G.C.* 1904, i. 142; *O.R.* 1904, 271.—Thwaites, 1904.

The first record erroneously gives L. Perrinii as the pollen parent.

16a. **L.** × **Ithone** (× Latona × purpurata).—Veitch, 1907.

L.-c. × Ithone, *O.R.* 1907, 152.—Veitch.

18a. **L.** × **Lawrencei** (grandiflora × purpurata).—Lawrence, 1907

L. × Purple May, *G.C.* 1907, ii. 116; *O.R.* 1907, 274.—Lawrence.

19a. **L.** × **Maroni** (acuminata ♀ × anceps).—Maron, 1904.

L. × acuminato-anceps, *J. S. H. Fr.* 1904, 24; *O.R.* 1904, 58.—Maron.

20. **L.** × **Minerva** (p. 91).

L. × Psyche, *G.C.* 1904, ii. 34.—Charlesworth.

22. **L.** × **Nemesis** (p. 91): *G.C.* 1906, i. 130, 131, **f.** 51 (Tring Park var.).

23a. **L.** × **Nora** (cinnabarina × xanthina), *O.R.* 1906, 252.—Clark, 1906.

30a. **L.** × **Sidneana** (cinnabarina × Jongheana), *G.C.* 1907, ii. 230; *O.R.* 1907, 315.—Tracy.

L. × (unnamed), *G.C.* 1907, i. 30; *O.R.* 1907, 50.—Potter.

32a. **L.** × **Statheræ** (flava × purpurata), *G.C.* 1907, i. 226; *O.R.* 1907, 147. —Stather Hunt, 1907.

21. LÆLIO-CATTLEYA (p. 93).

2a. **L.-c.** × **Adelina** (Cattleya Percivaliana × Lælia harpophylla), *G.C.* 1907, i. 195; *O.R.* 1907, 117.—Lucas, 1907.

3a. **L.-c.** × **Ægina** (C. × Hardyana × L. Perrinii), *G.C.* 1904, ii. 355. *O.R.* 1904, 367.—Veitch, 1904.

6a. **L.-c.** × **Alcyone** (C. Schilleriana × L. flava), *G.C.* 1904, ii. 293; 1905 ii. 254; *O.R.* 1904, 339; 1905, 309; 1906, 278.—Charlesworth, 1904.

6b. **L.-c.** × **Alexanderi** (C. granulosa × L.-c. × elegans), *O.R.* 1905, 317. —Sander, 1905.

L.-c. × (unnamed), *O.R.* 1905, 212.—Sander.

7a. **L.-c.** × **Alpha** (C. Schrœderæ × L.-c. × Ernesti).—Cookson, 1905.

L.-c. × Oakwood Alpha, *G.C.* 1905, i. 107; *O.R.* 1905, 75.—Cookson.

L.-c. × Oakwood Delta, *G.C.* 1905, i. 107; *O.R.* 1905, 75.—Cookson.

7b. **L.-c.** × **Amarylloso** (C. Harrisoniana × L. flava), *Rev. H. Belge*, 1905, 277.—Pauwels, 1905.

L.-c. × (unnamed), *G.C.* 1905, ii. 414.—Pauwels.

8. **L.-c.** × **Amazone** (p. 93).

L.-c. × Williamsoni, *Gard.* 1904, ii. 53.—Sander.

12a. **L.-c.** × **Andromeda** (C. Dowiana × L. flava ♀), *G.C.* 1904, i. 30; *O.R.* 1904, 50; 1905, 89; *Gard.* 1907, ii. 323, suppl. **pl.**—Charlesworth, 1904.

15. **L.-c.** × **Aphrodite** (p. 94).

Cattleya × Regnieri, *G.C.* 1905, i. 334.—Regnier.

15a. **L.-c.** × **Arethusa** (C. × Harrisoniana × L.-c. × exoniensis), *G.C.* 1907, ii. 153; *O.R.* 1907, 276.—Holford, 1907.

15b. **L.-c.** × **Ariel** (C. Dowiana × L. Cowanii), *G.C.* 1907, i. 61; *O.R.* 1907, 52, 62.—Holford, 1907.

17. **L.-c.** × **Astoriæ** (p. 95).

L.-c. × (unnamed), *Wein. Il* 265, **t.** 3.

19a. L.-c. × **Aureole** (C. × Iris × L.-c. × Truffautiana), *G.C.* 1907, ii. 285; *O.R.* 1907, 343.—Charlesworth, 1907.

22. L.-c. × **Ballii** (p. 95).

L.-c. × M. Seguin, *J. S. H. Fr.* 1905, 213.—Seguin.

22a. L.-c. × **Barbarossa** (C. Trianæ × L.-c. × callistoglossa), *G.C.* 1907, ii. 380; *O.R.* 1907, 373.—Holford, 1907.

22b. L.-c. × **Beauclerkiæ** (C. Trianæ × L.-c. × Ingramii).—Wellesley, 1906.

L.-c. × Mrs. de Vere Beauclerk, *G.C.* 1906, ii. 201: *O.R.*, 1906, 309: *J H.* 1906, ii. 291, f.—Wellesley, 1906.

27. L.-c. × **Bertha** (p. 96).

L.-c. × Rocksand, *O.R.* 1904, 158.—Miller.

27a. L.-c. × **Beta** (C. × Rothschildiana × L.-c. × callistoglossa).—Cookson, 1905.

L.-c. × Oakwood Beta, *G.C.* 1905, i. 107; *O.R.* 1905, 75.—Cookson.

The previous records inadvertently give "L.-c." instead of C. × Rothschildiana as the first parent.

28. L.-c. × **Bievreana** (p. 96).

L.-c. × De Bievreana, *Rev. H. Belge*, 1905, 48.—Praet.

30a. L.-c. × **Birkbeckii** (C. Mendelii × L.-c. × Greenwoodii).—Wigan, 1905.

L.-c. × J. F. Birkbeck, *O.R.* 1905, 178.—Wigan.

31. L.-c. × **bletchleyensis** (p. 96); *G.C.* 1904, i. 88, suppl. f. (v. Ruby King); *Gtfl.* 1906, 505, t. 1555.

31a. L.-c. × **Blountiæ** (C. Gaskelliana × L.-c. × Schilleriana).—Wellesley, 1907.

L.-c. × Mrs. Gilbert Blount, *G.C.* 1907, ii. 116; *O.R.* 1907, 275.—Wellesley.

33a. L.-c. × **Bradeæ** (C. Schrœderæ × L.-c. × Aphrodite).—Wellesley, 1905.

L.-c. × Mrs. Reginald Brade, *G.C.* 1905, ii. 16; *O.R.* 1905, 211.—Wellesley.

39. L.-c. × **Canhamiana** (p. 97).

L.-c. × Rex, *Flora & Sylva*, 1904, 264, t.

L.-c. × Mme. Réné Oberthür, *J. S. H. Fr.* 1905, 470.—Maron.

39a. L.-c. × **Capartii** (C. × Hardyana × L. purpurata).—Duchesne, Lanthoine & Co., 1906.

L.-c. × Dr. Capart, *Rev. H. Belge*, 1906, 95.—Duchesne, Lanthoine & Co.

L.-c. × George Woodhams, *G.C.* 1907, ii. 153; *O.R.* 1907, 278, 341.—Armstrong & Brown.

40. L.-c. × **Cappei** (p. 98); *J.H.* 1904, ii. 452, 453 f. (Charlesworth's var.).

41. L.-c. × **Cassiope** (p. 98).

L.-c. × Angela, *G.C.* 1904, ii. 355; *O.R.* 1904, 366.—Lucas.

44a. L.-c. × **chardwarensis** (C. dolosa × L. cinnabarina ♀), *G.C.* 1905, ii. 74; *O.R.* 1905, 247.—G. F. Moore, 1905.

45. L.-c. × **Charlesworthii** (p. 98).

L.-c. × Ibis Rose, *J. S. H. Fr.* 1904, 661, 662.—Lesueur.

45a. **L.-c. × chocophylla** (C. quadricolor (chocoensis) × L. harpophylla) *J. S. H. Fr.* 1905, 106.—Beranek, 1905.

47. **L.-c. × Cicero** (p. 98).

L.-c. × Gertrude, *Gard.* 1904, i. 297.—Clarke.

L.-c. × inter-elegans, *G.C.* 1904, i. 270; *O.R.* 1904, 140.—Mond.

57a. **L.-c. × Cordelia** (L. Dayana × L.-c. × bella), *G.C.* 1904, ii. 355; *O.R.* 1904, 366.—Lucas, 1904.

62a. **L.-c. × crispo-Hardyana** (C. × Hardyana × L. crispa ♀), *G.C.* 1905, ii. 254; *O.R.* 1905, 308, 317.—Holford, 1905.

65a. **L.-c. × Denisii** (C. Lueddemanniana × L. superbiens ♀), *O.R.* 1906, 135.—Denis, 1906.

70. **L.-c. × Deweyi** (p. 101).

L.-c. × Admiral Decocq, *Rev. H. Belge*, 1906, 219.—Hye.

71d. **L.-c. × Dicksoniæ** (C. Gaskelliana × L.-c. × Wellsiana).—Wellesley, 1906.

L.-c. × Mrs. W. J. Dickson, *G.C.* 1906, ii. 360; *O.R.* 1906, 366.—Wellesley,

72. **L.-c. × Dido** (p. 101).

L.-c. × Skinnerobarina, *J. S. H. Fr.* 1905, 106.—Beranek.

74a. **L.-c. × dolstene** (C. dolosa × L. tenebrosa).—Peeters, 1904.

L.-c. × (unnamed), *J. S. H. Fr.* 1904, 564.—Peeters.

77. **L.-c. × Doris** (p. 101).

L.-c. × (unnamed), *O.R.* 1907, 158, 159.—Clark.

77a. **L. c. × Duchess** (C. × Hardyana × L.-c. × Hippolyta ♀).—Sander, 1905.

L.-c. × The Duchess, *G.C.* 1905, ii. 382; *O.R.* 1905, 367; 1907, 342.—Sander.

77b. **L.-c. × Dumatii** (L. tenebrosa × L.-c. × elegans).—Marcoz, 1906.

L.-c. × Ingenieur Paul Dumat, *J. S. H. Fr.* 1906, 752.—Marcoz.

77c. **L.-c. × Duncanii** (C. × Hardyana × L.-c. × Gottoiana), *G.C.* 1905, ii. 316; *O.R.* 1905, 340.—Lucas, 1905.

L.-c. × Miss Mary Froude, *O.R.* 1906, 43.—Wellesley.

77d. **L.-c. × Duquesnei** (L. purpurata × L.-c. × warnhamensis), *O.R.* 1907. 92.—Cappe, 1907.

79a. **L.-c. × Elba** (C. Warscewiczii × L.-c. × Ingramii), *G.C.* 1907, ii. 77; *O.R.* 1907, 246.—Charlesworth, 1907.

83. **L.-c. × Emiliæ** (p. 102).

L.-c. × Aclandio-purpurata, *J. S. H. Fr.* 1904, 159.—Duval.

84. **L.-c. × epicasta** (p. 102); *G. Alb.* 1906, 15, f. (Gatton Park var.); *G.M.* 1907, 804, 824, f. (v. The Premier).

85. **L.-c. × Ernesti** (p. 102); *Dict. Ic. O.* L.-c. hyb. t. 32.

90. **L.-c. × Eva** (p. 102).

L.-c. × Endymion, *G.C.* 1905, ii. 254; *O.R.* 1905, 309.—Sander.

93. **L.-c. × Fascinator** (p. 103); *J.H.* 1904, ii. 5, f. (v. King Edward); *G.M.* 1907, 231, f. (v. splendens).

L.-c. × dourdanense, *J. S. H. Fr.* 1904, 107.—Doin.

95a. **L.-c.** × **Firmin** (C. Warneri × L.-c. × Hippolyta).—Lambeau, 1907.

L.-c. × Firmin Lambeau, *Rev. H. Belge*, 1906, 45 ; *Trib. H.* 1907, ii. 371, t. 48.

97. **L.-c.** × **Fournieræ** (p. 103) ; *Dict. Ic. O.* L.-c. hyb. t. 37 (v. obscure-purpurea).

L.-c. × Imperator, *G.C.* 1904, ii. 309 ; *O.R.* 1904, 330.—Peeters.

99a. **L.-c.** × **Gamma** (L. Jongheana × L.-c. × Ernesti).—Cookson, 1905.

L.-c. × Oakwood Gamma, *G.C.* 1905, i. 107 ; *O.R.* 1905, 75.—Cookson.

L.-c. × Millie, *O.R.* 1907, 311.—Keeling.

99b. **L.-c.** × **Ganymede** (C. Schrœderæ × L. × Latona), *G.C.* 1907, i. 290 ; *O.R.* 1907, 151.—Holford, 1907.

99c. **L.-c.** × **gattonensis** (C. Lawrenceana × L.-c. × Schilleriana).—Colman, 1907.

L.-c. × (unnamed), *O.R.* 1907, 251.—Colman.

101. **L.-c.** × **Gemma** (p. 104).

L.-c. × Schilleriano-xanthina, *J. S. H. Fr.* 1904, 159.—Duval.

101a. **L.-c.** × **Geoffrey** (C. Warscewiczii × L. longipes ♀), *G.C.* 1905, ii. 74 ; 1906, ii. 139 ; *O.R.* 1905, 247 ; 1906, 276.—Lucas, 1905.

101b.—**L.-c.** × **Georgina** (C. Dowiana × L.-c. × Leeana ♀), *J. S. H. Fr.* 1905, 659.—Maron, 1905.

102a. **L.-c.** × **Gilberta** (C. × Mantinii × L.-c. × Ingramii).—Wellesley, 1905.

L.-c. × Miss Gilberta Blount, *G.C.* 1905, ii. 348 ; *O.R.* 1905, 364, 373.—Wellesley

Later references (*G.C.* 1906, ii. 98 ; *O.R.* 1906, 247) give L.-c. × epicasta and C. Dowiana aurea as the parents, but it is difficult to say which is correct.

103a. **L.-c.** × **Glycera** (C. Trianæ × L. rupestris), *O.R.* 1904, 111.—Young, 1903.

L.-c. × (unnamed), *G.C.* 1904, i. 205 ; *O.R.* 1904, 118.—Hon. W. Rothschild.

103b. **L.-c.** × **Golden-Beauty** (× Ernesti × Greenwoodii), *G.C.* 1906, ii, Nov. 10, suppl. 4 ; *O.R.* 1906, 364.—Sander, 1906.

103c. **L.-c.** × **Golden-Belle** (C. Dowiana × L.-c. × Ernesti).—Holford. 1907.

L.-c. × Golden Beauty, *G.C.* 1907, ii. 347 ; *O.R.* 1907, 364.—Holford.

This should be compared with the preceding, as it is not quite clear whether the two are distinct.

103d. **L.-c.** × **Golden-Glory** (C. Mossiæ × L.-c. × Zephyra), *G.C.* 1906, i. 348, 349 ; 1907, i. 352, 353, 357, f. 152 ; *O.R.* 1906, 181 ; 1907, 174.—Sander, 1906.

103e. **L.-c.** × **Golden-Oriole** (C. Dowiana × L.-c. × Charlesworthii), *O.R.* 1907, 373.—Holford, 1907.

103f. **L.-c.** × **Goodsonæ** (C. Schrœderæ × L. Perrinii), *G.C.* 1905, ii. 381 *O.R.* 1905, 366.—Goodson, 1905.

103g. **L.-c.** × **Goodsoni** (C. Mendelii × L.-c. × Hippolyta), *G.C.* 1905, i. 332 ; *O.R.* 1905, 172.—Goodson, 1905.

103h. **L.-c. × Goodyi** (C. × Wendlandiana × L.-c. × Clive), *G.C.* 1906, ii. 265; *O.R.* 1906, 339.—Colman, 1906.

104a. **L.-c. × Gouldiæ** (C. × intertexta × L. tenebrosa).—Wellesley, 1905.

L.-c. × Mrs. Freke-Gould, *G.C.* 1905, ii. 34; *O.R.* 1905, 243.—Wellesley.

105. **L.-c. × Greenwoodii** (p. 104).

L.-c. × Géneral Voyron, *J. S. H. Fr.* 1904, 565.—(Maron) Peeters.

L.-c. × Mme. Karthaus, *J. S. H. Fr.* 1904, 565.—Maron.

108a. **L.-c. × harpo-aurea** (C. Dowiana × L. harpophylla), *G.C.* 1906, i. 110; *O.R.* 1906, 85.—Charlesworth, 1906.

107a. **L.-c. × Hardieri** (C. Warscewiczii × L. × juvenilis).—Cahuzac, 1906.

L.-c. × Réjane Hardier, *J. S. H. Fr.* 1906, 751.—Cahuzac.

110. **L.-c. × Helena** (p. 104); *G.M.* 1906, 514, **f.** (Westfield var.); *Gard. W.* 1906, 129, **f.**

114. **L.-c. × Hermione** (p. 105); *G.C.* 1905, ii. 275 (Westfield var.).

117a. **L.-c. × Hildegard** (C. Warscewiczii × L.-c. × Decia), *G.C.* 1907, ii. 318; *O.R.* 1907, 362.—Holford, 1907.

118. **L.-c. × Hippolyta** (p. 105).

L.-c. × Phœbe, *Gard.* 1906, ii. 17, **f.** (Gatton Park var.).

120a. **L.-c. × Hopkinsii** (L. tenebrosa × L.-c. × Pallas), *J.H.* 1906, i. 361, **f.**; *G.C.* 1906, i. 223; *O.R.* 1906, 146.—Wellesley.

127a. **L.-c. × illustris** (C. Dowiana × L. × Latona), *O.R.* 1904, 364; *Gard.* 1904, ii. 320; *G.C.* 1906, i. 190.—Charlesworth, 1904.

Lælia × illustris, *G.C.* 1904, ii. 324.—Charlesworth.

127b. **L.-c × ilsingtonensis** (C. × Brymeriana × L. xanthina).—Brymer, 1907.

L.-c. × Powellii, *G.C.* 1907, ii. 254; *O.R.* 1907, 341.—Brymer.

Re-named because of an earlier L.-c. × Powellii.

133. **L.-c. × Ivernia** (p. 107).

L.-c. × Prof. Fritz Röber, *G.C.* 1904, ii. 212; *O.R.* 1904, 311; *J. S. H. Fr.* 1904, 564.—Charlesworth.

133a. **L.-c. × Ixion** (C. Lueddemanniana × L.-c. × Myra).—Maron, 1905.

L.-c. × (unnamed), *J. S. H. Fr.* 1905, 477.—Maron.

133b. **L.-c. × Jason** (C. × Hardyana × L. × Latona), *O.R.* 1907, 316.—Jessop, 1906.

136a. **L.-c. × Kelpie** (C. Dowiana × L.-c. × Cranstounæ), *G.C.* 1906, ii. Nov. 10, Suppl. 4.—Wellesley, 1906.

136b. **L.-c. × Kitcheneri** (C. Schilleriana × L.-c. × elegans).—Sander, 1904.

L.-c. × Lord Kitchener, *O.R.* 1904, 181.—Sander.

L.-c. × Admiral Togo, *G.C.* 1904, ii. 156; *O.R.* 1904, 270.—Ingram.

137a. **L.-c. × Kronprinz** (C. × flavescens × L.-c. × Fournieri).—Maron, 1904.

L.-c. × Kronprinz Frederick Wilhelm, *G.C.* 1904, i. 296.—Maron.

L.-c. × Kronprinz Wilhelm, *J. S. H. Fr.* 1904, 465; 1906, 113.—Maron.

139a. **L.-c. × Lambeaui** (C. dolosa × L.-c. × elegans).—Lambeau, 1905.

L.-c. × (unnamed), *Rev. H. Belge*, 1905, 212.

139b. **L.-c. × Laura** (× elegans × Martinetii).—R. H. Measures, 1904.

L.-c. × Laura Gilbert, *Gard.* 1904, i. 425.—R. H. Measures.

139c. **L.-c. × Lawrie** (C. Lawrenceana × L.-c. × warnhamensis), *G.C.* 1907, i. 226; *O.R.* 1907, 146.—Lucas, 1907.

140a. **L.-c. × Leeseæ** (C. × Murrayi × L. tenebrosa).—Wellesley, 1907.

L.-c. × Miss Leese, *G.C.* 1907, i. 427; *O.R.* 1907, 213.—Wellesley.

142a. **L.-c. × Lesueuri** (C. Schrœderæ × L.-c. × Hippolyta).—Lesueur, 1907.

Cattleya × Fascinator, *J. S. H. Fr.* 1907, 338.—Lesueur.

146a. **L.-c. × Linnæus** (C. Warneri × L.-c. × Gottoiana).—Lord Rothschild, 1904.

L.-c. × Charles Linnæus, *G.C.* 1904, ii. 14; *O.R.* 1904, 213.—Lord Rothschild.

147a. **L.-c. × Lucasii** (C. Warscewiczii × L. × Iona), *G.C.* 1906, ii. 139; *O.R.* 1906, 276.—Lucas, 1906.

L.-c. × George Branch, *O.R.* 1906, 320.—Lucas.

148. **L.-c. × Lucasiana** (p. 108).

L.-c. × Fabia, *J. S. H. Fr.* 1906, 778.—Magne.

151a. **L-c. × Lusitania** (C. × Iris × L.-c. × Phryne), *G.C.* 1907, ii. 285; *O.R.* 1907, 343, 346.—Charlesworth, 1907.

151b. **L.-c. × Lustre** (C. Lueddemanniana × L.-c. × callistoglossa), *G.C.* 1907, ii. p. 254; *O.R.* 1907, 341.—Holford, 1907.

153. **L.-c. × Lycidas** (p. 108).

L.-c. × Isabelle, *J. S. H. Fr.* 1907, 429.—Maron. The parentage was inferred by the raiser.

153a. **L.-c × Lydia** (C. Gaskelliana × L. Cowanii ♀), *O.R.* 1904, 30.—Charlesworth, 1903.

154. **L.-c. × Mabel** (p. 109).

L.-c × Fanyauana, *J. S. H. Fr.* 1905, 229; *Rev. H. Belge*, 1905, 118.—Fanyau.

157. **L.-c. × Marguerite** (p. 109).

L.-c. × Mrs. Measures, *Gard.* 1905. i. 280.—R. H. Measures.

158. **L.-c. × Marica** (p. 109).

L.-c. × Proteus, *G.C.* 1905, i. 6.—Veitch.

158a. **L.-c. × Marnhami** (× Aphrodite × callistoglossa), *G.C.* 1906, i. 158; *O.R.* 1906, 108.—Wellesley, 1906.

161a. **L.-c. × Martiniæ** (L. grandis ♀ × L.-c. × Ascania).—Maron, 1905.

L.-c. × Madame Bienvenu Martin, *J. S. H. Fr.* 1905, 324.—Maron.

161. **L.-c. × Martinetii** (p. 109).

L.-c. × Pommerie, *J. S. H. Fr.* 1905, 375.—Beranek.

163. **L.-c. × massiliensis** (p. 109).

C. × massiliensis, *Dict. Ic. O.* Cat. hyb. t. 21.

164a. **L.-c. × Mazharata** (L. × Latona × L.-c. × Gottoiana), *J. S. H. Fr.* 1907, 405.—Beranek, 1907.

164b. **L.-c. × Measuresiæ** (L. xanthina × L.-c. × elegans).—Sander, 1906.

L.-c. × Mrs. Robert Measures, *G.C.* 1906, ii. 169; *O.R.* 1906, 278.—Sander.

165. **L.-c. × Measuresii** (p. 110).

L.-c. × bellula, *G.C.* 1906, ii. 234; *O.R.* 1906, 312.—Schuster, 1906.

165a. **L.-c. × Melina** (L.-c. × Ernesti × L.-c. Lucasiana), *J. S. H. Fr.* 1907, 191, 212.—Maron, 1907.

165b. **L.-c. × Memnon** (C. × Mendelii × L.-c. × elegans).—*G.C.* 1907, ii. 318; *O.R.* 1907, 362.—Holford, 1907.

166. **L. c. × Mercia** (p. 110).

L.-c. × Mona, *G.C.* 1904, i. 238; *O.R.* 1904, 139.—Veitch.

166a. **L.-c. × Merciana** (C. amethystoglossa × L. flava), *G.C.* 1905, i. 318; *O.R.* 1905, 174.—Lambeau, 1905.

169a. **L.-c. × Milo** (C. Mossiæ × L.-c. × Hyeana).—Beranek, 1907.

L.-c. × (unnamed), *J. S. H. Fr.* 1907, 337; *Rev. H. Belge*, 1907, 254.—Beranek.

170a. **L.-c. × Mitchelliæ** (C. Warscewiczii × L.-c. × Martinetii).—Wellesley, 1906.

L.-c. × Mrs. R. A. H. Mitchell, *G.C.* 1906, i. 158; 1907, i. 195; *O.R.* 1906, 108; 1907, 117.—Wellesley.

172a. **L.-c. × Mount-Ophir** (C. flavescens × L.-c. × Ernesti), *J. S. H. Fr.* 1906, 113.—Maron, 1906.

174. **L.-c. × Myra** (p. 110); *G.M.* 1904, 330; f. (v. pallida).

183a. **L.-c. × Olivia** (C. Schrœderæ × L. Jongheana), *G.C.* 1907, i. 195; *O.R.* 1907, 116.—Holford, 1907.

184a. **L.-c. × Oracle** (L. pumila × L.-c. × Schilleriana), *O.R.* 1904, 247.—Sander, 1904.

184b. **L-c. × Orestes** (C. intermedia × L.-c. × warnhamensis ♀), *O.R.* 1904, 271.—Cappe, 1904.

184c. **L.c. × Oriens** (C. Trianæ × L. Cowanii), *G.C.* 1906, i. 110; *O.R.* 1906, 80.—Thwaites, 1906.

L.-c. × Paradise (C. Mendelii × L. flava).—Sander, 1904.

L.-c. × Bird of Paradise, *G.C.* 1904, i. 269; *O.R.* 1904, 141.—Sander.

187a. **L.-c. × Peetersii** (C. Lawrenceana × L.-c. × callistoglossa).—Peeters, 1907.

L.-c. × (unnamed), *Rev. H. Belge*, 1907, 211.—Peeters.

188. **L.-c. × Percibarina** (p. 111).

L.-c. × Adelina, *G.C.* 1907, i. 195; *O.R.* 1907, 117.—Lucas.

188a. **L.-c. × Perrigottoi** (L. Perrinii × L.-c. × Gottoiana).—R. I. Measures, 1905.

L.-c. × (unnamed), *O.R.* 1905, 357.—R. I. Measures.

188b. **L.-c.** × **Perrilosa** (C. granulosa × L. Perrinii), *G.C.* 1906, ii. 265; *O.R.* 1906, 338, 350, 375.—R. I. Measures, 1905.

L.-c. × (unnamed), *O.R.* 1905, 357.—R. I. Measures.

188c. **L.-c.** × **Perseus** (C. × Minerva × L.-c. × Clive), *O.R.* 1905, 23; 1906, 29.—Chamberlain, 1904.

191. **L.-c.** × **Phryne** (p. 111); *O.R.* 1906, 339 (Gatton Park var.); 1907, 8, f. 2. **[See Fig. 97.**

Fig. 97. LÆLIOCATTLEYA × PHRYNE.

L.-c. × Mademoiselle Hilde Beyrodt, *J. S. H. Fr.* 1904, 565.—Maron.

196a. **L.-c.** × **Priam** (C. Harrisoniana × L.-c. × callistoglossa), *G.C.* 1907, ii. 347; *O.R.* 1907, 364.—Holford, 1907.

199a. **L.-c** × **Pujeti** (C. Trianæ ♀ × L. superbiens), *J. S. H. Fr.* 1904, 105. —Maron, 1904.

199b. **L.-c.** × **Purple-Emperor** (C. Warscewiczii × L.-c. × callistoglossa), *G.C.* 1904, ii. 82; 1905, ii. 218; *O.R.* 1904, 248; 1905, 307.—Sander, 1904.

L.-c. × (unnamed), *Rev. H. Belge*, 1907, 211.—Peeters.

L.-c. × Caligula, *G.C.* 1907, ii. 77; *O.R.* 1907, 245.—Holford.

206a. L.-c. × **rouselensis** (C. Forbesii ♀ × L. cinnabarina), *G.C.* 1904. ii. 433; *O.R.* 1905, 21.—Wavrin, 1904.

L.-c. × (unnamed), *Rev. H. Belge*, 1905, 23.—Wavrin.

210. L.-c. × **Ruby** (p. 113).

L.-c. × Beyrodtiana, *J. S. H. Fr.* 1905, 213.—Maron.

Fig. 98. LÆLIO-CATTLEYA × STATTERIANA.

211a. L.-c. × **Salus** (C. superba × L. crispa ♀), *O.R.* 1905, 286.—R. Young, 1905.

213a. L.-c. × **Schiffmanii** (C. Mendelii × L.-c. × callistoglossa).—Sander, 1904.

L.-c. × Dr. R. Schiffman, *G.C.* 1904, i. 76; *O.R.* 1904, 53.—Sander.

214a. L.-c. × **Schneideri** (C. Dowiana × L.-c. × Amelia ♀), *J. S. H. Fr.* 1904, 762; 1905, 699; *O.R.* 1905, 23, 368; *G.C.* 1905, ii. 382.—Cappe, 1904.

215. L.-c. × **Schrœderæ** (p. 113).

L.-c. × Baroness Schröder, *G.M.* 1907, 239, f. (Westonbirt var.).

216. **L.-c. × Schulzeana** (p. 113).

L.-c. × Fraulein Lotte Abeken, *Dict. Ic. O.* L.-c. hyb. t. 38.

222a. **L.-c. × Sheila** (C. Percivaliana × L. pumila), *G.C.* 1907, i. 161; *O.R.* 1907, 115.—Charlesworth, 1907.

222b. **L.-c. × Sirius** (C. Mossiæ × L.-c. × highburiensis).—Lambeau, 1905.

L.-c. × (unnamed), *Rev. H. Belge*, 1905, 190.—Lambeau, 1905.

222c. **L.-c. × Soulageana** (C. Eldorado × L. Perrinii), *J. S. H. Fr.* 1905, 797.—Ginot, 1905.

223. **L.-c. × Speranskyæ** (p. 114).

L.-c. × Hurstii, *O. R.* 1906, 221.—E. F. Clark.

224. **L.-c. × Statteriana** (p. 114); *O.R.* 1906, 361, f. 46 (v. oculata).

[See Fig. 98.

225a. **L.-c. × stellata** (C. intermedia × L. xanthina), *G.C.* 1907, i. 259; *O.R.* 1907, 149.—Wellesley, 1907.

227a. **L.-c. × Sunset** (C. Percivaliana × L. Jongheana), *G.C.* 1906, ii. 201; *O.R.* 1906, 308.—Holford, 1906.

227b. **L.-c. × Templeana** (C. Lueddemanniana × L.-c. × elegans), *O.R.* 1907, 150.—Lawrence, 1907.

227c. **L.-c. × tene-Gottoi** (L. tenebrosa × L.-c. Gottoiana).—R. I. Measures, 1906.

L.-c. × tene-Gottoi, *G.C.* 1906, ii. 265; *O.R.* 1906, 338, 350.—R. I. Measures.

227d. **L.-c. × Tenos** (C. Bowringiana × L.-c. × Nysa), *Gard.* 1904, ii. 320; *O.R.* 1904, 364.—Veitch, 1904.

228a. **L.-c. × Thetis** (C. Harrisoniana × L.-c. × Nysa), *O.R.* 1907, 84.—Veitch, 1907.

231. **L.-c. × Topaz** (p. 114).

L.-c. × cinno-Warneri, *G.C.* 1905, i. 62; *Rev. H. Belge*, 1905, 48.—King of the Belgians.

L.-c. × cino-Warneri, *Rev. H. Belge*, 1906, 71.—King of the Belgians.

234a. **L. c. × Tunis** (C. Warscewiczii × L. × cinnabrosa), *G.C.* 1905, ii. 218; 1906, ii. 234; *O.R.* 1905, 307; 1906, 310.—Holford, 1905.

236a. **L.-c. × Ursula** (L. crispa ♀ × L.-c. × Leeana), *O.R.* 1907, 157.—Clark, 1907.

236b. **L.-c. × Veisenpachii** (C. Trianæ × L.-c. × warnhamensis), *O.R.* 1907, 92.—Cappe, 1907.

238a. **L.-c. × Veronique** (C. Mendelii × L. × cinnabrosa), *G.C.* 1905, i. 205; *O.R.* 1905, 117; *G.M.* 1906, 355, f.—Charlesworth, 1905.

238b. **L.-c. × vesinetensis** (L. flava × L.-c. × Cappei).—Cappe, 1907.

L.-c. × (unnamed), *O.R.* 1907, 92.—Cappe.

241. **L.-c. × Vinesiæ** (p. 116).

L.-c. × (unnamed), *Rev. H. Belge*, 1905, 213.—Lambeau.

241a. **L.-c. × vivicans** (C. Eldorado × L.-c. × elegans ♀), *O.R.* 1905, 286.—Sander, 1905.

244a. **L.-c.** × **Whiteleggei** (C. × Hardyana × L.-c. × callistoglossa).—Bradshaw, 1906.

L.-c. × G. G. Whitelegge, *G.C.* 1906, ii. 265; *O.R.* 1906, 338.—Bradshaw.

246. **L.-c.** × **Wiganiæ** (p. 117); *J.H.* 1907, ii. 315, **f.**

248a. **L.-c.** × **Wellesleyæ** (L. xanthina × L.-c. × callistoglossa).—Wellesley, 1907.

L.-c. × Lady Leese, *G.C.* 1907, ii. 254; *O.R.* 1907, 341.—Wellesley.

249. **L.-c.** × **wisetonensis** (p. 117).

L.-c. × W. Balmforth, *G.C.* 1907, ii. 221; *O.R.* 1907, 308.—Ogilvie.

249a. **L.-c.** × **Wolteræ** (C. Loddigesii ♀ × L. anceps), *O.R.* 1907, 39, 40, 145, **f.** 15.—Wolter, 1907. **[See Fig 99.**

249b. **L.-c.** × **woodfordiensis** (L. crispa × L.-c. × Roeblingii), *G.C.* 1906, ii. 201; *O.R.* 1906, 308.—Fowler, 1906.

Fig. 99. LÆLIOCATTLEYA × WOLTERÆ (with its parents).

253. **L.-c.** × **Zixa** (C. Mendelii × L.-c. × bella), *G.C.* 1904, ii. 395; *O.R.* 1905, 19.—Veitch, 1904.

254. **L.-c.** × **Zoroaster** (L. × Latona × L.-c. × Canhamiana), *O.R.* 1906, 135.—Holford, 1906.

21. LYCASTE (p. 119).

1. **Lycaste** × **Balliæ** (p. 119).

L. × Mary Gratrix, *Flora & Sylva*, 1904, 120, **t.**

23. MASDEVALLIA (p. 120).

25. **Masdevallia** × **Kimballiana** (p. 121).

M. × Pourbaixii, *G.M.* 1904, 373, **f.**

38a. **M.** × **Veitchio-fragrans** (fragrans × Veitchiana ♀), *G.C.* 1904, ii. 156; *O.R.* 1904, 270.—R. I. Measures, 1904.

24. MILTONIA (p. 123).

1. **Miltonia** × **Bleuana** (p. 123); *J.H.* 1904, ii. 47, f. (v. splendens).

2. **M.** × **Hyeana** (× Bleuana × vexillaria), *G.C.* 1906, ii. 139; *O.R.* 1906, 276.—Hye, 1906.

24a. ODONTIODA.

A genus established to contain the hybrids between Cochlioda and Odontoglossum.

Fig. 100. Odontioda × Bradshawiæ.

1. **Odontioda** × **Bohnhoffiæ** (Cochlioda vulcanica × Odontoglossum cirrhosum), *G.C.* 1906, ii. 234; *O.R.* 1906, 311.—Charlesworth, 1906.

2. **O.** × **Bradshawiæ** (C. Nœtzliana ♀ × O. crispum), *G.C.* 1907, i. 30, 36, f. 21; *O.R.* 1907, 40, 50, 81, f. 9; *G.M.* 1907, 41, f.; *Gard.* 1907, i. 55, f.; *J.H.* 1907, i. 113, f.—Charlesworth, 1907. **[See Fig. 100.**

3. **O.** × **Devosziana** (C. Nœtzliana × O. Edwardii), *G.C.* 1907, ii. 318; *J.H.* 1907, ii. 529, f.; *O.R.* 1907, 363; 1908, 41, f. 6.—Graire.

4. **O.** × **heatonensis** (C. sanguinea × O. cirrhosum), *G.C.* 1906, i. 158; *O.R.* 1906, 108, 118; *B. M.* t. 8133; *J.H.* 1907, i. 157. f.—Charlesworth, 1906.

5. **O. × Vuylstekeæ** (C. Nœtzliana × O. nobile), *G.C.* 1904, i. 360, f. 159; June 4, Suppl. 2; 1906, ii. 47, ff. 21, 22; 1907, ii. 63; *O.R.* 1904, 181, 189, 209, f. 34; 1906, 217, f. 26; *G.M.* 1904, 376, f.; *J.H.* 1904, i. 487, f.; *Gard.* 1904, i. 433, f.; *B. M.* t. 7990; *Rep. R.H.S. Conf. Genet.* 264, 272, f. 83; *Rev. H. Belge*, 1907, 169, f. 39, t.—Vuylsteke, 1904. [See Fig. 101.

Fig. 101. Odontioda × Vuylstekeæ.

25. ODONTOGLOSSUM (p. 123).

Oa. **O. × Adrianæ** (crispum × Hunnewellianum), *G.C.* 1907, i. 108, 161; *O.R.* 1907, 83, 93, 115.—Crawshay, 1907.

Originally figured and described in 1897 (*Lindenia*, xiii. t. 590), when it appeared in Messrs. Linden's establishment as a natural hybrid (though the fact was not stated). See also *O.R.* 1898, 5, 179.

Ob. **O. × Albertii** (× armainvillierense × Denisonæ).—Sander, 1907.

O. × Prince Albert, *G.C.* 1907, i. 289; *O.R.* 1907, 172.–Sander.

O. × laudatum, *Rev. H. Belge*, 1907, 366.—Vuylsteke.

Oc. **O. × Aliceæ** (Edwardii × spectabile), *G.C.* 1907, i. 26, f. 15, 31; *O.R.* 1907, 41, f. 5; 49; *G.M.* 1907, 41, f.—Bull, 1907. [See Fig. 102.

Od. **O. × altum** (× armainvillierense × Hallii), *Rev. H. Belge*, 1906, 48; *O.R.* 1906, 241, f. 34 (v. Bellone); 242.—Vuylsteke, 1906.

Oe. **O. × amabile** (crispum × spectabile), *G.C.* 1905, June 3, Suppl. 2, f. 143 (v. Ixion); 1905, ii. 414; 1906, i. 254; ii. 152, f. 61 (v. Royal Sovereign); *O.R.* 1905, 182; 1906, 150, 241, f. 35 (v. Goliath); 242; *G.M.* 1905, 367, f. (v. Ixion); *Gard.* 1905, i. 360 f. (id.); *J. H.* 1905, ii. 3, f. (id.); 1906, i. 491, f. (v. J. Bradshaw); *Rep. R.H.S. Conf. Genet.* 243, f. 56 (v. Ixion); 272, f. 88 (v. Royal Sovereign).—Vuylsteke, 1905.

Fig. 102. ODONTOGLOSSUM × ALICEÆ.

O. × (unnamed), *G.C.* 1905, i. 60; *O.R.* 1905, 54.—Vuylsteke.

O. × Elinor, *O.R.* 1906, 369.—Thompson.

Of. **O. × amandum** (× Denisonæ × nobile), *Rev. H. Belge*, 1904, 138; *G.C.* 1904, i. 296; *Sand. O. Hyb.* 36.—Vuylsteke, 1904.

Og. **O. × Amneris** (× Crawshayanum × cristatellum ♀), *G.C.* 1907, ii. 178; *O.R.* 1907, 264.–Crawshay, 1907.

I. **O. × amœnum** (p. 123).

O. × concinnum, *G.C.* 1904, June 4. Suppl. 2; *O.R.* 1904, 181, 201, f. 33. v. lætum).—Vuylsteke.

O. × insignitum, *G.C*, 1904, June 4, Suppl. 2; *O.R*, 1904, 202.—Vuylsteke.

1a. **O.** × **Amonasro** (× cristatellum ♀ × Harryanum), *G.C.* 1907, ii. 178; *O.R.* 1907, 264.—Crawshay, 1907.

1b. **O.** × **Ariadne** (nobile × Wattianum), *G.C.* 1907, ii. 101; *O.R.* 1907, 263.—Crawshay, 1907.

2. **O.** × **armainvillierense** (p. 124); *O.R.* 1907, 155, 241, f. 28 (v. Robsonæ).

O. × ardentissimum, *G.C.* 1904, i. 260, f. 114 (v. Cooksonæ); *G.M.* 1905, 285, f. (v. Sibyl); *Rep. R.H.S. Conf. Genet.* 244, 246, f. 57; *J.H.* 1907, i. 431, f. (v. Herbert Goodson); *Rev. H.* 1907, 231, f. 5 (v. Esperance).

2a. **O.** × **ashlandense** (× Adrianæ × Kegeljani), *G.C.* 1906, i. 349; 1906, ii. 78; *O.R.* 1906, 179, 180, 249.—R. Ashworth, 1906.

Fig. 103. ODONTOGLOSSUM × BEAUTE-CŒLESTE.

2b. **O.** × **Astarte** (Harryanum ♀ × tripudians), *G.C.* 1907, ii. 42; *O.R.* 1907, 253.—Crawshay, 1907.

2c. **O.** × **Astræa** (× Fascinator × Wattianum), *G.C.* 1907, ii. 42, 43; *O.R.* 1907, 254.—Crawshay, 1907.

2d. **O.** × **auriferum** (crispum × Halli-xanthum), *G.C.* 1907, i. 108; *O.R.* 1907, 85, 90.—Linden, 1907.

3a. **O.** × **Beaute-Cœleste** (× armainvillierense × crispum), *G.C.* 1907, i. 59, f. 28; *O.R.* 1907, 48, f. 6.—Vuylsteke, 1907. **[See Fig. 103.**

O. × ardentissimum v. eximium, *O.R.* 1906, 240, 241, f. 30.—Vuylsteke.

O. × armainvillierense var., *O.R.* 1907, 26, 48.—Vuylsteke.

O. × eximium, *O.R.* 1907, 209, f. 24 ; 210 (v. King Edward) ; *Rep. R.H.S. Conf. Genet.* 247, 268.—Vuylsteke.

O. × cœruleum, *O.R.* 1907, 178, 209, 210, f. 25.—Vuylsteke.

The history of this hybrid has been much confused, owing to the absence of records, and if the above are all forms of one O. × eximium will be the name to be adopted, a point which was overlooked until Part I. was printed.

4a. **O. × Bertii** (× Adrianæ × Rossii).—Bert, 1907.

O. × (unnamed), *J. S. H. Fr.* 1907, 143, 198.—Bert.

4b. O. × blando-nobile (blandum × nobile), *G.C.* 1907, ii. 190 ; *O.R.* 1907, 307.—Sander, 1907.

5a. **O. × Brandtiæ** (luteopurpureum × nobile), *Rep. R.H.S. Conf. Genet.* 247 ; *O.R.* 1905, 171.—Charlesworth, 1905.

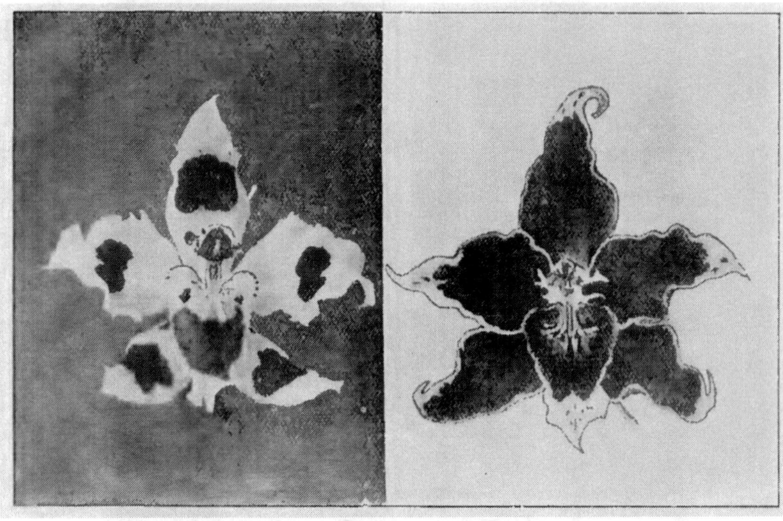

Fig. 104. O. × CRISPODINEI. Fig. 105. O. × THOMPSONIANUM.

5b. **O × caloglossum** (crispum × Vuylstekeæ), *G.C.* 1907, i. 62, 76, f. 33 ; *O.R.* 1907, 53.—Vuylsteke, 1907.

O. × Ruby, *G.C.* 1907, i. 62, 76, f. 34 ; *O.R.* 1907, 53.—Vuylsteke.

These two appear to us to be forms of the same hybrid.

5a. **O. × Cambria** (× Rolfeæ × spectabile).—Sander, 1907.

O. × Prince Edward of Wales, *G.C.* 1907, i. 290, 302, f. 124 ; 303 ; *O.R.* 1907, 152, 180, 181.—Sander.

6. **O. × Charlesworthii** (p. 125).

O. × Queen Alexandra, *G.C.* 1906, i. 426 ; ii. 13, f. 7 (v. Carmen) ; *O.R* 1906, 214 ; *J H.* 1906, ii. 51, f. (v. Carmen) : *Rep. R.H.S. Conf. Genet.* 254, f. 68 (id.). —Charlesworth.

O. × Harryano-triumphans, *O.R.* 1907, 181.—Crawshay.

6a. **O.** × **Cooksonæ** (× armainvillierense × percultum), *O.R.* 1907, 176.—Sander, 1907.

7. **O.** × **Cooksoni** (p. 125).

O. × Hallio-crispum, *Rep. R.H.S. Conf. Genet.*, 247, 266, **f.** 86 (v. Theodora).—Crawshay.

Fig. 106. ODONTOGLOSSUM × EURYDICE.

7a. **O** × **crispodinei** (× Coradinei × crispum), *G.C.* 1905, ii. 34; *O.R.* 1905, 241, **f.** 59; 243, 373, 374; *Rep. R.H.S. Conf. Genet.* 258, 270, **f.** 72.—Crawshay, 1905. **[See Fig. 104.**

9. **O.** × **Denisonæ** (p. 125).

O. × Wilckeanum, *O.R.* 1906, 241, **f.** 32 (v. Thalia); 242.—Vuylsteke.

9a. **O.** × **Elaine** (cirrhosum × Harryanum), *G.C.* 1906, i. 190; *O.R.* 1906, 111, 118.—Charlesworth, 1906.

10a. **O.** × **Ernesti** (× Adrianæ × triumphans), *O.R.* 1907, 158.—Charlesworth, 1906, Thwaites.

O. × Adriano-triumphans, *G.C.* 1906, i. 110; *O.R.* 1906, 85.—Charlesworth.

10b. **O.** × **Euphrosyne** (sceptrum × spectabile), *G.C.* 1906, ii. 239.—Peeters, 1906.

Fig. 107. ODONTOGLOSSUM × PHŒBE.
Fig. 108. O. × OTHELLO. Fig. 109. O. × FASCINATOR.

10c. **O.** × **Eurydice** (cirrhosum ♀ × hastilabium), *G.C.* 1906, ii. 36; *O.R.* 1906, 245, 265, f. 36.—Charlesworth, 1906. **[See Fig. 106.**

11a. **O.** × **exultans** (crispum × excellens), *G.C.* 1907, i. 226; *O.R.* 1907, 147.—Bert, 1905, Linden.

O. × (unnamed), *J. S. H. Fr.* 1905, 213.—Bert.

11b. **O.** × **Fascinator** (× Adrianæ × crispum), *O.R.* 1905, 201, f. 43, 202; 1906, 122; *Rep. R.H.S. Conf. Genet.* 252, 269, f. 66.— Peeters, 1905. **[See Fig 109.**

O. × (unnamed), *O.R.* 1905, 174.—Peeters.

O. × Hesperides, *J. S. H. Fr.* 1906, 240.—Boullet.

11c. **O.** × **Fletcherianum** (cirrhosum × Edwardi ♀), *G.C.* 1906, ii. 98; *O.R.* 1906, 248, 255.—Sander, 1906.

11d. **O.** × **formosum** (nobile × Rolfeæ), *G.C.* 1904, i. 296; *O.R.* 1905, 182, 297, f. 65; 1906, 240, f. 29 (v. Diana); 241; *J. S. H. Fr.* 1904, 465; *Rep. R.H. S. Conf. Genet.* 246, 247, f. 59.—Vuylsteke, 1904. **[See Fig. 110.**

Fig. 110. ODONTOGLOSSUM × FORMOSUM.

11e. **O.** × **Fowlerianum** (cirrhosum × Rossii), *G.C.* 1906, i. 158, 163, f. 65; *O.R.* 1906, 108; *G.M.* 1906, 181, f.; *Gard.* 1906, i. 173, f.; *Rep. R.H.S. Conf. Genet.* 247, 248, f. 60.—Sander, 1906.

11f. **O.** × **fuscum** (× Denisonæ × sceptrum), *G.C.* 1904, i. 296; *Sand. O. Hyb.* 37.—Vuylsteke, 1904.

11g. **O.** × **gandavense** (× armainvillierense × Vuylstekeæ), *G.C.* 1907, i. 353; *O.R.* 1907, 178, 209, f. 23; *Rev. H. Belge*, 1907, 84 (v. cœruleum).—Vuylsteke, 1907.

11h. **O.** × **Gardneri** (cordatum × nobile).—Gardner, 1902.

O. × Pescatoreo-cordatum, *Rep. R. H. S. Conf. Genet.* 247, 269.—Gardner.

11i. **O. × Gladys** (cirrhosum × spectabile), *G.C.* 1906, i. 157; *O.R.* 1906, 108.—Charlesworth, 1906.

11k. **O. × Hallio-Adrianæ** (× Adrianæ × Hallii), *G.C.* 1906, i. 110; *O.R.* 1906, 85.—Charlesworth, 1906.

11l. **O. × Halli-xanthum** (Hallii × Kegeljani).—Crawshay, 1906.

O. × Hallio-xanthum, *Rep. R.H.S. Conf. Genet.* 247, 269.—Crawshay.

Originally appeared as a natural hybrid in Messrs. Linden's establishment at Brussels in 1895. See *Lindenia*, x. t. 467.

12a. **O. × heatonense** (Hallii × hastilabium).—Charlesworth, 1907.

O. × (unnamed), *G.C.* 1907, ii. 37; *O.R.* 1907, 177, 244.—Charlesworth.

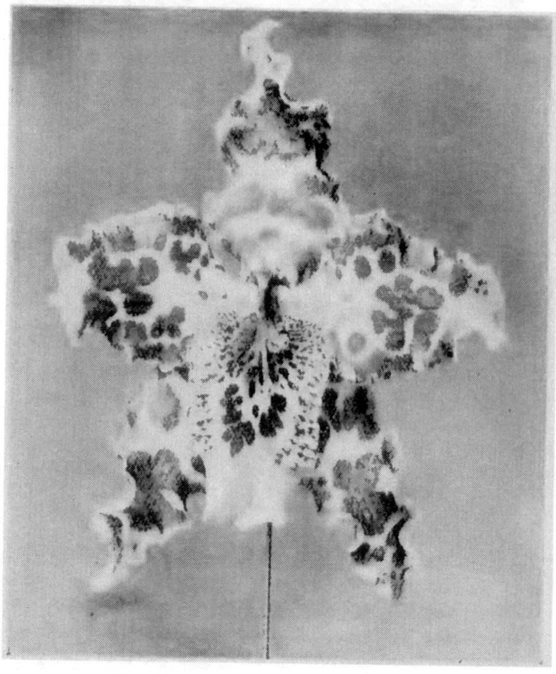

Fig. 111. ODONTOGLOSSUM × JAPONAIS VAR. EXQUISITUM.

12b. **O. × hellemense** (crispum × harvengetense), *J. S. H. Fr.* 1905, 324; *O.R.* 1905, 176.—Fanyau, 1905.

O. × Galpinianum, *J. S. H. Fr.* 1907, 143.—Peeters.

O. × (unnamed), *G.C.* 1907, i. 61; *O.R.* 1907, 53.—Sander.

O. × Watsonianum, *O.R.* 1907, 57.—Linden.

13. **O. × Hyeanum** (p. 126).

O. × Souvenir de Victor Hye de Crom, *Rep. R.H.S. Conf. Genet.* 247, 257, f. 71.

13a. **O. × Iago** (Harryanum ♀ × Hunnewellianum), *G.C.* 1907, i. 259; *O.R.* 1907, 149, 158.—Crawshay, 1907.

13b. **O. × Japonais** (crispum × Rolfeæ), *G.C.* 1904, June 4, Suppl. 2; *O.R.* 1904, 180, 201, f. 32.—Hye, 1904. **[See Fig. 111.**

O. × (unnamed), *O.R.* 1905, 174.—Peeters.

O. × Lambeauianum, *G.C.* 1905, ii. 324, f. 126; 434, f. 162 (v. exquisitum); *O.R.* 1906, 57, f. 7 (id.); 96; *Dict. Ic. O.* Od. hyb. t. 12; *J.H.* 1906, i. 229, f.; 1907, i. 273, f. (v. The Idol); *G.M.* 1907, 106, f. (id.); *Rep. R.H.S. Conf. Genet.* 247, 249, f. 61.—Peeters.

13c. **O. × Jorisianum** (luteopurpureum × triumphans), *G.C.* 1907, i. 226; *O.R.* 1907, 148.—Linden, 1907.

Fig. 112. Odontoglossum × Lairessei (with O. Cervantesii parent on left).

14a. **O. × Lairessei** (Cervantesii ♀ × Edwardii), *O.R.* 1905, 81, f. 21; *Rev. H. Belge*, 1906, 94; *Rep. R.H.S. Conf. Genet.* 247, 265, f. 85.—Lairesse, 1905. **[See Fig. 112.**

14b. **O. × Lambeauiæ** (Harryanum × sceptrum).—Sander, 1907.

O. × memoria Lambeauiæ, *G.C.* 1907, ii. 77; *O.R.* 1907, 247.—Sander.

14c. **O. × lapidense** (Hallii × Rolfeæ), *G.C.* 1905, ii. 36; *O.R.* 1905, 213.—Thompson, 1905.

14d. **O. × Lawrenceanum** (× Rolfeæ × triumphans), *G.C.* 1905, i. 174, 197, f. 86; June 3, Suppl. 3; *O.R.* 1905, 115, 182; *Gard.* 1905, i. 207, f.; *G.M.* 1905, 366, f. (v. Adonis); *Rep. R.H.S. Conf. Genet.* 247, 250, f. 62.—Vuylsteke, 1905.

14e. **O. × Leo** (Hallii × triumphans), *G.C.* 1907, i. 326; *O.R.* 1907, 199.—Crawshay, 1907.

14f. **O. × Lobbii** (× amabile × nobile), *G.C.* 1907, i. 109.—Fowler, 1907.

O. × Cobbiæ, *O.R.* 1907, 83.—Fowler.

14g. **O.** × **Lucasianum** (× cristatellum × Hallii), *G.C.* 1905, i. 333 (v. heatonense); *O.R.* 1905, 172 (id.).—Schröder, 1905.

15. **O.** × **mirificum** (p. 126); *G. World*, 1905, 455, **f.**

O. × Annie Louise, *G.C.* 1904, i. 239; *O.R.* 1904, 142.—Law-Schofield.

16a. **O.** × **moortbeekiense** (× Denisonæ × harvengtense).—Linden, 1907.

O. × (unnamed), *O.R.* 1907, 57.—Linden.

16b. **O.** × **Mossiæ** (× Denisonæ × Kegeljani), *G.C.* 1907, ii. 3.—Moss, 1907.

Fig. 113. ODONTOGLOSSUM × SMITHII.

16c. **O.** × **Nemesis** (× Coradinei × triumphans), *O.R.* 1907, 199.—Crawshay, 1906.

16d. **O.** × **Nesta** (× Andersonianum × luteopurpureum), *Gard.* 1904, i. March 26, Suppl. 10.—Bischoffsheim, 1904.

16e. **O.** × **nitidum** (× Denisonæ × spectabile), *G.C.* 1904, i. June 4, Suppl. 2; *O.R.* 1904, 181, 201, **f.** 30.—Vuylsteke, 1904

O. × lactum, *Rev. H. Belge*, 1906, 48.—Vuylsteke.

16f. **O. × Oberthuri** (× Adrianæ × harvengtense), *J. S. H. Fr.* 1907, 337. —Beranek, 1907.

The above is the recorded parentage, but M. Duval suggests O. sceptrum as the second parent.

16g. **O. × Ossultoni** (nobile × spectabile), *O.R.* 1905, 189; 1907, 171 (Glebelands var.); 180; *G.M.* 1906, 419, **f.**; *G.C.* 1907, i. 323; *Rep. R. H.S. Conf. Genet.* 251, **f.** 63 (v. W. H. Hatcher).—Charlesworth, 1905.

O. × W. H. Hatcher, *G.C.* 1906, i. 254; *O.R.* 1906, 150, 157.—Charlesworth.

16h. **O. × Othello** (× Adrianæ × Harryanum), *O.R.* 1905, 179, 201, **f.** 42; 202; 1907, 148; *G.C.* 1907, i. 259; *Rep. R.H.S. Conf. Genet.* 247, 252, **f.** 65.—Charlesworth, 1905. [See **Fig. 108** (p. 286).

Fig. 114. ODONTOGLOSSUM × STEWARTIANUM.

16i. **O. × percultum** (× armainvillierense × Rolfeæ), *G.C.* 1904, i. June 4, Suppl. 2; *O.R.* 1904, 181, 202; 1905, 273, **f.** 63 (v. Cybele); 1906, 240, **f.** 31 (v. Orion); 242; *Rev. Hort.* 1907, 231, **f.** 3; *J.H.* 1906, i. 537, f. (v. Orion); *Rep. R.H.S. Conf. Genet.* 247, 253, **f.** 67.—Vuylsteke, 1904.

16k. **O. × Phœbe** (cirrhosum ♀ × crispum), *G.C.* 1905, June 3, Suppl. 2; 1907, i. 355. **f.** 151 (v. magnificum); *O.R.* 1905, 179, 201, **f.** 41; *Rep. R.H.S. Conf. Genet.* 247, 252, **f.** 64.—Charlesworth, 1905. [See **Fig. 107** (p. 286).

17. **O. × Rolfeæ** (p. 127); *G.C.* 1904, i. 261, **f.** 115 (Oakwood var.): *Rep. R.H.S. Conf. Genet.* 247, 255, **f.** 69 (v. majesticum); *Rev. H.* 1907, 231, **f.** 4.

17a. **O. × Smithii** (Rossii ♀ × spectabile), *G.C.* 1905, ii. 411, 427, f. 158; 1907, ii. 62, 63; *O.R.* 1906, 9, f. 1; 11; *Gard.* 1905, ii. 400, 401, f.; *G.M.* 1905, 805, f.; *J.H.* 1905, ii. 541, f.; *G. Alb.* 1906, 12, f.; *Rep. R.H.S. Conf. Genet.* 247, 256, f. 70. **[See Fig. 113.**

18. **O. × spectabile** (p. 127).

O. × crispo-Harryanum, *G.C.* 1905, i. 276, f. 114 (v. King Edward); 1907, i. 142, f. 61 (v. F. Sander); *Rep. R.H.S. Conf. Genet.* 245, 247, f. 58 (Rosslyn var.).

O. × Bingelianum, *G.C.* 1905, ii. 348; *O.R.* 1905, 364; *G.M.* 1908, 69, 70, f. —Schröder.

18a. **O. × splendidissimum** (× armainvillierense × nobile), *G.C.* 1907, i. 352; *O.R.* 1907, 176.—Sander, 1907.

Fig. 115. ODONTOGLOSSUM × VUYLSTEKEÆ.

18b. **O. × Stella** (sceptrum × triumphans), *O.R.* 1905, 82.—Thompson, 1904.

18c. **O. × Stewartianum** (× Andersonianum ♀ × crispum), *O.R.* 1906. 120, f. 14.—Fanyau, 1905. **[See Fig. 114.**

O. × (unnamed), *J. S. H. Fr.* 1905, 213.—Fanyau.

O. × Watsonianum, *Rev. H. Belge*, 1907, 20.—Linden.

18d. **O. × Sylvia** (cirrhosum × Rolfeæ), *G.C.* 1907, i. 225; *O.R.* 1907, 147, 154.—Charlesworth, 1907.

18e. **O. × Terpsichore** (Kegeljani × nobile), *O.R.* 1906, 146, 221; 1907, 181.—Crawshay, 1906.

18f. **O. × Thompsonianum** (crispum × Edwardii ♀), *G.C.* 1905, i. 268, 285, f. 117; *O.R.* 1905, 149, 175, 241, f. 60; *Gard.* 1905, i. 290, f.; *Dict. Ic. O.* Od. hyb. t. 13 (v. M. Osc. Fanyau); *Rep. R.H.S. Conf. Genet.* 247, 258, f. 73.—(Rappart) Thompson, 1905. [See Fig. 105 (p. 284).

18g. **O. × tigrinum** (× Fascinator × Harryanum ♀), *O.R.* 1907, 158.—Thwaites, 1907.

18h. **O. × Una** (crispum ♀ × nevadense), *G.C.* 1906, ii. 265; *O. R.* 1906, 339, 349.—Crawshay, 1906.

18i. **O. × Urania** (crispum ♀ × cristatellum), *G.C.* 1906, ii. 298; 1907, i. 322; *O.R.* 1906, 342, 349; 1907, 170.—Crawshay, 1906.

18k. **O. × venustulum** (× armainvillierense × spectabile), *G.C.* 1904, i. June 4, Suppl. 2; 1905, ii. 2, f. 2; *O.R.* 1904, 181, 201, f. 31, 202; 1907, 82 (v. Apollo), 180.—Vuylsteke, 1904.

18l. **O. × Vuylstekeæ** (× spectabile × Vuylstekei), *G.C.* 1905, ii. 348; *O.R.* 361, f. 72; *Rep. R. H. S. Conf. Genet.* 247, 259, f. 74.—Vuylsteke, 1905.

This hybrid was omitted from Part I., owing to the absence of any record of parentage. That here given has been inferred, and requires confirmation.

[See Fig. 115.

19. **O. × Vuylstekei** (p. 128); *G.C.* 1904, i. 3, f. 3 (v. vivicans); *J.H.* 1904, i, 5, f. (id.); *G.M.* 1904, 59, f. (id.); *Rev. Hort.* 1907, 230, f. 1 (id.); *Rep. R.H.S. Conf. Genet.* 247, 260, f. 75 (id.).

20. **O. × waltonense** (pp. 128, 129, f. 44); *O.R.* 1904, 168, f. 27 (v. rosefieldiense); *G.C.* 1904, i. 331, f. 144 (id.); *J.H.* 1904, i. 335, f. (id.)

20a. **O. × warnhamense** (Hallii × nobile), *G.C.* 1905, i. 268; *O.R.* 1905, 148, 157.—Lucas, 1905.

O. × Phædra, *G.C.* 1906, ii. 234; *O.R.* 1906, 311; 1907, 176.—Charlesworth.

21a. **O. × Wiganianum** (× harvengtense × Rolfeæ), *G.C.* 1905, i. 237. 274, f. 112; 1906, i. 132; *O.R.* 1905, 146, 157; *J.H.* 1905, i. 333, f.; *Rep. R.H.S. Conf. Genet.* 247.—Wigan, 1905.

25a. ODONTONIA.

A genus established to contain the hybrids between Miltonia and Odontoglossum.

1. **O. × culiginosa** (Miltonia Warscewiczii × Odontoglossum nobile).—Vuylsteke, 1906.

Odontoglossum × culiginosum, *Rev. H. Belge*, 1906, 189.

2. **O. × Ellwoodii** (Miltonia Roezlii × Odontoglossum cirrhosum), *G.C.* 1907, i. 108; *O.R.* 1907, 84, 90.—Charlesworth, 1907.

3. **O. × Lairesseæ** (Miltonia Warscewiczii × Odontoglossum crispum ♀), *G.C.* 1905, i. 398; ii. 2, f. 1; *O.R.* 1905, 211, 217, f. 47; *G.M.* 1905, 412, f.; *Rev. H. Belge*, 1905, 277.—Lairesse, 1905. [See Fig. 116.

26. PAPHIOPEDILUM.

9a. **P. × Aitchisonæ** (Charlesworthii × Lucie).—Rogerson, 1907.

C. × Mrs. Aitchison, *O.R.* 1907, 366.—Rogerson.

18. **P. × Allanianum** (p. 130).

Cypripedium × Spicero-Curtisii, *G.C.* 1905, ii. 269; *O.R.* 1905, 343; *Rev. H. Belge*, 1905, 239.—Draps-Dom.

19. **P. × allertonense** (p. 130).

C. × Tressilian, *Rev. H. Belge*, 1906, 23.—Lambeau.

20a. **P. × altrinchamense** (× aureum × callosum).—Robson, 1905.

C. × (unnamed), *G.C.* 1905, ii. 383; *O.R.* 1905, 368.—Robson.

27. **P. × Angeliæ** (p. 131).

C. × Elvira, *G.C.* 1905, ii. 269: *O.R.* 1905, 344.—Stepman de Messemæcker.

Fig. 116. ODONTOGLOSSUM × LAIRESSEÆ.

35a. **P. × Argo-Youngii** (Argus × Youngianum).—Draps-Dom, 1905.

C. × Argo-Youngii, *Rev. H. Belge*, 1905, 239; *G.C.* 1905, ii. 269.—Draps-Dom.

54. **P. × aureum** (p. 135).

C. × Souvenir de Draps, *Rev. H. Belge*, 1905, 72.—Lambeau.

C. × La Candeur, *Rev. H. Belge*, 1906, 23.—Makoy.

58. **P. × Bala** (p. 136).

C. × Valleti, *Jard.* 1905, 104, f. F.; *J.S.H.F.* 1905, 31.—Cappe.

62a. **P. × Barclayæ** (Godefroyæ × Rothschildianum).—Fowler, 1905.

C. × Daisy Barclay, *G.C.* 1905, ii. 34; *O.R.* 1905, 242; *G.M.* 1905, 469, f.; *G. World*, 1905, 975, f.—Fowler.

62b. P. × **Baron** (× Hitchinsiæ × nitens).—Sander, 1905.

C. × The Baron, *G.C.* 1905, ii. 382, 405, f. 153; *O.R.* 1905, 367; *Gard.* 1905, ii. 369, f.—Sander.

65a. P. × **Beauclerkiæ** (ciliolare ♀ × Fairrieanum).—Wellesley, 1905.

C. × Mrs. de Vere Beauclerk, *G.C.* 1905, ii. 446; *O.R.* 1906, 13, 28.—Wellesley.

66a. P. × **Bella** (philippinense × vexillarium), *O.R.* 1905, 70, f. 17.—Wellesley, 1904.

C. × Bella, *G.C.* 1904, ii. 156; *O.R.* 1904, 270.

73a. P. × **Black-Prince** (× Hera × Rothschildianum).—Sander, 1906.

C. × Black-Prince, *G.C.* 1906, ii. 97; *O.R.* 1906, 248.—Sander.

73b. P. × **Blanche** (Charlesworthii × Niobe).—Goodson, 1905.

C. × Lily Blanche, *G.C.* 1905, ii. 381; *O.R.* 1905, 366.—Goodson.

75. P. × **Bollerillæ** (p. 138).

C. × Headlandianum, *G.C.* 1906, i. 30; *O.R.* 1906, 51.—Headland.

78a. P. × **bowdonense** (× nitens × triumphans).—Robson, 1907.

C. × bowdonense, *O.R.* 1907, 368.

79a. P. × **Braceyanum** (× Mabeliæ × superbiens).—Armstrong & Brown, 1907.

C. × Braceyanum, *G.C.* 1907, ii. 153; *O.R.* 1907, 278.—Armstrong & Brown.

80. P. × **Bræckmanii** (p. 139).

P. × Bridge Hall Seedling, *O.R.* 1907, 93.—Wrigley.

81a. P. × **Bridgei** (Argus × Godseffianum).—G. F. Moore, 1906.

C. × Bridgei, *G.C.* 1906, i. 63; *O.R.* 1906, 53.

81b. P. × **bridgense** (Argus × Schlesingerianum).—Wrigley, 1904.

P. × (unnamed), *O.R.* 1904, 371.—Wrigley.

81c. P. × **Brilliant** (× Buchanianum × Calypso).—Sander, 1904.

C. × Brilliant, *G.C.* 1904, i. 109; *O.R.* 1904, 83.—Sander.

83a. P. × **Brunette** (× Lathamianum × Wottoni), *O.R.* 1905, 190.—Wrigley, 1905.

89. P. × **Bullieri** (p. 140).

C. × Theodore Bullier, *Lind.* xvii. t. 814.

101. P. × **calloso-barbatum** (p. 141).

C. × mirabile, *G.C.* 1905, i. 31; *O.R.* 1905, 55.—Statter.

115. P. × **Celia** (p. 143).

C. × Mme. Jules Hye, *Rev. H. Belge*, 1905, 97, t. f. 3.

116. P. × **Chamber-Leeanum** (p. 143).

C. × Morteni, *G.M.* 1905, 103, f.; *J.H.* 1904, i. 113, f.

P. × Mariæ, *O.R.* 1904, 101.

116a. P. × **Chameleon** (× chloroneurum (Williamsianum) × nitens).—Lucas, 1904.

C. × Chameleon, *G.C.* 1904, ii. 293; *O.R.* 1904, 339.—Lucas.

117. P. × **Chapmanii** (p. 143).

C. × Chapmanii, *Rev. H. Belge*, 1904, 97, t. f. 1.

C. × memoria Aug. Lemoinier, *Rev. H. Belge*, 1904, 70.—Lemoinier.

118. P. × **Charlesianum** (p. 143).

C. × variabile, *Jard.* 1905, 104, f. A. (v. punctatissimum).—Cappe.

C. × Ami Treyve, *Jard.* 1905, 104, f. C.

C. × Ed. Deemunter, *Rev. H. Belge*, 1905, 96.—Lambeau.

C. × The Marchioness, *G.C.* 1906, i. 29 ; *O.R.* 1906, 51.—Sander.

120. P. × **chloroneurum** (p. 144).

C. × melanopthalmum, *O.R.* 1905, 349.

123a. P. × **claptonense** (Chamberlainianum × ciliolare).—Low, 1907.

C. × (unnamed), *G.C.* 1907, i. 62 ; *O.R.* 1907, 54.—Low.

124a. P. × **Clarkii** (Charlesworthii × Swanianum).—Clark, 1906.

P. × (unnamed), *O.R.* 1906, 348.—Clark.

134. P. × **Colesii** (p. 145).

C. × Grace Ruby, *G.C.* 1905, i. 141 ; *O.R.* 1905, 78.—McBean.

137. P. × **Colossus** (p. 145).

C. × Mahlerianum, *G.C.* 1904, i. 66 (Feiling's var.).

143a. P. × **conco-tonsum** (concolor × tonsum).—R. I. Measures, 1906.

C. × conco-tonsum, *G.C.* 1906, ii. Nov. 10, Suppl. 4. ; *O.R.* 1906, 363, 375. —R. I. Measures.

149a.—P. × **Cooksoni** (Druryi × Rothschildianum).—Cookson, 1905.

C. × Drurio-Rothschildianum, *G.C.* 1905, ii. 218 ; *O.R.* 1905, 306.—Cookson.

153a. P. × **Cravenianum** (× Hera (Lucienianum) × Spicerianum).—Charlesworth, 1904.

C. × Cravenianum, *G.C.* 1904, i. 174 ; *O.R.* 1904, 116.—Charlesworth.

160a. P. × **Cypheri** (Curtisii × Mastersianum).—Cypher, 1904.

C. × (unnamed), *G.C.* 1904, ii. 293 ; *O.R.* 1904, 340.—Cypher.

171. P. × **decipiens** (p. 151),

C. × Penelope, *G.C.* 1904, i. 78 ; *O.R.* 1904, 52.—Singer.

172. P. × **decorum** (p. 151).

C. × Mrs. Butterworth, *O.R.* 1904, 247.—Sander.

C. × Reygærti, *G.C.* 1905, ii. 269 ; *O.R.* 1905, 343.—Stepman de Messemæcker.

173a. P. × **dellense** (Mastersianum × Rothschildianum).—Schröder, 1907.

C. × dellense, *G.C.* 1907, ii. 153 ; *O.R.* 1907, 277.—Schröder.

175. P. × **Descombesii** (p. 152); *O.R.* 1905, 189 (v. marlfieldiense).—Le Doux.

175a. P. × **De-Vere** (× aureum × Charlesworthii).—Wellesley, 1905.

C. × De Vere, *G.C.* 1905, ii. 316 ; *O.R.* 1905, 340.—Wellesley.

175b. P. × **Dicksonianum** (× Hera × villosum).—Wellesley, 1905.

C. × Dicksonianum, *G.C.* 1905, i. 60 ; 1906, i. 63 ; 1907, i. 161 ; *O.R.* 1905, 53 ; 1906, 43, 53 ; 1907, 115.—Wellesley. Originally recorded as from × Savageanum (memoria Mœnsii) × villosum, but afterwards corrected.

C. × Countess of Carnarvon, *G.C.* 1907, i. 61, 226 ; *O.R.* 1907, 54, 147.—Veitch.

176. **P. × Dido** (p. 152).

C. × Sandero-selligerum, *G.C.* 1904, ii. 432 ; *O.R.* 1905, 20.—Lawrence.

176a. **P. × Dom-Carlos** (Godefroyæ × Lawrenceanum).—Beranek, 1904.

C. × (unnamed), *G.C.* 1904, i. 109 ; *O.R.* 1904, 84.—Beranek.

C. × Dom Carlos, *G.C.* 1904, ii. 433 ; 1905, i. 333 (v. Rex) ; *O.R.* 1905, 20, 172 (id.).—Cookson.

C. × Don Carlos, *J.H.* 1905, i. 529, f. (v. superbum) ; *Gard.* 1905, i. 376, f. (id).—Cookson.

180a. **P. × Dorothy** (insigne × Victoria-Mariæ), *O.R.* 1904, 102.—Appleton, 1904.

C. × (unnamed), *O.R.* 1904, 344.—(G. F. Moore) Colman.

180b. **P. × dourdaniense** (bellatulum × Io).—Doin, 1904.

C. × Dourdanianum, *J. S. H. F.* 1904, 211.—Doin.

C. × Isis, *G.C.* 1905, ii. 383 ; *O.R.* 1905, 368.—E. Ashworth.

180a. **P. × Draco** (× Hera × insigne).—Holford, 1906.

C. × Draco, *G.C.* 1906, ii. 298 ; *O.R.* 1906, 341.—Holford.

182a. **P. × Duchess** (× aureum × insigne).—Sander, 1906.

C. × The Duchess, *G.C.* 1906, i. 29 ; *O.R.* 1906, 51.—Sander.

184. **P. × Duvalii** (p, 153).

C. × Talisman, *Rev. H. Belge*, 1906, 96.—Hye.

184a. **P. × Earl** (× œnanthum × selligerum).—Sander, 1907.

C. × The Earl, *O.R.* 1907, 368.—Sander.

186. **P. × Edith** (p. 153).

C. × Nuyensii, *G.C.* 1905, ii. 269 ; *O.R.* 1905, 343 ; *Rev. H. Belge*, 1905, 239.—Draps.Doin.

187a. **P. × Edwardianum** (× nitens × Rothschildianum).—Wellesley, 1904.

C. × King Edward VII., *G.C.* 1904, ii. 293 ; *O.R.* 1904, 339 ; *G.M.* 1904, 772, 773, f. ; *J.H.* 1905, i. 231, f.—Wellesley.

189. **P. × Eira** (p. 154). **[See Fig. 117.**

C. × Miss Daisy Druce, *G.C.* 1904, i. 302 ; *O.R.* 1904, 171.—Druce.

P. × Miss Daisy Druce, *O.R.* 1904, 329, f. 46.

There seems to be a doubt as to whether P. × Eira was raised from P. Chamberlainianum and P. concolor, but materials are wanting to clear the matter up.

194. **P. × Elsie** (p. 155) ; *O.R.* 1904, 101.

194a. **P. × Emile** (× Hera × Lathamianum ♀).—Cappe, 1905.

C. × (unnamed), *J. S. H. F.* 1905, 31.—Cappe.

C. × Emile Cappe, *J. S. H. F.* 1906, 193.—Cappe.

C. × Minos, *Jard.* 1905, 104, f. J.—Cappe.

200a. **P. × epicasta** (× œnanthum × vexillarium).—J. W. Moore, 1906.

C. × (unnamed), *G.C.* 1906, ii. 328, Suppl. 4 : *O.R.* 1906, 364.—J. W. Moore.

C. × epicasta, *G.C.* 1907, i. 132.—Wellesley.

203a. **P. × Ethel** (Chamberlainianum × Stonei), *O.R.* 1904, 102.—Appleton, 1904.

204. **P. × Ettyi** (p. 156).

C. × Dowlingianum, *O.R.* 1904, 19.—Appleton.

P. × Dowlingianum, *O.R.* 1904, 101.—Appleton.

The second record gives P. × Psyche as the pollen parent.

205. **P. × Eucharis** (p. 156).

C. × Chantino-Lawrenceanum, *Lind.* xvii. t. 812.—Linden.

215a. **P. × exquisitum** (Argus × Godefroyæ).—R. H. Measures, 1904.

C. × exquisitum, *Gard.* 1904, i. Jan. 9, Suppl. 8.—R. H. Measures.

215b. **P. × exul-concolor** (concolor × exul).—Charlesworth, 1907.

Fig. 117. Paphiopedilum × Eira var. Miss Daisy Druce.

C. × exul-concolor, *G.C.* 1907, i. 61 ; *O.R.* 1907, 53.

217a. **P. × Fabiola** (× Niobe × villosum).—Wellesley, 1904.

P. × (unnamed), *G.C.* 1904, i. 194.—Wellesley.

217b. **P. × Fairrieano-Io** (Fairrieanum × Io).—Sander, 1905.

C. × Fairrieano-Io, *G.C.* 1905, ii. 446 ; *O.R.* 1906, 14.—Sander.

219a. **P. × fastuosum** (× augustum ♀ × Rothschildianum).—Peeters, 1904.

C. × fastuosum, *J. S. H. F.* 1904, 564 ; *Rev. H. Belge*, 1905, 190.—Peeters.

220a. P. × **Faunus** (Charlesworthii × purpuratum ♀), *O.R.* 1905, 304.—Young, 1905.

224. **P. × Figaro** (p. 158).

P. × Fitzus, *Rev. H. Belge*, 1906, 21.—Lambeau.

227a. **P × Fletcherianum** (Godefroyæ × Mabeliæ).—Low, 1906.

C. × Fletcherianum, *G.C.* 1906, ii. 234, 254, f. 103; *O.R.* 1906, 311; *J.H.* 1906, ii. 339, f.—Low. Raised from P. Godefroyæ leucochilum.

232a. **P. × Frankeanum** (Curtisii × tonsum ♀), *O.R.* 1908, 29.—Duquesne, 1904.

C. × (unnamed), *J. S. H. Fr.* 1904, 22.—Duquesne.

M. Duquesne's plant apparently agrees with the one which afterwards appeared with M. Th. Franke among imported plants of the parent species.

232b. **P. × Fred** (× Annie × bellatulum).—Sander, 1904.

C. × Fred. K. Sander, *G.C.* 1904, ii. 293, 307, f. 139; *O.R.* 1904, 340; *Gard.* 1904, ii. 293, f.—Sander.

246. **P. × giganteum** (p. 161).

C. × Dr. Allix, *Jard.* 1905, 104, f. B.—Cappe.

C. × Rene, *O.R.* 1907, 345.—Rogerson.

250. **P. × Goodsoni** (p. 161).

C. × H. G. Goodson, *G.M.* 1905, 136.—Goodson.

252. **P. × Goultenianum** (p. 162).

C. × Madame Alfred Janssens, *Rev. H. Belge*, 1904, 48.—Janssens and Putzeys.

254. **P. × Graceæ** (p. 162).

C. × W. H. Page, *G.C.* 1904, i. 109; *O.R.* 1904, 82.—Moore.

262. **P. × Greyi** (p. 163).

C. × Miss M. Sillem, *G.C.* 1905, ii. 115; *O.R.* 1905, 274.—Wellesley.

C. × Miss Sillem, *G.C.* 1906, i. 425; *O.R.* 1906, 214.—Wellesley.

263. **P. × Grovesianum** (p. 163).

C. × Gravesianum, *Rev. H. Belge*, 1907, 35.—Praet.

263a. **P. × Hackenschmidtii** (× Eismannianum × insigne). — E. Ashworth, 1906.

C. × George Hackenschmidt, *G.C.* 1906, i. 158; *O.R.* 1906, 108.—E. Ashworth.

267. **P. × Harri-Leeanum** (p. 163).

C. × Harri-Leeanum, *G.C.* 1906, ii. 166, f. 67 (Park Lodge var.).

269. **P. × Harrisianum** (p. 164).

C. × Harrisianum, *G.C.* 1904, ii. 411, f. 175 ("twofold").

271a. **P. × Haywoodiæ** (bellatulum × Haywoodianum).—Mrs. Haywood, 1905.

C. × Haywoodianum, *G.C.* 1905, i. 174, 195, f. 80; *O.R.* 1905, 114.—Mrs. Haywood.

272. **P. × Haywoodianum** (p. 165).

C. × Fanny, *G.C.* 1905, ii. 414.—Lambeau.

272a. **P. × Healei** (Druryi × Youngianum).—Drewett, 1905.

C. × John Heale, *G.C.* 1905, ii. 446; *O.R.* 1906, 13.—Drewett.

275. **P.** × **Helena** (p. 165).

C. × Tressilianum, *Rev. H. Belge*, 1905, 22.—Lambeau.

C. × Helen, *G. World*, 1904, 379, 381, **f.** (Oakwood var.); *G.M.* 1905, 169, **f.** (v. Fascinator).

279. **P.** × **Hera** (p. 166).

C. × Euryades, *G.M.* 1904, 255, **f.** (v. excellens).

C. × Henriette Cappe, *Jard.* 1905, 104, **f.** D.—Cappe.

C. × Hera, *Jard.* 1905, 104, **f.** G. (v. grandiflorum).—Cappe.

C. × punctatum, *Rev. H. Belge*, 1906, 70.—Lambeau.

279a. **P.** × **Herbert** (Sanderianum × Youngianum).—Tracy, 1905.

C. × Herbert Goodson, *G.C.* 1905, ii. 254; *O.R.* 1905, 309.—Tracy.

282. **P.** × **Hitchinsiæ** (p. 167).

C. × Elmireanum, *Rev. H. Belge*, 1905, 97, **t. f.** 4.

283. **P.** × **Hobartii** (p. 167).

C. × Nina E. Hollond, *G.C.* 1904, ii. 355; *O.R.* 1904, 366.—Hollond.

C. × Stottianum, *G.C.* 1906, i. 30; *O.R.* 1906, 55.—Law-Schofield.

286a. **P.** × **Honnoriæ** (Druryi × Godefroyæ).—Appleton, 1905.

C. × Honnoriæ, *G.C.* 1905, i. 108; *O.R.* 1905, 75; *G.M.* 1905, 133, **f.**—Appleton.

286b. **P.** × **Hopkinsianum** (bellatulum × Mastersianum ♀).—Wellesley, 1904. **[See Fig. 118.**

C. × Hopkinsianum, *G.C.* 1904, i. 333; *O.R.* 1904, 173.—Wellesley.

C. × Louise, *Sand. O. Guide*, 336.

P. × Louise, *O.R.* 1907, 169, **f.** 21.—Scott.

287a. **P.** × **Humbertii** (Mastersianum × niveum).—Sander, 1904.

C. × Prince Humbert, *G.C.* 1904, ii. 230; *O.R.* 1904, 309; *Gard.* 1904, ii. 283.—Sander.

290a. **P.** × **Iacchus** (Dayanum ♀ × Gowerianum), *O.R.* 1905, 283.—Young, 1905.

292. **P.** × **Ian** (p. 168).

C. × John Hamilton, *G.C.* 1905, ii. 414.—Lambeau.

293. **P.** × **I'Ansoni** (p. 168); *O.R.* 1905, 281, **f.** 64.

294. **P.** × **Ilione** (p. 168).

C. × Clio, *Gard.* 1904, i. 158; *G.C.* 1904, ii. 323; *O.R.* 1904, 364.—Sander.

295. **P.** × **illustre** (p. 168); *O.R.* 1904, 156.

295a. **P.** × **Imogene** (× Arthurianum ♀ × ciliolare), *O.R.* 1905, 103; 1906, 136, **f.** 16.—(Charlesworth) Wellesley, 1905.

296a. **P.** × **imperiale** (Rothschildianum × Stonei).—Sander, 1906.

C. × imperiale, *O.R.* 1906, 216.—Sander.

297a. **P.** × **ingens** (insigne × Rothschildianum), *O.R.* 1904, 103.—Appleton, 1904.

There appears to be some doubt about the parentage of this hybrid.

299a. **P.** × **Io-Argus** (Argus × Io).—Cookson, 1907.

C. × Io-Argus, *O.R.* 1907, 343.—Cookson.

300. **P. × Iphis** (p. 169).

C. × Argo-tonsum, *G.C.* 1904, ii. 324 ; *O.R.* 1904, 363.—Goodson.

307. **P. × Jeanette** (p. 169).

C. × Grace Pitt, *G.C.* 1905, ii. 218 ; *O.R.* 1905, 307.—Pitt.

C. × Closonianum, *Rev. H. Belge*, 1906, 23.—Lambeau.

308a. **P. × Jerninghamiæ** (Spicerianum × Winnianum).—Wellesley, 1905.

C. × memoria Jerninghamiæ, *G.C.* 1905, i. 15 ; *O.R.* 1905, 50 ; *G. World*, 1905, 69, 73, f.—Wellesley.

The parentage of this hybrid was unrecorded, but it apparently belongs here.

317. **P. × Kamilii** (p. 171) ; *O.R.* 1904, 101.

Fig. 118. Paphiopedilum × Hopkinsianum var. Louise.

318a. **P. × keighleyense** (× Arthurianum × nitens).—Craven, 1907.

C. × keighleyense, *O.R.* 1907, 346.

329. **P. × Lasellei** (p. 172).

C. × Alcibiades magnificum, *G.C.* 1905, i. 15, 16 ; 1906, i. 30, 52, f. 27 ; *O.R.* 1905, 50 ; 1906, 43, 50 ; *G.M.* 1906, 55, f. ; *Gard.* 1906, i. 55, f. ; *G. Alb.* 1906, 28, f.—Holford.

330. **P. × Lathamianum** (p. 172, fig. 62).

C. × Lathamianum, *Lind.* xvii. t. 808.

C. × Janssensii, *G.C.* 1905, i. 62; *Rev. H. Belge*, 1905, 47.—Janssens and Putzeys.

. C. × (unnamed), *Die Gart.* 1906, 386, **t. f.** 4.

330a. **P. × Laura** (× Arthurianum × œnanthum), *O.R.* 1905, 103.—(Bleu) Wellesley, 1905.

C. × Albert Westendorp, *Rev. H. Belge*, 1905, 273.—Deschryver.

332. **P. × Lawrebel** (p. 173).

C. × Lawrebel, *Gtfl.* 1906, 225, **t.** 1550.

332a. **P. × Lawregower** (× Gowerianum × Lawrenceanum).—Cypher, 1906.

C. × Lawregower, *O.R.* 1906, 183.—Cypher.

333. **P. × Leander** (p. 173).

P. × Leeanum, Cambridge Lodge var., *O.R.* 1907, 92.—R. I. Measures.

337. **P. × Leeanum** (p. 175).

C. × Drapeau Blanc, *Draps Dom. Cat.* 1904.

C. × Leeanum, *Amer. G.* 1904, 668, **f.** (v. Gravesianum); *G.C.* 1905, i. 27, **f.** 14 (v. giganteum); 88, suppl. **t.** (v. J. Gurney Fowler); *G.M.* 1905, 97, **f** (id.); 1907, 103, **f.** (v. Clinkaberryanum); *Gard.* 1905, i. 105. **ff.** (v. J. Gurney Fowler); *J.H.* 1906, ii. 569, **f.** (v. Corona).

C. × Confetti, *G.C.* 1905, i. 62.—Janssens and Putzeys.

C. × (unnamed), *Die Gart.* 1906, 386, **t. f.** 1.

339a. **P. × Leon** (× Leeanum × gigas? (Prewettii).—Pauwels, 1906.

C. × Leon, *Chron. O.* ii. 74.—Pauwels.

340. **P. × Leonæ** (p. 176); *O.R.* 1905, 153, **f.** 34 (v. Craveniæ).

342a. **P. × leyburnense** (Charlesworthii × Haywoodianum).—Mrs. Haywood, 1904.

C. × leyburnense, *G.C.* 1904, ii. 212; *O.R.* 1904, 310.—Farrer.

C. × Mrs. Haywood, *G.C.* 1904, i. 31; *O.R.* 1904, 50.—Mrs. Haywood.

C. × Firmin Lambeau, *Rev. H. Belge*, 1905, 239; *G.C.* 1905, ii. 269; *O.R.* 1905, 343.—Duchesne and Lanthoine.

345. **P. × Lincolnii** (p. 176).

C. × Abraham Lincoln, *O.R.* 1905, 106, 373.—Wellesley.

350. **P. × longwoodense** (p. 176).

C. × Standard, *Gard.* 1904, ii. 320.—Low.

C. × Lord Ossulton, *G.C.* 1904, ii. 323; 1905, ii. 317; *O.R.* 1904, 364. ("Lord Coulson"); 1905, 339.—Charlesworth.

C. × Sunray, *G.C.* 1904, ii. 432; *O.R.* 1905, 21.—Charlesworth.

C. × Standaert, *Rev. H. Belge*, 1905, 263.—Peeters.

C. × Margaritæ, *Jard.* 1905, 104, **f.** H.—Cappe.

C. × Padgeni, *G.C.* 1905, ii. 381; *O.R.* 1905, 367.—Goodson.

350a. **P. × Lonsdaleæ** (× Arthurianum × Lathamianum).—Wellesley, 1907.

C. × Mrs. Robert Lonsdale, *G.C.* 1907, i. 132.—Wellesley.

353a. **P. × Lubbersii** (barbatum × calophyllum (politum).—Draps Dom, 1904.

C. × Lubbersii, *J. S. H. F.* 1904, 465; *Rev. H. Belge,* 1905, 278; *G.C.* 1905, ii. 414.—Draps Dom.

353a. P. × **Lucasiæ** (× Clinkaberryanum × insigne).—Lucas, 1905.

C. × Edith Lucas, *G.C.* 1905, ii. 218; *O.R.* 1905, 307.—Lucas.

353b. P. × **Lucasii** (× Berkeleyanum (Beekmanni) × Swinburnei).—G. F. Moore, 1907.

C. × Chas. Lucas, *G.C.* 1907, i. 195; *O.R.* 1907, 117.—G. F. Moore.

356. P. × **Lumsdenii** (p. 178).

C. × Madame Bette, *Rev. H. Belge,* 1904, 120.—Lambeau.

C. × Henri Duval, *J. S. H. Fr.* 1904, 417, 418.—Debille.

358a. P. × **luxembergense** (Argus × Fairrieanum).—Opoix, 1907.

C. × Marguerite Opoix, *J. S. H. Fr.* 1907, 540.—Opoix.

364a. P. × **Madame** (× Calypso × Figaro).—F. C. Young, 1907.

C. × Madame Lloyd, *G.C.* 1907, i. 62; *O.R.* 1907, 54.—F. C. Young.

376a. P. × **Margery** (exul × tonsum), *O.R.* 1904, 102.—Appleton, 1904.

376b. P. × **Marjorie** (× Leeanum × Simonii).—Bromilow, 1907.

C. × Marjorie, *O.R.* 1907, 368.—Bromilow.

379. P. × **Marwoodii** (p. 181).

C. × Gloriana, *G.C.* 1904, ii. 43; *O.R.* 1904, 243.—Alcock, 1904.

381a. P. × **Mastersio-exul** (exul × Mastersianum).—Cypher, 1907.

C. × Mastersio-exul, *G.C.* 1907, i. 108; *O.R.* 1907, 84.—Cypher.

381b. P. × **Mastersio-villosum** (Mastersianum × villosum).—Sander, 1904.

C. × Masterso-villosum, *G.C.* 1904, i. 30; *O.R.* 1904, 50.—Sander.

382. P. × **Matthewsii** (p. 182).

C. × Lawro-Mastersii, *Rev. H. Belge,* 1905, 239; *G.C.* 1905, ii. 269.—Draps Dom.

383. P. × **Maudiæ** (p. 182).

C. × Maudiæ, *Amer. G.* 1904, 210, f.; *Amer. G.C.* 1905, 54, f.

390. P. × **Melia** (p. 183).

P. × Victorinus, *O.R.* 1904, 58.—Young.

C. × Briton, *G.C.* 1905, i. 110; *O.R.* 1905, 79.—Mrs. Gratrix.

392. P. × **Menelik** (p. 183).

C. × Mrs. W. Mostyn, *Gard.* 1905, i. 121.

392a. P. × **Mercatellii** (Lowii × Stonei ♀), *O.R.* 1905, 38.—Linari, 1904.

C. × Memoria Mercatelli, *Bull. Soc. Tosc.* 1904, 257.—Linari.

397a. P. × **Minerva** (exul × superbiens).—Lambeau, 1904.

C. × Minerva, *O.R.* 1904, 331; *Rev. H. Belge.* 1905, 22.—Lambeau.

C. × Minervæ, *G.C.* 1904, ii. 309.—Lambeau.

399. P. × **Minnie** (p. 184).

C. × Sophie, *Rev. H. Belge,* 1904, 70.—Lemoinier.

403a. P. × **Moloch** (Charlesworthii × Hera).—Holford, 1907.

C. × Moloch, *G.C.* 1907, i. 61; *O.R.* 1907, 52, 62.—Holford.

C. × Dante, *O.R.* 1907, 341.—Holford.

403a. P. × **Mooreanum** (× Evelyn × nitens).—(Moore) Holford, 1904.

C. × G. F. Moore, *G.C.* 1904, ii. 432; 1905, i. 61; *O.R.* 1905, 20, 52.—(Moore) Holford.

C. × George Moore, *G.C.* 1907, i. 61; *O.R.* 1907, 53.—Cypher.

403b. P. × **Moorei** (Godefroyæ × tonsum).—J. W. Moore, 1906.

C. × (unnamed), *G.C.* 1906, ii. Nov. 10, Suppl. 4; *O.R.* 1906, 364.—J. W. Moore.

405. P. × **Morganiæ** (p. 185); *O.R.* 1904, 41, f. 15.

C. × Morganiæ, *J.H.* 1905, i. 49, f.; *G.C.* 1907, i. 66, f. 29.

C. × Mme. Coffigniez, *J. S. H. Fr.* 1905, 477.—Opoix.

406. P. × **Moussetianum** (p. 185).

C. × callo-Veitchii, *G.C.* 1905, ii. 269.—Stepman de Messenmæcher.

407a. P. × **Muriel** (Chamberlainianum × tonsum), *O.R.* 1904, 102.—Appleton, 1904.

414a. P. × **nigratum** (Argus × Swinburnei).—Stanley, 1907.

C. × nigratum, *O.R.* 1907, 344.

415. P. × **Niobe** (p. 188); *O.R.* 1905, 41, f. 9 (v. Oakwood seedling).

C. × Niobe, Westonbirt var., *G.M.* 1904, 812, f.; *J.H.* 1904, ii. 519, f.

416. P. × **Niobe-Leeanum** (p. 188).

C. × Cecil Dickson, *G.C.* 1906, i. 63; *O.R.* 1906, 53.—Wellesley.

C. × Diomede, *O.R.* 1907, 364.—Veitch.

417. P × **nitens** (p. 188).

C. × (unnamed), *Die Gart.* 1906, 386, t. f. 3.

C. × Hector, *G.C.* 1907, i. 31; *O.R.* 1907, 55.—Keeling.

C. × Queen of Yellows, *G.C.* 1907, i. 62; *O.R.* 1907, 53.—Armstrong and Brown.

425. P. × **œnanthum** (p. 189).

C. × œnanthum, *Orchis*, i. 52, ff. 25, 26 (v. superbum).

435. P. × **orangense** (p. 191).

C. × Nora, *G.C.* 1906, ii. 299; *O.R.* 1906, 344.—Thompson.

445. P. × **Parkerianum** (p. 192).

C. × Geneviève Opoix, *J. S. H. F.* 1904, 22.—Opoix.

C. × Admiral Togo, *G.C.* 1905. i. 62; *Rev. H. Belge*, 1905, 47.—Janssens and Putzeys.

452a. P. × **Pelican** (× Andromeda × Rothschildianum).—Cookson, 1904.

C. × The Pelican, *G.C.* 1904, ii. 324; *O.R.* 1904, 363.—Cookson.

457a. P. × **Pharos** (Godefroyæ × Hookeræ).—Sander, 1906.

C. × Pallas, *G.C.* 1906, i. 109; *O.R.* 1906. 85.—Sander.

460. P. × **Phœbe** (p. 193); *O.R.* 1904, 101.

460a. P. × **Phryne** (Argus × exul).—Wrigley, 1907.

C. × (unnamed), *O.R.* 1907, 93.—Wrigley.

476. P. × **Priam** (p. 196).

C. × Leucas, *G.C.* 1905, i. 60; *O.R.* 1905, 54.—Veitch.

487. P. × **Pytho** (p. 197).

C. × Masterso-callosum, *G.C.* 1905, i. 268; *O.R.* 1905, 150.—Sander.

490. P. × **Rachel** (p. 198).

C. × May Proctor, *G.C.* 1904, ii. 157; *O.R.* 1904, 271.—P. Smith.

492a. P. × **Rajah** (callosum × triumphans).—Sander, 1906.

C. × Rajah, *G.C.* 1906, i. 109; *O.R.* 1906, 85.—Sander.

493. P. × **Rappartii** (p. 198).

C. × King Carlos, *G.C.* 1904, ii. 355.—Low.

C. × Don Carlos, *O.R.* 1904, 367.—Low.

The parentage of this hybrid requires confirmation.

493a. P. × **Readii** (callosum × Matthewsii).—Fowler, 1907.

C. × Readii, *G.C.* 1907, i. 30; *O.R.* 1907, 49.—Fowler.

503a. P. × **Rhesus** (× Harrisianum × Winnianum ♀), *O.R.* 1906, 60.—Young, 1906.

505a. P. × **Riddifordii** (× Atys ♀ × calloso-barbatum), *O.R.* 1905, 119.—Clark, 1905.

507a. P. × **Robbinsii** (× Calypso × Godseffianum ♀), *O.R.* 1904, 120.—Vanner, 1904.

509. P. × **Robinianum** (p. 200).

C. × Lowio-Parishii, *G.C.* 1904, i. 270; *O.R.* 1904, 140.—Drewett.

509a. P. × **Robsoni** (exul × insigne).—Sander, 1905.

C. × Robsoni, *G.C.* 1905, i. 174; *O.R.* 1905, 119.—Bostock.

C. × exquisitum, *G.C.* 1905, i. 15; *O.R.* 1905, 52—Sander.

The parentage of this hybrid requires confirmation.

512. P. × **Rolfei** (p. 200).

C. × Rolfei superbum, *G. World*, 1904, 1041, f.

C. × Rolfeanum, *J. S. H. F.* 1904, 777.—Beranek.

C. × Souv. de Düsseldorf, *G.C.* 1904, ii. 309; *O.R.* 1904, 331.—Beranek.

513. P. × **Romulus** (p. 200).

C. × Archimedes, *G.C.* 1904, i. 14; *O.R.* 1904, 21.—Warburton.

C. × Amy Moore, *G.C.* 1905, i. 15; *O.R.* 1905, 51.—G. F. Moore.

C. × The Czar, *G.C.* 1905, i. 31; *O.R.* 1905, 55.—Gratrix.

C. × Nogi, *G. World*, 1905, 29, 37, f.—Cypher.

C. × Albertiano-nitens, *G.C.* 1905, i. 62.—Lambeau.

C. × Damyre, *G.C.* 1905, i. 62.—Janssens & Putzeys.

C. × eboraicum, *G.C.* 1906, ii. 414; *O.R.* 1906, 19; *J.H.* 1906, ii. 589, f.—Craven.

513a. P. × **Rose** (× Haywoodianum × Spicerianum ♀).—Rogerson, 1907.

C. × Rose, *O.R.* 1907, 310.—Rogerson.

515. P. × **Rosita** (p. 201).

C. × Stanley Rogerson, *G.C.* 1904, ii. 323; *O.R.* 1904, 364.—Sander.

518. P. × **Rossii** (p. 202).

C. × Baron Kuroki, *G.C.* 1904, i. 398, 410; *O.R.* 1904, 213, 215.—Low

There appears to be some doubt about the parentage of this hybrid.

524a. P. × **Sally** (barbatum × nitens), *O.R.* 1904, 102.—Appleton, 1904.

525. P. × **Salomonæ** (p. 202).

C. × H. S. Goodson, *G.C.* 1906, i. 158; *O.R.* 1906, 108.—Goodson.

525a. **P. × Sanacderæ** (insigne × Sanacteus).—Wellesley, 1905.

C. × Sanacderæ, *G.C.* 1905, ii. 348; *O.R.* 1905, 364.—Wellesley, 1905.

525b. **P. × Sanacteus** (insigne × Simonii).—Cookson, 1905.

C. × San-Actæus, *G.C.* 1905, i. 61; *O.R.* 1905, 52; *G.M.* 1905, 821, **f.**—Cookson.

C. × Mrs. Robson, *G.C.* 1907, i. 62; *O.R.* 1907, 54.—Robson.

The record of this hybrid is probably imperfect.

· 525c. **P. × Sanarthur** (× Arthurianum × insigne), *O.R.* 1905, 373.—Wellesley, 1905.

C. × San-Arthur, *G.C.* 1907, i. 132.—Wellesley.

526. **P. × Sanderi** (p. 202).

C. × Boadicea, *G.C.* 1904, ii. 293; *O.R.* 1904, 340.—Sander.

530. **P. × Schlesingerianum** (p. 203).

C. × alportense, *G.C.* 1904, i. 125; *O.R.* 1904, 87, 344.—Gratrix.

C. × fulshawense, *O.R.* 1907, 368.—Bromilow.

531. **P. × Schrœderi** (p. 204).

C. × Mme. Hustin, *J. S. H. F.* 1904, 670, 778; *O.R.* 1905, 137.

P. × Baron Schröder, *O.R.* 1905, 136, **f.** 30 (v. Germaine Opoix), 137, **f.** 31 (v. Gaston Bultel).

C. × Germaine Opoix, Westfield var., *G.M.* 1906, 766, **f.**; *J.H.* 1906, ii. 475, **f.**; *G.C.* 1906, ii. 410, 411, **f.** 154; *Rev. H.* 1906, 328, **t.**

533a. **P. × Scipio** (× nitens × Schlesingerianum).—Holford, 1904.

C. × Scipio, *G.C.* 1904, i. 174; *O.R.* 1904, 115.—Holford.

536a. **P. × Seraphis** (× œnanthum × Orpheus ♀), *O.R.* 1906, 60.—Young, 1906.

536b. **P. × Seymouri** (callosum × gigas? (Prewetti).—Low, 1907.

C. × E. J. Seymour, *G.C.* 1907, i. 259; *O.R.* 1907, 149, 150.—Low.

536c. **P. × Shaferi** (× Leeanum × Medeia), *O.R.* 1905, 95.—(Roebling) Shafer.

536d. **P. × Sheila** (× Harrisianum × triumphans).—Thompson, 1906.

C. × Sheila, *G.C.* 1906, ii. 78; *O.R.* 1906, 249.—Thompson.

C. × Sheba, *G.C.* 1906, ii. Nov. 10, Suppl. 4 (Westfield var.).—Wellesley.

540. **P. × Simonii** (p. 206).

C. × Mme. Chas. Dietrich, *G.C.* 1905, ii. 414.—Lambeau.

C. × Viola Lee, *G.C.* 1905, ii. 446; *O.R.* 1906, 13.—Drewett.

C. × F. H. Cann, *G.C.* 1905, ii. 447; *O.R.* 1906, 15; *G.M.* 1906, 44, **f.**—G. F. Moore.

C. × Putzeysi, *Rev. H. Belge*, 1905, 22.—Lambeau.

C. × Sidneyanum, *G.C.* 1906, i. 23.—Tracy.

C. × Actæus, *G.C.* 1907, i. 12, **f.** 10 (v. langleyense).

C. × xanthinum, *G.C.* 1907, i. 30; *O.R.* 1907, 51.—Tracy.

C. × (unnamed), *Die Gart.* 1906, 386, **t. f.** 2.

540a. **P. Singeri** (× conco-bellatulum × insigne).—Low, 1906.

P. × G. Singer, *O.R.* 1906, 90.—Low.

547a. **P. × St.-Albans** (× Aphrodite × Harrisianum).—Sander, 1905.

C. × St. Albans, *G.C.* 1905, ii. 446; *O.R.* 1906, 24.—Sander.

549a. **P. × Statherianum** (Chamberlainianum × Mastersianum).—Armstrong & Brown, 1907.

C. × Statherianum, *O.R.* 1907, 178.

550a. **P. × Stephanos** (× œnanthum × Pollettianum).—Fletcher, 1906.

C. × Stephanos, *G.C.* 1906, ii. 360; *O.R.* 1906, 366; *G.M.* 1906, 798, **f.**—Fletcher.

562a. **P. × Tankervillei** (exul × nitens).—Sander, 1906.

C. × Earl of Tankerville, *G.C.* 1906, i. 30; *O.R.* 1906, 51.—Sander.

564. **P. × Tautzianum** (p. 210).

C. × Tautzianum, *Gard.* 1907, i. 89, **f.** (v. nigricans).

566. **P. × tessellatum** (p. 210).

C. × tessellatum, *G.C.* 1906, i. 19, **f.** 13 (v. rubens).

566a. **P. × Thais** (insigne ♀ × Orpheus), *O.R.* 1905, 157.—Young.

567. **P. × Thalia** (p. 210).

C. × Thalia var. Mrs. Francis Wellesley, *G.C.* 1906, i. 5, **f.** 2; *Gard.* 1906, i. 9, **f.**; *G.M.* 1906, 84, **f.**; *J.H.* 1906, i. 111, **f.**; *O.R.* 1906, 28.

569a. **P. × Thornianum** (Charlesworthii × nitens).—Appleton, 1904.

C. × Thornianum, *G.C.* 1904, ii. 433; *O.R.* 1905, 20.—Appleton.

C. × (unnamed), *O.R.* 1906, 369.—Low.

C. × (unnamed), *O.R.* 1907, 85, 93.—Wrigley.

570. **P. × Thorntoni** (p. 211).

C. × Katherine, *G.C.* 1905, i. 108; *O.R.* 1905, 75.—Goodson.

571. **P. × Thyades** (p. 212).

C. × (unnamed), *O.R.* 1907, 178.—Armstrong & Brown.

572a. **P. × tonso-superbiens** (superbiens × tonsum).—Goodson, 1904.

C. × tonso-superbiens, *G.C.* 1904, ii. 343.—Goodson.

572b. **P. × Tracyanum** (× aureum × Leeanum).—Tracy, 1904.

C. × Tracyanum, *G.C.* 1904, ii. 433; *O.R.* 1905, 21; *G. World*, 1905, 159, **f.**—Tracy.

575a. **P. × Trippiæ** (× Harrisianum × Hera).—Mrs. Haywood, 1905.

C. × Lady Tripp, *G.C.* 1905, ii. 411; *O.R.* 1906, 11.—Mrs. Haywood.

576. **P. × triumphans** (p. 212).

C. × triumphans, *J.H.* 1905, ii. 495, **f.**; *G.M.* 1905, 742, **f.**; *G.M.* 1904, 794, **f.** (v. magnificum).

C. × Fairlawn, *O.R.* 1906, 366.—Goodson.

583a. **P. × Upcheri** (Argus × Mastersianum).—Upcher, 1905.

C. × Argo-Mastersianum, *G.C.* 1905, i. 245.—Upcher.

584. **P. × Urania** (p. 213).

C. × Urania, *G.C.* 1904, ii. 152 (Rehder's var.).

C. × M. Martin Cahuzac, *Jard.* 1905, 104, **f.** I.—Cappe.

586a. **P. × Vanessa** (præstans × villosum), *O.R.* 1905, 216.—Mrs. Ross.

590a. P. × **Venilla** (Victoria-Mariæ ♀ × villosum), *O.R.* 1904, 58.—Young.

592a. P. × **Vera** (Godefroyæ × Spicerianum), *O.R.* 1904, 102.—Appleton.

C. × (unnamed), *G.C.* 1904, i. 109; *O.R.* 1904, 84.—Beranek.

597a. P. × **Victory** (× Euryale × triumphans).—Sander, 1906.

C. × Victory, *G.C.* 1906, ii. 234; *O.R.* 1906, 311.—Sander.

600. P. × **Villeboisii** (p. 216).

C. × Miss Annie Goodson, *O.R.* 1906, 366.—Goodson.

601a. P. × **villma** (× Norma × villosum).—Drewett, 1905.

C. × villma, *G C.* 1905, ii. 446; *O.R.* 1906, 13.—Drewett.

606a. P. × **Webbiæ** (× Minos × nitens).—Wellesley, 1907.

C. × Miss Dora Webb, *G.C.* 1907, i. 132.—Wellesley.

606b. P. × **Wellesleyæ** (× Gowerianum × Sanderianum).—Wellesley, —1905.

C. × Mrs. Francis Wellesley, *G.C.* 1905, i. 60, 83; 1907, i. 161; *O.R.* 1905, 53; 1907, 115.—Wellesley.

606c. P. × **Wellesleyi** (Lawrenceanum × Niobe).—Wellesley, 1906.

C. × Lawrenceano-Niobe, *G.C.* 1906, ii. 224; 1907, i. 132.

606d. P. × **Wendigo** (callosum ♀ × nitens), *O R.* 1905, 120.—Young.

607a. P. × **westfieldiense** (× Leeanum × Pollettianum).—Wellesley, 1904.

C. × westfieldiense, *G.C.* 1904, ii. 432; *O.R.* 1905, 21, 50; *G. World*, 1905, 69, f.—Wellesley.

611a. P. × **Whiteleggei** (bellatulum × Euryale).—Sander, 1905.

C. × G. G. Whitelegge, *G.C.* 1905, ii. 316; *O.R.* 1905, 341.—Sander.

612a. P. × **Williamsonianum** (× Leeanum × Rothschildianum).—Sander, 1904.

C. × Williamsonianum, *G.C.* 1904, ii. 118; *O.R.* 1904, 268.—Sander.

612b. P. × **Willoughbyæ** (Chamberlainianum × Charlesworthii).—Strickland, 1907.

C. × Mrs. Sutton Willoughby, *G.C.* 1907, i. 66.—Strickland.

C. × Cynthia, *O.R.* 1907, 308.—Holford.

620. P. × **Wottoni** (p. 218).

C. × westpointense, *G.C.* 1905, ii. 447; *O.R.* 1906, 16.—Gratrix. Raised from P. bellatulum album and P. callosum Sanderæ.

622a. P. × **Wrigleyi** (p. 219).

C. × Wormsæ, *J. S. H. F.* 1904, 105; *Jard.* 1905, 104, f. B.—Cappe.

C. × (unnamed), *O.R.* 1904, 92.—Craven.

C. × Elsie, *G.C.* 1906, ii. 360; *O.R.* 1906, 366.—Appleton.

625a. P. × **Yolande** (barbatum × exul), *O R.* 1904, 102.—Appleton, 1904.

627. P. × **Youngianum** (p. 220).

C. × Youngianum, *G.C.* 1906, ii. 439, f. 165 (v. superbum).

629. P. × **Zampa** (p. 220).

C. × hirsuto-Leeanum, *G.C.* 1905, ii. 414.—Stepman de Messemæcher.

632. P × **Zollingeri** (p. 632).

C. × Gordoniæ, *Rev. H. Belge*, 1906, 47.—Lambeau.

27. PHAIOCALANTHE.

3a. **P.-c. × Colmanii** (Calanthe Regnieri (Stevensii) × Phaius Cooksoni (Norman), *G.C.* 1907, i. 31 ; *O.R.* 1907, 49, 89, f. 10.—Colman, 1907.

29. PHAIUS.

4. **P. × Chapmanii** (p. 222) ; *O.R.* 1907, 221.

5. **P. × Clive** (p. 222) ; *G. World*, 1904, ii. 670, suppl. f.; *G.C.* 1907, i. 343, f. 144.

Fig. 119. PHAIOCALANTHE × COLMANII.

6. **P. × Cooksonæ** (p. 222) ; *O.R.* 1907, 189, 221.

7 **P. × Cooksoni** (p. 222) ; *G.M.* 1907, 134, f.

P. × Norman, *G. World*, 1904, 670, suppl. f. ; *G.C.* 1907, i. 343, f. 144.

8a. **P. × Doris** (× Cooksonæ × oakwoodiensis), *G.C.* 1906, i. 350 ; *O.R.* 1906, 180 ; 1907, 221, 222.—Cookson, 1906.

9. **P. × Harold** (p. 224) ; *G. World*, 1904, 670, suppl. f. ; *G.C.* 1907, i. 343, f. 144 ; *O.R.* 1907, 188.

12. **P. × Marthæ** (p. 224) ; *Gtfl.* 1904, 449, t. 1530.

13. **P. × oakwoodiensis** (p. 224) ; *O.R.* 1907, 189.

16. **P. × Phœbe** (p. 224) ; *O.R.* 1907, 188.

31. PHRAGMOPEDILUM.

5. P. × **Brysa** (p. 227).

Selenipedium × Pallene, *G.C.* 1905, i. 60; *O.R.* 1905, 54.—Veitch.

17. P. × **giganteum** (p. 228).

S. × Mme. Linden, *G.C.* 1904, i. 238; *O.R.* 1904, 139.—Linden.

Cypripedium × Gottianum, *G.C.* 1904, ii. 293; *O.R.* 1904, 340.—Sander.

18. P. × **grande** (p. 229).

C. × grande, *Die Gartenw.* x. 77-79, f.

23. P. × **nitidissimum** (p. 229).

S. × nitidissimum, *Dict. Ic. O.* Sel. hyb. t. 3.

32a. P. × **torconiense** (caricinum × Lemoinierianum).—Lemoinier, 1906.

S. × torconiense, *Rev. H. Belge*, 1906, 268; *Dict. Ic. O.* Sel. hyb. t. 4.

31a. PROMENÆA.

1. P. × **Rollissoni** (stapelioides ♀ × xanthina).—Crawshay, 1905.

P. × Crawshayana, *O.R.* 1905, 222, 262.—Crawshay, 1905.

Zygopetalum × Crawshayanum, *G.C.* 1905, i. 333; *O.R.* 1905, 172; *G.M.* 1905, 561, f.—Crawshay.

Originally described as a species under the name of Maxillaria Rollissoni, *Lindl. Bot. Reg.* sub. t. 1986, and subsequently figured (*l.c.* 1838, t. 40), but now believed to be a natural hybrid with the above parentage.

33. SOBRALIA.

1a. S. × **dellensis** (leucoxantha × Lowii), *O.R.* 1907, 196. —Schröder, 1907.

34. SOPHROCATLÆLIA.

1a. S.-c.-l. × **Medeia** (Cattleya bicolor × Sophrolælia × Orpeti), *G.C.* 1907, ii. 318; *O.R.* 1907, 362.—Holford, 1907.

1b. S.-c.-l. × **Phyllis** (C. Lawrenceana × S.-l. × læta), *G.C.* 1907, ii. 191; *O.R.* 1907, 306, 315.—Holford, 1907.

35. SOPHROCATTLEYA.

0a. S.-c. × **Antiochus** (C. Warscewiczii × S.-c. × Cleopatra), *G.C.* 1907, ii. 221; *O.R.* 1907, 309.—Charlesworth.

0b. S.c. × **Atreus** (C. Lawrenceana × Sophronitis grandiflora), *G.C.* 1904, ii. 324; *O.R.* 1904, 365.—Veitch, 1904.

4a. S.-c. × **Doris** (C. Dowiana × S. grandiflora), *G.C.* 1904, ii. 327; 1905, ii. 412; *O.R.* 1904, 342, 344; *G.M.* 1906, 209, f.—(Bull) Leemann.

6a. S.-c. × **Heathii** (C. Schrœderæ × S. grandiflora ♀), *O.R.* 1907, 85, 91. —Heath, 1907.

7b. S.-c. × **Marcus** (C. Enid × S.-c. × Calypso), *G.C.* 1907, ii. 221; *O.R.* 1907, 309.—Charlesworth, 1907.

9a. **S.-c. × warnhamensis** (C. amethystoglossa × S. grandiflora), *G.C.* 1904, ii. 355; 1906, i. 158: *O.R.* 1904, 366; 1906, 108; *J. H.* 1906, i. 295, **f** (v. Cerise); *G.M.* 1906, 547, **f.**—Lucas, 1904.

36. SOPHROLÆLIA.

3. **S.-l. × læta** (p. 236); *J. H* 1905, ii. 99, **f.** (v. Orpetiana).

Fig. 120. SPATHOGLOTTIS × COLMANII AND ITS PARENTS (S. × Veitchii (see p. 238) to left and S. aurea to right).

5a. **S.-l. × Phroso** (Lælia Jongheana × S.-l. × læta), *G.C.* 1906, ii. 98; 1907, i. 259, 281, **f.** 118 (v. superba); *O.R.* 1906, 252; 1907, 148, 158 (v. superba).—Holford, 1906.

7a. **S.-l. × Leda** (L. pumila × S.-l. × Gratrixiæ), *G.C.* 1907, ii. 221 ; *O.R.* 1907, 309.—Charlesworth.

37. SPATHOGLOTTIS.

Oa. **S. × Colmanii** (aurea × Veitchii), *O.R.* 1906, 80, 83.—Colman, 1906.

38. STANHOPEA.

2a. **S. × Wolteriana** (Martiana × tigrina ♀), *G.C.* 1905, ii. 102, f. 35 ; *O.R.* 1905, 272 ; 1907, 255 ; *Gartwelt.* x. 200, f.—Wolter, 1905.

44. ZYGOPETALUM.

1. **Z. × Clayi** (p. 237) ; *J. H.* 1905, i. 399, f.

1a. **Z. × Gottianum** (maxillare × Perrenoudi), *G.C.* 1904, i. 270 ; *O.R.* 1904, 141 ; 1906, 112.—Sander, 1904.

2a. **Z. × maxjorisi** (Jorisianum × maxillare), *G.C.* 1904, ii. 192 ; *O.R.* 1904, 306 ; 1906, 44, 53.—R. I. Measures, 1904.

6. **Z. × secundum** (p. 238).

Z. × Mackayo-crinitum, *G.C.* 1905, i. 78.—Sander.

INDEX OF SYNONYMS.

AS the names of the parents in Part I, and the adopted names of the hybrids in Part II, are in alphabetical order, it has only been thought necessary to give an Index of Synonyms. A name which does not appear in the Index should be found in the body of the work, and *vice versa*. The Addenda to each part should, of course, be consulted. The names are generally cited in the Index in the same form as in the text, but a few modifications have been made. For example, the article "the" has been uniformly omitted, and thus such a name as "Cypripedium × The Duke" appears as "C. × Duke." A few abbreviated words have also been modified in form where diversity of practice would have separated those that recur in different forms under the same genus, as "Madame," "Mme.," &c. In a few cases the repetition of a specific name is indicated by the initial letter, thus Cypripedium × Harrisianum, C. × H. v. lineatum, C. × H. v. robustum, and C. × H. v. Wallærtianum, which so-called varieties of C. × Harrisianum really belong elsewhere.

Cypripedium—

Cypripedium—

Cypripedium—

Cypripedium—

LIST OF ILLUSTRATIONS.

Future Supplements.

IT is inevitable that a work of this kind, dealing with a subject which is progressing with such rapid strides, should very quickly become out of date. The preceding pages contain the hybrids recorded up to the end of 1907, so far as their history could be ascertained, but a large number have been recorded since, and almost every meeting of importance brings additions to the list.

As stated at page v. of the Preface, it is intended to publish future additions in the ORCHID REVIEW, so as to prevent the work from falling out of date. Those for 1908 have already been collected, and a first instalment will appear in an early number of that work, after which the records will be continued from time to time as the materials accumulate. This will also afford an opportunity of correcting any errors that may be pointed out, and of including any hybrids that have been omitted for want of information. It is quite probable that materials exist which will enable the origin of some of these doubtful hybrids to be cleared up, and it is hoped that any such information will be forthcoming.

In order that future records may be as complete as possible, it is hoped that raisers will forward the necessary information respecting their productions, as they reach the flowering stage, accompanied by a flower as a voucher of authenticity, and this remark applies equally to any old hybrid which has been overlooked or omitted, or whose origin has been incorrectly given. If raisers will compare the work with their own private records, and let us know the result, some important information may be elicited, for we have reason to believe that there are hybrids in existence whose origin has never been properly recorded. Hybrids that have not yet reached the flowering stage are outside the scope of the work.

On the opposite page is printed a schedule showing the kind of information required, and it would facilitate the work if raisers will arrange the information forwarded on the same plan.

The information should be addressed to—

The Editor of the ORCHID REVIEW,
12, Lawn Crescent,
Kew Gardens,
London, W.

Schedule for Information respecting Additional Orchid Hybrids.

1. Seedparent.
2. Pollen parent.
3. Name (if any).
4. Raiser.
5. Exhibitor.
6. Date of first flowering.
7. Record of publication or exhibition (if any).
8. Any additional information.

Example:

1. Calanthe Masuca.
2. Calanthe furcata.
3. Calanthe × Dominyi.
4. Veitch.
5. ———.
6. October, 1856.
7. *Gard. Chron.* 1858, p. 4.
8. The first hybrid Orchid raised by hand.

The above is only intended as a rough guide as to the kind of information desired, and its arrangement. Some of the points may not be known, and others will necessarily in some cases have to be left blank. If, however, there are doubts about the actual parentage, it is hoped, in the interests of accuracy, that this will be pointed out. The exhibitor is not always the actual raiser, and sometimes the latter is not certainly known, but the complete record is desired as often as possible.

The above form is obviously not suitable for corrections and criticisms of existing records, which when necessary we hope to receive.

EDUCATION IN INDIA

Editor

R.K. Rao

KALPAZ PUBLICATIONS

DELHI-110052

EDUCATION IN INDIA

(Education)

ISBN: 81-7835-006-8

Published in 2005 in India by
Kalpaz Publications
C-30, Satyawati Nagar
Ashok Vihar Phase-III
Delhi-110052
E-Mail: kalpaz@hotmail.com

Laser Typeset at A.S. Printers
Printed at Mehra Offset Printers, New Delhi

Preface

Educational status in India is constantly changing as per the needs and capabilities of the nation. Now a days education has transgressed national boundaries and acquired a global dimension. National education systems and policies governing them are constantly changing in an attempt to meet the challenges of globalisation. Continued stress is being placed on restructuring of curricula, teaching technologies, planning, management mechanisms, and procedures for generating resources. Paradigm shifts are apparent, and the situation demands a relook at the higher education system and its management. This set of two volumes explains how the educational process in India is marching ahead in different fields employing the services if different agencies.

Before 1976, education was exclusively the responsibility of states, the Central Government was only concerned with certain areas like coordination and determination of standards in technical and higher education, etc. In 1976, through a Constitutional amendment, education became a joint responsibility. Decisions regarding the organisation and structure of education are largely the concern of the states. However, the Union Government has a clear responsibility regarding the quality and character of education. In addition to policy formulation, the Ministry of Human Resource Development, Department of Education shares with the states the responsibility for educational planning. The Central Advisory Board of Education (CABE), set up during the pre-Independence period in 1935, continues to play a lead role in the evolution and monitoring of educational policies and programmes, the most notable of which are the National Policy on Education (NPE), 1986, Programme of Action (PoA), 1986 and a revised NPE and PoA.

National Policy on Education, 1986 and the Programme of Action (PoA) 1992 envisage that free and compulsory education of satisfactory quality should be provided to all children up to the age of 14 years before the commencement of the 21st Century. The NPE visualised education as a dynamic, cumulative, lifelong process, providing diversity of learning opportunities to all segments of society. It envisaged improvement and expansion of education in all sectors; elimination of disparities in access and stresses on improvement in the quality and relevance of education at all levels—from primary to higher education along with technical and professional education. It is perhaps the first systematic effort on educational policies and programmes in India and should be useful to administrators, teachers and researchers alike.

Editor

Contents

Educational status in India is constantly changing as per the needs and capabilities of the nation. Now a days education has transgressed national boundaries and acquired a global dimension. National education systems and policies governing them are constantly changing in an attempt to meet the challenges of globalisation.

Continued stress is being placed on restructuring of curricula, teaching technologies, planning, management mechanisms, and procedures for generating resources. Paradigm shifts are apparent, and the situation demands a relook at the higher education system and its management.

This set of two volumes explains how the educational process in India is marching ahead in different fields employing the services if different agencies.

1
Evaluation of Education

The strategy of evaluation seeks to make a virtue of necessity, by looking at the patterns of intervention and trying to find whether any systematic changes in pupil, teacher, or school behaviour occur in conjunction with these. The results of these enquiries may only point to better questions around which future evaluations might be designed. We now take the main objectives of change in turn, explain the method of data collection, and present the results where data could be collected. In referring an individual pupil, a teacher is suggesting that this pupil's behaviour causes difficulties to a significantly greater extent than that of other pupils, without prolonged observation, it is impossible to determine the nature of the behaviour and the circumstances in which it arises. It is necessary to rely on the teacher's perception of the pupil's behaviour.

To accept that a record of behaviour is a perception creates one difficulty and solves another. The difficulty which it creates is that if the concern is not just with the behaviour at the time of referral, but also in the change in behaviour over time, then another record of behaviour must be made after a certain period of time, possibly as short as six months. For the second record to be comparable to the first, it needs to be completed under the same sort of circumstances, and with the same sort of perceptions. Ideally, the same person would make the second record as made the first. Since this is not always possible, a safeguard is to choose a means of recording which has been shown to be reasonably reliable when used by different people. The fact that the record may be as much of perception as of behaviour means that it might actually be a good indication of classroom disruption. As was emphasised, whether a classroom activity is determined to be disruptive depends largely on the attitudes and tolerance of the teacher involved, that is on the teacher's perception of the behaviour.

Disruption, then, is a construct which is a product of the behaviour, the situation, and the teacher's perception. In which case, a record of behaviour which includes these elements may be a helpful measure of disruption. The main requirements of a record of behaviour, in summary, include: It should be as precise as possible in specifying the disruptive behaviour in a variety of school situations: it should be capable of being used reliably on a second occasion, if necessary, by a different teacher: It should be simple and quick to complete. We found that the choice of available records was sparse, and settled for the Bristol Social Adjustment Guide (BSAG).

The Advantages of BSAG

In addition, we developed an instrument of our own. We were aware of the limitations of the BSAG, and particularly that the original reliability and validity studies were not convincing. Its widespread use by the National Child Development study had at least made it familiar to some teachers, and a degree of validity had been established in later studies. We later conducted a small reliability and validity study of our own, and concluded that the BSAG May be reasonably reliable for the same pupil across teachers, provided that they knew the pupil across teachers, provided that they knew the pupil well. The BSAG had two other advantages which persuaded us to adopt it. Firstly, it had an established scoring system and so, provided that we used the raw scores and not the standard scores, we could compare the records across time and derive means and standard deviations for groups of pupils in order to carry out statistical procedures.

Secondly, it contained positive, as well as negative, statements concerning a whole range of school situations. Because of this, most teachers were able to find some positive statements which applied to the referred pupil, thereby providing a more balanced account. The BSAG covers the following aspects of a pupil's school life: interaction with teachers, attitudes to school work, other children, games and play, personal ways, physique, general health and school achievement. (One variable which it does not cover and which we omitted to monitor independently was attendence.) Each of these aspects has a set of statements which sometimes describe behaviour, sometimes interactions and sometimes personal attitudes.

The teacher is asked to underline the statements which apply to the pupil. The guide is then scored on two main scales: one covers behaviour which is generally over-reactive and so called overact; the other covers behaviour which is generally under-reactive and so called Unract. (Since we were interested in Changes in Perceptions, it was possible to ignore any theory behind these concepts.) Both Ovract and Unract are divided up into sub-scales.

In practice, we have found that the two next important sub-scales, that is those which best indicate the nature and severity which comprise Ovract, These two sub-scales are called Inconsequence and Hostility. Inconsequence includes behaviour which seems to indicate that the pupil is relatively unaffected by consequences (pleasant or unpleasant). Examples of this would be: acting on impulse, restlessness, persevering with something in the face of pressure to stop, responding to correction fined, since it implies that, in the circumstances, hostile reactions are not reasonable.

The sub-scale covers hostility to both peers and adults. Examples of this would be: spoiling work on purpose, insulting remarks, easily provoked into a temper, moody. We were not satisfied that the BSAG would meet all our requirements either as an assessment instrument or for evaluation purposes. In particular, the BSAG was not specific enough in describing disruptive behaviour in the classroom, either in its exact nature or in its frequency. We did not find it as helpful to be informed by the BSAG that the child was "Moody" or "unconcerned about approval or disapproval" as to know exactly what the child did, in whose presence, and how often that prompted the teacher to make these inferences about his/her mental state. In order to catalogue the behaviours which lay behind these inferences we attempted to compile a list of behaviours about which teachers had complained.

It should be remembered that the evaluative model is essentially a multiple case study design. Individual detailed case studies may arguably be as important an aspect of evaluation of pupil behaviour change as summative statistics, in that they provide insights into the nature and process of change in the sort of detail that can prove illuminating for practice. The case studies and the summative data actually complement one another. The summative statistics show trends and patterns which can then be highlighted by case studies. This information is to help with our assessment procedure and will also form part of the data used in the ongoing evaluation of the School Support Unit project.

Teachers tended to make their ratings not according to some notion of a national average, nor an average of all pupils in the school, but actually according to an average for that particular class. In this case, a pupil in a difficult class might engage in disruptive behaviur, but have it only rated zero, since it was no more than average of the class. The difficulty was in deciding whether the disruptive behaviour was that of an individual, of a small group, or of the whole class.

It was, therefore, found to be necessary to modify the Behaviour Checklist to include a fourth rating option for the teacher. This was 'nn' (nothing noticeable) which allowed the teacher to indicate that the behaviour in question did not apply to any pupil in the class. The only reliablity and validity study which has been conducted in the checklist was the one mentioned above in connection with the BSAG. The Checklist was found to correlate significantly with classroom observation, and to be reliable across different teachers. Its validity was also strengthened by the findings that it discriminated well not only between disruptive and non-discriminated, but also between pupils who were referred because of their disruptive behaviour and those whose behaviour was disruptive but not so severe as to be referred.

A score can be derived from the Behaviour Checklists by giving two points for a behaviour rated two, and one point for a behaviour rated one, and then adding up the points. Clearly, some of the behaviours such as throwing furniture are more severely disruptive than others such as tapping a pencil. However, in scoring any behaviour one or two a teacher is indicating that its frequency is severe enough to be a problem, even though the behaviour in itself may seem innocuous.

The third means of measuring change in pupil behaviour was the first part of the Post-Intervention Questionnaire (PIQ). This questionnaire is given to the teacher in a school with whom the team has worked on a case, as soon as it has been closed. The first section deals with pupil behaviur. The first question asks the teacher from the school to list up to five disruptive behaviours upon which work has been done, and then to rate them on a scale of minus two (much worse) to plus two (much better).

Since the number of behaviours rated varied between one and five, then in order to compare outcomes on different cases or to derive average scores for groups of cases, a score had to be calculated from this first PIQ section, known as the "average behaviour rating". This was obtained for each case by adding up the ratings (e.g. +1, +1, O, +2] -1= 3) and dividing by the number of behaviours rated (in this example = 5) to give an average rating (= + 0.6). The data collected on the behaviour change of individual pupils may now be summarised. At the time of referral, a teacher in a secondary school who knew the pupil well, or the class teacher in a primary school, was asked to complete a BSAG (1st BSAG) and a behaviour Checklist (1st BC).

When the case was closed, the same teacher (or if she/he no longer tought the pupil, another teacher) Was asked to complete a 2nd BSAG, a 2nd BC, and a post-Intervention Questionnaire (PIQ). Finally, a 3rd BSAG and a 3rd BC were requested at least six months after closure as a means of follow-up. Rates of return on second, and particularly third BSAC's and 2nd BC's were collected, did we request 3rd BSAG's and 3rd BC's. Completing questionnaires on pupils who are no longer presenting problems is clearly not rewarding, since only 58 were retrieved. The missing data open the possibility of bias in the evaluation. An attempt to check for this was made by comparing cases with missing data with cases with complete data.

There have been two main changes in age distribution over the five years of the Team's operation. Firstly, them amount of work in infant schools stayed creased. The results of the first evaluation had been the encouraging results on infant pupils led to an increase in referrals from that sector. Secondly, the proportion of 14- and 15- year-olds has dropped in relation to the 12-and 13-year-olds. The other basic variable of the referral population is gender.

The proportion of boys referred as against girls has consistently remained 3:1 in ravour of boys. Moreover, this proportion does not vary significantly according to age. The consistency of this finding tallies with proportions of boys compared to girls judged by their teachers to show maladaptive behaviour in the National Child Development study. The consistency of this result, however, should not imply that further research is not required in the whole area of how boys receive disproportionate amounts of teacher attention through engaging in disruptive behaviour. We turn now to changes in the behaviour of referred pupils. Two BSAG's were collected on 177 pupils who were referred and worked with between September 1979 and February 1984.

The work with some lasted no longer than one term, with others it lasted up to two years. The average length of intervention was 35 school weeks, which, if holidays are included, is approximately one year. The 1st BSAG was collected of intervention.

The important point to bear in mind is that a difference in scores reflects a change in the type of statements that are underlined by a teacher with respect to the pupil. Since some of these statements, as indicated above, can cover quite general aspects of behaviour, then a small difference in score may represent quite a substantial change in the teacher's perception of the behaviour change. A significant change evidently takes place in the teacher's perception of pupil behaviour between the time of referral and the end of intervention, BSAG. It should be noted that the severity of the under-reactive behaviour is not as great as for the other scales, according to the percentile ranks.

The scores also show that the behaviour at the end of intervention (2nd BSAG) is not perceived to be angelic, that is with very low scores, but rather it represents a level with which the teachers in school feel they can cope, otherwise they would presumbly not have agreed to the ending of the intervention. Indeed, after the end of intervention, the class teachers can do more than cope. They can actually prevent the behaviour from worsening and, in some cases, of course, the behaviour continues to become more acceptable. The slowing down or, in the majority of the 58 cases with 3rd BSAG's, the flattening out of the rate of behviour change gives some evidence that the change between the flattening out of the rate of behaviour change gives some evidence that the change between the 1st and 2nd BSAG is a result of intervention, and not just an effect of the passage of time, or the maturation of the pupil.

It would be wrong, however, to expect the rate of behaviour change to be smooth. Our impression is that initial change is difficult to achieve, since that team teacher is usually called into a worsening situation. Stopping the slide can be an achievement in itself. Achieving change in a desired direction is another step. Once some change has started, further progress may actually be easier to achieve, but then there may be setbacks as this often necessitates changes in the behaviour of the rest of the class or of the teacher. If this happens, the pace of change may accelerate again, until all parties concerned (pupil, peer group teacher) find one another's behaviour more or less acceptable. At this stage, the motivation and the space for further change is reduced to the extent that the rate of change flattens out. When the pattern of scoring is analysed in terms of the shift in the numbers of 2's and 1's between same number or ones are scored on the first and second Checklists. The difference is that some of the 2's become 1's and some of the 1's become O's.

In other words, some of the behaviours which were rated as occuring much more frequently than average (2) did not reduce right down to an average level (O), but, more frequently, to a more than average level (1), since the checklist refers specifically to observable classroom behaviours, then the significant reduction in the scores represents less behaviour that is potentially disruptive, and a classroom in which the flow of the lesson is interrupted less. As with the BSAG scores, this flattening out of the rate of reduction is a strong argument for the existence of a true intervention effect: the change seems to be due to the intervention and not to chance factors, or simply the passage of time. It is encouraging, however, that the reduction is maintained after the end of intervention, even though the reduction does slow down, thus, intervention is not just like putting a finger in the dyke, It actually seems that some real behaviur change takes place.

The third measure of behaviour change which was obtained was from the first section of the PIQ which was completed by the key teacher in the school with whom the team had worked, the team teacher listed up to five behaviours on which she/he had been working with the referred pupil. The school teacher then rated each of these on a five-point scale of +2 to -2, according to whether the behaviours had become much less acceptable (-2), less acceptable (-1) stayed the same (O), become more acceptable (+1), or much more acceptable (+2).

The first behaviour listed was the most important to change as far as the teachers in the school were concerned. On 6 cases only one behaviour was indicated, but the majority had at least three listed. 74.4% of the cases were rated as having improved on the first (most important) behaviour originality specified as a basis of referral. In only 9 (4%) cases was any deterioration noted, which is all the more remarkable since referrals often arise from a worsening situation. An average behaviour change rating was computed for each case, This was the average rating for up to five possible behaviours that were rated. Because of the averaging, scores are not whole numbers; therefore following figure shows that in 81.5% of cases some improvement was noted by the teachers in schools, and that, in one third of the cases, this improvement was rated to wards the +2 end of the scale, implying considerable improvement.

In considering these ratings, it is necessary to be clear that they are likely to be influenced by the school teacher's feelings about, among many things, his/her own confidence, the pupil, and the team teacher. The school teacher is being asked to compare a pupil's behaviour in the present with his/her behaviour at the time of referral. Clearly, the memory will fade and some will exaggerate, and some will underplay the behaviour in recalling it. Possibly, over a large number of cases these distortions will cancel one another out. But, in another sense, the distortions do not matter, since the decision a teacher makes to refer a pupil will depend partly on some feeling that he or she regulars help in meeting the child's needs.

The rating at the end of intervention is perhaps some

subjective measure of the extent to which the teacher now feels confident to meet the child's needs, in terms of behaviour, independently. As argued previously disruption is a relative concept, partly constructed by teachers' perceptions. Having changed teachers' perceptions of the level of disruptive activity is in many ways tantamount to changing the 'real' level of disruptive activity. If the teachers are no longer finding a pupil's behaviour to be unacceptable, then disruption may be said to have ceased. Whether to ask for help from the Support Unit will depend on a variety of factors amongst which will be how desperate the teachers are, whether they believe intervention will help, or whether they merely treat it as a ritual act better done than not done. The ratings at the end of intervention may reflect whichever of these factors were in play. The results from the PIQ's show that something has changed, at least in the teachers' judgements, but also probably in the pupils' behaviour (as confirmed by the results from the BSAG's and BC's), to make the situation more acceptable.

The Performance of Other Children in the Class

It was necessary to be mindful of the amount of work which would be entailed for teachers in supplying data. Furthermore, if measures of attainment and behaviour were simply taken at the beginning and end of the team's involvement, any changes could hardly be attributed to the intervention of the team on disruptive behaviour. To make such inferences with any degree of confidence would necessitate an elaborate, experimental model with control groups to allow for other inputs apart from the team's intervention.

The most straightforward and economical method seemed to be to include a section in the Post-Intervention Questionnaire for teacher in schools to complete. This section simply asked for a rating on a five-point scale of the effects of intervention on the rest of the class, in terms of a) their educational achievement, and b) their behaviour. On this scale a rating of +2 indicates 'much better', +1 'better', 0 'the same', -1 'worse' and -2 'much worse'. It would be quite possible for teachers to rate the effect of intervention on the educational levels of the rest of the class as making things worse, if the interventions were such that the teachers had to devote so much time to the referred pupil(s) that the rest of the class were neglected.

On the other hand, following the rotten apple analogy, it is possible that the rest of the class is contaminated, as it were, by the behaviour of one or two pupils. In such a case, improvements in the behaviour of these pupils could lead to improvements for the whole class. But we were interested in the education and behaviour of the rest of the class for more practical measures than examining the hopes and fears of parents and teachers based on reference to barrels of apples. According to the social learning perspective espoused by the team, the attainment and behaviour of the rest of the class would be crucial in helping to maintain the behaviour (acceptable or otherwise) of the referred pupil. Indeed, peer pressure and response might have played a part in generating the behaviour in the first place.

The rotten apple analogy is, then, deceptive since the interaction between a pupil and the rest of the class is not one-way, but two-way. Indeed, social learning theory would only see a pupil's behaviour as comprehensible within the context of the rest of the class. Following this argument, the team's interventions were often as much with the context as with the referred pupil. Inter-ventions can involve teachers and, indeed, a pupil's peer group. For these reasons, interventions might be expected to have effects on the rest of the class as well as on the referred pupil.

The teachers felt that the intervention had a positive effect on the behaviour and attainment of the rest of the class. The importance of this perception cannot be over-emphasised, as it means that the policy of keeping a referred pupil in class rather than segregating him or her, far from holding back or contaminating the rest of the class actually benefits them, as a spin-off from support unit intervention.

The effect on the behaviour of the rest of the class might have been readily predicted, since this may be directly influenced by much of the Support Unit's work with teachers in school. The effect on attainment is more surprising, yet of such significance that it perhaps warrants a larger research project with control groups in order to test this finding as stringently as possible.

The evaluation was limited, therefore, to asking teachers with whom the team had worked to assess themselves, on a case by case basis, on the extent to which their confidence had increased or decreased as a result of working with a team teacher. A section of the Post-Intervention Questionnaire asked "If similar behaviours, occurred in the future, would you feel more or less confident of being able to handle them?" The questionnaire provided a rating scale of -2 to +2. On the PIQ's over 57% of teachers stated that they would be more confident in handling similar disruptive behaviour in the future. This is perhaps surprising, in that with team teachers, supposedly having been appointed for their expertise with disruptive behaviour, coming into their classrooms, the teachers in schools might be expected to feel de-skilled. One of the aims of the team has always been to share skills both within itself and with teachers in schools.

Unless in-service training is explicitly requested by a teacher or group of teachers, or unless it is agreed followed a formulation, then it is usually an aim implicit in working in schools rather than one which is overtly stated. So, if teachers in schools actually feel more confident as a result of intervention, this is an important vindication of the method of support evolved by the team. The spread of results indicates that the results have some validity, despite the limitations of being based on teachers' self-assessment: some were not inhibited from reporting a loss in confidence and a sizeable proportion (nearly 40%) reported no change. The validity of the results was further enhanced when data from the PIQ were cross-tabulated: one finding was that the greater the behaviour change reported for the pupil, the greater was the likelihood of the teacher's reporting increased confidence.

There were many aspects of school organisation and policy which could have been incorporated in a data collection before the team ever began its work. Pressure to begin casework, as well as ambivalence towards the putative policy of the Support Unit on the part of schools, made any systematic data collection of these variables impossible. Nevertheless, the team were interested in how schools explained the causes of disruption, the relative emphases placed on the urban environment, parent, peer group, curriculum, personality, classroom organisation, school rules, and teaching style.

The item also examined the different ways the schools organised themselves to help reduce disruption, since it was possible that effective ideas and good practice could be passed between schools. Some schools provided information on these matters in their school booklets. Most secondary schools had a system where-by a pupil was sent to a series of teachers, usually head of department, year, or house, and then on to a deputy or the head teacher for serious incidents which might warrant exclusion or suspension.

Schools differed according to who was informed about disruptive behaviour: some insisting that the head teacher was told about every incident where parents were informed, others leaving it to the discretion of the head of house or year. In primary schools, the arrangements for dealing with disruptive behaviour were more likely to be centered on the head.

Some primary and secondary schools had well defined criteria for what disciplinary action should be taken for what behaviour; other schools operated on a more informal basis. At least one school saw the formulation of the Support Unit as a response to the abolition of corporal punishment, and many were working out alternative strategies to caning. Various systems of report books, detentions, house marks, letters home, interviews with pupils and/or parents, and time-out rooms were being evolved.

Most of the information about these aspects of school organisation, however, was gathered informally, and was far from systematic. Limited in terms of systematic data collection on this aspects of the team's work, initial concentration was confined to examining time spent by different members of staff on disruptive behaviour. A distinction was made between class or subject teachers and senior teachers (heads of house/year/department, deputies and head teachers). In one section of the PIQ teachers were asked to rate an increase or decrease in time spent by the class teachers and senior teachers on each pupil with whom the team worked, both during the period of intervention and after it. The ratings were on a scale of -2 to +2.

After three years of the team's operation, it was felt appropriate to look in more detail at how schools dealt with disruptive behaviour. Interviews, rather than questionnaires, were chosen as yielding richer information, despite the fact that the time commitment involved meant that only a sample of cases could be taken. One of the authors took twenty random cases from those referred after September 1982, and independently approached the school teachers with whom the team worked on these cases. A structures interview schedule was devised, after some piloting, so that answers could be compared across interviews. In this way a picture was built up of how a school had organised itself to handle behaviour problems, and of how the work of a team teacher had interposed itself into that organisation.

One feature of the interviews was that three perspectives on the same situation were sought. For each of the twenty cases, the pupil, the team teacher and a key teacher in the school were interviewed. It was not possible, however, for most of the pupils to comment in much detail on the school organisation. The key question is whether the time spent by staff on the referred pupil was positive or negative. Even if there was no change in time spent during the course of or after intervention, there might have been a change in the quality of the contact-from negative to positive, or vice versa.

The information obtained from the PIQ does not allow assumptions about the quality of the contact to be made, though information on this is available from the results of the interviews. On the assumption that this does not mean that the teacher is actually spending less time with that pupil than, proportionately, with others (which is fairly unlikely), then the reduction in time spent is probably desirable. Disruptive behaviour is often time-consuming, and it often directs teachers' time and attention disproportionately to a few pupils, particularly boys. It is, then, desirable to reduce the time spent by staff on referred pupils closer to levels appropriate to other pupils in the class or school.

The amount of time spent with other pupils would then seem to be suffering, and their education not to be disrupted by the behaviour of the referred pupil. The interviews conducted in 1983 gave more detailed insight into the part that support team intervention played in the way schools conceptualise and deal with disruptive behaviour. One interview question asked the teacher to state what behaviour the pupil under discussion exhibited that was considered a problem.

A subsequent question asked the teacher to generate hypotheses about how pupils who behaved in such a way were different from those who did not. The responses to this question were analysed and placed into categories. Where a teacher offered more than one response, each was given equal weighting in assigning them to categories. Thus, the categories were derived from responses to open questions and were not suggested to the teachers. The categories are not quite mutually exclusive, and conceal many shades of meaning. However, they point to differences in the ways in which the two groups of teachers examine a problem, look for intervention, and determine who is responsible.

Thus, the team teachers tended to look first for within-child factors: learning ability, social learning, behavioural characteristics (such as paying little attention to consequences or restlessness). Since all of these may be improved by providing a learning environment appropriate to the pupil's needs, the responsibility for change rests clearly with the teacher and the pupil. The school teachers, on the other hand, tended to look first at home factors. Lack of parental care, changes of address, "unstable home life", "upsetting childhood" were all ideas which were put forward.

The responsibility for change, here, is shifted away from the school and the teachers. In the course of collaboration, school teachers and support teachers must negotiate their different accounts of disruptive behaviour. In Studying the twenty cases in detail, it became clear that the role of the team teacher varied considerably from case to case. In terms of contacts and communications the team teacher could be involved with any combinations of up to five or more participants: pupils, teacher, senior teacher (head), pastoral teacher (tutor in a secondary school) and parent(s). Detailed account of two of the cases illustrate these varying patterns of communication. The first case is that of a boy in junior school who refuses to conform to class rules and, if he wants attention from the teacher, simply shouts out. The class teacher is exasperated. She keeps the head teacher informed about the boy. The head informs the mother about him and she, in turn, gets angry and exasperated with her son.

Classroom Practice

There is an image of autonomy often connected with the professionalism of teachers whereby, once the door of the classroom is closed, what goes on inside it is the teacher's business an no-one in a school may meet in departmental groups to discuss their curriculum plans, guidelines may be issued by the LEA or by the DES, advisers may be asked into or sent into the school for specific curriculum areas, by these sources of outside input may do no more than make superficial changes in the actual substance of lessons. With regard to disruptive behaviour, this autonomy may become an embarrassingly serious issue. If teachers in a school know that one or two of their colleagues are having difficulties with classroom behaviour, then they may not necessarily mention it to the teachers themselves, nor bring it to the attention of those in authority.

On the one hand, this might be seen as interfering with the professional autonomy of a colleague, on the other as causing him or her difficulties with the head teacher. A further consideration is involved here in that, for many teachers, the admission of difficulties with classroom control, is perceived to be a form of failure. Even those most committed to the teaching profession seem to find it hard to discuss their part in classroom difficulties with colleagues on the staff. They will discuss what they perceive to be personality attributes of individual children, or the merits or otherwise of curriculum material. But to mention their own teaching behaviour is somehow to break a conspiracy of silence. This is clearly and exaggerated picture of what is nevertheless an extensive practice, which any amount of management courses, school conferences, creation of special posts in schools, has not succeeded in overcoming.

There is, indeed, a danger that those most in need of tangible assistance with classroom disruption will be the ones least likely to receive it, because to mention that such help were needed would be to come out from behind the shield of teacherly professional autonomy. Given this, there are obvious obstacles to the work of the support team teachers. Since these teachers themselves are on Scale 3 and, in some cases comparatively young, they re within a familiar hierarchical pattern and yet, being outside the structure of the school, they do not fit.

A youngish teacher from outside the school, who claims some expertise on such a highly sensitive issue as disruption, may well be perceived as a threat. What the team teacher needs to do is to offer help without implying criticism, to share professional notions of autonomy rather than to offer a defence, to encourage clear accounts of events without seeming to pry or to be likely to report back harmfully to senior colleagues. This seems like a fairly tall order. Whatever the state of personal relationships between a team teacher and teachers in schools, this knife edge between trust and mistrust remains in the background. It may, on the other hand, be what keeps the relationship alive and working, whereas staff within schools quickly discover how far their own personal relationships can go and settle into established patterns.

The question of how team teachers present themselves in schools and how they maintain positive and productive contact with all sorts of staff is as much a matter for team policy as it is for individual members. Indeed, in our case, we saw from the outset that getting to a position to be able to do the job was actually an important part of it. Indeed, many of the skills of tact and diplomacy necessary to get to that position were closely related to those likely to result in the job being performed with any success.

The policies which the team adopted concerned staff selection and training, the public relations of the team as a whole, an adherence to an overt professionalism and specifically formulated procedures. To take each of these briefly in turn, staff selection and training is vital. Team teachers need to have both professional experience and personal qualities that gain credibility with teachers. The critical professional background would appear to be some solid experience of mainstream schools as well as of some aspects of special education. Some qualification or confirmed interest in educational psychology or the sociology of education is also advantageous.

Further, no-one would be likely to be appointed who did not have a clear and enthusiastic commitment to the work of the team, and who did not accept the significance of the training and supervision procedures. These qualities would be in addition to the sine qua non that they would be able to manage most disruptive behaviour in a positive and successful way. These criteria seem hard enough to meet, but gaps can partly be filled by training. What is more difficult to select for and train for are those more indefinable attributes that so many interviewers seek. It is essential to send into schools people who can present themselves with both confidence and modesty, without appearing threatening or threatened, people who can deal with emotion, embarrassing or challenging situations with other adults, and respond with calmness, positive suggestions and humour. What is sought and what is encouraged through role-play and simulations in in-service training is personal style and presentation which gives team teachers at leas some skills and confidence in overcoming uneasiness or defensiveness when they encounter teachers in schools.

The profile of the Support Team in schools was always fairly high. This was adopted as a deliberate but high-risk policy in the face of not a few schools who would have preferred the conventional sin bin to a peripatetic team. The risk was that the team would not live up to its publicity. If such a team were established with less controversy, then it may not be necessary to adopt a high profile. Whatever the case, the aim is to provide some credibility for team teachers. As isolated teachers working in a variety of schools, often with people of higher status than themselves, they need to show support and a certain measure of authority from the public image of the team as a whole.

Of course, the maintenance of this image and credibility must be based on real achievement and is the responsibility of all members of the team. However, it is possible for certain members of the team, particularly the teacher in charge, to cultivate a high profile as a matter of policy. This can be done by giving staff meetings in schools to explain the team's work and to attempt to answer any questions on difficulties. This can be a productive way of facilitating a team teacher's work in a school by clarifying the role and by deflecting any criticism. It is a practice that needs to be repeated periodically in order to review objectives in a given school, and to re-negotiate roles if necessary. Another way of developing the team's profile is to run courses in schools or teachers' centres, by contributing to the induction of probationary teachers, and by playing a significant role in local educational policy discussions.

The encouragement of professionalism among team teachers is in some ways an attempt to meet those difficulties in intervention concerned with teacher autonomy in their own terms. Professionalism can often mean simply what one approves of, so it is as well to be specific. In addition to aspects of demeanour and social skills, touched on earlier, confidentiality is an important element of the team teacher's professionalism. This does, of course, apply equally to relationships with pupils and parents, but it is crucial when working with teachers.

Teachers and heads need to be assured of two forms of confidentiality: firstly, that team teachers can be given some information in absolute confidence, and secondly that information that is passed on, especially outside the school, will be for professional purposes only, and will not be debased into gossip or negative talk about their difficulties either with other members of staff or in other schools. Thus, it is good practice for team teachers to discussed cases amongst themselves without giving names of pupils, schools, or teachers. This is part of the process of treating colleagues in school with respect. This respect acknowledges and even expect as a commensurate professionalism on their part. Thus, the class teacher's autonomy mentioned above is always respected: a team teacher would never enter a classroom either for observation or intervention without first having obtained the consent of the class teacher.

Another way of demonstrating professionalism and of eliciting the same is to talk in strictly educational terms, to see difficulties as not to do with personalities, or success and failure, but rather with educational variables–curriculum, grouping seating, pupils' skills - which teachers are admirably suited to discuss and resolve.

Clearly, in time formality does relax and personal relationships do develop. But they are always best maintained if simple signs of professionalism remain — punctuality, responding to letter and phone calls promptly, brief and accurate record keeping. The procedures which the Support Team adopted, were designed to be of assistance in casework. They have the further advantage, however, of helping of provide rituals for formalising interventions in schools. Teachers must ask for assistance by completing a referral form or suggesting to a colleague that one is completed before any intervention is possible. The referral form always asks for the name of a teacher recommending the referral, as well as the signature of a senior member of staff. This gives the team teacher two points of contact in the school, one at a teacher level, the other at an administrative level.

There are further stages of questionnaire completion and discussion, providing opportunities for starchy politeness, relaxation, or resistance, before potentially more threatening matters arise. The process of joint formulation of the problem between team teachers and school teachers is particularly helpful in this respect. The bureaucratic task of jointly completing a form to summarise the assessment provides a structure for discussion and concentrates minds on areas of agreement and positive action.

Evaluation and review procedures likewise provide

a formal and pre-planned opportunity where, if necessary, disagreements and disappointments can be brought to light and alternative responses considered. It is important to stress the innovative nature of this work. Certainly, other groups of professionals, such as educational psychologists, regularly work as teams intervening in schools. But they ave certain status advantages over a groups of Scale 3 teachers, and they have an area of expertise and professional procedure on which to rely which is substantially different form the skills of the teachers with whom they are working.

The Support Team teacher, by contrast, may be regarded as just another teacher with little to offer beyond the expertise which already exists in the school. Indeed, this is an image which the support teachers are likely to encourage. If their expertise is seen as being educational and what they have to offer consists of a bit of time, a certain degree of experience and access to back-up services, then they can hope to assist in the business of teaching in schools.

Furthermore, if their skills are regarded as part of good educational practice, and not a matter of mystique or esoteric in schools will see these skills as something they can legitimately and with out too much difficulty develop themselves.

A further differences between he work of the team teachers and that of educational psychologists is that the latter can often focus their attention firmly on the referred pupil. They are then not seen as a threat to teachers. On the contrary, the model of individual casework and the high possibility of referral to segregated special provision is likely to confirm teachers' views that the difficulties are centered in the child and are not something to do with the functioning of specific teaches or the school as an institution. By contrast, the aim of the team teachers is to discourage the process of attributing all the difficulties to the child, and to try to develop in schools and teachers the skills and flexibility to advocate the referred child successfully without recourse to a segregated placement. In many ways the team teachers, far from relieving the school of difficulties, are likely to turn them back upon the class teachers and the head teacher—although with some tangible assistance.

In stressing these excitingly innovative features of the support teachers' work, there is a risk of describing it as a series of con-tricks. The above paragraphs could be read as depictions of methods of encouraging servility, fawning and devious manipulation among the team teachers, as if the main component of the team's in-service training was learning how to chat up school personnel. In fact, this is not the case. In order to work effectively in schools it is necessary to establish positive relations with the people who work there. If this is not done, there are risks of not receiving further referrals of having proposals vetoed and casework made almost impossible, of becoming a figure of suspicion or contempt in the staffroom.

Working as an outsider in schools is never easy, and haphazard attitudes to the regularity, etiquette and formalities of visiting are unlikely ever to develop the credibility needed to perform effective work with teachers and children. It is the nature of this work on classroom disruption that we now go on to describe.

It is possible to intervene on the case of a referred child and to diminish appreciably his or her participation in classroom disruption without ever having face to face contact with the pupil. Indeed, the pupil need never know that anyone other than his normal teacher(s) have been working with him or her. The focus of intervention is not the pupil but he teacher(s). The aim is to develop skills, confidence and flexibility whereby the teacher continues to educate the pupil without any more tangible assistance than discussion and advice. There are three major advantages to this method of working. Firstly, with regard to the referred pupil, it causes the very minimum of disturbance to the pattern of his or her education. He or she is not singled out and stigmatised, nor made to feel special either in his or her own eyes or in those of peers.

The opportunities to develop a deviant reputation with family, school staff or other pupils are severely diminished. Secondly, if a teacher or group of teachers can develop the skills and confidence successfully to educate a referred pupil, then there is a high likelihood that these skills may generalise. This is particularly likely since, as we describe below, these skills are not esoteric or specialised, but part of the normal repertoire of many positive teachers. If such skills can be developed, then this will be to the benefit of the teacher and colleagues as well as the referred pupil and the rest of the class. It will also be beneficial to all those children who will not subsequently be referred: that is, when such a teacher comes across difficulties of classroom disruption in the future, one may hope that he or she will be able to deal with them confidently without extensive external assistance, and without the possibility of children being referred to segregated provision. Thirdly, this type of intervention is exceedingly cost-effective as it need not consume too much of the team teacher's time. Given that the teamworks to a hierarchy of intervention, then this method of working is preferred option.

Having stressed the difficulties, the advantages and the innovative nature of working with teachers, it is now necessary to describe different ways of working with them, and to elaborate more precisely on the necessary skills and flexibility. This brings us then to the subject of the title of this chapter and, indeed, to one of the central contentions of the book. If the argument is accepted, that classroom disruption should be seen in a classroom context and not as a dimension of the personality of any of the participants, it follows that changes in that context may be able to do much to alter the pattern do disruption.

As we have emphasised throughout, our notion of effective classroom organisation is not based on any claim to esoteric knowledge or skills, but on the systematic, positive approach of many practising teachers. The main concern of this section is with pedagogy, although we do conclude with some remarks on the curriculum. Indeed, a main principle for avoiding classroom disruption is to keep pupils busy with curriculum work. Where teachers are approaching pupils with curriculum material which demands, excites and challenges, there is less chance that they will need a retreat with comments and complaints about behaviour.

The curriculum demands obviously need to be appropriate to the pupils in the group, but it is also helpful to have a range of teaching styles and tasks within any lesson. A varies sequence of activities helps to retain interest and momentum as well as offering opportunities for different individual skills. This, however, needs organisation and smooth management. Pupils need to be told in advance how the time is to be divided up, and transitions between tasks need to be handled smoothly and firmly.

Classroom Rules

Classroom rules should be precise and consistent. It is probably best not to have unnecessary rules: the fewer there are, the more likely they are to be observed. What rules there are need to be understood by pupils and, if possible, endorsed by them too. This tends to involve repetition with younger children, and may well lead to a certain degree of moral discussion with secondary classes. In both cases this is probably educationally worthwhile as well as being effective. This is not to say that exceptions cannot be made, but where this is done the reasons need to be made clear to all the pupils. Flexibility within a framework of consistency is necessary with regard to both the curriculum and standards of behaviour.

The alternative can be a series of unnecessary confrontations brought about by the teacher's insistence that every child must perform and behave up to some abstractly determined set of standards. A major element whereby a teacher can impart a positive influence on lessons is by control of the classroom environment. Factors within the teacher's control include the seating of pupils and him/herself, displays on walls and tables, the general tidiness and appearance of the classroom, the positioning of equipment which pupils are likely to use. Lack of time can make a considerable impact on a lesson and they need to be planned and adjusted according to the group and the curricular material.

A few minutes of routine activity at the beginning of a lesson can help to calm a class after a hectic playtime. A dull and qrumpy class can often be improved by the even simpler expedient of opening a window. This concern for the classroom environment should also include the physical organisation or lessons. Queues at a teacher's desk are a further example of this.

Many children are probably wasting time in them, waiting instead of working. They also block the teacher's vision and attention from the rest of the class who are thus more likely to stray from their tasks. The positioning of the teacher and the teacher's desk are important, as is freedom for the teacher to move effectively about the classroom. The sedentary teacher can rarely be as effective as one who spends at least some of the time on the move. If the teacher is mobile in the classroom reading and attending to children's work, initiating and contributing to discussion, praising and encouraging good work and helping to remove difficulties, then the pupils are more likely to be responding positively. Issues of the lesson can then be dealt with before boredom or frustration compound them into disruption. As an overall strategy, then, it is better for the teacher to the approaching rather than retreating, better to be setting, supervising and assessing work than complaining about misbehaviour, better to be among the pupils' desks that sitting behind one at the front of the room, better to be aware of everything happening in the classroom than being glued to one spot in the hope that everything is going well elsewhere.

It is more effective to reward than to punish, and a readily available reward in the classroom is praise from the teacher. This is most effective when directed towards the details of academic performance; not just a vague "good", but a precise definition of what has been successfully achieved. The quicker the praise or any reward follows the successful performance, the more effective it is likely to be. More tangible rewards are available to teachers, such as allowing pupils time at preferred tasks or activities.

Rather than a straight trade-off, it may be preferable to reward a small group for the successful attainment, thereby gaining the support and encouragement of the group for the specified and encouragement of the group for the specified task. More detailed and programmed reinforcements are discussed later in this chapter, but at this stage it is worth noting that where tangible rewards are used, it may be necessary to offer some explanation to the rest of the class, though children are rarely unaware of the different personalities with in their groups and the accordingly different demands these place on the teacher. Where this awareness appears to be lacking, or the singling out of a specific child even for reward seems to be inappropriate, it is possible to make a treat for the entire class contingent on successful performance by one child.

Although group pressure may assist a teacher's aims in such a case, it is rather a strong force to call upon and may work against the long term interests of the pupil, either because it may subject him or her to undue pressure, or it may lead to he role of the class baby. Such procedures are best used to with caution, and only when praise and encouragement have seemed to fail. If a team teacher were to suggest much a course to a class teacher, it is likely that the intervention would cease to be exclusively centered on the teacher. Inappropriate classroom behaviour may parado-xically be maintained by the teacher attention it generates, even where this is negative or actually punitive. At this stage matters become rather complex, and yet the policy of ignoring such behaviour is rarely practicable, and in a secondary classroom it could indeed prove disastrous. It may, however, be possible to minimise the attention received as a result of such behaviour.

Quietly spoken, but firm, rebukes to individual pupils are thought to be more likely to improve behaviour than loud, public, negative comments. It is, however, probably best for the teacher always to be seen to be aware of what is going on in the classroom, and to be seen to disapprove of what is not appropriate. However, punitive methods rarely work unless they form part of a well established pattern of reward and punishment for which there is a strong consensus
punishment for which there is a strong consensus

amongst staff and pupils. In particular, corporal punishment is not recommended. Apart from being inhumane, it provides pupils with an undesirable example of violent authority. The fact that the same pupils are often the recipients of repeated use of corporal punishment is a testimony to its ineffectiveness. Other punishments are also going to run the danger of becoming undermined by overuse or resentment if their effectiveness is not carefully monitored.

The most successful punishments are usually those imposed in an atmosphere of reward, when it is enough to punish by withholding reward. Other punishments—detentions or making good lost time or damage—are probably more effective if they are not delayed, if the pupil understands the reasons, and if the teacher ensures that it is properly carried out. If appropriate curriculum and pedagogy are used, it may be possible to avoid many confrontations, in which a teacher seeks recourse to threat or punishment. Confrontations in the classroom are an indication that inappropriate behaviour has become more important than the academic progress of the lesson.

However, if a confrontation with a pupil has occurred, it is essential to spend some time calming down afterwards, and to speak to the rest of the class about it. If emotions remain high, chain reactions of confrontations can occur. It may also be helpful to see the individual pupil or pupils concerned later. It is tempting then to reason with the pupil or extract promises, or to harangue them. Unless this happens in the context of a strong positive personal relationship, it is likely to be counter-productive. The reasons for this are that the individual attention may actually be rewarding, because that is the only form of individual attention the pupil receives or, if it is definitely not rewarding, the pupil may say the right things simply in order to get away.

Instead, a brief but firm statement of disapproval of the behaviour may be enough. Some pupils may need the reassurance that while the teacher may disapprove of the behaviour, he or she does not dislike them as persons. In case it should be thought that the team teacher only has to hand a distressed teacher a list of the above do's and don't's of classroom management, it ought to be stressed that these are principles which they bear in mind.

Most teachers know them in any case, but some lack the confidence or opportunity to practise them. The team teacher's job is to help the school teacher create the opportunity and to encourage the gradual steps towards changes in practice. The procedures of the team should help both the school teacher and the team teacher to establish a climate in which change can take place. The school teacher has asked for some help with difficulties. The team teacher asks the school teacher to do some work by completing questionnaires and by discussion in sharing in an assessment process.

Usually the team teacher will ask to do some classroom observation and so gain first-hand experience of the context, even if, as sometimes happens, the difficulties do not appear so extreme during observation. The process of assessment and, in particular, of feeding back observations is vital. Firstly, it builds in a systematic and objective approach and, secondly, it is gradual.

We have already described the assessment process in some detail and mentioned classroom observation as part of that process. It is rather the use that is made of certain kinds of observation, and the nature of the feeding back, that are important in working with teachers. When feeding back, the team teacher needs to make sure that there is something positive to say, and to be entirely neutral in the way the difficult events have been recorded. This is so much easier if the class teacher has understood beforehand the nature of the observation and the method of recording. For example, it may have arisen from the assessment and formulation process, in which the class teacher has shared, that one of the objectives for intervention was work on classroom management. The first step in such an intervention may be to observe more closely what the pupil does, and how the teacher responds. This may take the form of a minute by minute record over a fixed period of time, or something more elaborate, with pre-designed codes for pupil behaviour, a and for teacher behaviour. Once the ideas behind systematic observation have been grasped, there is no limit to the invention. Some teachers become adept at observing themselves.

More important, the whole process sensitises them to observing informally, but more keenly, the chain of reactions in their classroom. In this happens the team teacher may not need to continue classroom observation, and the class teacher may embark on the process of change through regular discussions with the team teacher about his or her classroom practice, or rather the particular aspects of it on which they are focusing. Thus, the whole process is a mixture of a certain amount of technique and method to which the team teacher has access, and a certain amount of support, in terms of two people sharing a difficulty.

A much less complex way of working with teacher sin schools is to centre the intervention on an individual child. This is likely to be more acceptable to teachers in school, as it does not assume that they play any part in classroom disruption. Collaboration is then any part in classroom disruption. Collaboration is then all the easier. However, the benefits of working directly with teachers outlines in the preceeding section are, in the main lost. Furthermore, this style of work is a move towards focusing the blame as well as the intervention of referred pupils. To a certain extent, this difficulty is inherent within a mode of working which is dependent on a referral system. On the other hand, since the work is with teachers as well as children, it need not be quite as referral-centered as that described in the next section.One way of keeping the work's emphasis as being that of collaborating alongside a teacher rather than targeted at a pupil is to work in conjunction with a particular teacher with a whole class.

There are several different ways in which this can be done once the class teacher has accepted the invitation to collaborate. One way is for the team teacher simply to offer to take the class for a regular session over a period of, say, a couple of weeks, to give the class teacher a break. This might be appropriate where there was a high degree of disruption and of teacher pressure. It certainly would provide the team teacher with a sharp insight into what was happening in the classroom. However, it has certain disadvantages. If the team teacher is able to work successfully with the class, then this is likely to prove de-skilling to the classroom teacher. It may become apparent to the class teacher, and perhaps to the pupils also, that there is considerably less disruption when he team teacher is taking the lesson.

Since a main aim of the Unit's work is to develop skills, flexibility and confidence among teachers, this would seem to be counter-productive. If the team teacher were to have as difficult a time with the class as their usual teacher, then it would be his or her position which would be undermined. This could hardly help the intervention, nor could the feeling, were it to develop among staff or pupils, that the class was becoming uncontrollable.

A more positive variation on this theme is effectively to reverse roles. Where a class teacher is insisting that it is just one or two children who are involved in disruption, that removing them from lessons would allow the others to proceed successfully, that this would also give the child or children some individual attention, it is possible to suggest that individual attention, it is possible to suggest that instead of the team teacher withdrawing the pupils, and the class teacher carrying on with the lessons, they simply change positions.

The advantages here are quite profound. It is surely better for the pupils to form a positive, close relationship with a teacher in the school whom they are going to see a lot, rather than with a peripatetic teacher with whom contact is necessarily limited. The positive relationship idea might work both ways, and some individual time with the referred pupil(s) may help the class teacher to develop a more positive view of them and to understand in more detail their needs and capabilities. Furthermore, it may well be possible to reintergrate the referred pupil(s) back into the class quite easily as they will be going back alongside the class teacher. If the pupils had been withdrawn to be taught by the team teacher, there could well have been difficulties of reintegration.

The only disadvantage of this method of work is that the team teacher is required to teach a class and probably a curriculum with which he or she is unfamiliar, and one which the class teacher is convinced will be free of disruption without the withdrawn pupils. It does require careful planning then and close collaboration over the curriculum. Another method of working with pupils in cooperation with the class teacher is simply to team teach. This can be done either by both teachers circulating the whole class, or by one of them taking a small group within the context of the general lesson.

The presence of two teachers is likely to diminish the opportunities for classroom disruption, and it may permit necessary attention and teaching time to be devoted to specific pupils who are likely to include those who have been referred. Team teaching also offers tangible support to class teachers within work of the rest of the class, but it may be appropriate sometimes to supplement this with material designed or chosen by the team teacher. Even where one of the objectives of the individual contact is to form a relationship with a pupil and perhaps proceed to some educational guidance and counselling, it is generally considered that this is best achieved on the basis of some tangible educational work. Even the most structured teaching, however, is likely to lead to broader discussion when it is carried out on a one-to-one or small group basis. Educational guidance is likely to form part of this discussion. This can range from how to get on better in Maths, to what options and exams to choose in the fourth and fifth year.

Some support teachers have been trained as counsellors, and they may sometimes make use of these skills with children. In these cases, the educational and personal guidance may be more formalised. The relationships team teachers develop with referred pupils are on the whole, however, rather different from those favoured by the publicists of school counselling.

If it means exploring with pupils issues wider that the formal curriculum, giving them a sympathetic hearing, and helping them to develop strategies to solve personal problems, then many effective teachers were doing this long before counselling was given diploma status. Again, the aim of intervention is to share skills with teachers and to exchange experience rather than to attempt to transform it into an exclusive domain. Nevertheless, counselling does have the advantage provided by more time and privacy which may all help more intimate discussion. If course, for a child to discuss his or her problems is by no means tantamount to their being solved, but it may be possible for the teacher and child at least to work out what areas are beyond solution and what to do about those that are not. In fact, the notion of using the counselling session to target in certain areas of behaviour is fundamental to what is known as behavioural counselling. A distinction between that and client-centered counselling is necessary. In the latter the client sets the theme of the discussion, and the counsellor reflects back feelings, contradictions, or diversions in it. It requires a degree of self-awareness and verbal fluency that is often lacking in a pupil whose behaviour is disruptive.

Behavioural counselling, however, takes as its focus the behaviour and not the client. Since behaviour is public, for all to see, them the counsellor may just as easily as the client point out that certain people find certain behaviours a problem. Of course, it is up to the client still to decide whether to accept that, and whether it is something on which he or she wants to work. Part of the counsellor's work initially may be to build up the counsellor's work initially may be to build up an awareness, through feeding back his or her own observations and those of others, of what behaviour is a problem and to whom, when, and how frequently, is a problem and to whom, when, and how frequently, it occurs.

The more the pupil is able and willing to take part in this information gathering, the more likely he or she will be to decide that alternative ways of behaving may be worth considering. The techniques of behavioural counselling, therefore, are those of behavioural analysis which have been described in the assessment stage of the team's work. The pupil learns how to analyse his or her own behaviour, just as the teacher learns to analyse the classroom situation. It should be clear, therefore, that, from the techniques of behavioural counselling, other more specific interventions with individual pupils may arise - the use of behaviour programmes, charts, contracts and social skills training. Indeed, these behavioural methods, all based on social learning theory, far from being manipulations of the individual for social control, only really work when the individual has been able to analyse his or her behaviour methods, all based on social learning theory, far from being manipulations of the individual for social control, only really work when the individual has been able to analyse his or her behaviour an fully agreed to work on certain aspects of it.

As long as the client is an active participant in the analysis, it is academic whether behaviour programmes are called behaviour modification. But it is important that the analysis is thorough and the programmes are called behaviour modification. But it is important that the analysis is through and the programmes well carried out. The basis of through behaviour analysis is observation. The team teacher's observations may form the basis of some discussion with individual pupils. Out of that, they may decide to focus on one, two, or sometimes three classroom behaviours. The first stage in this is often for the pupil to make his or her own monitoring booklet in which the day or the week is divided into appropriate time periods.

As an initial exercise, it may be best to start with a short period divided into short intervals. If the interval is not less than about 15 minutes, the teacher could be asked to find the time to record with a tick or cross in the pupil's monitoring booklet, whether or not the target behaviours have occurred. These behaviours usually include doing something positive, e.g. on task, sitting still, completing work being quite, etc., and refraining from the context where they consider themselves most to need it. Where the class teacher is less experienced than the team teacher at dealing with classroom disruption, it may provide opportunities for him or her to learn some skills from the model of a colleague actually in the same classroom. Since it is always the class teacher who is in control of the curriculum and the structure of the lesson, then it is probable that the team teaching situation will not be seen as a threat to his or her authority.

Team Teaching

Team teaching is a complex activity even in the best of circumstances so that, if it is to be attempted, it does need some firm organisation in advance. For two teachers to go into a lesson without having worked out what their roles are going to be or without both being familiar with the curriculum could well be a recipe for disaster. Team teaching is an intervention which is quite costly in terms of time, since it must continue over a period of at least weeks, but it may be effective in that it provides a tangible opportunity to assist both pupils and teacher. It may be possible to intervene more economically than this if both teachers can see the class to have a conversation about classroom behaviour, how it needs to be, and can be, improved.

The presence of a teacher from outside the school may provide a suitably chastened atmosphere in which such a discussion can take place and can, indeed, lead to improvements. There is, however, the risk that in the context, the team teacher will be perceived by the context, the team teacher will be perceived by the pupils either as a body man or as some kind of authority figures with unknown powers. This would make any further intervention either with the referred pupil(s) or with the whole class more complicated.

A final way in which class teacher and team teacher can collaborate in work with pupils is for the former to be involved in the work with individual referred pupils which is described in the next section. It may be essential to the success of an intervention for the class teacher to be involved in monitoring, rewarding and modifying any intervention and in explaining it to other teachers. It is desirable that the class teacher should be involved as closely as possible in the intervention, as without his or he co-operation it is unlikely to succeed.

Further more, the team teacher will need eventually to taper an terminate the intervention, an done way of doing this is to hand it over to the class teacher. Again, close involvement of the class teacher in interventions with pupils is likely to develop his or her skills and confidence. It is highly desirable, then, that the education programmes, charts and contracts described below should be designed and implemented with the closet possible collaboration of class teachers.

In turning to work done with individual children, it is stressed that on-one has a monopoly on such work. The techniques described below can be used by teachers in mainstream schools. The peripatetic support team is only one way of making such services more available to teachers. The interventions described below could perhaps as easily be carried out by a specialist teacher within a school. They are indeed interventions which class teachers can and do learn themselves and subsequently use. As such they may form a useful practice to aid discussion. At the basis of the team teacher's work with pupils is education and their skills in curriculum and pedagogy.

If the decision is taken to remove a child from a class for certain times in the school week to be seen by the team teacher either individually or as part of a group, the bases of their contact is likely to be educational work. In some cases it may be found that the pupil has 'fallen behind' with a subject or has been at pains to acquire basic skills. Indeed, there could be a close relationship between academic frustration and involvement in classroom disruption. In these circumstances it could well be that some remedial help from the support teacher would help a successful reintegration back into class. Normally, the curriculum for such withdrawal sessions would be supplied by the class teacher, so the pupil retains contact with the something negative, e.g. not shouting out, not running around, not fighting, etc.

For shorter intervals, the task is too much for the teacher who is teaching at the same time, and so the pupil can monitor himself or herself, or arrange with other pupils for them to do so. If a reciprocal monitoring system can be worked out, it is amazing how accurate and dedicated pupils can be. Another monitoring system that has been tired is a combination of self-monitoring and teacher monitoring. Whatever the results of the observations, it is best if the pupil's observations agree with the teacher's. After this initial stage of monitoring, the team teacher and the pupil can set targets for the next few days or weeks to increase the frequency of some behaviours or reduce others. The pupil may need some specific reward for achievement, but always praise and sometimes only praise.

On the subject of rewards, each pupil is different, and they will soon find what suits them best. The younger child will need more frequent rewards and a chart, which is a method of visibly plotting progress towards a reward, may be the best method. The object of rewards, however, is that as appropriate behaviour becomes more frequent, it will bring its own natural rewards—the satisfaction of achievement, the approval of others and the need for special rewards will diminish.

That is why the essence of a behaviour programme should aim to increase appropriate behaviour and not just decrease inappropriate behaviour.

Sometimes, when the curriculum is inappropriate for the child, the opportunity for appropriate behaviour may be limited. The principles and practice of behaviour programmes have been well described elsewhere. Although they are an important part of many interventions, it is the flexibility to adapt support to the climate of a particular school and the needs of a particular situation that we wish to emphasise in this chapter. Other behavioural techniques include charts, behaviour contracts, and social skills training.; Charts have the attraction of engaging the pupil's imagination and creative ability, as well as reasoning, in the process of change.

The chart is a visual representation of a pupil's progress towards a behavioural goal. It is helpful to take a child's interest, and help him or her to design and make a chart. Examples that we have seen include filling in one segment of web by Spiderman for every 10 minute period working, completing stages of a rocket for star Wars, hooking paper fish out of a three-dimensional model of a river, filling in scales of snake skin with the reward of someone bringing a live python to school. The activity itself of completing some of the more ingenious charts can be a sufficient reward.

Sometimes, the chart is a private matter between the child and the team teacher, sometimes shared with a class teacher, and sometimes the sole responsibility of the class teacher. If the chart sole responsibility of the class teacher. If the chart is public to the class, other pupils may want one. The solution to this is either to build a class reward into the individual chart, or to give those who want one a chart. Those who actually need one will benefit, those who do not really need one will usually not ask for a second. Behaviour contracts are an extension of charts in some ways, except that they move form a mainly visual to a mainly verbal format, and in that sense may be more likely to appeal to the older child. A contract is simply an agreement that if the child does X, the adult will do Y. It is making clear the connection between two behaviours and making one dependent on the other. When a contract is kept, it teaches a child two things: firstly, that the adult's behaviour does depend on his or hers, and secondly, that adults do what they say they are going to do.

The behaviour in the contract is reinforced and keeping a contract is reinforced. If the contract is not completed successfully, this is regarded as a failure of the contract, and not of the pupil: this means that an alternative more feasible document can then be drawn up. Sometimes a pupil may progress from one contract on several others—usually either more demanding or extending over more time. Though, as with all such programmes, the most definite reward that pupils receive is more positive access to their curriculum and the raised esteem of teacher and peers. Everyone is rewarded by having classrooms which are appreciably less disrupted.

Beyond these interventions in schools, the Unit has recourse to placing individual secondary aged children part-time and for a short specified period in its own class. This is not to say that involvement with the school and the class teachers ceases at this point. Pupils usually attempt to follow their mainstream school curriculum whilst at the Unit. It is, therefore, necessary to keep close contact with the school, so that the class teacher is informed of the curriculum and provided with the relevant materials. The teacher of the Unit's class may well make contact with the school in addition to their usual team teacher in discussions before placement.

Likewise, the team works during the time the pupil is at the unit to ensure that reintegration can go ahead with out difficulties. It is rarely wise to return a pupil back into the context where there has previously been disruption. Attempts are often made to change curriculum, class groups, subject teachers, or staff attitudes towards a pupil before he or she returns to his or her school full-time. Paradoxically then, when a pupil is placed in the Unit's class, this may actually involve more contact with the school rather than less. A curricular element which team teachers do frequently add to the education of young pupils concerns social skills training. The idea behind this is that behaviour causing trouble in school may result from lack of skill in social interaction—e.g. in asking for something, or in conveying anger without violence. A socially skilled person can influence their social interactions to bring about a rewarding outcome.

The aim in social skills teaching is to teach 'getting on with people' as a collection of skills with the intention of enabling pupils to increase the range and quality of their social interactions. It has recently earned rather an unfortunate reputation for itself, as it has become a component of YTS courses. There is genuine and justifiable anxiety lest social skills training be a direct form of social control and manipulation of young people, teaching them how to be subservient and uncomplaining wage fodder. This may be countered by discussing the content of the social skills session with the pupils before hand. They can first of all, identify through small group work and personal questionnaires their own areas of skill and deficiency. They can then determine what skills, either related to schools or to the wider world, they think that it would be helpful to learn.

The analysis of social skills which we have found the most useful involves 'micro' or basic skills and 'macro' or complex skills. Thus, qualities like eye contact, posture, voice quality, and perception of facial expressions are micro skills. More complex interactions like apologising, making friends in a new place, temper control, collaborating, are macro skills. Each session follows a broadly similar pattern: introduction of theme, instruction and discussion, modelling of behvaviour, practice and feedback. All the work is done in small groups of no more than either. The theme is often a macro skill within which one or two micro skills may be picked out for certain individuals.

2 Primary Education

Primary Schools as Personality Developing Centres

The concept of 'primary education' as a distinct area of development was fully established five years before the next report of the Consultative Committee appeared. Certainly the Board did everything it could to keep the concept alive, and after its publication in 1928. *The new Prospect in Education,* L.E.A.s drew up schemes for the full provision of 'post primary' education for children of 11+ along with the lines indicated in the Hasow Report. There can be little doubt that the later Hasow Report of 1931, *The Primary School,* was one of the most important that the Consultative Committee produced. There is a tendency to look upon it as little more than a historical curiosity; certainly beside the Plowden Report of 1967 it appears a very slim and modest volume, indeed, and although it took two years to produce its gross cost was minute compared with the cost of Plowden.

After a fairly lengthy introduction on general principles, the report provided a historical sketch of the development of the idea of primary education from the beginning of the nineteenth century. It went on to describe the physical and mental development of children between the ages of seven and eleven; and it is interesting to note that, just as Plowden leans quite heavily upon Piagetian thought, the 1931 report used and quoted Piaget's *Le Language et la Pensee chez l'Enfant,* published in France in 1923 and translated into English in 1926.

The report then went on to consider the age limits for the upper stage of elementary education, which it felt should be fixed at the age of eleven; that is, the transfer from the primary to the secondary school should take place between the ages of eleven and twelve. It went on to discuss in some detail the arguments against separate 'infant' and 'junior' schools, but finally recommended that, in those areas where it was possible, there should be separate schools for children below the age of seven, and that in all primary schools there ought to be a well-defined line of education between the younger and older children.

The report made it pellucidly clear that the primary school should not be regarded merely as a `preparatory department for the subsequent stage': primary school course were to be planned and conditioned by the specific needs of the child at that particular phase in his development, both physical and mental. Its attitude towards promotion to the secondary stage was made quite an examination at the age of eleven', were not to control primary schools curricula or activity.

The internal organization of primary schools was next discussed, including such problems as the size of classes and co-education at the upper stage or primary education. The report adduced evidence from a variety of sources to establish that classes in junior schools should be kept small, preferably about thirty five, and it further made the point that it would be impossible to put into operation many of its suggestions if large classes were retained in primary schools. The size of primary classes was indeed one of the most urgent problems facing education administrators. Concerning co-education the conclusion was that there was no valid objection on general or sociological grounds, provided due regard was paid to the differing needs of girls and boys in games and physical activities generally.

Problems of mental and educational retardation were considered in detail, and the chief causes, detection, diagnosis and treatment dealt with. Retarded children required special attention between the ages of seven and eleven, and it was recommended that special classes should be organized for this purpose and that they should be small.

The traditional curriculum of the public elementary school was next analyzed, and the general principles on which the upper stages of primary education should be based were elicited. The report considered the complexity of 'modern industrial civilization' and the bearing this has upon the work of the primary school. It emphasized the uselessness, as well as the innate danger, of seeking to inclucate what A.N. Whitehead has termed "inert ideas'; and it deplored and deprecated the fact that, whilst a great deal of teaching was good in the abstract, too little of it directly assisted children to enlarge and vivify their instinctive hold on the condition of life by enriching, illuminating and giving point to their growing experience.

In its further consideration of curriculum detail the report emphasized the desirability of devising new methods on approaching its various branches, and in particular dealt with the project method and 'centres of interest' as set against the traditional practice of treating the curriculum in terms of 'subjects'. It warned, however, against the dangers of such methods when used without due consideration or caution-music and drama were often merely 'dragged in' in order to fulfill what were regarded as the claims of a a principle. The staffing of primary schools and the training of teachers were next considered, and it was argued that teachers with general qualification rather than specialists were best suited for work in primary schools.

A brief survey was made of school premises, equipment, school and class libraries, visual and auditory aids to teaching, school visits and playing fields. There followed a discussion of examinations in primary schools and it was recommended that, in classifying pupils leaving the infant school, of consultation between the teachers concerned. Any classification should be merely provisional, and should be subject to frequent revision.

The council felt that as the provision of various types of secondary education was extend in the way proposed in the report on *The Education of the Adolescent,* the need for selecting by competition those children who would pass on to grammar and selective modern schools would diminish. It was convinced, however, that some sort of qualifying test or examination would always be required for the purpose of calssifying pupils, and argued for the use of written papers in English an arithmetic as a basic test of capacity and attainment of children at the age of eleven, together with carefully devised group intelligence tests. Throughout the report of *The Primary School* there was a lively sense of the needs of the children themselves. It considered that what any wise and good parent might desire for his own children was precisely what the nation as a whole must desire for all children.

The primary school was on the way to becoming what it should be, namely, the common school of the whole population, 'so excellent and so genrally esteemed that all parents will desire their children to attend it. In

1933 the Hadow Report on the *Infant and Nursery school* was published and, like its predecessor, it emphasized the need to build new schools for young children more on an open-air plan. It also made it clear that the best place for very young children was in the home; but if this were not possible there was a great deal to be derive from attending nursery schools.

There is a recognition of the child as a total being who has specific and differing needs within the realms of character and intellect, and additionally the need to be initiated into the world of work and life itself in such a way as to be able to cope practically as well as intellectually. Eaglesham may be right when he comments that whilst there is to be preparation for life there is to be no vocational education.

The children are to be trained in habits of careful observation and clear reasoning so that they may gain san intelligent acquaintance with some of the facts and laws of nature and this is hardly 1foliowership'! The school must further arouse in its pupils a lively interest in man's ideals, achievements, literature and history; it must give them 'some power over language as an instrument of thought and expression'—surely more keeping with education for leadership! All sound education should make pupils and students aware of the limitations of their knowledge and encourage a due sense of humility within the realms of learning-whether they are leaders of followers.

The code consequently adds that, while the school should make pupils conscious of their limitations it should, thoughtful study as will enable them to increase that knowledge' when their school career is over, and by their own efforts. This, indeed, is still one of the prime purpose of education-to demonstrate to pupils how to acquire knowledge and learning for themselves. The influence in practice of the 'sloyd' movement is to be seen in other elements of the introduction which suggests that the school should encourage the natural activities of th child's hand and eye 'by suitable forms of practical work and manual instruction'; and the general, though gradual, movement towards hygiene and health is suggested by the training of pupils in physical exercises, organized games and the simple laws of health.

It is true that the code saw the possibility of discovering 'individual children who show promise of exceptional capacity', and that such children should be qualified to pass at the appropriate age into the secondary schools and there be enabled to derive the maximum benefit from the education offered them. Whilst this was a recognition that some children rather that others were fitted for further education it is worthy of note that there was a clause in parenthesis which had in mind the sort of contention which many educators have put forward in more recent years against the streaming of children in primary schools for the 11+ examination, and the gearing of the whole of the primary curriculum for the benefit of the academic few to develop their special gifts. The introduction was not an exhortation to industry, respect and reverence in quire the same sense as that implied in pervious codes and reports.

There was little or no suggestion of 'followship' subservience in the terminology of th code. It was implied that there was a great responsibility on the part of the teachers to lay the foundations of conduct; and by their influence, example and personal sense of discipline, which should pervade the school, to inclucate in the children 'habits of industry, self control, and courageous perserance in the face of difficulties' training suited, surely, to the middle and upper classed as well as the working classes. Reverence was to be taught, not for the nobility bur for what was noble; and children were to be ready for self-sacrifice and to strive to the uttermost for purity and truth. The respect which was to be fostered was not that for 'their betters', but for others, 'which must be the foundation of unselfishness and the true basis of all good manner's. The corporate life of the school was the basis for the development of the instinct for fair play and sense of loyalty to one another-the very 'germ of a wider sense of honor in later life'.

Some of the introduction, for good or ill, reads almost like a public school code. The introduction concludes that school, parents and home should all unite in an effort to enable the children to reach their fullest development a individuals, and also to become useful and upright citizens in their community. Whether Morant was interested in forwarding elementary education or not, there was a certain liberalizing and humanizing purpose expressed in this introduction. And this was supported by the Blue Book issued by the Board of Education in 1905, which was a handbook of suggestions for teachers involved in the work of public elementary schools.

Uniformity of practice throughout such schools was not desirable, but rather that each teacher should think for himself and work out his own methods according to the school's conditions and requirements. Above all the teacher should know and sympathize with the children he was teaching. The entire process of education was viewed as a 'partnership for the acquisition of knowledge'.

Facts were not to be dealt with in isolation but in relation to the total experience of the child 'each lesson must be a renewal and an increase of that connected store of experience which becomes knowledge' The Blue

Book was in line with the introduction to the code in that it insisted that the latter should fully realize his duty to use his innate powers to the best advantage.

Life must be presented as something at once pleasant and serious, and in consequence the work being pursued in the schools was in a real sense a preparation for life. Moreover, the teacher's influence in all this was a very vital one, however short the period of influence might be. The First Education Act of 1918 enforced compulsory attendance at school up to the age of fourteen years, and it also underlined the need for a complete re-organization of what today is more specifically referred to as primary education, that is, the education of young children below the age of eleven years.

Officialdom had learned a lot form the less orthodox and more progressive movements already mentioned, but despite all this many of the school buildings were inadequate and unhygienic. And despite the general desire expressed to make the primary school curriculum free from the pressures of selective examinations at the upper end of the school, in practice their classes were geared largely to preparation for secondary school work at the subject level and to some sort of 'scholarship' examination at 11+.

The White paper on *Education Reconstruction* which appeared in 1943, suggested in particular that children of 11+ should not be classified on the basis of a competitive test, but rather upon the assessment of their aptitudes based largely upon school records and intelligence tests. It felt that competitive examinations at the age of eleven were wrong in principle, not only because of the strain to which children were subjected but also because the future schooling and careers of children were largely decided at this one point in time. An age when children's minds were nimble and receptive, when their imagination and curiosity were strong and fertile, they were subjected to a cramping and stultifying curriculum in which considerable emphasis was placed upon 'ways and means or creating the examiners. The White Paper also stated that there should be separate schools for infants and juniors; and, whilst attendance was not compulsory before the age of five, L.E.A.s must make adequate provision for either nursery schools or, where these were considered expedient, nursery classes in infant schools.

The Butler Education Act of 1944 gave the primary school statutory authority in this country, and it defined primary education in Section 8 as 'full time education suitable to the requirements of junior pupils', who in years. The Act forced a clear break between primary and post-primary education: between primary and secondary schools, We are not here secondary education, the developing tripartite system, put ever-increasing pressures upon primary schools to act as forcing-grounds for grammar schools.

The aims, so clearly expressed in the Hadow Report on *The Primary School*, were very soon forgotten in the cut-throat competition for grammar school places, and the more enlightened development of primary school methods was somewhat delayed. There was a very real sense in which the firm, separate, statutory establishment of primary and post-primary educational institutions postponed the liberation of primary school methods for some years; and the Central Advisory Council for Education was probably not being over-pessimistic when it stated in 1947 that the gap between a reasonable provision of primary schools and the existing provision was formidable" 'half a century's unremitting efforts will be required before we can hope to have good primary schools for all'. A lot, of course, depends on the connotation of the word 'good' in this context: the verdict of the Plowden Report, twenty years later, was quite simply expressed in th words, 'the primary schools are giving good value for the inadequate among of money spent on them'. But it made it quite clear tha the financial inadequancies has severe educational repercussions, as we shall presently see.

In August 1963 the Central Advisory Council for Education was asked by Sir Edward Boyle, then Minister of Education, 'to consider primary education in all its aspects, and the transition to secondary education'. Their report was concluded in October 1966 when it was presented to Anthony Crosland, Secretary of State for Education and Science, and it was published in january 1967. Volume 1 presented the report, and Volume II the statistics derived from a national survey of 20,00 schools. The total cost of the report was slightly over 120,000. Part one formed an introduction to the whole investigation and referred in particular to the close association between the home background and academic achievement.

The importance to individual of his family and social background was emphasized, and among question raised in general terms was that of whether 'finding out' had really proved to be better than 'being told'. The growth of the child, and stressed the enormously wide variability in physical and intellectual maturity amongst children of the same age, particularly during adolescence, and the tendency for children to mature physically earlier than formerly.

It went on to discuss the interaction of heredity and environment, the stages of child development as outlined by Jean Piaget, and the measurement of I.Q. It found a correlation between children's I.Q.s and parental occupations-the children of professional parents have an average I.Q. of 115, emphasized that the child was a total personality, and that its emotional, social and intellectual aspects were closely intertwined.

Some of the implications of this section include the fact that individual variations between children of the same age are so great that any class, however apparently homogeneous, must always be treated as a body of children needing individual and different attention. Until a child is ready to take a particular step forward, it is useless to try and teach him to take it. Since any child grows up intellectually, emotionally, and physically at different rates, his teachers need to know and take account of his'developmental age' in all three respects.

The child's physique, personality and capacity to learn will develop as a result of continuous interaction between his genetic inheritance and his environment. Whilst the genetic factors are not as yet under our control, the environmental factors largely are, part Two of the report, therefore, suggested the need of a very personal approach to the pupil in the primary school, with a special study of each child's 'readiness' for any particular form of learning or operation; and, at the same time, the provision of a sound, healthy, amenable sort of environment in order to present the best learning situations and conditions.

A minimum programme was suggested for the participation of parents in the education of children—a welcome to the school, meetings with teachers, open days, information for parents via brochures about the organization of the school, and reports for parents. There should be a concerted that the primary school should be used as fully as possible, out of ordinary school hours, as a sort of community centre. Community schools should be developed in all areas, but particularly in educational priority areas, where there was need for constant communication between parents and teachers if the schools' aims were to be completely understood. The report emphasized the need for colleges of education to have stronger and more efficient links with such schools and to develop courses to meet the needs of immigrant children in particular.

There was a very strong suggestion that the training of teachers genrally should take more account of those social factors which affect school performance, and also of the structure and functions of the school services. It recommended the initiation of experimental schemes in the joint training of teachers and social workers, and already there are colleges of education which are devising courses for social and youth wing work as well as general welfare work. The report made it very clear indeed that the primary school has a social role in the community, as well as an immediate and individual adductive role.

There should be *three* years in the infant school and children should not be transferred until the age of 8 years; this would permit both children and teachers to work steadily and without anxiety. The age for admission to a secondary school was suggested as 12+, since this would give a *four-year* course in the junior or middle school, with a median age range from 8 years 6 months to 12 years 6 months. It should be noted here that the definition of primary education provided by Section 8 of the 1944 Education Act was amended by Section 3 of the 1948 Education Act.

Primary education was there defined as 'full time education for children below 10 years 6 moths and children above that age but below 12 years who it is expedient to educate with them'; whilst the 1964 Education Act allowed proposals to be submitted to the

Secretary of State for the establishment of new schools with age limits below 10 years 6 months and above 12 years. the report emphasized the need for the fullest possible documentation of each pupil before transfer to the secondary school, and it detailed the type of contents that a folder on each child should contain.

The ill effects upon primary education of selection for secondary schools were lessening, and the council recommended that authorities still employing selection procedures should no longer rely on an externally imposed battery of attainment and intelligence tests. Part five dealt with the children in the schools, with curriculum and internal organization. Among a large variety of aims and purposes mooted, and dangers to be avoided, the following aims of primary education were accepted in somewhat general terms, with the provison that generalities have limited value and can quickly become little more than platitudes; it was agreed that 'a pragmatic approach to the purposes of education was more likely to be fruitful'.

(a) Adaptability-to fir children for the society into which they will grow up, and to train them to be capable of adjusting to their changing environment.

(b) The all-round development of the individual child.

(c) The acquisition of the basic skills necessary in contemporary society.

(d) The religious and moral development of the child.

(e) Physical health, intellectual development, emotional and moral health, aesthetic awareness, a valid perspective, practical and social skills, and personal fulfilment.

(f) Values and attitudes must be mediated to the children. The school is not merely a teaching shop but a living community in which pupils learn primarily to live as children and not as future adults.

The work of Piaget was emphasized as a sound developmental approach to children's learning, and the importance of children's 'cultural' play was made clear. The report went on to consider certain particular aspects of the curriculum, and throughout there was an enlightened approach to both content and method, and a balanced attitude towards heuristic principles.

The council has no doubt that 'children's questions about sex ought to be answered plainly and truthfully whenever they are asked'. It gave validity to the modern, both relaxed and friendly, approach within the primary schools as a much better preparation for life in contemporary society than th old authoritative one.

Whilst accepting 'discipline", the council were clear that this connoted neither heavy punishment nor soft and flabby relationships; discipline, it felt, was impaired by such elements as disorder, untidiness and slackness—it could flourish only in an ethos of order an purposefulness, in which boredom had been eliminated. There must be, in all this, a healthy combination of individual, group, and class work and learning. Due consideration was also given to the education of both handicapped and gifted children. The role of the teacher was discussed, and it was argued that teachers must enlarge their endeavors and enlist to a greater extent parents' interest in their children's education. It was extremely important to diagnose the child's needs and potentialities and there would be increasing demands on the knowledge of the teacher, whether literary, scientific or mathematical.

Teachers, said the Report, 'cannot escape the knowledge that children will catch values and attitudes far more from what teachers do than what they say.

unless they are courteous, they cannot expect courtesy from children: when teaches are eager to learn and turn readily to observation and to books, their pupils are likely to do the same'. The report, in effect, asked not only for more teachers but also for better quality ones. It went on to discuss teachers' aides, or trained ancillaries, who might give substantial help to teachers inside and outside the classroom, and who would have equal status with nursery assistants and have comparable training.

The council considered that colleges of education, in general, were too remote from the problems of the school; it recommended a full inquiry into the system of training of teachers, and suggested that there should be more joint appointments to college and school staffs. Further, a network of residential teachers' courses should be developed.

(i) The Department of Education and Science should consider taking steps which would require all independent schools to state on their prospectuses whether the schools were recognized or registered and what this implies. The Department of Education and Science should reconsider the terms "recognized" and "registered" and try to devise more informative ones.

(ii) The Secretary of State's powers to serve Notices of Complaint on independent schools should be based on more stringent criteria. The construction of "objectionable" should be widened to include any conditions, physical or educational, in which children's welfare was not thought to be adequately safeguarded.

(iii) All head teachers of independent schools should be qualified teachers. After a data to be specified, only qualified teachers should be appointed as heads in new schools, or when there is a change of head teacher.

(iv) In-service courses should wherever possible allow some places for teachers from independent schools. The independent schools themselves should take through their professional organizations to "increase the facilities for in-service training for teachers in independent schools'

The primary schools were giving good value for the inadequate amount of money spent on them, and went on th state that teachers were too few in number and too unevenly distributed to do the job adequately.

The first priority was the establishment of education priority areas; the recruitment of teachers' aides would be an essential and immediate source of help to the schools everywhere, the essential improvement of bad primary school buildings must be undertaken as soon as possible wherever they existed; and nursery education must be extended through increased accommodation and staff. Planning should begin on changes in the national dates of entry, and also on the ages of transfer between the different stages of primary education.

The Plowden Report represents one of the most through investigations into any area of education over produced. Perhaps not least of its achievements was its virtual unanimity, which is reflection on the goodwill and singleness of purpose of its twenty-five members over a period of three years of intensive work and study. Out of every 100 women who enter our colleges of education, only 47 will be in the schools after three years of teaching; and after six years of service only 30 will remain. Perhaps the most sanguine way to look at the figures is simply to argue that 70 women out of every 100 so trained have, at least, qualified in a profession to which they may later return, but in any case they have found one way of obtaining higher education, with often minimum of entry qualifications; and as mothers, in the majority of cases, they will have a better understanding of educational problems.

Primary curriculum

The problems that arose for those charged with managing the curriculum at the school level can be analysed in three discrete categories: curriculum time allocation, teacher expertise, and resources in primary schools. The first reason for unmanageability is the apparently simple matter of *time allocation:* how much time is needed for each subject and for the whole curriculum. The problem has been commonly represented as the quart of the statutory orders and the pint pot of the teaching week. If you are sitting on a national committee inventing or revising the statutory curriculum, it must appear merely a mechanical matter. Reduce the content until the whole curriculum matches, or is slightly less than, the time available.

The second reason concerns the *task demands on class teachers* attempting to deliver the whole curriculum—most obviously the range and level of subject knowledge required, the pedagogical skills necessary, including differentiation, the sheer detail and number of Statements of Attainment, and techniques necessary for reliable assessment. These have now been seen as unrealistic demands to make upon normal classroom teachers by all save the dismal succession of Ministers of State parading before us to assert that primary teaching, especially at Key Stage 1, is not a particularly demanding job, needing for its successful performance neither graduate knowledge nor long training.

The third reason concerns *resources.* Primary schools are staffed less favourably than secondary schools, even when the comparison is based on only Key Stage 3, yet the range and demand of their educational activities, and therefore their staffing needs, are almost identical. When Kelly ran a computer model of Stockport's curriculum led staffing, she found that it led to staffing needs that were more-or-less identical across the five to sixteen age range.

The first difficulty faced by teachers was simple; there was too much curriculum for the time available. One reason commonly given for this was that the statutory curriculum had been invented by means of committees of subject enthusiasts who were unable to consider how their subject had to fit into the whole curriculum.

There was some truth in at least the first two of these sentences, but the extent of policy error was substantially greater than Graham and Tytler allow. First, at an early stage Ministers had worked on a broad view that the Education Reform Act would create a curricular framework in which the national prescription should cover substantially less than the whole curriculum. This was because Religious Education and other important curricular areas such as health education and moral development were conceived of as lying beyond national prescription. The consultative document suggested that in schools were there was 'good practice' the National Curriculum subjects would occupy 70-80 per cent of curriculum time.

Three implications arose for curriculum management from the notional time allocations in this table. The most important is that they represented an error that was to have disastrous effects as the curriculum was implemented. The notional time for English and Mathematics combined, was dramatically lower than was conventionally provided by primary teachers, according to every study that had examined time allocations in the post-war period.

A summary covering much of the relevant research in the last fifteen years showed that 50 per cent of time was typically given to English and Mathematics, excluding their application to other subjects. Empirically, the phenomenon of 50 per cent of time on these two subjects—what we might call the 'basic instinct' in the primary curriculum—is firmly established. Indeed, a study by Meyer *et al.* which is an examination of official elementary and primary curricula world-wide across this century until the late 1980s, argues that the phenomenon has been a global constant—irrespective of region, political economy or state of development.

The second point refers to the time available for the whole curriculum. It relates to 'evaporated time', a term coined in a professional development programme and used by Campbell and Neill to indicate time technically available for teaching but used for non-cognitive purposes such as supervising children changing for PE, moving them from one location in the school to another, lining up and clearing away.

It is important because it is assumed to be available for teaching, but the studies referred to above that took account of this time by excluding it from teaching time, showed that something between 22 per cent of teaching time evaporates in this way, the amount depending upon the age of the pupils and the physical layout and size of the school and the methodology of time analysis. In general, younger pupils and those in open-plan settings experience more evaporated time. It occurs in small units of time in any one day, but in Campbell and Neill's research, based on time logs of over 3000 days from over 300primary teachers, the average evaporated time per week was calculated at nearly two hours per week, equivalent to nearly 10 per cent of the teaching time available and equal to the notional time allocated for at least one of the non-basic subjects, in the National Curriculum.

Long hours spent on repetitive computation exercises do not necessarily mean challenging learning for bright pupils any more than do long hours spent by low-attaining pupils on tasks too difficult for them. Nonetheless, the conclusion from the research findings on time showed no general problem in primary classrooms about the adequacy of time being spent on teaching and learning the two basic subjects. Evidence after the introduction of the National Curriculum suggested that little had changed, with Campbell and Neill showing 51 per cent and 49 per cent of time devoted to the basics. The reasons for this state of affairs are three well-known ones.

First, as Ashton's research showed, drawing on a national sample of 1500 primary teachers in the early 1970s, the highest curricular priority was given to the basic skills of Reading, Oracy, Mathematics and Writing. Art. PE, Music, Sex Education, Science and Technology and a second language were given low priority. A follow-up study by Ashton with a less representative sample at the end of the 1970s, showed, if anything, higher priority placed on Mathematics and formal language competence. Thus, commitment to the basics has always been at a premium in the professional culture. Second, parents and governors place highest curricular priority on the basics also, as Thomas's investigation of London schools showed, and the Government has required greater teacher accountability to parents and governors. Third, there has been a long tradition, stretching was back before 1988, of formal testing focused on Reading Comprehension and Mathematics, a tradition reinforced by National Curriculum assessment arrangements, though it is now slightly broadened by the inclusion of Science in the core. Such testing washes back into curriculum priorities.

The basic instinct is sustained and reinforced by the workplace culture in primary schools. Thus it becomes startlingly clear that the National Curriculum in primary schools, introduced by a series of Secretaries of State who had constantly banged on about the need to get back to basics and to raise standards of literacy and numeracy, put in place policy guidance designed to reduce the time typically spent by primary teachers on the basics, and especially on English, where the astonishing reduction of about one-third of existing time was proposed.

With respect to time allocations, the policy guidance outstripped the practice in the schools for liberality and breadth. It offered a fundamentally different concept and ideology of curriculum balance. The guidance given to the working group devising the English curriculum was such as to encourage infant teachers to reduce the time they typically spent teaching children to read and write from about seven hours to little over four hours a week. No wonder there was widespread stress at Key Stage 1 with infant teachers accurately reporting that, against their own professional judgment, they were having to reduce the time on hearing children read in order to fit in everything else. As if to confirm this interpretation of the general policy, the National Curriculum Council issued guidance on planning the Key Stage 2 curriculum in which three presumably recommended case studies of school planning were provided: two of them (year 6 and 5 classes) suggested that the basics should be planned to occupy 41 per cent and 37.5 per cent of curriculum time respectively.

The Year 5 class plan was developed into a yearly programme in which Mathematics and English occupy 316 out of the 846 hours available, some 37 per cent of curriculum time in their terms. Schools are urged by the NCC to review the exercise, including reviewing whether the time allocations are appropriate. In this context, it is interesting, but confusing, to see that in the summer *Update* from the NCC, the curriculum planning in a Coventry primary school was celebrated; it initially used a plan which involved only 40 per cent of time on basics, but after trilling, it changed to 50 per cent.

There was thus built into the curriculum at national level a four-pronged problem for every primary school: too much planned prescription overall; too much content in the statutory orders for each subject: not enough flexibility to allow for evaporated time; a pretence or assumption that there would be more time available for the non-basics than there was in actuality. The task demands placed on class teachers by the National Curriculum have been analysed by Thomas, who shows that in the slimmed down curriculum, teachers at Key Stage 2 had to be familiar with about 500 statements of attainment, detailed and confusingly presented programmes of study, poorly defined cross-curricular themes and religious education.

In addition they would have to posses subject knowledge in the ten subjects up to about Level 6, or to be able to differentiate the planning, teaching and assessment across at least 4 levels or the curriculum in each subject. To achieve all this they would need to be the curricular school equivalent of Albert Einstein. Marie Curie and Linford Christie rolled into one. The evidence about subject expertise sometimes takes a narrow view of the concept but the review of research by Bennett and S

There are serious deficiencies in individual primary teachers' understandings, especially but not exclusively in the science and technology areas. Graduate students training for primary teaching provide no greater reasons for being sanguine, if those studied by Bennett and Carre are typical. They brought with them to their PGCE courses misunderstandings of everyday phenomena, such as the energy in a sledge moving down a hill, the explanations for night and day, and basic arithmetic competencies such as expressing $18 as a percentage of $120. Bennett and Carre's research used tests in Mathematics, English and Science based on National Curriculum levels 4, 5 and 6, and Assessment of Performance Unit (APU) tests. In some of these latter, the top 20 per cent of primary pupils scored higher than the average of the PGCE students.

Technically, of course, the curriculum demands are placed on the whole school rather than the individual teacher, but in practice for the medium term further, most teachers will remain responsible for teaching most of the curriculum for the pupils in their class. Given the research findings, Alexander, Rose and Woodhead's assertion that, 'Teachers must possess the subject knowledge which the statutory orders require' sounds like a plea of desperation.

A major management issue therefore becomes how the specialist expertise in the whole staff group can be deployed to extend the work of class teachers, with the overarching purpose that, as Richards argued, such deployment should 'support not undermine' the class teacher's role. The previous two problems for manageability apply to all schools irrespective of location, size or other factors. Resource issues affect schools differentially, depending upon funding formulae, school size or pupil characteristics. There is however one key resource issue—the level of staffing. The disadvantage for primary schools of historic staffing allocations has been acknowledged for almost a decade, although the difficulty of translating the acknowledgment into staffing resources has been enormous, particularly since the acknowledgment occurred in a period of public expenditure restraint.

If primary schools are to develop more specialist approaches to the curriculum, if class size should rarely exceed 30, and if teachers are to have some time free of class teaching in the school day; if, in short, the schools are to be enabled to implement the National Curriculum witnout stress and overload remaining a chronic feature of teachers' work, some improvement in the resourcing of schools is required. Acknowledgment is no longer enough. The funding formula at local level and the approval of schemes of devolved management at national level will need to be based on realistic assessment of the work activities now required of teachers in modern primary schools. Without the development of such national or local policies there will remain constraints on the extent to which the curriculum reform policy can succeed.

For the management of primary schools, the Dearing review's interim report appeared to hold out seductive promises to make the curriculum manageable by sliming it down. In terms of the analysis provided so far, however, it was limited to the issue of time allocations, and my evaluation of Dearing start form this recognition; the review had nothing to say about subject expertise or resourcing, perhaps more fundamental problems than time allocation. Even the restricted problem-solving of the final report is a sleight of hand in respect of the 'curricular arithmetic' of time allocations, according to Alexander and Campbell.

Dearing's approach was to allocate 20 per cent of curriculum time for discretionary use by the school and to free two weeks of the school from any curricular prescription, and then to offer guidance on time allocation for the remaining time, viz for 80 per cent of thirty-six weeks. In discussing his own arithmetic, Dearing acknowledged that it was difficult to apply it to apply it to primary schools: 'Specific time will have to be set aside for work in English, but the full 30 per cent (KSI) and 25 per cent (KS2) does not have to be found in addition to time given to other subjects.' Perhaps too defensively Dearing added, "This is not sleight of hand; it is a statement of fact based on the realities of teaching expressed by teachers'. His own arithmetic was presented in a table in para, 4.20. With the bracketed figures referring to cross-curricular application, and therefore not counted in the total. Added percentages based on the total annual hours of 612 and 675 for which national prescription was envisaged, and these percentages appeared to reflect the historic practices of teachers, at least at KS1, with about 50 per cent given over to the basics.

There was however an assumed reduction in the proportion given to English at KS2. Alexander and Campbell however provide an alternative arithmetic, based on the overall time, not just the 80 per cent. Their arithmetic is given. Expressed this way, Dearing appears to have rendered almost a quarter of the school curriculum year discretionary, and therefore to have solved the manageability problem. However, as Alexander and Campbell show, there are five reasons why this has not really happened. First, the percentages for English and Mathematics are dramatically lower then previous or current practice, and time will have to be taken from the allegedly discretionary time to restore the basic instinct of 50 per cent time on them. Second, there is no educational or research-based justification for Dearing's assertion that as primary children become older they need less time on English.

The DES Primary Staffing Survey found 27 per cent allocated to English in the junior stage, and while it is obvious that the nature of English at KS1 is different from that at KS2, it is not clear why is should take less time. Nor has it done so in practice. Third, time on science has been reduced from what was previously proposed as necessary and the 10-15 per cent of time that was actually needed for the science curriculum. Fourth, national testing remains focused on the core subjects, pressing in on school management to ensure that teachers give priority to them in time allocation.

Alexander and Campbell calculated that all discretionary time would have to go to the core. Fifth, the time remaining for the other subjects will be inadequate, especially for those that are time consuming, such as PE, Music, Art and Technology. Sixth, without good reason, excessive time has been set aside for RE. As a consequence, the only way the curriculum will become manageable is if it is recognized for what it is, underneath the Dearing rhetoric a return to the elementary curriculum of the basic and RE updated with some Science and Information Technology. But manageability will have been gained at the expense of breadth and balance.

Management implications of the argument is based on two assumptions about the relationship between a national quango and individual schools. National quangos are not good at details, and have little competence in respect of the curriculum organization of individual schools. For example, within the space of nine months the National Curriculum Council and the School Curriculum and Assessment Authority could not even agree on the simple technical matter of how many hours per year should be considered as available for instruction.

Second, as Thomas pointed out, the National Curriculum was established by reference to the best practice in each subject. To be 'best' or even good at everything is not common in individual human beings or their institutions so that there was and is a certainly that virtually and schools would, to some degree, fail to meet the statutory requirements. He added that 'Schools in other countries commonly fail to meet the requirements of their national curricula'. If these two assumption are confirmed, the first lessons for school management are that it is in the individual school, not a national agency, that will create a curriculum that can be made to work for the school concerned; and that concern to cover the whole curriculum will have to be tempered by consideration of quality and standards in pupils learning. This latter goal might be more readily arrived at by the school establishing its curricular priorities than by attempting to deliver every statutory prescription equally well.

It was, after all, the quango charged with the inspection of schools that first made clear that coverage had been achieved only at the cost of depth in pupil learning. To restore confidence in their own professional judgment, it may first be necessary for teachers to lose faith in the ability of the national agencies to manage the curriculum implementation process sensibly. Dependency on external forces is as counter productive for the whole school staff as it is for the head and is likely to reduce rather than increase empowerment and accountability. On this basis six possible ways forward may be identified, though each will be contested by some teachers because of the value assumptions it contains.

First, in respect of time allocation, there is the possibility that much more of the teaching of English and Mathematics than currently might be planned, delivered and assessed through their application to other subjects. This is a position advocated for at least fifteen years by HMI, but has been found problematic in practice.

The problem is not helped by the framing of the curriculum in single subjects, nor by the tendency for mathematics and English schemes to be subject-specific. It is a good example of how a staff would have to have confidence as HMI had, that standards in the basics would improve by their being applied to other subjects. Unfortunately, it may be easier for staff in schools where pupils already have high achievement to develop such confidence than for staff where pupils appear to need substantial amounts of time on basic skills. Second, schools might consider the use of homework as part of their overall policy, especially perhaps at KS2. If there is shortage of time for English, part of the solution might be to cease to consider the pupils' curriculum time as synonymous with the timetabled school day.

Successful experience at S1 with parental partnerships provides exemplars for developing similar approaches at KS2. Some opposition might be raised by those who would see such a systematic approach to homework as increasing the disadvantages of pupils who live in unsupportive families or physical conditions unconductive to doing homework. School-based provision for facilities for doing homework, while a contradiction in terms, might go some way to mitigating the difficulties, though at a cost in staff supervision time.

A third solution to the problem of curriculum time might be to extend the school day, week or year. This is clearly sensible for those schools who currently spend less than the minimum expected weekly hours on instruction. It will be opposed on grounds of workload and of inappropriateness in rural areas where pupils have to travel long distances. It might also be surmised that while the current assessment and testing policy remains in place, any extra time would be devoted to the core and thus not release time for the non-core, which is the problem. A solution to teachers' lack of confidence and competence in subject expertise could be remedied by a greatly expanded. In-service training programme along lines similar to the DES twenty-day courses. This is obviously true, assuming that the courses are effective, and that their effects are long-lived, an assumption that Bennett and Summer's review of research questions in part. However, the problem for primary schools is that extensions of In-service training programmes are also extensions of the times when teachers have to be away from school and their class, so that a substantial programme of In-service Training in the school day may have disadvantages for pupil learning where schools do not have access to good quality supply cover.

A second possibility lies in suggestions that schools should deploy their staff in ways that enable their subject expertise to be exploited more effectively to the benefit of the school as a whole, whether as specialists, semi-specialists or as coordinators. Again, within limits, this might offer gains to some schools, especially those with staffing allocations that permit some flexibility of deployment. For most schools, however there is almost no flexibility, and, as school size reduces, the range of subjects in which there is staff expertise also reduces.

A third possibility is that more use should be made of class texts in which the teachers can have confidence that the intellectual content is reliable, freeing them to concentrate more upon planning for how pupils may learn more effectively from the texts. There may be some reluctance in the profession to the purchase of texts for whole classes, since it is seen as at odds with concepts of good practice which stress learning from first hand experience, building on pupils' interests, and practical investigation. While recognizing that purchasing class texts will not solve all problems, perhaps influenced by past images of whole classes sitting reading class textbooks at the same pace, each pupil being asked to read aloud with the rest of the class following. The way texts are used with primary classes is obviously an important matter, but the adoption of good quality class texts would be the quickest way of helping class teachers cope with both the cognitive demands of the whole curriculum and the time demands of preparing all learning materials for their pupils.

There is something puritanical in a professional culture which implies that the virtuous teacher is the one who prepares every worksheet herself. One of the few ways that a national quango could make itself useful to teachers would be to issue 'kitemarks' to texts to indicate that the statutory orders were accurately and adequately covered by them and that there were useful assessment activities integrated into them. This is, politically speaking, quite different from requiring that schools use one particular prescribed text.

Little useful can be added about the formulate by which, externally, resources are allocated to schools, beyond what has been argued earlier. On the internal allocation of the resources when allocated, one further point needs to be raised. In most primary schools lack of time, especially lack of time in the school day, has been a major obstacle to effective delivery of the curriculum. Yet Campbell and Neill showed that teachers spent about eighteen house a week teaching, and between five and six hours a week on low level routines, such as mounting displays, supervision, moving pupils round the school, registration, and collecting dinner money, etc. Where teacher had more time with a non-teaching assistant, they tended to spend more, not less time on such routines, probably because of the 'collaborative cultures' operating in them.

Yet there is something unsettling about the picture of teachers naming lack of time as the main obstacle to achieving the cognitive objectives of the curriculum while spending so much time on non-cognitive routines. Given that teacher time is the most valuable and most expensive resource available to a school, it is worth the management of the school exploring the advantages of re-thinking the use of time of all adults on the staff of the school, to see whether the non-teaching assistants' time might be used imaginatively to free up teachers' time. Professional groups validate their professional claim by reference to 'expert' knowledge, supposedly hard-won and rigorously tested, but few people are naive enough to believe that in a job as complex as teaching such formal training provides the sole resource for subsequent professional thought and action.

Experience plays a substantial part. 'On the job', teachers develop skills and insights through constant interaction with children; they come to recognise patterns, commonalities and recurrences in behaviours, situations and problems and thereby develop habits of diagnosis and response whose practical effectiveness they can confidently demonstrate. similarly, to an extent perhaps not sufficiently recognised, teachers draw on their pre-training experience; for, uniquely among professionals, they are engaged in a process with which they have already been involved, continuously and unremittingly, since the age of five or earlier. Their teacher training course is but a brief part of this total, cumulative educational experience and the latter, as much as the specifics of the one to four year training course, shapes the view of the educational process and its purposes within which they operate as teachers. It is a commonplace that many young teachers teach as they were taught in school rather than as they were urged to teach in college. Significantly too, teachers themselves display ambivalent attitudes towards initial training.

In the context of debate and negotiation about salary and status the teacher is a 'trained professional' in possession of expertise denied to all but those who submit themselves to the rigours of Certificate, BEd, or PGCE. But in everyday discourse, good teachers are 'born, not made' and that same expert knowledge may be dismissed as 'irrelevant' theory.

The truth is that it is empirically impossible to isolate initial training from earlier, contemporaneous or subsequent experience for the purposes of demonstrating its precise impact on the way a teacher performs in the classroom. It seems sensible to assume that it does have an impact, but to avoid the extremes of the grandiose strategic claim prepared for negotiation with Burnham on the one hand, and the dismissiveness of teacher folklore and staffroom conventional wisdom on the other.

Instead, two hypotheses can be supported. One is that by incorporating in its emphasis on certain sorts of knowledge and skill particular views of the teaching role, the nature and needs of young children, the initial training course tends to facilitate some lines of subsequent professional development and to discourage others. Second, initial training influences subsequent development as much by what it omits or does badly as by what it treats positively; or, to use for the sake of convenience some mild jargaon, a course may 'de-skill' as well as 'skill'. This latter point is particularly apposite in the present context, given that we have seen how primary ideology may relate to professional insecurity. the ideology, it will be recalled, is most strongly focused and most forcibly expressed in relation to those aspects of primary teaching where empirical study shows the greatest weakness.

Therefore, is not firm evidence of behavioural casuality—element *x* in initial training produces action *y* in the classroom—so much as a succession of positive and negative correspondences between training and subsequent practice which are sufficiently pervasive and exact as to leave little doubt about a causal relationship of some sort, albeit diluted by the power of experience, circumstance and contingency, and mediated through each individual's unique combination of personality, intellect and worldview. To provide a framework for the analysis which follows it is necessary at this point to give a brief resume of the overall structures and contexts of courses. There are two main routes into primary teaching, the four year BEd and the one year PGCE. The former is a post 'A' level undergraduate course and the latter, self-evidently, is taken by graduates in subjects which could equally well lead to other careers.

Deferred student choice and flexibility were major aspirations; this was the era of the 'container revolution', of courses which students put together from a wide selection of units and modules, and which often meant that professional study and work in schools were deferred until the second or even the third of four years. By the late 1970s, deferred choice, consecutive training and modularity were running into the logistical problems attendant upon contraction, for such courses had to be large to be viable. there were other criticisms. chiefly revolving round the continued lack of sufficient professional emphasis, the perceived divorce of theory and practice and the split between subject and professional study.

A large number of institutions had transferred from university to CNAA validation and alternative notions of 'degree-worthiness' had begun to be explored. Mark III BEds lasted the full four years, were usually honours only, and included serious attempts to put professional concerns at the centre of the course and at last to break down the barrier between subject and professional study. But by that time, the early 1980s now, there were countervailing pressures.

Successive HMI surveys, of primary and secondary schools had identified what were regarded as major weaknesses in serving teachers' professional expertise, above all in their curriculum knowledge. First HMI, then central government then ACSET, the teacher education advisory body—less from conviction than recognition of the irresistibility of political dogma backed by landslide election success—and finally and DES again proposed that all BEd students, whether primary or secondary, should spend half their course on main subject study in order to remedy these curricular deficiencies.

The inadequacy of the models of primary curriculum, primary teaching and initial training thereby encapsulated will be discussed. Courses are not disembodied artifacts but events and ideas which acquire their reality from particular institutional contexts. The majority of today's established primary teachers not only trained by the 2-3-4 year route but did so in a distinctive sort of institution, the college of education, which preserved a culture of remarkable homogeneity and historical persistence until the institutional reorganisations of the 1970s forced many of the surviving colleges into a usually reluctant alliance with mainstream higher education institutions.

While the PGCE was located mainly in the universities and—until the rude advent of compulsory initial training, comprehensive schools and mixed ability teaching—prepared its students for grammar and public schools, the 3-4 year course reflected the requirements of a less prestigious tradition, that of secondary modern and primary schools. Thus the two routes embodied and reinforced the mutual exclusiveness of the two central traditions in British education: minority/elitist/academic, and mass/elementary/utilitarian. Like primary schools, the colleges' origins were humble and impoverished. Like primary schools, they acquired a substantial contrary ideology—idealist, romantic, espousing values of self-actualization, individualism and student/child-centredness. By the 1950s and 1960s, the professionally formative years for the deputy heads, heads and advisers of the 1970s and 1980s, the college ethos was predominantly one, in Taylor's often-quoted words, of 'social and literary romanticism'.

Partial rejection of pluralism: suspicion of the intellect and the intellectual; a lack of interest in political and structural change; a stress upon the intuitive and the intangible, upon spontaneity and creativity... a hunger for the satisfactions of interpersonal life within the community and the small group, and a flight from rationality. The extent to which this incorporates caricature is debatable, but when one considers the institutions into which most of the products of these colleges went—primary schools—the correspondence is irresistible.

Specific manifestations and echoes of these values will continue to emerge from our discussions. We turn now, however, from general background to the first of several specific aspects of initial training; the means whereby it seeks to generate that 'understanding of children' required for primary class teaching and pre-eminent in the class teacher's professional claim.

In most post-war teacher education courses the intending teacher's capacity to understand and relate to children has been seen as the virtually exclusive concern of two elements:

(a) *academic*—courses in what until the 1960s were termed 'principles of education', subsequently the separate 'disciplines' of psychology and sociology of education, but more recently somewhat disguised within integrated, thematic education/professional courses;

(b) *experiential*—teaching practice and other school-based activity.

Little or no overlap of function is envisaged or, in terms of academic territoriality, allowed. there is assumed to be an exact correspondence between professional attribute and course component so that each becomes the 'property' of a particular department or group of staff. Thus 'understanding of children' is the concern not of anyone with insights to offer but of just two academic disciplines, psychology and sociology.

Psychology is relatively well-established in initial teacher education. The MCNair Report's 'principles of education' included; physiology and physical education, psychology, 'great classical writers on education', history of the education system, and appreciation of the 'home circumstances of the pupils'. This approach lasted well into the 1960s: Taylor, Tibble, Browne and others record the dominance of the 'mother hen'—the education tutor dispensing a mixture of 'method', history of educational ideas and, above all, psychology. The 1960s witnessed the coming of age of the 'four disciplines' of education, but this strengthened the position in primary training, where the 'child development' course continued to rule supreme. Despite this relatively long-established pre-eminence in teacher education, it must be recalled that as an academic discipline psychology is young, and sociology younger.

Through a combination of empirical research and theory-generation they seek to offer descriptions and explanations of individual and collective human behaviour which must be regarded as tentative, provisional and incomplete. Theories and models are frequently put forward, or at least received by students, as unassailable truths about the real world, their status as such apparently confirmed by the strong positivistic orientation of a good deal of the research drawn upon and by the convenient tendency of such work to offer quantified findings. Wilson showed how the very examination questions BEd and PGCE students were required to answer presumed their tacit acceptance of a wide range of concepts and constructs. That claim is readily substantiated.

Equally unsatisfactory, none of the questions invites application to the task of the teacher. Assuming the intending teachers duly demonstrate that they have committed the various theories, facts and arguments to memory,what then? What are they supposed to *do* with this knowledge? If it is seriously intended that it should inform their thinking about the job of teaching, why is no opportunity given for this capacity to be demonstrated? Or is it more important that they have knowledge than that they can use it? Taking their lead from this style of questioning, essays are peppered with the catch-phrase 'Research has proved that....' without apparent regard for the need for all proof claims to be probed, for the provisionality of scientific findings. The connection with everyday professional practice is evident.

The same formulae re-emerge in much of the published work exemplified in, and in the written and spoken utterances of some serving teachers. Here, however, their linguistic hardness may be duly softened to match the gentler, familial ambience of child-centred discourse, and with the 'authority' now accorded a hushed, parent-surrogate,almost Messianic reverence: 'Piaget has shown us that...'. In both contexts such unconditional deference, by negating the element of natural scepticism combined with informed critique vital to academic study and the proper use of academic research, effectively invalidates the latter's claim: for it is no longer knowledge—open, provisional, challengeable—but dogma.

Conversely, the students are exhorted not trust 'mere opinions', to have a higher regard for academic than common sense modes of analysis and explanation, and to prefer the 'objective' data of the social sciences to their or an experienced teacher's subjective' judgement. Understanding oneselves and others has probably always been a human preoccupation. Certainly from the time when the first written record was produced we have shown a deep interest in human and animal behaviour. Yet our ideas have been almost entirely unsystematic and unrepresentative.

Even now we casually watch others or listen with prejudiced ears to conversation and from this evidence build up distorted rules of thumb about human nature. It is of course highly probable that our 'interest in human and animal behaviour' predates written records, but that is to quibble. More problematic, it seems to me, is the implied dismissal of all but the psychologist's way of doing things as 'unsystematic', 'unrepresentative', 'casual', 'prejudiced', and 'distorted': clearly not the author's intention, but open to that interpretation by someone new to the discipline.

Thus may be generated or reinforced a basic epistemology to which the polarising of 'objective' and 'subjective', of 'fact' and 'value', of 'truth' and 'falsity', of 'knowledge' and 'belief', are fundamental. If internalised, this simplistic conceptual map is able and likely to provide signposts for a wide range of contexts: the teacher's subsequent response to educational research and theory most obviously, but also other situations in which knowledge claims are significant—record cards and diagnostic or attainment tests for example, and the wide and crucial range of claims which teachers make about children, their abilities, their potential, their home background and so on. The other context where this epistemology bears fruit in a palpable way is the primary curriculum. Its most public and assertive face is the view of curriculum in general and knowledge in particular which we explored—for example the way a view of knowledge as brute 'fact' can be used as a justification for rejecting knowledge in any guise.

Less obviously, but perhaps in the end more significant, the framework may influence the way in which different curriculum experiences are presented for the child, and the view of knowledge the child thereby acquires: art at the 'soft',, 'subjective', 'value' end of the continuum science at the 'hard', 'objective', 'fact' end. Moreover, by according experientially derived insight lower status an initial training course misses an obvious and significant opportunity. Given that it is at the commonsense, intuitive level that the student/teacher is frequently forced to operate once under the pressure of everyday classroom circumstances, it is precisely these sorts of judgements which should be exposed and explored during initial training, with a view to refining them and making them as reliable and reflexive as possible.

The psychologist's rejection of such perspectives is the more emphatic for being made on methodological grounds: personal knowledge is counted not so much less significant as inadmissible. Psychology has sought to replace commonsense theories about mental processes with propositions derived from the application to human nature of the methods of the natural sciences. Pre-eminent in this methodology is the charting of observable behaviours.

The 'introspective' method which seeks to uncover individuals' private knowledge, beliefs, attitudes and so on by eliciting these by word of mouth, is considered by the behaviourist majority to be inconsistent with the scientific claim. Thus because by the canons of a particular methodology such date is deemed inaccessible, as the object of study it ceases to be of interest. This raises broader issues concerning the historical development of psychology—its origins in the philosophy of mind, the late 19th century rejection of mind in favour of 'scientific' study of the brain and the central nervous system, the consequent issue of the distinctiveness of psychology vis-a-vis neurology and physiology, and the continuity of the behaviourist/ introspectionist debates. Such issues are beyond the scope of this book, but what is important for teachers and teacher educators is an awareness of the consequences for the way their task is defined in initial training. For teachers are not neuro-surgeon: their main focus of concern is that elusive entity, which causes psychologists such difficulty, the human mind.

Alternative perspectives on children which would complement the portrayal of the behaviourist psychologist—from literature, drama, philosophy and pre-eminently, everyday discourse—are explicitly rejected. Apart from its tendency to impoverish the teacher's professional development and classroom thought, this monopoly reveals the extent to which the view of teaching as science has pervaded academic and professional opinion, even including groups—like literature teachers and tutors—who might be expected to be more resistant. Perhaps, as academics so often do, they fail to make the connection between the claim that the arts offer unique and profound insights into the human condition and the obvious fact that teaching itself is nothing if not concerned with that condition. Three provisos must, however, be expressed, lest it be thought that this chapter's discussion stems basically from an anti-psychology standpoint. The first is that the teacher education community as a whole, rather than its psychologists alone, have to take responsibility for excluding alternative sources of insight into children in general and into their mental processes in particular. There has been large-scale connivance at this needless impoverishment of the training process. Second, arguing for courses as a whole to include addition perspectives not for psychologists to do what artists do.

The third proviso is that the psychology component of teacher education courses, particularly until, in the mid 1970s, it began to be taught by graduates with a board psychological training, may have been singularly unrepresentative of the parent discipline. It might, for example, over-emphasis Skinnerian behaviourism or developmental psychology; it might neglect study of the unconscious mind or of the social dimension of behaviour. It might fail to develop in students a proper consciousness of the extent to which a psychological model is a metaphor for behaviour, not the behaviour itself nor ever necessarily a particularly accurate representation of it.

Above all it might fail to convey the necessary sense of psychology, as of every discipline, as variegated, contentious and changing. The extent to which psychology of education courses directly reinforce the 'sequential developmentalism' element in primary ideology, which—drawing on King and others—provides a good example of several of the points above, particularly those concerning distortion in content and methodological oversimplification.

The central theme or core of such courses has traditionally been a chronological treatment of child development. Here 'development' is conceived as a matrix with norms for ages and stages providing one axis and various categories of human development—'intellectual', 'social', 'emotional', 'moral', 'physical' etc.—the other. This developmental matrix, open to fundamental criticism as it is provides a basic, widely accepted structure for primary discourse, curriculum planning and pupil assessment: the firmly fixed reference points on an otherwise shifting and undifferentiated map.

The ages attached to stages postulated by Piaget are approximate, and that the inevitability of the sequence and the state-independent processes and mechanisms of cognitive development—equilibration, assimilation, accommodation—are more significant than any inferred chronology. Yet it is notable that in student essays, as in professional discourse and teachers, books and curriculum materials,the stages as such feature more prominently than the stage-independent theory, despite the fact that an understanding of the latter is essential to using the undoubted insights of Piagetian theory to promote or accelerate learning. A Piagetian approach to HMI's concept of 'match', for example, would demand that children encounter learning tasks which are slightly, but not excessively, more complex than their present understanding, and that without this element of 'stretching' the disequilibration necessary for learning will not be produced. Where students or teachers perceived development in terms of states rather than processes they will tend to wait for learning to occur 'spontaneously' or 'naturally' rather than seek as teachers to advance it, on the grounds that the child has to be 'ready'.

Just as the dominance of developmentalism in everyday practice is matched by the dominance of the developmental 'matrix' in educational psychology courses, so the traditional fare of sociology of education courses corresponds strongly with another element in professional discourse, the family and home as the prime or even sole causes of the child's difficulties or failures at school.

Until the early to mid-1970s sociology of education courses were dominated by the issue of the effect of family and social-class factors on the child's attainment at school. Early studies of streaming pointed the way to the possibility that the school itself might be a contributory factor in the under-achievement of working-class children, but research on class-related socialisation practices, parental attitudes, language and so on tended to swamp such relatively slender evidence. Only with the 'new' sociology of education, with its two-pronged, ideologically committed concern to explore first the cultural loading of the school and its curriculum in favour of certain groups of pupils and, second, the nature of everyday classroom life, did alternatives to the family/home deficit model present themselves with much credibility.

A substantial literature concerning the effect of teacher expectations on pupil performance, teacher constructs and typifications, classroom interaction and teaching styles, now permits a more balanced appraisal of the relative impact of family and school, parents and teachers, on the child's educational career. Some of this work was referred. The shift, however, is recent, and everyday primary discourse, in as far as it is demarcated and to some extent controlled by senior members of the profession such as heads and advisers, still appears to display fairly unreserved affiliation to family/home theories; certainly the confident professional assertions about 'good' and 'poor' parents and homes are part of the essential fabric of both staffroom discussion and pupil record cards. What will be worth monitoring is the extent to which the 'new' sociology of education produces a discernible shift in the way children's learning difficulties or lack of motivation are explained as students of the 1970s gain headhips in the 1980s and 1990s and seek to influence their school's 'philosophies'. If, however, the family/home background theory is such an indispensable element in professional ideology—in that, for the weaker teacher in particular, it is fundamental to the preservation of his self-esteem—we can anticipate little movement overall.

Theories of child development and educability, it will be apparent, not only have ideological potential but need to be simplified, and perhaps even distorted, to achieve that potential. Thus, Piagetian theory may be interpreted as confirming a doctrine of 'readiness' rather than as challenging the teacher's ingenuity to provide the child with appropriately structured and sequenced learning experiences. Similarly, the complexity and tentativeness of, say, Bernstein's work on language and social structure may be ignored in preference for gross polarisations of 'restricted' and 'elaborated' codes which may confirm a student's or teacher's existing cultural stereotypes and prejudices. Both theories exemplified can be invoked to justify low expectations of children - on the 'grounds' of age, or of social class.

In fact, much of the theoretical material regarded as indispensable in initial training is intrinsically extremely elusive and difficult to understand, let alone to apply, and especially so for the 18-21 year old with neither professional experience of schools and children nor a background of introductory study in the social sciences. However, its misinterpretation could be reduced or offset if the typificatory process which it appears to reinforce were itself the object of scrutiny on initial training courses. But it is a characteristic of mainstream education courses in initial training that, more recent sociology and social psychology perspective apart, they tend to devote little attention to the teacher as such. This particularly true of psychology of education courses: an examination of student texts and course syllabuses will reveal that most deal not so much with the psychology of *education* as with the psychology of the *child*, and that child's education is treated only in so far as it can be conceived independently of the person who is its chief architect, the teacher.

The child emerges with an identity shaped by a combination of heredity and environment, having characteristics which are given and immutable. There is little or no psychological analysis of adults in general or teachers in particular; nor of the teacher's contribution to that classroom character of the child which serves as the basis for the teacher's appraisal of him or her. The child's actions are presented, if only by default, as independent of the teacher's; a conception of the child is encouraged which is somehow independent of the person, the teacher, who does the conceiving. These tendencies can be illustrated by comparing two recent psychology of education textbooks.

The model is not of the interaction of minds and personalities, still less of teaching as dependent on teacher qualities as well as child attributes, but of the operating theatre: the teacher, as complete person and competent professional, works on the child's mind with the detachment of the surgeon working on the anesthetized body of the patient. Skill is presumed; the sole knowledge required is of the mental anatomy of the child. Fontana's *psychology for Teachers* stresses in its introduction that 'no child's behaviour can be fully understood unless we study also the behaviour of others—teachers, parents, school friends—towards him', and subsequently argues that within the context of the school the teacher is the most important influence upon the child. Despite this promising beginning, and the author's reservations elsewhere about traditional psychology of education courses, twelve of the sixteen chapters are devoted to the pupil, only three to interaction and teacher-child relations, and just one to 'teacher personality and characteristics'.

The latter is a brief summary of research on the behavioural characteristics of 'effective' teachers, contextualised in an acknowledgement of some of the problems involved in defining teacher effectiveness: about a page each on the teacher's emotional security, attitude, styles and classroom talk—all crucial issues but far too briefly dealt with.

In the economic climate of recent years, publishers have been increasingly reluctant to take on other than obviously marketable basic texts and course readers in education. The original or unusual is squeezed out and the second- or third-hand comes to rule supreme. Primary education has suffered particularly from the flood of edited 'readers', many of them drawing repeatedly on the same rather limited pool of 'safe' articles. Thus, though one must not overstate the case, the public teachable, examinable face of the educational process is increasingly defined by a combination of academics' personal interests and market forces: the research which, fortuitously, happens to be feasible, interesting, fundable or available, and what publishers and entrepreneurial editors or authors see as likely to sell.

But that is to digress. 'Understanding children' is an attribute not of the object of that understanding but of the teacher who claims it. The teacher will perceive a child in a particular way not only because of the sort of person that child is but because of the sort of person the teacher is.

In the primary school, we remind ourselves, the class-teacher system ensures that a child is so perceived for educational purposes for a whole year by just one person: with that much at stake it seems indefensible for initial training courses to neglect the psychology of the teacher. Four shifts are indicated therefore. First, the inclusion, as argued, of a substantial focus on teachers and their impact on those various aspects of the learner conventionally treated as independent of them.

Second, a deeper exploration of the ways individual behaviour—whether the child's or the teacher's—can be understood in the context of, and sometimes explained as a consequence of, interaction, possibly through the use of transactional analysis techniques applies in industrial psychology and psychotherapy, as well as interaction analysis schedules and theoretical perspectives of social psychology and interactionist/phenomenological sociology. Third, a preparedness to explore the irrationality which frequently characterises human actions and interactions, not least in the classroom; the dominant psychological tradition in teacher education, as we have seen, takes the teacher's total rationality for granted and moreover imposes a sometimes over-tidy, predictive framework on the child. Fourth, just as theoretical study of children in teacher education is required to be supported by work with children in classrooms, so teachers in classrooms and above all students themselves would need to be the object of practical study.

If self-exploration is now included in the training of other professional groups whose job involves the management of people and relationships, it can surely be justified in the training of teachers. The second major context a course provides for developing the student's understanding of children is school experience. Again, a historical perspective on this part of the course is helpful because it character and purposes have changed in recent years, through not as radically as some current advocates of 'school-based' courses would have us believe.

To make use of schools not merely as a context for practising executive skills but as a prime means for developing the student's capacities to observe, understand and relate to children is a *sine qua non* of teacher education. It has to be asked, however, whether the opportunities are fully exploited. This is only partly, as we have seen, a procedural matter; what needs closer attention is the teacher educators' and course validators' view of what this 'understanding' might mean.

At present, and certainly during the decade when today's primary teachers and heads trained, the interpretations, explanations and hypotheses of students and serving teachers have been under-valued and therefore insufficiently pursued and tested. And while a somewhat restricted canon of child-related theories has been, in comparison, over-exposed, it has been the exposure of obeisance, rather than critique.

Some of the consequences, or correspondences, suggested by this restricted epistemology have been outlined in this chapter and exemplified more fully. There seem to be a number of ways the situation can be improved, of varying degrees of radicalism:

(a) the focus for 'understanding' can be broadened;

(b) better use can be made of existing education disciplines;

(c) additional (academic) sources of insight can be explored;

(d) 'everyday' modes of understanding can be more fully exploited;

(e) different conceptions of professional theory for teaching can be applied.

In an obvious sense, by definition, students are the main concern in a course of initial training: the qualities, skills and knowledge which they are deemed to need are the course's raison d'etre.

So in arguing that the course needs to focus more explicitly on the student and on the serving teacher, am arguing for a specific kind of attention with which this self-evident concern is not to be confused. Courses are premised on the importance of teachers' mastery of certain executive skills, their manifestation of particular personal qualities and their possession of certain kinds of knowledge. Pre-eminent among the latter is that academic knowledge about children which we have explored in this chapter, and which they may or may not make significant use of in practice. What, by and large, are neglected are the many layers or facets beyond these generalised propositions which combine to create the particular ways individual students and teachers actually view, or 'understand', the children they teach in particular classroom settings: teachers' actual and tacit, as opposed to preferred or espoused or idealised, knowledge of children, and the biographies which produce this knowledge: their subjective realities, as opposed to the quasi-objective ideas or the educational situation with which they are presented in training.

Merely to offer to the student a set of propositions from psychological/sociological theory or research—this is the way children are, this is what they are like, this is the reality to which your decisions must be addressed—is to ignore, or at least to fail to acknowledge sufficiently, two basic arguments concerning children in classrooms in which much of this book's discussion has been grounded. First, regardless of generalised principles of child development, motivation and so on, children are 'as they are' in classrooms, in part at least, because of the actions of the teacher; they respond, as in interaction all humans respond, to personality, to climate, to tacit or explicit signals, attitudes and expectations from a variety of sources, but chiefly, in the educational context, from the teacher.

Second, though individual children are viewed differently by each of those with whom they interact, and their self-concept indeed in part evolves from a consciousness of these various perceptions, in the educational context the teacher's view of them is the most significant. It is the teacher who defines their abilities, their potential, their personality, their attainment and their attitudes, for the purposes of making curricular decisions, evaluations and predictions, and, as we have seen, in a way which is consistent with their ideology. Such is the nature of the educational process, and the classroom power relationship, especially where young children are concerned, that the central assumption in child-centredness, of the child's autonomy, is not only fallacious but dangerously so.

It can never be the case that on the one hand we have the child, about whom there is pre-existing objective knowledge, and on the other the teacher, who simply has to acquire that knowledge. The teacher's knowledge of the child is subjective, it is created by the teacher, its character is therefore as strongly conditional on the way the teacher is as the way the child is. The theme for initial training, which should complement 'understanding children' is 'understanding how teachers "understand" children'. And if it is indeed students understanding that we wish to promote rather than their capacity merely to parrot the prepositions and formulae of others, the source as well as the character of such 'understanding', on the basis of which students and teachers act, needs to be explored; this necessitate attention to the unique individual biographies of each students as well as to the more generalised analysis of the professional, historical and ideological situation of the particular groups of teachers offered. The outcome of this process should be to sensitise the student to the possibility of a much wider range of diagnoses and explanations. The fact that introspective methods are unacceptable to some psychologists is worthy of debate in this context but is not grounds for rejecting the perspective defined. The course aims to train teachers, not professional psychologists, and if a perspective is helpful it should be included, methodological qualms notwithstanding. Thus the scope of 'understanding children' in initial training needs to be broadened chiefly by taking in *teachers'* influence on both the children and their 'understanding' of them.

Equally important, and more easily enunciated, is the need to allow existing perspectives on children offered by psychology and sociology to be supplemented by alternatives from within those disciplines. Clearly, given our discussion of the complementary relationship between ideology, professional theory and practical situation, the introduction of less comfortable psychologies and sociologies might be resisted, but perhaps we can begin to accept that our comfort may well be secured at the expense of the quality of the child's education. This shift has already begun in the sociology of education: the sociology of knowledge and of classrooms has provided the needed counterbalance to the family/home educability preoccupations of the 1950s and 1060s. We now need a 'new' psychology of education which more fairly represents the richness of mainstream psychology.

The newer perspectives offer both alternative focuses and tools for analysis. Centre-stage are not only classroom processes and the interactions of teachers and children which feature in 'objective' study in the Flanders tradition, but also the meanings which the teachers and children themselves assign to those processes. The underlying assumption here is that human actions can be properly understood only if one uncovers these meanings, since 'action is forged by the actor out of what he perceives, interprets and judges... The "objective" approach holds the danger of the observer substituting his view of the field of action for the view held by the actor.

In studying classrooms it becomes important to understand pupils' as well as teachers' definitions of the situation, and the extent to which the latter are not autonomous but are influenced by the former; at the same time the power differential in classrooms makes the impact of teachers' meanings on children and classroom life considerable. This perspective prominently informs the classic and comprehensive exploration of school interaction by Hargreaves and specific studies of primary classrooms like that of Berlak et al. The study of infants' classrooms by King, to which I have made frequent reference, is eclectic: it is critical of phenomenological, interactionist and Marxist perspectives yet is also influenced by them. It belongs to the 'family' in so far as it is grounded in close and sustained observation which is interpreted by reference to actors' perceptions and explanations rather than observer preconceptions.

At the same place time it places these in broader frameworks of ideology and social structure. These developments are recent: empirical study of primary classrooms, of whatever methodological complexion, is still relatively thin. Nevertheless, in terms of what by this book"s analysis seems to be needed—far greater attention to how teachers 'understood' children and teaching —the growth points are now significant, diverse and rich.

The last point notwithstanding, we also need to ask whether the monopoly by psychology and sociology of insights into children and classrooms is to be desired or supported. The other two disciplines in the educational studies pantheon are philosophy and history. Philosophy of education—whether so defined or used thematically in an integrated course—tends to concern itself with broad non-contextualised questions about aims, the nature of knowledge, the justification for particular educational concepts and activities, the ethics of reward and punishment.

Frequently it is conceived as a tool of encouraging a sharper, more reflexive and considered mode of analysis than the easy, instant judgement, as a basis for critique of teachers' and students' 'commonsense' statements. This is undoubtedly necessary, but it is also the case that by such means, intentionally or unwittingly, is the status of academic thought preserved, for philosophical analysis ought equally to be applied to the statements, judgement and explanations offered by psychology and sociology of education: conceptual analysis should have no boundaries.

Especially, a concern with epistemology ought not to start and finish with the school curriculum, but should encompass the knowledge and truth claims of the teacher training curriculum as well, the ways of making sense of and understanding children, teaching and learning which the initial training course expects the student to internalise and subsequently 'apply' in the classroom. In other words, 'ways of knowing' about educational processes should be subjected to the same level of scrutiny as are the ways of knowing which constitute the school curriculum out there in the school. To fail to do this is to miss an opportunity to give the student a working understandingof epistemological issues; and it could be construed as hypothetical to subject to critique the school curriculum but not that of teacher education. A similar argument applies in the case of history of education.

We saw that how usefully a historical awareness of the institutional and ideational background of primary education both illuminates and provides a basis for critique of present-day ideas and practices, particularly in respect of the ways of the child is viewed and the curriculum defined in the context of the class-teacher system. We also saw how primary professional discourse with its 'cocoon' imaginary and polarising of the child and society, seems resistant to a sense of the interplay of historical events, cultural values and educational ideals.

Conventionally, history of education courses have done little to remedy this. Courses in 'the educational system of England and Wales' can still be as normative, functionalist, systemic and superficial as they were in the years following the NcNair Report: resumes of the clauses of education acts and the recommendations of major reports, but rarely interpretations or explanation beyond a sort of sub 'O' level 'seven causes of the Boer War' variety, and certainly little real delving into the pedagogy and curriculum experienced by previous generations of children and the justifications offered by teachers and others in support of these.

Of course academic monopolies are not fortuitous: the one under discussion reflects aspirations to make teaching a 'science' grounded in a set of empirically derived principles and so to demonstrate the 'expert knowledge' basis of the teacher's professional claim. However, we might try asking afresh, with no preconditions, the open question: 'What is the best way to develop the young adult's capacity to understand other human beings, especially pre-adolescent children?'in pursuit of an answer we might attempt to catalogue those ways which humans have learned to understand each other and themselves. On the one hand, and prominently, there is the pervasiveness and potential of insight grounded in individual and collective experience.

Meanwhile, we concentrate more on academic or public modes of personal and inter-personal exploration, we have to acknowledge that the field can encompass, at least, literature, art, music, drama and religion as well as the social sciences; and that even the latter can extend much further than teacher education has allowed. The modes of inquiry we actually make available to the student are from one small spectrum of human knowledge, and, as it happens, they are from one of the newest and—to workers in the physical sciences and the arts alike—one of the most suspect in terms of its claims to represent humans as they are. Putting into operation such extended concepts of 'understanding children and teachers' is not necessarily easy, but the issue needs to be faced. As presently conceived, teacher education courses place arbitrary and unnecessary restrictions on this aspect of the student's development.

The most basic reappraisal would concern the academic/professional distinction, and, as a consequence, the common ground between subject studies and education theory as regards each's capacity both to generate professional insight and to met 'personally educative' functions might be disconcerting. However, the most substantial and necessary shift in this context is towards the exploration and use in initial training of non-academic, everyday, subjective professional knowledge. The arguments seem inescapable: such knowledge is pervasive, inevitable and influential in everyday practice and therefore requires exploration; it is effective in that it is the basis for teaching of a high quality and therefore may encapsulate ideas worthy of emulation; it is also, conversely, the basis for weak teaching and therefore its limitations as well as its strengths need to be exposed. Where, as in this context, the everyday knowledge in question concerns children, it taps, or may tap, insights stemming from one of the most fundamental of human relationships: it cannot simply be disregarded on the grounds of arbitrary stimulative definitions of what constitutes 'science' and 'objectivity'. This is not an argument for rejecting academic inquiry, or for a revival of apprenticeship approaches to teacher education.

Rather, the case is made for recognising the strengths and limitations of any mode of understanding pursued in overmuch isolation—particular disciplines, academic study in general, personal, experientially grounded everyday knowledge—and for acknowledging the advantage of using these in combination and juxtaposition, particularly in pursuit of that understanding of ourselves and others which educationists seem happily prepared to lay claim to, despite the fact that the rest of humanity has found it rather more elusive. Such eclecticism as is argued here would be conditional upon courses sensitising students to the epostemological problems raised. It is not adequate to 'raid the disciplines', or rather to 'raid' all available and potentially productive sources of insight, without also understanding the nature of the truth claim each makes and the limitations thereof.

Traditionally courses have tended to treat academic sources as given the experiential sources as suspect or unacceptable: all are problematic, though in different ways. It will be apparent by now that, in combination, the ideas above require not minor adjustment to the content and pedagogy of initial training courses, but a more fundamental shift..

'School-based curriculum development' is a clumsy term, used to refer to activities which, because they take place in the unique contexts of individual schools, are necessarily diverse. This chapter attempts to place some structure on the idea of school-based curriculum development by linking material from four relevant areas. First, *theoretical concepts* are outlined; second, these concepts are qualified by reference to the *practice* of curriculum development in primary schools; third, *contextual factors* influencing the nature of such development are examined; and finally, the *values* underlying school-based curriculum development in primary schools are briefly elaborated.

One of the problems faced by anyone attempting to understand school-based curriculum develop-ment as an idea is that it is used very much as a catch-all concept. For example, as illustrated by Mitson, it means something as substantial as groups of secondary school pupils, together with appropriate staff training and resources development; or it may be small-scale revision of a language programme in a primary school, such that described by Timms and Lees.

The DES has stressed the significance of school-based approach, but two writers in particular have helped to sharpen the formulation of ideas about them. Eggleston's introduction to six case studies provides a useful starting-point. Although it is unclear whether Eggleston was describing school-based curriculum development or prescribing a particular way of doing it, four features of his definition are worth picking out:

1. It is *particularistic*: The curriculum-development activity is focused upon the diagnosed, or perceived, needs of the specific school or part of it.
2. It is *process-oriented*: In the terms of 'strategies for the curriculum' intended, the process by which these are developed in important in itself.
3. It is *participatory*: The appropriate style for developing the curriculum is cooperative, that is, staff working together to produce plans for change.
4. It is *preliminary*: The curriculum developed is to be seen an experimental, in the sense that it is open to evaluation and appraisal after its implementation.

One of the interesting things about this definition is the stress, not on the curriculum as such, but on the *roles* that teachers have to play in the process of its development, and the attitudes that are required to underpin it. This characteristic is also central to the analysis offered by another writer, Skilbeck. He identified three models of school-based curriculum development—the *rational-deductive*, the *rational-interactive* and the *intuitive*—and located them within differing politico-educational frameworks.

The first operates in centrally directed educational systems, where the task of the school is to 'interpret central directives' and the role of the teacher is as a mere functionary in a bureaucratised educational service. The second emerges in mixed systems, such as those in England and Wales, which stress the active role of teachers in adapting the curriculum at school level within rather broad general outlines of national policy. Teachers working within this kind of framework have a more complex role than in the rational-deductive model and have more demands made upon them; they 'have to act as course assessors, to help construct syllabuses, to select learning materials and to devise learning systems'.

The third model stresses the individual teacher's decision-making and creativity, and leads to great diversity between teachers between schools, and to inconsistency between 'normal policy and individual school programmes'. Although school-based curriculum development may share elements from all three, the rational-interactive model represents the style and values most appropriate to contemporary English schools, especially because of the stress put upon the range of roles expected of teachers, and the assumption that teachers have to negotiate the fine details of their roles by working in partnership with each other. Thus in this formulation also, school-based curriculum development is as much about changing roles and relationships among a school staff as it is about changing schemes of work or methods of teaching and learning. A major goal of school-based curriculum development in Skilbeck's terms is the continuous adaption by teachers of externally defined curricula into forms of educative experiences unique to the teacher and learner. We need a system for curriculum development that combines the advantages of national policy making, national centres for the production of materials and for research and development, with the flexibility, adaptability, and professionally satisfying features of local initiatives and creativity.

Thus school-based curriculum development is predicated upon the concept, admittedly idealised, of teachers who creatively reconstruct the curriculum within a recognised framework of local and national expectations; it is not predicted upon passive acceptance of external definitions of the curriculum, or the myth of the 'autonomous' school, existing independently of its political and economic context.

Given the political development, outlined, of a national framework for the curriculum, the relevance of Skilbeck's model for teachers in England and Wales has increased considerably. Skilbeck's analysis enables us to add two further characteristics of school-based curriculum development to the four identified earlier. These concern the relationship between the school's curriculum and national or local guidelines, and the view taken of the role of the teacher.

The distinctive arena for school-based curriculum development is the staffroom rather than the classroom, and the distinctive discourse is concerned not only with the surface details of curriculum practice, but also with the assumptions underlying it. The theoretical analyses discussed above are necessarily generalised, and need to be qualified somewhat in the light of the practice in the Warwick inquiry schools.

Brief outlines of the programmes have already been provided, which suggest two characteristics that are perhaps distinctive to primary school curriculum development. They can be considered under two headings, namely *gradualism* and *specialism*. To dichotomise rather too simply, gradualism qualifies the idea of 'development', while specialism qualifies the idea of 'curriculum'. By gradualism, three related features of the notion of 'development which stress the limited expectations that may be held for it. These three limitations may be thought of as the *problematic*, the *unpredictable* and the *incremental* qualities of curriculum development in primary schools.

The problematic nature of curriculum development derives from the fact that there is a conceptual difference between development and change. The latter is neutral and implies merely that practice has altered, not that it has been improved. 'Development', 'renewal' and probably 'innovation' imply not merely change, but change for the better. What counts as a change for the better in education is problematic.

An analogy with the practice of medicine may he helpful. If a doctor diagnoses, say, constipation in a patient and prescribes a change of diet as a remedy, there is not much professional or lay disagreement about what would constitute a change for the better in the patient's condition. Not being constipated is generally regarded as an improvement on being so. But the school curriculum is a more difficult area for diagnosis, with less sure a basis for agreement about what constitutes improvement.

A curriculum where there has been, so to speak, little movement for a number of years is not necessarily in a worse condition than one in which there has been a great deal of it. One of the points that follows from this is that, although the term 'curriculum development' is widely used throughout the literature and in this book, in practice it cannot be shown in advance, and often it is not known even in retrospect, whether changes are actually developments. At best it is commonly a matter of belief, intuition and professional judgement of those involve.

Indeed, to return to Eggleston's emphasis on the *process* of development, it was quite striking to note how frequently the teachers in the Warwick inquiry reported that the major benefit, for them, of school-based development activities had been the experience of being involved in the process rather than, or in addition to, any changes in actual curriculum practice. It was as though they were hedging their bets on the curricular outcome of the initiatives. Second, there is *lack of predictability* in outcome.

Given the experimental approach characterised by Eggleston as 'discussion, planning, trial and evaluation', there is the built-in risk that the evaluation might show no tangible development in the desired direction. This seems to have been the case in the Oxfordshire primary school reported in a case study for the Open University prepared by Clift. He reported a self-evaluation exercise by the school staff, lasting over a year, and involving at least seven in-school staff meetings, to prepare a review of the school's policy, provision and practices across a range of activities, including the curriculum. It appears to have been characterised by serious, professional involvement by the staff, and to have been efficiently and yet flexibly organised. It covered, among many other matters, problems or curricular aims and how they should be described, curricular practice, including the grouping of pupils and catering for individual differences, and the provision of curricular guidelines, and was carried out by effective teacher collaboration.

The kind of sweeping changes in curricular aims and practices currently being promoted for the 14-19 years-olds, for example, could not easily be developed in the school-based mode precisely because they are predicted upon external intervention fundamentally to redefine curricular aims at least in the innovation period. School-based curriculum development is a more modestly conceived activity, designed to build upon existing mainstream curricular practice, and predicated upon the assumption of a curricular framework about which there is already consensus, or which can be taken for granted. It is incremental, not radical, change in the curriculum, with slow, small-scale, granted. It is incremental, not radical, change in the curriculum, with slow, small-scale, almost routine, benefits, accruing over time from a school staff gradually building upon its collective strengths and, where possible, remedying weaknesses.

There should be little of the heady rhetoric associated with large-scale national projects of the 1960s and early 1970s, not just because such rhetoric tends to lack credibility in the routine of school life, but because school-based approaches are designed to improve the normal curriculum, not graft abnormal practices on to it. Discussions with teachers in the Warwick inquiry illustrated the incremental quality in an interesting way, showing the mundane and highly pragmatic nature of what was involved. In School 1, a staff group met to review their curricular policy in social studies, and attempted to revise an existing scheme by constructing it around some basic concepts and skills, drawn partly from some Schools Council curriculum materials and partly from their experience with the previous scheme. No grand claims were made, or were felt necessary to be made, about either the changes that might follow or the process itself. Many frameworks were tried in private and rejected; it was felt important to demonstrate that the content..could be organized-conceptually.

To test this we developed a matrix, setting four broad conceptual areas of Environmental Studies across four conceptual themes from 'Home and Family'. When we did this, we simply jotted down in the matrix what we thought would work, given that had worked before, and the overall conceptual scheme we were developing. And then we met and locked at what we'd written down and tried to sort it our from there.

What strikes one about these statements is their very ordinates, their tentativeness and the absence of extravagance is what is being claimed. They are the voices of routine improvement not radical, or even substantial, change, expressing the gradual, incremental quality of school-based curriculum development at primary-school level. They embody the view of HMI that: A slow but steady build up from the points of strength of individual teachers is probably the only way forward.

Specialism refers to the exploitation of expertise in a subject or, more accurately, in a curriculum area. This exploitation took a variety of forms in practice but three can be distinguished: specialist teaching, subject teaching and subject diffusion. Specialist teaching occurred in two cases, with teachers used to teach a number of classes and having no class responsibility themselves. The two cases provide ambivalent evidence, limited though it is, for the idea of specialist teaching as a basis for in-school development. Both teachers taught their subject to all the older children in the school, but non the less needed to influence the quality of work with the younger children, who were taught by class teachers. They exercised responsibility for raising the quality of work done throughout the school, though they also acknowledged a reduced impact upon the younger classes. They appear to have experienced little of the conflict and strain that other postholders felt, as reported. This was probably because teaching one subject and not having class responsibilities dramatically reduced the range of the other demands made upon specialists.

On the other hand, as suggests, the two teachers used as specialists tended to have involved their colleagues less in the process of curriculum development than did other postholders. Furthermore, the specialist teachers did not involve colleagues in evaluation of their programmes. This suggests, accepting that these are two cases only, that specialist teaching, whatever its merits in classroom practice of the specialist, may, in terms of initiatives of a school-wide kind, tend to produce leadership of a more isolated, less collective style than would otherwise be the case. Subject teaching occurred when teachers with specialist subject knowledge taught one or two other classes on a regular basis, while retaining a generalist class-teaching role with their own class. This occurred in two cases.

A related version of subject teaching was when a teacher irregularly, and for limited specific purposes, taught alongside colleagues, or swapped classes, in order to teach a specialist topic or skill or to demonstrate a skill and show the quality of work that could be expected. This happened in three other cases. Subject diffusion occurred in all the programmes, when teachers with expertise were consulted by others who needed advice, or when they took a lead in curriculum planning and review groups. It was the main mechanism for spreading specialist knowledge from the post-holder to the other staff. It was what the Inspectorate meant when they talked of postholders' having an 'influence' on the work throughout a primary school. With organisational arrangements reflecting the class-teacher principle, even where some subject teaching occurred, this diffusion model was the dominant style of in-school development.

The stress on the use of teacher specialism in the curriculum development programmes is largely explicable in terms of the political analysis. All the programmes were focused on issues raised in the Primary Survey, which stressed the need to provide for greater progression and continuity, to cater for able children, to fill the gap in science, to extend advanced reading skills, and so on. Although it may not be a permanent characteristic of primary school curriculum development, it probably provides quite strong evidence of the impact of the survey, an impact followed up in two later surveys by HMI in which 'specialisation' and its contribution to curriculum development in first and middle schools were further examined.

There is an ecology of curriculum development. Just as certain kinds of plant and animal life flourish in favourable conditions of soil, light, temperature and the balance of relationships in their overall environment, so the context of primary schools inhibits or encourages the growth of the kind of curriculum development discussed above. Factors in this context can be considered as *external* to the school or *internal* to it, although the distinction is not clear cut.

External factors are those derived from the educational system itself, from its administration, finance, demography and from teacher career opportunities. Internal factors include the role relationships of teachers and the ways in which authority is exercised by the headteacher.

More important, however, overall staff expertise may be affected, because the impact of falling rolls will lead to loss of flexibility in the ways that staff can be used, and sometimes to arbitrary loss of specialism. Even if staffing is reduced in line with pupil numbers, a school's ability to deploy teachers in ways that can effectively exploit their skills and expertise will become limited and, most crucially perhaps, the opportunities to free teachers for necessary curriculum development activities in school time will be lost. It is for this reason that some local authorities have developed what they refer to as 'curriculum-led' staffing policies.

Although there is a suspicion that such policies could be used primarily to decide that small schools are not viable, an interesting consequence of them is that the local authority has to make clear what its conception of an adequate primary school curriculum is, for curriculum-led staffing policies in effect move from a ratio as an index of staffing policy which emphasised.

The minimum number of classes that each type of primary school ought to be able to form if a satisfactory curriculum is to be available to pupils. It went further towards defining the curriculum by which is staffing policy should be led. If an adequate middle school curriculum is to be provided... then the staffing must provide some who are capable of specialising in science, craft, foreign language and music. Thus, in theory at least, staffing allocations, and curriculum-led staffing policies, can be seen as supporting school-based curriculum development. Precisely because, having broadly defined the curriculum provision thought to be appropriate, they highlight the need to identify, develop and exploit staff expertise in order to maintain and renew the local authority, conception of the primary school curriculum. This still obtains as a principle, even where teacher-redeployment strategies adopt criteria other than curricular specialism. At the present time it is unclear whether decisions about which teachers should be redeployed are based on curricular demands, degree of seniority or local political pragmatism; probably all three are involved to differing degrees. There is no logical reason why redeployment of staff should in itself reduce curriculum development possibilities, assuming that the nettle of curriculum-led staffing priorities can be grasped. Put at its most basic this would mean that a teacher with essential specialist curricular expertise would not be redeployed simply because he or she might be the youngest, or the most vulnerable, or the least likely to cause a fuss, or a part-timer.

Equally, it might mean that a teacher with expertise in a shortage area might work in two schools rather than, as is normal, only one. In the recent past the real value of capitation resources allocated to schools has fallen quite substantially, and in some local authorities the reductions were regarded by HMI as endangering educational standards. Although it is a truism to say that such reduction adversely affect the potential of a school staff to improve their curricular provision, the effects will vary greatly according to the nature of the particular curriculum development programme.

There is a great difference in impact of resource expenditure upon a programme requiring for its introduction in a school the purchase of new sets of materials and equipment and one requiring different applications of existing materials and approaches. It has been argued earlier that school-based approaches in primary schools tended to be developments of existing practices, and resource reductions may go some way towards explaining that feature. If so, it suggests that such reductions will influence the nature of school-based development, rather than stifle its growth entirely.

The objective experience of contraction may not necessarily be the most powerful constraint upon development; the ways in which such contraction is perceived subjectively by teachers may be a far more important determinant. Put crudely, curriculum development depends much more upon the ability of a staff to harness its collective energy and enthusiasm than upon marginal reductions in staffing, or even real reductions in resources. It is upon teacher morale that the progress of innovation hangs, and morale itself has been damaged by contraction.

In part, the impact of contraction has been cumulatively routine, with teachers coming in each morning to uncleaned rooms, dusty desks and other evidence of reduced expenditure, which has nothing directly to do with the curriculum, but which effectively eats away at teacher enthusiasm. But the dramatic impact is upon the teachers' perceptions of reduced career and promotion opportunities, which are real enough and may help to discourage innovation amongst career-minded teachers. This is, however, very much a two-edged sword.

Under an expanding system, teachers were sucked up into senior posts by a kind of capillary action and, having obtained their promotion, would demonstrate their merit afterwards. They would be given their special-responsibility allowances and then earn them. In a contracting system such promotion as there is will have to be earned in advance. As a local-authority adviser put it. Previously we promoted Mrs X in order that she would develop science in a school; now we may be able to reward her if he has developed it. And this has to apply to Scale 1 teachers as well—they will have to learn to lead other teachers in an area of the curriculum before they get a responsibility post.

Of course the degree of certainty of promotion differed in the two situations. However, the point about shrinking career opportunities is that they too will be perceived differently; some teachers will doubtless be confirmed in their view that there is no point to curriculum development if it is not certain to be rewarded, whilst for others it will at least be a surrogate for, and at best a precursor to, promotion. It would be unrealistic to ignore such a factor in examining the context of primary school curriculum development, and it may be for that reason that a number of recent commentaries have, included the notion that it should help to raise morale and channel the professional energies of teachers who would previously have been promoted more easily. There is, however, a small irony in the situation.

Whatever the general disadvantages of reduced promotion opportunities, from the point of vies of school-based development there is one advantage. For development of this kind to be originated, implemented and above all maintained requires, a relatively permanent, or at least stable, staff group. Frequent and widespread teacher mobility is not conducive to school-based approaches to curriculum development.

The impact of the external factors, even in a contracting system, upon a school's ability to develop its curriculum is not overwhelmingly and inevitably adverse. Perhaps the most optimistic element is that primary pupil rolls are expected to stabilise in the mid-1980s and arbitrary loss of specialist skills within a staff group will occur less often. A further issue in the next decade, currently being canvassed in some local authorities and nationally, is the idea that INSET could become part of the contractual obligation of teachers. If this were to be successfully negotiated it would give considerable impetus to school-based curriculum development, especially if, as is also being considered, it is allied to earmarked resources and a re-aligned career structure for teachers.

Much of the discussion in the literature about school-based curriculum development is implicitly about secondary schools, so that internal issues raised are problems of relationships between subject departments, of development 'across the curriculum' and of managing large institutions. For primary schools the internal factors pressing upon change are different.

Recognised authority, in respect of the primary school curriculum, is nearly always perceived as residing in the office of headteacher. There is a legal basis for this, but in an age when a broad liberal curriculum in mathematics, English, Science, art, music, craft, physical education and social and moral understanding is expected to be offered to all children, the notion of the headteacher as an authority in all these fields is no longer credible, if it ever was. There is therefore a mismatch between authority and responsibility for the curriculum in primary schools, with teachers who are responsible for developing aspects of the curriculum in which they are the 'expert' having little in the way of formal authority ascribed to them, and the headteachers, who have the authority, lacking the expertise.

Lack of formal status is compounded for postholders by lack of informal recognition from their colleagues, according to HMI, who found few primary schools in which the postholders had a school-wide influence in their subject. It is disappointing to find that the great majority of teachers with posts of special responsibility have little influence at present on the work of other teachers. There are some practical implications of this comment for the primary school post-holder's workload, but the major issue concerns the attitudes of primary school staff toward curricular authority.

Some shift towards a kind of collaborative decision-making about curriculum matters has been proposed by a number of commentators on primary schools, including Coulson and Razzell, although the latter appears, as Harling shows, to understate the obstacles to such an approach being adopted generally. The problem may not be so much the attitudes of headteachers as those of other teachers. When headteachers delegated responsibility and authority to their deputies, according to Coulson and Cox, the problem was that other teachers did not accept the transfer of authority as legitimate. This brief review of the internal factors has been deliberately uncritical of them in order to report in summery form the prevailing view of the internal culture of primary schools. This internal culture is seen as structuring both teacher relationships in primary schools and teacher perceptions of curricular authority in classrooms and schools so as to provide a major constraint on postholder-led curriculum initiatives development.

3

Change and the Primary School

Circumstances—norms of professional discourse, initial training, the organisation and culture of the school—combine both to discourage a constant and critical perspective on change and to deny access to the requisite knowledge and skills. This is certainly not to say that such capabilities do not exist, but rather that the many teachers who seek and gain such a perspective do so often in the face of considerable contrary norms and constraints.

Their resources are personal rather than situational, and their insistence upon swimming against the tide and valuing reading, theorising, ideas and argument can cause them acute problems in certain school settings where, perhaps. They risk the charge of 'airy-fairy' indulgence or of encroaching on the territory of the head as the school's resident and sole philosophiser. Handling change within schools depends on comparable abilities—the teacher needs to be able to analyse situations, diagnose needs, conceptualise and appraise alternative strategies and solutions, and evaluate their implementation.

The organisational and interpersonal skills of 'making things happen' are central, a *sine qua non,* but have no role without a framework of educational justification. We shall need to bear this last point in mind as we consider now various emergent mechanisms whereby schools are being encouraged to cope with change—mandatory management courses for heads and deputy heads, the enhancement of posts of responsibility, the rehabilitation of curriculum schemes and guidelines, and the proliferation of procedures for evaluation and self-evaluation, for example. In respect of each such strategy we shall need to consider not only its practical efficacy but its conceptual and ethical basis and the kinds of intellectual as well as organisational demands it places on the teachers concerned.

Primary heads have substantial power is not to say that all primary heads are autocratic, still less that the power is abused. It is a concomitant of the possession of power that its holders can choose to exercise it in different ways, to the point, indeed, of introducing widespread delegation and power-sharing. But it is also a function of power that the choice in this matter is the head's alone, and he has no formal obligation to account to a school's staff for the way he decides to conduct the decision making process. Thus the pivotal point in the matter of how a school copes with change is the *leadership* provided by the head. Studies of leadership tend to use two or three 'ideal types'. Lewin's early typology—'autocratic', 'democratic', and 'laissez-faire'—has proved durable and influential, though, as Nias points out, such terms are capable of many interpretations and are rendered particularly problematic by their evaluative connotations.

Thus 'automatic', in a society whose leaders constantly invoke their 'democratic' credentials, soon acquires dictatorial overtones. Similarly, 'democratic' can sustain many different interpretations, from 'popular power in the majority interest' to 'representative democracy conditional upon open elections'. In turn both such poles have variants; witness; witness the arguments about proportional representation. So a stimulative and neutral definition of such terms is needed if they are to be useful. We also used the terms, 'instrumental' and 'expressive'. These terms can also be applied to leadership, as indeed they were by Etzioni. Commenting on the various studies and the problems they arise, Nias suggests that quite apart from the value-connotations, such 'ideal-type' approaches have tended to be rather one-dimensional.

A point is made by Whitaker when he identifies 'concern for people' and 'concern for task' as the two central dimensions of leadership and by the use of a grid argues that the optimum position is for a head to score high on both dimensions rather than pursue tasks at the expense of people. This juxtaposition of positive leadership and involvement is a useful antidote to the kind of argument which equates school democracy with purposeless chat or even anarchy, a sort of leaderless confusion. This characterisation is popular among 'bourbon' heads anxious to resist participation, In fact it is a characterisation not of democratic but of laissez-faire regimes.

The few people who have written analytically about primary headship tend to conclude that since something approaching Nias's 'positive' leadership both works in practice and is preferred by teachers, it provides the best basis for development. HMI in the middle school survey link the head's positive leadership, high expectations and exemplary teaching with 'higher standards'. Coulson, Nias and the Schools Council all argue, for example, for 'collegiality': the head, are accountable for the various and specific responsibilities they exercise. The head would become a chief executive, but the right single handedly to determine or dominate policy and decision making would cease.

On the face of it this may seem a sane and civilised development, but in fact transition is fraught with difficulty, attitudinal as well as procedural, and for the staff as much as the head. For while collegiality requires that a head treats the staff as 'professionals' rather than 'employees', it also necessitates that staff too see themselves as —in Hoyle's terms—'extended' rather than 'restricted' professionals, concerned with the school as a whole rather than their own classroom only. And while the kind of paternal/maternal role complementarity we explored may discourage the development of true intellectual autonomy, it could be argued that at least, after a fashion, it works.

To argue that collegiality is desirable is thus to miss the point that some class teachers themselves - rather than, exclusively, the head—may prefer paternalism as long as it is reasonable and benevolent, since it absolves them of responsibilities over and above that of running their class. That this point does not emerge from Nias's study may reflect a typicality of her respondents. They were young PGCE trained graduates, whose educational background, it seems fair to assume, would tend to predispose them towards intellectualist views of teaching and school decision-making. It could also be argued that as a distinct, and privileged, minority, PGCE—trained teachers might feel this made them 'different to the point, perhaps, of tending to reject the dominant professional culture which they might perceived by other staff— whether they were or not—as stand-offish or 'superior'. Consciousness of this perception would compound the difficulty.

Three points of some importance emerge from the discussion so far. The first is that positive leadership, participation and individual autonomy are not—as they are often held to be—mutually exclusive: on the contrary, each seems to be an essential ingredient if a school is to continue to grow and to cope with changes. Second, the matter of leadership is not merely one of style, still less of mere procedures but revolves fundamentally round the question of attitudes to and perceptions of the respective roles of a head and a class teacher, and to/of the characteristics of a community of professionals. Third, that though the head's leadership is pivotal, the attitudes on such matters held by class teachers are as significant for the 'health' and effectiveness of the school as those of the head.

Internal Accountability

Discussion of accountability tends to focus on extra-institutional relationships, on the public accountability of whole institutions to the outside bodies who have a claim to know how they are performing. In the present political climate such concern is understandable, but it rather detracts from the equally pressing matter of a school's internal accountability relations and procedures. Collegiality, participation, 'positive', 'passive' and 'bourbon' leadership all generate a fundamental question concerning the extent to, and manner, in, which head and staff should or should not be accountable to each other.

We have established, however, that so one-dimensional a view of professional relationships is inadequate because teaching is complex and value-saturated, and happens to involve children and parents as well as employers. Acknowledging these complexities, therefore, we might consider not one mode of accountability but five.

Professional accountability within the school: five 'ideal types. *Managerial* reflects the assumption that individual teachers are exclusively accountable to those who administer and control the school and who allocate human and other resources to their work. What goes on in their classroom, therefore, is of legitimate concern to such 'managers' and to them alone.

Consultative reflects the view that, as professionals, teachers in a school hierarchy have a right to be involved in discussions about their work but that the form of such involvement and the control decisions still rests with the head. It is the version of 'democratic' decision-making operated in many educational institutions and is a familiar response at local and national government levels to pressure for public 'participation' in decision-making.

Autonomous reflects the assumption that what goes on in a particular school or classroom is the sole responsibility of the professional most immediately concerned. It rests on a view of individuals—whether teachers, or heads—as professionally competent over the full range of activities they undertake, and this competence includes the necessary knowledge and skills to make or seek insightful and valid appraisals of their work and to act on those appraisals. Their status as 'professional' is a guarantee of the integrity of their work. The teachers, or heads, then, are accountable chiefly to themselves.

Mutual reflects the view that education has to be conceived as a collective enterprise, so that all who participate directly in a particular educational activity have a legitimate interest in its quality and progress; that such quality and progress being the result of the particular contribution which each participating individual makes, participants should account to each other for their various contributions.

Being the most public and open form it is some distance from 'autonomous accountability' at the individual teacher level, though in fact it is essentially a model for professional autonomy at the whole profession level. It does not necessarily incorporate any particular structural view of school decision-making it allows for continued role and status-differentiation, such as is probably inevitable in schools. It is egalitarian only in the sense that it requires that all participants, regardless of role or status, see themselves as equally accountable to each other for their particular contributions to the educational process.

Proletarian is the exact reverse of managerial accountability in that the accounting relationship is downward from those given managerial responsibility to the 'workers'. At the same time it is neither an 'autonomous' model nor 'autonomous' model. This, since it implies grass-roots staff control is the least likely in the British educational context, but it is a theoretical possibility, and of course, like all the other models it has its counterpart, as a working out of the relationship of the individual to the state, in national political systems.

'Managerial' and 'consultative' accountability assume accounting upwards only; 'proletarian' assumes downwards only; 'autonomous' denies accountability, other than contractual, to others; and 'mutual' assumes omni-directional ready comparison with situational realities explored in this book. 'Autonomous' is that privatisation most prevalent in primary classrooms and university departments. While it may not necessarily include the kind of intellectual autonomy needed to justify the extent of executive freedom claimed, it is on intellectual autonomy that the claim rests.

Strict 'managerial' and its perhaps commonest variant 'consultative' accountability are the traditional models for primary headship. 'Proletarian' is there as a theoretical possibility, but rarely emerges in practice—some of the 1960s/1970s 'free schools' may be the nearest. This leaves 'mutual' accountability. The case for mutual accountability in primary schools is strong. Strict 'managerial' accountability can alienate staff in the way explored earlier and deskill them in terms of the kinds of cultural and educational awareness the class teacher needs. The privatisation of 'autonomous' accountability may offer the freedom which creative teaching needs, but in so extreme a form may feed the curriculum incoherence and inconsistency as between teachers and classes which emerges from recent surveys.

A 'while curriculum' as we have considered it can exist only in a climate of mutuality, with openness, the sharing and comparing of ideas, and the dovetailing of schemes and practices. And if primary schools are serious in their commitment to educational goals for the child like co-operation, the development of empathy, inter-personal skills and so on, they need to acknowledge the force of the hidden curriculum in such matters whereby the behaviour of adults in the school towards each other is as significant a learning resource as, say, group work in the classroom. The espousal of curricular goals for the child of holism and social inter-dependence is not compatible with either autocratic management for teacher privatisation.

Curriculum Schemes and Guidelines

'Schemes' were once universal in primary schools: the head presented the teachers with a set covering all or most aspects of the curriculum, and expected them to teach to its prescriptions. The weekly record-book or forecast enabled the head to monitor the teachers' adherence to the schemes. Such devices were viewed as inconsistent with the openness and flexibility required by 1960s progressivism, and indeed in many schools planning in any form became anathema. Record-books listing intentions were replaced by retrospective diaries of events, and schemes fell into disuse, though rarely completely so in the case of mathematics and reading.

The 1982 survey found most schools using 'guidelines' of some sort for language and mathematics, but the former tended to be restricted to reading, and perhaps writing, and to ignore spoken language, literature, poetry and drama.

In other areas of the curriculum the situation was variable, and more than half the schools visited had no guidelines at all in areas other than mathematics, language, physical and religious education. Where schools had guidelines these were rarely exemplary in HMI's terms, but tended to contain merely lists of items to be taught and to offer little on ways of organising learning experiences. HMI viewed the connection between guidelines which were ill thought-out or absent altogether and curriculum superficiality, unevenness and inconsistency as a causal one.

The situation may not be that clear cut, not least because the absence, presence, on quality of curriculum guidelines can be viewed equally as a symptom rather than a cause of a school's outlook on a number of issues: the desirability of forward planning: the extent needed of such planning: the balance between individual class-teacher freedom and collective adherence to common procedures. It is this important to avoid naive overestimation of the impact of guidelines.

They are only written words after all, a 'paper curriculum' rather than a curriculum in action, and the relative privacy enjoyed by primary teachers permits the possibility of a substantial gulf between words and deeds, even if the guidelines do not actively suffer the fate noted by teacher folklorists of 'gathering dust in the stock cupboard'. This would suggest that if guidelines are to have any value they should be constructed on the basis of attention to strategies for their use as well as to their content. HMI seem to imply that quality of content is sufficient guarantee of success. The question of strategy be considered before the guidelines are written, not, as commonly happens, afterwards, since the characters of guidelines must obviously be consistent with their intended manner of use.

The central question is 'How can a written document influence class teacher practice?'. The usual answer is 'By being as comprehensive and a prescriptive as possible' and armed with this precept post-holder produce immaculate documents which may or may no have the impact they seek. We are bound to consider the possibilities: (a) that a scheme may be partly or even wholly unworkable for a particular teacher; (b) that, specialist expertise notwithstanding, a document may not be perfect; (c) that the more comprehensive it is, the more it may be seen to cast doubts upon the class teacher's competence. Even if these are possibilities rather than actualities, they could suggest that the imposition of a 'definitive' scheme upon a group of teachers is an unwise strategy.

In any even, apart from the practical, interpersonal and political objections, such an approach runs counter to the view of teacher autonomy postulated in this book which requires close intellectual engagement by the teacher in the activities relevant to his task, and to the notion of a dynamic and responsive curriculum. A curriculum can never be 'definitive': nor therefore can a curriculum document. It would seem that it may be more sensible to consider an alternative strategy whereby no scheme produced by one individual has more than 'working paper' or 'draft' status, and the nearest a school comes to a definitive statement is a document which is the product of substantial collective discussion and is subjected to regular review and modification in the light of both the experience of implementing it and of changing circumstances. It is worth noting that HMI views on this matter in the latest of the succession of phase surveys, that on 9-13 middle schools, shifted towards a greater concern with strategy. They too now argued for 'working documents' rather than polished 'schemes'. This is not to argue that the content of a curriculum scheme should be vague or meagre.

On the contrary, provided its status is understood, the more detail it offers the higher the level of debate it can provoke. In this respect HMI are right to castigate those schemes which provide subject-matter checklists and give no attention to pedagogy. Equally, however, we must be alive to the conceptual and ideological dimensions of curriculum documents: they embody views of the children and the education process. All such views are inherently challengeable.

We should recognise that this essentially means-ends view of learning is not the only one available and, at the very least, it must cause us to ask, along with the critics of behavioural objectives, whether it is either desirable or possible to specify learning objectives and strategies in advance in this way for all pupils and for all areas of the curriculum.

If there is to be prescription as to what a curriculum document should include it should be self-conscious and open-ended: a rationale for a curriculum area, which may or may not include specific aims and objectives; a statement of the possible content or subject-matter to be encountered rather that, necessarily, a list of concepts to be 'covered'; indicators as to alternative teaching and learning strategies—which focus teachers' attention on the decisions to be taken in matters like children groupings, the uses of individual, group and class work, the use of resources, but do not pre-empty those decisions; and suggestions as to criteria, means and purposes of evaluating children's learning which do not necessarily presuppose testing and allow for the appraisal of learning processes as well as outcomes.

A curriculum working paper, then, might best be conceived as incorporating what Stenhouse terms 'principles of procedure' whereby decisions may be taken and justified with respect to intentions, the selection of content, the development of a teaching strategy, the sequencing of learning, the diagnosis of individual children's needs, strengths and weaknesses. Such an approach is some way from the definitive and authoritarian uses of guidelines implied in the two HMI primary surveys.

Staff meetings, whether in connection with curriculum documents or for other purposes are another current growth points. The relative intimacy of primary schools has sometimes served to justify heads' avoidance of formal staff meetings: HMI criticised the heavy reliance on 'informal gatherings at break or launch times'. But formal meetings may have been resisted by heads for other reasons, to do less with school size than the assumption that curriculum and policy matters where not open to debate and that residual matters—like arrangements for Christmas parties, sports days and playground supervision—could be dealt with either informally or by the issuing of directives and notes. HMI, however, clearly regarded formal meetings as an essential ingredient of curriculum planning, consistent with their view that teachers should play a greater part in the formulation of school policy. As with schemes and guidelines the issues here are both practical and conceptual.

Staff meetings can engender a sense of collective commitment; they can help teachers towards an understanding of and involvement in whole school concerns; open up the individual teacher to alternative arguments and ideas; stimulate intellectual engagement; minimise curriculum in coherence and inconsistency: in short, staff meetings are potentially one way of realising both the concept of a 'whole curriculum' as discussed in these pages and the notion of the autonomous teacher.

Equally, staff meetings can consist of headteacher monologues, aimless and trivial anecdote-swapping or opinion-parading, frustrating to staff and head alike. This kind of scenario prompts some to emphasise efficiency and instrumentality in respect of staff meetings: the need for a clearly defined and realistic agenda, circulated in advance; the need for input to meetings, to avoid off-the-top-of-the-head discussion, in the form of previously circulated discussion or working papers; the need for meetings to be firmly chaired so as to ensure progress through the agenda, to enable all staff to contribute and achieve a tangible outcome; the need for decisions to be ratified and minuted.

Such procedural aspects are undoubtedly important. At the same time, the act of formalising professional discourse politicises the process to an extent which those steeped in the relatively informal primary tradition may not apprehend. Procedures facilitate manipulation of the direction of discussion and decisions. They promote the stronger divergence of the two levels of discourse and meaning to some extent present in most human interaction—the spoken and the unspoken, the text and the subtext. They provide fertile ground for rhetoric and populism, for what Bailey in his anthropological study of committees, calls 'The tactical uses of passion'.

The formal meeting adopts par excellence the trappings of rationality, but it feeds and legitimises irrationality, cynicism, insincerity and manipulation. It requires polite consensus. Yet it may deal with issues on which consensus is unachievable: in which case votes have to be taken and dissent to the tune of 49.9 per cent can remain as an unresolved embarrassment, a reminder not so much that the decision was 'right', or had 'majority support', as that the issue was of such complexity or controversy that to force a vote was the least appropriate way to deal with it: a vote 'for' or 'against' implies the existence of only two points of view.

Such consequences of bureaucratising human interaction are especially marked in large institutions where an added complexity is that the few individuals gathered together may represent or claim to represent many others, so that the committee or broad manifests the maneuvering or sectional interests, the problem of the real or claimed mandate from absent constituents, and the heightening of the power and game-playing dimensions of the whole process. Committees in this charecterisation are an overwhelmingly male preserve. That being so, many women teachers may be instinctively less comfortable in such circumstances than men, who may actually revel in the ritualised aggression and sometimes bogus instrumentality. They may feel themselves disadvantaged by the style of the procedure to an extent which they would not in a less circumscribed situation, and therefore unable to make the kind of contribution of which they are capable.

We have characterised curriculum issues as having several dimensions: cultural, epistemological, psychological, pedagogical, planning and evaluation, and value. It will perhaps be acknowledged by now that the last is the most fundamental and pervasive in that value-issue underpin all the others. This is a diagnosis shared by Reid who sees curriculum problems as predominantly *practical*, yet in a *moral* rather than a *technical* sense, so that few of them yield ready certainties. He criticises mainstream curriculum theory for its pursuit of rationalism at the expense of proper exploration of the moral dimension, and bureaucratic decision-making for forcing curriculum debate into a mould where 'procedure, majority votes and authoritative pronouncements have... usurped the place of appreciation, deliberation and judgment'. Each of these latter three words is used carefully: *appreciation* of a problem demands analysis of its many facets and possibly a variety of 'expert' perspectives to elucidate these; *judgement* invokes both a practical capacity and a sense of and discrimination among differing values; *deliberation* is used in preference to 'debate' because the latter presumes the existence of final and correct answers.

One might add that 'debate' also suggests a contest between a maximum of two viewpoints, one usually the antithesis of the other. Deliberation, in contrast, is a multi-faceted collective process of seeking to understand complexity; its practical essence is informality and the absence of threat so that members will be prepared both to risk and context assertions. Deliberation is the collective pursuit of that 'theorising' which should come to replace 'recipe theory' in both initial teacher training and everyday teacher discourse. Reid's notion of 'deliberation' is consistent with the approach to curriculum this book has taken, to an extent that bureaucratised discourse is not.

On the other hand 'deliberation' is vastly more disciplined and informed than that which highly formalised staff meetings seek to replace, namely random, anecdotal chat. There has to be a middle ground between inhibiting structure and debilitating flaccidity. Equally pertinent is Reid's suggestion that the optimum group number for deliberation is ten or twelve people in that it enables different sources of expertise to be represented without the tendency to excessive formality associated with larger groups. A medium-sized primary school has that number of staff, and it could be argued in any case that the size and cultural tradition of primary schools makes them less vulnerable to the bureaucratic excesses of, for example, higher education institutions. Difficulties arise, however, in relation to the view that deliberation requires a range of expertise. For as long as primary teachers define themselves as experts only on primary children this diversity may be unavailable. But the gradual legitimation of specialists, in the wake of the 1978 HMI survey, may make for conditions in which the specialist contribution to policy is accepted and indeed forestered, provided that the threat potential to head and class teacher can be neutralised.

Perhaps, therefore, in the allocation of responsibility posts schools should attend to four further than two types of responsibility. First, the curriculum areas, second, a particular age-range of children, third, one of the central dimensions of curriculum analysis and planning, and fourth, various school odd jobs. Thus through selective study and experience an individual teacher might claim general proficiency as a class teacher together with specialist expertise in, for example, environmental studies, the education of 7-9-year-olds, and curriculum evaluation; or in mathematics, the education of 9-11-year-olds, and pedagogy/classroom organisation. The 'odd jobs' can surely be fairly distributed on the basis of choice or rotation: 'notice broads' hardly requires a course o advanced study. This line of speculation is one which schools might profitably pursue: in any case it could be argued that, regardless of the meetings/deliberation issue, the concept of 'specialist' adduced by HMI should not be accepted at face value since it is very narrowly premised.

Evaluation

On the one hand we have increasingly elaborate documentary procedures for providing information about pupils, teachers and curriculum to heads, LEAs, parents and other schools: and, on the other, procedures for generating individual or collective review of teaching, curriculum and policy as a basis for change and development.

One responds to external demand, the other to what are seen as fundamental professional imperatives; one provides information for consumption outside the school, the other is an internal matter. Despite these essentially different purposes and requirements the two activities are frequently treated as necessitating identical or similar procedures. The commonest such procedure is the checklist, which in recent years has become such an ubiquitous feature of the educational scene that many find it hard to accept that it is neither necessarily the only nor the best way of meeting accountability requirements, let alone of promoting professional development.

Checklists are now constructed by LEAs and schools as a basis for three sorts of evaluation: pupils, of teachers and of schools. Their essence is a set of questions or items requiring answers or scores; sometimes, as in the case of pupil records, in the form of ticks or literal/ numerical grades-scores; elsewhere, as with some of the school self-evaluation checklists, they are more agenda for discussion. Thus, while most LEAs have recorded cards. Rochdale LEA has a book for each pupil which has to be completed for each school year in respect of detailed lists of concepts, skills and qualities. Inner London LEA, one of the pioneers of school self-evaluation, has its now widely used document 'Keeping the school under review' which offers an extended list of questions about children, parental involvement, curriculum, organisation, staffing and staff roles 'to assist a school to examine its organisation, its resources, its standards of achievement and its relationships'. Another pioneering LEA, Salford, shifted from an overt accountability approach, with a detailed primary school self-evaluation booklet requesting the transmission to 'the office' of regular detailed information on facets of schools life from the state of the buildings to curriculum areas, resources, community relations and management, to a version which combined accounting to the LEA with school self-assessment 'as a contribution to staff development ... and ... curricular and organizational developments'.

Detailed analysis of the contents and procedural implications of such documents is now available elsewhere; the most extensive are by Elliott, and by Clift, Weiner and Wilson. Much of the discussion is concerned with technical aspects—format, categories of questions, intended mode of use, problems of clarity, ambiguity, time required for completing checklists and record cards/books, and so on. Because checklists and elaborated record-keeping systems are now a fact of school life it is inevitable that such factors should weight heavily, for above all these procedures are time-consuming.

Becher, Eraut and Knight, dealing specifically with these practices as used in primary schools, are among the commentators who draw attention to some rather more fundamental problems of this approach. One is the checklist or record card's implicit view of whatever is being reviewed—children's language, teacher's use of resources, schools' relationships with parents, for example. By asking, or giving priority to, some questions rather than others, the head or LEA responsible implies a preferred model. Thus, as we saw, LEAs like Avon expect teachers to rate children's writing in terms of the Bullock Report's categories of 'transactional', 'expressive' and 'poetic' and to appraise children's use of language (oral) in terms of Joan Tough's categories of 'elf-maintaining', 'directing', 'reporting', 'reasoning', 'predicting', 'projecting' and so on. Apart from the fact that these are indeed only models of language, it appears to be tacitly assumed that teachers completing the cards have the requisite understanding of what such categories mean. In this regard the danger in such approaches is their apparent but often spurious objectivity. Putting a tick or a number against a word like 'predicting' may seem to some teachers to be more objective than writing an opinion in an empty box.

In fact, both activities are heavily value-laden, the letter in an obvious way, the former more profoundly so because the vagaries of personal opinion are compounded by another person's values and by problems of interpretation, meaning and judgement. In contrast some such devices are so obviously tendentious as to be ludicrous and therefore, paradoxically, less dangerous in use. An example is the checklist sent to me in place of the more usual invitation to write a reference on a teacher. This required ratings on a five-point scale on such items as: 'skill in putting into practice good principles of teaching, judged largely by results; energetic, even-tempered; pleasing, attractive, appropriately dressed, wholesome influence; success in making social contacts; aggressiveness and initiates; intellectual alertness—native mental endowment as distinguished from acquired abilities; freedom from social indiscretions...'.

The second problem is the lack of attention in some such documents to strategy. As Becher, Eraut and Knight remark. To the outside world, checklists to offer an interesting compromise between external guidance and authority and internal choice and responsibility. But within the school itself their strong management-orientation can seem to belie their declared purpose of guiding self-evaluation. This dilemma is not necessarily resolved by stressing the development function while elaborating the preferred strategy., The strength of the Schools Council/Bristol University 'GRIDS' approach is that it provides detailed guidance on school self-review strategy as a cyclic process and specifies the various steps and tasks to be undertaken. This contrasts with the more familiar LEA approach of merely sending the school a list of questions to be answered.

The GRIDS booklet also emphasises the importance of grounding strategy in key principles or commitments in areas like consultation and staff involvement. In this respect it is comparable to this author's development of an evaluation 'constitution' for a Manchester college', though the latter was considerably more detailed and covered issues like confidentiality, dissemination and the vital matter of who controls the various decisions which an evaluation requires.

Where GRIDS fails to escape the dilemma is its tacit vesting of such control with the head, so that although there is consultation about topics for review and the implications of view for development these are firmly circumscribed by the head's decision over who should be involved and in precisely what capacity. Formalised self-evaluation them, is not simply a matter of asking and answering questions, completing forms and cards: it requires elucidation of more fundamental matters concerning schools' and teachers' value-systems in respect of children, curriculum and teaching on the one hand, and school decision-making, and professional relationships and responsibilities on the other.

The external accountability functions of evaluation procedures can be reduced in favour of 'development', but the internal accountability dimension remains pervasive. Formalised evaluation is pre-eminently a management tool and underpinning every style of management is a view of the accountability relations and obligations of the institution whose members and affairs are begin managed. Thus we could, and should, extend our list of the dimensions of formalised evaluation, by analysing the kinds of decisions which all such evaluation necessarily entails.

The development of procedures for formal evaluation, we have seen, may all to frequently neglect the central issues discussed above, but even more fundamentally, it may tend to imply two questionable assumptions: first, that such procedures constitute the most valid forms of evaluation; second, that their arrival heralds the end of an earlier era of non-evaluation.

Throughout the discussion we have used the adjective 'formal' or 'formalised' in order to emphasise both the official and artificial character of such evaluation procedures, and to allow for a contrast with other sorts of evaluation which can reasonably be termed 'informal'. We can define evaluation in the curriculum theorist's terms as 'information for decision-makers' or as 'measurement of the extent to which objectives are achieved' (both of them problematic and prescriptive rather than neutral and descriptive); or we can seek a more open definition like 'making judgements of worth or effectiveness'. Note, as against this, how limited are the first two definitions in terms of our eight evaluation decisions listed above: one views evaluation mainly in terms of decisions and the other terms of decision.

Both neglect the vital areas of values, criteria, control and accountability. If we adopt the third definition, it allows for three extensions to our conceptual framework. One is to project to centre-stage the actual *judgemental process* at the heart of evaluation; the second is to free it from presuppositions about particular methodologies, contexts or uses; the third is to prompt a sense of evaluation as a continuum of many diverse types and modes of judgement, all of which can make a claim to be taken seriously, not because they are 'formal' rather than 'private' or 'informal' but because they happen, they occur in real life. This judgemental continuum, in schools and classrooms, overwhelmingly comprises evaluations which are nearer its 'informal' than its 'formal' pole.

Teachers and heads use of tests, checklists, profiles and so on constitutes a minute proportion of the evaluation on which their most important everyday decisions are made. The *focus* is children's personalities, their potential, their behaviour, their educational progress. The *aims* are diagnosis, making necessarily rapid decisions as a basis for further action. The *criteria* are personal, experimental, value-loaded, sometimes idiosyncratic, sometimes collectives evolved.

The *methods* are watching, talking, listening, giving out and receiving non-verbal cues and signals, reflecting, hypothesising, discussing... Evaluation in this sense is of fundamental importance in schools and classrooms because it is basic to human behaviour and interaction. It is a process of immense subtlety and, for the child or teacher being evaluated, of profound consequence. And it works no less effectively than tests and checklists in providing a reliable basis for diagnosis and action. Indeed, HMI argue in the 9-13 survey that such formal procedures tend to neglect this latter, diagnostic, dimension and concentrate overmuch on generalised and summative judgements of attainment.

Nor is it the case as we have seen that 'formal' procedures necessarily have a stronger claim to 'objectivity' than informal: formal procedures are more accessible to public scrutiny than informal and thus can more readily be checked for bias, but this does not of itself guarantee their objectivity. The realistic approach in this matter would seem to be not to replace everyday informal evaluation but to refine it. It may or may not be always valid or reliable, but its ubiquity and dominance demand our attention.

School self-evaluation, then, would seem to require first that teachers and heads develop a proper self-consciousness about their everyday appraisals and judgements, then that they device ways of refining them further, supplementing them where appropriate by more formalised procedures. The questions for schools are less 'How *shall* we evaluate?' than 'How *do* we evaluate?' and 'How valid and effective is our evaluation?'

The focus of such appraisal then becomes the schools central evaluations: the everybody, minute-to-minute ways in which teachers assess children's progress, define their needs, judge their potential, and decide what curriculum experiences to provide; the ways heads determine curriculum policies and priorities, and assess staff competence and progress. The dimensions of this appraisal can be those same decisions of which 'formal' evaluation is constituted—aims, focus, content, criteria, methods and so on. The processes under scrutiny, in effect, are those we have examined in this book, though the word 'evaluation' was not necessarily used: the teacher's judgements about the nature and purposes of primary education, about childhood and individual children, about teaching strategies, about appropriate curriculum experiences; teachers' and heads' judgements about the whole curriculum, school staff' individual or collective judgement about school policy and decision-making.

A large part of this chapter is essentially an examination of evaluations and evaluation capacities in primary education. All this implies an important shift in consciousness. The evaluation movement has seemed to imply that hitherto teachers did not evaluate, or at least did so inadequately. The parallel with initial teacher education is not coincidental: there the assumption, we saw, was that teachers operate without theory, without a valid view of children, curriculum teaching and learning. In teacher education a recipe theory has been imposed on students and teachers without regard to existing everyday theories and theorising process.

In evaluation a predetermined set of focuses, criteria and methods is imposed without regard for existing evaluative processes. Both tendencies are a consequence of factors we have touched on at various points in the book: the failure of the primary teaching profession to develop an adequately rational and generalisable language of discourse about its tasks and activities which could hold its own against that of academics, researchers and policy-makers; the acquiescence of the profession in the elevation of the one sort of language and the one sort of activity over their own; their acceptance of an over-simplified and scientistic view of knowledge which unduly favoured the claims to 'fact' and 'proof' of social scientists and evaluation technists; the power differential in such matters between the class teacher on the one hand, and the academic researcher, LEA adviser to administrator on the other; the presumptuousness of some in the latter groups concerning the relative merits of their own and teachers' procedures; the exacerbation of these tendencies (a) by a dominant primary school culture which isolates and parochialises the class teacher and (b) by teachers' lack of influence, relative to other groups in the educational world, on the vehicles for generating and disseminating ideas—books, journals, conferences and professional networks.

4
Problems and Solutions in Higher Education

The need for greater flexibility in patterns of teaching and learning was, therefore, highlighted, as was the adoption of a more market-oriented system. Greater emphasis was also to be placed on quality assurance to ensure the enhancement of the quality of both teaching and learning. Thus, the ground rules were set out for a model of mass HE. There has since been fairly widespread discussion and debate about how to cop with expansion on the scale proposed and within the context of an overriding concern to maintain quality.

Some efficiency gains, and hence some savings, might be achieved by squeezing more teaching into the working day and by extending the academic year, many vice-chancellors and senior managers realized that traditional patterns of education provision would not enable HE institutions to meet the expansion of student numbers envisaged in the White Paper, while at the same time maintaining academic standards and the quality of the provision. In 1993, there was a reprieve when a halt was called on the rate of expansion; but since then there have been further, significant reductions in the unit of resources. To cope with such unwelcome changes and establish sound, long-term strategies, a fairly fundamental review of existing systems is needed, including a consideration of the possible contribution of more flexible patterns of teaching and learning. During the 1980s, a degree of awareness about flexible approaches to education was beginning to percolate through HE. This may in part be attributed to the work of the Open University (OU), which employed a number of part-time tutorial and counselling staff from within the ranks of HE lecturers.

More recently, a number of institutions became involved in the hundred or more Open Tech projects that were funded by the then Manpower Services Commission. The impact of such developments was, however, fairly limited. For many HE lecturers, it was against the uncertain background of expansion and resource constraints that they first encountered any serious discussion of open learning. It was, therefore, hardly surprising that the initial reaction of many individuals to the idea of exploring alternative approaches to teaching and learning was sometimes less than enthusiastic: many were fearful for their jobs and hence were suspicious of motives.

As educationalists first and foremost, teachers in HE are understandably and rightly suspicious of any approach which appears to spring from mere expediency rather than from a sound and principled educational foundation. Hence the importance of starting any debate about the possible contribution of OL by exploring some of the educational reasons for adopting alternative approaches to teaching and learning and by considering the possible advantages and disadvantages of particular approaches. Since my work in the OL field has mainly been in this area, whenever the points that are raised apply equally to other subject areas.

Traditionally, the organization of HE has been largely course-based, and as a consequence most educational activities have centred on the course. The past decade, however, has seen the introduction of a number of educational initiatives designed to enhance the accessibility and flexibility of HE, bringing with them a number of significant benefits for both students and employers. The main innovations include the following:

Modularization

Students are no longer expected to commit themselves to entire courses that may last several years. Rather, they can enrol on individual modules and can shape their programme by selecting subsequent modules with the benefit of the experience gained.

Credit accumuation and transfer scheme (CATS)

With modularization,it became necessary to develop a system that enabled academic credits to be 'banked' and recognized by other institutions, allowing students to transfer more easily between institutions than had traditionally been the case. Between 1986 and 1991, the Council for National Academic Awards spearheaded the development of CATS, thereby helping to change the culture of HE by enhancing flexible provision and structures. This scheme has now been adopted by many universities.

Accreditation of prior learning/prior experiential learning (APL/APEL)

This increased student mobility between education institutions through CATS required, in its turn, the establishment of a formal system to assess and accredit prior leaning. Only thus could it be ensured that students received both full, formal academic recognition for previous learning, and appropriate guidance about what modules needed to be successfully completed in order to gain a particular award.

For many students, traditional and methods of teaching raise enormous difficulties. Taken together, the above developments lead to an increase in accessibility an flexibility. They open up HE opportunities to a wider section of society including part-time and mature students, and remove many of the barriers of inflexible structures previously encountered by many students.

As a corollary, increasing numbers of institutions are realizing the need to explore new approaches to teaching and learning, and are beginning to explore how OL materials might be incorporated into new and existing modules to enhance the flexibility afforded by modularization, CATS and APL/APEL. If, OL is merely regarded as offering a pragmatic solution for some of the practical difficulties currently facing HE, then it is unlikely ever to be regarded as a mainstream educational activity. If it is to succeed, OL must be fully integrated into course provision and its contribution needs to be evaluated.

Open learning

The OL approach brings together sound educational principles and an organizational framework which is practical and suited to the needs of our times. Its success depends on the provision of effective learning materials which have been specifically designed to enable students to take responsibility for their learning. It is characterized by the flexibility, adaptability and responsiveness of organizational structures and - not least—by the reduced reliance on teacher availability at specific times and places. In all these respects, OL provides a significant alternative to conventionally taught courses within traditional HE structures. Within a programme that uses OL materials, there can, of course, be substantial differences in the amount of openness and control offered to students.

In addition, students may be involved in decisions such as the kind and amount of support needed and who might provide it and whether the learning will be assessed and, if it is, how it will be assessed and when. At the other extreme, lecturers may wish to exert far more control over the learning process, determining what is studied, broadly when it is studied, and how and when learning will be assessed.

However, even when such parameters are defined at the outset, the use of learning materials which encourage active learner involvement and which can be studied away from an educational establishment may still allow students greater flexibility and control over learning than is usually possible in conventionally taught courses offered within traditional educational structures.

Finally, the middle course between teacher control and student autonomy is readily achieved by the inherent flexibility of an approach in which OL is given a significant role. At present, despite the success of local schemes, the use of OL still appears to be somewhat marginal. It is largely confined to areas where access to conventional education provision is problematic, or where a student population tends to be scattered over a fairly wide geographical area. In order to examine the case for open/distance learning, it may be helpful to explore some of the potential advantages and disadvantages.

From a teacher's perspective, there would appear to be a number of potential advantages in using OL. First, the continuing move for providers of HE to widen access faces teachers with the challenge of meeting the learning needs of increasingly large, heterogeneous groups of students who may also be at different starting points in terms of background knowledge, needs and academic ability. The use of learning materials can help cope with larger student numbers while still maintaining the quality of educational provision. Taking an example from the area of health and nursing, one can look to the uptake of the OU's programme.

A Systematic Approach to Nurising Care to see how a set of learning materials written on a core topic has been used on a large scale to meet a particular education need. In just the first four years of its presentation, the OU claimed to have sold over 20,000 copies, and it has been estimated that the actual usage increases this figure by at least a factor of three. Since teacher contact time tends to be a relatively small proportion of total study hours, the use of OL materials to cover much of the core 'information giving' can free lecturers from that role, enabling them to focus more on facilitating the learning process and providing guidance and support to individual students and small groups of students.

In this way, available contact time may be used to ensure that individual learning needs are met, and to focus on learning activities that cannot be achieved by materials-based learning. Indeed, by combining the advantages of materials-based learning and face-to-face contact in mixed-mode modules/programmes, it is possible to capitalize on the advantages of each.

Published learning materials have usually been written by experts in their field, and during the developmental process are reviewed by further subject experts and groups of students who work through the materials, providing detailed feedback regarding their relevance an usefulness from a user's perspective. With such systems in place to ensure quality, a programme that incorporates effective learning materials may offer better experience than an equivalent taught course, particularly when teacher contact hours are limited. For some lecturers, however, the possibility of using learning materials either produced in house or by major producers such as the OU and the National Extension College raises the crucial issue of the 'not invented here syndrome'.

If one is prepared to accept these arguments, the use of such learning materials can save education institutions considerable development and course planning time, although any learning materials that are used do, of course, need to be fully and carefully integrated into the overall educational philosophy and structure of the programme in which they are used.

Meanwhile, the shift of emphasis for the lecturer from primarily a teaching/lecturing role to one of facilitating learning can be enormously rewarding, reminding one perhaps of halcyon days when considerable periods of time were spent with students on an individual basis or in small groups.

In addition to the use of OL materials to meet the needs of large numbers of students. OL can also enable lecturers to offer options to small groups that might otherwise not be regarded as economically viable when face-to-face teaching costs are calculated. There is also evidence, which may surprise some educationalists, suggesting that OL materials can provide an effective means of changing attitudes. For those HE lecturers involved in delivering programmes of professional education, this is an important consideration. The benefits of OL do not, therefore, appear to be restricted solely to the cognitive domain.

The application of theoretical and conceptual issues to work experiences is also of central importance for teaching groups such as social workers, nurses and midwives, teachers and managers. Lawrence et al. found that through the use of carefully designed activities, OL materials can provide an effective means of helping students to relate theory to practive, thereby bridging the theory-practice gap that dominates much of the literature on professional education. Perhaps not surprisingly, there are also some potential disadvantages. The cost of the learning materials can be high, whether they are developed in-house or bought in from an external producer. This may require pump-priming funds, or some form of loan, since in HE fees follow student enrolments, and this can make it more difficult to fund any new development that is front-loaded in terms of costs.

If money is borrowed to purchase learning materials or to develop them in-house, and has to be repaid from income derived from running the programme, a sound business-planning approach is vital. There may also be additional costs incurred in adapting or augmenting the materials so that they can be used within a particular programme to ensure that learning outcomes are full addressed. An even greater disadvantage in some areas is that suitable learning materials simply do not exist, forcing lecturers to consider whether they should become involved in developing them in-house. With just this reason in mind, the Open Learning Foundation was established in 1990, encouraging its 23 founder members to collaborate in the development of core learning materials that would meet their needs.

The change in role to 'facilitator of learning' may initially seem rather threatening to some lecturers in HE. This feeling is clearly reflected in one of the findings of the survey of OL undertaken by Lawrence *et al*: 'Teachers frequently expressed the need for training in the use of learning materials and for the development of the facilitator role. There is a sense of anxiety about the loss of control of the learning experience in many of the statements made.....by teachers, which may reflect their uncertainty about their own future roles.'

Initially, the use of OL may involve a period of considerable uncertainty for some lecturers while they adjust to the shift in emphasis from the role of teacher to that of facilitator of learning and to a perceived loss of control over the learning process. To address this issue, some producers offer their learning materials on a computer disk to enable teachers to select particular sections, adapt the text and add local examples, case material, etc., prior to reproducing the material for use with their own students, the rationale being to increase the sense of ownership.

Some teaching staff will, therefore, need additional preparation to develop the skills, attitudes and confidence required to facilitate learning and to encourage students to become more self-directed. They may initially require considerable help and support from more experienced OL tutors. Initial staff development and institutional development needs can incur high start-up costs which need to be regarded as a long-term investment. Although, in the long run, effective, supported use of OL materials within an educational programme can enable students to become more self-directed, this can take time to develop.

Teaching staff must realize that, initially, some students may need considerable time and support during their early exposure to OL until they have developed sufficient confidence to work with reduced teacher input, direction and control, and patterns of independent learning have been established. In addition, lecturers may need to adopt more flexible working hours to meet student' needs, particularly those of students studying part time. To sum up, for lecturers and students alike, the underlying aim and basic principle can be seen to be increased autonomy and self-direction. In some respects the student perspective has much in common with that of the tutor who is introducing the principle of self-directed learning - both may have new habits, skills and attitudes to learn! Depending on the openness of the system. OL can allow students to shape their own learning programme by defining their own learning outcomes and working through learning materials at their own pace. The use of individually negotiated learning contracts can help ensure that learning meets the specific needs of individual students, although this is essentially a two-way process. It aims to help students avoid repetitious learniing and build on existing knowledge and skills.

A further benefit is that students can study in ways that are best suited to their individual circumstances, and make optimum use of available time to meet their own particular learning needs. As a practical consequences, opportunities may be increased for those who, due to unsocial working hours and personal commitments, might otherwise be unable to attend a more traditional programme. In addition, there is also the important educational gain in the understanding of, and commitment to, the learning process.

We have seen that OL offers flexibility and the scope for individuals to study different topics at different depths and different speeds according to specific interests and needs. The use of learning materials can allow learners to exert greater control over the pace, place and time of learning. These benefits are nicely summarized for us by the Open Tech slogan of the mid-1980s: 'OL enables people to learn at the time, place and pace which suits them best.' Given the stages through which quality learning materials must pass during development, they can offer students exposure to the ideas and teaching of nationally recognized experts who might not otherwise be available to lecture in their local institutions.

The use of good learning materials can help to ensure quality education provision that is not dependent on who is teaching, how the teacher is feeling and other factors that can affect the quality of face-to-face provision, such as unsuitable teaching accommodation and the like. If the quality and suitability of learning materials are carefully evaluated prior to their use, an OL programme can be of a very high quality. Not only may the use of such learning materials raise the morale of hard-pressed lecturers who are committed to the delivery of quality learning opportunities for their students, but they can also help to engage the understanding of students and thus motivate the learner.

Among the advantages perceived by students is also the choice of working either alone or in small groups, depending on preference and on individual learning styles. The use of learning materials need not, therefore, necessarily imply isolation. Moreover, learning materials are always available to the student for reference in a way that a teacher cannot be. As a further benefit, it can be easier to make up for lost study time if a student is absent due to illness or some other reason.

Students can also become more self-directed and begin to acquire the habit of lifelong learning that is all-important when working in environments that may constantly be changing. It can help to empower students to take charge of their own learning through greater control and ownership of the learning will process. Students who are able to organize and structure their own learning will have developed the key skills of self-motivation, self-discipline and self-management that are now required in so many work contexts.

Turning now to the major potential disadvantages, some students may experience isolation if they are not able to attend regular, scheduled face-to-face sessions during which ideas can be exchanged and the enthusiasms of others shared. Mann argues that student support by teacher's is the key to motivating students to ensure that they successfully complete a programme of learning. Negotiated access to tutorial support at specified times/places is crucial, as is the installation of direct telephone lines with answerphones.

A student whose interest and motivation may be failing is unlikely to persist in trying to get in touch with his or her totor if the swichboard is always slow to answer a call, or if an individual is constantly unavilable. Due to the problems associated with isolation, students will often welcome a mixed mode of delivery, whereby OL materials are integrated within a module that includes some scheduled face-to-face sessions that allow students to benefit from the advantages of both modes of delivery.

The creation to self-help groups can also provide a valuable source of peer support that can help to reduce the sense of isolation. Students need to feel a high level of commitment and internal motivation to succeed, since much more is left up to the learner. It has to be acknowledged, therefore, that OL may not suit all individuals at the outset: some students may need considerable support initially before they begin to feel comfortable and confident with a more self-directed mode of learning. This point is reflected in one of the findings reported by Lawrence *et al.* who state that 'not everyone responds to this learning approach, it may be that some degree of preparation is needed to cope successfully with this learning method'. OL producers believe that although not all students respond well at the outset, the vast majority can be helped to understand OL and value a more student centred approach. Increasingly, industrial and commercial organizations are looking to OL to help meet the education and training needs of the workforce Those HE teachers who are offering education and training programmes for either the public or private sectors should be aware of the reasons why an increasing number of employers are finding that the use of OL materials can help meet their needs.

A major issue in the minds of any potential user is that of affordability. Cost effectiveness is often assumed to be one of the main benefits of open/distance learning and, indeed, it may turn out to be highly cost effective. At present, however, there is insufficient evidence either to support or to challenge this assumption. It can be difficult to measure in any meaningful way the full costs of providing an OL programme and compare these with the full costs of an equivalent conventionally taught course. When costing any education programme, it is necessary to calculate both the fixed costs and the variable costs, which will vary depending on the number of students.

Fixed costs for OL include items such as the cost of accommodation, publicity material, scheme managers and administrators, institutional overheads, and developing or purchasing the learning materials. Variable costs include tutorial time, copies of material, computers, etc. Some preliminary costings from Highland College of Nursing an Midwifery suggest that 'OL is a cost effective method of delivering continuing education to nursing when compared with conventional methods'.

Finally, if OL is to become more widely used within HE, and if it is to offer a good educational experience for every open learner, we need to consider a number of key issues in relation to staff and institutional development. David Baume 'Staff Development for Open and Flexible

Learning', also considers possible approaches to staff development for those using OL and the need for institutional development.

Staff development

Any systematic evaluation of learning materials will need to assess the extent to which they meet an agreed set of criteria, including the learning outcomes for a particular education programme. Robinson and Clark suggest that a minimum of 10 per cent of the total study hours may be required to evaluate a set of materials.

If the evaluation suggests that the materials are not entirely appropriate either to student needs or to the desired learning outcomes, then additional time and resources will be required to adapt or supplement the materials. In addition, some teachers may need considerable support while adjusting to a shift in their role from teacher to facilitator of learning, as well as help in encouraging students to become more self-directed. Some may also want to acquire further skills in guidance and counselling in order to provide better student support, and to help students to formulate their own objectives and plan how these might best be met.

Some teachers will also need specific preparation on the use of the learning materials, telephone tutorials and the management and administration of an OL system. Thus, a programme of staff development will usually be required to develop a critical mass within the overall population of teaching staff with the necessary attitudes and commitment to implement OL successfully. And, even if there are already significant numbers of teaching staff who are experienced in using OL. They will need time to become thoroughly familiar with the learning materials that form the basis of a specific module or programme.

Recognizing this, the OU pays a staff development fee to all tutorial staff who are new to a particular programme to cover the cost of this all important familiarization period. Once successful OL schemes have been established both within and beyond mainstream undergraduate provision, they can be set up as demonstration projects within an institution, or even within the HE sector as a whole, to help raise the level of awareness among colleagues. The use of demonstration projects, coupled with work-shops and more widespread dissemination of ideas through publications such as the Times Higher Education Supplement and journals such as Open Learning, can go a considerable way to further the debate about the potential value of introducing more flexible patterns of teaching and learning.

Regulation issues

Internal debates may be needed within an institution about the proportion of the total number of study hours that can be dedicated to OL and still contribute towards an award previously based on fixed number of hours of classroom teaching. The concept of minimum course attendance requirements would obviously need to be reassessed. This in turn raises the question of whether it is necessary to specify minimum time periods for the achievement of particular learning outcomes.

Some students may be capable of achieving specific learning outcomes in a considerably shorter time than other students and should perhaps be allowed to complete summative assessments whenever they are ready, rather than at fixed points in a module or programme. The emphasis needs, therefore, to be shifted away from specifying numbers of study hours, module/ programme duration and/or minimum attendance, and towards the development of more flexible means and timescales for students to demonstrate the achievement of specific learning outcomes at predefined academic levels. In some institutions, there may be concerns about how to weight students who do not attend programmes in a traditional manner. Indeed, OL students may be weighted differenly in statistical returns, making it less beneficial for staff members wishing to incorporate OL materials into their programmes for sound educational reasons. If, under a modular scheme, one student full-time equivalent is regarded as equivalent to a student enrolled on six modules, then one student enrolled on one module equals one-sixth of an FTE. If the same criterion were to apply to OL students, then six OL module registrations would equal one FTE. Thus, OL students can be recognized in the same way as, and given the equivalent weighting to, any other student in the institution.

Student support is recognized to be crucial to the success of any programme incorporating OL materials. Students need to be provided with clear information about the availability of tutorial support when undertaking any programme of self-directed learning: the use of OL should not be viewed simply as a means of reducing the amount of teacher contact or teaching hours. As already suggested, students should also be encouraged to set up self-help groups or study pairs to help reduce the sense of isolation that some may feel. In the first instance, students may also require special preparation to help them to appreciate and take full advantage of the flexibility afforded by OL and to seek tutorial or peer support when needed.

By comparison, conventional teaching requires relatively little administrative support and, as a consequence, there is a tendency to underestimate the amount of administration time needed to establish and manage an effective OL system, and the cost of providing that support. Administrative support is needed to deal with enquiries, and to ensure the avialability of learning materials which need to be ordered, checked, logged in, stored and issued. If a loan scheme is in operation for the learning materials, returned items also need to be checked, and non-returned items need to be chased to ensure their availability for future students.

The establishment and maintenance of accurate and up-to-date records is also essential, particularly if assessment does not occur at fixed points in the programme or at fixed points in the year, and if a large number of students have enrolled. A crucial aspect of any OL system is, therefore, an efficient administrative system. In my experience, many course/programme leaders have, at the outset, seriously under-estimated the amount of administration time needed to run a programme involving OL, and this element needs to be adequately costed. As OL operations develop within a school, department or faculty, it may become necessary to appoint an administrator with special responsibility for OL. Moreover, this person may be required to work flexible hours to ensure that adequate administrative support is available to both students and staff during periods when OL students come into the institution.

Existing institutional validation procedures may not readily accommodate the special needs of a programme with a substantial OL component, and may need to be adapted. Members of a validation panel for an OL programme must be familiar with the specific issues that would need to be addressed in both the supporting documentation and during the validation event, to ensure that sufficient attention is paid to all aspects to the OL system that could affect the overall quality of the student learning experience. This should include the provision of flexible student support and also adequate administrative support for both students and teachers. Whenever published learning materials are to be used, evidence would be required that a systematic evaluation of the materials has been undertaken to establish their suitability for the proposed use. In a mixed-mode module/programme, validators must ensure that the various components are well integrated, and that a consistent educational philosophy is maintained throughout and is clearly understood by all members of the course planning team.

Where learning materials are being developed in-house, it should be noted that it would be entirely inappropriate for validators to require to see all the learning materials prior to validating the course. They should, however, reassure themselves that sound procedures have been implemented, by requesting a clear description of the stages of materials development and the steps that have been taken to assure quality, together with a sample of the learning materials that have been developed.

5
Adult Education

There are many individuals who are chronologically adult but who show a marked disinclination to behave in anything approaching a self-directed manner in many areas of their lives. Self-directedness is rather being advanced as a prescriptively defining characteristic of adulthood. Hence, for an act of learning to be characteristically adult, it will have to exhibit some aspect of self-directedness. But before examining further the nature and form of self-directedness, let us consider the range of theoretical perspectives that have been elaborated with regard to adult learning. To specify generic principles of learning is an activity full of intellectual pitfalls.

Even if we leave aside the variables of physiology, personality, and cultural background, we still have to consider the implication of those developmental theories that hold that adults function in very different ways when responding to the societal and personal imperatives required of them in young adulthood, midlife, and old age. This suggests that the generic concept of adulthood is so broad and oversimplified as to be of limited use as a research construct. Nonetheless, in the last twenty-five years a number of respected theorists have made an attempt to identify generalizable principles of adult learning in their quest to build a theory of adult learning that would aid practice. The earliest of these attempts was that of Gibb, who presented the following principles of adult learning as the basis for a "functional" theory:

Learning must be problem centered, learning must be experience centered, experience must be meaningful to the learner, the learner must be free to look at experience, goals must be set and pursued by the learner, and the learner must have feedback about progress toward goals. As with other specifications of principles of adult learning, however, what Gibb actually offers is a mix of pedagogic procedures and learning theory. Following on from Gibb, Miller identified six crucial conditions for learning premised on the belief that at the higher levels of human development in adulthood cognitive models of learning, rather than behaviorist ones, were necessary.

Miller argued that students must be adequately motivated to change behavior, they must be aware of the inadequacy of present behaviors, they must have a clear picture of the behavior required, they must have the opportunity to practice required behaviours, they must obtain reinforcement of correct behaviour, and they must have a sequence of appropriate materials. Despite Miller's emphasis on cognition, however, the conditions he specifies actually appear to fit the behaviorist paradigm. In this review of theories of learning and their applicability to adulthood, Kidd identified the concepts that he felt informed the efforts of researchers into adult learning. These concepts were derived from the changing conditions of the adult's life-span, role changes required by changing societal imperatives, the egalitarian nature of adult student-teacher relationship, the greater differentiation of the organs and functions of adults, the self-directing nature of the adult, the physical, cultural, and emotional meaning of time, and attitudes surrounding aging and the prospect of death.

The learning context of the physical, social, and personal characteristics sorrounding the learning act, as well as the content and pace of learning, also affect the learning achievement. Knox also concludes that adults tend to underestimate their abilities and by over emphasizing school experience and interests, often perform below their capacity. Longitudinal studies show a retention of, and sometimes increases in learning abilities during adulthood, though cross-sectional studies tend to contradict this finding.

Fluid intelligence decreases and crystallized intelligence increases in adulthood, and adults are able to learn as well in their forties and fifties as in their twenties and thirties, when and if they can control the pace of learning. Knox found the level of formal education to be associated much more with learning ability than with age, and recency of participation in formal education to be correlated with more effective learning. This finding, incidentally,was supported by earlier studies of Knox and Sjorgen and Knox, Grotelueschen, and Sjorgen. Other findings from Knox's survey were that effective learning entailed an active search for meaning in which new tasks were somehow related to earlier activities.

Knox found that short-term memory held stable until late adulthood and that long-term memory apparently improved with age. In terms of the mechanics of learning, practice was deemed to be initially important for the reinforcement of learning. Prior learning experiences had the potential to enhance or interfere with new learning. Older adults were able to learn most effectively when they set their own pace, when they took periodic breaks, and when learning episodes were distributed according to a rationale dictated by content. Knox found learning transfer to decrease with age, though his findings on problem-solving abilities were ambiguous, with a decline according to cross-sectional studies and a holding steady with longitudinal studies. The same difference was evident in studies undertaken of critical thinking.

Task complexity and creativity were found to reflect individual differences and to be related only marginally to age. Knox concluded his summary in an optimistic vein, declaring that individual differences in learning were mostly unrelated to age and that "almost any adult can learn anything they want to, given time, persistence, and assistance." One of the most ambitious attempts to identify the cardinal principles of adult learning and to put these to practical use is that of Brundage and Mackeracher. These writers identify thirty-six learning principles and draw from each principle facilitating and planning implications. For example, Brundage and Mackeracher believe that adults are able to learn throughout their lifetimes. Their past experience can be a help or hindrance to learning. It is through such experience, however, that individuals construct the meanings and value frameworks that in turn determine how they code new stimuli and information.

Brundage and Mackeracher declare that past experience needs to be respected by teachers and that it can be directly applied to current situation for good educative effect. Those adults with positive self-concepts are thought to be more responsive to learning. Environments that reinforce the self-concepts of adults, that are supportive of change, and that value the status of learner will produce the greatest amount of learning. These writers judge adults to be strongly motivated to learn in areas relevant to their current developmental tasks, social roles, life crises, and transition periods. The development of skills requires adults to have a clear perception of desired behaviors. Reinterpreting past experience is time consuming and requires a redefinition of values and meanings. In Brundage and the Mackeracher's view, voluntary participation in education and training is likely to create a nonthreatening climate of instruction that will result in a greater amount of learning.

Learning will be further enhanced by regular feedback on progress, and positive feedback will act as a reinforcer for the pursuit of more learning. They think that a certain degree of arousal is necessary for learning to occur, whereas stress acts as a major block to learning. Brundage and Mackeracher also think adults learn best when they can control the pace of their learning and when they enjoy good health. However, because each individual will have an idiosyncratic learning style, it is dangerous to prescribe one mode of learning for all adults.

Typical points of personally significant transition occur at the ages of twenty, forty, and sixty, and adults are said to be most responsive to learning programs that are related to these transition. Collaborative modes of teaching and learning will enhance the self-concepts of those involved and result in more meaningful and effective learning. A blend of learning for autonomous mastery of life with participation in groups is said to provide the greatest satisfaction for the learner.

As a result of a career-long exploration of the development of adults' learning-to-learn capacities, Smith has identified six general observation concerning the nature of learning: It is lifelong, it is personal, it involves change, it is partially a function of human development, it pertains to experience, and it is partially intuitive.

Adult learners, however, also exhibit four essential characteristics. First, they have multiple roles and responsibilities, and this results in a different orientation to learning from that of children and adolescents. For example, they wish to make good educational use of the finite time they invest in education, they often take responsibility for identifying what they wish to learn, and they have a partially or fully formed self-concept Second, adults have accumulated many life experiences, and these result in distinct preferences for modes of learning and learning environments, such modes and environments comprising the essentials of individual learning styles.

Third, adults pass through a number of developmental phases in the physical, psychological, and social spheres, and the transitions from one phase to another provide for the reinterpretation and rearrangement of past experience. Finally, Smith argues, adult experience anxiety and ambivalence in their orientation to learning. In particular, attempts to become more autonomous and self-directed are likely to involve threatening elements.

Anxiety and stress may also be the result of job pressure, relational problems with significant others or of the adult's recalling the anxiety produced by earlier schooling experiences. These four characteristics of adult learners-their special orientation to learning, their experiential base, their particular developmental changes and tasks, and their anxiety regarding learning generate, according to Smith, certain conditions for learning. Adults learn best when they feel the need to learn and when they have a sense of responsibility for what, why, and how they learn.

Adults use experience as a resource in learning so the learning content and process must bear a perceived and meaningful relationship to past experience What is to be learned should be related to the individual's developmental changes and life tasks. The learning method used wil foster, to different degrees, the adult's exercise of autonomy.

Adults will, however, generally learn best in an atmosphere that is nonhreatening and supportive of experimentation and in which different learning styles are recognized. Darkenwald and Merriam present a list of eight principles of learning derived from learning process research that they believe can serve as guidelines for effective facilitation. They surmise that adults' readiness to learn depends on the amount of their previous learning, that intrinsic motivation -produces more pervasive and permanent learning, that positive reinforcement is effective, that the material to be learned should be presented in some organized fashion, that learning is enhanced by repetition, that meaningful tasks and material are more fully and easily learned, that active participation in learning improves retention, and that environmental factors affect learning.

Adults learn throughour their lives, with the negotiations of the transitional stages in the life-span being the immediate causes and motives for much of this learning. They exhibit diverse learning styles-strategies for coding information, cognitive procedures, mental sets and learn in different ways, at different times, for different purposes. As a rules, however, they like their learning activities to be problem centered and to be meaningful to their life situation, and they want the learning outcomes to have some immediacy of application. The past experiences of adults affect their current learning, sometimes serving as an enhancement, sometimes as a hindrance.

Effective learning is also linked to the adult's subscription to a self-concept of himself or herself as a learner. Finally, adults exhibit a tendency toward self-directedness in their learning. Such conclusions constitute a catechism familiar to educators and trainers of adults, as well as to learning theorists. They support Simpson's contention referred to at the outset of this chapter that adult learning theorists most commonly emphasize the experiential dimension of adult learning and stress the self-directedness of adults.

Self-directedness is seen both as an empirically observable trait and as a propensity that should be encouraged. We should note, however, that the samples for the studies on which these generalizations concerning the nature of adult learning are based are culturally specific. To this extent, the research on adult learning is no different from that on its childhood equivalent, where, as a massive comparative study of primary school quality recently acknowledged, "With less than 5 per cent of the world's school population, the United States accounts for the majority of the world's empirical research on education".

In research into adult learning, moreover, the adults who form the sampling frames are for the most part ethnically homogeneous; that is, they are Causasian Americans. They are also drawn chiefly from middle-class or upwardly mobile working-class families, since this is the foremost clientele of continuing education programs. To base a comprehensive theory of adult learning on observations of white, middle-class Americans in continuing or extension education classes in the post-Second World War era is conceptually and empirically naive. It is, admittedly, cumbersome to preface every comment regarding adult learning theory with a caveat concerning the cultural and class specificity of one's sample and, hence, the limited generalizability of one's conclusions. Nonetheless, we fall far too frequently into the mistake of declaring that research reveals that adults, in a generic sense, learn in a certain way.

The eagerness to construct an empirically verifiable theory of adult learning is inextricably bound up with the quest for professional identity on the part of adult educators. As much as we would like to believe that the conduct and dissemination of research are motivated by an intellectually altruistic search for truth, it must be recognized that the definition of research "problems" and the selection of appropriate topics for investigation often reflect wider societal or professional imperatives. In this case, the reality is that the discovery of a set of learning behaviors that are unmistakably adult would be a cause for substantial professional celebration. If we could discover certain empirically verifiable differences in learning styles between children and adults then we could lay claim to a substantive area for research that would be unchallengeably the property of educators and trainers of adults. Such a claim would provide us with a professional identity. It would ease the sense of insecurity and defensiveness that frequently assails educators and trainers of adults in all settings when faced with the accusation that they are practicing a nondiscipline.

The discovery of an empirically discrete domain of adult learning would grant to us an intellectual and professional raison d'etrae. Such a revelation is unlikely to transpire for some considerable time, and it may be that the most empirically attestable claim that can be made on behalf of adult learning style concerns their range and diversity. Certainly we should be wary of claiming too high a level of generalizability for theories and concepts of adult learning derived from studies of white Americans in the lower-middle, amiddle and upper classes.

The body of research literature discussed in the preceding section is one characterized by a mixture of speculation and empirically observed features of adult learning. The studies cited use a variety of methodological approaches and survey different samples, with the result that baseline comparisons are extremely hard to make. In recent years a number of researchers and practitioners have sought to synthesize the findings of this body of research into some framework of central adult learning principles. These central principles have then been converted into various research instruments that their designers believe can be applied to examining the extent to which principles of adult learning are being exemplified in any given practice setting. Two of these instruments the Principles of Adult Learning Scale (PALS) and the Andragogy in Practice Inventory (API)-were designed to test the presence of effective facilitation in practice rather than to provide empirical measures of forms of adult learning. In other words, both these instruments can be used to determine whether or not teachers or programmers are behaving as effective facilitators.

The PALS was devised by Conti to measure the extent to which practitioners supported the collaborative mode of teaching-learning that is usually cited by writers in the field as an exemplification of good practice. Conti surveyed a number of highly regarded theorists, including Freire, Lindeman, Houle, Knox, Kidd, Knowles, and Bergevin, to discover what they held to be the basic assumptions of adult learning. Not surprisingly, his findings are similar to those identified by the theorists revieed in the present chapter and to the central principles of effective facilitation.

Hence, Conti found these writers to argue that "the curriculum should be learner centered, that learning episodes should capitalize on the learner's experience, that adults are self-directed, that the learner should participate in needs diagnosis, goals formation, and outcomes evaluation, that adults are problem centered, and that the teacher should serve as a facilitator rather than as a repository of facts". For his doctoral dissertation, Conti determined "to develop and validate an instrument capable of measuring the degree to which adult education practitioners accept and adhere to the adult learning principles that are congruent with the collaborative teaching-learning mode".

Drawing on Flanders's Interaction Analysis Categories that were established to assess student initiating actions, Conti constructed a five-point Likert scale to record practitioner responses on a number of items that were based on collaborative principles but "reworded in behavioral terms compatible with realistic experiences of practitioners". For each of the items said to describe actions congruent with the collaborative mode, a separate item was included to describe mode. The PALS instrument was tested for construct, content, and criterion-related validity by two juries of adult education professors and fifty-seven practitioners in six separate programs.

Testing for reliability was undertaken in phase two of the field testing by twice administering the scale to twenty-three adult basic education practitioners in chicago and comparing the congruence of the scores. The outcome of the study was a forty-four-item rating scale that Conti believes can be used to assess the effectiveness of collaborative modes in producing significant learning gains or to identify themes and topics around which in-service training activities could be designed for staff development.

Since its initial framing, Conti reports that the PALS has been used in numerous training workshops and that it has formed the basis for three research studies. Dinges used the instrument to study 265 Illinois ABE teachers in a staff development needs assessment, Pearson administered PALS to 99 midwestern training directors to investigate the relationship between managerial style and the adoption of collaborative modes of facilitation, and

Douglass used it to examine the relationship of professional training in educating adults to the degree of support granted to the collaborative mode by 204 hospital educators and cooperative extension educators in the state of Washington.

In addition, scores have been collected from 153 Texas practitioners in adult basic and allied health education. Not surprisingly, perhaps, the research of Pearson and kouglass indicates that the chief variable positively correlated with the adoption of a collaborative approach in management training, hospital education, and cooperative extension is the amount of previous formal education undertaken by these practitioners. It seems, from these studies at least, that those who are trained as educators of adults do indeed incorporate collaborative principles into their subsequent professional activities.

After Conti's presentation of the PALS research at a recent conference of university adult educators in Britain, we can expect some cross-cultural validation of this instrument through comparative analyses of educators' use of the collaborative mode in Britain and North America. Turning to the API, which was devised by Suanmali on the basis of Mezirow's interpretation of andragogy and his specification of a charter for andragogy, we find that it is a ten item inventory of educator practices. To help adults enhance their capability to function as self- directed learners, the education must:

1. progressively decrease the learner's dependency on the educators;
2. help the learner to understand how to use learning resources-especially the experiences of others, including the educator, and how to engage others in reciprocal learning relations;

3. assist the learner to define his/her learning needs—both in terms of immediate awareness and of understanding the cultural and psychological assumptions influencing his/her perceptions of needs;
4. assist learners to assume increasing responsibility for defining their learning objectives, planning their own learning programs and evaluating their progress;
5. organize what is to be learned in relationship to his/her current personal problems, concerns and levels of understanding;
6. foster learner decision-making-select learner-relevant learning experiences which require choosing, expand the learner's range of options, facilitate taking the perspectives of others who have alternative ways of understanding;
7. encourage the use of criteria for judging which are increasingly inclusive and differentiating in awareness, self-reflexive and integrative of experience;
8. facilitate problem-posing and problem-solving, including problems associated with the implementation of individual and collective action; rocognition of relationship between personal problems and public issues;
9. reinforce the self concept of the learner as a learner and doer by providing for progressive mastery; supportive climate with feedback to encourage provisional efforts to change and to take risks; avoidance of competitive judgment of performance; appropriate use of mutual support groups;
10. emphasize experiential, participative and projective instructional methods; appropriate use of modelling and learning contracts;

This instrument was examined by 147 members of the American Commission of Professors of Adult Education. The professors interviewed displayed a remarkable degree of agreement concerning the extent to which the practices identified above were indicative of good andragogical practice.

Manley's review of the literature and her survey of eighteen members of the American Commission of Professors of Adult Education yield a familiar cluster of categories. The professors surveyed agree that adult learning is best facilitated when learners are engaged as participants in the design of learning, when they are encouraged to be self-directed, when the educator functions as a facilitator rather than didactic instructor, when individual learner needs and learning styles are taken into account, when a climate conducive to learning is established, when learners' past experiences are utilized in the classroom, and when learning activities are deemed to have some direct relevance or utility to the learners' circumstances.

In a more ambitious study, similar to Conti's researches, James devised the following set of basic principles of adult learning after a team of researchers had undertaken a search of articles, research reports, dissertations, and textbooks on adult learning.

1. Adults maintain the ability to learn.
2. Adults are a highly diversified group of individuals with widely differing preferences, needs, backgrounds, and skills.
3. Adults experience a gradual decline in physical/sensory capabilities.
4. Experience of the learner is a major resource in learning situations.
5. Self-concept moves from dependency to independ-

ency as individuals grow in responsibilities, experience and cconfidence.

6. Adults tend to be life-centered in their orientation to learning.
7. Adults are motivated to learn by a variety of factors.
8. Active learner participation in the learning process contributes to learning.
9. A comfortable supportive environment is a key to successful learning.

All nine principles were validated by a jury of national adult education leaders, and from these principles a questionnaire was constructed comprisig forty-five statements. The questionnaire was then administered to educators in five settings: hospital patient education, university extension programs, community colleges, business and industry, and agricultural extension.

Some interesting differentials emerged in the study. Hospital patient educators, university extension instructors, community college instructors, and agricultural extension instructors all perceived themselves as implementing all the principles identified "frequently," while business and industry personnel perceived themselves as implementing principles one, two, and eight "sometimes" but the others "frequently." An interesting difference was also revealed regarding the principle ranked highest by these practitioners. In hospitals, universities, community colleges, and agricultural extension, principle nine "a comfortable, supportive environment is a key to successful learning"-was ranked as the most important.

In business and industry, however, principle three "adults experience a gradual decline in physical/sensory capabilities"-was ranked highest. In contrast to the findings of Conti's PALS research, the principle referring most explicitly to collaborative modes of teaching and learning was ranked relatively low by instructors in all five settings. In particular, a number of studies of how practitioners do or do not conform to principles of good practice in real life program development settings will be examined. For the present it is enough to say that the foregoing instruments all represent contributions toward building a body of research on principles of good practice.

Development

Published accounts of the adult learning process nearly always make reference to life-span developmental stages, the life cycle of the 'phases' of adult life. In a similar way many policy documents in adult and continuing education stress the importance of addressing the needs associated with adult development and growth. Allman sets out the case for this interest in adult development. She observes that studies of adult life reveal it to be a period of change and development, much like that of childhood and adolescence.

She argues that the results of such studies serve notice on the prevailing assumptions about adulthood—that it is a long period of stability where previously learned capacities, skills, attitudes and values are applied to one's activities at work, in the family, in leisure and in civic life. These assumptions need to be challenged because they 'clearly affect decision makers in the field of politics, education and social policy'. In education they are linked to the conventional view that the period of initial education equips young adults for the remainder of their working lives—a view which continues to inform political debate on educational priorities.

Arguments like these are convincing and we do need to revise our outmoded views about adult life. But, as we shall argue we need to proceed with caution, otherwise there is a risk of replacing one set of false beliefs with another equally false set of beliefs about adult development. This chapter reviews some of the connections which have been made between adult development and adult education. The second part focuses on evaluating the adequacy of existing theory and research in this area. A question commonly posed by those with an interest in adult learning is 'What are the implications of adult development for adult and continuing education practitioners?' Knox outlines three possible implications:

1. To predict and explain success in education: 'Practitioners are typically interested in developmental generalizations regarding performance or personality in order to predict and explain successful participation in educative activity'.
2. To help people adapt to changing adult roles: 'Adult life cycle trends in performance in family, occupational and community roles suggest ways in which continuing education participation might facilitate adaptation and growth related to each role area'.
3. To improve the effectiveness of marketing and instructional activities: 'From time to time, the stability of adulthood is punctuated by role change events such as the birth of the first child, a move to another community or retirement... Such change events typically produce heightened readiness to learn which, if recognized, can contribute to the effectiveness of marketing and instructional activities'.

The whole tenor of the above implications indicates a view about adult development and an attitude to adult education. That is, that the various 'roles' of adult life are inevitable and people must learn to cope with them as they arise; and that adult education agencies, if they wish to be successful, should gear their marketing and instructional activities to cater for the different needs of adults at different life-stages. There is no sense in which adult roles are portrayed as arbitrary or even oppressive, or that alternative roles and options are possible for a given life period. In this sense adult education contributes towards the maintenance of social norms and structures. One need not look very far to find other instances of this type of approach.

A significant example can be found in McCoy's tabulation of 'Adult life cycle tasks and educational program responses' which is reproduced in Chickering's influential volume The Modern American College. McCoy identifies seven developmental stages, each of which is characterized by a set of common tasks. For example, the 'leaving home' stage has the associated tasks of 'break psychological ties','choose career','enter work', 'manage time' and so on. Each stage is then related to an appropriate range of programme responses, with a final column indicating the outcomes sought from the educational re-programme. The table is too lengthy to reproduce here but a cross-section of one stage only will be sufficient to illustrate the general strategy.

A casual glance at the list of tasks and how each of them relates to specified programmes confirms my general point about adult education supporting the status quo. Even a non-specific 'task' such as 'achieving autonomy', is interpreted in the most narrow sense possible—that is, as the capacity to 'live alone successfully'. It is unnecessary to elaborate further, the tabulation speaks for itself. What is surprising, and disappointing, is that anyone in adult education would take such an analysis seriously as anything other than a narrow descriptive exercise.

Yet there is a strongly held view among adult educators that the everyday reality of learners should be acknowledged, no matter how culturally specific that reality may be. The reader may remonstrate that McCoy is simply following this precept—what, then, is so objectionable? There are two objections. The first of these is that there is no acknowledgement of the narrow culturally specific 'tasks' which are identified. Quite the opposite, the 'tasks' are presented as a generalizable framework to be used by adult education agencies in formulating their programmes. There is no sense in which McCoy is using her analysis as a case study of a process for others to emulate in a different cultural context. The second objection, already mentioned in relation to Knox, is that the response of adult education is depicted as solely adaptive.

There is no scope for questioning and challenging the tasks—they constitute the taken for granted reality of the learners and the adult educators. There are many adult educators who, being dismissive of the above approach, nevertheless subscribe to the view that adult development is a central concept in adult education. An interest in adult development stems quite naturally from a commitment to the notion of lifelong learning and the associated concepts of 'lifelong education', 'recurrent education' and *'education permanente'*.

The policy and research documents of UNESCO, the OECD and the Council of Europe, which are the major sponsoring bodies of these concepts, frequently cite adult development as a central concern of any lifelong learning strategy. However, they do not understand adult development to be an immutable sequence of stages through which people pass at more or less predictable ages. Indeed, they challenge the concept of the 'typical' life cycle and support their view with an analysis of contemporary social and economic change.

Most likely, the crucial factors behind changes in the individual's life-cycle pattern will be the economic and employment conditions that the industrialized countries will face during coming years. Recurrent education, and its closely related concepts, accepts the diversity of life-cycle patterns and the need for educational institutions to respond to and foster this diversity through a diversity of provision. It supports the notion that individual options should be extended, especially the way in which paid work, education and leisure are combined. The principles espoused can be seen as a response to the effects of social, economic and technological change.

Changes in demographic patterns, the sexual division of labour, the length of working life, hours spent at work, retirement age and so on, are all seen as relevant to the proposition that educational opportunities should be distributed, in a recurring way, across the life-span. Recurrent education also embodies the notion of social justice, and its evolution as a concept from the late 1960s has been linked with a host of terms implying broad social reforms: industrial democracy, participation in planning, social equity, decentralization, links between education and work and between younger and older generations, and concern with the disadvantaged. An underlying value in all this is a humanistic concern for the individual.

The idea of self-development, which is based on notions of individuality and growth, is contrasted with the opposing notions of enslavement, alienation and stagnation—which are the psychological consequences of clinging to an outmoded conception of the 'normal' life cycle. There are two persistent problems which are a feature of adult developmental psychology. The first is that there are insurmountable methodological difficulties in establishing 'phases' or 'stages' of adult life.

The second is that much of the literature is historically and socially rooted and lacks any worthwhile generalizability. Not all adult development studies adopt a stage-sequence approach; nevertheless, they usually have a stake in making comparisons between different 'ages', 'phases' or 'stages' of life. Leaving aside the problem of deciding what type of data to gather, the common methodological problem is to construct a research design which generates comparative data.

Many of the most influential studies in adult development use research design which fail to do this. Three basic research designs are the 'cross-sectional', 'longitudinal' and 'time-lag' designs. Perhaps the best known example of this technique is to be found in the research of Gould. In an initial study Gould observed and recorded the concerns expressed by a number of psychiatric outpatients. He hypothesized that these concerns differed among different age groups. He then used these expressed concerns to construct a questionnaire which contained 160 questions divided into ten areas of life. This questionnaire was then administered, in a later study, to a sample of 524 non-patients, who were white middle-class men and women aged 16-50 years.

The difficulty with a research design such as this is that the observed differences in 'concerns' may be due to the different life experiences of the different age cohorts. For example, the life history of a 5-year-old in 1972 would necessarily include the 'great depression' of the 1930s and the experience of the Second World War. This would be quite different from the life history of 22-year-old in 1972 who would have experienced the economic boom of the post-Second World War years and the social changes of the 1960s. It seems reasonable to assume that such historical events and trends affect people's 'concerns'. Indeed they may be more significant in explaining the different concerns of different age cohorts than any hypothesized notion of the life cycle. One way to avoid making comparisons between different cohorts is to investigate a single age cohort over a number of years. Ninety-four college graduates from the early 1940s were followed through until 1969. They were part of an initial study of 268 male undergraduates who were given extensive physiological and psychological examinations early in their college years. A

fter graduation the sample of 94 graduates completed annual questionnaires untitled 1955, and every two years after that date. They were interviewed in their homes twice, between 1950 and 1952 and in 1969. Vaillant reports the results in detail, but his thesis is simple: that ego defence mechanisms mature through the life cycle and that healthy adults progress through a hierarchy of adaptive mechanisms as shown in Table.

Hierarchy of adaptive mechanisms

Level I:	Psychotic mechanisms (common in psychosis, dreams, childhood)
	Denial (of external reality)
	Distortion
	Delusional projection
Level II:	Immature mechanisms (common in severe depression, personality disorders and adolescence)
	Fantasy (schizoid withdrawal, dental through fantasy)
	Projection
	Hypochondriasis
	Passive-aggressive behavior (masochism, turning against the self)
	Acting out (compulsive delinquency, perversion)
Lvel III:	Neurotic mechanisms (common in everyone)
	Intellectualization (isolation, obsessive behavior, undoing, rationalization)

	Repression
	Reaction formation
	Displacement (conversion, phobias, wit)
	Dissociation (neurotic denial)
Level IV:	Mature mechanisms (common in 'healthy' adults)
	Sublimation
	Altruism
	Suppression
	Anticipation
	Humor

There are some well-documented problems with long and practice effects and time-of-measurement effects. A significant problem, and one often overlooked, is that over, say, a 30 year period, there are bound to be shifts in the theoretical perspective of the theory upon which the research is based. This often means that the initial questions and modes of analysis become obsolescent and are replaced by more contemporary techniques.

In the late 1930s at the University of California Erikson had begun the work that in 1950 was to culminate in 'Childhood and Society'-providing convincing evidence that adults mature as well as children. During the same period, the Grant Study staff, like their colleagues elsewhere, saw psychodynamic maturation as being largely completed by adolescence. Even though longitudinal studies overcome the problems of comparing different cohorts, they nevertheless remain historically bound. This means that generalizations to different cohort groups can only be made on the assumption that historical variation is unimportant. Is it possible to avoid the influence of historical variation? The answer to this question rests heavily on one's analysis of how history and culture influence the psychological make-up of individuals. From a research design of view it is certainly possible to control for historical effects by using some combination of longitudinal and cross-sectional designs. Vertical columns in Figure would represent a cross-sectional sequence where all four cohort groups are investigated twice, once in 1970 and again in 1980.

Similarly, combining the bottom two rows would represent a longitudinal sequence, where two cohort groups are investigated simultaneously over a number of years. Though such techniques it is possible to obtain data about the effects of cohort differences, time-of-easurement differences and age differences. For example, the differences between 20-year-olds can be compared with the differences between 30-year-olds in order to gauge the effect of cohort membership on the general difference between 20-and 30-year-olds.

This, in effect, is a way of 'controlling' for historical variation. But the control gained through such a practice is very limited. First, it depends on whether the changes being monitored are easily quantifiable. In fact, most of the studies of this kind have been developed by those with an interest in measuring the development of human abilities, especially intellectual development. The research designs employed were initially intended to partial out the historical effects of improvements in educational provision during or between the lifetimes of the subjects being studied. This is easy to do when it is simply a matter of comparing test scores, but it is a dubious task to take such comparisons with qualitative data of the king found in adult personality development.

Second, there is an assumption that the impact of histories linear and cumulative. But this is an untenable assumption. Another way of minimizing the impact of historical variation on developmental research is to gather 'data' of a high level of generality. For example, Lowenthal et al. used a cross-sectional technique to investigate the adaptive processes of men and women across the life-span. In their study they documented such general psychological qualities as complexity, self-image, expressiveness and perceptions in continuity of value structure. The biographical interview technique of Levinson was primarily aimed at elucidating changes in the relationship between self and world throughout the life course.

Loevinger was also concerned with the rather abstract notion of ego as a central frame of reference for understanding self and others. However, a closer look at this research will still reveal its social and historical specificity. Research in adult development, especially the genre concerned with life 'stages' or 'phases', seems prone and historical bias. This is evident in four ways; the existence of purely descriptive inventories of life 'tasks', the selection of subjects for research, the data gathering techniques, and the way in which the concept of the 'healthy' personality is constructed.

Descriptive inventories, whereby an inventory of life tasks is constructed, has its origins in Havighurst's Developmental Tasks and Education which was written in the early 1940s. It is similar to the inventory of McCoy and the same objections apply here. It is worthwhile noting, however, Havighurst's comments on his original inventory. The tasks the individual must learn—the developmental task of life-are those things that constitute healthy and satisfactory growth in our society. They are the things a person must learn if he is to be judged and to judge himself to be a reasonably happy and successful person.

A developmental task is a task which arises at or about a certain period in the life of the individual, successful achievement of which leads to his happiness and to success with later tasks, while failure leads to unhappiness in the individual, disapproval by the society, and difficulty with later tasks. Thus the developmental tasks of life amount to a socially approved timetable for individual growth and development. In a pluralistic society this timetable will differ between social groups.

While it may be useful to identify the developmental tasks of particular social or community groups, as Tucker and Huerta have done in their study of Mexican-American females, it is dangerous to generalize about the developmental tasks of society as such. Table sets out the sample, method and developmental processes identified by each of six well-known adult developmental psychologists. Five of these gathered data prior to formulating their views about adult development.

An impressionistic description of the samples used is that they consisted of North American, white, middle class, better educated, predominantly male subjects. The techniques for gathering data were the structured interview, questionnaire, self-rating checklist, standard psychological test and observer rating. But one should be wary of accepting reported results without a detailed knowledge of how these techniques were applied in each case.

Development implies growth and progress, not merely change. But growth and progress towards what end? The answer to this question is often the starting point for theories of adult development, and it is the conception of the end point of development, the 'mature' or 'healthy' personality which frequently governs how progress and growth is monitored and explained within a given theory. Many developmental psychologists construe the end point of development with terms like 'individuality', 'autonomy' and the 'integrated self'. But do such descriptions represent a particular way of looking at the world which excludes certain cultures or sections of the population? A closer look may help to resolve this issue. Levinson, for example, makes the following remarks about the 'individuation' prices:

Throughout the life cycle, but especially in the key transition periods such as infancy, pubescence and the Mid-life Transition, the developmental process of individuation is going on. This term refers to the changes in a person's relationship to himself and to the external world. These changes are part of the individuation process.

In successive periods of development, as this process goes on, the person forms a clearer boundary between self and world. He forms a stronger sense of who he is and what he wants, and a more realistic, sophisticated view of the world: what it is like, what it offers him and demands from him. Greater individuation allows him to be more separate from the world, to be more independent and self-generating. But it also gives him the confidence and understanding to have more intense attachments in the world and to feel more fully a part of it. This emphasis on 'separateness', 'independence' and 'self-generation' is the language of the ethic of individualism, it is worthwhile noting the claims of at least one commentator, Gilligan, that the emphasis on the development of individual identity among developmental theories is an aspect of gender bias which pervades the literature. She begins her analysis by referring to the work of Chodorow, who observes that, in general, girls are parented by a person of the same gender while boys are parented by a person if the opposite gender.

The significance of this is that the identity of boys is built on the perception of contrast and separateness from their primary caregiver, while the identity of girls is built upon the perception of sameness and attachment to their primary caregiver.

Consequently, relationships, and particularly issues of dependency, are experienced differently by women and men. For boys and men, separation and individuation are critically tied to gender identity since separation from the mother is essential for the development for masculinity. For girls and women, issues of feminity or feminine identity do not depend on the achievement of separation from the mother or on the progress of individuation. Since masculinity is defined through separation while femininity is defined through attachment, male gender identity is threatened by intimacy while female gender identity is threatened by separation. Thus males tend to have difficulty with relationships, while females tend to have problems with individuation.

The quality of embeddedness in social interaction and personal relationships that characterizes women's lives in contrast to men's, however, becomes not only a descriptive difference but also a developmental liability when the milestones of childhood and adolescent development in the psychological literature are markets of increasing separation. Women's failure to separate then becomes by definition a failure to develop.

Gilligan then proceeds to cite evidence of the undervaluing of female characteristics—the concern with relationships and responsibilities, empathy and attachment-among developmental theories. For example, Freud considered the persistence of women's pre-Oedipal attachment to their mother to be linked with their failure to resolve completely their Oedipal feelings and their consequent failure to develop a strong superego. This developmental failure in women results in their having little sense of justice:

The fact that women must be regarded as having little sense of justice is no doubt related to the predominance of envy in their mental life... Another example comes from Jean Piaget, who observed sex differences in the way children engage in games. Girls, because of their more flexible attitude towards rules and their enforcement were considered to have a less developed legal sense than boys—which is the cornertone of corstone o moral development.

The rule is no longer an imperative coming from an adult and accepted without discussion, it is a means of agreement resulting from co-operation itself. But girls are less explicit about this agreement and this is our reason for suspecting them of being less concerned with legal elaborations. A rule is good so long as the game repay it. Kohlberg too is open to the same criticism. Gilligan observes that his empirical work, which led to the formulation of moral development stages, was based on a sample of boys only.

According to Gilligan, this is because the higher stages of kohlberg's scale are constructed from what are traditionally 'male' qualities—the concern with justice and rights rather than with responsibilities and relationships. The thrust of Gilligan's argument is that womanhood is rarely equated with mature healthy adulthood in much of the adult developmental literature. This is because the healthy personality is too often portrayed from a male perspective, with an emphasis on individuation and autonomy.

The elusive mystery of women's development lies in its recognition of the continuing importance of attachment in the human life cycle. Woman's place in man's life cycle is to protect this recognition while the developmental litany intones the celebration of separation, autonomy, individuation, and natural rights.

An alternative to documenting the 'stages' and 'phases' of adult life is to understand development as an ongoing dialectical process. The basic notion here is that there is a constant 'dialectic' between the changing or developing person and the changing or evolving society. That is, the person creates, and is created by the society in which he/she lives. Accompanying this notion is the rejection of those psychological approaches which search for stability, equilibrium and balance in the life course.

The person is construed as a changing person in a changing world, and the dialectical approach is very much concerned with the dynamics of change. The preference for an equilibrium model in the behavioral science has been as firmly established as has the preference for abstract traits or competencies. Without any debate it has been taken for granted that a state of balance, stability, and rest is more desirable than a state of upheaval, conflict and change. Thus we have always aimed for a psychology of satisfaction but not of excitement. This preference has found expression in balance theory, equilibrium theory, steady state theory, and indirectly in the theory of cognitive dissonance.

With the possible exception for the latter, these interpretations fail to explore the fact that every change has to be explained by the process of imbalance which forms the basis for any movement. Once this pre-requisite is recognized, stability appears as a transitory condition in the stream of ceaseless changes.

One source of such change is the historical change in one's culture, the other source is the change associated with one's age-related social category. Such changes are primarily mediated through people interacting in everyday life—thus an investigation of developmental change will entail an analysis of common, everyday interactions and the dialogues contained in them.

Rriegel's position has much in common with Berger and Luckmann's exposition for how personal identity is shaped, maintained and transmitted within a given social order. Their analysis offers a powerful account of how personal identity is a social construction which, especially in a modern pluralistic society, is constantly open to change and transformation. What is meant by the proposition that personal identity is a social construction? Put simply, the idea is as follows:

1 We do not have biologically determined identities;
2 We are all born into a particular social world which has been constructed by humans;
3 We develop a notion of who we are from the way 'significant' others;
4 These 'significant' ohters represent the social world and mediate it to us.
5 We take on the roles and attitudes of significant others, internalize them and make them our own;
6 We extend our identification with significant others to an identification with society as whole: 'Only by virtue of this generalized identification does his own self-identification attain stability and continuity. He now has not only an identity vis-a vis this or that significant other, but an identity in general...'

Identity, as a social construction, needs to be maintained through social interaction. The routines of everyday life serve to confirm the reality of the world and our place in it. In particular, the language used in everyday conversations confirms for us the silent, taken-for-granted world that forms the foundation of our personal identity.

In modern pluralistic society, however, there is a multiplicity of world views or realities. Because there is no common social reality there is no socially produced stable structure of personal identity. This means that achieving a stable personal identity in modern society becomes an individual, private enterprise. Moreover, the possibility of transforming one's identity is always present. Indeed, one could argue that many life events require a change or re-orientation of identity. Berger and Luckmann maintain that any transformation of identity requires a process of re-socialization. In extreme cases, such as with religious conversion, there may be a complete dismantling of one's former identity. This would require the following:

1 Affiliation with the new community;
2 Segregation for the individual from the inhabitants of other 'worlds', especially those from the 'world' being left behind;
3 A reinterpretation of the old 'reality ' in terms of the new 'reality'

Each of these steps can be recognized as extreme versions of what happens to many adults as they develop new personal, family, work and leisure pursuits. The difference between this analysis and the life-span development literature is that transformation does not imply a move towards some state of maturity—it simply means change, not improvement.

There are no propositions about the regularity and predictability of change—only that personal identity is open to change, subject to the existence of a community of others who maintain the change through discourse in everyday life. The idea of the malleability of personal identity is both a source of hope and an occasion for despair. Hope, because it means that change is always possible' despair, because it implies that a belief in the real, true, authentic self is a fanciful indulgence.

Adult development is, in principle germane to anyone with an interest in adult education. Too often, however, people with an applied intent will latch on to an easily assimilated theory, one which clearly differentiates and orders the 'phases' or 'stages' of life and which advances an unambiguous account of the process and end point of development. Adult educators may find such theories useful but they need to be wary of the methodological and conceptual difficulties. They also need to be mindful of the impact such theories have on shaping and maintaining conventionally held views about what it means to be a mature, healthy adult.

Purposeful, enlightening, and personally significant discussion is not only possible without previously specified learning objectives, it actually requires that no such specifications be made. As Paterson cogently argues, to engage in the collaborative exploration and interpretation of individual experience is the most meaningful form of discussion for adults. But such discussion cannot be tied to previously determined objectives. It must be open and subject to continuous negotiation.

Teachers and learners will often hold conflicting beliefs, values, and notions of importance. The most illuminating encounter is one in which these beliefs, values, and notions are externalized and subjected to collaborative analysis and in which participants are always ready to alter lines of inquiry on the basis of newly realized insights or interests. Our sfinal criticism of previously defined objectives in programme development for adults concerns the question of unplanned, incidental learning.

If we use the attainment of previously specified learning objectives as the evaluative criterion for judging the success of an educational effort then we must logically relegate unplanned, serendipitous, and incidental outcomes to a position of secondary importance. Indeed, we may consider such learning to have no real value at all. This idea, however, has provided so repugnant to some educational evaluators that a whole school of goal-free evaluation has developed as a counter to it. Here, we might simply note that several writers have questioned the idea that the only learning outcomes of any value are those that correspond to previously specified objectives. Apps points out that it is impossible for educators to anticipate all the learning that will result from participation in adult education classes.

Jones declares that "the unintended consequences of a learning situation are often much more important than the original restrictive catechism of goals which invariably assumes an instrumental role for learning". Some empirical support for the view that learners may perceive the unplanned outcomes of course participation to be of considerable significance is presented by Fodor. In her investigation of incidental learning occurring in structured educational experiences, she surveyed 246 adult accounting students in three different colleges.

The study confirmed the ubiquity of incidentally learned information, skills, and attitudes in a set of circumstances designed for purposeful learning. Particularly important was the encouragement for such learning received from peers. Fodor advised adult teachers to arrange for informal interactions among peers as part of the course experience, to give greater attention to the cultivation of incidental learning in study skills courses, and to direct students to materials or resources that could help them develop independence and self-knowledge.

It is evident, then, that no programmer can predict the range of learning outcomes that are likely to arise from participation in one class session, let alone from membership in a course lasting several months. When the difficulties of trying to arrange learning outcomes for one adult are multiplied many times, the irrelevance of the predefined objectives approach for most programs becomes immediately apparent. That we still persist in using this approach to guide our program planning style irrespective of the nature of our clientele or our educational purposes is an extreme example of the "emperor's clothing" syndrome.

If, as programmers, we assume that the only valid learning is that which corresponds to some specific format we have previously arranged,then we are guilty of an unusually high degree of intellectual arrogance. Such arrogance is not uncommon, however. For example, if a learner leaves a programme before the end of the course, such withdrawal is almost always regarded as symptomatic or failure—failure by the learner who did not apply his or her talents with sufficient industry or failure by the teacher who possessed inadequate pedagogic skills.

An equally plausible interpretation, however, is that the learner feels that she has gained what was most valuable from the course and decides that, with limited time at her disposal, she would be better advised to pursue other avenues of learning. Indeed, withdrawal might sometimes be interpreted as a sign of the success of the course in that it has so animated a learner's interest in a field that she commits herself to a sustained and independent exploration of its boundaries. It is timely to remind ourselves, then, that we cannot prescribe for our diverse clienteles the exact range, from, and number of learning outcomes that will result from their participation in our programmes.

Learners' perceptions of what valuable learning may bear little relation to the previously determined objectives that we prescribe to determine instructional design, course content, and evaluative procedures. Learners will frequently take from course participation various skills, insights, and information that have nothing to do with the activities and outcomes initially intended by the educator. In every learning group there may well be an optimal balance that can be attained among facilitators' purposes, participants' expectations, flexibility of format, and sense of overall direction. In the most satisfying of group transactions, this balance will be negotiated continually. This, of course, is not to advocate an abandonment of the concept of educational purpose, whether this be expressed in broad philosophical aims or in terms of specific behavioral or other performance objectives.

Although various encounter or support groups may decide to meet for no other reason than to make contact with others of similar outlook and may be able to spend a great deal of time negotiating purposes, for many learning groups this will not be realistic. Community action groups, engaged in advocacy, work-study groups seeking to acquire occupational skills, and groups meeting to undertake hard intellectual analysis will most likely not wish to spend more than a small part of their time engaged in an initial negotiation of purpose. They will probably benefit from a regular formative evaluation session, in which progress is discussed and fundamental purposes reiterated, but the majority of participants' time will be spent in purposeful learning.

The point is, however, that incidental learning, unplanned acquisition of skills and knowledge, or unanticipated insights should not be regarded by participants or facilitators as somehow innately less valid than previously specified learning outcomes. A sense of common purpose is probably a precondition of effective group interaction and development of a moral culture within group. But it should not become reified to such an extent that deviations from the previously agreed-upon purpose are condemned as irrelevant even before they occur. This, in effect, may block off fruitful avenues of intellectual exploration and act against participants' making meaningful connections between learning activities and their own experiences. The last comments on this question behavioral objectives might profitably be left to Eisner. As he remarks, "In thousands of ways, teachers draw on images of human virtue as criteria for the direction of their activity as teachers and for the directions they should take with their students.

The storehouse of such images is large, and it needs to be. It is modulated according to the circumstances and context and with regard to the particular student with whom the teacher interacts". Why, then, should we regard it as unprofessional or irresponsible for facilitators to encourage learners to explore feelings, perceptions, and avenues of inquiry that were not originally specified as part of the learning group's activities? Arguably, the most exiting, memorable, and profound moments in learning are those in which individuals stumble into insights and perceptions of which they had previously been unaware. Such moments can rarely be planned beforehand in precise terms, though the facilitator can encourage a learning group culture that will make the likelihood of such moments occurring much stronger.

A facilitator who can make unexpected connections between participants' contributions or who encourages learners to depart from the "script" of the sessions's activities to explore themes that were unanticipated but that engage and excite is the most valuable. The needs revealed by a needs assessment are what provide the goals an daims of the programme, which are then translated into specific objectives curricula, and evaluative criteria. Griffith, however, has called the concept of need an adult education shibboleth in that the favored answer to questions concerning the function of an educational programme is that isit is meeting learners' needs, meeting adults needs or meeting the needs of the community

The concept of need also functions as a "premature ultimate" in discussions concerning the proper role of education and training programmes. A premature ultimate is a concept or term that provokes such reverence and contains such cannective potency that its invocation tends to silence any further discussion on a matter.

Lawson points out that the term need functions in this manner when question concerning the curricula of training and education programmes are raised. Hence, to say that one is meeting needs in a programmes is to state a case rather than to argue a viewpoint. Discussion on the merits of the case comes to be seen as inappropriate. But to say that as a programmer one is meeting needs is somewhat akin to politicians saying that an action or policy is democratic. In both instances the justification invoked for the decisions taken is ambiguous, while at the same time it forecloses further discussion. What is important to realize is that many different interpretations can be made of the concept of need and that the concept is irrevocably value laden.

The value-laden aspect of the concept has been discussed in several analyses. As these writers all recognize, those who invoke the concept of need to justify their decisions should specify whether the needs in question are felt by learners or prescribed by educators. It is unpardonable to confuse the two, yet such confusion is frequently evident in the writings and conversations of educators and trainers. The difference between felt needs and prescribed needs has been discussed by the writers cited above and also by this writer. Felt needs are equivalent to the wants, desires, and wishes of the learner. They are perceived and expressed by the learners themselves. Examples of commonly felt needs of adult learners might be how to use microcomputers, how to lose weight through aerobics, how to speak a foreign language, or how to cook in a certain style.

Prescribed needs arise when an educator decides that an individual, group, or community falls short of some ideal identified by that educator. Monette calls such a need a normative need that entails three propositions on the part of the educator: "that someone is in a given state, that this state is incompatible with the norms held by some group or by society, and that therefore the state of that someone should be changed".

Felt needs, then, are expressions of preference or desire by learners. Prescribed needs are premised upon educators' beliefs concerning the skills, knowledge, behaviors, and values that they feel adults should acquire. To base education and training programmes on a mix of felt and prescribed needs causes some educators to feel uncomfortable. It seems arrogant and authoritarian compared to the apparently democratic process of responding solely to the felt needs of learners.

Nonetheless, it is my contention that a total subscription to a felt needs approach to programme development condemns education to an adaptive, reactive mode and turns educators into mere providers of consumer goods. The exact form of these goods, according to this rationale, is to be determined by the market forces of expressed learner preferences.

The educator becomes an automation of functionary, a technician responding to expressed desires but with no responsibility for suggesting alternative curricula or activities. Such a view absolves the educator from ever having to make value choices or from having to prompt learners to consider the possibility of other ways of thinking, feeling, and behaving. This is entirely unacceptable as a way of viewing an educator's professional responsibilities. Those who behave in this manner and who equate the sum total of education with reacting to expressed learner needs are technicians, not educators.

The element of felt needs will determine some of the courses offered in every programme. It would be hard for educators and trainers of adults to survive in most institutional settings if their programmes did not clearly satisfy the felt needs of a reasonably large number of adults in the vicinity. Programmes will frequently be mounted to attract large numbers of participants so as to allow programmers to engage in educationally crucial but economically unviable work. For example, the price of my running a free Educational Advisory Service for adults in the community was my arranging courses on popular subjects.

The service was established to assist adults in charting a path through the bewildering range of formal educational opportunities open to them and to discuss general learning difficulties they were experiencing in their intellectual pursuits. No fee was paid for this service, and it was open to adult who were not enrolled in courses at my center, as well as those who were. Courses on yoga or on Vegetarian Cooking attracted large numbers of participants and made it easier for me to argue that the Educational Advisory Service should be continued, despite its not generating revenue for the college, since this was offset by the fees collected from yoga and cooking classes.

The danger, however, is that courses dictated by the felt needs rationale will come to comprise the total programme offering. If this happens, then the programmer will be discouraged from engaging in provocative, controversial, or unpopular alternative programming. Encouraging adults to consider alternative ways of conceiving their world and acting within and upon it often involves a painful readjustment of perceptions. It is a threatening and traumatic experience to be prompted to reinterpret on's dearly held belief systems, value frameworks, and common behaviors from another perspective.

We often bridle against being asked to consider the possibility that we might be operating under false assumptions or ignoring important realities. A practical example may illustrate may point. It is my firm relief that every publicly funded adult education programme should sponsor some kind of political discourse, whether by setting up a formal course or by providing resources for groups already engaged in such activity in the community.

Adult Life

In a commonsensical way, we are inclined to take them for granted rather than posing them as problematic. This essentially pragmatic mental stance that accompanies our everyday adult activities is described by Alfred Schutz as the natural attitude in which we suspend all scepticism during the pursuit of our daily affairs about the immediate events, environmental effects, and societal contexts in which we are involved. Unfortunately, this necessary pragmatic stance of the natural attitude leaves us increasingly vulnerable to the harmful consequences of decisions steered predominantly by technical rationality and of ill-conceived technological innovation.

It becomes more and more an imperative for adults to acquire the capacity to put aside the natural attitude of their everyday life-world and adopt a sceptical approach towards taken-for-granted innovations 'necessary for progress', supposedly 'acceptable' impositions as the price of progress, and seemingly authoritative sources of information that describe for us the landscapes of contemporary social reality.

Clearly, if the concerns of this book are taken seriously, a critical capacity of this kind cannot be engendered on a wide scale by the deployment of courses on critical thinking skills and essays on how to think critically. Such instrumentalization of the problem, in a taken-for-granted manner, defeats its purpose. A capacity to replace the mental stance of the natural attitude in relevant situations that are presently taken for granted requires an unrelenting pedagogical effort. Only through a commitment to embracing a continuing critical reflection on practice and a determination to incorporate critical though (not merely debating pros and cons) within all education settings can adult educators help counter the debilitating consequences to our life-world of an ideology of technique reinforced by its taken-for-granted acceptance.

Through legalistic means, professionalization has resulted in the transference to experts of many vital activities that were, and can still be, adequately performed within the domain of the everyday life-world.

Rather than questioning and offering informed resistance to a trend that has led to a significant de-skilling within life-world contexts, the modern practice of adult education has lent its weight to the world of the specialists the system-world. To the simplistically offered objection that one would not go to a non-specialist for surgery, antibiotics, or advice on litigation, there is an obvious response that the retrieval and development of competence in personal care home economics, and community based services would considerably, reduce dependence on surgeons, pharmaists, lawyers, and other specialists. Apart from engendering critical discourse among professionals about professionalization and identifying problems induced through an unexamined technical rationality that undermines vital aspects of our everyday life-world adult educators can light upon locations and concerns where a thoughtful pedagogy would help sustain life-world interests.

Neighbourhood issues, the relationship between adults and children, concerns about health, ecology, concerns about military installation—these are all cooled out by the taken-for-granted encroachment of a technical rationality that can still be made problematic through an informed, critical pedagogy. Nor need pedagogical involvement with these concerns be confined to informal community-based contexts. Schools, colleges, prisons, the work-places-most formal institutional settings, in fact—are locations where practical critique can be undertaken through a pedagogy favouring the enhancement of communicative competence over educational strategies merely intended to alleviate concerns of the non-experts.

Clearly, there are difficulties in practising such a pedagogy within the very institutions from which threats to life-world values emanate, but the stresses and crises of modern institution always provide opportunities for alternative kinds discoursse where management does not shortsightedly favour a degree of authoritarianism that becomes dysfunctional to its own interests. It is important for adult educators to foster alternative discourses within large scale institutionalized settings because the preservation of what is vital in our everyday life-world depends upon the fostering of its vital, communicative, constituents within the system-world. The task is to humanize the latter so that it enhances rather that depletes the former. Adult educators, then, have a significant role to play in taking a piece of the 'commons', so graphically described by Ivan Illich, into contemporary society's industrialized, commercialized, and bureaucratized organizations, although Illich himself would maintain that we should look exclusively to alternative community-based arrangements for the preservation of traditional values.

Despite the relevance for us of Illich's notions of the 'commons' and 'vernacular values', a hardier, less romanticized, pedagogy in line with the theoretical and practical commitments of Gramsci and Hsbermas holds out more promise of social transformation, since it extends to the institutions of the system-world from which we cannot entirely escape. Unlike Illich these two theorists and activists recognize that industrial and bureaucratic organizations, though steered by an ideology of technique, provide significant locations for retrieving genuinely democratic communicative value.

At the same time, the predicament of the family in contemporary society presents a challenge for adult education to create learning situations, transcending class, socio-economic and ethnic boundaries, that explore how men and women can live together and, more importantly, raise children in caring relationships. The typical family unit headed by a patriarchal male as sole bread-winner becomes increasingly less typical while it is idealized by state interests wich undermine traditional family autonomy through reformist interventions.

Even those middle-class families which seems to approach the ideal are subject to external influences and intrusions that serve to erode traditional patriarchal and domestic functions, add to the emotional turmoil of growing children, and bring further ambiguity to the roles of wife and mother. Clearly, the retention of an idealized typical family unit from which all other domestic arrangements for living together are defined is now extremely problematic.

A concerned pedagogy can scarcely escape from the critical everyday life-world considerations touched upon here. They are situated within what Habermass describes as 'the new problem zone'. Much more research is required to reveal the full extent of problems that suggest a diminishing ability to inculcate future generations into a community ethic and value-oriented action that will sustain it. Adult education has a role to play in examining, and offering, options to nihilistic tendencies that cannot now be fully countered by the disappearing traditional family unit.

A useful start in a hopeful direction could be made by incorporating a critical dimension to, and completely re-conceptualizing, the subject that takes the family and domestic arrangements as its focus-home economics. Government and corporate interests are now having to confront increasing alarm about the destruction of valuable environmental non-renewable resources. The extent of the crisis presses for relevant involvement of adult educators within the environmental movement which is gaining momentum on a global scale as governmental and corporate efforts to alleviate puhlic concerns without dealing with their vilidity are being systematically challenged.

Apart from bringing their organizational capacities to bear through direct participation in the movement and through dissemination of information to critically engage complacent, but methodically presented, corporate public relations reports, adult educators have a significant role to play in introducing ecological themes into regular educational programming and cladssroom teaching.

Similar opportunities exist for the development of a more thoughtful pedagogical involvement with anti-nuclear and peace movements, with alternative community-based, non profit, initiatives such as food coops, credit unions, co-operative housing and alternative technology, and with movements committed to the preservation of cultural, linguistic, and regional identities. These alternative spheres of resistance to both corporate and state capitalism make problematic areas of concern that are otherwise overlooked by an overly technocratic orientation to progress. In view of their healthy practical concern for the well-being of the species and the survival of our planet over capitalistic or state-determined politico-economic imperatives, these spheres of resistance are eminently progressive.

It is to be hoped that in subsequent phases of their development, and this is where adult education can surely help, they will place more emphasis on transforming bureaucratized and governmental structures into a means for supporting and enhancing precious dimensions of the life-world exemplified by genuinely democratic interactions. People create the structures of the system-world; people can bring them in hand. Adult educators in many parts of the world already incorporate the kind of commitments outlined above into our pedagogical practice.

The International Council for Adult Education, in particular, publishes accounts of initiatives consistent with a transformative pedagogy sensitive to adult life-world concerns and the protection of the commons. Insights and imaginative contemporary strategies directly relevant to a transformative practice of adult education can be derived from essays on community development initiatives, of then'grass-roots' genre rather tha 'top-down' approaches, and from the activities of popular movements which are not yet overly attentive to all the significant dimensions of their adult educational function. There is, then, a discernible and active arena in which careful work is undertaken on behalf of collective and public concerns rather than those of corporate and individualistic interests, and where transformative pedagogy already manifests itself.

No adult educator needs to be talking about transformative practice of critical theory in isolation from some relevant location where the discourse can be put to the test. An optimistic perspective, supported by an enlightened pedagogy envisages the life-world and system-world acting upon each other to mutual benefit. Initiatives to protect life-world interests can add greater democratic communicative capacity to the system-world of corporate and bureaucratic decision-making, which thus becomes more readily inclined to act rationally in conserving the 'commons' of Illich's metaphor. But the educational effort is necessary.

There are still may influential people who find no problem at all with the notion of constructing mines and corporate enterprises in wilderness parks which, in effect have already been legally designated as 'commons'. Some may even resort to violence in asserting a right to savage the 'commons'. While this chapter was being written, the Manchester Guardian Weekly reported that Francisco Mendes, internationlly known defender of the Amazon rain forests and aboriginal rights, had been murdered. The man who surrendered himself to the police is said to have been a rancher opposed to the struggle to the rain forest.

Francisco Mendes, among others, has established how wasteful and destructive ranching is of rain forest resources and the extent of involvement in forest devastation on the part of large corporations such as Xerox, Georgia Pacific, the Dutch company Bruynzeel and the Japanese Toyomenka. As a result of his educational activities, the World Bank and the Inter-American Regional Bank were persuaded in 1988 to withhold financing from the region until serious environmental protection measures had been taken'. But the stakes are high.

Implicit in the alternative orientations described in the previous section is a strong affinity with moves towards decentralization and against further centralization. It is in this regard that adult education can well afford to examine its own practice, where prevailing trends to centralize the curriculam in line with a management perspective calls for continuing scepticism.

In addition to advancing critiques concerning ethical and practical claims which accompany the deployment of centralized curriculum disigns, adult educators should make every reasonable effort to be meaningfully involved in curriculum initiatives. Meaningful involvement would require resistance to suggestions that a mere endorsement of already determined criteria and frameworks is sufficient. Failure to realize meaningful participation does not necessarily incapacitate adult educators working in formal institutional settings, but a disinclination to struggle for such involvement and to question top-down centralizing initiatives scarcely qualifies them to talk about teaching critical thinking to their students.

While the trend towards centralized administration and design of the adult education curriculum has encountered critical assessment, other centralizing measures within adult education agencies seem to have been accepted in a taken for granted manner. Sometimes, they are readily embraced by those who ought to be asking the questions. In any event, if the widely espoused notion of 'empowering adult learners' through the teaching of critical thinking is to be taken seriously, adult educators must attend to the way that top-down initiatives within their own organizations effectively curtail prospects for genuine dimocratic discourse and for the relevant participation in decision-making that this implies.

A careful analysis of the context and the motivations from which these initiatives emerge usually reveals some possibility of less formalized appropriate communicative discourse that sustains countervailing strategies. The latter, viewed individually and in the short run, may not seem immediately significant, but they do shape the course of events even in quite authoritarian institutions where adult educators work such as prisons, the military, hospitals, and public schools.

Alternative strategies that do arise as part of an informal communicative structure cannot be totallly eliminated or completely steered through a heavily centralized administrative format unless the right to question and resist, even in subtle forms, is surrendered. Some initiatives towards centralization and management of resources do, of course, make sense. This is the case with distance education programmes created to meet the needs of people who do not have ready access to format learning opportunities in line with their educational needs.

Here too, through, careful involvement is required of the part of committed adult educators to ensure that enthusiasm for the available technology and a capability to neatly pre-package learning materials at central locations do not supersede the need for locally oriented educational support. Without the latter, which usually means provision for some face-to-face interaction between educator and students, distance education can become a vehicle for a kind of cultural invasion in which communities are envisaged as 'reception sites' for the technology and methodological approaches of distance education specialists. This is most evident, for example, where distance education courses emanate from a central location within the dominant culture for delivery to aboriginal people in remote areas.

More critical analysis is needed to assess the homogenizing effects of distance education and its potential as a delivery system to serve governmental and large scale corporate interests rather than those of people in their community settings. In the meantime, adult educators should be on guard to ensure that distance education is not shaped largely by technocrats and those with those with a bent for implementing overarching curriculum design.

Issue has to be taken with those who claim that the price of genuine participatory democracy in our institutional arrangements is continuing inefficiency. This book is not a plea for the relegation of a concern for efficiency, for the complete abandonment of technical rationality, or for a bizarre, romanticized stance against technological development of any kind. A technical rationality, tempered by careful consideration, practical, ethical, and aesthetic in line with Habermas's notion of a superior rationality embedded in genuinely democratic communicative action, is conducive to the sustenance of vital life-world interactions and to the protection of the 'commons'. As an integral aspect of a more wholesome communicative action, is conducive to the sustenance of vital life-world interactions and to the communicative rationality, which it seeks to support rather that determine, technical rationality becomes most relevant in the development of more benign technologies that serve, first and foremost, democratically conceived community needs rather than those determined predominantly by state and corporate interests.

6

Dynamics of Professional Education

The future of continuing education appears to be headed toward rapid growth and development. Many people believe that systems of continuing education will be built that rival the professional preparation programs now in existence. The leaders of most professions would probably agree that "what we hardly dare prophesy today will be seen by later generations as efforts to achieve a manifest necessity". This increasing attention in seen by many as a positive development of continuing education. This focus has also magnified the widespread shortcomings in the practice of continuing professional education.

Houle does not overstate the problems of continuing education today when he describes this typical program: "Faculty members who can be persuaded to do so give lectures on subjects of their own choosing to audiences they do not know, who have assembled only because they want to put in enough hours of classroom attendance so that they can meet a relicensure requirement". Furthermore, these simple activities are expected to improve the performance of professionals whose practices are full of complexities, uncertainty, and judgments. Given these conditions, the great concern in the professions with the quality of continuing education should not be surprising. Due to the increasing attention given to continuing education in the professions, a new field of educational practice has come into existence. This field is becoming increasingly differentiated from the educational practices of preprofessional education. For example, many people think of themselves and are considered by others to be continuing medical educators or continuing engineering educators, when, in fact, they may not have had any experience in the preprofessional education of the groups with whom they work.

The evidence for this movement is unmistakable. For example, several journals in North America are devoted exclusively to the theory and research of continuing education for specific professions. There is the Journal of Continuing Education in the Health Professions, the Journal of Continuing Social Work Education, the Journal of Continuing Education in Nursing, and the Journal or Nursing Staff Development. In addition, there is a trend for continuing educators in specific occupation to form interest groups within their national professional organizations, such as the American Nurses Association. Other educators choose to form their own associations, such as the Society of Medical School Directors of Continuing Medical Education, the Society for the Advancement of Continuing Education in Ministry, and the National Association of State Judicial Educators.

Within the professions the traditional view has been that the continuing education function must be directed by its own members, while the emerging view is that individuals trained in the field of continuing education have the most appropriate background for this function. While there is an increasing movement toward the emerging view, its adherents are still in a significant minority. One estimate is that of all the people who perform continuing education functions within the professions, 95 percent have been trained only in the content of their own profession. The remaining 5 percent either have their formal training only in education or have been trained both in their profession and in education.

Continuing education for the professions as a field of educational practice is quite young. As such, it is guided by concepts that have not been fully thought through or adequately tested. In fact, many of these concepts are holdovers from the models of preprofessional education, which should not be surprising given the academic background of most educators. However, with the entry of more individuals trained in the field of adult education, increasing attentiveness is being given to models and concepts of educational practice from that field.

The most effective way to improve practice is for educators to understand the assumptions and principles that guide their work, examine whether they are the most useful ones, and change them when necessary. A small but growing literature base in continuing professional education itself serves as a useful point of departure for analysis. This literature has begun to synthesize the voluminous material that describes the research and practice base of continuing education for the individual professions. The literature in the individual professions additionally constitutes a rich resource for the study and practice of continuing professional education. This material is used selectively to illustrate the major issues that are common in the practice of continuing education across the professions.

As first step toward analyzing practice, it is necessary to make explicit the approaches being used to understand both the professions and continuing education. There is no commonly accepted way to approach these concepts; thus it is imperative that the assumptions underlying this book be stated that for the reader to evaluate. In order to talk intelligently about continuing education for the professions as a field of practice, the differences between professions and other occupations must be examined. Without making this distinction, educators would be practicing in continuing occupational education or continuing education because their clientele would be undifferentiated from adult learners in general.

The problem of defining professions has a long and controversial history. The earliest effort to define a profession is generally considered to be by Flexner in 1915, and the most recent comprehensive analysis was by Friedson. As anyone who has examined the literature on the professions will readily attest, there is no commonly agreed upon answer to the question of what constitutes a profession.

Rather, schools of thought with different approaches yield different answers. Because sociologists are no closer to an accepted definition now than in 1915, many have suggested that it makes no sense to try define the professions at all. Avoiding a conscious attempt at definition would promote the belief that professions are simply those occupations which have gained professional status. This determination is unacceptable to those who wish to think clearly and systematically about continuing education for the professions.

The central tasks are to identify the major approaches to a definition, select one, and provide a rationale for the choice. Three approaches that have been identified in the literature are static, process, and socio-economic. The oldest definitional approach was pioneered by Flexner, who believed "there are certain objective standards that can be formulated" that distinguish professions from other occupations. He identified the following six characteristics as essential for an occupation to claim professional status. Professions must (1) involve intellectual operations, (2) derive their material from science, (3) involve definite and practical ends, (4) possess an educationally communicable technique, (5) tend to self-organization, and (6) be altruistic. Others over the years have compiled the lists of attributes of a profession. Today many occupations are still applying these generic criteria to decide whether their occupation is a profession. This is particularly true for occupations that are striving for higher status, such as social work, school teaching, nursing, and early childhood education. This is called the *static approach* because objective criteria firmly discriminate between those occupations which are inherently a profession and those which are not. Once this distinction is made, it is unlikely that those which are not could ever develop into professions. Since the 1960s the static approach has received such criticism that almost no one uses it who seriously studies professions as a concept.

The major problem with this approach is the persistent lack of consensus about the criteria that should be used to define professions. For example, Millerson found twenty-three elements that were included in various definitions. Of the twenty-one authors used in his analysis, no single criterion was common to all of them. Furthermore, no two authors agreed that the same combination of criteria should be used to define a profession.

Johnson provides a systematic treatment of the reasons for this lack of consensus. In his view the fundamental problem arises at the starting point of this approach, which is that there are "true" professions that exhibit all of the criteria to some degree. The procedure of listing criteria without any explicit theoretical framework means that it is possible to apply particular criteria arbitrarily. The implication for continuing education is that, without any way to agree on the criteria that mark a profession, educators cannot have a clear idea of which occupations are professions and which are not. Because of the problems inherent in the static approach, a different way of thinking about professions developed in the early 1960s. Hughes put in this way: "In my own studies I passed from the false question 'Is this occupation a profession?' to the more fundamental one, 'What are the circumstances in which people in an occupation attempt to turn it into a profession?". This *process approach* came into full flower then Vollmer and Mills used it as the organizing principle for their book on professionalization. This approach differs from the all-or-nothing-at-all style favored in the static approach by viewing all occupations as existing on a continuum of professionalization.

The relevant question became Hoe professionalized is an occupation? It has been argued that all occupations go through a natural sequence in their passage to professional status although there is no consensus on this point. Another possibility raised by the process approach is that occupations can deprofessionalized, suggesting that the continuum is not a one-way street. A number of authors have explored this possibility for even the most professionalized occupations such as medicine and law. Kleinman argues that liberal protestant clergy have deprofessionalized their own role as a response to modernization, secularization, and religious pluralism. They have rejected the idea that ordained clergy are experts in religious matters and have replace it with a role that accepts egalitarian relationships with lay people.

Although the process approach assumes that it is possible for a profession to deprofessionalize, it is generally not viewed as desirable. An important assumption of the process approach is that no clear-cut boundary separates professions from other occupations. Vollmer and Mills state that professionalization is a process "that may affect any occupation to a greater or lesser degree". This is important for continuing professional educators because "all occupations seeking the ideals of professionalization are worthy of sympathetic study...". This approach avoids many of the pitfalls of the static approach because it recognizes the dynamic conditions of contemporary occupations structures.

By claiming that professions never reach a point of becoming an ideal profession, the rationale is established for both constant improvement and continuing learning. Another positive aspects of the process approach is its emphasis on understanding the professions in relation to society. The process approach is based on the premise that the professions are necessary to the smooth and orderly functioning of society. In turn, society provides professionals with relativity high levels of money and status as a way of rewarding their highly valued with.

However, by stressing the socially functional value of professional activity, this approach does not recognize the social inequalities that are a result of these rewards. These inequalities are usually interpreted as natural and even necessary to support professional work. Because it does not deal critically with the social and economic consequences of professionalization, the process approach has been criticized as "a distortion of reality because it neglects a historical explanation which indicates that any given reward structure is the result of arrogation by groups with the power to secure their claims....". That is, the process approach does not seek to understand the professions in terms of their power in society. By failing to account for the processes by which professions gain and use their power and authority, it does not explain how occupations can come to be viewed as more professionalized. Friedson concludes that the difficulties encountered in using the static and process approaches to define a profession stem from the same fundamental problem. Both attempt to treat a profession "as if it were generic concept with particularistic roots in those industrial nations that are strongly influenced by Anglo-American institutions".

Several theorists argue that occupations in England and the United States have sought to be classified as professions since the late nineteenth century, whereas in western Europe, and even more so in eastern Europe, this activity has been nearly nonexistent. Friedson notes that the newer occupations of Europe "did not seek classification as professions to gain status and justify a market shelter; such an umbrella title inputting special institutional characteristics to them was not employed to distinguish them". Rather, the status and security of these occupations were gained by other means, such as protections provided by their governments.

Instead of striving to find a scientific concept that would apply to a wide variety of settings, several analysts have concluded that any profession is a "folk concept" that is historically and nationally specific. This approach contrasts dramatically with both static and process approaches and that no set of criteria is necessarily associated with it. There are only those occupations which are commonly regarded by the general public as professions and those which are not. As Becker argues: "Such a definition takes as central the fact that 'profession' is an honorific title...a collective symbol and one that is highly valued."

A profession is determined by which occupations in a specific society of at a given historical time have achieved professional status and privileges. Although this approach assumes that reality and meaning are socially constructed, it emphasis that "social construction is not a random process but a political war". Relatively high degrees of social and economic rewards are accorded they winners of this war.

Professionalization is the process by which producers of special services constitute and control the market for their services. In this process, occupations attempt to negotiate the boundaries of a market for their services and establish their control over it. For this professional market to exist a distinctive commodity must be produced. Unlike industrial labor, most professions produce intangible goods in that their product is inextricably bound to the person who produces it.

Therefore, the producers themselves have to be "produced" if their products are to be given a distinctive form. In other words, professionals must be adequately trained and socialized to provide recognizably distinct services. This process has been institutionalized in the modern university, which gives professions the means to control their knowledge base as well as to award credentials certifying that practitioners possess this recognizably distinct type of knowledge. Therefore, an occupation's level of professionalization can be assessed by the extent to which and political authorities accept its credentials as necessary to provide a specific type of service. One approach to determining which occupations are accepted as professions by the public in the United States has been to use the categories developed by the federal Bureau of the Census.

Although there is some disagreement about how to use census categories, the debate has been framed in such a way as to produce a least-restricted and a most-restricted approach to defining professional occupations. By presenting both of these approaches, the range of occupations that might be considered as clientele for continuing education for the professions can be delimited. Much of the literature on census definitions has used the categories as they were defined in the 1970 census. Attention was focused on two major categories: (1) professional, technical, and kindred workers and (2) managers and administers, except farm workers. Some definitions in the literature use all of the occupations in both categories to represent the professions. Some use "new class" theory to identify the existence of a "professional-managerial class", while others attempt to formalize the perceptions of the general public. These definitions are the least restricted ones commonly used to identify professions in the census data.

Some assumptions must be made when extrapolating these definitions to the most recent census figures, because these two categories were rearranged for the 1980 census. In that census a new category was created: managerial and professional speciality. This classification combined the two previous categories, except that technical occupations were moved to another major category. Because the technical occupations have been used in much of the literature, they are included here.

Applying the least-restricted definition to the 1986 census figures produced an estimated of nearly 30 million professionals in the United States. Some of the more populous occupations, totaling over 1 million practitioners, are accountants and auditors, engineers, registered nurses, teachers, and health technologists and technicians. This collection of occupations made up 27 percent of the employed work force in 1986. In comparison to the total work force, of which 44.4 percent were women, women made up 43.8 percent of the professions. Friedson criticizes this broad definition of the professions because of the great heterogeneity in these census categories in terms of educational background, income, and prestige. In its place he offers a more restrictive definition of the professions. For many of these occupations, particularly in the "executive, administrative, and managerial" category, very few had training or educational requirements that were mandatory. He argues that to be able to identify a reasonably homogeneous group of occupations as professional, a more restrictive criterion is necessary. Friedson proposes that for an occupation to be classified as a profession, some amount of higher education must be a prerequisite to employment.

The rationale is that "formal knowledge creates qualification for particular jobs, from which others who lack such qualification are routinely excluded. Such a circumstances is likely to mean that those occupations have developed a coherent organization....that succeeds in carving out a labor-market shelter.....". Using this criterion, most of the occupations in the "professional specialty" category are included, except for "writers, artists, entertainers, and athletes." Some of the occupations command high prestige and income, such as law and medicine, while others score relatively low in these areas, such as school teaching.

Nevertheless, whether high or low in prestige, they have almost a complete labor-market monopoly for their services. In the "executive, managerial, and administrative: category, only three occupations are actually professions, according to Friedson: school administrators, including principles and superintendents; health administrators; and accountants. In the technical category, only health, engineering, and science technicians are included; airline pilots, computer programmers, and legal assistants are excluded. These occupations are not considered a profession, according to Friedson, because working in them does not depend on possessing higher education credentials. Applying this more restrictive criterion produces an estimate of 16.2 million professionals in the United States, almost 14 million fewer than produced by the least-restrictive definition. Without a doubt, professions are an important social reality in American society. While there is no agreement on which occupations constitute that reality, we know its parameters. Somewhere between 16 and 30 million people in this country given the label of professional by the general public. This book is devoted to the practice of continuing education for this group of occupations.

In the rapid growth of continuing education, most educators have relied for guidance and models on the distinctive knowledge base and structures of a particular professional group. For example, most physicians, accountants, and lawyers would claim that continuing education should keep them up to data, a concept that is consistent with their preservice training in which they were given large amounts of information to remember for application in their practice setting. By relying on preprofessional training, each profession naturally concludes that its continuing education programs are unique to its own profession.

Mmany people have noted the similarities of the continuing education efforts of individual professions in terms of goals, processes, and issues. Thus, the concept of "continuing professional education" begin to be used in the late 1960s to describe an identifiable field of study and practice. The early advocates for this *comparative approach* were adult and continuing educators who were struck by the similarities in the educational processes used by the different professions with which they worked. Houle's comparative study of seventeen professions convinced him that "certain dominant conceptions guide all of them as they turn to the task of educating their members and that they tend to use essentially the same kinds of facilities, techniques, and thought processes".

The most important rationale for this movement is that the study of similarities across the professions can yield a fresh exchange of ideas, practices, and solutions to common problems. The comparative approach to continuing education for the profession has a base in the literature as well as in the social organization of educators. Several books, numerous articles, and many conference reports have been published on the topic of continuing professional education.

The way in which professional organizations organize themselves reflects an increasing awareness of continuing professional education. For example, two major associations of adult educators have specialized divisions devoted to continuing professional education. Finally, many graduate programs in adult and continuing education have a course or sequence of courses devoted to the special knowledge, skills, and issues necessary for effective practice in continuing professional education.

Continuing educators see professionals as learners and as participants as they develop and evaluate programs, which they do within an institutional context and a particular ethical framework. Because these elements operate simultaneously in most practice situations, they must be synthesized into a coherent whole to understand and to improve practice. In this chapter these various elements are synthesized into a unified picture of effective practice in continuing professional education. The purpose is to offer a comprehensive statement of what constitutes effective practice, thereby providing the criteria to evaluate and improve current efforts in continuing professional education. These criteria may be used to evaluate individual or collective activities of many continuing educators working with any of the professional groups identified.

The identification and analysis of the elements of effective practice flow from the assumption that continuing educators are engaged in a form of professional practice. Seven when program development was described as a form of professional work. This premise is now made explicit in order to explore its implications. The foundations of this exploration are the discussions of professional practice and knowledge. Thus, an understanding of effective practice for continuing professional educators should be consistent with the view of effectiveness in all forms of professional practice.

The functionalist, conflict, and critical viewpoint provide three fundamentally different understandings of professional practice. It was argued that the critical viewpoint offers the most accurate understanding of professional practice and should form the foundation of understanding continuing professional educators' practice. In choosing the critical viewpoint the functionalist and conflict viewpoints were rejected because they offer incomplete descriptions of practice.

Functionalist prescriptions for effective practice offer suggestions for good practice in such areas as assessing needs, developing objectives, assessing learning outcomes, and administrating institutional units. These prescriptions are generally in the form of guidelines or principles that are to be applied to situations faced by continuing educators. Take, for example, that shibboleth of good practice, assessing the needs of learners. The principle is often stated something like this: Sponsors of continuing education programs should utilize systematic processes to define and analyze the issues or problems of individuals, groups, and organizations for the purpose of determining learning needs. While this may seem like a worthwhile goal for practice, it offers little in the way of guidance to practitioners because it ignores the crucial element of institutional context.

To be sure, there is no shortage of statements of good practice that provide what must seem a rather obvious list of things continuing educators ought to be able to do. However, the existence of such lists assumes that there are standard contexts and problems to which these principles can be applied. Herein lies the fatal flaw, as discussed, continuing educators work in a variety of different situations that make radically different demands on their skills, knowledge, and judgment.

One of the fundamental problems in conceiving of effective practice as the application of principles to situations is that each principle means different things and emerges as different practices in varying contexts. A major reason, then, that continuing educators reject textbook prescriptions for exemplary practice is that the principles are either vacuous or limited, or both. To illustrate these points, take the example in which the continuing educator is planning a program for engineers on new techniques for designing nuclear power plants. The question to answer is: What would effective practice look like in terms of assessing the needs for this program?

An important consideration in answering this question is the type of institution in which the continuing educator works. The context of a university continuing education unit provides a different set of constraints and opportunities for the educator than the power plant does for the training director. For example, the training director has direct access to the learners themselves, as well as records of their performance. Another consideration is the level of resources that the educator has available to conduct the needs assessment. Suppose the university continuing educator responds to a request from the training director for a program on the newest techniques in designing power plants. The educator knows that the training director did not conduct a systematic needs assessment and that no university resources are available to conduct one. Should his practice be judged as ineffective in this situation? What criteria would be used to do so? The critical viewpoint asserts that practice cannot be understood as the application of standardized principles to well-formed problems because most situations faced by continuing educators are characterized by uniqueness, uncertainty, or value conflict.

Like other professionals, continuing educators must make choices about the nature of the problem to be solved as well as how to solve it. Because continuing educators are continually making choices, as opposed to simply applying principles, the critical viewpoint stresses the need to be aware of the range of choices open to educators and the ways in which these can be made. The critical viewpoint provides a framework within which to describe effective practice in continuing professional education. It offers a rich account of practice and one that can help continuing educators to improve their work.

Continuing educators' practice must be rooted in a coherent account of its ethical, contextual, and epistemological bases. All of these bases of practice are interconnected and are implicit in all forms of practice in which continuing educators engage. Because they seek to change individuals through their programs, continuing professional educators, like all educators, are engaged in a normative enterprise. Any attempt to change professionals is based on ideals of what they ought to be, to know, to do, or to feel. These ideals are rooted in continuing educators' beliefs about the goodness or rightness of the new course of action. Herein lies the ethical nature of practice, for educators continually make choices, often implicitly, about the ideals toward which their activities are directed. Therefore, practice can be judged as effective only with respect to a particular ethical framework, and it can be judged as ineffective if it is inconsistent with the tenants of the framework by which it is being evaluated. Many continuing professional educators act as if there is consensus about the proper ends of professional practice. As a result, there is rarely any discussion of the ethical dimensions of their practice.

Continuing educators are often blinded to the ethical implications of their work by the homogeneous value orientations of the environments in which they work. They are often unaware that they make ethical choices in their practice because everyone who may be involved in a particular situation agrees with those choices. Stripped of this ethical understanding, continuing educators are limited to using a paratechnical language to describe their practice, using words such as needs assessment, performance objective, collaboration, and teaching style. This provides at least a partial explanation for the current dominance of the functionalist understanding of professional practice. In all professions there are differing, if not conflicting, ethical frameworks that guide the work of practioners.

Every educative activity for which continuing educators have responsibility is a statement about the need for a particular form of technical knowledge, as well as a statement about the proper ends of professional practice. The ethical questions that are central to educational practice are: Why should professionals have this knowledge? To what ends will this knowledge be put? and What model of the learner should guide educational decisions? The most important decisions continuing educators must make in order to answer these questions are: Who should decide on the content of the activity? and On the basis of what criteria? These ethical choices are not some abstract ideal, but are embedded in the very fabric of practice. Let us return to the continuing engineering education example in which the training director has asked the university continuing educator for a program on the newest techniques in designing nuclear power plants. By agreeing to deliver this program, the educator has made a series of ethical choices. For example, he believes that building power plants is a good thing and that the engineers need new knowledge to build them. He may not acknowledge having made these choices; instead, he might say he is basing his decision to offer the program on the need to generate income for the university continuing education unit.

However, he cannot deny that the content of the program is consistent with a particular ideal about what society needs. His practice would be seen as effective if one agreed with this ideal and if the engineers attended the program and learned the new engineering techniques. However, his practice would be seen as ineffective if one did not agree with this ideal; for example, if participation in the program facilitates the goal of building nuclear power plants, and if one were opposed to nuclear power, then this practice would be seen as ineffective.

Our understanding of continuing education practice is impoverished by not discussing its ethical dimensions. Ethical understanding is central to the practice of all professionals and is an important criterion by which decisions are made in many situations. If continuing educators are to adequately understand and improve their practice, its ethical dimensions must be made explicit in the context of own practical knowledge, as well as in the ongoing of good practice in the continuing education literature. Continuing education practice is not conducted in a laboratory where all conditions are controlled except for the educator's actions. If this were true it would be reasonable to construct a description of ideal practices, the completion of which would produce specified results.

However, practice is always conducted in a context composed of varying personalities, shifting expectations, conflicting goals, and limited resources. Because continuing educators' practice is rooted in particular sets of circumstances, it would be inappropriate to judge their efforts against some fixed ideal of good practice. Rather, to know whether practice is effective it must be judged by what is best in a given set of circumstances. Excellent practice cannot be characterized by a discrete set of knowledge of skills, but rather by an understanding of why educators do what they do when they do it. At the root of practice is not measurable techniques but judgment, which is itself a from of knowledge. The primary context for continuing educators is provided by the institutional setting in which they practice.

Continuing educators are not independent agents developing educative activities in ways they alone believe to be the most appropriate. Rather, their concepts of a target audience, how best to serve it, and what resources are available are conditioned by their particular institutional contexts. Their work is conducted within a discretionary framework set up by the goals and resources of the agency in which they work. There are four principal types of institutional contexts in which continuing professional education is provided. The continuing education unit in which practitioners work will have different functions depending on the type of institution in which it is located. Thus, its effectiveness will be judged in different ways. For example, many employing agencies use continuing education to improve professionals' performance, while others use it to generate income. Some functions may not seem ideal and may even contradict an educator's vision of what constitutes effective practice.

Within an institutional context, these different functions help to define the circumstances within which educators practice. The contextual relativity of practice does not mean that all practice is equally good. It dies mean that practice can only be judged against what is best under the circumstances in which it occurs. Returning to the continuing engineering education example, let us ask whether the university-based continuing educator should have assessed the learning needs of the target audience. Let us assume that the training director asks for a program on the newest techniques of nuclear power plant design. To whether and what kind of needs assessment is required in this situation, more information is required. That alone illustrates the contextually relevant nature of the decision. It is easy to conceive of a set of circumstances in which the educator should have done a systematic needs assessment but did not.

Perhaps a course is taught on techniques that cannot be implemented in the engineers; work setting. This continuing educator clearly can be judged as having engaged in ineffective. It is possible to develop guidelines that can serve as orienting principles for effective practice. However, these guidelines must be *models of* practice in the sense that are taken from studies of actual practice. The guidelines will prove useless if they are *models for* continuing practice, in the sense of prescriptions of how educators ought to conduct themselves regardless of the specific context. If guidelines are to be used to judge practice, evaluated. Context is not an adjunct to understanding effective practice; rather, it is woven into the very fabric of practice. To fully explain effective practice, continuing educators must be able to describe how they do what they do. This description provides an understanding of the epistemological basis of their practice. The question that is of central concern here is: "What kind of knowledge or knowing characterizes effective practice? Another way to say this is: What does one need to know to be an effective practitioner? Schon has answered these questions by offering an epistemology of professional artistry.

An epistemology that can only offer an account of the declarative knowledge possessed by continuing educators is inadequate as a tool for understanding the complexity of practice. This type of epistemology does not adequately describe the forms of knowledge that distinguish the excellent educator from the merely adequate, or in Benner's terms, the expert from the notice. For example, many expert continuing educators cannot describe any one of the planning frameworks, whereas many novices can describe them in great detail. A more appropriate epistemology is needed to connect continuing educators' plans, techniques, ideals, and knowledge to the real judgments made in the unique, uncertain, and changing contexts of practice. Schon responds to this need by suggesting that two forms of knowing are central to effective practice: knowing-in-action and reflection-in-action.

In contrast to the epistemology that views practice as the application of knowledge, Schon assumes that continuing educators' knowing is in their actions. Many of their spontaneous actions do not stem from a rule or plan they were conscious of before their action. That is, continuing educators constantly make judgments for which they cannot state a rule or theory. In many cases this knowing-in-action does not solve a particular problem because the situations faced by continuing educators are unique, uncertain, or marked by conflicting values. Therefore, they need to construct the situation to make it solvable. The ability to do this, to reflect-in-action, is the core of effective practice.

The continuing educator's goal is to change this situation into a determinate one, one in which he is relatively certain about the correct course of action. Based on past experience, the educator has built up a repertoire of examples and understandings of situations like this. This repertoire of practical knowledge is used to make sense of the current situation, to see it as some prior situation in which his actions were successful. Once the current situation is framed in such a way as to make it solvable, the educator would probably conduct an on-the-spot experiment to test its appropriateness. This might be done during conversations with others, such as the training director or the head of the continuing education unit, to determine their satisfaction with the potential course of action. If effective practice is not to be utterly context-dependent, its epistemology must account for a kind of knowing that can be used in most or all situations.

Reflection-in-action is such an epistemology. Its use is a key to understanding effective practice in continuing professional education. This epistemology describes how continuing educators make decisions in areas such as developing and evaluating educative activities, fostering participation in such activities, and forming interrorganizational relationships. For instance, the entire program development process may be viewed as a form of reflection-in-action in which educators are continually framing ambiguous situations so as to make them solvable.

The interrelationship of the ethical, contextual, and epistemological bases of effective practice can be articulated as follows: Effective practice in continuing professional education means making the best judgment in a specific context and for a specified ethical framework. These judgments, which are made as a result of knowing-in-action and reflection-in-action, are evaluated as best against what is possible in the specific circumstances in which they occur and what is desirable within a particular ethical framework. To improve practice, the abilities of continuing educators to make their "best judgments" must be facilitated. How can the ability to judge be facilitated by those who train continuing professional educators and by those educators themselves? To improve suggests a process of learning and thus, as discussed, this facilitation must be based on a model of continuing educators as learners. As with other professionals, it is essential to specify how they know and how they acquire this knowledge.

Continuing educators' knowing-in-action is acquired from their reflection-in-action undertaken in the indeterminate zones of practice and from the theory and research developed in continuing education and other fields. Reflection-in-action generates new knowledge by contributing new examples, understandings, and actions to educators' already existing repertoires. The acquisition of reflection-in-action appears to be less straight forward than the acquisition of knowing-in-action. Continuing educators reflect-in-action as matter of course in their everyday life and use these same processes in their practice.

However, to improve this ability continuing educators must reflect on their reflection-in-action by describing what they have done. As they can more consciously describe how they reflect and what that teaches them, continuing educators can more readily employ that form of knowing in new situations. Practice can also be improved by participating in formal educational programs. In formal educational settings, such as conferences, workshops, and graduate programs in continuing education, declarative knowledge about continuing professional education is most often stressed. To increase the likelihood that this knowledge will be incorporated into continuing educators' practice, it must be presented in such a way that continuing educators will use it to reflect on their own practice situations in the presence of the instructor. This type of process can build the educators' repertories of practical knowledge. Experientially based methods, such as case studies, simulations, and role plays, are useful for developing this kind of knowledge.

Practice can also be improved in these settings by helping continuing educators increase their ability to reflect-in-action. Schon's suggestive account of how this process can be coached, but not taught, is useful. Faculty in graduate programs and workshop presenters, for example, can assume the role of coaches by explaining how they would perform in given practice situations and by reflecting with participants on the ways in which they approach similar situations. The primary responsibility for improving practice in work settings falls to continuing educators themselves.

The major strategy is for continuing educators to see themselves as researchers of their own practice. Their goal should be to understand how they frame problems and their own roles, to uncover their own practical knowledge and the processes by which they use that knowledge. Individual reflections on practice can be fostered by institutionally supported activities, such as staff meetings where practitioners discuss how their practice is affected by the constraints of their organizational settings. A tremendous amount of practical knowledge generally exists in a collection of continuing educators at the workplace, which unfortunately is often not fully tapped by others. Supervisors often have a wealth of uncovered practical knowledge among their staff that is not systematically made available to everyone. Finding ways to identify and share this knowledge would offer many ways to improve the practice of individual educators, as well as the collective work of a given continuing education unit. Continuing professional education researchers also have a role to play in improving practice.

Their theoretical formulations and empirical studies have an important role in improving practice. However, much more effort and resources need to be expended in these efforts in order to improve practice. More research and development units need to be developed, such as the one at Pennsylvania State University, where a collection of researchers focuses on a particular area of continuing professional education. This could be done by any one of the four principal providers of continuing professional education or through the collaborative efforts of several providers. Some of their work should begin to focus on continuing educators' practical knowledge and the processes these practitioners use to make the best judgments, the effect of context on these judgments, and the ethical frameworks in which these judgments are made. Researchers can do this by examining their own practice as continuing educators or by working collaboratively with practitioners. Benner, Elbaz, and Schon have offered useful ways to conduct this type of research.

Although the responsibility for improving practice must rest ultimately with individual continuing educators, the achievement of this goal can be facilitated by individuals who see themselves as part of the collective enterprise of continuing professional education. Continuing educators see professionals as learners and as participants as they develop and evaluate programs, which they do within an institutional context and a particular ethical framework. Because these elements operate simultaneously in most practice situations, they must be synthesized into a coherent whole to understand and to improve practice. In this chapter these various elements are synthesized into a unified picture of effective practice in continuing professional education.

The purpose is to offer a comprehensive statement of what constitutes effective practice, thereby providing the criteria to evaluate and improve current efforts in continuing professional education. These criteria may be used to evaluate individual or collective activities of many continuing educators working with any of the professional groups identified. The identification and analysis of the elements of effective practice flow from the assumption that continuing educators are engaged in a form of professional practice. Seven when program development was described as a form of professional work. This premise is now made explicit in order to explore its implications.

An understanding of effective practice for continuing professional educators should be consistent with the view of effectiveness in all forms of professional practice. The functionalist, conflict, and critical viewpoint provide three fundamentally different understandings of professional practice. It was argued that the critical viewpoint offers the most accurate understanding of professional practice and should form the foundation of understanding continuing professional educators' practice. In choosing the critical viewpoint the functionalist and conflict viewpoints were rejected because they offer incomplete descriptions of practice. Functionalist prescriptions for effective practice offer suggestions for good practice in such areas as assessing needs, developing objectives, assessing learning outcomes, and administrating institutional units. These prescriptions are generally in the form of guidelines or principles that are to be applied to situations faced by continuing educators. Take, for example, that shibboleth of good practice, assessing the needs of learners. The principle is often stated something like this: Sponsors of continuing education programs should utilize systematic processes to define and analyze the issues or problems of individuals, groups, and organizations for the purpose of determining learning needs. While this may seem like a worthwhile goal for practice, it offers little in the way of guidance to practitioners because it ignores the crucial element of institutional context. To be sure, there is no shortage of statements of good practice that provide what must seem a rather obvious list of things continuing educators ought to be able to do.

The existence of such lists assumes that there are standard contexts and problems to which these principles can be applied. Herein lies the fatal flaw, as discussed, continuing educators work in a variety of different situations that make radically different demands on their skills, knowledge, and judgment. One of the fundamental problems in conceiving of effective practice as the application of principles to situations is that each principle means different things and emerges as different practices in varying contexts. A major reason, then, that continuing educators reject textbook prescriptions for exemplary practice is that the principles are either vacuous or limited, or both. To illustrate these points, take the example in which the continuing educator is planning a program for engineers on new techniques for designing nuclear power plants. The question to answer is: What would effective practice look like in terms of assessing the needs for this program?

An important consideration in answering this question is the type of institution in which the continuing educator works. The context of a university continuing education unit provides a different set of constraints and opportunities for the educator than the power plant does for the training director. For example, the training director has direct access to the learners themselves, as well as records of their performance. Another consideration is the level of resources that the educator has available to conduct the needs assessment. Suppose the university continuing educator responds to a request from the training director for a program on the newest techniques in designing power plants.

The educator knows that the training director did not conduct a systematic needs assessment and that no university resources are available to conduct one. Should his practice be judged as ineffective in this situation? What criteria would be used to do so? Even this brief example should be sufficient to point out the shortcomings of the functionalist understanding of continuing education practice. Instead, continuing professional educators must operate within the critical viewpoint in order to provide a comprehensive understanding of continuing education practice and the means to improve it. The critical viewpoint asserts that practice cannot be understood as the application of standardized principles to well-formed problems because most situations faced by continuing educators are characterized by uniqueness, uncertainty, or value conflict.

Like other professionals, continuing educators must make choices about the nature of the problem to be solved as well as how to solve it. Because continuing educators are continually making choices, as opposed to simply applying principles, the critical viewpoint stresses the need to be aware of the range of choices open to educators and the ways in which these can be made. The critical viewpoint provides a framework within which to describe effective practice in continuing professional education. It offers a rich account of practice and one that can help continuing educators to improve their work. Continuing educators' practice must be rooted in a coherent account of its ethical, contextual, and epistemological bases. All of these bases of practice are interconnected and are implicit in all forms of practice in which continuing educators engage. Because they seek to change individuals through their programs, continuing professional educators, like all educators, are engaged in a normative enterprise.

Any attempt to change professionals is based on ideals of what they ought to be, to know, to do, or to feel. These ideals are rooted in continuing educators' beliefs about the goodness or rightness of the new course of action. Herein lies the ethical nature of practice, for educators continually make choices, often implicitly, about the ideals toward which their activities are directed. Therefore, practice can be judged as effective only with respect to a particular ethical framework, and it can be judged as ineffective if it is inconsistent with the tenants of the framework by which it is being evaluated. Many continuing professional educators act as if there is consensus about the proper ends of professional practice.

As a result, there is rarely any discussion of the ethical dimensions of their practice. Continuing educators are often blinded to the ethical implications of their work by the homogeneous value orientations of the environments in which they work. They are often unaware that they make ethical choices in their practice because everyone who may be involved in a particular situation agrees with those choices. Stripped of this ethical understanding, continuing educators are limited to using a paratechnical language to describe their practice, using words such as needs assessment, performance objective, collaboration, and teaching style. This provides at least a partial explanation for the current dominance of the functionalist understanding of professional practice. In all professions there are differing, if not conflicting, ethical frameworks that guide the work of practioners. In the same way, continuing educators' practice is embedded in a variety of ethical frameworks.

Every educative activity for which continuing educators have responsibility is a statement about the need for a particular form of technical knowledge, as well as a statement about the proper ends of professional practice. The ethical questions that are central to educational practice are: Why should professionals have this knowledge? To what ends will this knowledge be put? and What model of the learner should guide educational decisions? The most important decisions continuing educators must make in order to answer these questions are: Who should decide on the content of the activity? and On the basis of what criteria? These ethical choices are not some abstract ideal, but are embedded in the very fabric of practice. Let us return to the continuing engineering education example in which the training director has asked the university continuing educator for a program on the newest techniques in designing nuclear power plants.

By agreeing to deliver this program, the educator has made a series of ethical choices. For example, he believes that building power plants is a good thing and that the engineers need new knowledge to build them. He may not acknowledge having made these choices; instead, he might say he is basing his decision to offer the program on the need to generate income for the university continuing education unit. However, he cannot deny that the content of the program is consistent with a particular ideal about what society needs. His practice would be seen as effective if one agreed with this ideal and if the engineers attended the program and learned the new engineering techniques. However, his practice would be seen as ineffective if one did not agree with this ideal; for example, if participation in the program facilitates the goal of building nuclear power plants, and if one were opposed to nuclear power, then this practice would be seen as ineffective.

Our understanding of continuing education practice is impoverished by not discussing its ethical dimensions. Ethical understanding is central to the practice of all professionals and is an important criterion by which decisions are made in many situations. If continuing educators are to adequately understand and improve their practice, its ethical dimensions must be made explicit in the context of own practical knowledge, as well as in the ongoing of good practice in the continuing education literature.

Continuing education practice is not conducted in a laboratory where all conditions are controlled except for the educator's actions. If this were true it would be reasonable to construct a description of ideal practices, the completion of which would produce specified results. As we know, however, practice is always conducted in a context composed of varying personalities, shifting expectations, conflicting goals, and limited resources. Because continuing educators' practice is rooted in particular sets of circumstances, it would be inappropriate to judge their efforts against some fixed ideal of good practice.

Rather, to know whether practice is effective it must be judged by what is best in a given set of circumstances. Excellent practice cannot be characterized by a discrete set of knowledge of skills, but rather by an understanding of why educators do what they do when they do it. At the root of practice is not measurable techniques but judgment, which is itself a from of knowledge. The primary context for continuing educators is provided by the institutional setting in which they practice. Continuing educators are not independent agents developing educative activities in ways they alone believe to be the most appropriate. Rather, their concepts of a target audience, how best to serve it, and what resources are available are conditioned by their particular institutional contexts. Their work is conducted within a discretionary framework set up by the goals and resources of the agency in which they work.

There are four principal types of institutional contexts in which continuing professional education is provided. The continuing education unit in which practitioners work will have different functions depending on the type of institution in which it is located. Thus, its effectiveness will be judged in different ways. For example, many employing agencies use continuing education to improve professionals' performance, while others use it to generate income. Some functions may not seem ideal and may even contradict an educator's vision of what constitutes effective practice. Yet, within an institutional context, these different functions help to define the circumstances within which educators practice.

The contextual relativity of practice does not mean that all practice is equally good. It dies mean that practice can only be judged against what is best under the circumstances in which it occurs. Returning to the continuing engineering education example, let us ask whether the university-based continuing educator should have assessed the learning needs of the target audience. Let us assume that the training director asks for a program on the newest techniques of nuclear power plant design. To whether and what kind of needs assessment is required in this situation, more information is required. That alone illustrates the contextually relevant nature of the decision. It is easy to conceive of a set of circumstances in which the educator should have done a systematic needs assessment but did not. Perhaps a course is taught on techniques that cannot be implemented in the engineers; work setting. This continuing educator clearly can be judged as having engaged in ineffective. It is possible to develop guidelines that can serve as orienting principles for effective practice. However, these guidelines must be *models of* practice in the sense that are taken from studies of actual practice. The guidelines will prove useless if they are *models for* continuing practice, in the sense of prescriptions of how educators ought to conduct themselves regardless of the specific context. If guidelines are to be used to judge practice, evaluated. Context is not an adjunct to understanding effective practice; rather, it is woven into the very fabric of practice.

To fully explain effective practice, continuing educators must be able to describe how they do what they do. This description provides an understanding of the epistemological basis of their practice. The question that is of central concern here is: "What kind of knowledge or knowing characterizes effective practice? Another way to say this is: What does one need to know to be an effective practitioner? Schon has answered these questions by offering an epistemology of professional artistry.

An epistemology that can only offer an account of the declarative knowledge possessed by continuing educators is inadequate as a tool for understanding the complexity of practice. The program planning frameworks does not adequately describe the forms of knowledge that distinguish the excellent educator from the merely adequate, or in Benner's terms, the expert from the notice. For example, many expert continuing educators cannot describe any one of the planning frameworks, whereas many novices can describe them in great detail. A more appropriate epistemology is needed to connect continuing educators' plans, techniques, ideals, and knowledge to the real judgments made in the unique, uncertain, and changing contexts of practice. Schon responds to this need by suggesting that two forms of knowing are central to effective practice: knowing-in-action and reflection-in-action. In contrast to the epistemology that views practice as the application of knowledge, Schon assumes that continuing educators' knowing is in their actions.

Many of their spontaneous actions do not stem from a rule or plan they were conscious of before their action. That is, continuing educators constantly make judgments for which they cannot state a rule or theory. In many cases this knowing-in-action does not solve a particular problem because the situations faced by continuing educators are unique, uncertain, or marked by conflicting values. Therefore, they need to construct the situation to make it solvable. The ability to do this, to reflect-in-action, is the core of effective practice.

Returning to our example, how did the university-based continuing educator decide whether or not to conduct a needs assessment for the continuing engineering education program? If Schon's analysis is correct, the continuing educator would make the best judgment under the circumstances if he were highly skilled at reflecting-in-action. What would this process look like? The assumption is that this is an indeterminate situation because it is not immediately obvious that a needs assessment should be conducted. The continuing educator's goal is to change this situation into a determinate one, one in which he is relatively certain about the correct course of action. Based on past experience, the educator has built up a repertoire of examples and understandings of situations like this. This repertoire of practical knowledge is used to make sense of the current situation, to see it as some prior situation in which his actions were successful.

Once the current situation is framed in such a way as to make it solvable, the educator would probably conduct an on-the-spot experiment to test its appropriateness. This might be done during conversations with others, such as the training director or the head of the continuing education unit, to determine their satisfaction with the potential course of action. If effective practice is not to be utterly context-dependent, its epistemology must account for a kind of knowing that can be used in most or all situations.

Reflection-in-action is such an epistemology. Its use is a key to understanding effective practice in continuing professional education. This epistemology describes how continuing educators make decisions in areas such as developing and evaluating educative activities, fostering participation in such activities, and forming inter-organizational relationships. For instance, the entire program development process may be viewed as a form of reflection-in-action in which educators are continually framing ambiguous situations so as to make them solvable.

The interrelationship of the ethical, contextual, and epistemological bases of effective practice can be articulated as follows: Effective practice in continuing professional education means making the best judgment in a specific context and for a specified ethical framework. These judgments, which are made as a result of knowing-in-action and reflection-in-action, are evaluated as best against what is possible in the specific circumstances in which they occur and what is desirable within a particular ethical framework. To improve practice, the abilities of continuing educators to make their "best judgments" must be facilitated. How can the ability to judge be facilitated by those who train continuing professional educators and by those educators themselves? To improve suggests a process of learning and thus, as discussed, this facilitation must be based on a model of continuing educators as learners.

As with other professionals, it is essential to specify how they know and how they acquire this knowledge. Continuing educators' knowing-in-action is acquired from their reflection-in-action undertaken in the indeterminate zones of practice and from the theory and research developed in continuing education and other fields. Reflection-in-action generates new knowledge by contributing new examples, understandings, and actions to educators' already existing repertoires. The acquisition of reflection-in-action appears to be less straight forward than the acquisition of knowing-in-action.

Continuing educators reflect-in-action as matter of course in their everyday life and use these same processes in their practice. However, to improve this ability continuing educators must reflect on their reflection-in-action by describing what they have done. As they can more consciously describe how they reflect and what that teaches them, continuing educators can more readily employ that form of knowing in new situations.

Practice can also be improved by participating in formal educational programs. In formal educational settings, such as conferences, workshops, and graduate programs in continuing education, declarative knowledge about continuing professional education is most often stressed. To increase the likelihood that this knowledge will be incorporated into continuing educators' practice, it must be presented in such a way that continuing educators will use it to reflect on their own practice situations in the presence of the instructor. This type of process can build the educators' repertories of practical knowledge. Experientially based methods, such as case studies, simulations, and role plays, are useful for developing this kind of knowledge. Practice can also be improved in these settings by helping continuing educators increase their ability to reflect-in-action.

Schon's suggestive account of how this process can be coached, but not taught, is useful. Faculty in graduate programs and workshop presenters, for example, can assume the role of coaches by explaining how they would perform in given practice situations and by reflecting with participants on the ways in which they approach similar situations. The primary responsibility for improving practice in work settings falls to continuing educators themselves.

The major strategy is for continuing educators to see themselves as researchers of their own practice. Their goal should be to understand how they frame problems and their own roles, to uncover their own practical knowledge and the processes by which they use that knowledge. Individual reflections on practice can be fostered by institutionally supported activities, such as staff meetings where practitioners discuss how their practice is affected by the constraints of their organizational settings. A tremendous amount of practical knowledge generally exists in a collection of continuing educators at the workplace, which unfortunately is often not fully tapped by others. Supervisors often have a wealth of uncovered practical knowledge among their staff that is not systematically made available to everyone.

Finding ways to identify and share this knowledge would offer many ways to improve the practice of individual educators, as well as the collective work of a given continuing education unit. Continuing professional education researchers also have a role to play in improving practice. Their theoretical formulations and empirical studies have an important role in improving practice. However, much more effort and resources need to be expended in these efforts in order to improve practice.

More research and development units need to be developed, such as the one at Pennsylvania State University, where a collection of researchers focuses on a particular area of continuing professional education. This could be done by any one of the four principal providers of continuing professional education or through the collaborative efforts of several providers. Some of their work should begin to focus on continuing educators' practical knowledge and the processes these practitioners use to make the best judgments, the effect of context on these judgments, and the ethical frameworks in which these judgments are made. Researchers can do this by examining their own practice as continuing educators or by working collaboratively with practitioners. Benner, Elbaz, and Schon have offered useful ways to conduct this type of research.

Continuing professional educators work almost exclusively in the context of institutional settings. Although these settings vary in size, complexity, and purpose, they have something in common that the above anecdote vividly illustrates: The institutional context is a major, if not *the* major, determinant of continuing educators' understanding of effective practice. Each organization shapes in powerful ways what continuing educators do and how they do it. For example, the conference coordinator in a for-profit continuing medical education organization knows that she will be judged by the number of conference registrations and the net profit from her educational programs. Her institutional context offers clear and explicit guidelines for her vision of effective practice. To the extent possible, she will perform in ways consistent with this vision. Likewise, the human resources director in a hospital has a vision of effective practice that is shaped by the context in which he works. He knows that he will be judged by how well his programs have improved the performance of the hospital's professional staff.

There are substantive differences in how these two continuing professional educators define effective practice. The purpose of this chapter is to examine how continuing educators' practice is shaped by the institutional context. Each specific institution has a unique set of values and resources and a particular history and culture. Continuing professional educators are attentive to these characteristics and guide their practice accordingly. Although each institution is unique, groups of institutions share similar characteristics. For example, continuing professional educators in different universities encounter similar opportunities and constraints in their practice.

Universities can be considered a type of provider of continuing professional education. An overview of continuing professional education providers is followed by a discussion of their strengths and weaknesses. The major institutional issues faced by continuing professional educators are explored, along with how the particular context frames its practice regarding these issues. Educators rarely carry out their work without recognizing what other providers are doing and how other institutions may help or hinder their own practice. As a result the issue of competition and collaboration among providers has become a preoccupation of many continuing professional educators.

Where data are available, the estimates vary so wildly that one cannot trust any one estimate. Thus, in trying to determine who the major providers are, Stern's advice will have to suffice: until statistics become available, "the experience of 'old hands'... will be a major resource". There is, however, consensus in the literature that the four major providers are universities and professional schools, professional associations, employing agencies, and independent providers.

Other types of providers that are described in the literature are government, foundations, autonomous groups such as teachers' centers, and purveyors of professional supplies and equipment. Within each of the types of providers many forms and subtypes can be identified. It is impossible to estimate which types of providers are the most or the least prominent in either the number of offerings or the number of participants. Arnstein notes that while the rules are reasonably well established for counting participants in continuing higher education, 'these rules do not extend to continuing education when offered by business and professional societies..." Also, the relative importance of each type of provider varies with the individual profession.

Whereas universities are major providers in medicine and engineering, they are second to professional associations in the field of certified public accountancy and provide virtually no continuing education in the field of real estate. Thus, even if we knew how many educational programs were offered by each type of provider, it is likely that estimates would vary by profession.

The provision of continuing education by this institutional type is characterized by great diversity in annual numbers of participants, size of budget, and staff. Programs may be sponsored by professional schools, colleges, or departments, or by a university wide continuing education unit. Houle describes the various ways in which professional schools and universities relate: "There are many kinds and levels of such schools;

some are free-standing and others are parts of larger entities, often universities". A recent development is the sponsorship of these schools by corporations, such as by Arthur D. Little and the Rand Corporation. Eurich has identified eighteen such "corporate colleges." The patterns by which higher education organizes its continuing professional education function vary a great deal.

The primary difference is whether it is coordinated into a single university function or administered separately by individual professional schools. An extreme example of the latter approach is that in 1977 a major university had thirty-eight separate administrative units responsible for the provision of continuing education. A major reason that decentralization is a desirable option for professional schools is that continuing education often generates a revenue surplus, which can be used to fund other projects.

The decentralized approach is favoured by those who insist that the programming function can be performed only by individuals who are trained in the specific profession. As a consequence of this approach, continuing educators, rather than faculty or clients, tend to be the central figures in the planning process. These continuing educators usually believe they understand the problems of their profession, academically and from practice, and do not need to rely on others for programming ideas.

The centralized approach is becoming a more viable option because it can provide programming in a more efficient manner. It seems inefficient for several professional schools at the same university to establish duplicative staffs and facilities. Houle notes that general extension divisions are building up staffs of competent programmers with advanced degrees in continuing education.

In contrast to the decentralized approach, faculty members and clients have central roles in the educational planning process. Because many people with advanced degrees in continuing education do not have a background in the content area in which they are providing programs, they rely on those who do have this background. Another plus for the centralized arrangement is that more physical resources may be available, such as residential centers, audiovisual materials, and computer-assisted instruction. A hybrid of the centralized and decentralized approaches has been implemented at Pennsylvania State University, where the professional school or department is the locus of the planning effort and technical support is given by a centralized university unit.

Higher educational institutions have a number of strengths as continuing professional education providers. Because of their research orientation, universities are the primary source of knowledge for most professions. It is appropriate, then, that the faculty members who originally develop and present this information should teach it to practitioners through continuing education programs. Universities are experienced with lengthy and complex forms of instruction, as delivered in preservice training, and can provide certification for the successful completion of such instruction. Unlike other providers that deliver relatively discrete forms of instruction over a short period of time, universities are more capable of offering lengthy types of learning experiences that lead to continuing education credits.

Unlike most other providers, universities have a large resident staff whose full-time responsibility is instruction. With the decline of the school-age population many of these faculty members have insufficient numbers of preservice students and thus are able to turn their energies to the education of practicing professionals.

Another strength is that these institutions ordinarily have more abundant and readily available physical facilities than other providers, such as housing, libraries, meeting rooms, state-of-the-art equipment, and food service. The problems faced by professionals are often complex and require interdisciplinary solutions. For example, members of several professional groups may be involved in a decision to remove life-support systems from a patient.

The university is in an excellent position to provide educational programs about this issue for representatives from all of these professions because of the comprehensive makeup of its faculty. Particularly when programming is done by the centralized approach, an individual professional, such as a social worker, might attend a program that has instructors from medicine and law as well as social work. Perhaps most important is the perception by most professionals that universities are a credible source of continuing education. The perception that "quality is higher education's most important attribute" predominates even among those who believe that higher education is losing its place as a major continuing professional education provider.

Higher education has a number of weaknesses as a provider. One is that continuing professional education is not a primary function of higher education institutions. One consequence is that substantial and reliable funding is not generally available. Primarily as a result of the lack of a funding base, "the university as an institution has no independent policy and no independent set of practical guidelines in continuing professional education".

The continuing education efforts at any one institution are often uneven because they rely upon an enthusiastic committee member, the ability of the programming staff to convince faculty to teach beyond their normal teaching load, or the presence of grant monies to support special programming. Knox found that almost all income comes from fees paid by participants, which contributed to instability in the programming unit. A second consequence of being a marginal university function is that professors view continuing education as ancillary to other work and responsibilities. Knox found a lack of incentives and rewards for faculty participation in one university's continuing education effort. Yet many faculty members will conduct programs for other providers, including other universities, for higher honoraria.

Experimentation at Pennsylvania State University has found that faculty members can be encouraged to be part of their university's continuing education effort when they see promise of joint publications, collaborative research, or opportunities for recognition from their peers. Universities generally do not have the ability to link what is taught to practice. Even the continuing education representatives of higher education recognize that universities are separate from professional work settings and thus cannot reinforce what is taught as well as other providers.

A notable exception is the "practice integrated learning sequence" developed by the Temple University Office of Continuing Medical Education. This office-based educational activity incorporates the actual practice of medicine into a formal educational program, with primary focus on the quality of physicians' practice behaviors. Several other weaknesses have been cited by a prominent leader among the independent providers of continuing education.

Universities are generally limited to their own faculty and facilities; are generally insensitive to instructional quality; have only limited ideas about how to price their product; lack proper marketing expertise; have internal organizational characteristics that are not conducive to developing, marketing, and administering programs; and tend to be rooted in traditional approaches to fields of knowledge. Nowlen estimates there are at least three thousand national professional associations. Many more state and local associations either are organized independently or are affiliated with a national body. Typically each profession is represented by at least several associations, while some associations have members from several professions.

Professional associations think about and deliver continuing education in considerably different ways, depending on the number of members, the scope of purpose, and the size and structure of staff. In many cases, however, the educational program is defined as having to do with the "accreditation of professional schools or other training programs, the issuance of publications, the sponsorship of conventions and conferences, and the operation of special training programs, such as courses, conferences workshops, and other activities clearly defined as instruction". A study done in 1977 showed that nearly all associations provided some form of continuing education for their members, and about one-third sponsored certificate, licensure, or degree programs.

One of the major strengths of associations is their ability to secure a wide array of talent, especially from their membership. Other providers are usually limited to members of their own staffs. In contrast, associations include among their membership many, if not most, of the professionals in the field, who can bring a variety of points of view to the educational programming. Additionally, because of "an association's breadth of service and continuity of coverage, its educational program has a special capacity to deliver discrete and not necessarily sequential messages". Associations are best at sponsoring conferences that build on this strength, as opposed to programs that require depth of coverage over a relatively long duration. Associations also have direct access to professionals who are seeking continuing education and are usually familiar with their learning needs.

Finally, associations are able to engage in some cost-effective strategies for delivering educational programms. For example, in comparison to private enterprises, associations enjoy a nonprofit status and thus have certain financial advantages, such as reduced postage expenses. Also, programs can be replicated within the levels of an association, thus amortizing the start-up costs over a number of offerings. For example, a program developed at the national level can be used by state and local affiliates for a relatively low cost.

A major weakness of professional associations is the organizational placement of the continuing education function. The educational function is typically shared by different divisions or committees responsible for publications, conventions, and the standard type of educational programs. The effect of this practice is that the educational program division may be responsible for only a few specific programs, which may not be considered important by the membership because they can find these programs elsewhere.

Continuing educators also are often at a disadvantage when they compete for internal resources with other association divisions, such as one dealing with legislative concerns that have greater public relations value. A second weakness stems from the role of association staff in carrying out the educational function. Staff members usually cannot take the leadership in programming because they are viewed as subordinate to volunteer committees of association members. Although they would like to have a more substantive role in programming, staff are often viewed as simply "seminar schedulers". Directors of education tend to be involved in many association responsibilities, limiting their ability to take a leadership role in the program development process. When educational programming is directed by a board that changes from year to year, long-term planning or future-oriented programming suffers. Several other weaknesses stem from the nature of professional associations.

Suleiman notes that associations typically lack marketing expertise and have only a limited idea about how to price their product. Associations may lack the physical facilities, such as a meeting space and a library, that are necessary for educational ventures. Finally, Nowlen argues that associations generally do not engage in interprofessional programming because they lack the political base to use association resources to address other professions. Employers such as hospitals, social agencies, business firms, and governments offer a tremendous amount of continuing education to their employees.

While estimates of the money spent by employers on the educational function vary, a commonly accepted figure is $60 billion annually. This may be compared to the $55 billion spent by all higher education institutions in 1981-82. Although not all of this money is spent on educating professionals, a reasonable hypothesis is that more continuing professional education is offered by employers than by higher education. Shelton and Craig cite recent evidence indicating that at least half of the continuing education in health care is provided by employers, in contrast with other providers, and that "most management education is done by employers and by the training industry."

The central task of educators in employment settings is to improve participants' performance with respect to the mission of the agency. The measure of success is the extent to which the problem that gave rise to an educational program has been remedied. The employers' ability to directly assess "specific inadequacies of personal or collective service" is perhaps the greatest strength of providing education within employment settings. Unlike any other provider, professionals' performance problems can be directly assessed on a regular basis and used to determine both the need for an educational program and the extent to which the program has made a difference in the workplace. Employers have fairly explicit performance expectations, which, when not met, can provide a powerful stimulus for effective educational programming.

Continuing educators in the employment setting are in a unique position to coordinate educational strategies with the daily work of employees, thereby increasing the likelihood that what was learned in a program is applied on the job. It is possible to involve members of several professions in a learning activity to solve a particular organizational problem. A good example is the hospital setting where increasing morbidity or mortality rates are often due to the collective rather than the individual failure of physicians, nurses, and allied health staff.

Another strength from the employer's viewpoint is the relative convenience of scheduling and the minimization of lost work time due to attendance at programs outside the work-place. However, keeping participants' attention when attending an educational activity at the workplace can present several problems that stem from their proximity to their work. It is difficult for employees to maintain their focus to remain present at an educational program when they believe it is more important to attend to their work.

The relative convenience of on-site training must be balanced against the relatively higher cost. In a national study of providers of adult education and training, Anderson and Kasl found that the average cost of a "participant learning hour" was $38 for employers, compared to $5 for colleges and universities and $15 for professional associations. Payment by employers for participants' lost work time accounts for some of these cost differences; when this cost is excluded the average cost of a PLH drops to $26. The other major cost difference is that instructors' salaries are much higher for employers than for colleges and universities and associations. Because education is subservient to the main goals of the employment setting, the education function often suffers from a lack of regular and substantial support from the parent body, particularly in difficult financial situations.

Most employers of professionals do not have a senior executive in charge of education. Most often the educational function is merged with the personnel function in a human resource development office. Nowlen points out that one result of this structure is that the quality of educational decision making by employers is no more sophisticated than that of other providers. Their educational planning is likely to be far less proficient than for primary organizational goals, such as providing health care or manufacturing consumer goods.

Finally, employers can promote only a limited vision of how to solve a work-related problem through learning activities. As Nowlen notes: "The educational strategy can become as incestuous and self-deceptive as the organizational culture which developed it." The providers in this category represent a wide range of institutions and constitute a growing segment of the field. Some of these providers are operated for profit and others are nonprofit, some are cooperative self-help ventures, and some are philanthropic organizations. Research organizations and consulting firms such as Arthur D. Little, accounting firms, and manufacturers/suppliers such as IBM often use seminars and conferences to gain exposure to customers and client groups. Publishers are also moving into continuing professional education as another way to serve well-defined audiences to whom they currently provide printed materials. There are also the "privates", institutions that are organized on a free-standing basis and treat continuing professional education strictly as a business.

The greatest advantage that independent providers have is program development. Suleiman argues that they can respond quickly to learners' needs, "with good instruction free from problems of faculty involvement, committee approvals, and other political considerations". Most private organizations offer programs nationally, which enables them to amortize development costs over a number of offerings. Because of their flexibility, independent providers have pioneered new formats and methods of instruction that have subsequently been adopted by larger and better established providers of continuing education.

The independent providers' major weakness is that, in general, they lack an automatic image of quality and thus are less credible to their audiences until they demonstrate otherwise. For example, a program sponsored by a manufacturer is generally suspect until it is clear that the educational format is not simply being used to promote products. Lacking a credible image is a problem partly because continuing professional education is a field that is easy to enter.

Many independent providers have exploited either professionals' desire to learn or their need to meet recertification requirements with programs that have promised more than they delivered. However, independent providers also have the freedom to create their own image. Unlike universities, which have a deeply rooted image independent providers can develop an image that is consistent with the educational product they wish to sell.

Ironically, a common strategy used to overcome this image problem is having faculty members form higher education institutions as instructors. In about 40 percent of the direct mail brochures received from independent providers by the University of Chicago's Office of Continuing Education, the instructors were university faculty members. Because "privates" are a single-item business they are extremely sensitive to downward swings in the economy because no other part of the business can pick up the slack when relatively fewer people attend their programs. They also usually lack the facilities necessary for extensive educational programming, such as libraries and many classrooms.

One primary goal of people working in institutions is to do what they do well, whether it is producing automobiles, offering health care, or providing education. If an organization is working well, all of its subunits ill be working together toward the same ends. The educational subunit is part of this larger institutional context, and helps to determine the way its members go about their work.

Continuing professional educators are not independent agents serving their audience in ways that only they believe is appropriate. Rather, their concept of which audience to serve and how to serve it is conditioned by the demands of the parent institution as it tries to survive and prosper. Continuing professional educators must constantly be sensitive to how their effort relates to basic organizational goals. Continuing professional educators practice in different types of institutional contexts and have different educational functions.

Effectiveness is judged in different ways. Some organizations use continuing education as a means of improving the performance of professionals, others use it to generate income, and still others use it as a public relations strategy. Some of these functions are not ideal and may contradict an educator's vision about the true purpose of continuing professional education. Yet these functions are powerful determinants of effective practice. If continuing professional educators are to survive and prosper, they must keep in mind the educational goals institutionally defined as effective.

The key question is: What is the relationship of the continuing education unit to the basic purposes of the agency of which it is a part? A broad classification scheme has been used to analyze the different forms that these relationships can take in other adult education agencies. Fundamental differences flow from these relationships regarding the audience and the mission of a continuing education unit. No matter what type of agency continuing educators work in, the key leadership challenge is to position "continuing education activities so that they come to be seen as actively contributing to the attainment of institutional goals".

Darkenwald and Merriam purpose that adult educational agencies relate to the purposes of their parent organization in four different ways. Based on this scheme, continuing professional education can be the primary function of an agency, a secondary function of an educational agency, a complementary function of a quasi-educational agency, or a supportive function of a noneducational agency.

The four major types of continuing professional education providers correspond fairly well to these four orientations. However, the boundaries between orientations are somewhat blurred and there is some difficulty in classifying all institutions into one orientation or another. In the following section, these orientations are arrayed on a continuum, beginning with the one in which continuing education is the most derivative of the parent's basic operating goals, and proceeding to the one in which it is central to the agency's basic purpose.

Noneducational organizations use continuing education to enhance the achievement of their fundamental mission. For example, the basic purpose of schools is to teach children, of architectural firms to design buildings, and of hospitals to restore patients to health. In these types of settings, continuing education is more a means than an end to its parent institution's goals.

Employing agencies were characterized as using education as a means of improving their primary service or product. In these settings, professionals' needs are usually of less concern than organizational needs in determining the content of continuing education programs. For example, the administrators of a hospital felt a need to help patients leave more quickly after surgery because its third-party payers would only reimburse a patient's stay for a specified number of days. The continuing education unit implemented program to teach nurses some physical therapy strategies that could be used with patients to promote a quicker recovery.

Continuing educators in employing agency settings usually need to demonstrate how their efforts relate to effectively providing the parent's basic service or product. Professional associations are an example of *quasi-educational organizations* in that continuing education is only one of their basic purposes. Associations are organized to advance the interests of their members. Most are devoted to their members' professional development, as well as to legislative lobbying, maintaining certification programs, and promoting the public image of the profession.

Associations vary in the importance they attach to education. Some consider continuing education one of their most important responsibilities and have a full-time educational director. Other associations attach little importance to education and thus have no one to handle it. Continuing professional education is a *secondary function* of universities and professional schools in which preparatory education is a primary function. In this position the heads of continuing education units are usually at a disadvantage in fighting for institutional resources. This is often true even for those units that have a long history, large staffs, and sizable budgets.

Continuing education units are marginal, and will continue to be so until the higher education faculty considers the instruction of practicing professionals a mainstream responsibility. Independent providers have two orientations to continuing education. Agencies such as pharmaceutical companies that use continuing professional education to market their products or services are noneducational providers. They use continuing education as a way to achieve another organizational end. In contrast, the business of selling continuing professional education programs is a primary function of the "private" providers, so the mission of the parent body and the continuing education unit is the same. Continuing educators in these agencies have a great deal of discretion in what they do because their work does not derive from the operating goals of a parent body.

The relationship of the continuing education unit to its parent body has important implications for how its market is defined. Moving on a continuum from noneducational to independent agencies, the audience or market for continuing education becomes increasingly external. The audience for continuing education in employing agencies, their employees, is almost completely internal.

There is little need to market these programs to professionals outside the organization. Some units do this only as a secondary activity to the education of the employees. Professional associations also have a constituency, their members and others in the profession who are not members. Association members have some affinity and allegiance to the programs of the association. However, the association has little formal control over its members and so must market these programs to them.

Universities and independent providers share a similar situation, in that they do not have a constituency for their programs. Thus, the market for both of these providers is totally external. The only part of the market that has some natural affinity to universities and professional schools is their own graduates. Independent providers generally have to start from scratch in building up a constituency. At least three types of providers serve external audiences that have varying degree of allegiance to them.

Azzaretto suggests that continuing educators must develop a competitive strategy in order to secure a sufficient number of participants from these audiences. He offers five components of a competitive planning model for continuing professional education providers. The first is that the provider must have an internal orientation to service excellence. First popularized by Peters and Waterman, the "customer-driven" organization is now seen as a key in any people-intensive business such as continuing professional education. Second, providers must attend to the processes of market segmentation and positioning.

Taken together, these two concepts provide a basis for developing instructional programs that meet client needs, are market competitive, and are based on what the provider does best. The third element is to develop a focused operating and geographic strategy. That is, providers should be clear about why and where they are serving their audience. The fourth part of the strategy is to establish partnerships and coalitions,.

Fifth, the ultimate test for a competitive strategy is that participants perceive the quality and cost effectiveness of the educational product as high. Taken together, these elements make up an organized plan to analyze a provider's existing strengths and resources. By using this plan to design and deliver programs, continuing educators can increase the likelihood of developing effective market relationships. The institutional context strongly influences the focus of continuing professional educators' practice. This occurs because the purposes of the parent agency determine to a great extent the mission of the continuing education unit or function.

7

Technical Education

Technical Education represents a complex of activities that include post-graduate courses and research; under-graduate course leading to a first degree or equivalent award: diploma courses; certificate courses; junior technical schools and technical studies at secondary school level; apprenticeship etc. The predominant characteristic of technical education is what may be called the "double finality" of educational development for the individual and the acquisition by him of techniques and skill. The emphasis on the one or the other may vary from course to course; the organisational arrangements may differ; or the types of institutions may be diverse. But both form essential components of technical education.

Technical institutions are sometimes referred to as engineering colleges; sometimes as technological colleges; and in some cases as colleges of engineering and technology. There is no doubt that a certain amount of terminological confusion exists, but this is more in usage than in basic concept. Historically engineering included only the more well-known fields such as Civil Engineering, Mechanical Engineering and Electrical Engineering. As the application of science to industry widened and the forces of Nature were harnessed increasingly for the material prosperity of man, a large body of applied scientific knowledge grew up and was called by the more comprehensive term Technology.

Technology, therefore, includes all fields of engineering and applied sciences that are responsible for present-day progress. Confusion has also arisen out of the fact that between the two words, Technologist and Technician which sound and look alike there is a wide difference though the words are often used synonymously. A trained technician may be defined as a person who, without aspiring ever to reach one of the directing positions in industry, is nevertheless fully competent to understand, control and maintain the technical processes committed to his charge.

A technologist, on the other hand, is a person capable of appreciating the latest progress in research laboratories and applying scientific knowledge and methods to industry. This distinction between a technologist and a technician is important since it determines the standard and scope of technical education at different levels.

Technical education in India is a four-tiered structure comprising post-graduate courses and research; first degree courses; diploma courses; and vocational or industrial training. Each tier is a self-contained aspect intended to serve a specific purpose and neither the diploma courses nor the industrial training courses are a preparation for the next higher tier. For post-graduate courses and research, however, only those candidates who have a first degree in the relevant subjects are admitted. The objective of the first degree courses is to train technologists, some of whom may eventually become designers, research engineers or specialists in various fields either after further studies at post-graduate level or experience in the profession. they are not concerned with preparing persons for specific positions or jobs in industry, but with giving them a broad-based education in the scientific principles and methods underlying technology. Equally, they are not concerned to develop particular technical skills in students but to acquaint them with various production methods in accordance with constructional requirements in a system that consists of an assembly of men, materials and machines.

First degree courses

Till recently, the duration of first degree courses was general four years with the Intermediate in Science as the minimum admission qualification. The Intermediate in Science, a preparatory stage for university courses was of two years' duration after a high school education that extended over a period generally of ten years. It therefore took six years for a student to complete the first degree after his high school education. Secondary education in the country is in process of re-organisation and the new pattern envisages an eleven-year schooling intended to prepare candidates for life and for direct entry to university.

The existing Intermediate course is being abolished. As a result of this change, the first degree course are being re-organised into a five-year integrated course after higher secondary education. The advantages of a five-year integrated course are: first, a more fruitful integration of fundamental sciences, technological subjects and liberal arts will be possible. Second, a higher level of scientific and technical competence may be expected since the students can absorb the different subjects in more suitable stages and in the right combinations. Third, a five-year tutelage will give the teachers an opportunity to reduce class work and to develop in the students a capacity for growth and maturity. Finally, in these days of specialisation, a five-year curriculum admits of introduction to different specialised fields and prepares the student for post-graduate studies or research.

Post-graduate courses leading to a Master's degree or equivalent award are generally of one or two years' duration, and provide for specialisation in a branch of a major field in formal instruction, project work and independent study of a chosen problem presented as a dissertation. Research degrees like the Ph.D. or D.Sc. are awarded on the basis of original research done by candidates at recognised centers. The normal period required is two to three years after a Master's degree.

Next to first degree courses, diploma courses occupy an important position in technical education in India. These courses are conducted by a large number of institutions called Polytechnics and Rural Institutes and are designed to train technicians who will eventually occupy supervisory positions like foreman, overseers etc., in industry and other technical organisations, in charge of engineering construction, production and operation and maintenance. Another function that the diploma-holders can perform is as engineer aide in design offices or on the shop floor or on field execution. The courses are three yeas long after a high school education and have a strong practical bias.

The view has, however, been advanced in recent years that the practical knowledge and experience required by a technician cannot be given to him in an adequate measure in a course that in wholly institution-based, and that the present three-year diploma courses do not always produced the right type of personnel. The All India Council for technical Education has therefore designed a Sandwich Course of four years for diploma in mechanical engineering. In this course, practical training in industry and institutional studies alternate in suitable layers. The student spends stated periods in industry and in an educational institution, throughout the course and fulfills the academic requirements for the diploma. He also gains the practical experience necessary for a supervisory position. The scheme has been introduced at selected centers in co-operation with industry.

The sandwich pattern is now the normal form of training technicians for mining industry, and has been adopted at all the mining schools. As training facilities in industry expand, the sandwich course will become an important feature of technical education in India. The diploma courses are offered in the main fields of civil, mechanical and electrical engineering. A few institutions also offer Textile Technology, Leather Technology,Mining Engineering and other fields according to regional requirements for technical personnel at this level.

As a matter of established usage, the term "Polytechnic" represents in India today technical institutions that conduct diploma courses chiefly in civil, mechanical and electrical engineering. It indicates at once both the standard of training and the main fields of study. Except for a few institutions that are under the direct control of universities, all polytechnics are affiliated to State Boards of Technical Education in different States. The State Boards prescribe the courses of study, conduct examinations and award diplomas. Uniformity of standards on an All-India basis is maintained through the All-India Council for Technical Education which has formulated National Certificate course to serve as a model for the diploma courses conducted at polytechnics.

The Indian Constitution makes it essential for the State to provide free compulsory education for all children up to the age of 14 i.e. up to three classes below the new higher secondary course that is in process of being introduced. The question is how to provide diversified opportunities for education and training to a majority of students after 14, for gainful occupation in life. The issue partly arises from the fact that secondary education is a terminus for a majority of students and so, has to be a self-sufficient and practical preparation for entry to life. It is partly due also to the fact that the present menace of large numbers of students crowding aimlessly into universities and other higher institutions has to be eliminated.

University education should be open only to those who can profit by it and have the necessary academic merit. For the rest, secondary education of diversified types that suits individual ability and aptitude should be provided. Therefore technical education and training at secondary level is of vital importance. The Junior Technical School, a special type of secondary technical school, is designed specifically for students who wish to enter industry and other technical occupations. It offers a three-year integrated course in general education, technical education and technical training in various engineering trades. It accepts fully the concept of 'Double Finality' within its curriculum of educational development of the student from 14 to 17 and of his effective preparation for a definite technical occupation in life. In each year, general education, technical studies and workshop training are so integrated that all three elements constitute the base for the total development of the young student.

The work-load is so designed that the technical school functions as a cross between a factory and a school. The workshop-training that constitutes over 55% of the total course and conducted in well-equipped shops provides a good foundation for the development of the student as a skilled worker of a high order. The development of technical skill is facilitated by training in engineering drawing and in elementary mechanical and electrical engineering included in the course. The occupational meaningof 'technical eduation' is still not well defined but the fact that occupational levels exist between that of skilled worker is obvious. In fact the gap s so wide that two intermediate levels are called for, which will be referred to as 'technician', originating in the industrial field, is now extended to denote a certain academic and social level intermediate between 'skilled worker' and 'engineer'.

During the nineteenth century scientific and technical education gradually evolved and increased in importance, largely as a result of the political and industrial revolutions which has spread throughout Europe. Life and philosophy can change society: and society can change life and philosophy. Steam and electrical power did more than revolutionize modes of transport: they changed men's minds, the way they thought and believed.

Mechanical devices in turn led to theological revision and uncertainty. The concept of evolution gradually led to concepts of control of evolution, control of life and death, increased control in agriculture, and control of disease. It was doubtful whether any other form of educational study offered the same advantages for 'training and developing the mental faculties.' However wrong the commissioners might have been in supporting the teaching of science on the basis of transfer of training and a faculty-psychology, they were right on more utilitarian ground concerning the need for developing scientific and technical instruction. They thought it highly important to introduce science into education at a very early stage; they argued that it was no more difficult to young pupils than grammar or arithmetic, and certainly more interesting. The Devonshire Commission did not mince matters when it came to a final judgment on the national position concerning the teaching of science. They felt compelled to express the opinion that the general position was extremely unsatisfactory, a matter for serious regret; and considering the increasing importance of science to the country form an industrial and economic point of view, in the context of expanding European economics, they felt that its exclusion from the education of the middle and upper classes was 'little less than a national misfortune'. The obvious concern felt by the Devonshire Commission was sustained both at the education and the industrial level.

Without education interest in technical education it became increasingly clear that industry would suffer, and so there began a mushroom growth of all sorts of institutions with pretensions to giving some form of technical instruction. This created further anxiety that such instruction might not be properly controlled nor, in fact, be adequate to deal with the actual industrial and social problems. It was largely with these questions in mird that a Royal Commission on Technical Instruction was appointed in 1881, under the chairmanship of Bernhard Samuelson who has served on the Devonshire Commission.

The Samuelson Commission was to inquire into the technical and other instruction provided for the industrial classes of certain foreign countries and then to compare such provisions with that made for the corresponding classes in this country. The commission was also asked to consider the influence of this instruction upon manufacturing an other industries at home and abroad. It was, in itself, a considerable and searching exercise to set any commission, and without the spadework and know-how of the chairman over the previous fourteen years it seems impossible that six men could have performed the task. The report itself appeared in several volumes during the years 1982-4; it felt, optimistically, that despite the progress of other countries Britain still held its position at the head of the industrial world; but

As a result of the contentions the report recommended that writing an rudimentary drawing should be developed as a single elementary subject, and that should be less part-time employment and more full-time education for children. The work of the Mechanics' Institutes came in for special mention, as well as a hint that many of them had fallen behind in their development of technical instruction. Many of them, however, has clearly seen that their teaching, both in content and method, was out model and unsuited to the needs and requirements of expanding industry. They were, therefore, revising their constitutions and their curricula. Particularly praised for taking the initiative in providing facilities for artizans to obtain instruction in art and science, whilst their was more than a suggestion that the trades' union has a duty 'to promote the technical education of their members'.

The commission strongly supported the further development of technical instruction in this country , but it felt equally strongly that the 'Imperial budget' was providing enough. There should be greater expenditure by local authorities on this type of education, and they should be empowered to establish more secondary and technical schools. There should exist opportunities for intelligent young artizans to gain scholarships to such schools. Also, it was important that the great mass of the working class should be given those basic elements of the sciences which has some bearing upon industry. The use of the rule and the compass was essential to all, as well as geography taught as a branch of elementary science, more object lessons from nature, more dimple agriculture and more craft work. The commissioners took the view that men selected as foremen in industry should not be entirely ignorant of the more theoretical side of their work; and since they were drawn from the working classes the later, as whole, must be better educated in technical matters as well as in general knowledge. Similarly, when it came to the education of the leaders of industry, the commissioners believed that no part of the national expenditure on education was more important that spent on their scientific culture and technical training.

Other recommendations of the report included the provision of works schools in which young workers might be trained in the shops and factories themselves. They cited as an example the workshop school of Messers. Mather and Platt, which was a private evening school providing technical education for the firm's apprentices. The firm worked on the basis that the school must be brought to the workshop and not the workshop to the school; not only was this a simple and inexpensive way of training workers, it also had the advantage of providing the work atmosphere and brought home the immediate utility of the technical theory.

Another recommendation concerned the training of teachers. If the children in elementary schools were to receive adequate tuition in technical subjects then teachers themselves also had to be taught more science and more art; this would mean changes in the curricula of the training colleges. Form their general tone, as well as from more specific recommendations, it was clear that the commissioners were in favour of modifying the more generally accepted curriculum of the secondary grammar-type school. They were not opposed to a broad culture, but they were opposed to what they considered the dead wood of a great deal of secondary education. They were in favour of dropping latin and Greek and putting in their place more study of modern languages, mathematics, science and technical drawing. This sort of educational programme reflected very much the interests of the chairman and the general trend of educational thinking at this time.

A number of Parliamentary Acts as well as grants now began to assist technical education, in however small a way. The setting up of county and county borough councils by the Local Government Act of 1888 delineated certain areas of responsibility for the development of scientific education, and the onus for the further organization and establishment of technical secondary schools was firmly laid on local authorities.

In 1889 the Technical Instruction Act was passed whereby the new organs of local government were empowered to spend a certain proportion of the rates on technical education and manual instruction. The local rates were further subsidized by grants from the Science and Art Department, as well as by the somewhat odd diversion of customs and excise 'whiskey money' to aid higher technical education. It was chiefly through such grants, and through the some-what *laissez-faire* attitude which inevitably arises when authorities are 'empowered' but not 'compelled' to do certain things, that the Science and Art Department appeared to be gaining more and more control of technical education, whilst the Education Department seemed to be getting less and less. It was for this reason that the Cross Report of 1888 had recommended that the responsibility for institutions which provided technical instruction should be transferred to the Education Department.

The Education Act of 1899 finally created the Board or Education, which became a central authority taking over the educational functions of the Charity Commission and the Science and Art Department. Whilst the 1902

Education Act represents a landmark in many ways in the history of the development and organization of education, it in fact paid very little attention to the pressing need to organize further technical education along sound lines. The science schools which had developed through the grants of the Science and Art Department were being gradually absorbed into the secondary system, or continued as higher elementary schools.

Once the Board began to function it produced some regulations for the running of schools of art, art classes and technical institutions. These regulations, which appeared in 1903 and 1904, made provision for day instruction for suitably qualified students who might profit from more advanced education. These students were being prepared specifically for work in industry and commerce, and therefore such day instruction as they received would naturally be geared to the work of life. This was a theme taken up by the *Introduction to the Elementary* code of 1904, where it was claimed that the purpose of public elementary education was to assist the pupils to fit themselves both practically and intellectually for the work of life. The *Regulations for Secondary Schools* of 1904 sought to distinguish very clearly secondary schools from technical institutes and classes which gave, almost exclusively, instruction and training in certain subjects to both adults and young people who had already completed a general education. Thus it was inevitable that the technical school should eventually emerge as a different breed of educational institution.

Junior Technical Schools

The accommodation and equipment, as well as the staffing, of the further education institutions were profitably used by the junior technical schools; whilst, starting as they did with virtually no tradition, they were able to diverge considerably in curricula from both the orthodox higher elementary school and the tradition-bound secondary grammar school. Employers became immediately interested in these schools because of their vitally practical nature, and because they would obviously began to supply a superior type of youth for apprenticeship—one already trained in certain skills as well as possessing clear aptitude for the practical work of the factory or workshop.

The various industries became sufficiently interested in this new educational project to make substantial grants towards their foundation and development, as well as providing staff to teach and train the pupils, and industrial equipment of very nature to give a sense of realism to technical education. In 1921-13 the Board of Education published *A Report and Regulations for Junior Technical Schools* where by such schools were officially recognized as a separate category which in future would 'receive aid from the state to a degree more commensurate with their importance'. This was double edged. It was obviously an attempt to gain a greater control over the proliferation of educational institutions through the outside efforts of industry and commerce; it was not a declaration of the supreme importance nationally and economically of the expansion of technical education.

In 1926 in the Hadow Report, on *The Education of the Adolescent,* there was the first organized attempt to define the origin, aim and province of the junior technical schools. Their chief purpose was to provide a course of instruction, extending over two or three years, for pupils who previously had attended elementary schools and had there received a general education. The curriculum of the junior technical school was designed to continue and expand this general education, whilst making provision for a special type of training for entry into some particular occupation or group of occupations.

The committee felt that it was inadvisable to place a pupil of the age of 11+ in a school planned specifically to provide a course of definitely vocational education, and so the normal age of entry to such schools was fixed at 13+. They argued, as many have argued since about the whole question of the 11+ selection procedure, that the arrangement whereby pupils were given admission to junior technical schools at the age of 13+ considerably reduced the risk of committing a pupil to a course of study and training which might ultimately prove to be completely unsuitable. From 1924 to 1928 Lord Eustace Percy, who was then President of the Board of Education, produced a number of surveys and reports on technical education, education for industry and commerce, and further education generally.

A very thorough investigator, Lord Percy examined the problem from the side of industry and commerce as well as from the side of education. In the process he consulted something like 500 firms, and opened up enquiries into the field of special education for industry and commerce. He reported in 1928 that about 80-90 per cent of those undertaking further education in industry and commerce attended evening classes, and he argued that it was of great importance to develop day courses for such students, both full-time and part-time.

In 1929 the Clerk Committee on Engineering Industries strongly commended the work done by junior technical schools, and underlined the importance of recruiting for the engineering industry those who had received full-time education in them. By then there were 108 officially recognized junior technical schools with something in the region of 18,000 pupils, including 4,600 girls. The next year the Board of Education published its report, *The junior Technical School.* In this it was stated that the growth and progress of this type of school was steady, although not considerable. Each school had less than 200 pupils, whilst some had even less than 100; this was uneconomical, particularly when one considered the costly equipment used and the problems of staffing.

The report emphasized the serious-mindedness of the pupils under instruction, and the fact that their concentration derived from a sense of the relevance and practicality of their work. They were learning for life and this provided the necessary motivation to tackle their studies. The 1930 report highlighted the real problem. The growth of these schools, like many before and since, had not in any way been planned; and lack of planning in any sphere can lead to considerable wastage. The Board realized that local authorities had to be encouraged to work together in the establishing of more technical schools, and so it issued in 1936 its *Circular 1444,* in which it stressed the need for co-operation between neighbouring authorities when planning such provision. During the same year the Board published *A Review of Junior Technical Schools in England,* a systematic survey of the way in which these schools were organized and distributed, the nature of their curricula, and their classification.

During that year there appeared a Board of Education conference report on *Co-operation in Technical Education.* The purpose of this again was to impress upon local authorities the need to co-operate in order to pool their technical resources and prevent unnecessary duplication. The Board was determined to accomplish three things: the expansion of technical education; strict economy in this expansion; and the maximum of co-operation between industry, the staffs of technical schools and colleges, and board inspectors. It was suggested that joint advisory committees should be formed.

Secondary Technical

The Spens Consultative Committee received its terms of reference in 1933 and published its report in 1938, which contained a number of recommendations about technical schools. It was felt that the word 'junior' in the name 'junior technical school' had misleading associations; and so it recommended that the expression 'technical school' should in future be used as a general term for all technical schools which recruited pupils at the age of 13+ and provided courses lasting for two or three years.

The committee urged to establishment of a 'new type of higher school of technical character quite distinct from the traditional academic grammar school'. To effect this it was suggested that a number of the already existing junior technical schools should be converted into technical high schools, and should be given in all respects equality of status with grammar schools. They would recruit their pupils at 11+, by means of the general selective examination, and provide a five-year course up to the leaving age of 16+. The committee felt that the curriculum for pupils between the ages of 11+ and 13+ in such schools should be, in general the same as that i other secondary schools of equal status, such as the grammar school. After thirteen there should be a liberal education informed by the spirit and practice of science. Subjects in the curriculum would include English, mathematics, history, geography, engineering drawing, practical crafts in the workshops, physical education and aesthetic subjects.

In addition, some pupils would continue with a modern foreign language if they showed some capacity for profiting from it. Wherever possible these schools should be housed in the premises of technical colleges or technical institutes in order to make full use of the equipment and staff which these had. The technical high school would be organized as a department of the college or institute; and the head of this department would be the headmaster of the school. The committee recommended that there should be a new type of school-leaving certificate for pupils in technical high schools on the basis of internal examinations. These would be founded on the curriculum of the school, but there would be external assessors, appointed by the Board of Education, who would ensure a uniform minimum standard of certification in technical high schools throughout the country.

The certificates would have an equal standing with the existing school certificates as fulfilling the first conditions for matriculation. Finally, the report recommended that there should be close relations between the newly-created technical high schools and grammar schools, so that there might be ease of transfer at 13+ for those pupils whose later development made it clear that they were more suited to an alternative form of education. The terms of reference supplied, in October 1941, to the Norwood Committee asked them to consider any changes they might suggest the curricula of the secondary schools, and also the question of any school examinations relating to them. The Norwood Report of 1943 largely supported the recommendations of the Spens Report, rather on the basis of a faculty-psychology which Dr Cyril Burt had already rejected in an appendix to that report. It argued that the relationship between local industry and the technical high school was an essential one which could not be maintained unless the school could freely control its own destiny. The report accepted a tripartite division of secondary schools, namely, secondary grammar, secondary technical and secondary modern, and opposed multilateralism as a general policy although it did not reject the possibility,, or even desirability in some instances, of bilateralism.

The technical high school, or secondary technical school, should give a general education, orientated from 13+ onwards towards special technical courses. Its chief function should be to provide a training for entry to industry and commerce at 16+, a training which met, at the same time, the demands of local industrial conditions. Facilities for more advanced work should also be offered from the ages of sixteen to eighteen.

In 1943 it was discovered, in the throes of a life and death struggle with Germany and her allies, that 'in the youth of the nation we have our greatest asset'. The White Paper on *Educational Reconstruction*, published in that year, recognized the need for some positive action if the country were to recruit more youths into industry and commerce through the technical schools, which it claimed held out great opportunities for pupils with a practical bent. It accepted the principle of the tripartite system laid down in the Norwood Report and set the general tone for further secondary development. The 1944 Education Act made it clear in Section 8 that it was the duty of every local education authority to make schools available sufficient in number, character and equipment so that all pupils, whatever their age, ability or aptitude, would have the most desirable form if instruction and education, including practical instruction. The parity of esteem and equality of status, which had been sought so long for all forms of 'secondary' education, were at least recognized in law by the 1944 Education Act, even if they did not exist in fact. A great deal of hard work was put into establishing in the public mind this equality of status, but parents remained, and remain, strangely unconvinced.

In 1945 a Special Committee on Higher Technological Education, under the chairmanship of Lord

Eustance Percy, reported on the needs of higher technical education in England and Wales, with regard to the requirements of industry and the contributions made by the universities and technical colleges. One of the committee's main considerations was the lack of liaison between the major technical colleges and the technological departments of the universities. Its chief recommendations included the establishment of regional Advisory Councils whose main purpose was to co-ordinate the technological studies and investigations in the colleges of technology, the universities and all other technical institues.

Coupled with the recommendation was the suggestion that the Ministry of Education should establish a standing organization known as the National Council of Technology, which should give advice on national aspects of all regional policy. It was further recommended that each Regional Advisory Council should establish an Academic Board to ensure that there existed co-ordination at the teaching level. At the same time adequate arrangements should be made for the representation of industry on both the Council and the Board, and for full consultation. The committee recommended that a selected number of colleges of technology should provide full-time courses of a university standard, as well as facilities for post-graduate work.

Links with industry could be strengthened if industry released some of its more articulated specialists as part-time teachers. It was also envisaged that in the future both technical colleges and universities should educate students with a view to becoming senior administrators and managers in industry rather than concentrating upon the production of science teachers, research workers and pure scientists by the universities, and upon the training of technical assistants and craftsmen by the technical colleges. The Percy Report further recommended that colleges of technology should conduct their own examinations and award their own qualifications. Courses of study would be approved and moderated by the N.C.T. through the Academic Board, who would also advise on equipment, accommodation and staffing. It was the function of the Board to ensure some parity of standards throughout the country and to select external examiners.

There was some disagreement over the actual title of the qualification provided by the major institutions, but nune concerning its nature. It was to be the equivalent of a university first degree, awarded with classified honours. But it was felt that the institutions involved should not be grated a charter to confer degrees, l and the award was therefore to be called a diploma in technology.

In 1948 the National Advisory Council on Education for Industry and Commerce was established. The Carr-Saunders Report of 1949 suggested that several defects existed in education for commerce. It was not based on a sufficiently broad study of the subject: it started vocational training, as distinct from vocational education, too early; and too much of the study took place in the evenings-there should be longer periods of full-time day study. With this in mind it recommended sandwhich-courses leading to new qualifications of degree standard.

The first report of the N.A.C.E.I.C. on *The Future Development of Higher Technological Education* appeared in 1950, and discussed technological education of first degree standard. The report recommended that there should be improvements in the financing of those colleges which provided such courses, and an improvement in their accommodation and equipment. It also proposed that a Royal College of Technologists should be establish, which would award associateships, memberships, and fellowships. In 1951 the Advisory Council produced a White Paper, which was a brief statement of the Government's policy for the development of *Higher Technological Education in Great Britain*. It stressed that in the university field the numbers of fulltime students in technology had increased from 5,288 in 1938-9 to 10,933 in 1949-50; and similarly the numbers of post-graduate students had more than doubled from 662 to 1,539. New building was in process.

The University Grants Committee was encouraging some universities to institute post-graduate courses in particular fields of technology, including mechanical, electrical, chemical, agricultural and civil engineering, metallurgy, mining and textiles. The committee was also considering the possibility of establishing a university of technology for two or three thousand students, but the government was satisfied that it would not be in the national interest to proceed with such a project at that particular point in time. The proposal to arrange for the establishment of a College of Technologists was later reversed. The Ministry of Education's *Circular 255* of 1952, however, provided for a special grant at the rate of 75 per cent in respect of approved advanced technological courses. In 1956 the White Paper entitled *Technical Education*, stated that the aim of the Ministry of Education was to increase by 50 per cent the output of students from advanced courses at technical colleges, and to double the number of part-time release students during the ay, thereby raising the number to 700,000. It clearly distinguished three grades of worker-technologists, technicians, and craftsmen; and it stated that the main road to the highest technological qualifications would be sandwich courses lasting four or five years with alternate periods in industry and technical colleges.

It was expected that the scheme would attract pupils leaving school at eighteen, most of whom would be concentrated in colleges of advanced technology which would be developed from existing technical colleges. In 1956 the Ministry also published *Circular 305, The Organization of Technical Colleges,* which delineated four main types. *Local colleges* provided, on the vocational side, courses which were mainly part-time and up to the level of Ordinary national Certificate or its equivalent. *Area colleges* provided, in addition to these courses, varying amounts of advanced work, mainly of a part-time nature and above Ordinary National Certificate and Diploma Level. *Regional colleges* were those which did a substantial among of full-time and sandwich courses involving advanced work.

The standard of staff and equipment made it unrealistic to spread this work over too many colleges. Finally, *colleges of advanced technology* would provide a broad range and substantial volume of exclusively advanced work, including post-graduate work. The terms of reference given to the Central Advisory Council for Education in 1956 were quite simply to advise the Minister on 'the education of boys and girls between the ages of fifteen an eighteen'. Part Six of the "Crowther Report, which was eventually published in 1959, was entitled 'Technical Challenge and Educational Response'. This section remarked on the need to produce far larger numbers of technicians and craftsmen.

Among a number of recommendations made was the desirability of a greater degree of integration between schools and further education, and the need to transform what was then a varied collection of plans for vocational training into a coherent national system of practical education. Whereas only about 12 per cent of fifteen to eighteen year-olds were in full-time education, it was suggested that 50 per cent at least should be the aim. There was a lack of integration between school and college education, and it was argued that there should be expanded provision for 'college based' sandwich courses for young people aged sixteen to eighteen, provided satisfactory arrangements could be made for training in industry.

The White Paper entitled *Better Opportunities in Technical Education* was published in 1961 and made some far-reaching proposals for a major reconstruction in the system of courses for technicians, craftsmen and operatives in technical colleges. The Government looked for a large increase in the number of students attending technical courses. It suggested a wider range of courses, an improvement in the methods of selecting students for courses, and more time for students to cover the necessary ground. There was an explicit desire expressed for more students to succeed, and for a reduction in the wastage rate through failure. Its chief proposals were that:

1. Student should begin at a technical college as soon as they left school, and preliminary courses in evening institutes should be discontinued.
2 The selection of students for courses should be undertaken with more care. The colleges should experiment with full-time induction courses and with tutorial methods.
3. Courses would include national Certificate and Diploma Courses for students aiming to become high-grade technicians at least; technician courses specifically organized for particular industries; craft courses and courses for operatives.
4. O.N.C. courses would last for two years and not three. Standards of entry were to be raised.

5. There would be new courses for four or five years specially for technicians.
6. New general courses would be introduced, which would lead to either technician courses or O.N.C. and O.N.D. courses.
7 Craft courses would be modified i various ways.
8 There should be a vigorous development of operatives' courses.
9 More time ought to be provided under day release schemes, and no student should have to rely entirely on evening study.
10 Sandwich courses and block release courses should be increasingly developed.

Thus, the White Paper sought to develop and implement some of the suggestions of the Crowther Report, particularly with reference to a greater variety of 'alternative routes', and a new form of full-time 'practical' education for those who were unsuited to the full-time academic route, or who would suffer from a wasteful part-time course.

The National Council for Technological Awards was established by the Ministry of Education in 1955. It was responsible for the award of the Dip. Tech., which was recognized as being of honours degree standard. The Robbins Report suggested that this council should be replaced by the Council for National Academic Awards which should cover the whole of Great Britain and might be established under Royal Charter. Its function would be to award honours and pass degrees to students in regional and are colleges. More will be said bout the development of the C.N.A.A. Later; it is sufficient here to say that it was established by Royal Charter in September 1964. In 1966, the Department of Education and Science presented to Parliament a White Paper entitled *A Plan for*

Polytechnics and Other Colleges. This was an attempt to discuss and make proposals about higher education in the further education system.

The colleges of advanced technology had now been transferred to the university sector of education, and the N.A.C.E.I.C. had emphasized the pressing need for further concentration of courses in order to achieve the most effective utilization of resources. The White Paper noted the rapidly increasing demand for higher education within the further education system, and the fact that the Government believed the demand could best be met by establishing a limited number of new, strong centres with adequate staffing, buildings, and equipment 'needed both to achieve and maintain high standards and to provide the right setting for an active community of staff and students'.

The Government considered the best results could be achieved by creating a number of polytechnics which would be comprehensive academic communities catering for students at all levels of higher education. In the appendix to the White Paper twenty-eight such institutions were proposed, although the final number was not precisely fixed in advance. Before a polytechnic was finally designated account would be taken of the possibility of associating a number of colleges by merger, or in some other way, in order to form the most effective unit possible. One of the proposals was to reduce substantially the number of colleges engaged in full-time higher education, but colleges which were not designated as polytechnics would continue to offer full-time courses of higher education provided they could satisfy the criteria for approval of course in force from time to time. Unless there were exceptional circumstances colleges not already engaged in higher education would not be expected to embark on it.

In January 1965 the Universities Central Council on Admissions reported that in pure science the universities would have admitted 1,080 more students if suitable candidates had presented themselves, and they could have also admitted 420 more students in technology. The Council for Scientific Policy was requested on February 25, 1965, 'to examine the flow of candidates in science and technology into higher education', and in consequence a working group was set up under the chairmanship of Dr F.S. Dainton, Vice-Chancellor of Nottingham University. In February 1966 the Group produced an interim report, and two years later, in February 1968, a full report. This made number of recommendations after stating that science and mathematics were, relatively, losing ground in the sixth form.

The proportion of school leavers specializing in them had declined in relation to other subjects of study since 1960. It was clear that there had been an increasing preference for the social sciences, and the report deprecated this relative decline in technology and science which it regarded as 'potentially harmful both to individuals and to society'. We cannot deal with the recommendations of the Dainton Report in any detail here, but briefly they included the following. It considered that in the sixth forms there should be a broad span of studies, and any irreversible decisions for or against science, technology or engineering should be postponed as long as possible. All pupils should, normally, study mathematics until they left school, and mathematics teaching should show some relationship to other studies, such as economics and the experimental and engineering sciences. The report felt that there was an urgent need to infuse into the teaching of science and its curriculum a breadth, humanity and up-to-dateness. It was the responsibility of schools and L.E.A.s to ensure that within five years of the report the majority of secondary pupils should come into early contact with sound science teaching.

There was a great need, especially in science and technology, for the participation of teachers in in-service courses; and the development of teachers should ensure that younger and uncommitted pupils received high quality teaching in science. Positive incentives should be offered to an increasing number of graduates of high ability in order to recruit them into science teaching. The responsibility should be firmly placed upon L.E.A.s to recognize the additional costs of curriculum reform, and to be prepared to finance promising new proposals. The universities were recommended to look again at their entry requirements and encourage a broad span of studies in the sixth form and to increase the actual flow of candidates intc science, technology and engineering. They should also experiment with new courses in these fields in order to attract into these disciplines able students who were uncommitted. Employers, in their turn, should recognize their own responsibility to ensure that careers in the areas already mentioned were made both possible and attractive to students.

The organisation of technical education in India characteristic features of the Indian Constitution and a strong bais in favour of central planning and co-ordination. India is a union of States that are autonomous in certain subjects that include education. The Union comprises 16 states, each with its own legislature and a government formed on the basis of universal adult franchise. It is, therefore, the primary responsibility of the States to organise, develop and administer technical education and training within their respective areas. The constitutional position notwithstanding, the organisational and administrative set-up in many States was till recently unsatisfactory. There was no single department in the state government fully responsible for technical education and a variety of a arrangements existed. In some states technical institutions were under the administrative control of Industries Departments; in some under the Public Works Departments; and in others under the Education Departments.

In a few states, Industries Departments and Public Works Departments performed overlapping functions. In ths same states, the Industries Department was in chanrge of others. Each department laid down its own standards for the courses conducted by non-unitersity institutions under its control, held examinations departmentally and awarded diplomas and certificates. As schemes for the expansion of technical education on a large scale were formulated under the Five-Year Plants, it was realised that a unified approach to the problems of organisation and administration of institutions was necessary at the State level.

More important, when a large number of institutions, especially polytechnics were established in all states, in became necessary to ensure that the institutions maintained high standards of instruction, and their examinations were conducted by an independent body on a uniform basis. The All-India Council for Technical Education, therefore, recommended that in each state there should be set up a Directorate of Technical Education in the Government and a State Board of Technical Education.

The State Board should include inter alia representatives of industry, commerce, universities, technical institutions and other interests concerned with technical education. it should prescribe courses of study for institutions not affiliated to universities, inspect institutions from time to time to ensure maintenance of standards, hold examinations and award diplomas and certificates. The Directorate, as the administrative agency of the government, should be in charge of the organisational and management aspects of the institutions.

The recommendations of the Council have been accepted generally by all states, which have set up their own State Boards of Technical education. In most states one single government department is now in administrative charge of technical institutions. The establishjment of this new organisational set-up for technical education in the states is of great importance. it has not only helped in ensuring uniform standards on an all-India basis, but in associating various interests with the development of technical education and co-ordinating their efforts.

The concept of central planning and co-ordination has resulted in the Central Government's playing an active role in the development of technical education and training in the cournty as a whole. This concept is justified by several important considerations. First, in any system of planned economic development a clear perspective of the different sectors is an essential pre-requisite to action, whether at local, regional or central level.

Second, when the programmes of economic development include large-sized projects for key industry, power, fuel, transport and communications etc. in the public sector, it is the primary responsibility of the Centre to ensure that the manpower required for the projects is made available. Third, on a national level, facilities for advanced technological studies and research can be organised satisfactorily only by the Centre, which has also to ensure that the institutions established for the purpose play their due role in the development of the country like India involves a heavy financial outlay that is beyond the resources of the states. The Centre, therefore, has to bear a major part of the expenditure both directly and as grants to the states. Fifth, the Seventh Schedule of the Constitution places upon the Centre the responsibibity for co-ordinating and determining standards in institutions for higher education or research and scientific and technical institutions.

In view of the above considerations, the Centre's role in technical education has a four-fold objective viz.

(a) to prepare an integrated plan of development of technical education for the country as a whole;

(b) to establish higher technological institutions, institutions for specialised courses and other institutions of all-India improtance;

(c) to assist financially and otherwise state governments, universities and other agencies in the establishment of technical institutions;

(d) to watch over the progress of technical education and to ensure the maintenance of high standards.

These are essentially in the nature of educational leadership which the Centre has to provide.

Council for technical education

As a national body, the All India Council advises the Centre, the states, University Grants Commission and other authorities on all aspects of improvement and development of technical education. its functions include inter alia, the preparation of plans for the development of technical education on an all-Inida basis; to assess the requirements for technical manpower of different types and to suggest measures required to meet them; to suggest improvements in the pattern of technical education from time to time to suit changing conditions; to establish liaison between industry, government departments an other organisations, on the one hand, and technical institutions, on the other; to co-ordinate the activities of State Boards fo Technical Education; to recommend grants and other forms of assistance that may be given by the Centre to the states, universities and other organisations in the development of technical education. presided over by the Minister of Scientific Research and Cultural Affairs and with the Minister of Scientific Research and Cultural Affairs as its secretariat, the Council functions with fewer handlicaps than most other advisory bodies, whose relations with the administrative authorities are not so very closely knit and whose recommendations are subject to further examination.

As a matter of convention the recommendations of the Copuncil are accepted by the Central and State Governments. The fact that technical education is not a controversial subject has facilitated the work of the Council. For the correct discharge of its functions the All-India Council for Technical Education has set up a Co-ordinating Committee, four Regional Committees and seven Boards of Technical Studies. The Co-ordinating Committee is the Executive Committee of the Council and co-ordinates the work of the Regional Committees and Boards of Studies.

The importance of Regional Committees in promoting a co-ordinated development of technical education in the different parts of the country cannot be overemphasized. The vastness of the country explains the number and variety of problems of development that require to be examined in the light of conditions and needs of each region. Schemes for the establishment of new and improvement and development of existing institutions have to be formulated and implemented on a regional basis.

A constant watch over the progress of institutions, spread over the whole country, has to be maintained and expert advice and assistance to them have to be provided. These and other tasks can be performed satisfactorily only through appropriate regional agencies specially set up for the purpose and working in close co-operating with local authorities.

The four Regional Committees of the All-India Council for Technical Education deal with the following areas:-

Northern Region: Jammu & Kashmir; Himachal Pradesh; Punjab; Rajasthan; Delhi; Uttar Pradesh.

Eastern Region: Assam; Manipur. Tripura; West Bengal; Bihar; Orissa; Andaman & Nicobar; Nagaland.

Western Region: Maharashtra; Madhya pradesh; Gujarat.

Southern Region: Mysore; Madras; Andhra Pradesh; Kerala & Pondicherry; Laccadive; Minicoy& Aminnidevi Islands.

Each Regional Committee consists inter alia of representatives of the state governments within its area, representatives of industry, commerce and labour, technical institutions, State Boards, universities and experts. Constituted in this manner the committees are fully representative of all authorities and interests concerned with technical education in their respective areas. Their main functions are:-

(a) to survey facilities for technical education at all stages and to make recommendations on the development of technical education, including the establishment of new institutions wherever necessary:

(b) to make a preliminary examination of any institution seeking recognition:

(c) to tender advice and guidance to technical institutions within the region;

(d) to promote liaison between technical institutions and industry;

(e) to assist the states and institutions in securing practical training facilities.

The Boards of Technical Studies advise the All-India Council on all academic aspects, viz. the pattern of technical education, duration, standard and contents of courses, admission requirements etc. They also lay down the minimum standards of instructional facilities required for the conduct of various courses by technical institutions.

In addition to representatives of technical institutions, universities, industry and commerce, each Board has experts appointed by the All-India Council in order to bring to bear on the work of the Boards, expert knowledge and guidance in various fields. In the 14 years that the Boards have functioned, much valuable work has been done in formulating courses of study in various branches, on an all-India basis that have served as a guide to technical institutions.

The standards of instructional facilities like buildings, equipment and staff suggested by th Boards have formed the basis on which the Regional Committees assess the requirements of institutions and recommend grants. The Boards have also advised the Council from time to time on specialised courses to meet the needs of industry and commerce and formulated various schemes for the purpose. Thus, with a Co-ordinating Committee, four Regional Committees and seven Boards of Technical Studies, the All-India Council for Technical Education has become a most effective national body for technical education in the country. Recently, a Board for post-graduate studies and research has also been set up.

The University Grants Commission set up by the Central Government in 1956 is concerned with the co-ordination of standards and development of university education as a whole.

Where technical education at universities is concerned as, for instance, post-graduate courses and research, first degree courses etc., the Commission acts on the advice of the All-India Council for Technical Education. This has ensured a unified approach to technical education in all sectors. In the Ministry of Scientific Research and Cultural Affairs, there is a separate Division for technical education to assist in the formulation and execution of policies and programmes.

The existence of advisory and administrative functions in the same organisation is a feature characteristic of the Ministry and one that have made for much progress in technical education. The Division has also four Regional Offices, at Calcutta, Bombay, Kanpur and Madras whose respective territorial coverage corresponds to that of the Regional Committee of the All-India Council. Working in close association with the state governments, and as secretariat to the Regional Committees, the offices are concerned with actual field work and provide the much-needed link between the Center and the States. Among their more important functions are making arrangements for the practical training of graduates and diploma-holders; keeping a close watch over the progress of development schemes approved by the All-India Council for Technical Education; providing assistance to technical institutions in various matters; ensuring the correct utilisation by institutions of funds provided by the Centre.

Developments

There are many reasons for the development of technical education during the past fifteen years. First, because the last war effort was retarded due to earlier neglect of technical education, a crash programme of intensive technical education and training was instituted; but after the war complacency returned. Faith rested on the knowledge that Britain had led the world in industrialization for a hundred years. When it became obvious by the mid-fifties that Britain was falling behind in the competition for world markets, immediate and long term action was required.

In order to produce the wealth which is needed to provide the needs and meet the obligations of an industrial nation, technical education had to be expanded. Past experience has proved that effective technical education depends on a sound foundation of primary and secondary education in mathematics, science, English, and in the development of creative imagination. It is for this reason that those responsible for technical education and industrial training what the school leaving age raised to 16 immediately, and to 18 in the fore-seeable future. More parents are recognizing the career value of longer education.

The number in sixth forms continues to increase. Firms are being persuaded, and are likely in the immediate future to be offered financial incentives, to train more apprentices. They are being urged to absorb larger numbers of school leavers without any fear that the nation will have an excess of skilled manpower.

Increasing productivity requires a more than proportional increase of technologists, technicians and craftsmen. Efficient British firms compare more than favourable in all respects with their foreign competitors. They have been quick to move forward with new ideas, to finance research, to modernize their equipment and organization to train the technologists and technicians. They insist on apprentices attending technical college courses to obtain the appropriate qualifications. They have efficiently staffed and equipped training workshops and schools. If factory training is not possible outside the production shops their apprentices attend apprenticeship courses centred on the local technical college.

At the opening of Churchill College in Cambridge, Sir Winston Churchill was specific about the urgent needs and aims of scientific and technological education. 'More than any other country in the world Britain had to rely on the enterprise and trained ingenuity of her people. Since we had neither the massive populations nor the raw material, nor yet adequate agricultural land to enable us to make our way in the world with ease, we had to depend for survival on our brains on skilled minds that were at least proportionately equal to those in the United States and Russia.

The quantitative target is far from being achieved. Let none believe that the lunar rockets are merely ingenuous bids for prestige. They are the manifestations of a formidable advance in technology. As with many vehicles of pure research their immediate uses might not be apparent. But I do not doubt that they will ultimately reap a rich harvest for those who have the imagination and power to develop them and to probe ever more deeply into the mysteries of the universe in which we live.'

The chief purpose of technical education is to enable industry to meet the challenge from competing countries. Technical teachers, therefore, have a number of aims by which to direct their teaching effort:

1. To support industry and business and as a consequence the national economy.
2. To help their students to become fully effective in the practice of their careers.
3. To continue their personal, scientific, technical and

general education as well as their knowledge of modern industry and business in order to be intellectually adequate to present their material in a realistic and interesting way.

4. To encourage clear thinking and flexible attitudes in their students to changing ideas in industrial organization and techniques.
5. To educate students to use their technological knowledge and skills for the common good.
6. To encourage a worthwhile use of leisure by helping students to widen their horizons.

A *technologist* has the scientific and educational background, the qualifications and the responsible industrial experience for membership of a professional institution. He can be a university graduate or he may have qualified at one of the technical colleges which at present produce two-thirds of the country's technologists. He has been referred to as the 'commissioned officer in the industrial army'. He functions at the higher levels of management and administration, applied research and development, design, production, planning and organization. It has been estimated to take ten years to produce a professional technologist.

A *technician* requires scientific and technical knowledge not far below that of the technologist, together with the skill of the craftsman. He is a specialist in a particular branch of an industry. He is likely to be employed as an assistant designer, senior draughtsman, stressman, specialist tester or inspector, supervisor of plant installation, maintenance specialist, junior manager or foreman on the shop floor or on a building site. He may be working under the direct guidance of a technologist or he may be working alone with sole responsibility for the operation of specialist equipment. This is a comparatively new function which has to be defined from industry to industry, so that special courses can be designed for his needs. He requires a good knowledge of mathematics and science which he can apply to industrial requirements. In some industries he may be doing almost the same work as university graduates and in others it may be little more than that of a craftsman. It is estimated that about five technicians are required for every technologist in industry.

A *craftsman* is a skilled worker who has normally completed an apprenticeship. Craftsmen represent over one-third of industry's manpower. The estimated demand is for ten craftsmen to every technologist in industry. As industry becomes more complex it is becoming necessary for crafts-men to learn why they use certain tools and machines, materials and techniques in particular ways for different operations on equipment such as the builder's tower crane or who carries out skilled operations in a foundry, in a textile mill, in a steel or chemical factory.

Although operatives do not serve a recognized apprenticeship they usually have special training varying from a few weeks to as many years as a craftsman. The four tier pattern of technical colleges consists of a top tier of ten colleges of advanced technology, then thirty-two regional colleges of technology, followed by an unspecified but considerable number of area technical colleges, and finally a large number of local colleges. In addition there are a very few national colleges each serving the needs of one particular industry.

Colleges of advanced technology

There are ten such colleges which were designated in the five-year period after the publication of the 1956 White Paper, *Technical Education*. They are independent of local authority control and are financed direct from the

Ministry of education. Each college has an independent governing body representative of industry, business, education and the college teaching staff. The teaching staff is highly qualified academically and is well experienced in top-level industrial management and usually has considerable research achievement.

The colleges are developing post-graduate studies and higher level research. They cater for University of London external degree courses and for the qualifications of professional bodies, but the main education is for the Diploma in Technology. At present according to official statistics 71 per cent of the courses for the Diploma in Technology are in Engineering and the remainder in applied science. A Diploma in Technology for business studies is to be introduced as a qualification towards a career in management.

The Diploma in Technology is a four-year course, admission to which requires tow or more General Certificate of Education passes at Advanced Level or an Ordinary National Certificate at a prescribed standard. About one quarter of the admissions are by the Ordinary National Certificate route. The courses are organized on a sandwich basis which usually means six months of the year in college and six months in industry. Students can be industry or college-based. If industry-based they are paid a salary by the firm, which also accepts responsibility for industrial training.

If college-based, maintenance grants are paid through local education authorities as for University students, and the college organizes the students' industrial training. Official statistics state that 80 per cent of all engineering and 56 per cent to all applied science students for the Diploma in Technology are works-based. The standard of the Diploma is equivalent to a university honours degree. The second main course at advanced colleges leads to the Higher National Diploma in technological or business studies and to professional qualifications of a similar level. Admission requirements are about the same as for the Diploma in Technology, but the course is for those who would be unlikely to attain honours degree standard.

The Higher National Diploma is considered to equate with a university pass degree. Study is on a full-time sandwich basis and students are based either in industry or college. These courses are considered to be appropriate to the regional and area colleges of technology which are the second and third tiers in the pattern.

Regional colleges of technology

The constitution of the governing bodies varies, but normally there is a considerable industrial and commercial element with representatives from neighbouring education authorities. In very few cases is there any significant teaching staff representation. The qualifications of some, but not all, of the teaching staff compare with those of colleges of advanced technology. Both kinds of college are expanding their premises, but at present only the colleges of advanced technology are building residential accommodation on a substantial scale.

The regional colleges provide some curses for the Diploma in Technology but only when these are specifically required, and where they are not in competition with a college of advanced technology. Ministry statistics show that in 1961, 4,969 students enrolled in 101 Diploma in Technology courses distributed over 26 colleges; for the 1962 session the number of enrolments was 6,201 in 108 courses at 28 colleges. The immediate aim is to have 15,000 college places as soon as possible for professional technologists, increasing to 27,000 in 5 to 10 years and to over 30,000 within 12 to 15 years. Some of the development is likely to be in the regional colleges which concentrate on work beyond Ordinary National Certificate, or its equivalent the General Certificate of Education, at Advanced level. Regional colleges also provide a large proportion of the courses for the Ordinary and Higher National Diploma and for the Ordinary and Higher National Certificate.

The difference between National Diploma and National Certificate courses is that the former require full-time study usually on a sandwich basis while the latter are part-time on a block or day-release basis. Day-release means that the student is released, at present as a privilege, by his employer for one full day a week to attend the college. In addition, attendance is normally required on two evenings per week. In many cases employers cease to grant day release after the age of 18, just when most students are about to take examinations for the Ordinary National Certificate or its equivalent in craft studies.

The student has then to continue to the Higher National Certificate standard usually by attendance at college on three evenings a week. Not all employers grant day-release up to the age of 18 and only a few grant it beyond the age of 21. Block-release from industry is a comparatively new experiment by which students attend college full-time for periods varying from two weeks to three or four months at a time. The most popular arrangement is for full-time attendance for a term of twelve weeks.

A sandwich course requires over eighteen weeks' continuous full-time attendance at a college and anything less, which is full-time, is labeled block-release. The arguments for block-release rather than day-release are that the teachers and students get to know one another better. There is more time for integrating English and liberal studies with technical studies, and there are more opportunities for developing interests in ar, music, drama, handicrafts, sport and corporate activities.

Firms which support block-release find it possible to make more effective use of training facilities because they can be used every day all the year round. It allows for larger intake of apprentices which is an important factor when trained manpower will be increasingly required in the years ahead. The educational arguments against block-release are not strong. It is said there could be such a lapse of time between blocks of attendance at college that the normal rate of forgetting would have taken its full toll.

Students could lose the benefit of the continuous urge to effort provided by regular, day-a-week attendance. Most of the weaknesses are being met in a variety of ways. For example, students are required to attend on one or two evenings a week, or to continue day release between each period of block-release. The additional time is devoted to tutorial work in which the teaching effort is concentrated on helping individuals rather than in class teaching. Perhaps a more serious observation about block-release is the possibility that theory and training could get out of gear, and the pauses result in some loss of skill and re-tradition of practical training.

A more general and controversial question is whether technical colleges should remain in session for forty-eight weeks a year in order to make the most efficient use of accommodation, equipment and industrial training facilities. Although admission qualifications to full-time National Diploma and part-time National Certificate curses are similar, the former is much broader in conception and treatment. This is likely to be reflected in two significant ways. Formerly, it was possible, for example, for an engineer having a Higher National Certificate to qualify in a fairly straight forward way for professional technologist status as an associate member of one of the professional status as an associate member of one of the professional engineering institutions-in fact the large proportion of associate members qualified in such a way. The route is still open but it is being made so much longer and harder that in the near future it will only be possible to qualify for membership of a professional institution via a university degree, a Diploma in Technology or a Higher National Diploma. The Higher National Certificate is being increasingly regarded as the qualification of top level technicians.

One qualification for admission to a National Certificate course is four passes in specific subjects at the Ordinary level of the General Certificate of Education. It is also the qualification required for direct admission to most of the new courses being designed for higher level technicians. One of the reasons why parents want their children to remain at school until they obtain Ordinary level passes is in order to qualify for a technician apprenticeship or its commercial equivalent. It is also a reason for encouraging General Certificate courses in secondary modern schools.

The second admission qualification to National and Technician courses is by a new kind of course, the General Course. It is of either one or two years' duration and it will usually be taken straight after leaving school at a local college or its equivalent, a branch college of further education. The regional colleges may have considerable numbers of craft students working for initial qualifications, but the aim and tendency is to shed such work, so that in future only craft students studying beyond an initial craft qualification for a technician qualification are likely to attend regional colleges. At present, however, some of the regional colleges are catering for all of work in technical, commercial catering and women's subjects from the Diploma in Technology at one extreme to pre-apprenticeship curses and General Courses at the other. It is difficult at this stage of development to distinguish major differences between area and regional colleges. In the future there will probably be no degree or post-graduate studies and little technical research work being done by the staff at area colleges.

A few area colleges still retain Diploma in Technology and Higher National Diploma courses. Regional Councils for Further Education, which are co-ordinating bodies, decide in which colleges higher level courses are to be held in order to make the best use of regional resources. The Regional Councils endeavour to ensure that such courses will survive into the foreseeable future. They try to avoid unnecessary duplication and to concentrate advanced studies mainly in colleges of advanced technology and to a lesser extent in regional colleges of technology.

Area colleges are likely to continue to have a range of Ordinary and Higher National Certificate and top-level technical courses in the technologies as well as in commercial and business studies. It may be, that, in the near future regional colleges will delegate all work below the Higher National level to area colleges.

An increasing proportion of the courses in area colleges is likely to be on a block-release basis particularly in the newer kinds of courses for agriculture, catering, hotel and other seasonal occupations where adequate practical training is only possible during certain times of the year. Block-release courses are likely to be normal practice for industries in which the trained manpower exists only in small units dispersed over wide areas. In addition to the advantages already discussed for block-release, it is also claimed that there is less student wastage than in day-release courses. Where experiments have taken place it would appear that more students complete courses successfully, in some cases obtaining two examination qualifications where previously by day-release few would have attained one qualification.

The argument would be relevant for students in seasonal occupations, who may both be able to attend regularly on the same day and same tow evenings every week and who, in any case, could be more subject to fatigue and more prone to minor illnesses by being over exerted during their busy seasons. The student from a small specialized firm may have to travel long distances for his day-release and two evenings' study. In such respects daily traveling to block-release would not necessarily be less unsatisfactory; hence the immediate locality to have hostels or approved lodgings.

In the past, many craft students did not proceed beyond the Intermediate stage of a City and Guilds of London craft course. It is a good qualification for the majority of craftsmen but the title is considered to be unsatisfactory and is being changed to Craft certificate. The previous higher qualification of final City and Guilds is being replaced by the Advanced Craft Certificate which is regarded as the qualification for a top-level craftsman.

To become a technician it will be necessary for a craftsman to obtain a higher qualification still, similar to the present full Technological Certificate of the City and Guilds. The courses for advanced craftsmen and for craftsmen wishing to quality as technicians are likely to be in area colleges. The range of courses in commercial, business and women's subjects in the area colleges is as comprehensive and covers the same wide field as in regional colleges.

Local colleges

Local colleges are suited to the further education needs of a small town catering for the majority of students up to the age of 18 or 19, by which time they will normally be expected to have reached the level of qualification required for attendance at an area or regional college. In larger towns and cities branch colleges are being established to deal with the same range of studies as local colleges in smaller towns.

The technical courses in local and branch colleges are likely to be up to Ordinary National Certificate and equivalent level for craft courses as well as for secretarial and domestic subjects. Because the local college is, for most students, the first stage of further education, it is probably the most important tier in the four-tier system. The educational aim is that pupils should go straight from school into further education. At present too many students have a year's interval after leaving school without any incentive either from parents or employers to attend a technical college. Among those who obtain apprenticeships at 16, many are not required by employers to attend college and as a result do not continue further study. Fewer still of those going into jobs not requiring apprenticeship attend a college.

Until the school-leaving age is raised to 16 it is hoped that more parents will persuade their children to remain in full-time education for an additional year. If suitable courses are not available in the schools the pupils can attend the local college courses leading to Ordinary and, if they wish, to Advanced level General Certificate of Education. Statistics show that courses in colleges are catering for increasing numbers of students.

Pupils remaining longer in full-time education in schools and students straight from school pursuing full-time General Certificate, pre-apprenticeship and secretarial studies in local colleges are mainly from the professional and upper-level occupational groups.

Mostly, from smaller families and, except for secretarial courses, enrolments show a great preponderance of boys, but this is a social problem requiring a political rather than educational solution. Another development is for industry to send its younger employees to the local college for a period of induction to further education extending from two or three weeks to as many months. The scheme, as with all educational release by industry, is entirely dependent on the attitude of employers, so that employers with economic vision are likely to adopt it while the others ignore it.

The broad aims of the induction course are to provide opportunities for educational and vocational guidance based on the techniques of diagnostic and prognostic testing; to experiment with methods of remedial and intensive teaching, particularly in mathematics and science; to work out devices for helping young people to understand the need of further vocational and general studies.

Industry is not enthusiastic about induction courses, but where pilot courses are being tried much is being learned by the staffs of local firms and local colleges. Industry as a whole is more enthusiastic about the recently introduced General Courses which are planned as an immediate educational follow-on from school, in order to maintain continuity of learning based on vocational interest. The General Courses are planned to take tow years for pupils who leave school at 15, and one year for those leaving at 16 and not possessing four appropriate passes at Ordinary level of the General

Certificate of Education. At present the courses are part-time day or block-release but there is increasing support for the idea that they should be on a sandwich basis. They are intended to replace any existing preliminary evening courses, because it is considered that evening study by itself is an unsatisfactory and wasteful way in which to introduce school leavers to intensive technical studies.

The general Course is designed as a period during which appraisals can be made about the kinds of special vocational education courses which students should follow. The studies concentrate on mathematics and science because there is evidence that successful study in mathematics and, to a lesser degree, in science is likely to lead to success in National Certificate and higher technicians' courses.

There are additional subjects including drawing and English studies. As in all technical college studies, the educational aim is to encourage intellectual versatility and the rational understanding of vocationally-relevant fundamental principles, rather than to provide industrial training in precise skills and techniques. At the end of the first year of the General Course a student may be transferred to the first year of a technician's course, or he may continue into the second year of the general course if he shows the ability for a National Certificate course.

At the end of the second year he may be transferred for example to the first year of a two-year Ordinary National Certificate or Diploma course, provided he has obtained credits in mathematics and engineering science and a pass in engineering drawing in the externally set and marked examinations. If he has passes in these three subjects he can be transferred to the second year of a technicians' course. The student who left school at 16 and is pursuing a General course can at the end of one year be transferred on the same basis to the first year of a National Certificate or the local college for two further years to obtain the Ordinary National Certificate, or for four or five years for the Advanced Craft Certificate or for a technician qualification. When the admission qualifications to National Certificate courses were accepted as either four Ordinary Level passes in specific subjects or passes with appropriate credits in the General Course, the duration of the Ordinary Certificate course became two years instead of three.

Experience had already shown that a two-year course based on adequate admission qualifications produced a greater success rate than a three-year course without such admission qualifications. Block-release and sandwich type courses raise the success are still further. Specialization is delayed beyond the Ordinary National stage which is usually at the age of 18 and is began at the Higher National Certificate stage. The aim is that higher technicians should have a sound understanding of fundamental principles which they can learn to apply in the automated workshops and offices designed for increased productivity.

Delayed specialization allows for greater career flexibility and for adaptability within a changing pattern of industry. Only a few Advanced Craft Certificate Courses have been introduced but as courses are being reviewed the new arrangement is being adopted. A craft student can transfer after the craft certificate stage to the first year of the National Certificate course, provided he reaches the required standard in the craft certificate examination. Specialist technician courses are being developed in association with the requirements of particular industries.

There are courses for technicians in telecommunications, electrical, mechanical and aeronautical engineering, metallurgical work, instrument maintenance and plastics technology. Technician courses based on further study, after final City and Guilds or Advanced Craft Certificate, are being planned for the building and furniture industries, for motor vehicle work and for printing technicians. They are known as 'end on' courses. Gradually specialist technician courses will be required and available for all industries. It is in the local colleges that new type courses for operatives are being developed. They vary in length and they are being worked out industry by industry. They are mainly on a day-release basis because it is accepted that no student on any course should have to depend entirely on evening study.

Operatives' courses have long existed in the textile, iron, steel, chemical, boot and shoe and the coal-processing industries. Special industrial safety courses for operatives are being developed at local colleges, for example in radiation safety practice, in order to reduce the accident rate of juveniles in industry. As an indication of the contribution by local colleges to industry, Ministry statistics show that 210 full-time pre-apprenticeship courses were arranged in 1961 by 82 local colleges for 4, 000 school leavers. Over 3, 200 apprentices, employed mostly in engineering, and some in mining and building, attended a total of 121 first year full-time industrial training and education courses arranged at 55 local and branch colleges. Each local college has a wide variety of secretarial and domestic courses.

Many of the local and branch colleges have as many students studying for General Certificate examinations at Ordinary and Advanced levels as are doing so in large-sized secondary grammar schools. The growth is being encouraged because full-time education to the age of 16 is regarded as the best preparation for technical studies. There has been tremendous emphasis in recent years on the need for closer co-operation between school, further education institutions and industry. Although philosophers have always propounded that education is for living, the tendency in the practice of the traditional education has been to ignore that living includes earning a living, and that education must include learning to earn a living. There is perpetual argument about 'living the good life' in an abstract way which ignores or is insensitive to the fact that to live the good life requires the economic resources to support all aspects of the good life.

Primary school-teachers tend to be out of touch with the social and occupational influences affecting the patterns of living of their pupils as children, as adolescents and as parents and workers. Secondary school-teachers do not seem on the whole, to be actively concerned that they are in large measure conditioning the technical education and career opportunities of their pupils. Although 34 per cent of boys and 7 per cent of girls leaving school go into apprenticeship and the great majority of the remainder into semi-skilled jobs, it is rarely that their teachers spend any length of time within the industries in which their pupils will spend much of their lives. It is equally rare for school-teachers to spend time in technical colleges. Some of them want to know about Diplomas in Technology, National Courses, craft qualifications, General and Induction curses, but they want to be told or to read about them. Because the pattern of technical education is larger than school education, but not by any means more complicated, school-teachers rarely make the effort understand it. In order to excuse this attitude they infer that technical education is a mystery.

The only way to learn about technical education, its aims, courses, qualifications and organization, is to become actively involved. The Ministry of Education has made many recommendations, but without much success, regarding integration of school, further educations and industry. They include: a greater emphasis on the theory and practice of technical education and training for student teacher sin university departments of education and training colleges; periods of industrial experience for all student teachers; fairly long exchanges between the staffs of schools and technical colleges; more frequent seminars, study groups, courses, conferences, and meetings between school and technical college teachers and their colleagues in industry.

The individual class teacher has little control over the present situation which perpetuates educational isolation. The initiative, better quality planning and detailed arrangement is required not from individual teachers but from organizers, advisers, inspectors and the large increasing body of administrative staffs who appear, in many cases, to be concerned with anything except educational thinking and teacher guidance. It is unfortunately true that few technical college teachers make or take opportunities for learning about secondary education. It is difficult to understand why this should be Most Principals, Heads of Departments and Headmasters have occasional meetings and maintain a kind of superficial, educational and social contact, but technical teachers rarely spend any long period with their colleagues in the schools.

It is equally difficult to understand how technical teaching can begin to be effective unless technical teachers are fully aware of the aims, content, curriculum, organization and methods of the immediately previous stage in students' education. School education is now linked very closely to technical education by the four tier system of colleges and the new kinds of vocational education courses. The best results from further education require more effective liaison to be created between colleges and schools.

Technical teachers need to learn how to use and interpret pupils' school record cards and reports, scores in tests of attainment, ability, aptitude and personal qualities and how to correlate results with further educational and vocational guidance. They need training in the use of diagnostic tests, remedial techniques, intensive teaching methods, tutorial methods and methods based on active individual and group learning. They will need time to go into schools to make a learning. They will need time to go into schools to make a trained study of schemes of work and teaching methods, and in particular of vocational courses including the business and industrial skill and craft subjects.

In order that they may continue 'education for life and living' technical teachers must have opportunities to learn about the experimental work being done in schools in all fields of education, but particularly in the 'creative' subjects, because the country requires people with developed creative ability in order to regain a significant place in the field of industrial design, and to maintain a good standard of national culture. It is doubtful if technical education can function effectively unless it is made easy for all technical teachers to take advantage of opportunities for professional training in one form or another. Teachers without training on the whole place too much reliance on methods of teaching and learning which have long been proved inadequate by any criteria.

8

Distance Education

Distance education has been in existence for about one hundred years. The different forms of distance education can be identified by their use of technical media and as the basis for the learning materials. By far the great majority of distance education programmes are print-based. The teaching basis of the Open University of the United Kingdom, for example, is approximately 80% print-based, 10% broadcasting (radio and television) and 10% face-to-face seminars and summer schools.

A real disservice has been done to the field of distance education by overemphasis on terms like 'University of the Air'. Educators, administrators and politicians, not only in developing countries but also in developed countries where finance for education is now being limited, should realise that the vast majority of distance education courses are print-based and will remain so. Exceptions to this in the foreseeable future will come only with populations for whom literacy is a problem and perhaps in those regions where there is traditional reticience about correspondence-type programmes.

Higher education in the United States of America is an area where an attempt to transfer emphasis to videotape-based or computer-based programmes might be worth considering because of the population's interest in technology and dislike of correspondence study. An interesting variant on print-based programmes are the courses by newspaper developed under the leadership of Martin N. Chamberlain, Dean of University Extension at the University of California, San Diego. The Deutsches Institutfur Fernstudien at Tubingen has recently introduced a similar programme in the Federal Republic of Germany.

Audio-based courses in which the educational content is carried by audio-cassettes or transmitted over radio and to which printed materials are peripheral, if used at all, have been used by distance educators. They are frequently cost-effective, can be used by people with literacy problems and may be a successful method of teaching languages. The University of Waterloo in Ontario is an extensive user of this method.

Distance education can be video-based when the basic educational content of the course is broadcast on television or contained on video-cassettes. Some printed materials containing background, further reading and assessment procedures often are supplementary, to the course. The development of cable television and the possibility of home ownership or rental of VCRs make this an area of interest in some cultures.

Series of programmes for television have already been developed by a number of groupings in America and elsewhere and a series of programmes based on video-cassettes is offered for credit by the independent study division of the University of Minnesota. Such programmes are to be regarded as distance education when they satisfy the characteristics outlined in the first section of this article. A variant of both audio and video-based programmes is the educational use of satellites.

Daniel presented an evaluation of the first attempts at satellite-based programmes to the 11th World Conference of the I.C.C.E. at new Delhi. Interest has also been aroused by the educational programmes of the Appalachian Area Satellite Project.

A computer can be the medium on which educational programmes that fall within the definition of distance education are based. A number of institutions have developed computer-based distance education programmes and the Fall Education Company lists over 300 computer-based courses already developed for the ATO system. They range from Accounting Fundamentals to Zeiss—a model Planetarium. It is known that in America negotiations are in progress for the accreditation of some of these computer-based programmes for college and university credit.

No evaluation of the relative merits of the media described nor of the possibility of developing a multi-media system by combinations of the various components is offered here. Nor can consideration be given to whether it is possible or desirable to combine distance education with on-campus education. That is the work of other studies.

Private, proprietary correspondence schools have made valuable contributions to this field of education since the last century. In recent years standards have been set by affiliation to national accrediting bodies: the National Home Study Council of the U.S.A., the Association of Accredited Correspondence Colleges of the United Kingdom. Some of these institutions are non-profit making and a number receive some government support and they are found throughout the world. Government sponsored schools, colleges and universities have played a role in distance education for the last seventy years. Many of these institutions are specially structured for distance education: Athabasca University, Edmonton; the Open College of Further Education, Adelaide; the Centre National de Tele-enseignement in France; the Fernuniversitat-Gesamthochschule in Hagen. Many other colleges and universities have a department which concentrates on the distance students : the independent study department of the University of Minnesota, Minneapolis; the external studies department of the University of Queensland, Brisbane.

Three forms of didactic structure characterise distance education institutions, especially when considered under the headings: provision for two-way communication and possibility of occasional seminars. Variations of the three models presented here are to be found employed by the different institutional types considered above in their effort to link learning materials to learning. The correspondence schools send learning materials by post to the student, the student studies the materials and posts assignment back to the institution which marks and comments upon them and posts them back to the student.

The correspondence element in distance education is here reduced to a minimum and once the learning materials have been developed and distributed to the students, the emphasis is placed on compulsory fortnightly two-to-three hour consultations. At these, groups of students meet their tutor for evaluation of their home study and for explanation and preparation of the next stage of learning materials. In the third and fourth year of study the frequency of the consultations is greatly diminished.

In a system similar to that of the Open University of the United Kingdom the link between learning materials and learning is promoted by as coherent a structure as possible. The student is supported by a wide range of activities, most of them optional unless the course team has decided otherwise. This tends to strengthen the possibility that learning takes place and that unnecessary drop-outs are prevented. From time to time distance education is described as the opposite of face-to-face education. This statement needs to be taken further as there are many forms of what may be considered the 'opposite of face-to-face' education that are not distance education.

Pamphlets, books and teach-yourself manuals fall into this category. The lack of an educational organisation is again the major factor which distinguishes these from distance education, together with the impossibility of two-way communication. It is clear that many people learn a great deal from these means, even though they may lack didactical structuring or even an educational goal.*Teaching kits.* In increasing use in face-to-face teachering are kits of various kinds containing samples, games and specimens on which students are invited to work without supervision.

When a lecturer communicates with a student by means of audio-visual aids: slides, film, audio and video-tapes, he is teaching indirectly. Depending on the structure of the programme within which they are being used, these forms of indirect teaching can form part either of face-to-face instruction or of a distance education programme. Many people learn a great deal from radio and television and sometimes those media are used in distance education programmes, Kenneth Clarke's Civilisation or Jacob Bronowski's The Ascent of Man were not conceived as part of a distance education programme. Nevertheless they have become part of both on-campus and distance education programmes when offered for credit with accompanying didactically structured assignment, reading and assessment materials.

Programmed learning, which was popular in the 1960s, is a form of indirect teaching which has many similarities to distance education. Both demand extensive preparation of learning materials, careful sequencing and tend towards the individualising of learning. Computer-aided learning is a recent form of indirect education and is used extensively in many conventional teaching programmes. Mention is made here of independent study and private study as two forms of education with similarities to the above. There are many forms of independent study amongst which can be classed study guided by a governess, tutor or counsellor and many contract, independent or external degree programmes in American colleges.

Private study can be seen as neither a form of direct, classroom education nor of indirect off-campus studies. It is widespread and devoid of institutional linkages, though it may be based on materials developed for use within an institution either for traditional classroom students or distance learners. There are certain forms of education which have some similarities to distance education but are not identical with it. Four of the most important are here presented for consideration: extension programmes, University Without Walls, experiential learning, the external degree. Three more general terms: 'non-traditional learning', 'off-campus studies' and 'open learning' are first considered briefly. One cannot define 'non-traditional learning' without first defining 'traditional learning' and that is clearly beyond the bounds of this article. It seems at times that in the United States any educational programme that is not a four-year, residential, university degree programme can be regarded as non-traditional learning, though there are clearly more restricted usages.

"Non-traditional learning' is to be regarded as a vague, generalised term of which distance education is one example. 'Off-campus studies' is another general term for any programme which does not take place on the central university or college campus—distance education is one possibility.

'Open learning' therefore, is a term that is not to be used in an administrative context; rather its context is philosophical to describe, for instance, colleges with 'open' administration policies or a special spirit like Paris VIII at Vincennes, I'Universite Ouverte. Some of these are face-to-face institutions, others teach at a distance. Extension programmes are ways of extending the expertise of a university or college to new populations. The terms can imply offering the same programmes as for full-time, day-time students by different means, at different locations or at different times.

An extra-mural department usually has a similar function of extending the expertise of the university to a broader community. Some of these programmes are for credit, others not. The range or extension and extra-mural programmes is very extensive and distance education can be regarded as one grouping of a number of possibilities of providing education outside the normal lecture room. Extension, especially as used in the United States, is a much broader term which can include part-time day or night, conventional lectures on campus.

University without walls implies the design of an individualised programme based on a learning contract for students with clear learning objectives who cannot realise their whole educational aspirations through existing programmes. A University Without Walls programme can include experiential learning credits, ordinary lectures, distance education elements, learning from community sources or job-related activities, all of which can be evaluated towards a college or university degree.

Experiential learning programmes are those which give credit for prior learning which did not take place in a lecture room setting and was not sponsored by an educational institution, but was acquired through work experience including volunteer work, co-operative education or self-study. A degree programme which can be completed in the following manner: a student entering the programme with the minimum entrance qualifications can complete it with less than 25 percent of the required work taking the form of campus-based classroom instruction.

In the attempt to place some conceptual order around the wide range of study programmes that are associated with non-traditional and distance education, the question of whether or not the external degree should be included within the concept of distance education is the one which poses the most precise definition and research problems. In so far as the external degree serves to describe the programmes whose primary function is to recognise education and attribute to it an appropriate qualification, it does not fall within the concept of distance education as it has been presented in this study.

If, on the other hand, it is used to describe programmes whose function is to provide education for students, then it may be identified with distance education providing it agrees with the descriptors given in the first section of this article. One hundred and eighty-three college and university degree programmes are classified as external in the American study referred to above.

Tele-enseignement 'distance teaching' is an influential term in French because of its use in the titles of the Centre National de Tele-enseignement, (C.N.T.E.), the Centres do Tele-enseignement Universitaire (C.T.U.) and the Tele-universite de Quebec. There are some who would argue that *formation a distance* 'education at a distance' reflects more closely modern pedagogical theories. The problem with *tele-enseignement* is that many do not realise that the root of *'tele'* is the Greek word *tele* 'from afar', 'from a distance' and does not refer to television. *Tele-enseignement* appears to be the generally accepted term. The words *education a distancia* in Spanish and *teleducacao* in Portuguese seem to be gaining acceptance as terms for 'distance education', side by side with the spread of influence of this type of education in Spanish and Portuguese speaking countries.

In English there are at least six major terms: correspondence study/education, home study, independent study, external studies, distance teaching, distance education. Correspondence study is not a suitable word for what has been described as 'distance education' in this article. It cannot describe radio-based programmes like *Ensemble,* television-based programmes like *The Great Plaine,* computer-based programmes in the PLATO series nor the Appalachian Satellite programme.

Communications theory experts tell us that words get tired and if they do then 'correspondence study' is a tired word. It is significant that when the directors of the correspondence schools of the United States of America came together in 1926 to form an association the title chosen was the National Home Study Council and not the National Correspondence Study Council.

Home study is used mainly in the United States of America and is there confined to further and technical education. The 1979 listing of approved members of the National Home Study Council contain 94 institutions, most of them proprietary. When the universities of the United States of American which teach at a distance wanted to form an association it is significant that they rejected the title 'Home Study' and chose instead

'Independent Study'. 'Home study' is thus unsuitable an a generic term for the wide range of teaching-learning activities which have been described.

Independent study is the term used in higher education in the U.S.A. The 1979 Guide to independent study through correspondence instruction lists 68 members of the Independent Study Division of the National University Extension Association. Nearly all of these are correspondence sections of extension departments of American universities. In addition to programmes for degree credit, may of the courses are at high school or certificate level.

External studies is the term most widely used in Australia, Its use is confined to that region where it well describes the essence of the 'integrated model' of distance education as found in many Australian institutions: 'external to' but not 'separated from' the faculty staff. It can have little claim to general acceptance because of this limitation and because of confusion with the American external degree. Whether or not the American external degree, especially those associated with Antioch and Nova universities, falls within the concept of distance education has already been discussed. *Distance teaching or teaching at a distance* has been the term most commonly used by the Open University in the United Kingdom.

Distance teaching is only half the process we are trying to describe: to distance teaching must be added distance learning. The description of distance education as a form of industrialized education will, among other things, be criticized as public opinion is a still influenced by anti-technical, or more generally, anti-industrial emotions which emerged in the context of the critique of our modern culture.

'The gospel of humanity cannot be separated from the critique of modern culture,' summarized Litt. In the second part of the nineteenth century cities of culture such as Ruskin, Hildebrandt, Nietzsche and Langbehn opposed industrialization, arguing mainly that it mechanizes and factionalizes man. Hans Scheuerl has described the damage done to man by industrialization as set forth by critics of culture.

According to these critics there is a fear that 'original individuality will decline in a mass culture' and will be summarized to mere functional efficiency, that 'the imitation, the mass production will make the deeper layers of soul waste away', that stressing external, values will result in the loss of interior values, that the materialistic attitude towards life will alienate man from spiritual contents and their requirements. Altogether, these critics believed that 'the originally wholesome nature' of man is not enriched by the artificiality of civilizatory achievements but 'alienated, endangered and suffocated'. These attacks of the critics of culture have become especially important as their fundamental attitude was mediated by the youth and school reform movements and had strong effects on the theory and practice of education in the first half of our country.

The attitude of several generations of teachers towards technical achievements, the mechanization of instruction, and, therefore, towards distance education as well was influenced by their critique of culture. In spite of this, the return to the critique of culture in order to find out the reasons for the reservations of present-day educationists to distance education seems to be a little inadequate at first glance. First of all, critical discussion of distance education has not yet started on a scientific level. And secondly, we have learnt that the opposition towards other forms of industrialized education, such as programmed learning and cybernetic pedagogy, has been less strong than was expected.

In the meantime, one is often prepared to view industrialization as an irreversible process. Nevertheless, it must still be supposed that the attitude of former critics of culture was handed down by the movement of neohumanistic education and is still potent in the educational world of today, even if it is mainly found below the level of scientific discussion. This may be the reason for the widespread sacepticism, lack of interest and even disdain for distance education. As evidence for this are the critics who readily concede that industrialization is, indeed, an irrevocable development, but at the same time consider it dangerous and disastrous.

Judgements of this kind can be heard from modern critics of culture in the conservative camp to the anti-authoritarian and progressive Marxist camp - where they are growing in numbers. Progressive Marxist examples are mainly the attacks on the cultural industry by Theodor W. Adorno, on the consciousness industry by Hans Magnus Enzensberger and Herbert Marcuse's description of the consequences of advanced industrialization on man. There is no doubt that many of the arguments set forth by critics of culture in three different historical periods apply also to industrialized education.

One is, for instance in line with the critics of culture of the second part of the nineteenth century when saying that the original individuality of the teacher and also of the students cannot express itself and is even lost over long periods of the teaching-learning process because of the use of technical media and of fixed goals and procedures of instruction. Teachers and students do not meet as fully developed individuals, but only as reduced and specialized functionaries.

Distance education produces neither funny teaching characters nor notoriously annoying types of students, as is often the case in face-to-face instruction. The systems of distance education are, it is true, 'standardized in order to raise their functionality', and 'production in series', 'mechanization', and 'functionalization' and 'functionalization' are their important structural traits. Finally, it should be mentioned that the motivation of many distant students derives from a 'materialistic attitude towards life'—that,is, that they strive to improve their conditions of life by obtaining higher qualifications. While this attitude may be a general one in our time, it seems, however, to be typical in a special sense for distant students.

When we consider new arguments - for instance, those of Jochen Kaltschmid, who has proved again in a profound analysis that 'the apparatus, the technicalization, mechanization, division of labour and organization' are all elements of the process of rationalization which shape the existence of man, and that the consequences of this rationalization are that our world is 'dominated by purposes', that we lose our 'inwardness', the 'immediacy of life' and the unity of our psychological faculties—then, of course, we have to see that these consequences, indeed, are very likely to be reinforced by industrialized education.

In fact, its rationalized systems of teaching and learning are, as we have seen, structured in such a way that the purposes—the defined teaching goals - are achieved in the best way, the 'inwardness' of the students and the teachers, which is normally preserved by their personal interaction, is more or less lost by the objectivation of teaching behaviour, the splitting up of teaching and learning functions, and by the use of technical media. Also, the 'closeness to life' of instruction is, naturally, reduced a great deal.Teachers and students are no longer involved as whole human beings. And the unity of our psychic faculties is broken up. There are also many current argument about the incompatibility of technical developments and education which are often emotive and relate to the concept of instrialized education, as this form of education is - as we have shown—a result of the general process technicalizing of society.

Ludwig Heieck has discussed some of these arguments. According to him, education gives way to the functionalist thinking in terms of expediency in our technical age and abandons man. He says: 'Education derives from history. It is determined by the view that man is a historic being. Technical progress, however, is a historic. Instruction and education, therefore, have not participated in technical progress as they have felt threatened by it'.

The problem cannot be solved in the theoretical framework used so far in other chapters of this book. We have to face the same situation which was characterized by Paul Heimann, when he defended his contention that 'film, radio, and television are the powerful educational institutions of the present'. The objections raised to their educational use in the past also apply top distance education, especially when it employs such mass media. According to Heimann, these critics were afraid of 'the furtherance of a receptive learning behaviour, an educational and instructional impressionism, the emergence of a dangerous conformism, the immobilization of creative imagination, the artificial increase of optical and acoustical stimuli, the reduction of primary experiences in favour of secondary experiences, the depersonalization, the mechanization of the relation between teacher and taught, and the leveling out of individual instruction'.

Heimann emphasized that these objections must by no means be trivialized, as some of them contain important arguments of educational philosophy. On the other hand, his reflections led to the conclusion that these objections can scarcely be refuted on the level of pure educational thinking. Therefore, he offered arguments dealing with problems of intellectual history and sociology. In this chapter a similar avenue is followed in order to invalidate possible objections of cultural critics to distance education or other forms of industrialized education.

The discussion will have four different starting points. First, the interpretation of a model of the historical development of instruction is to clarify whether distance education really distinguishes itself structurally to such a great extent from traditional education that the teacher and the students are placed in an entirely new existential situation which is not in line with the general historic trend and which must be considered as a development which fundamentally fails to reach the goal of humanity. Secondly, a number of socio-cultural preconditions of distance education and developments in the history of ideas are dealt with, in order to find out whether the objections of the critics of culture remain feasible.

Thirdly, it will be proved by comparing traditional instruction in the classroom with distance education that it integrates into the process of general change of social subsystems and into the present inevitable development of society, whereby many of the norms defended by the critics of culture appear to be unreal. Fourthly, distance education is interpreted in anthropological terms. It is to be expected that dealing with it in such a way will result in further general arguments for judging the objections of the critics of culture.

If we consider the context of the origin of distance education not in a concrete socio-economic, but in a more general, far-teaching sense, then a new dimension emerges for the understanding of distance education. In order to achieve this it is, however, necessary to describe some structural elements of historical forms of instruction.

If one relates this initial situation of instruction to our distance education today, a historical model of instruction can be constructed which shows that instruction has fundamentally changed in a development of several thousand years. The dimensions of this change can be determined by the following extreme parameters; the elitist instruction becomes egalitarian, its sacral contents and procedures become profane, the government of the teacher is substituted by the self-government of the student, the intimate group becomes a larger and less intimate group or even an anonymous mass of students, the personal interaction between teacher and students becomes mechanized and automated, and the traditional ties of instruction to a special teacher, a special place and a special time are removed. It is evident that developments have taken place in the dimensions referred to whereby it is not necessary to consider their division into periods or their delays in certain cultural areas.

The entire extent of these changes could be demonstrated on a bipolar scale. Distance education would arrive at the extremes in all cases. However, if one also assesses the present instruction in classrooms it becomes apparent that his form of education has not developed accordingly. A closer examination will show that there is a correlation between the different stages of development and the extent to which principles of industrialization have been applied in each case. Analogously to the historical process of the democratization of political power, which passed through several stages, there was also a process of continued democratizing of political power, which passed through several stages, there was also a process of continued democratizing of teaching and learning and of knowledge. One can ever—parallel to the political development—distinguish priestly-aristocratic, bourgeois and democratic forms of teaching and learning and of knowledge.

Whereas in the beginning of the cultural development only small groups handed down their knowledge, which was often kept secret, to the chosen ones, now a phase is reached in which in many countries of the world knowledge is in principle accessible by everyone, whereby traditional ethnic, religious, social and regional boundaries, which still make education privilege to many, can be surmounted—due to the availability of industrialized education. The latest and most convincing steps in this direction have been taken by the Open University in the United Kingdom.

Consequently, in many countries educational politicians consider distance education as a means for equalizing educational opportunities. Such a way of thinking, it is true, overlooks the enormous socio-cultural barriers on the way to education and surely underestimates the real difficulties. Nevertheless, it must be admitted that distance education provides at least necessary technical and organizational preconditions for a universal admission to continued and higher education. An analysis of statistics about distance education reveals that millions of distant students do indeed profit from this industrialized way of education.

Often enough it offers them the only way towards the desired education as all other ways are barred by lack of funds or by other circumstances. Comparison with the conditions under which face-to-face-instruction takes place in the schools of the Federal Republic of Germany as well as in those of other countries can be used to show that we are dealing with school systems organized according to class structures in which access to secondary schools and universities remains restricted, so that people continue to suffer from the inequality of educational opportunities. The sacral character of instruction can be related to the fact that at the beginning of our cultural development the knowledge and skills which were handed down from one generation to the other were priestly wisdom and ritual ceremonies. Only later were the various scientific disciplines differentiated from the knowledge of the priests. In ancient Babylon the priests were physicians and teachers in one person.

The Indian Veda consisted at first of hymns, teachers in one person. The Indian Veda consisted at first of hymns, prayers, wordings and proverbs which were important in sacrificial ceremonies. Only later varying systems of interpretation and research approaches developed out of them and disciplines like law, logic and dogmatics branched off. The Egyptian priest caste also imparted collections of hymns as part of the holy literature.

The scientific disciplines could emancipate themselves from mythical ideas and ritual reinforcements only later. This applied of course, to the respective instruction as well. In the beginning, however, the forms of instruction corresponded to sacral contents. Everything we still can learn shows us that the priest-teacher was venerated by the students and that the instruction and examinations were permeated by a ceremonial solemnity.

It is obvious that most forms of our present instruction have left those sacral origins far behind them, of course. However, on looking more carefully one can see that the process of secularization has not yet ceased everywhere. As distance education is mainly dependent on indirect interaction and communication it has, so to speak, completed its seculization. The interaction between teacher and student is objectified by rational teaching techniques and the use of technical media to such a degree that even relicts of archaic attitudes are no longer possible. In instructional face-to-face situations, however, one can still find them. In fact, rudiments of an originally sacred teaching-learning behaviour can be identified in the following circumstances:

— teachers - be they in the classroom or lecture hall - see themselves as the source of knowledge;
— the teacher dominates the students verbally in such a way that the intended dialogue between the student which is structurally similar to that of a priest in the pulpit preaching to the faithful;
— the students rise from their seats when the teacher enters or leaves the classroom;
— there are ceremonial greetings and forms of dismissal;
— the teacher—for example, in English public schools and colleges—still wears a gown which recalls a clergyman's vestments;
— the school continues to stick to certain rituals as, for instance, prayers at the beginning of the school day or hymns and other ceremonies during inauguration and graduation;
— school celebrations assume a special significance in the educational process.

These and other aspects of face-to-face instruction have been handed down by tradition. In distance education, however, this tradition is discontinued because of the technological revolution in the methodology of teaching.

The original communicative stance of teachers and students is substituted by a technologically medicated interaction between the two of them. The process of secularization could, therefore, go further than in face-to-face teaching. Under the aspect of hierarchy it can be stated that the structure of all early forms of instruction was characterized by the fact that the teacher assumed the role of the old man, the father, which was connected with wisdom, authority and power. His power derived often from the knowledge of the power bringing formulas and from his knowledge of the tradition. But above all, it was derived from the power of God. *Hieros* means 'holy'. Accordingly, a hierarchy was originally a 'holy rule'.

The students, who also waited on their teachers, were expected to respect and venerate them. Brunner reports on ancient Egyptian education how the power of the teachers resulted in the punishment of the students. The students were subjected to corporal punishments, were put in the stocks, threatened, admonished, but never praised. In the Middle Ages the status symbol of the teacher was, typically enough, a rod, which he was to hold upright, as may be seen in contemporary pictures. Sometimes, the teacher was supported in his punishing activities by the *locates,* a school janitor who also carried a rod as a token of his dignity, but—for hierarchical reasons—with the tip facing downwards.

Generally, people were of the opinion that, for instance, in the education of artisans as well as of knights, learning and serving went together. The master-servant relationship which was constituted during the training ceased only when the apprentice was formally released from this relationship after having qualified as a journeyman. The development which started off with the student who was ruled and maltreated in the ways described comes to an end with a student who is able to identify his learning needs and who decides himself which learning goals he wishes to reach and in which way or with the university student who applies the concept of learning by researching. Both approaches orientate themselves to the model of the self-determined and self-governing student. Both of them advocate domination-free learning. There are several reasons why distance education has developed structural approaches for forms of learning which are free from teacher dominance and the influence of the teacher's authority and why, hence, distance education would have its place at the end of this dimension:

— The increased availability and accessibility of distance education enables the learner for the first time to check through the learning material of a number of respective courses and make decisions himself when selecting one of them. The necessary qualification for doing so may still be lacking with most learners as, so far, usually other persons have decided what is to be studies and when and where the studying will take place. It can, however, be acquired with the help of systems of distance education and their counselling services.

— Normally, the teacher is not physically present when the student learns. He effects his learning only indirectly. In the same way as in the political sector the personal power of the king was objectified as soon as his personal exercising of power with the help of written documents which then led to bureaucracy, the personal interaction between teacher and student became objectified by the written word and the use of other media. Thus a scope of independence and freedom came into being, which, indeed, is used and appreciated by the students.

— The student takes over the control of the time, the frequency and the duration of his learning.

— Very often adults begin to study a course in distance

> education by their own free decision. In such cases, the relation between the teacher and the student is entirely different from the corresponding relationship in the traditional and institutionalized schools, where the teacher is usually the representative of the power which makes students attend the school and even controls their learning behaviour and school life.

However, the simple fact that a student learns relatively independently does not allow the conclusion that distance education already gives rise to absolutely dominance-free learning. In particular, if distance education is organized as a part of compulsory general education—as, for instance, in Australia, Canada and the United States, with the military services or in vocational training—repressive effects of those who have the power are not removed, but only distributed in another way and sublimated. Their power cannot be done away with simply by replacing face-to-face instruction by distance education.

In spite of this, it must be stressed that the objectivation of learning processes offers more scope for independent learning than instruction tied to special teachers in special situations. Above all, it enables the critical cooperation of students when instruction is evaluated even if this happens only in a representative form. When, for instance, selected students are members of the course team their influence upon the intended teaching-learning process can be increased.

Here, dominance-free learning might, indeed, have more scope for its development in distance education than in face-to-face instruction. At the extreme point of this dimension one can place learners who identify their learning goal themselves, select and handle the respective system of industrialized teaching expertly, and also control the outcomes of their learning themselves.

Obviously, face-to-face instruction is still far from this extreme point, as the learning process is often not only influenced by the teachers' dominance and predilections, as A. and R. Tausch have shown so impressively in their research on the language behaviour of teachers and students, but also by traditional and institutional constraints.

Criteria of repressive teaching behaviour are : corporal punishment of pupils which is still preserved in many primary schools, various forms of disciplinary action at secondary schools, and sending down from universities. In these cases the teaching-learning process is still connected to the process of disciplining the students. The double meaning of 'discipline' is, indeed, telling and applicable even today.

The social pattern of instruction was originally modelled after the social interaction in the family. Keay and Brunner agree in that in ancient times instruction began in the family on the basis of the farther-son relationship. Obviously, teaching started in the intimacy of a father-son relationship and in the form of private tuition. Thinking in ideal types, one can assume that there was a an initial period in which private tuition dominated; for instance, when a priest introduced his successor into the procedures of secret sacral ceremonies, or when children of aristocratic families were carefully prepared for their future role in society. Our knowledge from history shows us that the subsequent periods must have been characterized by the following communication structures between teachers and students :

— group instruction;
— classroom instruction;
— large group instruction;
— instruction of mass audience.

It must be added that each period continued to exist and could even assume new importance in later periods. The changes, however, which came to pass when one period replaced the other must have been considerable, and were, obviously, caused by certain societal necessities. Brunner, for instance, reported that in ancient Egypt private tuition changed to classroom instruction as early as the beginning of the second millennium—that is, at a time when a rigid administration was established and a technically and ethically well-educated civil service was highly valued.

The ability to rationalize instruction with the help of better organization is obviously a precondition for proceeding from one period to the next one. If one asks how distance education relates to these periods, and especially distance education in the multimedia form which has developed during the last fifteen years and which has already integrated radio and television, the answer can only be that it belongs to the final period. The extreme of mass education has been reached fully. Some projects of this kind provided tuition for groups counted in tens of thousands and even a hundred thousand students.

The traditional instruction in the classroom, however, originated at a very early period. It is, strictly speaking, still closely attached to individual instruction, as classroom instruction is basically often still merely an extended and schematized individual instruction—if one disregards the many efforts to change it into group instruction. Educational theorists, who stressed the individuality of the single pupil, Locke, Rousseau, Herbart, Weniger, Bollnow and Buber may have supported this practice. The traditional teaching and learning behaviours are obviously so stable that they resist the use of technical media and the application of principles of industrialization.

The communicative structure of traditional instruction in the classroom depends on limited number of students. Probably 120 students would be the largest possible number in a lecture hall. A radical new approach was needed to overcome this limitation and to make possible the instruction of large and extremely large groups of students which appeared when the general level of education had to be raised as a consequence of industrialization. Distance education is such an approach.

The archaic forms of imparting knowledge and skills could be characterized with regard to their media structure by the negative statement that they functioned without any technical medium. This means that the teachers relied on the medium of the words spoken directly to the student. Whether the teacher was a medicine man, a prophet, a shaman or a priest, he or she always communicated knowledge orally.

The oral teaching of those priest-teachers must, however, not be understood in a modern (that means more or less abstract) sense, as the words were not yet isolated from their original context. For a long time it remained part of the redeeming actions of the priest. The student experienced his speaking as his action. This means that the student not only took in the words, but was also included in the actions. This alone shows why the students had to be taken into the teacher's house. And it becomes clear why the spoken language could not just be substituted by written language at that time as this would certainly have reduced the global context of those actions.

The spoken language of the early forms of instruction was, so to speak, only a medal *pars pro toto.* It was connected to the personality of the teacher—who was considered to be a medium himself. Oral instruction consisted of the teacher's saying a text and the student's repeating. A comprehensive and reliable memory was required for both of them. The oral form of instruction prevailed after writing and reading had been introduced. In ancient India they were used first for commercial and trading purposes, and it took a long time before they were accepted by the teachers. Keay assumes that the tests were considered to be too holy to be handed down in writing. Teachers might have also been afraid that such written texts could be used by unauthorized persons. He reports that in India the old forms of instruction have been preserved longest and have remained unchanged. The Veda are still handed down orally today, although they are, of course, also available in print. And it is not unusual that students succeed in learning whole textbooks by heart.

Distance education, especially in its form of integrated multimedia systems, will again have to be placed at the present end of this line of development. With regard to the decreased importance of the physical presence of the teacher it is surpassed only by programmed instruction. Traditional face-to-face instruction, however, must be classed with an earlier stage of this development, especially when the teacher and his spoken words dominate.

In spite of the use of technical media such as paper, books, blackboards, pictures or even film, the basic communicative structure has not detached itself from the original oral form of instruction. Linking instruction to a special place is also of sacral origin. If a place had proved to be holy, because the effects of the divine power were repeated there, it became a 'special place'. This could be a grove, a grotto, but also a house or a temple. Obviously, temples were the first places where the priests accumulated wisdom, and, hence, the first places of instruction. Just as there was in archaic thinking—no idea of a homogeneous space, there was also no idea of a uniform time. Rather, each time had its own significance. This suggests that the early forms of instruction did not take place at fixed times in the sense of an abstract regularity. This became possible only after a first and very important phase of rationalizing in which it was considered to be possible to isolate time from its close connection to traditional places and actions which up to then were experienced as a global unit. Such an abstracting of traditional places and times became necessary when, as in ancient Egypt, one teacher had to teach several students or even larger groups of students at a time. In such a situation he was compelled to invent group instruction. It was characterized by a certain regularity and by the unity of place, time and persons. In fact, this structural unity was to become a traditional constant of all face-to-face instruction to this day.

In a second phase of rationalizing the teaching-learning process, this unity of place, time and persons disintegrated as a consequence of the application of principles of industrialization. This means that a long tradition, was discontinued. The significance of this break in the tradition of instruction may be indicated by a parallel in the arts: when dramatic presentations on the stage were substituted by dramatic presentations in film, space lost its static condition, and time its continuity. In distance education as well, the unit of place and time, constitutive of face-to-face instruction, as has been shown, ceases to exist.

As the teaching is objectified in the form of course material or educational film several teachers who live far apart from each other and from the students can impart their knowledge one after the other, or even simultaneously, and in a sequence quite different from face-to-face teaching. Time as well is taken out of the context of traditional instruction. The course team can manipulate the stimuli and thus organize the presentation according to new ideas of the dramaturgy of teaching, and the students are free to develop their own learning strategy by fixing their individual times of study. Seen in this way, the break of tradition mentioned appears to be a singular event in the history of instruction.

If one assesses the described stages of development of face-to-face instruction and distance education in this sixth dimension, one cannot but see that face-to-face instruction has not come further than the special conditions of group instruction in ancient Egypt; that is, instruction with fixed times and places and persons. Distance education, however, developed considerably further by becoming largely independent from these ties. This opens up new perspectives which have not yet been noticed and new problems which have not yet been tackled by experts of the methodology of teaching and learning.

Distance education provides for instruction in which teaching and learning have been *secularized* to a high degree, as the relation between teacher and students has been isolated from its traditional social context and objectified. Teacher and students do not interact as persons in their totality, but as special teaching and learning functions which operate only in order to reach the defined goals. The numinous, however, needs the social context in order to be able to express itself. Distance education enables and facilitates *instruction without repressive actions* in the sense that arbitrary acts of teachers—as well as of students—are cut out as technical mediation and the required division of labour have objectified instruction.

If there are institutional or direct dependencies, as, for instance, in the military services and in vocational training, they will be less effective for the same reasons. Distance education is a form of instruction which is capable of catering for great numbers of students and even *mass audiences*. Such a form of instruction would be impossible without the techniques of industrial mass production and without the help of mass media and the computer. Distance education is principally mediated instruction. It cannot take place without the help of *technical media*. Without the mechanization of the presentation of the contents of instruction and of the feedback activities it would not be possible to start, optimize and control it.

Distance education has *cut the three bonds which ties face-to-face instruction to special places, special times and special persons*. The industrial approach of objectifying teaching and learning behaviour and of storing, transporting and reproducing it was the required precondition for this. It has made distance education the most accessible and flexible form of teaching and learning. On the whole, and with regard to the objections of the cultural critics referred to at the beginning, the interpretation of the historic model of instruction results in the conclusion that the tradition of instruction has not been disturbed or even neutralized by the advent of industrialized education.

On the contrary, it subsequently developed along the lines of development in the history of instruction. Distance education is, therefore, not something entirely new, different and strange in the world of education. It cannot be placed beside face-to-face teaching, but rather belongs to the hitherto final stage of the developments of instruction, as it has overtaken face-to-face teaching on the six lines of development, in part even considerably and distinctly. This means that distance education is, structurally speaking, ahead of face-to-face teaching. Clearly, this is the result of its industrialization.

In socio-cultural and intellectual preconditions, the hypothesis to be established and substantiated is that distance education can be assigned to the era of industrialization not only because of the availability of the necessary material and technical conditions, but also because of particular socio-cultural and intellectual developments which are imperative before distance education can emerge.

If in our society many adults and adolescents decide to study at a distance and not in the traditional way, if they manage to go their own way and do not depend on the traditional educational institutions, they must have qualities which distinguish them from people who lived in earlier eras. It is elucidating to analyse these qualities. A first precondition is a particular relationship between humans and their environment. Human consciousness of the environment has changed in along process which stated with archaic-mythological ways of thinking which were gradually replaced by empirical-realistic ideas and concepts. This process was accentuated by the Renaissance and the Enlightenment as they helped to emancipate human thinking from earlier limitations. At this point it is sufficient to indicate which of these developments were important in the context of the hypothesis presented at the beginning.

In the Renaissance, many people became aware for the first time that education can be also used for secular purposes. There was a growing need for the establishment of town schools and of an urban education. In the era of the Enlightenment, teaching and learning were secularized even further. People were inspired by the image of the individual who is able to change unsatisfactory conditions of society by means of reason. For the first time reason was attributed to everyone. And there was an eagerness to educate people in such a way that they learned how to use reason in an efficient way.

There was a widely published popular literature in the form of moralizing periodicals and scientific treatises at that time. The enlightened individual was to become emancipated. He was to learn 'to use his reason without the guidance of anybody else'. It is evident that teaching and learning received new directions in this era. For the hypothesis mentioned it is important to note that the inner relationship between instruction and practical and useful activities was seen. Instruction assumed a rational-utilitaristic meaning.

It is remarkable that in people's conceptions of life, vocational efficiency and success in practical life became significant—an idea which was propagated in Germany above all by the philanthropic movement. Only then did it become possible for long-term systematical work in an occupation to be valued and considered to be a 'sense of life' and 'a standard for success in one's life'. Seemingly, this is one root of the motivation for vocational qualification which was to become so important for distant students in our time. Further preconditions have been described by David Riesman in his theory of various constants of social behaviour which can be identified in European and American societal development. According to this theory, people in pre-industrial society were tradition-directed; that is, that their observation of the external rules of behaviour was regulated and forced upon them down to the last details by customs, habits, ceremonies, rites and etiquette.

When society became industrialized, however, it developed entirely new mechanisms of maintaining conformity. In childhood or adolescence, people now internalized specific principles of the desired behaviour which took effect on the whole of their lives like a steering gear. In this way, types of persons emerged who succeeded in determining their lives without a strict and obvious direction by tradition. They became inner-directed. Only now did they become able to act on their own discretion. And only in the industrialized society did they have options of doing so, as traditions fragmented, many new goals of life emerged, and conditions of life changed increasingly. Those who intended to realize the career prospects provided by the new society had to learn to take the initiative and to disentangle themselves from tradition-directedness.

Whereas the tradition directed individual could not choose between work and spare time, as their lives were regulated by tradition with regard to this as well, the inner-directed persons had the possibility of separating leisure time from working time and being able to have it at their disposal. Under the influence of the Protestant success ethic this happened increasingly in favour of useful activities, for the endeavour to be efficient, to control oneself permanently and to fight the 'demon of indolence' was religiously motivated. The then popular motto *per aspera ad astra* was internalized by the inner-directed person. This led to a striving after vocational success never known before, and partly even to a 'passionate drive to earn and gain'. At the same time the individual in the inner-directed society 'was dissociated and sheltered from others' and became, thus, isolated and more vulnerable. The relevance of such developments for the emergence of distance education can easily be seen. It is evident that distance education would have been unthinkable in a tradition-directed society.

Only the inner-directed society provided the necessary subjective preconditions for it. Every characteristic trait used by Riesman to describe the inner-directed person can also contribute to the explanation of the situation of distant students. Their decision to enrol in a distant study course is already behaviour according to their own direation. Their strongest motivation is derived from vocational career prospects. When they study a t a distance they dispose of their leisure time, make sacrifices, have many difficulties and are typically 'dissociated and sheltered from others'. Hence, it can be assumed that the phenomenon of the adult distant student is in accordance with an inner law of development of our culture in the era of industrialization. It influenced the student's socio-cultural and intellectual development in such a way that the motivation of millions of distant students became strong enough and their inner-directedness so stable that it caused them to stay outside of the institutions of traditional education and to commit themselves to an unorthodox way of teaching and learning.

Furthermore, it can be postulate that the individual's consciousness is also influenced by life in an industrialized society itself. These influences prepare the individual for being able to study at a distance in special ways, as can be illustrated by reference to the following four experiences:

1 the practice of dealing with people, who - in a given situation are charged with the performance of single functions only;
2 the adjustment to the permanent reception of coded information;
3 the development of attitudes towards substitute persons;
4 the orientation towards new basic personality types.

In agrarian society people lives in villages and had relatively few interpersonal relations, which, however, were long-lasting, emotional and integral. No matter what the reason for their interpersonal relation was, the persons involved were expected to be dealt with as total personalities. If, for instance, someone did business with someone else, it certainly mattered whether the persons involved had a liking for each other, whether they were of the same religious faith, how they had led their lives so far, whether they enjoyed a good reputation, and so on. In such a village, a teacher, for instance, played a role which exceeded that of just teaching pupils, and which affected the adults also. His impact was a unique one. Hence, he considered no exchangeable.

Man in the industrialized society is, on the other hand, typically a town-dweller and has a such usually many interpersonal relations, which, however, are relatively short, not emotional, and used for specific purposes. Even with an unusual transaction such as the purchase of an automobile the interaction between the customer and the salesman will, as a rule, no longer be influenced by their personal likings, their religious beliefs, their political leanings, their family situations or their social status.

Customer and salesman interact merely as .persons who serve in a specialized function, and the two expect from each other that this function be performed well. This means that only a small fraction of one person interacts with a small fraction of another person. Each person is fragmented and consists of many functional parts. This reduction of person can be demonstrated by referring to be example of a teacher in a city school; that is, to a teacher specializing in one or two subjects. It is true he teaches pupils, but, as a rule, he cuts out his personal background in this process. He separates official and private functions sharply. As he is reduced to someone who serves certain functions only, it is easier to imagine that he could be replaced. In comparing him to the teacher in a village school it can be seen how far this process has gone.

At the same time it must be seen that the teacher in a city school is still a partner in a continued process of communicative acting which induces him to perform more functions that a teacher in a system of distance education. Considering the stages of development from the teacher in a village school to a teacher in distance education, the teacher in the city school can be classed somewhere in the middle between the extremes.

As individuals in industrial society are able to make contact with many persons in order to perform special functions, they enjoy a freedom never known before. They have disentangled themselves from old bonds which involved their emotions as well, and even the totality of their persons. Now, they are principally also ready to approach complete strangers and to communicate with them—if it is necessary for objective reasons—without doubt, a new human skill. This freedom must have been a favorable precondition for readiness to teach and to learn at a distance, if a specific educational need could not be satisfied otherwise. If the individual, in doing so, did not meet 'real' teachers and 'real students, but only persons charged with the performance of often highly specialized functions, this experience was not new to them, as it was in harmony with so many patterns of interaction which are taken for granted in industrialized societies.

Individuals in industrial society distinguish themselves from persons in pre-industrial society by their ability to receive and to work with information which is technically mediated. First of all, they are reading men.

The mass media with their modern methods of production and distribution enable them to take part in the doings around them and in the world in a very specific way. As oral forms of information were more or less substituted by printed ones they got used to their presentation by technical means. At the same time, in industrial society people see and listen to many things which remained closed to them in agrarian society.

A permanent supply of information from radio and television has certainly an effect on them, whereby the same information can be coded in different ways; for instance, by newspaper, radio or television. In order to acquire the ability to study at a distance—that is, to work with mediated instruction—it may be very important that people have already gained the experience of receiving many pieces of coded information which are independent from the persons and occurrences in their immediate neighborhood. This experience is new, for pre-industrial man received typically only relatively few pieces of information, which were accidental, not coded, and connected to persons and events. The difference is obvious. Through his daily experience, industrial man has learnt to use purposeful (that is, constructed) communications which tend to be concentrated and concise. Such communications are intentional to a high degree, they avoid unnecessary repetitions, and try each time to reach the highest level of information.

Evidently, experiences of this kind are better preconditions for learning at a distance than oral communication as practised nearly exclusively in agrarian societies. The ideas and the behaviour of persons in industrial society are not formed and shaped by their interaction with their primary and secondary groups only, but also by their relations to human beings whom they know exclusively from the mass media: sports idols, film stars, politicians, scholars, authors. They learn about their developments and their life style, observe how they react to actual occurrences, and even develop a lasting attitude towards them. Thus, they are already used to dealing with 'substitute persons' and have accumulated a considerable skill in this respect.

In distance education the students meet, so to speak, 'vicarious teachers' whom they know only from printed texts or aural and visual presentations. This shows again that people in an industrial society are prepared for distance education to a higher degree than those in a pre-industrial society, in which corresponding relations were established by myths, legends and rumours, and remained, therefore, vagues and uncertain.

A corresponding sociological analysis shows that industrial society has also developed new models of human development. With regard to this Richard W.Behrendt speaks of a 'change of basic types of man' which was caused by the industrialization of society. Referring to pre-industrial time, he speaks, for instance, of the ruler, the subject, the patriarch, the heroic warrior, the missionary, the wise man and the scholar. In industrial society, however, these lose their importance and are substituted by types; as, for instance, the conscious man, the emancipated man, *Homo faber*, the technically competent man and the mobile man.

Further types are 'the radically organizing and manipulating man' on the one hand and 'the radically organized and manipulated man' on the other. This change of basic types of human is a profound one, and so serious in its consequences that one can consider it a major transformation in the development of mankind. This transformation has been already dealt with in regard to its relevance in intellectual history. At this point it can be postulated that only human beings who can be classed with the basic types in industrial society are ready for teaching and learning at a distance. That is to say, if one scrutinizes these basic types, one cannot but agree that all of them have a special affinity to industrial education.

Conscious man, who tries successfully 'to become aware not only of the physical and societal world around him, but also of his inner psychic structure, which is often still unconscious', is more easily ready to assess himself and his abilities and, hence, make decisions with regard to realistic educational or training goals. In addition, he is presumably also more likely to assume responsibility for his learning. Emancipated man, 'who has disentangled himself from transcendental and traditional ties' and 'claims an original and autonomous orientation in new situations of life', is certainly more easily motivated to acquire new qualifications which he needs to adjust to such new situations.

Only *Homo faber*, the type of man, 'who considers the world in all its non-transcendental aspects and also man himself as producible or at least malleable', has self confidence enough to be able to change an unsatisfactory situation of life purposefully by learning. Technically competent man is 'the archetype of an era with a relatively developed technology'. He no longer carries loads and no longer eats his bread in the sweat of his brow. Instead, he operates machines, whereby his work is mostly reduced to the control of mechanical energy. This deliverance from heavy manual work and involvement with machines and technical appliances, which save time and energy, is a good precondition for learning, and especially for dealing with technical teaching-learning systems.

Mobile man, who no longer accepts being rooted for his lifetime, geographically speaking, in his native country, in the spiritual sense in this religious belief, and with respect to society in specific social strata, but claims a maximum of mobility according to his abilities and opportunities is emancipated enough to be able to learn without the local, temporal, and personal ties which are usually necessary in face-to-face instruction.

Finally, the negative types of Radically organizing and manipulating man and Radically organized and manipulated man can be applied to distance education organizers and to distant students too. Here it becomes evident that industrialized education brings forth dangers of its own. The structural roots of it will be dealt with later, in the discussion of the language as a medium. On the whole, the special aspects referred to so far facilitate the formulation of the hypothesis at the beginning of this chapter in more concrete terms: the establishment of distance education and the teaching and learning in this type of industrialized education require that a certain intellectual development and the orientation to new types of man have already taken place.

The ability to detach oneself from the direct guidance of a personal teacher and from the social inspiration and pressure of the learning group, and to determine oneself the time and place of study, the amount of study, and possibly even the ways in which it is controlled, is obviously based on intellectual and socio-cultural experiences which build up enough self-confidence and self-assurance in the individual learner in such a way that he or she can, indeed, 'use reason without the guidance of anyone else'. If such a stage is reached, a barrier has been overcome. This event can be compared with overcoming the barrier of illiteracy, as it has a similar importance in setting free intellectual potentialities and for the further development of the educational system. It may even be thought that an 'absolute threshold of culture' has been crossed.

The discussion on the intellectual and socio-cultural preconditions of distance education shows that possible reservations of the critics of culture with regard to this form of industrialized education can be modified in so far as individuals of the European-American industrial visualization are much better prepared for this form of education that people in preceding eras ever could have been. In other words: persons who teach and learn in the industrialized way are basically different human beings. In many ways - it has been possible to name only a few aspects - they are prepared and ready to benefit from abstract, objectified procedures of imparting knowledge. Furthermore, the constructed, abstract relation between teacher and student fits into net of manifold abstract social relationships, which together form a kind of 'secondary system'.

Man in industrialized societies is used to assimilating 'secondary experiences' instead of making the respective experiences himself. He does not live any longer in 'primary, organic, natural relationships, but in a produced, planned, organized, and very often manipulated world'. Those who accept the changes of man's consciousness caused by industrialization because they think that these intellectual and socio-cultural adaptations are indispensable for coping with the economical, political and cultural tasks of the future will see that the objections of the critics of culture lose some of their significance.

Possibly, they will even become critics of culture the other way round, as they might think that the persistent adherence of traditional schools to preindustrial methods of teaching and learning can be considered as a serious dysfunction of the educational system—an age which is already developing structural elements of a post-industrial society. As industrialization is at the centre of sociological research and as dealing with it has grown from the need for orientation and understanding in view of the rapid changes in our time, which were caused and accelerated exactly by this industrialization, it will be advantageous to analyse and characterize the concept of industrialized education in its sociological aspects as well.

Many sociologists even think that industrialization has caused such far-reaching processes of cultural change that they interpret it as the beginning of a new cultural era in the history of mankind, quite comparable in importance with former cultural eras—for instance, those of the hunting and gathering society and the agrarian society. And—still more important—the blending of technology and the production process is considered an absolute pre-condition for the continuation of the existence of mankind.

In view of such a fundamental philosophy one is not surprised to learn that the industrial production of goods is considered one of the dominant shaping powers of modern society. Helmut Schelsky emphasizes that 'there is practically no sector of life of modern man in which the industrial production has not caused decisive changes of behaviour'. The analysis of distance education has shown that the educational sector has not altogether been left out of this development. Comparing the sociological interpretation of the industrial era with the superficial and dilatory way in which, for instance, technical media are dealt with by didactical experts—to say nothing of the rationalization of instruction by planning and organizing it professionally—the different approach of the two disciplines becomes evident.

Advocates of the use of technical media for instruction have only been marginal in the theory and practice of education. Educational technology has not become a central issue in the methodology of teaching and learning, and did not even get belong the beginnings. The general attitude in this matter is that technical media are merely added to traditional instruction.

The insight is lacking that in view of the changes of the consciousness of modern man, the enormous impact of the teaching capacity of industrialized mass media, which so far have only been used to a small extent, and the enormous increase of teaching and training tasks—

taken altogether—will make new structural forms of teaching and learning imperative. Only such an approach would correspond with the tendencies of industrialization in our present society. Only in such a way could 'cultural lag' in this sector be reduced.

The methodology of teaching and learning has, so far, not been in position to describe the social change caused by a form of instruction in which the teaching is transported to the student, and to clarify the social conditions in it which are structurally quite different. Typically, enough, when trying to explain the teacher-student relation in programmed instruction some authors refer to old, traditional patterns of instruction such as the individual instruction is substituted by industrialized instruction. This change can be identified on several levels. Max Weber, Ferdinand Tonnies and other representatives of the older sociology have described at an early stage the changes which took place under the dominance of purposeful, rational action and as a consequence of the scientific-technical permeation of traditional social subsystems.

Accordingly, one could understand face-to-face instruction in a classroom as a traditional social subsystem; distance education, however, as a 'modern' one. Thus, distance education would be characterized as a system based on rational planning and development just like the organization of industrialized work processes.

On the other hand, face-to-face instruction in the classroom would then be a system handed down by tradition which is not, or is only slightly, affected by the consequences of industrialization. This would mean traditional instruction in a class room could be classed with the category of *gemeinschaft*, as there is a special type of closeness or familiarity between the teacher and the students as well as among the students. The persons involved are also more or less conscious of this familiarity. They approve of it and try to deepen it in order to profit from the solidarity of *Klassengemeinschaft*. It can be assumed that in such groups of students 'archaic personal relations' are fostered. According to Tonnies, the learning group in the classroom would be founded on 'a *gemeinschaft* of place and spirit'.

Subjectively experienced forms of action and their traditions and rites play an important role. In each group a balance of power is developed, a process which might become so dominant that the original objectives for bringing together teacher and students temporarily lose some of their significance. If the concept of *gemeinschaft* is applied to teaching and learning in a class room, the following categories could be subsumed: organic solidarity which can develop in direct social interaction, informal grouping, the dominance of primary social relations, and traditional forms of control, which, for instance, are mirrored in the hierarchy of principal-teacher-student.

If, one the other hand, the concept of *gesellschaft* is applied to distance teaching, the following categories help to explain its structure: mechanical solidarity—that is, the artificial solidarity which is brought about by means of technical media: formal groups—that is, the importance of the formal organization of the learning groups in individual distance study courses; secondary relations with little intensity and without familiarity of the participants, and bureaucratic control which helps to maintain the contacts between school, teachers and students. However, be mentioned that the characterization of distance education with the help of the category 'secondary relations' does not apply to all cases. Fairs has shown that an emotional relationship can be maintained in spite of physical separation, whereby he explicitly mentions the medium of correspondence. Therefore, elements of primary group relationships can also be found in distance education - whereas, the other way round, emotional closeness can be missing even under favorable face-to-face conditions. Jurgen Habermas has observed that Talcott Parsons' catalogue of possible alternatives of value-orientation can also be used to characterize the change of dominant attitudes as a consequence of the transition from traditional to modern society.

Distance education is normally characterized by affective neutrality—as here the teaching and learning is not achieved by an interaction of persons, but, strictly speaking, of isolated functions. As Fairs also suggested, this does not necessarily mean that technically mediated instruction cannot be affective at all. Now and then one can find initial stages of it. Generally speaking, however, it remains safe to say that in distance education the social relations tend to be neutral.

Traditional instruction in the classroom is oriented to a particular frame of reference: a given teacher teaches a given learning group in a given temporal and locational situation. Industrialized instruction, on the other hand, disregards particular conditions of this kind, as it has a more general, if not principally universal frame of reference. Distance education tends, indeed, towards universal application.

With traditional instruction in the classroom teacher and students orientate themselves to certain ascribed qualities. Students, for instance, are 'diligent', 'good companions', 'well-behaved', 'cheeky', or 'exercise restraint'. Teachers are 'strict, but just' or 'soft'. The orientation in this dimension may become more important than the original objectives of instruction. A proof of this is the student who is the best one with regard to his school work, but plays openly a peripheral part in the dynamics of the learning group. With industrialized instruction, however, students and teachers orientate themselves exclusively towards the achievements which are assessed with the help of tests. Traditional instruction can be characterized by diffuse value-orientations. The reason for this is that the norms of the learning group and the experience of 'group life' are usually not considered and, therefore, made conscious to a slight extent only. They become effective in direct social interaction in a global-holistic sense.

Correspondingly, the teachers often think that precise objectives of instruction cannot be described, the methods to be chosen cannot be predicted and the sequencing of instruction cannot be fixed in advance. In contrast to this, in industrialized instruction the indirect interaction is orientated towards the specific qualities of teachers and students in the sense that these are characteristics which are of great importance for the actual achievement of the intended learning process. This tendency for clear determination corresponds with the efforts to lay down detailed definition of learning objectives and to acquire as much relevant empirical data as possible for the learning process in each case.

Even a rough comparison shows that the two forms of instruction could, indeed, be compared with each other with the help of these seven pairs of categories. It is evident that instruction in the classroom is regulated by norms. The direct interactions of teachers and students are more or less caused by binding expectations or value concepts developed by the learning group, the school, the families and society. How much this is, indeed, the case can be seen from the fact that there are often conflicts of norms in classrooms which lead to critical intensifications of social interactions.

As societal norms determine the actions of the teachers and students, their interactions are influenced by socio-cultural traditions, whereby they themselves become part of the socio-cultural life of society. Distance education, however, is basically determined by technical rules. Most behaviour possibilities for the teachers and the students are carefully planned, calculated, formalized and standardized.

Originally global and complex behaviour patterns are reduced to the setting and control of specific functions. The students are informed about the rules of the teaching-learning system, and these rules must be followed. Instruction in the class room is a system of 'communicative acting' and uses intersubjective divided colloquial language. This language is characterized by the traits of special persons, groups of persons, places and times. Thus, in a special sense each communicative situation is experienced as being unique. Distance education, however, uses a language which is taken out of its originally associated surroundings, and is thus free of its context.

The technically mediated communication of necessity remains unaffected by particular circumstance, as it addresses students everywhere. In the classroom the communicative acting is determined by reciprocal expectations of behaviour. This means that the teacher who acts expects the students to react in a special way and vice versa.

The expected reactions take place with a higher degree of probability the more the interacting persons have internalized a role consensus and the more the expected behaviour has become ritualized by habit. In industrialized distance education the segments of interaction are constructed on the basis of conditioned prognoses and conditioned imperatives. Again, particular sequences of a global behaviour become objectified and isolated. In face-to-face instruction the dominant mechanism of acquisition is the internalization of roles. The students live up to expectations by internalizing the norms of the group. Knowledge and skills are transported by means of this particular role identification, role taking and role performance.

In distance education, however, the teaching-learning process is reduced to the learning of skills and qualifications. Every measure in this system has the sole function of achieving this goal. Communicative action and role performance are cut out. In face-to-face instruction the social interaction helps to maintain the institution. Teachers and students are subject to external and internal control. In distance education, however, the indirect interaction is subject to the attainment of the learning goals by using means to an end. Correspondingly, the reactions to breaches of the rules are different in the two subsystems. In face-to-face instruction, the students are punished by conventional sanctions; they fail because of the authority of the institution.

In distance education, however, they fail because of lack of success; that is, they fail because of reality. Finally, the two subsystems also differ with regard to their particular ways of 'rationalizing'. Face-to-face instruction leads to the emancipation of the student, to his individuation, and to the extension of 'dominance-free communication'. Distance education leads to an increase of effectiveness by using technical devices. In the result of this comparison are summarized.

With regard to the objections of cultural critics it must be stated here that the described change of behaviour is, indeed, a deep one, and therefore, full of consequences for the didactical structure of distance education. The fears of negative consequences, for instance, the mechanization, functionalizing and depersonalization of instruction are real. Obviously, these processes are inevitable in such a specialized system of teaching and learning. And important educational goals such as individualization and the extension of the domination-free communicative action cannot be reached. A critic who compares distance education with face-to-face instruction will consider these deficits as really serious ones.

The considerable structural difference between the two forms of instruction, however, suggests that such a comparison is not really helpful. Thus it must be regarded as inappropriate to want to use the new systems of rational thinking in instruction to achieve exactly what was possible with the system of communicative action. It would be more appropriate to ask whether the standards of communicative action must and may still be valid reference points for the evaluation of the social relationships between teacher and taught.

We must also teat whether the gains in teaching capacity in the reproducible system of rational thinking are not so great that deficits in the case of certain learning objectives of the type referred to can be regarded as acceptable. In this context the basic question has to be put once again whether all mediation of knowledge and skills has to be a priori permanently connected with forms of communicative action, or whether the socialization and cultural effects—the acquisition of norms, values and symbols either consciously or unconsciously—cannot take place in other experiencing and practical contexts as well. If, in addition, when answering this question we start from requirements made of people living in industrial societies today, there is another aspect which plays a part.

People in industrial societies have had to find their way around the secondary system referred to, and make good use of the subsystems contained in this system. This ability can obviously only be imparted by a form of instruction which is not based on communicative action alone. Exaggerating only slightly, it can be said that a form of instruction based exclusively on communicative action, which by nurturing the 'innerliness' of teachers and students enables them to develop complete, individual personalities, cannot achieve a current generally applicable learning objective, because it well not teach students how to manage the 'apparatus of existence' of the 'secondary school system' in an advanced industrial society. Reflections of this nature can lead to the conception of a dual educational system in which it will be possible for students to relate communicative and rational actions to one another in lessons.

On the other hand, it is necessary to relate the differences between the two subsystems brought out so far to a more fundamental problem. With an analysis of its particular structural elements, distance education can be seen as a system for the extension of our disposal of technical means in education. Therefore, it must be related to another analytical level than face-to-face instruction which is based on the ways groups of persons see themselves and their traditions. Following Habermas, it could be stated that the increasing application of techniques of distance education results in a variation of the general problem of how usable knowledge can be employed in a social world.

Obviously, there is a clash of two different intellectual traditions: the hermeneutical interpretation of the contexts of life, and empirically obtained and technically used knowledge. In a similar context Helmut Schelsky distinguished between science as reflection and science as technology. The juxtaposition of two respective different forms of teaching and learning has not yet been theoretically incorporated. It conveys a 'life problem of our civilization' namely, how the relations between technical progress and the social world, which are today still natural, can be reflected and controlled by a rational discourse. This will become a central problem of the new didactics.

If one relates distance education as a form of industrialized education to anthropological terms of reference, the question arises how to interpret the phenomenon that man uses technical media in order to be able to teach and learn at a distance. To answer this question requires consideration of two general features which were very important in human development: people's attitude towards technology and their ability to be challenged by new conditions of their environment and to renew themselves through it.

On the many anthropological models of interpretation that of Arnold Gehlen seems to be most suitable for the purpose of this discussion. Following Herder and Schemer, he sees man as a being characterized by biological deficiencies, lacking specialize4d organs and instincts, and not adapted to a particular species-specific environment. This means that he must necessarily rely on his own cautions and must make his environment himself. In order to achieve this, people need technology, which compensates for their deficiencies in the sense of the substitution, intensification and relief of their organs.

Technology had a determining influence on man's interaction with nature throughout his development. In a general sense, technology belongs to him and technology mirrors his being. Technology is, as it were, the 'great being'. The 'continuously increasing substitution of the organic by the inorganic can be considered a relevant result of our cultural development'. This is a process which began as early as the anthropogenesis and which has accelerated increasing during the last centuries and decades.

In a long course of development man had to get used to handling these and other substitute organs and to learn how to use them; that is, how to substitute by tradition what heredity had withheld from him. In the context of this argument it is important to note that the substitute organs are media which are also used in instruction, and that tools, language and thinking are assigned to the same categorical level. In order to stress the importance of these media, one of the first substitute human organs—language—will be discussed in a preparatory digression as it shows paradigmatically to what degree even anthropogenesis depended on a medium which first had to be created. Furthermore, with the help of this medium, effects can be identified which are comparable to those which are achieved by the mechanization and industrialization of instruction.

Finally, language is chose as an example as it is certainly above suspicion for even the most severe critics of culture, as it is not considered a part of technology, but rather a part of culture which is allegedly in opposition to technology. Marshall however, typically enough, called language a human technology. By referring to a quotation from Bergson's *L'Evolution creative*, emphasized that it enabled the human intellect to separate real objects from its environment. Without language, he explain, human intelligence would have remained totally involved in the objects of its attention. A short reflection shows, indeed, that people can distance themselves from an object only if they have found a word for it—the pre-condition of any detached consideration.

Kurt Strunz characterized this development in this way: 'Man is released from the prison of the here and now of his environment'. And he added that it was only through language that man was able to give an overview and ordered analysis of reality, including past events and distant phenomena. The fundamental importance of language is further clarified by McLuhan's comparison: 'Language does for intelligence what the wheel does for the feet and the body. It enables them to move from thing to thing with greater ease and speed and ever less involvement'. The reference to a lesser degree of involvement can be judged positively and negatively. On looking more carefully one can see that already this early use of a medium necessarily connects the advantages mentioned with important disadvantages.

As language extends and amplifies man's thinking, and as man learns to handle it as a technical extension of consciousness, it also diminishes his originally very important intuitive awareness of collective consciousness. Thus, 'speech acts to separate man from man, and mankind from the cosmic unconscious'. Strunz observes that the spoken word changes human inwardness as it objectified it. And here he sees dangerous implications.

The verbal fixation of contents of the world and the inwardness blinds him with regard to the things we do not understand. His detachment alienates him from reality, its contents are 'talked to death'; and, finally, there is also the misuse of the word, in false gossip, in the distortion of the truth, and in lying. A further danger is that language tends to become independent, to develop in its own way, and thereby to assume an inadequate importance which is separated from reality. This may render communication more difficult, or block it or make it open to manipulation. The example shows the enormous adaptations which became necessary when humans learned how to use the medium of language.

Their structures of consciousness changed to a high degree. One might assume that people acquired language only reluctantly and that they refused to use it in some areas of their life altogether, as they were afraid that, for instance, religious and social relations would become stunted.

Even today there are situations in which the exchange of feelings is so subtle that the persons involved believe that talking about them would destroy everything. The use of the medium of language was, on the one hand, an important gain for the development of mankind and, on the other, a considerable loss. The same can be said about the use of newer media in instruction; namely, writing, and later print, and still later electronic media. And the same holds true for industrialized education. It must, however, be acknowledged that the losses were by far outweighed by the extraordinary and even epoch-making advantages.

In all cases the use of media made it possible to solve educational tasks which so far had been insoluble. For the interpretation of industrialized education it is important to see that there are similarities in the consequences of the use of the medium of language and of modern technical media. The following insights have been gained: (1) instruction has been removed from its close attachment to given places, times and persons; (2) teachers and students become detached from reality—that is, from the life of the learning group; (3) as the teaching behaviour is objectified the students have it practically at their disposal.

They can actualize the teaching with greater case and speed whenever they wish to learn. Thus, instruction is released from the prison of the here and now and of a given environment. This opens it up for further developments in new dimensions. Considering the structural similarities conveyed by this analogy, the question suggests itself whether industrialized instruction can release, intensify and differentiate intellectual faculties in the same way as language has done as it is also no longer tied to fixed places, times and persons.

If we follow Gehlen's approach, industrialized instruction can be understood as a complex technical system of teaching and learning which man is forced to develop as he is no longer able to cope with all the instructional and training tasks of the advanced industrial society by means of his natural organs. In the same way as technology was called 'the great teacher'. In order to be able to fulfill its tasks, the great teacher operates with the help of substitute organs which are to intensify and extend the following human organs or faculties:

— The voice of the teacher, which can scarcely fill a large auditorium, is intensified and extended by media such as audio tapes, records, television, and in a coded form as printed material. In this way it can reach practically every home of this globe - and with the help of radio waves, even out into space. Some of these media transmit the teacher's picture as well and even their gestures and body language, so that the teacher's total teaching behaviour can reach practically everyone.

— The forefinger, an organ which is so unspecified and so deficient that it had already been extended by the pointer in the pre-industrial era, is extended and intensified by graphical representations, careful camera work, and the application of multisensoric stimuli techniques. The camera, for instance, can be directed to the object to the shown in such a way that it appears more precisely than in reality. With the help of cinematographic techniques, for instance, focusing, close-up, microscopic filming, slow motion, quick motion and trick filming, it becomes possible to present the object to the student, didactically speaking, much more effectively than it is possible in reality.

— The eyes and ears of the teacher which inform her or him about the learning behaviour of his students are substituted and intensified by the empirical collection of data and their evaluation with the help of the computer. In this way tens of thousand of students can be observed at once with regard to their particulars, their relevant previous qualifications, their entrance behaviour, their gains in knowledge and skills, the results of specific tests, and possibly also the change in their attitudes.

— The memory of the teacher, which is often not as firm and infallible as he or she might wish and which is in addition often also tied to certain situations, is extended by powerful external data banks and computer programs and thus becomes extraordinarily exact.

— The art of teaching - that is, the didactical decisions which are necessarily tied to given persons and situations in face-to-face instruction - is substituted by strategies and technologies which address all students wherever they might live.

In general, the following statement can be made: Human organs can be substituted, intensified and relieved in the ways described in an industrial society only, and the extent to which this happens will increase together with the further industrialization of society. The new possibilities for teaching and learning resulting from this development are not yet fully foreseeable. Having interpreted the technically designed distance teaching system as equipping the teacher with artificial organs, thus enabling him or her to tackle instructional and training tasks of unprecedented magnitude, reasons why the decisive changes which industrialized instruction brings about have to be accepted now have to be given from an anthropological aspect. Present-day man can be characterized by the fact that he is challenged in an unprecedented way by the extreme disproportion between the possibilities of his natural body and of his teaching and learning habits handed down by tradition—and the immense increase in instructional and training needs.

With regard to these needs, which are very likely to increase in the future, the individual, indeed, proves to be a biological deficient being who, because of his morphological helplessness, is bound to fail in his efforts to cope with them. Since the natural teaching capacity is already at a premium in traditional forms of education and since it will be lacking even more drastically when it has to fulfil the needs of the disadvantaged in industrial as well as developing societies, the only way out is to teach and to learn in an industrialized way. This is a pre-condition for enabling as many people as possible to take part in the emerging industrial world civilization.

Heinrich Roth in his *Pedagogical Anthropology*, summed up his discussion about the biologically caused release of man from his environment by saying that man is 'world-open', in the sense that he is not tied to his environment, not adjusted to adaptation, but rather to change. This means that he actively organizes his environment. In fact, he is 'the only being who is able to react to change of his environment and who is best in experimenting with it'.

Industrialized education must be seen as the result of such a basic disposition as well as of an epoch-making thrust in the development of mankind. Now, people face the necessity of coping with 'a new and greatly advanced situation'. If they employ industrialized forms of education they will surely have to bear grievous losses of traditional forms of life. But this happened again and again in the history of mankind whenever new media were used.

The design and the implementation of further forms of industrialized education will also be risky. However, the difficulties to be expected are part of those critical developments typical for our time of transition from the last phase of the last western visualization to the first phase of the emerging global industrial civilization. This development may raise mankind to a high general level of civilization never reached before. Seen anthropolo=-gically, man is also 'a being open for the future'.

As such he will be able to overcome the critical structural changes which result from such transformations of civilization and in education especially from the juxtaposition of traditional occidental forms of instruction and the industrialized forms of teaching and learning in the coming world civilization. History has shown that 'man has repeatedly been able to overcome extremely advanced alienations which were caused by transformations of humanity'. The arguments of the critics of culture that the humanity of education is threatened by the use of rational planning and organization, and of technical media, no longer hold true in the light of this anthropological discussion.

Seen in a larger context the construction of complex technical systems of teaching and learning and their successful implementation must be interpreted as a real proof of man's capacity to react to fundamental changes of society. It is a building block for the 'secondary environment' which people must create in order to survive. In the same way in which technology was not anything strange or even hostile to the inner nature of man in the anthropogenesis, their efforts to industrialize instruction, their ability and skill to instruct extremely large groups of persons with the help of technology can be interpreted as a condition for the possibility of survival in the forthcoming industrial world civilization.

THEORY

The statements depend upon political as well as philosophical views about education. So development is for Man, by Man, and of Man. The same is true of education. Its purpose is the liberation of man from the restraints and limitation of ignorance and dependency. Education has to increase men's physical and mental freedom - to increase their control over themselves, their own lives, and the environment in which they live. The ideas imparted by education, or released in the mind through education, should therefore be liberating ideas; the skills acquired by education should be liberating skills. Nothing else can properly be called education.

The way in which education is expanded is also important. Expansion of schooling is of limited value if it simply reinforces the ideas that learning is a valuable possession, held by the teacher or shut within the covers of a textbook, that can be acquired provided the student listens or reads diligently and respectfully. Instead, with many educators, we would stress the importance of dialogue.

There are, however, both weak and strong forms of the argument for making it central to a theory of education. The weak form of the argument points out that expression helps learning and that dialogue, giving an impression of human warmth and interest, encourages it. Learning is more effective if, through dialogue between student and teacher, the student can be shown how the new matter he is learning relates to what he already knows, and relates to his environment. And dialogue has an important checking function: it enables the tutor to check the student's progress, the tutor to check her method of presentation by seeing whether the student understand her, and the student to check the tutor, in case the tutor has actually got things wrong.

The strong form of the argument goes much further and claims that, unless there is dialogue, education changes to indoctrination: dialogue is here seen as a necessary condition of an education which respects the humanity of student and teacher. This view is reinforced in much out-of-school education, where it is clear that the student's knowledge of the world in which he had grown up merits respect and attention along with the tutor's knowledge of her own specialism.

If those, then, are our aims—of expanding education and of stressing the importance of dialogue—then a theory of distance teaching should illuminate the ways in which it does, or does not, lead towards them. The ways in which distance teaching is used are, of course, politically and culturally determined. If, for example, society rewards credentials and the diploma disease is rife, then it is extremely difficult for a distance-teaching institution to set off in a different direction.

Distance-teaching institutions inevitably reflect the values of their societies. The experience of *Telescundaria*, or of the Free University of pre-revolutionary Iran, which was seen as a device to prevent students coming together, can be contrasted with the radio campaigns of the United Republic of Tanzania, which reflect something of the political philosophy of TANU in their attempt at mass involvement. The success or failure of a distance-teaching project will, therefore, depend at least as much on its political context as on its methods. Our arguments about method inevitably rest on political assumptions.

Experience enables us to make five hypotheses, our first five 'statements', about the way n which distance teaching can be used to maximize education. Chu and Schramm exhaustively analysed the literature on the comparative methods of different media, seeking differences between print, radio, film, television, classroom teacher and so on.

Most of the research suggests that there are no significant differences between them in their educational effectiveness. Trenaman similarly found in comparing radio, print and television that 'the three media communicate a wide variety of material with roughly equivalent efficiently.' While differences between students or audiences, and differences between subjects, have a major effect on how easily something is learned, differences between the media seem to be far less important? Making the point very broadly, then, Statement 1 is: *you can use any medium to teach anything.* Much flows from this hypothesis; it has consequences for our methodology, considered below, and for our desires to expand education.

For, if we can use a variety of media secure in the knowledge that they are comparable in their effectiveness, then we can examine how to use audio-visual media like radio and television, which enable us to reach audiences who could not get to school or college. And we can go on from considering the qualities of individual media to decisions about using a variety of media, and decisions about combining print or broadcasts with some face-to-face study. It follows from Statement 1 that the face-to-face teacher is not unique in his/her ability to teach. And so we can depose teacher: distance teaching can break the integuments of fixed staffing ratios which limited the expansion of education when teacher and student had to be in the same place at the same time.

Traditionally the expansion of education has demanded an expansion in the number of teachers; if that constraint is removed by distance teaching then the prospects for expanding education may be enhanced, provided that distance teaching is no more expensive than teaching through orthodox methods.

The prospect would, on the other hand, be no brighter if distance teaching were necessarily more expansive than orthodox education. Economic forces would then press any reasonable person into expanding ordinary schools and colleges. But distance teaching can be cheaper. With broadcasts, as with print, one teacher's words can reach a much larger audience than world ever be possible face-to-face so that economies of scale are possible. There is empirical evidence of such economies being attained. Jamison and Orivel, for example, considered twelve distance-teaching projects for which cost data are available and found that 'most of the projects studied here are less expensive than equivalent traditional methods of education'.

At primary level, most teachers are paid so little that it is difficult to find any cheaper way of educating small children. At the other extreme, tertiary education is often so expensive that it is much easier to come up with a cheaper, distance, alternative. At any level it is fairly easy for distance teaching to work out as an expensive alternative if only a handful of students follow any one course or (if we are concerned with the number of students who successfully complete a course and not just with the number of enrollments) if the drop-out rate is high.

And at any level costs per student are sensitive to the choice of medium. This can vary widely, so that one could conceive of the costs, for the same programme, of print, radio and television being in the ratio of 1:10:100.

Statement 4: the economies achievable by distance education are a function of the level of education, size of audience, choice of media and sophistication of production. If these hypotheses are true then we have established that distance teaching can be effective and that its costs can compare favourably with those of orthodox education.

Universal post, and radio with its seven-league boots, thus make it possible to increase access to education, while the social constraints on the use of telecommunications are at least slightly different from those on the use of schools. The relevance of distance teaching to the expansion of education is clear, and our key Statement 5 is: distance teaching can reach audiences who would not be reached by orthodox means. So distance teaching may help us towards our first objective. What of the second, to encourage dialogue? We are faced with a dilemma here. If teaching through broadcasts and print is linked with face-to-face study then dialogue is, of course, possible within that face-to-face element. It is far easier to envisage dialogue, if we use the term to mean our strong form or in the sense that Freire uses it, in face-to-face discussion, than through print or broadcasts.

As educators, discussion, than through print or broadcasts. An educators, therefore, we are constantly under pressure to increase the face-to-face component of distance teaching. But, as well saw, the economic attractiveness of distance teaching springs from the economies of scale which it makes possible; we are equally under pressure to limit the size of the face-to-face component. A central problem therefore, concerns the balance between economic arguments, of crucial importance to us if we wish to widen access to education, and educational arguments, of equal importance if we want to emphasize dialogue.

The way that dilemma is resolved, between quantity and quality, will vary from time to time and place to place; we return to it below when considering the methods of distance teaching. In struggling with the dilemma, it is worth remembering that much orthodox education is not based on dialogue. Children are taught to learn things by heart; much agricultural extension assumes that the farmer should simply do what the extension agent tells him.

In practice we cannot learn everything, in school or out, by discovery and dialogue. The tough challenge for distance teaching, then, is provide not merely as good opportunities for dialogue as orthodox education, but more such opportunities. Distance teaching has long been criticized for encouraging rote learning. Of its nature, correspondence education demands a respect for the printed word which is at odds with the sort of scepticism implicit in our view of education. Even a distance-teaching institution as sophisticated and generously endowed with arrangements for dialogue as the British Open University has not always overcome the problem:

But many correspondence-based courses, at the Open University and elsewhere, do encourage dialogue of one kind or another. The radio campaigns of the United Republic of Tanzania and Botswana set up dialogue between village learning-group members and both educators and government; Radio Educative Senegal has used feedback from radio groups to change government policy.

Students in National Extension College correspondence courses confirm that dialogue, on paper and face-to-face, forms a central part of their experience, even though they learn mainly at a distance. Despite the inherent problems, therefore, of arranging dialogue when learning is based on materials produced in advance and distributed on masse, there is empirical evidence for tour key Statement: It is possible to organise distance teaching in such a way that there is dialogue. That dialogue may be on paper, or may be through occasional face-to-face sessions between tutor and student, or may be organized through group discussion of one kind or another. But its existence suggests a change in the function of the teacher, the function of a teacher working in distance education is different from that of a classroom teaching.

If the distance teacher is writing lessons; or making broadcast programmes, her function can be quite easily compared with that of a teacher standing before a class. But even here there are important differences: the kind of explanation which is appropriate to a class often needs to be transformed in one way or another if it is to be recorded. In just the same way as, to turn a play into a film, you need to do more than put a cine camera in the auditorium, so the teacher producing educational material needs to do something different from recording just that she says or does before a class.

Once that job of recording the factual information which is to be used by students has been done, then the role of a teacher in a face-to-face session for distance students becomes markedly different from that of an ordinary teacher. She is no longer the means of passing on information; rather she is there to help students learn information brought to them from outside. That Copernican revolution is one that many teachers in regular schools already welcome.

Where a tutor meets distance students face-to-face, her role is changed from being a communicator of information to that of a facilitator of learning. Dialogue between a student and tutor is only one kind of dialogue. There is extensive evidence that, where distance teaching materials are available, students can help each other to solve problems which in an ordinary class they would put to their teacher. This is the normal method of working for distant students in farm forums or radio schools; more surprisingly, perhaps, children learning from television in Niger found that they could and would solve each other's learning problems when there was no adult present. In formal education, then, there is a place for class work or group work, along with distance study.

Group work looks even more important in adult education. A whole range of group-learning projects, from the radiophonic schools of Latin America to the farm forums of Africa and India, confirm that group learning can be effective, and can lead to group activity. The finding is buttressed by communication theory: the two-step and multi-step theories of human communication suggest that we are more likely to adopt an innovation if we discuss it with friends or colleagues than if we simply learn about it individually and passively.

The combination of local interest and knowledge, possessed by a group of people meeting together, and information from scholars recorded in print or on tape, is a potent one: group discussion is an effective method of learning when distance teaching is used to bring relevant information to the group. Distance teaching, then, can be effective and can stimulate dialogue. Linked with group study, it can extend education far beyond the confines of schools or colleges and can be related to community needs and interests. It can do all these things cheaply. But it will not do so cheaply if we have to provide anew the schools, the libraries or the network of teachers or extension agents which orthodox education and extension requires. We need to use what is already there. And experience of many projects suggests that, in many communities, there are resources which are under-used.

Tevec, a distance teaching project in a poor area of Quebec, for example, had as an explicit aim to enable its students to make use of its resources in the community, nominally available to them, which they lacked the knowledge or confidence to take advantage of.

Obviously the resources available will vary immensely from place to place, from time to time, and in their relevance to any particular educational programme. In most communities there are resources which can be used to support distance learning, to its educational and economic advantage. We started with 'method' in order to establish that distance teaching could face the major educational problems of access and of dialogue. But considerations of 'method' lead in another direction, too, into decisions about the best way of organizing distance teaching.

If statement is accepted, and a range of media are available to us, then there is no easy way of deciding which medium to use, in what way, for which purpose. But there is evidence to believe that several media are better than one. This may simply mean that to use more than one medium makes learning more fun, and therefore, perhaps, more effective, or that it enables information presented in one medium to reinforce that in another, or that individuals learn more easily from one rather than another. There is evidence that, in the United Kingdom, if we measure the proportion of people following a course, a multi-media approach is superior to one that relies on a single medium.

A multi-media programme is likely to be more effective than one which relies on a single medium. This does not solve our problems of choice. Distance teaching remains, for many educators and scholars, an uncharted area. We have very few years' experience of combining print, broadcasts and face-to-face learning in contrast with the centuries of experience of orthodox teachers, working with schools and books. We cannot - for better or worse - teach just as we were taught if we are to teach in a new medium; we need to plan to do something different. Experience so far suggests Statement 11: a systems approach is helpful in planning distance education. The problems of students at a distance drive us on to three further statements. We have already stressed the importance of dialogue to the student. But the benefits to the tutor are also important, and the problems for the tutor separated from her students are different from those of classroom teachers. Unless the tutor has some means of knowing how her students are working, she has no means of helping them and she cannot discover how successful are the materials she has created. Feedback is a necessary part of a distance-learning system.

Feedback can be of various kinds: the term embraces both feedback to the student, showing where he has understood or misunderstood, and feedback to the tutor or course writer. Some of the feedback to the student is immediate—if answers to questions in a correspondence course are printed at the back of the book, for example. But some is necessarily delayed and the distant student faces particular problems in learning by himself. It is peculiarly easy not to learn when studying by correspondence, or by following broadcasts. One can concentrate on the material, feeling that one is working hard, but remembering little of what one experiences. Even with generous opportunities for face-to-face learning, most distance study involves individuals working their way through material, and we cannot assume that tutorials will ensure learning.

To help the student learn, the materials he is to use must be designed so that he does more than read or listen to them or watch them. To be effective, distance-teaching materials should ensure that students undertake frequent and regular activities over and above reading, watching or listening.

Feedback and active learning, the, are necessary for effective distance education, but a concentration on them does not answer the opening question about which medium to use for which purpose. If we group the media roughly into three—print, broadcasts (including recordings) and face-to-face meetings of any kind—then face-to-face communication has two qualities which differentiate it from the others. It makes possible immediate feedback between student and tutor, or dialogue between student and student, and its costs rise proportionately with the number of students, whereas economies of scale are possible with both print and broadcasts. It is this which, as we saw above, leads to central problems for us in reconciling the demands of education and economy.

Bibliography

Central Schools: Run by Kendriya Vidyalaya Sangathan, an autonomous organisation of the Department of Education of MHRD. These schools have been set up to meet, the needs of Central Government employees who are liable to be transferred to any part of country.

Concurrent List: Subjects included in list on which both Centre and State legislate.

Dey Smarajit, A Computerised Information System for Off-Campus Educational Administration, Doctoral Thesis submitted to BM, Pilani in May, 1989.

Education Commission (1966), Government of India. Set up under the chairmanship of Dr. D.S. Kothari which examined all levels and all aspects of education in depth and made comprehensive recommendations for the reconstruction of the educational system.

Education Commission 1964-66, Ministry of HRD, Government of India, (Department of Education), New Delhi.

Education Policy, 1968, Ministry of HRD, Government of India, (Department of Education), New Delhi.

Fifth All India Educational Survey, NCERT.

Goa Report (1987) *Management of Distance Teaching Institutions, CIET, NCERT*, unpublished,

Ministry of Education, Govt. of India—*Challenge of Education—A Policy Perspective*, 1985.

Ministry of Human Resource Development (1986), *National Education Policy*, New Delhi, Deptt. of Education.

Ministry of Human Resource Development (1990), *Selected Educational Statistics* 1988-89, New Delhi,.

Mitra, CR and others, *Challenge and Response—Towards a New Education Policy and Beyond*, 1986, Wiley Eastern W. (India).

Naik J P and Nuniffah Sayed, *A Students History of Education in India*, 1800-1973.

National Policy on Education (1986), Government of India. Envisaged national system of education whereby all students, irrespective of caste, creed, location or sex, have access to education of a comparable quality.

National Policy on Education-1986, Ministry of HRD, Government of India, (Department of Education), New Delhi.

Navodaya Vidyalaya: Run by Navodaya Vidyalaya Sangathan, an autonomous organisation of the Department of Education of talent with a special provision for SCs, STs and girls.

NIEPA (1990) Education for All by 2000, New Delhi, National institute of Educational Planning and Administration. Institutions, CIET, Perry, Walter (1976) Open University, Walton Hall, The Open University. Press.

Ram Reddy, G (Ed) (1988) Open Universities: *The Ivory Towers Thrown Open*, New Delhi, Sterling Pub.

Ramamurti Committee Report (1990) *Towards an Enlightened and Human Society*. Final report to Review NPE 1986.

Report for the Committee for Review of National Policy on Education, Government of India. Set up under the chairmanship of Prof. Ramamurti which has made very concrete recommendations for the universalisation of education.

School Education—After Independence, NCERT.

Secondary Commission (1952), Government of India. Set up under the chairmanship of Dr. Laxmanaswamy Mudaliar. It made a number of recommendations for the reorganisation and restructuring of secondary education. Some of the important recommendations included: diversification of courses after the middle stage, establishment of multipurpose schools, improvements of textbooks and qualitative improvements in teacher-training programmes.

Statistical Outline of India, 1988-89, Tata Services Limited.

University Commission (1948), Government of India. Set up under the chairmanship of Dr. Radhakrishnan which reviewed the state of university education and brought out deficiencies, of the secondary education.

INDEX